MW01012712

The Wiley Handbook of Home Education

The *Wiley Handbooks in Education* offer a capacious and comprehensive overview of higher education in a global context. These state-of-the-art volumes offer a magisterial overview of every sector, sub-field and facet of the discipline—from reform and foundations to K-12 learning and literacy. The *Handbooks* also engage with topics and themes dominating today's educational agenda—mentoring, technology, adult and continuing education, college access, race and educational attainment. Showcasing the very best scholarship that the discipline has to offer, *The Wiley Handbooks in Education* will set the intellectual agenda for scholars, students, researchers for years to come.

The Wiley Handbook of Learning Technology
Edited by Nick Rushby and Daniel W. Surry

The Wiley Handbook of Cognition and Assessment
Edited by André A. Rupp and Jacqueline P. Leighton

The Wiley Handbook of Home Education
Edited by Milton Gaither

The Wiley Handbook of Home Education

Edited by

Milton Gaither

WILEY Blackwell

This edition first published 2017

Registered Office
John Wiley & Sons, Ltd, The Atrium, Southern Gate, Chichester, West Sussex, PO19 8SQ, UK

Editorial Offices
350 Main Street, Malden, MA 02148-5020, USA
9600 Garsington Road, Oxford, OX4 2DQ, UK
The Atrium, Southern Gate, Chichester, West Sussex, PO19 8SQ, UK

For details of our global editorial offices, for customer services, and for information about how to apply for permission to reuse the copyright material in this book please see our website at www.wiley.com/wiley-blackwell.

Library of Congress Cataloging-in-Publication data applied for

Hardback ISBN: 9781118926932

A catalogue record for this book is available from the British Library.

Set in 10.5/13pt Minion by SPi Global, Pondicherry, India
Printed and bound in Malaysia by Vivar Printing Sdn Bhd

10 9 8 7 6 5 4 3 2 1

Contents

Notes on Contributors

Henk Blok is a senior researcher at the Kohnstamm Instituut, the University of Amsterdam's knowledge and research center in the fields of education, child-rearing, and child welfare. His research interests include early childhood education, literacy education, and home education. Together with Sjoerd Karsten, he authored a review of home education in Europe, published in the *European Journal of Education*, 2011.

Christine Brabant is professor of Educational Foundations and Administration at the University of Montreal (Quebec, Canada). Her research interests include educational innovations, governance and change management. Her book *L'école à la maison au Québec: un projet familial, social et démocratique* (Presses de l'Université du Québec, 2013) presents her home education research since 2002. She is a founding member of the International Center for Home Education Research and associate researcher at the Center for Philosophy of Law at Université Catholique de Louvain.

Marine Dumond is a Masters student in Educational Administration at the University of Montreal. Her research investigates parental autoregulation of home education practices within home education support groups.

Cheryl Fields-Smith is an associate professor of elementary education at the University of Georgia's College of Education in the department of Educational Theory and Practice. She earned her degree in 2004 from Emory University under the direction of Dr. Vanessa Siddle Walker. While conducting a study to replicate her dissertation, titled, "After 'It takes a village': The Attitudes, Beliefs, Practices, and Explanations for Parental Involvement among Upper and Middle Income African American Families in Elementary School Settings," Dr. Fields-Smith encountered a Black family who homeschooled their children. From 2006–2008 she conducted a study of Black homeschooling among forty-six families with support from a

Spencer Foundation Grant. Dr. Fields-Smith is the 2014 recipient of the College of Education Carl Glickman Faculty Fellow Award.

Wills Emilio Alejandro Fonseca is an independent scholar with a degree from the University of Los Andes. He has an MSc in Information Technology for Education.

Milton Gaither is a professor of education at Messiah College. He has authored two books, including the 2008 *Homeschool: An American History*, the second edition of which is in press. He is a founding member of the International Center for Home Education Research (ICHER) and maintains the Center's reviews of recent home education research at icher.org/blog.

Christine E. Gleim is a senior at Messiah College, majoring in biology with minors in education and criminal justice. She also works as a research assistant to the faculty in the education department. After graduation, she plans to earn a Master's degree in forensic science and then hopes to work in a forensics lab and someday teach high school science classes at a small Christian school.

Karen Hurlbutt-Eastman, PhD, is a professor at Minnesota State University, Mankato in the department of Special Education. Her areas of expertise and focus of research include autism spectrum disorders, intellectual disabilities, the transition from high school, and pre-service teacher education.

Eric Isenberg, a senior researcher in the Chicago office of Mathematica Policy Research, has studied homeschooling, access to effective teaching for low-income students, teacher labor markets, teacher evaluation systems, alternate certification, and induction programs. He has authored many articles, reports, and working papers on subjects ranging from the methodology of value-added models to a large-scale randomized evaluation of Teach For America. He has also advised public and charter school leaders in the District of Columbia on teacher evaluation systems.

Glenda M. Jackson is the director of Australian Home Education Advisory Service. She maintains a regularly updated list of all available Australian and New Zealand research on home education/homeschooling that is published through major Australian home education networks, titled "Summary of Australian and New Zealand Home Education Research." She was recently invited to write submissions to NSW Parliamentary Select Committees on Home Schooling and Vocational Education (2014, 2015) and to appear before the NSW Parliamentary Select Committee on Home Schooling (2014) to review Australian research on home education and home-educated student use of Technical and Further Education colleges (TAFEs).

Sjoerd Karsten is professor emeritus of Policy and Organization of Vocational Education, Adult Education, and Life Long Learning at the University of Amsterdam, the Netherlands. He has served as an advisor to the Dutch ministries of Education and of Social Affairs, the national Education Council, and the national Inspectorate of Education, and as an external expert for the European Union. His research centers on education policy, vocational education, parental choice, and home education.

Elife Doğan Kılıç is associate professor and doctor of education administration at the University of Istanbul. Her research interests include organizational behavior, learning organization, leadership, organizational cynicism, and organizational citizenship. Together with Özgür Önen, she authored a study of home education in Turkey, published in the *US-China Education Review*.

Antony Barone Kolenc is a professor at the Florida Coastal School of Law, where he teaches Constitutional Law. His scholarly research focuses on homeschooling, constitutional law, and military policy. He also writes a legal column in *Practical Homeschooling Magazine*. He retired as a Lieutenant Colonel from the US Air Force Judge Advocate General's (JAG) Corps, where he litigated civil and criminal cases before trial and appellate courts, and taught at the Air Force Academy.

Yvona Kostelecká, PhD, is assistant lecturer at Faculty of Education, Charles University in Prague. Her research interests include home education, the integration of foreigners into the Czech school system, and international migration of researchers and skilled workers.

Robert Kunzman is a professor of education at Indiana University and the managing director of the International Center for Home Education Research (ICHER). He is the author of more than a dozen publications on homeschooling, including *Write These Laws on Your Children: Inside the World of Conservative Christian Homeschooling* (Beacon, 2009).

Helen E. Lees is a lecturer in Education Studies at Newman University, Birmingham UK and a researcher of the theory and practices of educational alternatives to mainstream school attendance. She wrote *Education Without Schools: Discovering Alternatives*, published by Policy Press, Bristol, UK (2014) and is co-editor with Nel Noddings of the *Palgrave International Handbook of Alternative Education* (2016). She is founding Editor-in-Chief of *Other Education – The Journal of Educational Alternatives* (www.othereducation.org).

Kyle Levesque is a PhD candidate in the Department of Psychology and Neuroscience at Dalhousie University, Nova Scotia. His research focuses on language and literacy development across the lifespan.

Jennifer Lois is professor of Sociology at Western Washington University in Bellingham, Washington. She studies gender, emotions, and identity ethnographically. Her first project examined these themes among search-and-rescue volunteers

(*Heroic Efforts*, 2003, New York University Press); her second project focused on homeschooling mothers (*Home Is Where the School Is*, 2012, New York University Press). She is currently researching the gendered culture of romance novel writers (with co-researcher Dr Joanna Gregson, Pacific Lutheran University).

Robert Lyon is a Spanish Education student from Messiah College in Mechanicsburg, Pennsylvania.

Erwin Fabián García López, MEd, is coordinator of the action-research group on descholarization, collaborative self-directed learning, homeschooling, and flexible forms of schooling in the Faculty of Human Sciences at the National University of Colombia.

Bryan Mann is a PhD candidate in the Educational Theory and Policy (EDTHP) program at Penn State University. His research focuses on organizational and institutional change, school choice, K–12 online learning, and educational policy in general. His dissertation, "Navigating the Web of School Choice: The Market, Institutional, and Environmental Pressures on School District Responses to Cyber Charters," considers how school choice policies interact with various environmental pressures to shape adoption or non-adoption of online learning in traditional school districts. Mann started his career as a teacher at Communications High School in New Jersey.

Sandra Martin-Chang earned her PhD from the Department of Psychology, Neuroscience and Behaviour at McMaster University, Ontario. She is now an associate professor and the Graduate Program Director in the Education Department at Concordia University, Montreal. Her main focus of research is on the development of skilled reading in home and school settings.

Michael S. Merry is professor of Philosophy of Education at the University of Amsterdam, the Netherlands. He is the author of *Culture, Identity, and Islamic Schooling: A Philosophical Approach* and *Equality, Citizenship and Segregation: A Defense of Separation*, and is co-editor of *Citizenship, Identity, and Education in Muslim Communities: Essays on Attachment and Obligation*, all of which are published by Palgrave Macmillan.

Joseph Murphy is the Frank W. Mayborn chair and associate dean at Vanderbilt's Peabody College of Education. His research focuses on school improvement, emphasizing leadership and policy. He has written and co-authored twenty-two books in this field and edited twelve others, including the 2012 title *Staying Home: Homeschooling in America*.

Fiona Nicholson is an independent home education consultant based in the North of England. Fiona analyses the diversity of policy and practice in local government's dealings with home educators and has provided evidence to a number of government committees. Fiona's research also informs the work of the All Party Parliamentary Group for Home Education at Westminster. She maintains several websites, including *Ed Yourself* (www.edyourself.org).

Michael Olalekan Olatunji holds a PhD in Education Foundations from the University of Port-Harcourt, Nigeria and specializes in Philosophy of Education. Over the years he has worked as a lecturer in universities and colleges of education in Nigeria, Zambia, and Botswana. He is accredited by the Botswana Training Authority (BOTA) as a trainer and is currently a senior lecturer at Botswana Institute for Leadership Development. His areas of research interest include Teacher Education, Philosophical Analysis, Critical Thinking and Professional Ethics.

Xiaoming Sheng, PhD, works in the area of sociology of education and has experience in social stratification, gender and women's studies, and homeschooling. She currently is on the Faculty of Education at the University of Cambridge, UK. She is the author of *Higher Education Choice in China: Social Stratification, Gender and Educational Inequality* and *Learning with Mothers: A Study of Home Schooling in China*.

Marc Snyder received his EdD in Higher Education Leadership from Nova Southeastern University, Florida, in 2011. He is currently Headmaster of True North Classical Academy in Miami, Florida and was previously the Upper School Principal of Aquinas American School in Madrid, Spain. His research interests are centered on homeschooling and its impact on higher education. His most recent publication, a study comparing the academic achievement of homeschooled students with that of traditionally schooled students attending a Catholic university, appeared in *Catholic Education: A Journal of Inquiry and Practice*.

Diego Fernando Barrera Tenorio is a lawyer, researcher, and member of the action-research team on homeschooling at the University of Colombia. In the action-research project, he contributed on the legal and political status of homeschooling in Colombia.

Kaitlin Wingert is a senior at Messiah College in Grantham, Pennsylvania. She is currently pursuing degrees in both English and French.

Introduction to The Wiley Handbook of Home Education

Milton Gaither

Home education, which is frequently labeled "homeschooling" (especially in the United States), "home-schooling," and "home schooling," has grown since the 1970s into an established phenomenon around the world. Given its dynamic growth, its intrinsic interest as an alternative to conventional schooling, and its association with political protest and countercultural ideologies, it has increasingly been attracting scholarly attention around the world. Scholarly study of home education has grown with the movement, from a small handful of studies focused almost exclusively on the United States in the 1980s to a sprawling literature today that varies profoundly by discipline, methodology, topic, geographic location, and academic quality. Twenty years ago scholars studying home education could without too much trouble stay abreast of the entirety of this literature on their own, but now the subject has matured to the extent that no single individual can master it all. The rapid proliferation of scholarship has also made it difficult for popular media outlets and interested citizens to know where to look for reliable and up-to-date information. Furthermore, ignorance of the scholarship already done has contributed to the unfortunate tendency of graduate students to conduct predictable studies on time-worn topics that merely replicate what others have done before. There is a clear need for a single, authoritative source that both synthesizes the extant literature and sets an agenda for future study. That is the purpose of this book.

This handbook comprises twenty original, newly commissioned essays, each one providing comprehensive coverage of a particular topic within the larger world of home education scholarship. Some of the chapters cover topics that have long interested both scholars and the general public, such as the demographic make-up of homeschoolers, motivations parents have for choosing home education, the academic achievement of home educated students, the performance of homeschooled children

The Wiley Handbook of Home Education, First Edition. Edited by Milton Gaither.

at colleges and universities, and the impacts of home education on children's socialization. Other chapters engage themes researchers have been studying with care but that have received less popular attention, including the impact of home education on family dynamics and mothers' lives, home education among minority populations, homeschooling of children with special needs, and the emergence of hybrid home–school arrangements abetted by technology. Still other chapters introduce to an English-speaking audience the scholarship available on home education outside of the United States. Throughout, all authors have sought to provide a roadmap to help readers develop the ability to be discriminating in their consumption of home education scholarship. It is unfortunately the case that for decades a good bit of what has passed for homeschooling research has been little more than thinly veiled advocacy or opposition. The goal of these essays is to summarize the best scholarship available on the widest range of topics possible to provide the reader with the most comprehensive and authoritative coverage of home education scholarship ever produced.

While each chapter functions as a stand-alone essay fully comprehensible on its own terms, there is a logic to the overall arrangement of the chapters. Home education emerged at roughly the same time in many parts of the world, but it has always been most popular and hence most studied in the United States. In the States the practice galvanized a powerful political movement by the late 1970s, attracting a wide range of anti-establishmentarian adherents from both the ideological Left and Right. The United States' decentralized educational laws blended with social trends ranging from Cold War-era animus against centralized government, to gains in women's education, to a resurgent religious right emphasizing the nuclear family, to suburban prosperity and privatization, all of which combined to produce a large population of (mostly) mothers able and eager to remove their children from public and private schools to teach them at home.

Because the home education movement has always been largest and strongest in the United States, the lion's share of the scholarship has been produced by scholars in the United States studying US homeschooling. Scholarship in other countries, while growing every year, has not as yet reached the volume and specificity of US scholarship, and in fact much of the literature coming from scholars around the world often draws heavily from US sources. Given this empirical reality it was deemed best to separate this handbook into two parts. Part I contains a series of chapters summarizing the academic literature on various topics related to homeschooling in the United States. Readers interested in home education in other countries, the subject of Part II, will likely find it helpful to become familiar with this US literature, for it often forms the contextual background of studies done elsewhere. Familiarity with the US literature also helps develop awareness of comparative possibilities. Despite the significant influence of the US homeschooling movement on other parts of the world, home education is not simply a North American export. It is a truly global movement, with each region developing its own unique legal and political framework, set of parent motivations, and familial/communal educational practices.

A second factor influencing the content and arrangement of these chapters is the fact that the scholarship on home education outside of the United States has not been equally distributed around the world. In some countries home education scholarship has been produced in significant quantities for many years. In others there is only a handful of scholarly works. It can roughly be asserted that the phenomenon of home education has been most popular in English-speaking countries like the United Kingdom, Australia, and bilingual Canada. Not surprisingly, the scholarship on the phenomenon in those countries is the most robust. In Part II, therefore, chapters covering Canada, the United Kingdom, and Australia precede those on other countries. Even the English-speaking countries, however, have not yet produced enough scholarship to justify several chapters devoted to separate topics as is done with the United States in Part I. In Part II each chapter will cover the totality of home education scholarship for the given country.

Home education has emerged in non-English speaking parts of the world as well. It has done so, however, on a smaller scale in some locales, in the more recent past in others, or facing effective opposition from government or the broader society in still others. As such there are both fewer practitioners and less scholarship to survey for many parts of the world. For many countries, in fact, there exists no scholarly literature at all. While the chapters included in this handbook do not cover every country, they provide as complete a survey as the current scholarly landscape permits of home education research for important parts of Central and South America, Western and Eastern Europe, Asia, and Africa. All of these chapters were either written by English-speaking scholars or translated into English, and in some cases scholarship that has heretofore been unavailable to an English-speaking audience is made accessible for the first time.

The authors of each chapter were given substantial freedom to construct their essays as they deemed best within the general parameters that each chapter synthesize the best scholarly literature on the topic and suggest needs and opportunities for future study. No singular organizational structure or criterion for selecting sources was imposed on the authors, largely because the topics engaged in this volume differ so widely in terms of the amount and level of scholarship devoted to them. In some cases authors have synthesized scores of peer-reviewed quantitative and/or qualitative articles and books. In others authors have had to dabble in more popular sources or unpublished primary references to provide the most complete picture possible. Each author's voice remains as well. Though spelling and punctuation were Americanized, effort was made not to edit out individual authors' rhetorical particularity. It is hoped that this approach results in a volume that can be read with benefit both in its individual parts and as a whole.

Part I

Home Education in the United States

1

The History of Homeschooling

Milton Gaither

Introduction

When discussing the history of homeschooling two distinctions need to be made at the very outset. First, it is important to distinguish, as some do not (Jeynes 2012; Hill 2000), between homeschooling as a deliberately chosen alternative to institutional schools on the one hand and, on the other, the pragmatic use of the home to educate children. The latter practice has been central to many if not most human societies from ancient times. In this chapter we will label this "domestic education" and only deal with it cursorily. What we are mostly concerned with is the self-consciously alternative practice, and this emerged only in the 20th century in reaction to compulsory school laws and public school bureaucracies, at first in isolated instances but coalescing into a discernible political movement by the late 1970s.

The second distinction that needs to be made is between history as an academic discipline and history as an argumentative tool. Many polemics by homeschoolers against schools and by advocates of schools against homeschooling include historical claims. Many scholarly articles on homeschooling, especially those making legal or philosophical arguments, include historical claims or narratives as part of their overall argument. But very few polemicists or academics have approached the topic of homeschooling history from within the discipline of historical study itself with its requisite attention to primary source documentation, its careful consideration of context, and its feel for nuance and complexity. The result has been a series of oft-repeated but false claims about the homeschooling movement or some aspect thereof. Many of the most egregious and frequently reiterated false claims pertain to the legal history of homeschooling, including inaccurate assertions about the degree to which homeschooling was illegal in the past (Somerville 2001), misleading claims

The Wiley Handbook of Home Education, First Edition. Edited by Milton Gaither.

about the basis for and easy acceptance of compulsory school laws (Curren and Blokhuis 2011), or misinterpretations of the meaning and scope of key Supreme Court cases such as *Pierce v. Society of Sisters* and *Wisconsin v. Yoder* (Kreager, Jr. 2010; Olsen 2009).

In what follows we will, after briefly discussing the historiography of home education outside the United States and the historiography of domestic education within the United States, survey all of the available scholarship on the history of the modern American homeschooling movement. We will not cover the many articles that contextualize their theme by providing a brief and entirely derivative historical introduction (e.g., Vieux 2014).

The History of Home Education Outside the United States

As of this writing no major work concerning itself exclusively with the history of the home education movement in any country outside of the United States has been published. As most European nations and their colonies had longstanding traditions of domestic education, there has been good recent work done on the pre-homeschooling period. English-language examples include articles about visual learning in the homes of early modern Italians (Evangelisti 2013), tutors in 19th century Brazil (Vasconcelos 2013), the British and French tutors and governesses of the Russian Aristocracy (Staroverova 2011) and rural Mongolia in the early 20th century (Marzluf 2015). Such work is typically performed by specialists in various historical fields and is typically not connected explicitly to home education movements in their respective countries today, though sometimes the connection is made (Staroverova 2011).

While we lack any complete account for a particular country, region, or continent, in general it can be asserted that movement homeschooling emerged in many countries outside the United States at roughly the same time as it did in the States, though usually on a much smaller scale. Occasionally the influence of the American movement was discernible; occasionally developments seemed to be more autochthonous. Until a fuller and richer historiography emerges it will be difficult to say with precision exactly what happened when and why. Until that literature emerges interested readers will have to make do with historical material that occasionally shows up in more general pieces about home education in particular countries. Recent examples of English-language works that include at least some information about the history of home education in a given locale include Olatunji's robust account of the emergence of home education in South Africa (2014), Paciorkowski's detailed description of the legal history of home education in Poland (2014), Drabsch's brief discussion of the history of home education in Australia (2013), Martin's summary of the history of the unique situation in Germany (2010), Staroverova's description of the reemergence of domestic education among the new Russian plutocrats who have emerged since the fall of communism (2011), and Zur Nedden's account of pioneering Canadian home educator Wendy Priesnitz (2008). This is not by any means an exhaustive list. It is very common for articles about home education in some country other than the United States to include at least a brief history of the practice in the region under discussion.

Domestic Education in the United States

Like their European, African, Asian, and South American counterparts, specialists in various periods of American history have occasionally studied the use of the home to educate children. Huge fields of historical inquiry devoted to the history of childhood, of the family, and of femininity and masculinity, have all on occasion explored the use of the home as an educative institution. Most of this historical scholarship was synthesized by Gaither in 2008 in what remains the most complete account of the home as an educational institution. The first three chapters of that book deal respectively with domestic education in the colonial period, the early national and antebellum periods, and the late 19th and early 20th centuries. This chapter will not review the secondary works upon which that synthesis was based. Interested readers are invited to consult the endnotes therein for the sources available as of 2008 for such an account (Gaither 2008).

Since 2008 a fair amount of high level scholarship has been published on related themes that adds even more to our knowledge of domestic education practices prior to the expansion of compulsory schooling in the mid-20th century. Herndon and Murray's 2009 book *Children Bound to Labor* brings together the work of thirteen scholars who collectively tell the story of pauper apprenticeships in early America. The book's many case studies draw on archival and other primary sources to bring the common practice of placing orphaned, neglected, or simply poor children in the homes of other families to be taught trades. One component of the apprenticeship model was the requirement that host families teach basic literacy and numeracy to their charges, and the book provides a more detailed look at how various families did and did not do this than anything before it (Herndon and Murray 2009).

Several other recent works have examined various aspects of family life, all of which have connections with domestic education. Wilson emphasizes the degree to which stepfamilies were a pervasive phenomenon in colonial New England due to frequent spousal death dislocation (2014). Glover provides rich detail about the family lives of many of the United States' founding fathers, many of whom were taught at home and/or had their own children taught at home (2014). Hyde provides a remarkable synthesis of the history of the American West, using the family as organizing principle and revealing along the way how fluid were the boundaries between home and school on the frontier (2011). King's revised and expanded version of her classic study provides much new information about the lives of slave children in both the South and North (2011). del Mar's sweeping synthesis of US family history provides a fitting context for both the domestic education of early centuries and the emergence of homeschooling in more recent times (2011). Hampel investigates the dramatic rise of correspondence study-at-home programs in the early 20th century, some sponsored by universities but many by profit-seeking firms often engaging in dubious practices (2010). Morice provides an early 20th-century case study of progressive home education as a reaction against industrialized institutional schooling (2012). Many other works could be listed, but these are standout examples of recent historiography with direct bearing on various aspects of domestic education.

History of The Homeschooling Movement – Early Contributions

For this chapter we will take Gaither's book *Homeschool: An American History* as a pivot point. Historical accounts written prior to Gaither's book will not be discussed in detail as they are all parsed and synthesized in that work (2008). Briefly, the most notable early works that tried to provide a history of the modern homeschooling movement fall into two categories. In the first place there are accounts of the early years of the national homeschooling movement or its manifestation in a particular locale by movement activists. While there is much of value in these memoirs and first-person narratives, they must be read with scholarly discernment. For the national movement standout examples of the genre include Klicka's celebratory account (2006) and Seelhoff's more critical appraisal (2000a, 2000b, 2000c, 2001a, 2001b, 2001c). Many local accounts by movement insiders, some book-length (Richman 1989; Meighan 2007; Griffith 2007), most brief (e.g., Lambert 1997; Smith 2007) have been published, though often only in a transient online format (Lepore 2015).

Very few scholarly works dealing exclusively with the homeschooling movement's history were published prior to 2008. Perhaps the most widely cited has been Knowles, Marlow, and Muchmore (1992), which laid out a five-phase model of the development of homeschooling in the United States. Their basic narrative structure was one of conflict between homeschooling advocates and public school personnel that gave way gradually to cooperation as laws were changed to make the practice more clearly legal, culminating in the consolidation of the movement as national networks emerged to group like-minded homeschoolers into rival camps. Carper's work, published in several articles, has also been influential, describing a grand, three-act historical arc beginning with educational pluralism in the colonial and early national periods, moving to the near-universal establishment of public schools in the mid-19th to mid-20th centuries, and concluding with a growing dissent against that establishment in the late 20th century (1992, 2000). Finally, a few early works provide good coverage of particular states or regions. McIlhenny (2003)'s study of the early history of Texas homeschooling is a standout example, as is Tyler and Carper's (2000) study of South Carolina.

Other scholarly works not explicitly devoted to history nevertheless contained a good bit of historical information or analysis. Influential examples include Van Galen's many articles laying out her landmark dichotomy between "ideologues" and "pedagogues" (1986, 1987, 1988, 1991) and Stevens' pioneering ethnographic study full of detail about homeschooler politics and practice in the 1980s and 1990s (2001). Provasnik's remarkable work on the legal history of compulsory education legislation is an important resource for the legal history of homeschooling in the United States (2006). Finally, a few of the many dissertations conducted on homeschooling during the 1990s and 2000s provided rich historical accounts of local homeschooling histories. Examples here include Bloodworth's study of North Carolina (1991), Cochran's study of Georgia (1993), and Kelly's study of Hawaii (2008).

All of this work and much else besides was synthesized in Gaither's 2008 *Homeschool: An American History*. The first three chapters of that book deal with domestic education in the colonial and early national periods and explain how and why nearly all Americans chose institutional schooling over the home in the 19th and early 20th centuries. Gaither draws on a wide range of historiography from various subfields of US social history to tell this story. Chapter four, with the help again of a large bibliography of US political and social history, lays out three broad contextual changes in the mid-20th century that set the stage for the homeschooling movement: the growth of the postwar suburbs and the anti-institutional ideologies they helped establish, the Civil Rights and women's movements, which popularized organized protest against the established order, and the polarization of the electorate into right and left wings in the late 1960s and 1970s, both of which were skeptical about established institutions like government schools. Chapter five provides detailed biographies of pioneer homeschooling leaders John Holt, Raymond and Dorothy Moore, and Rousas J. Rushdoony. Chapter six chronicles the rise of the Home School Legal Defense Association (HSLDA) in the mid-1980s and the fissuring of the homeschooling movement into rival camps of conservative Christians and everyone else. Chapter seven details the history of the legal and legislative battles fought over homeschooling in the 1980s and 1990s, and a final chapter describes trends in homeschooling up to 2008 (Gaither 2008).

Since Gaither's book a small but significant number of works on the history of homeschooling in the United States have been published. The rest of this chapter will summarize them. Some of the most interesting works in this regard make broad theoretical arguments. Historians regularly deal with the tension between constructing a coherent narrative or argument on one hand and faithfully reproducing the complexity and detail of the past on the other. In the next section we will summarize works that provide some sort of overarching argument or master story for the history of homeschooling. In subsequent sections we will turn to works that emphasize various details.

The Homeschooling Movement, Theoretical Constructs

Jones (2008) examines three traditions of private education crafted in opposition to the dominant US Public School system – 19th century Catholic parochial schools, mid-20th century Jewish day schools, and the contemporary homeschooling movement. For each his claim is that arguments made for and against the practice have been remarkably consistent over time. Jones' account of the history of homeschooling in chapter one offers nothing new, but situating it in a longer tradition of oppositional education movements is enlightening, most notably his finding that for all three of his examples large, nationwide organizations and leadership were crucial for success.

Chapter two finds two common philosophical assumptions to undergird all religious private education, be it Catholic, Jewish, or Protestant homeschooling. First, all groups have argued that their faith traditions give them unique access to truth, for truth comes from God. Second, all of these religious traditions believe that God has charged parents, not the State, with the task of educating their young.

Chapter three looks at the continuity over time of arguments made against private religious education. There are two basic arguments. First, it has consistently been argued that private schooling and homeschooling pose a threat to public education by taking away both fiscal resources and social support from public schools. Second, critics claim that sectarian religious education poses a threat to the nation by isolating and segregating young Americans by creed even as it prepares these divided children to hate and fear people who disagree with them, and possibly to try to take over the country and impose their theocratic vision on all.

Chapter four shows that the various religious groups have responded to the arguments summarized in chapter three in remarkably similar ways over time. Catholics, Jews, and Protestants have all made the case that their efforts in no way drain resources from public schools. They have always argued, on the contrary, that they pay taxes to support public education even though they do not use the benefit. Their lack of support for public education is actually a civic good, they argue, for government-run public education is inefficient and ineffective. As for the charge that religious education threatens to balkanize and radicalize the country, private advocates have typically responded in two ways. They first point out that public schools are by no means models of diversity themselves – they are often just as segregated by race and class as are private schools. Advocates also argue that in fact it is they who are safeguarding the heritage of American democracy by "providing competition to the government monopoly" and thereby "protecting and ensuring" diversity and freedom (Jones 2008, 101–102).

Chapter five finds another longitudinal continuity in popular history textbooks from all three traditions, all of which both celebrate the United States and celebrate the particular religion's contributions to that greatness. For homeschooling Jones provides a careful examination of A Beka and Bob Jones, two of the most popular Christian curricula among homeschoolers. These books, like the Catholic and Jewish texts before them, encourage children reading them to believe that their particularistic tradition was "an integral part of American life all along" and that they are therefore "every bit as American as [their] public school counterparts" (Jones 2008, 131).

Andrade (2008) tests the thesis that homeschooling might not really have been a movement at all but was perhaps simply an inevitable outcome given "convergence of several global forces" (Andrade 2008, 12). Some of these forces include the rising cost of schooling, the emergence of radically individualist notions of intelligence and self-fulfillment, the politics of privatization, the evolution of copyright law, and the changing status of women. But the changes in information and communications technologies that have transpired in the past three decades are Andrade's main target.

To justify his suggestion that homeschooling emerged not out of the dedicated work of grassroots organizers but as the inevitable outcome of social changes, Andrade notes that many countries outside of the United States have seen a sharp rise in homeschooling as well. He describes in great detail the rise of the post-industrial, communication technology-driven workforce and its trenchant critique of industrial-era public schools. He also cites much secondary literature that has stressed the technological savvy of homeschoolers.

To test his technological change hypothesis Andrade does not engage in conventional historical inquiry but conducts focus-group and individual interviews with 27 New York homeschoolers, carefully compiling and coding their responses. Few of those in his sample began homeschooling prior to 2000, and none of them mentioned technology as a factor in their journey to homeschooling until prompted by the researcher. Once prompted, many of his subjects did acknowledge the role computers played in teaching them about the topic of homeschooling, in connecting to other homeschoolers, and in providing some curriculum options. Veteran homeschoolers on the whole acknowledged the complementary role technology has played in helping homeschooling flourish, but they tended to cite other sources for the movement's true power.

Even with this lackluster finding in his own data Andrade persists in his deterministic conviction that technological change is what really caused homeschooling to emerge when it did. Andrade makes this claim despite the fact that his own subjects (none of whom were homeschooling when the movement really took off in the 1980s and early 1990s) failed to cite this as a factor and despite his lack of attention to forms of evidence most historians would find imperative for such a thesis as this – things like documents, visual and material culture, oral histories of actual participants in the period under discussion, and so forth, all of which would show that back when the movement was changing state laws and winning court cases all around the nation it was phone trees, mailing lists, newsletters, and conventions that informed and connected people, not personal computers.

Greenfield (2009) recapitulates the thesis of Ferdinand Tönnies, who argued that modernization causes society to move from what he termed *Gemeinschaft*, or tribal codes of honor and status appropriate to rural, agricultural living, passed down from generation to generation through osmotic folkways, to *Gesellschaft*, or modern, industrialized, urban codes of living premised on individualism, acquired through deliberate and systematic cultivation of the young in formal institutions. Greenfield summarizes many anthropological studies conducted among a wide range of population groups and finds that in general as societies move away from *Gemeinschaft* to *Gesellschaft* family practices shift significantly, profoundly affecting child development. Family size shrinks. Nuclear family is less connected to extended family.

Formal schooling increases. Literacy rates climb. IQ scores go up. Children's individuality is nurtured even as familial commitments (such as that older children care for younger or that children care for elderly relatives) wane.

The shift from *Gemeinschaft* to *Gesellschaft* does not occur overnight. It has a generational component. Adults who were raised in a more *Gemeinschaft* context often try to parent in the old way even though the broader social context has shifted. This can lead to tensions within families. For example, parents may seek to perpetuate the ethos of a subsistence village by requiring all sorts of chores of their children when what the children really want is remunerative work so they can buy consumer goods. As the cultural shift takes place, children change. *Gesellschaft* children become better at recognizing abstractions (as opposed to memorizing details), handle novel situations more nimbly, think of themselves more as individuals (especially the girls, whose life choice options are significantly expanded), value sharing less and ownership more.

If Greenfield's grand theory is correct, homeschooling turns out to be a rear-guard effort by partisans of various *Gemeinschaft* virtues to pass those on to children who inhabit an increasingly *Gesellschaft* world. This explains in good measure both the countercultural vibe of so many homeschoolers and their political anxieties. It does not, however, apply to those families who choose homeschooling for its curricular flexibility and technological opportunities. For such "Creative Class" families, homeschooling more fully embodies *Gesellschaft* values than industrial-era formal schools (Gaither 2009; Griffith 2007). Another potential problem for this analysis is in its forecasting implications. Though Greenfield is clear in her text that she does not see *Gesellschaft* as inherently superior or historically inevitable, the general tenor of this distinction does suggest that *Gemeinschaft* practices are residual and headed for extinction. Yet homeschooling continues to grow every year. There must be more going on than mere pastoral nostalgia.

Wilhelm and Firmin (2009) provide a brief and derivative synthesis of the history of homeschooling in the United States. Given their audience in a journal devoted to Christian education, they stress the Christian foundations of both early American schooling and the public schools that emerged in the 19th century. In the late 19th century, however, bureaucratic and industrialized trends began to corrode this Christian influence, at least in some locales. It was not until the 1960s, however, especially with the key Supreme Court cases declaring school-sponsored prayer and devotional Bible reading unconstitutional, that Biblical authority was truly abandoned. As a result, homeschooling emerged as an alternative, first among leftists led by John Holt but then by a growing group of conservative Christians fleeing secularism, values-clarification, and other ills of the public schools.

Krause (2012) draws on literature about dissent traditions to argue that the homeschooling movement is a democratizing trend in an educational landscape that has in the past several decades grown increasingly bureaucratized and alienated from participation by ordinary citizens. She makes this argument by emphasizing two domains. First, she provides detailed examination of much of the legal and legislative history of the movement, with a special focus on the *Leeper* case and the experiences of homeschooling pioneers in Texas, all of which show the power of grassroots activism and networking. Second, she provides a close reading of several Christian curricula, including Diana Waring, Beautiful Feet, Cadron Creek Christian Curriculum, and Cornerstone Curriculum, arguing that these illustrative cases represent homeschoolers' spirit of dissent against the system and repudiation of elite management. Homeschoolers' refusal to accept dominant epistemologies puts them at the heart of the democratic tradition, according to Krause.

Murphy (2012) is a book-length review of the scholarship on every aspect of the modern homeschooling movement. Though elements of the history of homeschooling can be found in other chapters, chapters three and four deal with history explicitly. In a separate article Murphy reprints his historical review, focusing especially on the material laid out in chapter four (2013).

In chapter three Murphy begins by explaining how most historians who have covered the history of homeschooling break the overall story down into three stages: a pre-compulsory school period characterized by institutional diversity and significant domestic education, a compulsory school period characterized by near-universal attendance at either public schools or private schools, and a post-compulsory period characterized by the growth of the oppositional homeschooling movement. Murphy does not engage in chapter three with the literature on stages one or two.

For stage three, Murphy explains that historians have consistently found two core founding traditions, each with its own key national leader. On one hand is the liberal left, whose founding father was John Holt. On the other is the conservative Christian right, whose founding father was Raymond Moore. Though they represented polar opposite political and often religious convictions, the two traditions in the early years of the movement worked hand-in-hand to facilitate homeschooler networking and to fight to make homeschooling easier to do by securing friendly court decisions and changing state laws.

After covering the founding generation, argues Murphy, historians tend to stress the increasingly mainstream nature of homeschooling in the 1990s and thereafter. By 1993 the legal battles were largely finished and homeschooling was accepted throughout the country. As more and more people turned to homeschooling, its public profile was raised, which led even more Americans to think of it as an acceptable educational option.

But why and how did this normalization occur? Murphy isolates five reasons from the historical literature. First, large social trends like the growth of privatization, localism, and deinstitutionalization have created a hospitable environment for homeschooling, as has the waning public commitment to the welfare state as the values of the market invade every sector of life, including education. Second, the growth of homeschooling has created for itself a sort of positive feedback loop, as more people are exposed to the phenomenon, leading some to embrace it, which exposes more to it, some of whom embrace it, and so on. Third, homeschoolers won their legislative battles decisively. This has given the movement a momentum and sense of inevitability that has enhanced its profile considerably.

Fourth, homeschoolers have generally had allies in the popular press, who typically love a good David and Goliath story, especially when David can be counted on reliably to win at the statehouse. Finally, homeschooling has grown because its product has been seen thus far to be a success – most Americans who know homeschooled children have found them to be responsible, hardworking, intelligent, and capable, which has only enhanced the movement's profile.

A good bit of homeschooling's normalization, therefore, can be attributed to the movement's success. But what gave the movement such success? Murphy points to the frequent finding among historians that homeschoolers were and are very good at grassroots organizing. Most homeschoolers have long been part of support groups that connect individuals at the local level, and many of these local groups are affiliated with state-wide and national umbrella organizations. The intense level of social capital among the homeschooling community has proven decisive over and over in battles with public school bureaucrats in legislatures around the country, since homeschoolers were able to overwhelm their critics both in number and enthusiasm. The group-forming tendencies of homeschoolers have the macro result of securing accommodating state legislation, and these tendencies also provide the micro benefit of meeting the social, academic, and spiritual needs of individual children and (usually) mothers.

Murphy next chronicles the legislative history of homeschooling, summarizing what many historians have explained as the remarkable victory of homeschoolers in state after state to change laws to make what they do clearly legal and relatively free of regulation, though some states regulate the practice more heavily than do others.

Chapter three concludes with a brief look at the growing diversity and hybridity of homeschooling, as more and more children experience a range of options such as dual enrollment programs, independent home-based public education (cyber charter schools, for example), and other alternatives.

In chapter four Murphy provides a summary of the various contextual factors and social forces that have combined to facilitate the growth of the homeschooling movement. He begins by returning us to the early days of the growth of public education, stressing how the changing economy, society, and politics of the 19th century were conducive to the spread of public schooling. Social, political, and economic changes in the late 19th and early 20th centuries, however, began to alter the character of the heretofore localized public schools in a more centralizing and bureaucratic direction. These developments in turn led to the growth of anti-statist ideologies and critiques of managerial expertise.

Just as economic, social, and political changes led to the rise of government schooling, so further changes in these three domains have contributed to the rise of homeschooling. Key political and social developments include decentralization, direct democracy, parental empowerment, and the ideology of choice, along with the rise of the religious right particularly and a more conservative national mood generally in the 1980s. The key economic factor is the rise of privatization and market-based ideologies and concomitant reduction of the public sector, a development frequently dubbed libertarianism.

Having canvassed all of the post-2008 scholarship that has attempted a grand narrative account, what can we conclude? With the exception of Andrade's technological determinism (2008), which on principle does not permit contingency, the macro historians tend to stress a combination of broad sociocultural forces *and* human agency when explaining the rise and growth of homeschooling in the United States. The difficulty for broad social forces-type arguments, however, is in demonstrating causality. The rise of homeschooling happened at the same time as or immediately after many social trends underway in the 1960s–1980s. But which of any of them were truly causal? History is not science and thus has a very difficult time proving causal assertions. It is much better at providing descriptive, evidence-based narratives about specific events in time, examples of which are discussed in the next several sections.

Specific Topics

Biography and autobiography

Since 2008 several biographies or autobiographies of significance for the history of US homeschooling have been published. This section summarizes some of the most important.

Aiken (2009) describes the childhood experiences of the renowned author Joan Aiken, emphasizing her early education at home between the years 1924 and 1936. She was taught by her mother, who emphasized a richly literary education. Transition at age 12 to institutional schooling proved a very traumatic experience, and the young Joan often retreated to the rich imaginative world she had formed during her childhood domestic education.

Rice (2010) is an autobiographical account by former Secretary of State Condoleezza Rice, the first African American woman to hold the position. She devotes a significant amount of time to her childhood in 1950s and 1960s Birmingham, AL, including material about her early childhood education in music and literacy and a first grade year taught at home by her mother. This was in 1960, well before the organized homeschooling movement, and in segregated Birmingham to boot. At the end of the year Rice took the school entrance exam and scored at the third grade level in math and the fifth grade level in reading, which more than qualified her to jump straight into second grade at her local segregated black school.

McVicar (2015) is a book-length, major study of one of the most important figures in the early history of American homeschooling, Rousas J. Rushdoony. Gaither (2008) had included Rushdoony in the pantheon of early homeschooling leaders alongside John Holt and the Moores, and for this he was criticized in a key review by Cochrane, who said:

> while Gaither makes a good case for Rushdoony's interest, promotion, and support of home education, and even his influence on some of its leaders, it remains questionable

> how much influence, if any, he had on parents' decisions to teach their children at home or to what extent his Christian Reconstructionist views were infused in the movement (Cochrane 2010, 69).

McVicar's book, far and away the most thorough and well-sourced account published on Rushdoony's life, work, and influence, lays the question to rest. In six powerful chapters grounded in a rich study of Rushdoony's personal papers and journals, oral histories, and other primary sources, McVicar explains in great detail the intellectual pedigree, connections and funding networks, and influence of Rushdoony and the Christian Reconstruction movement he founded.

Chapter one briefly covers Rushdoony's early life as his family narrowly escaped the Armenian genocide during World War I and as Rushdoony began his ministry among American Indians in Nevada. While on the reservation he established a wide-ranging correspondence with various Protestant thinkers, most notably Cornelius Van Til, whose Biblical Presuppositionalism proved foundational for Rushdoony's Reconstructionist vision. McVicar masterfully situates Rushdoony's intellectual development within the broader intellectual context of mid-20th century American life.

Chapter two chronicles Rushdoony's growing radicalism, as his unabashed sectarianism put him at odds both with the Presbyterian Church USA, under which he was ordained, and with the broader conservative movement developing in the 1950s and 1960s. Instead, Rushdoony allied with groups that have been little studied by historians but very influential among conservative intellectuals, groups like Spiritual Mobilization, the William Volker Charities Fund, and the Center for American Studies.

Chapter three explains Rushdoony's expanding reach as he worked with grassroots organizations in California and obtained funding from individuals like Walter Knott and groups like Women for America that enabled him to found the Chalcedon Foundation and to devote himself full time to writing and activism.

Chapter four provides an excellent summation of Rushdoony's Christian Reconstructionist philosophy, which seeks to write Biblical Law into American government so as to return the nation to what Rushdoony believed to be its historic founding mission as a Protestant Nation God intended to use to usher in the Christian Millennium.

Chapter five is perhaps the most significant for the history of homeschooling, for it explains the wide reach of Rushdoony's ideas among his many followers and imitators. McVicar is very clear on how the family was at the very heart of Rushdoony's project, and how many in the homeschooling movement understood what they were doing through his framework. Key figures in popularizing Rushdoony's vision among homeschoolers included the influential lawyer John W. Whitehead and Franky Schaeffer, son of the famous Christian apologist Francis Schaeffer, along with their financial backer, billionaire heir Howard Ahmanson. Through these and other second-generation reconstructionists thousands of Christian homeschoolers became exposed to Rushdoony's ideas. His books and speeches became fixtures of many Christian homeschooling curricula, and Rushdoony was called upon many times to offer expert witness at key homeschooling court cases across the country.

Chapter six and a brief conclusion detail the sordid history of the various schisms, personality cults, and extremist factions that emerged out of Reconstructionism. Many of these movements emphasized and continue to emphasize homeschooling, and their radical brand of patriarchal sectarianism has exerted much influence among Christian homeschoolers, particularly those frequently dubbed "Quiverfull" (Joyce 2009).

Curriculum

Since 2008 several publications have shed light on the history of homeschooling curriculum. This section summarizes some of the most important.

Laats (2010) uses a rigorous historical methodology of intensive examination of archival primary sources, oral histories, and contextual historiography to tell the stories of the three most influential and long-lasting Christian curricular options. All three began as curricula for Christian day schools but eventually spread to homeschooling as well. All three were self-consciously created as alternatives to the "secular humanism" and "progressivism" of public education curriculum. Yet for all their similarities the three curriculum providers were often very forthright in their denunciations of one another for various transgressions.

The oldest, Accelerated Christian Education (ACE), consisted mostly of a series of workbooks students worked through at their own pace with only minimal supervision. Its low cost, early availability, and limited need for teacher supervision made it very popular, especially in the 1980s, though some criticized it for its dependence on tedious worksheets and others for its occasional use of non-Christian figures (Confucius, for example) or progressive-sounding language.

A Beka, a curriculum created by Arlin and Beka Horton originally for their Pensacola Christian Schools, became a popular alternative to ACE among fundamentalists looking for a more self-consciously conservative and Protestant alternative. Influenced by conservative educational theorists like Max Rafferty and Rudolph Flesch, the Hortons emphasized phonics, rote memorization, and authoritarian teachers to help students discipline their sinful natures. Entire lessons were scripted so that no open-ended discussion leading to questions that might challenge the Truth would occur. The Hortons rejected progressive ideals like critical thinking and learning by doing, arguing that such things are actually a by-product of subject matter mastery. The actual content of A Beka consisted largely of out-of-print textbooks from a time when American schools inculcated heavy doses of Protestant morality and patriotism.

In direct contrast to ACE's drill-and-kill worksheets and A Beka's "no fun" direct instruction in dated texts by unquestioned authorities, the Bob Jones curriculum was an original product, emanating from the professors at Bob Jones University (BJU). The guiding spirit of the endeavor was Walter G. Fremont, dean of BJU's School of

Education from 1953 to 1990. BJU affirmed the importance of well-educated teachers, of conceptual learning in addition to memorization, of thoughtful discussions, field trips, and flexibility. BJU's school of education taught its student teachers Bloom's taxonomy, class management skills, and how to make school fun. Many homeschooling families have used BJU's complete curriculum, though homeschoolers have even more frequently chosen to do exactly what many Christian day schools did – choose eclectically from these and other curricula to suit their needs.

Krause (2012), whose theoretical argument was summarized earlier in this chapter, should also be mentioned in this section on curriculum. Her insightful history of the early years of Christian homeschooling curricula begins with the paucity of options in the early 1980s and the lack of openness to homeschoolers by established Christian curriculum providers like A Beka and Bob Jones. Many mothers during these early years created their own curricula, and some of them went on to publish and market their products to other homeschoolers. Krause pays special attention to four such products: Cornerstone Curriculum, Beautiful Feet Books, Diana Waring Presents, and Cadron Creek Christian Curriculum.

Cornerstone Curriculum, created by David and Shirley Quine for their own use and first sold to others in 1983, was heavily influenced by the popular worldview perspective of Francis Schaeffer, who believed that Christianity should be integrated into all areas of life and hence into every subject in the curriculum. Schaeffer also believed that the United States was founded as a Protestant nation with a special mission to the world, and Cornerstone's history curriculum reflects that conviction as well. Beautiful Feet Books, created by Rhea Berg, drew inspiration from 19th century British educator Charlotte Mason to bring out-of-print "living books" to children. Berg began selling her collection of old books in 1984 and quickly organized them into several comprehensive historical curricula whose purpose was to use mostly 19th century works of historical fiction to teach both historical understanding and Christian character. Diana Waring, also influenced by both Schaeffer and Mason, began creating her own history curriculum in 1992 and selling it in the late 1990s. Her histories emphasize the Providential direction of history by God from ancient times to the present, and she too draws upon a wide range of historical fiction and Christian biography to bring the story to life. Cadron Creek, created more recently by Margie Gray, takes a Unit Studies approach that unites all subjects around one common theme or text. For example, Gray's first curriculum grounds study of every subject in the famed *Little House* books. In her analysis Krause unpacks significant differences in tone and sense of Christian mission in these curricula.

Mazama and Lundy (2013, 2014) do not engage explicitly with the history of curriculum, but given the uniqueness of their subject some of the data they provide can help historians get purchase on one aspect of the phenomenon. In a series of five articles that were eventually combined into a book, Mazama and Lundy describe and analyze the results of a large-scale study they performed on a geographically diverse sample of African American homeschoolers. Two of those articles discuss how some African American parents approach curriculum.

In their 2013 article Mazama and Lundy reveal that about one quarter of their sample were explicitly Afrocentric in their pedagogical orientation. The authors provide a solid history of the fraught relationship between African Americans and the public school curriculum and include many engaging quotations from Black homeschoolers about why they find both the public school and much private Christian school curriculum unacceptable. These homeschooling parents are able to use their own home space to inculcate a more positive sense of self and of race consciousness in their children.

In their 2014 article, in contrast, Mazama and Lundy reveal that about 15% of their sample explicitly repudiated this Afrocentric perspective, describing their homeschooling motivations and practices in ways that were nearly indistinguishable from those of white conservative Christians. Though they do not discuss the precise curricular content of this group's homeschooling lives, the revelation that there is a significant group of African American homeschoolers who speak in color-blind terms and reject African heritage is of great historical significance.

Regions

Since 2008 several publications have shed light on the history of homeschooling in specific locales. This section summarizes some of the most important.

Millman and Millman (2008) includes an important chapter on the history of homeschooling groups in New Jersey. It begins by connecting homeschooling to the "emergence" scholarship of John H. Holland, explaining that homeschooling is an unplanned and uncontrolled system of networks built "from the bottom up by thousands upon thousands of individuals making free choices about education" who nevertheless coalesce into "educational communities that are as stable and distinctive" as the city neighborhoods studied by Jane Jacobs or the leaderless ant colonies studied by Deborah Gordon. The Millmans also draw on the "social capital" framework of Robert Putnam's influential *Bowling Alone*. They explain how homeschool groups provide rich social bonds of connectivity and reciprocity for their members.

After laying out this context, the Millmans narrate the history of some of New Jersey's most important homeschooling groups. Details are provided for Nancy Plent's founding of the Unschoolers Network in coordination with John Holt in the late 1970s, one of the most important organizations of its kind until the early 2000s, when it faded from the scene. The Millmans also describe the much larger and tightly organized Friendship Learning Center, an exclusively Protestant organization. The Millmans conclude that despite ideological differences, when threats to homeschooler freedoms appear, as they did in 2004 in the New Jersey State Legislature, homeschoolers quickly put aside differences and rally to the cause with shows of such overwhelming force that regulators quickly back down.

Coleman (2010) provides a detailed account of the history of homeschooling in Delaware County (which includes the city of Muncie), Indiana, explaining how a few isolated homeschoolers from very different perspectives came together in the early 1980s to secure homeschooling legal freedom. They did this through a favorable Seventh Circuit Court of Appeals ruling in *Mazanec v. North Judson-San Pierre School Corporation* (1985), which found that the Indiana school law's "instruction equivalent" language applied to homeschooling. Coleman describes how early Muncie-area homeschoolers were influenced by John Holt and Raymond Moore and worked together across religious lines. But by the 1990s those lines had hardened considerably. In 1993 the Delaware County Christian Homeschool Association (DCCHA, later changed to DCCHC) was formed exclusively for Christians. In 1998 this already conservative Christian group amended its statement of faith to make it even more exclusive. Some disgruntled homeschoolers left and tried unsuccessfully to found an alternative group, but DCCHC continued to grow until its peak in 2001 with about 300 families in Delaware County, dominating the homeschooling scene and serving as the public face of homeschooling in the county and first contact for families thinking about starting. The DCCHC worked closely with the exclusively Christian state-wide Indiana group, which itself was closely affiliated with the Home School Legal Defense Association (HSLDA).

But then came the internet. By 2005 the internet had transformed the way homeschoolers communicated, and especially the way prospective homeschoolers got information. The DCCHC's monopoly was broken. In 2005 the DCCHC disbanded, partly because its key leaders had graduated from homeschooling, partly because the internet took over its functions. As Coleman puts it, the internet has "democratized the flow of information, eliminating the role once played by gatekeepers such as the DCCHC" (81). It has also fragmented the homeschooling community in Delaware County. Upon the demise of the DCCHC, many smaller cooperatives and support groups have been formed, often along religious lines.

Krause (2012) has already been mentioned twice in this chapter, but it is worthy of inclusion in this section as well for its many revealing quotations from pioneer homeschoolers in Texas and its extensive coverage of the *Leeper* case and other aspects of Texas homeschooling in the 1980s and 1990s.

Hoffman and Hoffman (2014) is an interesting book-length collection produced by a mother–daughter homeschooling team that relates some of the history of homeschooling in Minnesota through first person accounts. The Hoffmans begin with a timeline of the history of homeschooling in Minnesota that, based as it is upon first person recollections and opinions, is not always accurate in its chronological details or legal interpretations. They next present twenty-seven chapters, each of which features an interview with one or more Minnesota homeschooling pioneers. The Hoffmans themselves are conservative Christians, so their timeline and contributor list stress that side of the movement, though they do include an interview with Jeanne Newstrom, a more left-liberal homeschooling mother who appealed her homeschooling conviction to the Minnesota Supreme Court, which declared in 1985 that the Minnesota Compulsory Attendance Law was unconstitutionally vague.

The interviews are arranged in a roughly chronological fashion and collectively tell the story of the separation in the mid-1980s of conservative Christian

Minnesotans from other homeschoolers as they founded and grew the Minnesota Association of Christian Home Educators (MÂCHÉ). Interviews with founders of other Christian Minnesota Homeschooling organizations and resources like Teaching Effective Academics and Character at Home (TEACH), Home Grown Kids, Heppner and Heppner Construction (1985–2006), and Heppner's Legacy Homeschool Resources (2006–present) are featured. The Hoffmans interview Michael Farris of HSLDA, who describes his early encounters with some key homeschoolers in Minnesota. They also interview State Senator Gen Olson, who was the central figure in the statehouse working to pass the first homeschooling law in Minnesota in 1987, to defeat a bill in 2001 that would have increased regulations, and to pass a bill in 2011 that significantly reduced regulations.

Legal

Martin (2010) offers a comparative study of the legal situation pertaining to home education in the United States and Germany. For this chapter we will ignore the Germany portion, which constitutes part one of Martin's study. Part two begins with a review of the history of compulsory schooling in the United States, drawn largely from very dated historiography. Martin next summarizes the history of homeschooling litigation and legislation. Throughout his discussions of the standard court cases typically covered in historical accounts, Martin offers interpretations and asides that make it clear that he is approaching the issue as a friend of homeschooling with a libertarian, parental-rights orientation. His historical account is also mostly provided as a means for situating his discussion of the current legal situation. Professional historians tend to frown on this sort of thing as it tends to reduce history to a servant discipline of policy and to produce anachronisms, but in general Martin's summaries are reliable despite his clear argumentative slant.

After providing the historical background, Martin investigates in more detail two recent homeschooling cases, the 2008 *Jonathan L.* decision in California that caused such an uproar and the 2008 *Combs* case in Pennsylvania that unsuccessfully sought to argue that homeschoolers with a First Amendment religious objection to regulations did not have to abide by them. Martin's careful examination of these recent cases and their implications for First Amendment jurisprudence need not concern us in this chapter on the history of homeschooling, though it is a notable contribution to the broader legal scholarship. Martin goes on to provide more analysis of parental rights jurisprudence and to offer predictions about future trends both in the United States and in Germany.

Waddell (2010), whose political outlook is the polar opposite of Martin's (2010), covers much the same ground as Martin's text just summarized. He begins with a history of the homeschooling movement itself, describing how activist homeschoolers have been so successful in transforming the legal and political landscape in their favor since the 1980s. He explains in some detail the key role of HSLDA in all of this, noting especially how they have claimed over and over, for years now, that the First and Fourteenth Amendments give parents a constitutional right to homeschool and that state regulations violate this right.

Next Waddell claims that we are perhaps in the midst of a gradual process of re-regulation, a claim that the last six years of legislative history have not borne out, as many states have in fact loosened regulations in recent years. But Waddell asserts that as homeschooling continues to grow the practice is coming under increased scrutiny. He mentions efforts (all unsuccessful) in New Jersey, Michigan, and New Hampshire to increase regulations and focuses especially on Washington, DC which in 2008 became "the first jurisdiction in the United States in over 15 years" to successfully increase regulations (2010, 554).

Like Martin, (2010) Waddell's history is simply a prop for his own arguments, but also like Martin (2010), he does a good job summarizing the major cases typically covered in historiography of homeschooling jurisprudence: *Meyer*, *Pierce*, *Yoder*. Like Martin, he wades into the murky waters of First Amendment jurisprudence that will not concern us here. Together Martin (2010) and Waddell (2010) illustrate an important stream of historiography of homeschooling, namely that of lawyers without historical training and not particularly interested in the fine contours of historical contingency nevertheless delving into the history of jurisprudence as prolegomena to their own proposals for the increased or decreased regulation of homeschooling today. This summary will not cover all of the recent legal articles in this vein. Martin (2010) and Waddell (2010) serve as exemplars of the genre, one advocating less regulation and the other arguing for more.

Krause (2012) should be mentioned yet again for its excellent and thorough treatment of the legal and legislative battles in Texas in the early and mid-1980s. Krause briefly compares developments in Texas with those in Oregon and Arizona, whose homeschooling activists employed different strategies but were no less successful.

In a lengthy footnote Krause offers helpful summaries of most of the early 20th century cases related to homeschooling, and in the main body of her text she analyzes thirty legal cases spanning twenty-two states from the late 1970s on, featuring cases with a human-interest element and a Religious Freedom claim. The general thrust of the decisions covered show that state courts have consistently found that the famous *Yoder* Supreme Court decision about Amish education did not mean that homeschoolers have a First Amendment free exercise right to flout government homeschooling regulations. Homeschoolers, having lost in the courts, turned to state legislatures to realize their deregulatory agenda.

Mawdsley and Cumming (2012) covers the background and current legal situation pertaining to state regulation of private schools, of whom homeschools are a part in many states. They begin with the famous *Dartmouth College* decision of 1819 and work through the other relevant Supreme Court cases to set the stage. They then offer a topical summary of several aspects of jurisprudence on private schools and homeschools: homeschooling regulations, participation by non-public school students in public school extracurricular and curricular activities, special education services, federal regulations (mostly pertaining to civil rights issues).

The general conclusion reached is that courts have generally upheld the state's right to regulate private (and home) schools, but that state legislatures have typically been very lax in their regulations and slow to prosecute violations. The one exception is in cases of race or gender discrimination, where courts and legislatures have generally held private entities to the same standards as public institutions even if religious belief is cited as the justification for violations.

Homeschooling Historiography – Needs and Opportunities for Study

In this section I would like to lay out nine topics in need of scholarly attention to enhance our understanding of the history of home education in the United States. I will work from the specific and limited to the grand and abstract.

1. **Biographies**. I described above McVicar's (2015) excellent recent study of Rousas J. Rushdoony. We need similarly rich and comprehensive biographies of Raymond and Dorothy Moore and of John Holt, studies that go beyond their published work to examine the fullness of their lives. Though no other figures loom so large in the history of homeschooling as Holt and the Moores, there are several second-tier individuals whose contributions merit serious academic study as well. Mary Pride, John W. Whitehead, Bill Gothard, Gregg Harris, Michael Farris, Cathy Duffy, Mark and Helen Hegener, David and Micki Colfax, Linda Dobson, and many other influential figures would be worthy candidates for biographical coverage that would shed light on their homeschooling practice and influence.
2. **State histories**. I noted earlier in this chapter that historians have provided excellent coverage of the legal and legislative history of the homeschooling movement in a few key states. Texas, Hawaii, Georgia, the Carolinas, and Indiana have all been studied in depth by at least one scholar. But the histories of the other states are wide open territory. Activists and insiders have published (sometimes self-published) accounts from their own point of view in some states, but for many states there is not even that. It would be a wonderful thing were every state's story to be covered by a historian dedicated to the topic. With such knowledge in place it would then be much easier to tell the national story, as chronology, themes, key individuals and organizations, and legal and legislative trends would be much easier to map out.
3. **Curriculum**. As described earlier, Laats (2010) provided excellent coverage of the early histories of the ACE, A Beka, and Bob Jones curricula, and Krause (2012) did the same for Cornerstone Curriculum, Beautiful Feet Books, Diana Waring Presents, and Cadron Creek Christian Curriculum. Though not described above, the classical education movement has received at least some historical assessment as well (Liethart 2008). Many other specific curricula and/or curricular approaches would be great topics for historical study. Potential

examples of specific curricula are legion, but they include Alpha Omega, Apologia, Sonlight, Rod and Staff, Tapestry of Grace, Saxon Math, Singapore, and Math-U-See. Potential examples of approaches whose histories need to be told include the Charlotte Mason Method, the Unit Study approach, and unschooling.

4. **Groups**. Much has been written about the Protestant Christian homeschooling community and movement. But far less is known about the histories of other groups of homeschoolers. A good study of the history of home education among Mormons would be most welcome, as would a history of homeschooling among Seventh-Day Adventists. Both groups have long utilized the home for the education of their children. While African American homeschoolers have been studied quite a bit, there has been little to no work, historical or otherwise, on homeschoolers of Latino/a descent or on Native Americans, Asians, Catholics, or Jews.
5. **Networks and strategies**. As with many other political issues, though the legal and legislative history of homeschooling took place largely at the state level, very similar developments happened in many if not most states at about the same time. Study of the political networks and organizations that fomented these trans-state developments is desperately needed. HSLDA, which became a significant player in such developments in 1985, is certainly an important part of the story, but, especially for the earlier period, we need to know more about how, and why homeschooling burst onto the scene like it did in the early 1980s, and who made that happen. How did state leaders keep track of what was happening in other states? How were the national networks of Holt, the Moores, and Rushdoony maintained? How did they change over time? How did the lawyers and lobbyists go about furthering their sides of the movement through establishing connections at the state and court houses? What role did churches and other community organizations play in it all?
6. **Domestic education**. Tutoring and other non-movement forms of domestic education did not disappear when homeschooling burst onto the scene in the late 1970s and early 1980s. Aside from the homeschooling movement itself, how was the home used to educate children and adults? Private, live-in tutors, online distance education, self-study using various forms of technologically mediated instruction, the architecture and geography of the home itself as education, and much else would fall into this broad category.
7. **Social history**. Scarcely anything has been written about such topics as the actual practices in which children and (usually) their mothers engaged as homeschoolers, the impact of the decision to homeschool on the family and the family's social networks, and the ways daily homeschooling changed over time within individual families and across the decades more generally. Little of the published scholarship from the past will be of much help here, for survey questions about parental motivations and so forth cannot take us very far. Oral histories, especially of adults who were homeschooled as children, will need to

be collected and analyzed. Visual and print media from old practical magazines might yield insight. Documentary evidence such as meeting minutes or other relics kept by some of the larger state-wide organizations (especially recordings of old sessions) could prove insightful.

8. **History of ideas**. Several overlapping ideological orientations have swept the Christian homeschooling movement. Though Joyce (2009) and others have begun to bring together the various strains that make up what she calls the "Christian Patriarchy movement," much more could be said about the intellectual roots of these beliefs and their connections to broader themes in American history. Even less has been written about the history of ideas like unschooling. Homeschooling's connection to so many diverse ideological orientations makes it a particularly fascinating subject for intellectual history.
9. **Longitudinal study**. Many if not most homeschooling parents choose this approach to education largely out of the desire to cocoon their children away from what they believe to be harmful outside influences emanating from the broader culture and to prepare their children to be faithful Christian adults (Vigilant, Trefethren, and Anderson 2013; Hoelzle 2013). Homeschoolers are not the first Americans to try to concoct a childhood educational experience that will ensure a desired adult outcome. A history of such efforts, whether through homeschooling or other strategies, would be most welcome.

A history like this could take several possible forms. It could consist of longitudinal studies of homeschooled children. Many of the qualitative studies done in the 1980s and 1990s would be wonderful bases for a follow-up study now or in the future. A very few studies of this nature have already been published, and the results are intriguing (Bolle-Brummond and Wessel 2012; Hanna 2012). Something similar was attempted by Bengtson and colleagues in a thirty-five-year longitudinal study of the religious beliefs and practices of three generations of families (2013). While generalizations about homeschooling as such cannot be made from what are essentially life-spanning or even generations-spanning anecdotes, if many small-scale studies come to similar conclusions then we are getting somewhere.

A second possible approach would be to look at the deeper history of American family life to see if there are discernable patterns in terms of what parenting strategies succeeded in passing on parental values to children and what failed. Specific subgroups like the Amish, Mormons (especially the FLDS (Fundamentalist Church of Jesus Christ of Latter-Day Saints)), Jehovah's Witnesses, and other religious outsiders would make for powerful cross-generational study. Population study using census data or ancestry databases might prove fruitful. Case studies of well-documented families might yield promising results. Such "collective biography" could shed important light on the likely impact homeschooling will or will not have on the children who experience it, making historical conclusions, if not actually predictive, at least suggestive of what the future might hold (Davies and Gannon 2006).

References

Aiken, Lizza. 2009. “Growing Up with Joan Aiken: A Daughter’s View.” *Horn Book Magazine*. May/June: 253–258.

Andrade, Albert G. 2008. “An Exploratory Study of the Role of Technology in the Rise of Homeschooling.” PhD diss., Ohio University, Athens.

Bengtson, Vern L. 2013. *Faith and Families: How Religion is Passed Down across Generations*. New York: Oxford University Press.

Bloodworth, Robert Harrison. 1991. “A Legal History of Home Schooling in North Carolina.” EdD diss., University of North Carolina, Chapel Hill.

Bolle-Brummond, Mary Beth, and Roger D. Wessel. 2012. “Homeschooled Students in College: Background Influences, College Integration, and Environmental Pull Factors.” *Journal of Research in Education*, 22: 223–249.

Carper, James C. 1992. “Home Schooling, History, and Historians: The Past as Present.” *The High School Journal*, 75: 252–257.

Carper, James C. 2000. “Pluralism to Establishment to Dissent: The Religious and Educational Context of Home Schooling.” *Peabody Journal of Education*, 75: 8–19.

Cochran, Casey Patrick. 1993. “The Home School Movement in the United States: Georgia as a Test Case, 1979–1984.” PhD diss., Emory University, Atlanta.

Cochran, Casey Patrick. 2010. “Homeschool.” *History of Education Quarterly*, 50: 97–100.

Coleman, Rachel E. 2010. “Ideologues, Pedagogues, Pragmatics: A Case Study of the Homeschool Community in Delaware County, Indiana” MA thesis, Ball State University, MA.

Curren, Randall, and J. C. Blokhuis. 2011. “The Prima Facie Case Against Homeschooling.” *Public Affairs Quarterly*, 25: 1–19.

Davies, Bronwyn, and Susanne Gannon, eds. 2006. *Doing Collective Biography*. New York: Open University Press.

del Mar, David Peterson. 2011. *The American Family: From Obligation to Freedom*. New York: Palgrave Macmillan.

Drabsch, Talina. 2013. “Home Education in NSW.” *NSW Parliament E-Brief*, NSW Parliamentary Research Service, 7: 1–15.

Evangelisti, Silvia. 2013. “Learning from Home: Discourses on Education and Domestic Visual Culture in Early Modern Italy.” *History*, 98: 663–679.

Gaither, Milton. 2008. *Homeschool: An American History*. New York: Palgrave MacMillan.

Gaither, Milton. 2009. “Homeschooling in the USA: Past, Present, Future.” *Theory and Research in Education*, 7: 331–346.

Glover, Lorri. 2014. *Founders as Fathers: the Private Lives and Politics of the American Revolutionaries*. New Haven: Yale University Press.

Greenfield, Patricia M. 2009. “Linking Social Change and Developmental Change: Shifting Pathways of Human Development.” *Developmental Psychology*, 45: 401–418.

Griffith, Mary. 2007. *Viral Learning: Reflections on the Homeschooling Life*. Morrisville, NC: Lulu Press.

Hampel, Robert L. 2010. “The Business of Education: Home Study at Columbia University and the University of Wisconsin in the 1920s and 1930s.” *Teachers College Record*, 112: 2496–2517.

Hanna, Linda G. 2012. “Homeschooling Education: Longitudinal Study of Methods, Materials, and Curricula.” *Education and Urban Society*, 20: 1–23.

Herndon, Ruth W., and John E. Murray. 2009. *Children Bound to Labor: the Pauper Apprentice System in Early America*. Ithaca: Cornell University Press.

Hill, Paul T. 2000. "Home Schooling and the Future of Public Education." *Peabody Journal of Education*, 75: 20–31.

Hoelzle, Braden R. 2013. "The Transmission of Values and the Transition into Adulthood Within the Context of Home Education." *Journal of Research on Christian Education*, 22: 244–263.

Hoffman, Given, and Eileen Hoffman. 2014. *The Voices of the Pioneers: Homeschooling in Minnesota*. Bloomington, IN: AuthorHouse.

Hyde, Anne F. 2012. *Empires, Nations, and Families: A New History of the North American West, 1800–1860*. Lincoln: University of Nebraska Press.

Jeynes, William. 2012. "The Rise of Homeschooling as a Modern Educational Phenomenon in American Protestant Education." *International Handbook of Protestant Education*, edited by William Jeynes and David W. Robinson, 77–92. New York: Springer.

Jones, Steven L. 2008. *Religious Schooling in America: Private Education and Public Life*. Westport, CT: Praeger.

Joyce, Kathryn. 2009. *Quiverfull: Inside the Christian Patriarchy Movement*. Boston: Beacon.

Kelly, Anita E. 2008. "Pioneers on the Home Front: An Exploratory Study of Early Homeschoolers in Hawaii." PhD thesis, University of Hawai'i.

King, Wilma. 2011. *Stolen Childhood, Second Edition: Slave Youth in Nineteenth-Century America*. Bloomington: Indiana University Press.

Klicka, Christopher J. 2006. *Home School Heroes: The Struggle and Triumph of Home Schooling*. Nashville: Broadman and Holman.

Knowles, J. G., S. E. Marlow, and J. A. Muchmore. 1992. "From Pedagogy to Ideology: Origins and Phases of Home Education in the United States, 1970–1990." *American Journal of Education*, 100: 195–235.

Krause, Jean M. 2012. "Homeschooling: Constructing or Deconstructing Democracy." MA thesis, California State University Long Beach.

Kreager, Ronald, Jr. 2010. "Homeschooling: The Future of Education's Most Basic Institution." *University of Toledo Law Review*, 42: 227–233.

Laats, Adam. 2010. "Forging a Fundamentalist 'One Best System': Struggles Over Curriculum and Educational Philosophy for Christian Day Schools, 1970–1989." *History of Education Quarterly*, 49: 55–83.

Lambert, Tim. 1997. "A Home School History Lesson." Texas Home School Coalition. Accessed April 29, 2016. http://www.jcharper.net/index.php/interesting-maybe-useful/17-home-school-history.html

Lepore, Jill. 2015. "The Cobweb: Can the Internet be Archived?" *The New Yorker*. 26 January. Accessed April 29, 2016. http://www.newyorker.com/magazine/2015/01/26/cobweb

Liethart, Peter J. 2008. "The New Classical Schooling." *Intercollegiate Review*, 43: 3–12.

Martin, Aaron T. 2010. "Homeschooling in Germany and the United States." *Arizona Journal of International & Comparative Law*, 27: 225–282.

Marzluf, Phillip P. 2015. "The Pastoral Home School: Rural, Vernacular and Grassroots Literacies in Early Soviet Mongolia." *Central Asian Survey*, 34: 204–218.

Mawdsley, Ralph D., and J. Joy Cumming. 2012. "Government Regulation of Nonpublic Schools in the United States." *International Journal of Law & Education*, 17: 39–55.

Mazama, Ama, and Garvey Lundy. 2013. "African American Homeschooling and the Question of Curricular Cultural Relevance." *Journal of Negro Education*, 82: 123–138.

Mazama, Ama, and Garvey Lundy. 2014. "African American Homeschoolers: The Force of Faith and the Reality of Race in the Homeschooling Experience." *Religion and Education*, 41: 256–272.

McIlhenny, Ryan. 2003. "The Austin TEA Party: Homeschooling Controversy in Texas, 1986–1994." *Religion and Education*, 30: 62–83.

McVicar, Michael J. 2015. *Christian Reconstruction: R. J. Rushdoony and American Religious Conservatism*. Chapel Hill: University of North Carolina Press.

Meighan, Roland. 2007. *John Holt*. London: Continuum.

Millman, Gregory, and Martine Millman. 2008. *Homeschooling: A Family's Journey*. New York: Penguin.

Morice, Linda C. 2012. "A Place Called Home: Educational Reform in a Concord, Massachusetts School, 1897–1914." *History of Education*, 41: 437–456.

Murphy, Joseph. 2012. *Homeschooling in America: Capturing and Assessing the Movement*. Thousand Oaks, CA: Corwin.

Murphy, Joseph F. 2013. "Explaining the Change in Homeschooling, 1970–2010." *Home School Researcher*, 29: 1–13.

Olatunji, Michael Olalekan. 2014. "Contemporary Homeschooling in the Republic of South Africa: Some Lessons for Other African Nations." *Middle Eastern and African Journal of Educational Research*, 9: 4–16.

Olsen, Chad. 2009. "Constitutionality of Home Education: How the Supreme Court and American History Endorse Parental Choice." *B.Y.U. Education and Law Journal*, 2: 399–423.

Paciorkowski, Szymon. 2014. "Homeschooling in Poland? Legal Status and Arguments Used in Polish Debate over Home Education." *Social Transformations in Contemporary Society*, 2: 153–162.

Provasnik, Stephen. 2006. "Judicial Activism and the Origins of Parental Choice: The Court's Role in the Institutionalization of Compulsory Education in the United States, 1891–1925." *History of Education Quarterly*, 46: 311–347.

Rice, Condoleezza. 2010. *Extraordinary, Ordinary People: A Memoir of Family*. New York: Crown Publishers.

Richman, Howard. 1989. *Story of a Bill: Legalizing Homeschooling in Pennsylvania*. Kittanning, PA: Pennsylvania Homeschoolers.

Seelhoff, Cheryl L. 2000a. "A Homeschooler's History, Part I." *Gentle Spirit Magazine*, 6(9): 32–44.

Seeloff, Cheryl L. 2000b. "A Homeschooler's History, Part II." *Gentle Spirit Magazine*, 6(10): 66–70.

Seelhoff, Cheryl L. 2000c. "A Homeschooler's History of Homeschooling, Part III." *Gentle Spirit Magazine*, 6(11): 38–47.

Seelhoff, Cheryl L. 2001a. "A Homeschooler's History of Homeschooling, Part IV." *Gentle Spirit Magazine*, 7(1): 54–60.

Seelhoff, Cheryl L. 2001b. "A Homeschooler's History of Homeschooling, Part V." *Gentle Spirit Magazine*, 7(2): 1–6.

Seelhoff, Cheryl L. 2001c. "A Homeschooler's History of Homeschooling, Part VI." *Gentle Spirit Magazine*, 7(4): 1–6.

Smith, Manfred. 2007. "A Lifelong Journey: Twenty Years of Homeschooling." Maryland Home Education Association. Accessed April 29, 2016. http://www.mhea.com/features/journey.htm

Somerville, Scott W. 2001. "The Politics of Survival: Home Schoolers and the Law." Home School Legal Defense Association. Accessed April 29, 2016. https://www.hslda.org/docs/nche/000010/PoliticsOfSurvival.asp

Staroverova, T. I. 2011. "Home Education in Russia." *Russian Education and Society*, 53: 23–36.

Stevens, Mitchell L. 2001. *Kingdom of Children: Culture and Controversy in the Homeschooling Movement*. Princeton, NJ: Princeton University Press.

Tyler, Zan P., and Carper, James C. 2000. "From Confrontation to Accommodation: Home Schooling in South Carolina." *Peabody Journal of Education*, 75: 32–48.

Van Galen, Jane Ann. 1986. "Schooling in Private: A Study of Home Education." Ph.D. diss. Chapel Hill: The University of North Carolina.

Van Galen, Jane. 1987. "Explaining Home Education: Parents' Accounts of Their Decisions to Teach Their Own Children." *Urban Review*, 19: 161–177.

Van Galen, Jane A. 1988. "Ideology, Curriculum and Pedagogy in Home Education." *Education and Urban Society*, 21: 52–68.

Van Galen, Jane. 1991. "Ideologues and Pedagogues: Parents Who Teach Their Children at Home." *Home Schooling: Political, Historical, and Pedagogical Perspectives*, edited by Jane Van Galen and Mary Anne Pitman, 63–76. Norwood, NJ: Ablex Pub.

Vasconcelos, Caria Celi Chaves. 2013. "Domestic Education in Nineteenth Century Brazil: Aspects of European Influence on the Performance of Tutors and Private Teachers." *Social and Education History*, 2: 1–22.

Vieux, Andrea. 2014. "The Politics of Homeschools: Religious Conservatives and Regulation Requirements." *Social Science Journal*, 51, 556–563.

Vigilant, Lee Garth, Lauren Wold Trefethren, and Tyler C. Anderson. 2013. "You Can't Rely on Somebody Else to Teach Them Something they Don't Believe': Impressions of Legimitation Crisis and Socialization Control in the Narratives of Christian Homeschooling Fathers." *Humanity and Society*, 37: 201–224.

Waddell, Timothy Brandon. 2010. "Bringing It All Back Home: Establishing a Coherent Constitutional Framework for the Re-regulation of Homeschooling." *Vanderbilt Law Review*, 63: 541–597.

Wilhelm, Gretchen M., and Michael W. Firmin. 2009. "Historical and Contemporary Developments in Home School Education." *Journal of Research on Christian Education*, 18: 303–315.

Wilson, Lisa. 2014. *A History of Stepfamilies in Early America*. Chapel Hill: University of North Carolina Press.

Zur Nedden, Natalie. 2008. "Reflections on Homeschooling, Mothering, and Social Change: The Life History of Wendy Priesnitz." PhD thesis, University of Toronto.

2

Using Survey Data Sets to Study Homeschooling

Eric Isenberg

I. Overview[1]

This chapter describes survey data available for studying homeschooling. The focus is principally on nationally representative cross-sections of US schoolchildren. In addition to describing the strengths and limitations of each data set, I discuss what is known about the number of homeschooled children in the United States, and how the number has changed over time. Finally, I discuss some suggestions for future research, drawing on the data currently available. In some respects, this chapter updates an earlier discussion in Isenberg (2007).

Survey data of US households may be used not only to estimate the total number of homeschooled children but also to develop a big picture of homeschooling by presenting information about both deeply committed homeschoolers and more transient cases of homeschooling. Much of the data on homeschooling are qualitative, based on a relatively small number of in-depth interviews with families that homeschool their children. By contrast, survey data can disclose several phenomena that are not discussed in depth in qualitative work. For example, it is common for families to homeschool one child but send other children to public or private school. As a second example, much homeschooling is short-lived, lasting just a year or two before children attend (or return to) a conventional school (Isenberg 2007).

Another advantage of survey data is that the data include comparable information on children who are not homeschooled. Such information is useful in understanding relationships between family characteristics and homeschooling. For

The Wiley Handbook of Home Education, First Edition. Edited by Milton Gaither.

example, a cursory study of homeschooling families may suggest that mothers with preschool children at home are also likely to homeschool older, school-age siblings. By examining families with preschool- and school-age children who choose both to homeschool and to send children to public or private school, one can estimate the degree to which the presence of preschool children at home makes homeschooling more likely. With survey data, one can also calculate straightforward tabulations of averages and categorical differences as well as rely on more sophisticated statistical modeling techniques. In this way, it is possible to compare homeschooling families to families that do not homeschool (without accounting for differences) as well as to non-homeschooling families when statistically accounting for observable differences.

Nonetheless, survey data sets also have limitations. First, even surveys with the most extensive modules on homeschooling lack the type of in-depth information that can result from individualized conversations with homeschooling parents and children. Second, data are scarce on academic outcomes for homeschoolers, leaving the biggest question about homeschooling – its academic effectiveness – unanswered. Finally, most data sets that include at least a modest number of homeschooled children are cross-sectional. They do not follow the same families over time, so it is not possible to track the development of individual homeschooled children.

Despite various limitations, research using large survey data sets complements the work based on in-depth interviews and other qualitative techniques. By combining insights from both methods, researchers can uncover a fuller picture of what motivates parents to homeschool their children and how homeschooled children are similar to or different from children who attend public or private schools.

II. Nationally Representative Cross-sectional Surveys

Researchers seeking to study homeschooling by using nationally representative cross-sections of households have two main options for data: (1) the National Household Education Survey (NHES) and (2) the National Survey of Children's Health (NSCH). The purpose of each data set is distinct. Accordingly, the types of research questions that may be asked depend on the data. The common thread between the two data sets is that they ask directly about homeschooling as a response to a question about school choice. The result is robust data as to which children are homeschooled versus those educated in public or private schools. In some other data sets, households' responses to questions about homeschooling help resolve missing data on school choice. In a third type of data set, homeschooled children are included with children attending private school rather than given their own category.

In particular, each survey collects information on school-age children from an adult in the household (generally one of the parents) and directly asks all respondents if a child is homeschooled. For example, the 2007 NHES asks the following question:

PB3. Some parents decide to educate their children at home rather than send them to school. Is (CHILD) being schooled at home?

YES .... 1 (GO TO PB4)
NO .... 2 (GO TO 2ND BOX AFTER PB6)

By contrast, the 2013 National Survey on Drug Use and Health (NSDUH) asks school-age youth directly about homeschooling as the second part of a two-question series:

YE09 [IF CURNTAGE = 12–17] Have you attended any type of school at any time during the past 12 months?
1 Yes
2 No
DK/REF

YE09a [IF YE09 = 2 OR DK/REF] Some parents decide to educate their children at home rather than send them to school. Have you been home-schooled at any time during the past 12 months?
1 Yes
2 No
DK/REF

By asking the homeschooling question only to those who have not attended any school in the last 12 months, the NSDUH likely misclassifies homeschooled children who might answer "yes" to the first question on the grounds that they attended school at home during the past year, as distinct from being dropouts or truants. Based on the same series of questions, another group of homeschooled children – those who attend school for a specific activity during the week – may not be labeled as homeschooled because an appropriate "yes" to the first question precludes them from being asked the second question. In addition, in some states, parents legally homeschool by registering as their own private school or as part of a private school. In this case, students may also be inclined to answer "yes" to the first question. In fact, the percentage of children classified as homeschooled in data sets based on a two-question approach has always been lower than that of a contemporaneous data set that uses a direct approach.

National Household Education Survey (NHES)

The NHES, authorized by the National Center for Education Statistics (NCES), is the closest source of "official" information about the characteristics of homeschooled children and their families. NCES routinely publishes estimates of the number of homeschooled children in the United States following the release of a new round of survey data (Henke et al. 2000; Bielick, Chandler, and Broughman 2001; Princiotta, Bielick, and Chapman 2004; Bielick 2009; Redford and Battle forthcoming).

The purpose of the NHES is to provide descriptive data on educational activities taking place within households, mostly focused on adult–child interactions. The NHES has been administered 10 times, starting in 1991. It was administered approximately every other year from 1991 to 2007 and then again in 2012. The one exception to "every other year" was that the fourth NHES was conducted in 1996 rather than in 1997. Otherwise, the NHES data were collected in every odd-numbered year from 1991 to 2007. Westat conducted survey administration and data collection through 2007; the US Census Bureau did so in 2012. Each administration of the NHES collects data through several surveys; there have been eight types of surveys in all.[2] The surveys vary by year. The two surveys with the most homeschooling data are the Parent and Family Involvement Survey (NHES-PFI) and the Before- and After-School Programs and Activities Survey (NHES-ASPA).[3] The NHES-PFI was conducted in 1996, 1999, 2003, 2007, and 2012 while the NHES-ASPA was conducted in 2001 and 2005. Even though each round poses many of the same questions, the survey has evolved, with some questions added, others deleted, and the wording sometimes modified based on experience. Each time, the survey collects information from a new nationally representative cross-section of the population; it does not track the same respondents over time. Thus, the surveys provide a snapshot of homeschooling during each year of collection but do not allow for the measurement of long-term outcomes for homeschooled children. Table 2.1 provides basic information about these two NHES surveys, along with the same information for the NSCH.

From 1991 through 2007, the NHES participants were selected through a process of random-digit dialing of landline telephones. However, reliance on the landline telephone methodology has become problematic for two main reasons: (1) people have become less willing to cooperate with telephone-based surveys, leading to lower response rates; and (2) as more households have moved to reliance on cell phones only (and no landline telephones), it has become more difficult to obtain a random sample of households. In particular, households that are younger and/or lower-income are disproportionately unlikely to have a landline telephone (Noel, Stark, and Redford 2015). Owing to these concerns, beginning in 2012, the NHES switched to an address-based sample and administered surveys by mail.

The administration of the NHES surveys involves a two-part process. Selected households first complete a screener survey that asks about household members' basic demographics (sex, age, and relationship to other household members) and

Table 2.1 National cross-sectional data on homeschooling.

Data Set	*National Household Education Survey: Parent and Family Involvement Survey*					*National Household Education Survey: Before- and After-School Programs and Activities*		*National Survey of Children's Health*		
Year Collected	**1996**	**1999**	**2003**	**2007**	**2012**	**2001**	**2005**	**2003**	**2007**	**2011–2012**
Total number of children in data	20 792	24 600	12 426	10 681	17 563	9 583	11 684	68 904	63 843	65 394
Total number of homeschooled children	251	301	262	311	397	195	269	1405	1530	1638
Purpose of data collection	The NHES-PFI survey is designed for students from kindergarten through grade 12 and focuses on parent involvement in homework, family activities, and involvement in school.					The NHES-ASPA survey collects information on student participation in care arrangements in private homes with relatives and with care providers not related to them, participation in school-based or center-based after-school programs, participation in after-school activities that were not part of a school- or center-based program, and self-care.		The NSCH is designed to collect information on the physical and mental health status of children, access to high quality health care, and information on the child's family, neighborhood, and social context.		
Outcomes	Current school status, school characteristics, student experiences, family/school involvement and school practices, family involvement in schoolwork, family involvement outside of school, health and disability, involvement of nonresidential parent.					Center- or school-based programs, arrangements with relatives, arrangements with nonrelatives, activities children participate in after school, and self-care.		Child's health and functional status, health insurance coverage, health care access and utilization, family functioning, parent health, and neighborhood and community characteristics.		
Background characteristics	Race, ethnicity, sex, primary language, parent education, parent employment status, public assistance, household income.					Race, ethnicity, primary language, parent education, household income, Census region.		Race, ethnicity, sex, primary language, parent education, country of origin, employment, public assistance.		

Restricted-use data available	Location data (ZIP code, state), verbatim strings of other specific categories.					Location data (ZIP code, state), verbatim strings of other specific categories.		ZIP code, key child health indicators.		
Data on religious participation	• Homeschooling for religious reasons • Frequency household adult attended religious services	• Homeschooling for religious reasons • Attended any religious events	• Homeschooling for religious reasons • Attended any religious events • Used curriculum or books from religious organizations • Used services or participated in activities provided by religious organizations • Participated in church or temple youth group or religious instruction			• Homeschooling for religious reasons • Participation in religious activities or instruction • Choice of after-school care based on religious reasons	• Participation in religious activities or instruction	• Participation in a religious group • Attended religious service	• Attended religious service	• Attended religious service
Homeschooling questions	• Reason for homeschooling	• Reason for homeschooling • All or some schooling at home • Number of hours attending school	*All questions in previous years, plus:* • Resources used • Used a tutor	*All questions in previous years, plus:* • Person providing instruction • Days, hours per day homeschooled • Interaction with other home-schoolers	*All questions in previous years, plus:* • Teaching style • Parent/family member preparation for home instruction • Internet course-taking • Subject areas of instruction	• Reason for homeschooling • All or some schooling at home • Number of hours attending school • Resources used • Used a tutor	• All or some schooling at home • Number of hours attending school	*None*	*None*	*None*

educational information, including whether school-age children are enrolled in public school or private school or are homeschooled. Some respondents refuse to respond to the screener, at which point their information is lost. Others are willing to complete the screener but do not complete the other surveys. For those who complete the screener, their answers determine eligibility for follow-up surveys. For example, households without school-age children would not be eligible for the NHES-PFI or NHES-ASPA. The subsequent surveys administered after the screener tend to focus on a specific individual within each family – a school-age child in the case of the NHES-PFI and NHES-ASPA. When there are multiple school-age children in a household, the NHES employs an algorithm for selecting which child is the focus of the follow-up survey(s). Starting in 1999, to save costs, the NHES allowed for the selection of several focal children within a family as long as they were in different age ranges.

Given that the screener data include basic information about each child's type of schooling – whereas the follow-up surveys ask only about particular children in each household – the screener data are of intrinsic interest. For example, Isenberg (2006) used screener data from the 1996 and 1999 NHES to document the frequency with which families homeschooled one child but sent another child to school. In addition, by providing more cases of homeschooled and non-homeschooled children, the screener data increase the statistical power of any analysis by bolstering sample size. Unfortunately, the screener data are publicly available only for the 1996 NHES as part of the Household Library Use survey. Isenberg (2006) obtained a restricted-use file of screener data through NCES to use with the 1999 NHES. These data are housed at NCES and may be available upon request. It is possible that comparable data for other years may be obtainable from NCES.

The NHES-PFI collects data on a host of factors measuring the involvement of parents and families in their children's education. The survey samples households with students from kindergarten to grade 12, accounting for students through age 17. In addition to questions about homeschooling, the survey focuses primarily on parental involvement in various aspects of their child's education, including student experiences and family involvement in the child's educational activities both in school and at home. The NHES-PFI also provides background information on the family from the screener, including the age, sex, and relationship of each member of the household. Additional demographic information includes state of residence, students' race and ethnicity, students' and parents' primary language, and parents' educational attainment as well as adults' employment status, hours worked, receipt of public assistance, and total household income.

In addition, the NHES-PFI asks questions about the religious activities of parents and children, always useful background information when investigating homeschooling. The most recent surveys ask about potential religious motivations for homeschooling, participation in religious events and activities, the use of curricula or books published by religious organizations, and participation in religious instruction (NCES 2012). Earlier versions of the survey delved less deeply into the religious aspects of the child's education.

In two years – 2001 and 2005 – in which the NHES-PFI was not administered, the NHES-ASPA was administered using the same process: a screener survey followed by a secondary survey targeted to a focal child. The NHES-ASPA inquired about participation in after-school programs among students in kindergarten through grade 8. In particular, it collected information on student participation in care arrangements in private homes with relatives and other care providers, participation in school-based or center-based after-school programs, participation in after-school activities that were not part of a school- or center-based program, and self-care. The survey collected similar household demographic information as the NHES-PFI. It also asked questions about religious activities, but the questions were less extensive than those in the NHES-PFI.

The NHES-PFI and the NHES-ASPA have been administered to samples that have ranged from 9583 to 24600 participants, depending on the year. Population weights are supplied to match the surveyed sample to the US population. For example, if the sample of rural participants were twice as large in the survey as in the US population, each rural household would receive a relatively low weight to account for oversampling. Across five administrations from 1996 to 2012, the NHES-PFI has included from 10 681 to 24600 children per survey, including 251 to 397 homeschooled children in each round. The NHES-ASPA included 9583 children in 2001, including 195 homeschooled children, and 11 684 children in 2005, including 269 homeschooled children.

Both NHES surveys ask questions about whether children are homeschooled, and, if so, why parents have chosen to homeschool them. In particular, each survey asks whether the child attends an assigned public school, public school of choice, or private school, or is homeschooled. Beginning with the 1999 NHES-PFI, the surveys also ask if the child is receiving instruction at home full-time or part-time and the number of hours they attended a school. In addition, with the exception of the 2005 NHES-ASPA, the NHES surveys ask parents to state the motivation for homeschooling and provide a list of options from which to choose. Parents are first asked to select all options that may apply, and, beginning in 2003, parents also identify the single most important reason for homeschooling. Choices have included factors such as the child's health or safety, approaches to instruction, special needs, concerns about the school environment, and religious or moral reasons. Such distinctions help differentiate between "ideologues" and "pedagogues," borrowing the terminology of Van Galen (1991).

Beginning in 2001, there are also questions about homeschooling practices, with questions becoming more detailed over time. The 2001 NHES-ASPA and 2003 NHES-PFI pose questions about resources used for homeschooling, including the use of a tutor or other outside instruction. Although the 2005 NHES-ASPA contained no additional questions about homeschooling, the 2007 NHES-PFI added questions on which parent or family member is the primary instructor, the hours per day and days per week spent homeschooling, and extended questions on interaction with other homeschoolers. The 2012 NHES-PFI has a particularly rich trove of data on homeschooling. In addition to covering all topics in previous years, this survey collected information on parental teaching style (how formal or informal), whether a family member has taken any courses to prepare for the child's home instruction, and subject areas of instruction, plus additional information on the use of internet course-taking.

In addition, each NHES-PFI except for the 1999 round has asked for retrospective histories of the grades in which children were homeschooled, both for children currently homeschooled and for those who were previously homeschooled. Although retrospective histories are subject to a greater number of errors than longitudinal data collected over the years in waves, the resultant data are valuable in that they provide information on the duration of stints of homeschooling. For example, analysis of data from the 1996 survey indicates that much homeschooling in the mid-1990s was short-lived (Isenberg 2003).

All of the data from 1999 to 2012 are available online, and earlier data are available on a CD-ROM that can be obtained from NCES. In addition, it is possible for researchers to request a restricted-use file that contains the ZIP codes of each household, permitting the data to be linked to external information on school and community characteristics. The process to apply for restricted-use data sets is described in NCES (2011).

National Survey of Children's Health (NSCH)

The other nationally representative cross-sectional survey that classifies children as homeschooled by asking a direct question is the National Survey of Children's Health (NSCH). This survey focuses primarily on the physical and mental health of children rather than on education.

The National Center for Health Statistics conducts the NSCH, which measures the prevalence of various physical, emotional, and behavioral health outcomes for children age 0 to 17. The survey was conducted in 2003, 2007, and 2011–2012. It uses random-digit dialing to sample households, with sample sizes considerably larger than the sizes associated with the NHES surveys. In 2012, the NSCH surveyed 95677 households. As with the NHES, population weights are provided at the household level to obtain estimates that generalize to the US population, and, for households with several children, the survey selects one focal child to be the subject of the interview. In another similarity to the NHES, the NSCH represents repeated cross-sections of the US population, not longitudinal data that track the same households over time. A restricted-use version of the data provides access to each household's ZIP code.

Given that the primary focus of the survey is to collect data on various health indicators, most questions in the NSCH pertain to physical health, mental health, and access to high-quality health care. In addition, the survey collects an array of demographic data, including race and ethnicity, parental education, employment and income, birthplace of children and parents, residential mobility, neighborhood conditions, and school enrollment. For children age 6 to 17, the survey asks whether a child is enrolled in a public school or private school or is homeschooled. In each round of the survey, there were between about 1400 and 1700 homeschooled children. However, the survey asks no questions about motivation for homeschooling, time spent in homeschooling, concurrent enrollment in a school, or other potential areas of interest. Cordner (2012) has used the data to describe homeschoolers' access to and utilization of health care.

Cardus Education Survey

The Cardus Education Survey is based on a national random sample, but, unlike the NHES or NSCH, the target population is not children but high school graduates age 24 to 39. Topics include educational and labor market outcomes, religiosity, and civic and political involvement. Since the purpose of the survey was to compare how graduates of private Christian schools compare to graduates of public schools, private school graduates were oversampled.

Cardus, a non-profit research organization, authorized the survey, which was funded by three foundations, conducted in partnership with the University of Notre Dame, and administered using a web-based platform to a standing panel of participants recruited by the survey firm GfK (formerly Knowledge Networks). The survey was first conducted in 2011 and repeated using a separate cross-section in 2014. (Cardus also conducted a similar survey of Canadian graduates in 2012 and a survey of private school administrators in 2011.) The survey included about 1500 participants in each round. Aside from the outcome data, the survey also collected data on the type of school attended, school experiences, family background, and current family status. The official Cardus report for the initial survey summarizes survey results for five groups of students – those who attended public schools, Catholic schools, Protestant schools, non-religious private schools, and religious homeschoolers (Pennings 2011). The official Cardus report for the second survey omits homeschoolers, but promises to analyze the data on homeschoolers in a separate report (Pennings et al. 2014). Although there are just 82 homeschoolers in the initial survey, Uecker and Hill (2014) use data to explore differences in family formation for people with different school backgrounds, and find that homeschoolers appear most similar to students who attended public schools.[4]

Other national cross-sectional surveys

Three other prominent surveys ask questions about homeschooling; however, the design of the question about homeschooling in the surveys likely results in misclassification of some homeschooled children.

American Community Survey (ACS) The American Community Survey (ACS) is a key data set administered by the Census Bureau and designed to provide data on the social and economic status of the American population. In asking whether school-age children attend public or private school, the ACS is an excellent source of data for enrollment in public and private school, but it does not ask separately about homeschooling. In fact, starting in 2008, the ACS has instructed respondents to classify homeschooling as a form of private school. Approximately 250000 households respond to the survey each month. The ACS replaced the long form of the Decennial Census, which was last administered with the 2000 Census. The Census Bureau provides data sets for one-, three-, and five-year estimates from the ACS. Due to the comparatively large sample size and compulsory participation, the ACS would be an ideal source of information about homeschooling if the Census Bureau were to decide it was worth the cost to collect homeschooling data. A group of students in the ACS appears to be homeschooled – those at an age to be required to attend school but who fall into the category of "neither public nor private school." In a typical year, about 2% of the overall sample of children age 7 to 14 fall into this category. However, for many of the same reasons that asking about homeschooling as the second of a series of two questions can undercount homeschoolers, one should not assume that this count necessarily captures homeschooled children accurately. This caveat applies even before the change in the regulations in 2008 that officially classified homeschooled children as attending private school.

The Current Population Survey (CPS) The Current Population Survey (CPS) is jointly sponsored by the Census Bureau and the Bureau of Labor Statistics. Approximately 60000 households participate each month. A household is surveyed for four consecutive months and then once more after a four-month period. The CPS is primarily a survey about labor force information – the data are used to construct the official monthly estimate of the national unemployment rate – but it asks supplemental questions about school enrollment each October. The CPS is thus another reliable data source for estimates of the overall population of children in public and private school (Davis and Bauman 2013). However, the CPS does not currently include any questions about homeschooling. Only in 1994 did the October supplement include questions about homeschooling. Unfortunately, survey respondents "backed in" to the homeschooling question; they provided information on homeschooling only when they replied "no" to an earlier question about school-age children attending school. Thus, some homeschooled children are likely to be misclassified as attending school (Henke et al. 2000). Despite these limitations, Bauman (2002) has analyzed the characteristics of students classified as homeschooled by using data from the October 1994 supplement to the CPS as well as two rounds of the NHES-PFI.

National Survey on Drug Use and Health (NSDUH) The National Survey on Drug Use and Health (NSDUH) is administered each year by the Substance Abuse and Mental Health Services Administration to approximately 18000 households. The NSDUH collects data on the use of drugs, alcohol, and tobacco as well as on mental health status among children age 12 to 17. The survey also includes a question about homeschooling, and, in 2013, the most recent year for which data are available, the NSDUH sample included 100 homeschooled students. As with the CPS, respondents backed into the homeschooling question (see the example at the beginning of section II of this chapter). Green-Hennessy (2014) has analyzed the homeschooling data in the NSDUH.

III. Other Types of Data on Homeschooling

Aside from data sets that survey individual households, three other types of data sets include information on homeschooling: (1) counts of the number of homeschooled students maintained by state education agencies, (2) SAT data from the Educational Testing Service, and (3) data from longitudinal surveys that track individuals over time, such as the National Longitudinal Survey of Youth and Religion. Each has its strengths and weaknesses, although in general the data sets are of limited use in answering research questions about homeschooling.

State education agency data sets

States vary widely in the degree to which they track the number of homeschooled children. Some provide annual counts by district and/or by grade. The quality varies widely and is typically related to how the state regulates homeschooling. The politics of homeschooling have made it difficult to collect accurate data (Isenberg 2007). In states that collect and publicize data on the number of homeschooled children, several complicating factors are at work. First, some states rely on local school districts to collect and then provide the data to the state education agency; the quality of data collection by local districts can be haphazard or can vary across districts or over time within a district. Another complicating factor in some states is the number of ways to homeschool legally such that data may not be collected uniformly for all methods. For example, in Florida, families may homeschool their children in one of three ways: (1) under the "homeschool law," (2) by operating legally as a private school, or (3) under the private tutor law (Home School Legal Defense Association 2016). Florida tracks the number of homeschooled children – officially 77054 for the 2013–2014 school year – but the number reflects only students homeschooled under the first option (Florida Department of Education 2015).[5]

By contrast, the state of Wisconsin is a model for collecting data on homeschooled children. To homeschool in Wisconsin, a family has traditionally needed only to fill out a simple form and return it to the state education agency – these days, a family submits the form online. The low-burden approach, combined with Wisconsin's laissez-faire attitude toward homeschooling and the bypassing of local school districts, makes the Wisconsin data among the cleanest homeschooling counts of any state. The data are publicly available on the website of the Wisconsin Department of

Public Instruction, and they track the number of homeschooled children by district and grade level annually since the 1984–1985 school year.

Although higher quality state data can be useful in documenting trends in the number of homeschooled children, they are more limited in their use for research. The data must be linked to other data to create a data set with the demographic and social characteristics of local communities. Due to the lack of high-quality data across states, it is generally not possible to link state data on the percentage of homeschooled children to other state data. Gordon (2009) uses data on homeschooling regulations to understand the relationship between demographics and regulations but sidesteps the issue of the percentage of homeschooled children.

An alternate strategy is to make use of variation in homeschooling within a state; however, such a strategy is limited because it is not possible to associate individual households with demographic characteristics when matching occurs at the district or county level. For example, Isenberg (2003) linked Wisconsin data on the percentage of children homeschooled, first, to district demographic data from the decennial US Census and, second, to decennial county-level data on religious participation collected by the Association of Statisticians of American Religious Bodies (and available at the website of the Association of Religion Data Archives). The main finding was that homeschooling was most likely in counties in which an intermediate percentage of the population was evangelical Protestant, but actually less likely in counties with the highest proportions of evangelical Protestants, either because evangelical private schools were easier to form or because public schools become more acceptable among potential (ideologue) homeschoolers when more likeminded people live nearby. It is more difficult to infer how household characteristics – such as a mother's level of education – relates to the likelihood that she homeschools a child because it is impossible to match individual mothers to the schooling choice for their children. Houston and Toma (2003) attempted to derive as much as possible from data in Kentucky and several other states.

SAT data from the Educational Testing Service (ETS)

The Educational Testing Service (ETS) administers the SAT for college-bound high school students, along with a battery of other national tests. The SAT has asked whether a student attends public school or private school or is homeschooled. Thus, ETS not only collects data on a large number of homeschooled students but also maintains data on achievement. A database on achievement is a rarity because homeschooled students are exempt from the state assessments that public school students take. Through a restricted-use agreement with ETS, Belfield (2004) analyzed the data to assess the relationship between homeschooling and the math and verbal ability of homeschooled children, finding that they perform about as well as observationally equivalent students enrolled in private school. Ray and Eagleson (2008) used these data to analyze the relationship between the regulation of homeschooling and SAT scores.

The SAT data have three inherent limitations. First, students elect to take the SAT. As a result, the students in the data set are not representative of public, private, or homeschooled students of high school age. Second, the schooling status is that which the student marked on the SAT form, presumably representing how the student was schooled at the time that he or she took the test. Given the substantial movement of students in and out of homeschooling and conventional schools (Isenberg 2007), these static indicators may mask the dynamics of a student's career. For example, a student who was homeschooled from kindergarten through grade 8 and then entered a public high school would mark "public school," whereas a student who spent 11 years in public school before opting to be homeschooled by the time of the test would mark "homeschool." Third, even though the SAT data provide information on achievement, there is no information on student achievement at an earlier time point. Both the lack of earlier test data and the lack of a record of years of homeschooling make it impossible to attribute learning gains to homeschooling.

National Longitudinal Survey of Youth and Religion (NLSYR)

Several longitudinal databases track a representative group of people, often beginning in their teens or younger and continuing into adulthood. Participants answer a wide battery of questions and/or take tests. For studying homeschooling, some researchers have used the NLSYR, administered by the University of Notre Dame and funded by two private foundations. The purpose of this survey is to better understand the religious lives of young people, from adolescence to young adulthood. The survey began in 2002–2003 with 3370 adolescents age 13 to 17. These participants were surveyed again in 2005, 2007–2008, and 2012 (at which point most were in their mid-twenties). Uecker (2008) used the first wave of the NLSYR to explore how school choice is related to later religious behavior and participation, and finds that, accounting for parental background, homeschoolers are similar to public school students. Hill and Den Dulk (2013) used the NLSYR to ask how school choice is related to volunteerism, finding that homeschoolers were less likely to volunteer than graduates of all other types of schools except for private non-religious schools.

Other longitudinal data sets

Another example of a longitudinal data set is the Early Childhood Longitudinal Survey, Kindergarten Class of 1998–99 (ECLS-K), collected for the National Center for Educational Statistics. This survey followed children starting in kindergarten in fall 1998 until grade 8 in spring 2007. Various researchers have used this data set and others like it to answer a wide variety of questions. One complication in the case of studying homeschooling is that some of the data sets – ECLS-K among them – select their initial sample by using a representative sample of schools. Because homeschooled children are, by definition, not in school, longitudinal surveys such as ECLS-K miss such children at the outset. Nonetheless, the ECLS-K does include homeschooled children by virtue of the fact that some of the students who attended a public or private school in kindergarten were homeschooled in later grades. However, the ECLS-K asked about homeschooling only in the final wave of data collection and found that 48 of 9725 students were homeschooled in grade 8, likely constituting too small a sample to have the power to detect statistically significant differences in outcomes between homeschooled and non-homeschooled children. In general, small sample sizes of homeschooled students, typical in many longitudinal data sets, can limit the usefulness of these data for studying homeschooling.

IV. Estimates of the Number and Percentage of Homeschooled Children

Two of the most basic questions about homeschooling concern the number of homeschooled children and how the number has changed over time. Given the volume of current and historical educational statistics, it would seem that an answer to these questions could be found after a brief online search. The results from various rounds of the NHES-PFI provide the closest source of an official answer: strong growth led to an increase from 1.4% of the total population of homeschooled children in 1996 to 3.4%, or about 1 773 000 children, in 2012. However, some caution is required in interpreting the data on growth over time.

The landscape for school choice has changed over the past two decades, with some changes promoting homeschooling and others discouraging it. On the positive side, homeschooling has gained social and legal acceptance during this period. At the same time, strictly residentially based public school assignments have been giving way to greater school choice, especially with the growth of charter schools. In addition, a small number of voucher programs have allowed families to obtain public money to pay tuition at private schools. It is not clear, however, how much these enhanced school choice options appeal to families that might be inclined to homeschool their children.

A direct count of homeschooled children is not available. Unlike the case of public schools, which must count students in part because public funding depends on enrollment, there is no such justification to count private school or homeschooled students. Although some states maintain tabulations of homeschooled students, the data are often incomplete and of uneven quality.

Consequently, national estimates of the number of homeschooled children derive from surveys of households. Given that the two main large-scale Census Bureau surveys used to estimate the number of children in public and private school – the American Community Survey and the Current Population Survey – do not ask about homeschooling, estimates of the number of homeschooled children may be derived from the two smaller surveys that ask directly about homeschooling – the National Household Education Survey and the National Survey of Children's Health.

To extrapolate from a sample to the broader population from which the sample was taken, each household is assigned a weight corresponding to the number of households it represents in the broader population. Not everyone contacted for the survey agrees to complete the survey. The response rate – the number of households completing the survey divided by the number who were contacted – typically varies for different types of households. Thus, the sample weights compensate for varying response rates to ensure that the population totals along various dimensions match the weighted totals from the sample completing the survey. The weights also compensate for random differences between the sample and the population. For example, in the 1999 NHES, the child-level sample was weighted up to the population total based on race, ethnicity, household income (across three categories), the four Census regions, urbanicity (urban or rural),whether the family owns or rents its home,and the child's age (US Department of Education 1999).

With the number of homeschooled children in any given survey relatively small – for example, across the five rounds of the NHES-PFI, it ranges from 251 to 397 children – a fair degree of uncertainty is involved when extrapolating from the sample to the population with respect to the exact number of homeschooled children in the population. The uncertainty is quantified as the confidence interval around the point estimate calculated for each year – that is, a range for which it is most likely to obtain the estimate of the number of homeschooled children.

Distinct from the precision of the estimates, a more difficult issue relates to the accuracy of the estimates. That is, if homeschooled children actually constitute, for example, 2% of all school-age children, are surveys likely to estimate that 2% of school-age children in the sample are homeschooled or will they systematically over- or underestimate this number? A key issue is the relative response rate of homeschooling families to other families with school-age children. If homeschooling families are systematically more or less likely to respond (or, given the selection methods of random-digit dialing, to be contacted in the first place), the national estimates may be too high or too low. On the one hand, given their sometimes insular nature, homeschooling families may resist a request for information by a company administering a federal survey. Particularly in the uncertain regulatory environment of the 1990s, homeschooling families may have been reluctant to participate in surveys addressing school choice. Even in the late 2000s, the Home School Legal Defense Association, a non-profit advocacy organization committed to seeing that homeschoolers are by and large free of regulation, has referred to the American Community Survey as "intrusive" and decries its "tendency to overstep Constitutional bounds" (HSLDA 2007). On the other hand, mothers who homeschool tend to work less than mothers who send their children to school, presumably leading to more flexible schedules that might better accommodate the ability to respond to a survey, all else equal. There is also evidence that in general survey respondents tend to be more inclined to respond to surveys that focus on topics they find salient to their own lives, which might incline homeschooling families to respond to the NHES (Groves, Stanley, and Dipko 2004). An additional concern is that the growing acceptance of homeschooling may have increased survey response rates over time, making it more challenging to calculate an accurate growth rate of the number of homeschooled students. An associated question is measuring the proportion of homeschoolers who do so predominantly for religious reasons rather than for educational or other reasons. Anecdotal data suggest that religious homeschoolers may be less inclined to answer national surveys than other types of homeschoolers. If so, this would lead to an undercount of religious homeschoolers in survey data, both overall and relative to other types of homeschoolers.

Evidence suggests that the NHES surveys before 2012 may have slightly undercounted homeschooling families, with larger gaps in completion rates on surveys in the earlier years. In the 1990s, homeschooled children were less likely to complete the youth components of the NHES surveys than children in public or private school. In 1996, 74% of homeschooled children in grades 6 to 12 completed a civic involvement survey following the completion of the NHES-PFI by an adult, compared to 80% of children in private school and 86% of children in public school (Collins et al. 1997). In the 1999 NHES, 74% of homeschooled children in the same grade range completed the youth component of the interview compared to 85% of private school children and 87% of public school children (Nolin et al. 2000). These gaps close in later rounds. In 2003, 82% of parents of public and private school students completed the NHES-PFI compared to 79% of parents of homeschooled students (Hagedorn et al. 2004). In 2007, 78% of parents of public and private school students completed the NHES-PFI compared to 74% of parents of homeschooled students (Hagedorn et al. 2008). Finally, in 2012, 79% of both groups completed the NHES-PFI (McPhee et al. 2015).

Differences in completion rates are suggestive of undercounting of homeschoolers in earlier years, but a potentially larger source of discrepancies is a difference in what is known as the cooperation rate – the proportion of contacted households that complete a screener survey. In other words, whereas the documented completion rates examine how likely households are to complete a follow-up interview after having completed the screener, there also may be differences in how likely families are to pick up the telephone in the first place or to refuse to complete the screener upon learning that an anonymous caller wished to ask them a battery of questions. Bielick et al. (2009) investigated the question of differing rates of cooperation by obtaining mailing lists of households that had purchased homeschooling materials, randomly sampling households from these lists, and calling them to ask them to participate in a screener survey under the same conditions as the households sought out for the 2007 NHES. This method did not yield an exact answer on whether homeschoolers are underrepresented in the 2007 NHES because just 42% of the households that responded had school-age children, and 30% of these households were currently homeschooling. Instead, the authors were able to identify the relationship between (1) the percentage of homeschooling households refusing to answer the survey (an unknown quantity) and (2) the cooperation rate. For example, if 30% of the refusals were homeschoolers, the cooperation rate among homeschoolers would be 76%. However, if 60% of the refusals were homeschoolers, the cooperation rate among homeschoolers would be 54%. By comparison, the cooperation rate on the 2007 NHES was 62%. Although the homeschooler cooperation rate cannot be pinned down with certainty, Bielick et al. (2009) interpret their findings as suggesting that at this time the cooperation rates of homeschooling households were similar to those of non-homeschooling households. This is not out of line with the evidence from the survey completion rates in the 2007 NHES-PFI, where parents of homeschooled children were just four percentage points less likely to complete the survey (after having started it) compared to parents of public and private school students. This study does not answer the question, however, of whether cooperation rates have shifted over time or whether cooperation rates are different for ideologues and pedagogues.

Taking the point estimates of the NHES-PFI at face value, there was steady growth in the population of homeschooled children, from 1.4% of schoolchildren in kindergarten to grade 12 in 1996 to 3.4% in 2012. Figure 2.1 shows the point estimates as the diamond in the middle of each vertical solid bar. To avoid confounding changes in the number of homeschoolers with changes in the overall population of school children, the figure focuses on the percentage of schoolchildren who are homeschooled rather than on the overall number of children. The confidence interval is shown by the length of the bar; it is about 0.6% in the first two surveys and 0.8% in the last three surveys.

The NSCH provides another estimate. Although not designed as a survey about homeschooling, the NSCH collects data on the schooling of each child and thus

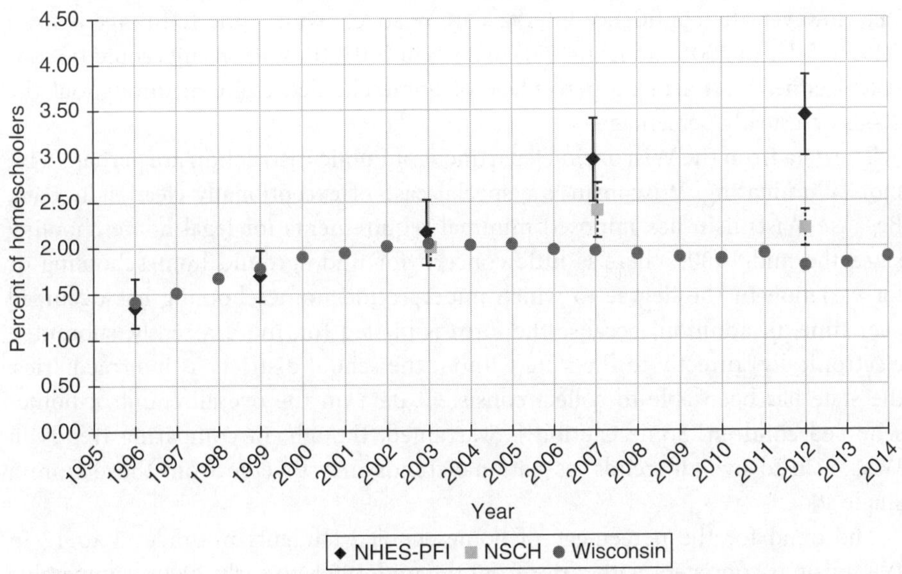

Figure 2.1 Percent homeschooled 1996–2014. Source: Author calculations based on Snyder and Dillow (2015), Henke et al. (2000), the National Survey of Children's Health (NSCH), and data from the Wisconsin Department of Public Instruction.

allows for an alternate estimate of the total number of homeschooled children in the United States. The overall sample size for the NSCH is larger than that for the NHES, making for more precise estimates and thus smaller confidence intervals. As shown in Figure 2.1, the point estimate of 2.0% homeschooled in 2003 is similar to and within the confidence interval of the estimate of 2.2% for the NHES that year. The discrepancy may be explained by sampling error – the departure from the truth generated because a finite sample of households is interviewed. Another reason why the NHES percentage may be slightly larger is that the NHES records children said to be homeschooled in kindergarten, whereas the NSCH begins with children at age six and thus does not include five-year-old kindergarten students.

Unlike the NHES data, the NSCH data show basically a flat trend in the percentage of homeschooled children, not robust growth. Accordingly, after 2003, the estimates begin to diverge. In 2007, the NSCH estimate is 2.4% compared to 2.9% in the NHES, out of the range of the NHES confidence interval. Finally, in 2012, the NSCH estimate of 2.2% is substantially lower than the 3.4% estimate based on NHES data collected in the same year.

The NHES-ASPA data from 2001 and 2005 also provide estimates of the proportion of homeschoolers. The NHES-ASPA data are limited to students in kindergarten through grade 8, although, as will be seen, there is no statistically significant difference in the percentage of the population of homeschooled children at the elementary, middle school, and high school levels. Therefore, the levels in the data are likely informative of overall trends that include older students. According to the data, about 2.6% of students were homeschooled in 2001 and 2.4% in 2005. Given the smaller sample size of the NHES-ASPA compared to that of the NHES-PFI, however, the confidence intervals are relatively wide – the full range is from 2.1% to 3.1% in 2001 and from 2.0% to 2.9% in 2005; thus, the results could be consistent either with a rising percentage of homeschooled children throughout the 2000s or a steady percentage.

The data from the Wisconsin Department of Public Instruction are perhaps a bit more illuminating. Wisconsin is a special case of exceptionally clean state data. Because Wisconsin has imposed minimal requirements for legal homeschooling since the mid-1980s, there is little concern for underground homeschooling or for variation in the degree to which underground homeschooling has occurred over time. In addition, because the form is mailed (or, more recently, submitted electronically) directly to the state without the school districts as intermediaries, the state has been able to collect consistent data on the overall count of homeschooled children. Some caution is warranted, though, in comparing trends in Wisconsin to overall trends, as national trends may diverge from those from a single state.

The trend for the percentage of homeschooled students in grades 1 to 12 in Wisconsin is consistent with a rise from the mid-1990s to early 2000s, comparable to that in the NHES data. As plotted on Figure 2.1 by the circles, the percentage homeschooled in Wisconsin in 1996 is nearly identical to the national estimate from the NHES: 1.4% (although the measure applies to slightly different populations because the NHES includes kindergarten while the Wisconsin data do not). By 1999, 1.8% of school-age children in Wisconsin were homeschooled, compared to 1.7% in the national estimate. In 2003, the national estimate had reached 2.2% compared to 2.0% in Wisconsin, but the Wisconsin percentage is well within the 95% confidence interval of the national estimate from the NHES and identical to the NSCH estimate to one decimal place.

After 2003, the percentage homeschooled in Wisconsin diverges from the NHES national estimate. Even though the NHES estimate continues to increase markedly, homeschooling in Wisconsin levels off. The percentage of homeschooled students reached its maximum in 2003, when 2.04% were homeschooled. By 2014, the percentage of homeschooled students was 1.89%. Despite a smaller percentage of students homeschooled in Wisconsin after 2003 than is reflected in a national estimate – even in the NSCH data – the flatter trajectory of the 2007 and 2012 data points for the NSCH is closer to the Wisconsin experience than the continually rising pattern of successive NHES estimates.

This leaves us with the puzzle of why the NHES-PFI estimates, particularly the 2012 estimate, diverge so strongly from other data sources. Has homeschooling taken off, or has it stagnated? To answer this question, it is illustrative to look at how homeschooling was defined in the 2012 NHES for the purpose of obtaining a national estimate. Recall that one significant design change from the earlier rounds of the NHES is that the 2012 NHES was a mail survey. Randomly selected families initially received a short screener survey in the mail asking them to enumerate the ages of household members and indicate whether any school-age children were in public school, private school, or were homeschooled. Based on this information, they received a longer follow-up survey that was geared either to students enrolled in school or to homeschooled children. According to official documentation from NCES, children may be counted as homeschooled if either (1) the family responded to the initial mailed screener survey by indicating homeschooling or (2) the family responded to the screener by indicating that a child attended public or private school, but marked that the child was homeschooled when asked about homeschooling for a second time on the follow-up survey for enrolled students (McPhee et al. 2015; Noel, Stark, and Redford 2015). After collecting these data, McPhee et al. (2015) report that 78% of children whose families responded to the follow-up homeschooling survey "fit NCES's definition for homeschooling for reporting purposes." (In the past, families could fail to meet this standard if they were homeschooling due to a temporary illness or if they combined homeschooling with enrolling the student in a school for the majority of the school week.) However, for students apparently homeschooled based on the follow-up survey intended for enrolled students, there are not the detailed homeschooling questions to make this determination. Therefore, NCES applied an ad hoc adjustment of multiplying the number of homeschooled children so identified by 78%, on the assumption that the same patterns were present for these households as was the case for households that received the homeschooling follow-up survey. NCES will release further details about the homeschooling population in Redford and Battle (forthcoming).

By contrast, the NSCH does not subsequently offer parents a second opportunity to identify homeschooling as the choice. This could lead to a downward bias in the NSCH estimate of homeschooled students if some of the students marked as enrolled were actually part-time homeschooled students who would have met criteria for inclusion as a homeschooler (or who for another reason might have changed the answer to "homeschool" if asked again). On the other hand, because NSCH does not ask any further questions about homeschooling, some homeschooled students who would not meet the NHES definition of homeschooled would be counted. If the NHES 2012 survey is representative, the overall direction of the bias would be downward – far fewer students dropping out for not meeting the homeschooling criteria than are added from a second opportunity to self-identify as homeschooled. In the 2012 NHES-PFI, 2.3% of children were said to be homeschooled on the basis of the screener survey (adjusting for sampling weights). This is comparable to the 2.2% estimate from the 2012 NSCH. This suggests that differences in survey design were responsible for differences in estimates of the homeschooled population, with the NHES estimate more likely to be closer to the actual population total, despite the need for an ad hoc adjustment to the estimate. In fact, although the differences between the NHES-PFI and NSCH were not as great in 2003 and 2007, in both years the NHES-PFI estimate was higher. It is a feature of the earlier NHES surveys as well that, even when administered by telephone, there were opportunities for parents to declare that their child was homeschooled in the screener and again in the follow-up survey (Nolin et al. 2000; Hagedorn et al. 2004; Hagedorn et al. 2008).

Finally, the data from the NHES-PFI, NHES-ASPA, and NSCH provide an age breakdown, showing minimal difference in the percentage of children homeschooled at the elementary school level (kindergarten to grade 5), middle school level (grade 6 to grade 8), and high school level (grade 9 to grade12). Results are shown in Table 2.2. For the NSCH, which reports ages rather than grades, the results are disaggregated by age 6 to 11 (roughly elementary school ages) and age 12 to 17 (roughly middle and high school ages combined). For example, averaging across the four NHES-PFI surveys, 2.0% of elementary school students are homeschooled compared to 2.1% of middle and high school students. It is important to note that the denominator for high school students for the NHES includes only students enrolled in school; it excludes dropouts. Therefore, the percentage of homeschooled adolescents (students plus dropouts) may be slightly lower than the percentage of homeschooled students. Including the two rounds of the NHES-ASPA in the average for elementary and middle school (high school students do not participate in the survey) shows that 2.3% of elementary students are homeschooled compared to 2.1% of middle school students. In the NSCH, 2.0% of students age 6 through 11 are homeschooled compared to 2.3% of children age 12 to 17.

By comparison, the Wisconsin data show an increase in homeschooling at the high school level. In the 1984–1985 school year, the first year for which Wisconsin tracked data on homeschooling, just 12.4% of all homeschooled students were in high school. The number increased steadily, hitting a peak of 34.5% in the

Table 2.2 Percent homeschooled by grade and age range.

		NHES-PFI (by grade)				*NHES-ASPA (by grade)*		*NSCH (by age)*		
Grade	*Age*	*1996*	*1999*	*2003*	*2007*	*2001*	*2005*	*2003*	*2007*	*2011–2012*
K-5	**6–11**	1.4 (0.2)	1.8 (0.2)	1.9 (0.2)	3.0 (0.4)	2.9 (0.3)	2.7 (0.3)	1.7 (0.1)	2.4 (0.2)	2.0 (0.2)
6–8		1.3 (0.2)	1.6 (0.3)	2.4 (0.4)	3.0 (0.5)	2.1 (0.2)	2.1 (0.2)			
9–12		1.6 (0.2)	1.7 (0.3)	2.3 (0.3)	2.8 (0.4)					
	12–17							2.2 (0.2)	2.3 (0.2)	2.4 (0.2)

Note: Standard errors are given in parentheses beneath each point estimate.
Source: Author calculations based on the National Household Education Survey–Parent and Family Involvement Survey (NHES-PFI), National Household Education Survey–Before- and After-School Programs and Activities (NHES-ASPA), and National Survey of Children's Health (NSCH).

2001–2002 school year. In the 2013–2014 school year, the most recent year for which data are available, 29.5% of homeschooled students were in high school.

Although the percentage of homeschooled students is similar at different grade levels, this does not imply that individual students are homeschooled continuously from kindergarten through grade 12 any more than it implies that the types of students who are homeschooled or parents who instruct homeschooled students are similar at different grade levels. Isenberg (2003, 2007) shows that most homeschooling is short-lived (based on the 1996 NHES). Isenberg (2006) also finds evidence that the characteristics of families differ across grade levels, and parent self-reports suggest different motivations at different grade levels as well, even if the percentage of homeschooled students appears to be similar.

In sum:

- The quasi-official estimate of homeschooling from multiple rounds of the NHES-PFI has shown growth each time the survey has been administered, from 1.4% of the total population of homeschooled children in 1996 to 3.4%, or about 1 773 000 children, in 2012.
- The estimates should not be treated as a census count of homeschoolers but as the midpoint of a range of plausible estimates. For example, the estimates from the 2012 NHES suggest that the percentage of schoolchildren who are homeschooled is likely to be within a range from 3.0% to 3.9%.
- Because homeschooling families have become more likely over time to complete the NHES follow-up surveys and possibly more likely to cooperate in taking the initial screener survey, the true numbers of homeschoolers (prior to 2012) may

have been a bit higher than the estimates provided by the NHES and the implied growth rate a bit lower.

- Data from the NSCH and the state of Wisconsin track the NHES-PFI estimates closely until 2007 and then diverge, with a flat or slightly downward trend in the NSCH and Wisconsin data from 2007 to 2012. One explanation for this discrepancy between the NSCH and NHES-PFI is that the NHES surveys provide a second opportunity for families to self-identify as homeschoolers.
- Children were equally likely to be homeschooled in the elementary, middle, and high school grades.

V. Avenues for Future Research

In general, the statistical data on homeschooling may find three applications: (1) descriptive information on a representative sample of homeschoolers; (2) examination of the decision to homeschool rather than enroll children in public or private schools; or (3) comparison of outcomes for homeschooled children versus children who attend public or private school. In all cases, one of the main concerns for using data on homeschooling has been statistical power. Given that homeschoolers typically represent 2–3% of any sample, any data set includes relatively few homeschooled students, sometimes making it difficult to distinguish true relationships from randomness. The traditional solution to such a problem has been to stack together several cross-sectional data sets.

For understanding the relationships between family and neighborhood characteristics and the choice of homeschooling versus public or private schooling, it would be possible to update current research by using additional data sets. Several rounds of the NHES-PFI and NHES-ASPA – which tend to have similar if not identical definitions of variables – could be stacked. The NSCH data might be added as well, with more attention to how variables are defined across data sets. Stacking data will allow not only for more precise estimates of overall results but also for more precise subgroup results – for example, disaggregating the sample into families with younger or older children or examining better-educated mothers separately from less well-educated mothers.

A second area that could be better understood with more recent data is the persistence of homeschooling. Hanna (2012) suggests that the internet has transformed how homeschooling is conducted, which might induce some families to continue homeschooling for longer stints. Isenberg (2007) has documented the short-lived nature of homeschooling by examining data in the 1996 NHES-PFI, but data from later rounds of the NHES-PFI should allow for documenting the degree of persistence among a larger set of homeschooled children from more recent years. Assuming that there has been growth in the proportion of children homeschooled over time, this would help us understand whether this has been driven by more families trying homeschooling or a similar number of families homeschooling but doing it for longer intervals. These data would also allow for conducting further investigation, including formal statistical modeling, into which types of families tend to persist and which types of families tend to drop out of homeschooling.

A third avenue for future research is to mine the 2012 NHES-PFI for a richer description of homeschooling than has previously been possible. Given the added questions to this round of the survey (as summarized in Table 2.1), this data set provides an unprecedented depth of information, which might be analyzed in various ways – for example, describing homeschooled students separately by age group. As a single data set, the main limitation may be statistical power. It is hoped that future rounds of the NHES-PFI continue to gather responses to these types of questions.

For comparing outcomes of homeschooled students to outcomes of public or private school students, researchers are hard-pressed to claim that existing cross-sectional data sets are sufficient for causally relating homeschooling to outcomes. The data sets simply do not contain enough information on how homeschooling families differ from other families. However, it might be possible to use the data sets to describe differences between homeschooled children and non-homeschooled children on health outcomes, based on the NSCH or a variety of family involvement outcomes (such as how often parents take their children to a museum) by using the NHES data sets. Researchers could tabulate averages across homeschooled and non-homeschooled children as well as account statistically for observable differences among children and families. In the future, to better understand whether homeschooling is educationally beneficial to students, it would be ideal to design a data collection effort that would obtain achievement outcomes for a random sample of students before they enter homeschooling and after they exit, along with comparable data on students who attend school.

Notes

1. The author acknowledges the excellent work provided by research assistant Nikhil Gahlawat, especially in creating the tables and figures. Sheila Heaviside provided valuable feedback.
2. The eight surveys are Adult Education, Before- and After-School Programs and Activities, Early Childhood Program Participation, Parent and Family Involvement in Education, Civic Involvement, Household Library Use, School Readiness, and School Safety and Discipline.
3. The Before- and After-School Programs and Activities survey was originally just the After-School Programs and Activities survey. NHES continues to use the acronym ASPA for the original name of the survey. I have followed that convention.
4. Cardus does not document the sample sizes for each type of schooling. Milton Gaither obtained the sample sizes via correspondence with the principal researcher of the quantitative portion of the study. See https://gaither.wordpress.com/2011/09/23/the-cardus-education-survey-and-homeschooling (accessed October 19, 2015).
5. See the website of the International Center for Home Education Research at http://www.icher.org/endata.html for an archive of state data on the number of homeschooled children.

References

Bauman, K.J. 2002. "Home Schooling in the United States." *Education Policy Analysis Archives*, 10: 1–26.

Belfield, C. 2004. "Home-Schooling in the US." (Occasional Paper No. 88). New York: National Center for the Study of Privatization in Education, Teachers College, Columbia University. Accessed October 19, 2015. http://ncspe.tc.columbia.edu/working-papers/OP88.pdf

Bielick, S. 2009. *1.5 Million Homeschooled Students in the United States in 2007* (NCES 2009–030). Washington, DC: National Center for Education Statistics, Institute of Education Sciences, US Department of Education. Accessed October 19, 2015. https://nces.ed.gov/pubs2009/2009030.pdf

Bielick, S., K. Chandler, and S.P. Broughman. 2001. *Homeschooling in the United States: 1999* (2001–033). Washington, DC: National Center for Education Statistics, US Department of Education,. Accessed October 19, 2015. http://nces.ed.gov/pubs2001/2001033.pdf

Bielick, S., L. Guzman, A. Atienza, and A. Rivers. 2009. "Using a Seeded Sample to Measure Response among Homeschooling Households." *Survey Practice*, 2: 1–8.

Collins, M.J., et al. 1997. *National Household Education Survey of 1996: Data File User's Manual, Volume I* (NCES 1997–425). Washington, DC: National Center for Education Statistics, Institute of Education Sciences, US Department of Education.

Cordner, A. 2012. "The Health Care Access and Utilization of Homeschooled Children in the United States." *Social Science and Medicine*, 75: 269–73.

Davis, J., and K. Bauman. 2013. *School Enrollment in the United States: 2011*. Washington, DC: US Census Bureau, US Department of Commerce, Economics and Statistics Administration. Accessed October 19, 2015. https://www.census.gov/prod/2013pubs/p20-571.pdf.

Florida Department of Education. 2014. "School Choice Fact Sheets: Home Education in Florida." Tallahassee, FL: Florida Department of Education. Accessed October 19, 2015. http://www.floridaschoolchoice.org/pdf/Home_Ed_Fast_Facts.pdf.

Gordon, N. 2009. "What Explains State Regulation of Home Schooling?" Unpublished working paper.

Green-Hennessy, S. 2014. "Homeschooled Adolescents in the United States: Developmental Outcomes." *Journal of Adolescence*, 37: 441–49.

Groves, Robert M., Stanley Presser, and Sarah Dipko. 2004. "The Role of Topic Interest in Survey Participation Decisions." *Public Opinion Quarterly*, 68: 2–31.

Hagedorn, M., J., et al. 2004. *National Household Education Surveys of 2003: Data File User's Manual, Volume I*. (NCES 2004–101). Washington, DC: National Center for Education Statistics, US Department of Education. Accessed October 19, 2015. http://nces.ed.gov/pubs2004/2004102.pdf

Hagedorn, M., et al. 2008. *National Household Education Surveys Program of 2007: Data File User's Manual, Volume I* (NCES 2009–024). Washington, DC: National Center for Education Statistics, Institute of Education Sciences, US Department of Education. Accessed October 19, 2015. https://nces.ed.gov/nhes/pdf/userman/NHES_2007_Vol_I.pdf

Hanna, Linda G. 2012. "Homeschooling Education: Longitudinal Study of Methods, Materials, and Curricula." *Education and Urban Society*, 20: 1–23.

Henke, R.R., P. Kaufman, S.P. Broughman, and K. Chandler. 2000. *Issues Related to Estimating the Home-Schooled Population in the United States with National Household Survey Data*

(NCES 2000–311). Washington, DC: US Department of Education, National Center for Education Statistics.

Hill, Jonathan P., and Kevin R. Den Dulk. 2013. "Religion, Volunteering, and Educational Setting: The Effect of Youth Schooling Type on Civic Engagement." *Journal for the Scientific Study of Religion*, 52: 179–97.

Home School Legal Defense Association. 2007. "HSLDA Examines the American Community Survey." Accessed October 19, 2015. http://www.hslda.org/docs/news/hslda/200104100.asp

Home School Legal Defense Association. 2016. *Home Schooling in the United States: A Legal Analysis,* 2015–2016 edition. Accessed October 19, 2015. http://www.hslda.org/laws/analysis/Florida.pdf

Houston, R., and E. Toma. 2003. "Home Schooling: An Alternative School Choice." *Southern Economic Journal*, 69: 920–35.

Isenberg, Eric. 2003. "Home Schooling: Household Production and School Choice." PhD diss., Washington University.

Isenberg, Eric. 2006. "The Choice of Public, Private, or Home Schools." (Occasional Paper No. 132). New York: National Center for the Study of Privatization in Education, Teachers College, Columbia University. Accessed October 19, 2015. http://ncspe.tc.columbia.edu/working-papers/OP132.pdf

Isenberg, Eric. 2007. "What Have We Learned about Homeschooling?" *Peabody Journal of Education*, 82: 387–409.

McPhee, C., S. et al. 2015. *National Household Education Surveys Program of 2012: Data File User's Manual* (NCES 2015–030). Washington, DC: National Center for Education Statistics, Institute of Education Sciences, US Department of Education. Accessed October 19, 2015. https://nces.ed.gov/nhes/pdf/userman/NHES_2012_UsersManual.pdf

National Center for Education Statistics. 2011. *Restricted-Use Data Procedures Manual.* Washington, DC: National Center for Education Statistics, Institute of Education Sciences, IES Data Security Office. Accessed October 19, 2015. http://nces.ed.gov/pubs96/96860rev.pdf

National Center for Education Statistics. 2012. *The National Household Education Survey: A Survey about Homeschooling in America* (NHES-31AE(INFO). Washington, DC: National Center for Education Statistics, Institute of Education Sciences, US Department of Education. Accessed October 19, 2015. http://nces.ed.gov/nhes/pdf/pfi/PFI_homeschool_2012.pdf

Noel, A., P. Stark, and J. Redford. 2015. *Parent and Family Involvement in Education, from the National Household Education Surveys Program of 2012* (NCES 2013–028.REV). Washington, DC: National Center for Education Statistics, Institute of Education Sciences, US Department of Education. Accessed October 19, 2015. http://nces.ed.gov/pubs2013/2013028rev.pdf

Nolin, M.J., et al. 2000. *National Household Education Survey of 1999: Data File User's Manual, Volume I* (NCES 2000–076). Washington, DC: National Center for Education Statistics, Institute of Education Sciences, US Department of Education. Accessed October 19, 2015. http://nces.ed.gov/pubs2000/2000076.pdf

Pennings, R. 2011. *Cardus Education Survey*. Hamilton, Ontario: Cardus. Accessed October 19, 2015. http://www.tpcs.org/about-us/Cardus-Cardus_Education_Survey_Phase_I_Report.pdf

Pennings, R., et al. 2014. *Cardus Education Survey 2014*. Hamilton, Ontario: Cardus. Accessed October 19, 2015. https://www.cardus.ca/research/education/survey_schedule

Princiotta, D., and S. Bielick. 2006. *Homeschooling in the United States: 2003* (NCES 2006–042). Washington, DC: National Center for Education Statistics, US Department of Education. Accessed October 19, 2015. http://nces.ed.gov/pubs2006/2006042.pdf

Princiotta, D., S. Bielick, and C. Chapman. 2004. *1.1 Million Homeschooled Students in the United States in 2003* (NCES 2004–115). Washington, DC: National Center for Education Statistics, Institute of Education Sciences, US Department of Education. Accessed October 19, 2015. http://nces.ed.gov/pubs2004/2004115.pdf

Ray, Brian D., and Bruce K. Eagleson. 2008. "State Regulation of Homeschooling and Homeschoolers' SAT Scores." *Academic Leadership: The Online Journal* 6. Accessed October 19, 2015. http://contentcat.fhsu.edu/cdm/compoundobject/collection/p15732coll4/id/303/rec/2

Redford, J. and D. Battle. Forthcoming. *Homeschooling in the United States: 2012 (NCES 2015-019). Washington, DC: National Center for Education Statistics*, Institute of Education Sciences, US Department of Education.

Snyder, T.D., and S.A. Dillow. 2015. *Digest of Education Statistics 2013* (NCES 2015-011). Washington, DC: National Center for Education Statistics, Institute of Education Sciences, US Department of Education. Accessed April 8, 2016. http://nces.ed.gov/pubs2015/2015011.pdf

Uecker, Jeremy E. 2008. "Alternative Schooling Strategies and the Religious Lives of American Adolescents." *Journal for the Scientific Study of Religion*, 47: 563–584.

Uecker, Jeremy E., and Jonathan P. Hill. 2014. "Religious Schools, Home Schools, and the Timing of First Marriage and First Birth." *Review of Religious Research*, 56: 189–218.

Van Galen, J. 1991. "Ideologues and Pedagogues: Parents Who Teach Their Children at Home." In *Home Schooling: Political, Historical, and Pedagogical Perspectives*, edited by J. van Galen and M.A. Pitman, 67–92. Norwood, NJ: Ablex.

3

Legal Issues in Homeschooling

Antony Barone Kolenc

No treatment of homeschooling would be complete without a discussion of the law. The two topics are inextricably linked, influencing and shaping one another. The "fundamental" parental right to educate one's children limits the State's ability to regulate homeschooling, while the interest of the State in the education of its citizens limits the exercise of the parental right. Where is the balance in this delicate system, especially in relation to legal rights protected by the United States Constitution? This chapter explores and evaluates the interplay of these concepts, as well as related legal issues. For instance, what is the connection between home education and the right of religious freedom under the First Amendment? Does the Fourth Amendment protect the privacy of homeschooling families during child abuse investigations? Does the law require states to give homeschoolers access to public school programs and extracurricular activities? Beginning with the legal roots of homeschooling, this chapter examines how the movement's struggles in both litigation and legislation eventually brought it into the legal and cultural mainstream of American society.

The Road to Legal Conflict

To understand the legal issues that impact homeschooling, one must first appreciate the historical and cultural roots from which the modern movement grew. Early in the history of the United States, no one would have suggested that educating one's children at home required government approval or that homeschooling might not be legal. In general, schooling was not compulsory in England, the colonies, or early America (Kaestle 2010; Steilen 2009). Although brick and mortar schools existed, most Americans were educated in their homes, producing such historical giants as

The Wiley Handbook of Home Education, First Edition. Edited by Milton Gaither.

George Washington, James Madison, Benjamin Franklin, Abraham Lincoln, Mark Twain, Andrew Carnegie, and Thomas Edison (Barnett 2013; Olsen 2009, 415).

There were few opportunities for legal conflict between parents and the government until the late 19th century, when states passed "compulsory education" laws that required children to attend school or else be considered truant (Provasnik 2006, 320). These laws sought to assimilate and teach "greater loyalty" to the waves of immigrants arriving in America from non-Protestant and non-English-speaking nations, who were often distrusted due to their religious and cultural differences (Steilen 2009, 305–309; Bartholomew 2007, 1179). With mandatory public schooling in full swing by the early 20th century, few parents still homeschooled. To comply with compulsory education, some (particularly Catholics and Lutherans) turned to private religious schools to preserve their traditions (Steilen 2009, 318–326). Others put their children in public school and conformed.

By the 1950s, this mass government-run system of education was drawing criticism, especially from "liberals and educational progressives" who viewed inept and constrictive brick and mortar schools as "too rigidly conservative" and harmful to the natural curiosity of children (Yuracko 2008, 125–127; Lines 2000). These parents – perhaps as many as 10 000 of them – turned to homeschooling in the same model as liberal educator John Holt (Lines 2000). In most states, these pioneering families risked fines and jail by violating compulsory education laws (Bhatt 2014). Despite the risks, the movement grew, with only "isolated examples of conflicts between homeschooling families and local school officials" (Gaither 2008, 120). Complex social, economic, and political factors combined to foster the tremendous growth of home education in the second half of the 20th century (Murphy 2012, 68–73); however, this chapter focuses on perhaps the two most important movements that coincided with the resurgence of homeschooling – one legal and the other cultural.

In the legal arena, after World War II the US Supreme Court began in earnest to enlarge the power of the Federal Judiciary by applying the Constitution against the states in revolutionary ways. The Court actively recognized new fundamental rights under the Due Process Clause of the Fourteenth Amendment (e.g., the Right of Privacy) and expanded First Amendment protections in such areas as freedom of speech and religion. This legal movement, focusing on individual liberties, eventually would fuel the claim by homeschoolers that states could not interfere with the parental decision to educate their children in whatever way they think best.

Developments in the law of individual liberties soon converged with cultural movements based on human rights. The revolutions of the 1960s – civil rights, feminism, anti-war speech – helped divide 1970s America on controversial moral issues: abortion, sexuality, the place of God in the public schools. Radical change generated a conservative backlash, including faith-based political groups such as Reverend Jerry Falwell's "Moral Majority" – a stepping-stone for one of homeschooling's most influential lawyers, Michael Farris (Gaither 2008, 159). This supercharged religio-political climate transformed home education over the next two decades as unprecedented numbers of religious families abandoned public schools they perceived as hostile to Christian faith and morals (e.g., banishing God from school while introducing sex education) (Murphy 2012, 87–92). The growing correlation between faith and homeschooling created further legal complexities, combining parental rights issues with the First Amendment freedom of religion. The interaction among these three movements (law, culture, and home education) formed fertile soil in which to grow a politically active Christian homeschool lobby.

During this time period, key lawyers such as Michael Farris and John Wayne Whitehead of the Rutherford Institute focused their legal talents on defending homeschoolers – especially Christian ones – from government persecution (Gaither 2008, 157–161). Beginning in earnest in the 1980s, religious parents and their advocates sought full legal recognition and complete freedom to educate their children at home without government regulation. The approach of these parents differed from earlier homeschool pioneers, who had often stayed underground to avoid fines or jail in states that did not accept homeschooling as compatible with compulsory education laws (Lines 2000). The founding of the Home School Legal Defense Association (HSLDA) and other advocacy groups across the nation accelerated the pace and scope of homeschooling and related legal issues (Lagos 2011, 99). Liberals and progressives still taught their children at home, but the surge of politicized, religion-based homeschoolers changed the face of the movement. Activism in the state legislatures and the courts ushered in a new era of engagement – and in many cases, conflict – between parents and school districts. The defining principle that drove this conflict was the belief by homeschooling advocates that parents possess a God-given, "fundamental" legal right to educate their children as they see fit.

Parents versus the State

The modern legal drama surrounding home education stems from a clash of ideas, pitting the rights of parents against the duty of the State. This battle first unfolded in State and Federal courts, with each side certain of the rightness of its cause. This section explores the arguments made by both sides of that fight, briefly recapping the historical and legal precedent supporting each position.

Both sides of the legal argument

Many homeschooling parents hold the core conviction that the US Constitution protects their fundamental right to educate their children in whatever way they please (Waddell 2010, 552). Building on decades of legal and cultural advances regarding individual rights, they contend that any government efforts to regulate homeschooling must be supported by "compelling" state interests – a difficult standard for regulators to meet. They at times locate this fundamental parental right in the Ninth Amendment, which declares that "the people" possess "other" rights that are not specifically enumerated in the Constitution (Lopez and Tsitouras 2008, 1251).

More often they look to the Due Process Clause of the Fourteenth Amendment as the basis for their position (Witte 1996, 193–194).

On the other side, state governments believe they owe a duty to educate their citizenry. They resist labeling the parental right as "fundamental" because parents do not raise their children in the state of nature but rather within the geographical boundaries of a political state, subject to regulation. Officials tout their role as *parens patriae* – a Latin phrase meaning "parent of the country." Under that legal doctrine, states "have the ethical responsibility and legal authority to care for and educate all children for the ultimate benefit of the state" (Cloud 2008, 708). States argue that their interest in an educated citizenry gives them the right to reasonably regulate homeschooling. Indeed, some view this as a governmental "custodial responsibility to *all* children within its jurisdiction" to ensure every child is treated "with equal respect and concern in its *parens patriae* capacity," regardless of the claims of parents (Blokhuis 2010, 203).

Both sides in this struggle have cited historical and judicial authority to support their positions, appealing to such doctrines as Natural Law and *parens patriae* to persuade the courts.

The historical basis for parental rights

The uncontroversial premise of the homeschoolers' position – that parents have primary authority over child-rearing and education – finds its roots in age-old tradition. Indeed, the near-universal global recognition of parental rights stems from both common sense and the common law. Shared biological and social human experience confirms that parents conceive their children and give them life, provide them life-sustaining benefits as infants, sacrifice for their needs as they grow, and afford them love, care, and a safe home. This pervasive nurturing vests parents with an inherent right to make key decisions regarding the care of their children.

Parental rights spring from Natural Law – principles embedded in nature itself that precede and supersede man-made laws. In the *Declaration of Independence*, Thomas Jefferson appealed to Natural Law by drawing from "the Laws of Nature and of Nature's God" the "self-evident" truths "that all men are created equal, that they are endowed by their Creator with certain unalienable Rights, that among these are Life, Liberty and the pursuit of Happiness." Though not listed in the *Declaration*, parental rights flow from this same wellspring, buttressed in western civilization by the Judeo-Christian recognition of a divine right of parents to raise and educate their children.

The foundation for parental rights goes beyond common sense and Natural Law, extending to the realm of man-made law. In nearly every culture this legal right went unchallenged for millennia, including in Britain, from which US law originated. Sir William Blackstone – the authoritative 18th century English jurist – described the parental right as "universal," and British common law saw it as a "sacred right with which courts would not interfere" (Witte 1996, 218). This legal view continued for all of US history, even to include the modern federal foray into the area of childhood education. For example, when re-creating the US Department of Education in 1979, Congress recognized the parental right, noting that "parents have the primary responsibility for the education of their children" and that "States, localities, and private institutions have the primary responsibility for supporting that parental role" (Schlueter 2001, 619).

The historical basis for state regulation

Some homeschooling advocates have argued that the government system of public education is based on the voluntary decision by parents to delegate their authority to the State to teach their children (Bartholomew 2007, 1194). They suggest this was the norm in colonial and early US history, and they view homeschooling as a "return to this nation's historical traditions" where early compulsory education laws existed merely "to assist parents in their duty of educating their children" (Page 2002, 185). Under this view, the right to educate has always belonged to the parents – the government has no role apart from the parents. On the opposite extreme, some supporters of state regulation have contended that the government holds all the power, passing on its education authority to parents (Yuracko 2008, 132). Neither one of these polarized positions can survive historical scrutiny.

As already seen, the historical evidence supporting parental rights is unassailable. Yet US history has also reserved a place for the State in childhood learning through its *parens patriae* power. From the beginning, government has played some part in encouraging and regulating education, both inside the home and in more formal settings (Wang 2011, 415). During the colonial period, officials "began to regulate to make sure that children received a basic education" (Moran 2011, 1073). The Massachusetts Bay Colony required families "to provide children the kinds of vocational and moral instruction they had previously provided in England" (Steilen 2009, 286–287). Although such laws existed, they were "weakly enforced;" in reality, "parents decided whether to send their children" to school (Kaestle 2010, 53; Steilen 2009). Still, history acknowledges by the existence of these policies that government had some *parens patriae* responsibility in ensuring the education process took place.

Parental rights and the courts

Although the Supreme Court has yet to take a case that expressly defines the limits of parental rights in the home education context, it has set precedent that strongly favors parental rights in general. The Court waded into the parental rights fray in *Meyer v. Nebraska* (1923), a case involving the prosecution of an educator who taught German in a Lutheran elementary school. His actions violated Nebraska's "English-only" law, which was passed as part of the "xenophobic hysteria" aimed at Catholics and German-Americans during the World War I era (Moran 2011, 1076).

Instead of focusing on the right of the teacher to teach, the Court decided the case by focusing on the right of the parents to decide that their children should be taught a foreign language. While striking down the law, the Court concluded that a person's right to "marry, establish a home and bring up children[, and] … give his children education suitable to their station in life" was a "fundamental" substantive due process liberty interest protected by the Fourteenth Amendment of the US Constitution, as applied against the States. Nebraska's restrictive law had violated the parents' rights.

Just two years later, in *Pierce v. Society of Sisters* (1925), a unanimous Supreme Court struck down an Oregon law that required children to be educated in *public* school – a policy that would have shut down all private schools in the state, including the Catholic schools run by the Society of Sisters. Of course that was the point of the law, due to Oregon's desire to assimilate immigrants, a practice which long had been tainted by "sometimes vicious anti-Catholicism" among the nation's school reformers (Moran 2011, 1077; Steilen 2009, 310–311). Again focusing on the rights of parents, the Court proclaimed, "The child is not the mere creature of the State." It acknowledged that parents have "the right, coupled with the high duty, to recognize and prepare [the child] for additional obligations." The State's attempt to force children out of private schools, in contravention to the will of their parents, had "no reasonable relation to some purpose within the competency of the State."

Over the next 80 years the Supreme Court addressed parental rights in various contexts. In *Prince v. Massachusetts* (1944), the Court declared that the "custody, care and nurture of the child reside[s] first in the parents, whose primary function and freedom include preparation for obligations the state can neither supply nor hinder." Twenty-eight years later, in *Stanley v. Illinois* (1972), the Court reiterated this idea: "The rights to conceive and to raise one's children have been deemed 'essential,' 'basic civil rights of man,' and '[r]ights far more precious … than property rights.'" This same line of cases provided the foundation for a variety of individual liberties, including the Right of Privacy, which undergirds the abortion line of cases after *Roe v. Wade* (1973) (Ross 2000, 179–180). A more recent pronouncement came from the Court in *Troxel v. Granville* (2000), overturning a judge's order that gave visitation rights to the paternal grandparents of two young girls, despite objections by the girls' custodial mother. A plurality of the splintered Court found that "the Due Process Clause of the Fourteenth Amendment protects the fundamental right of parents to make decisions concerning the care, custody, and control of their children." The plurality called the *Meyer–Pierce* parental right "perhaps the oldest of the fundamental liberty interests recognized by this Court."

Parens patriae and the courts

Although parental rights have a strong judicial pedigree, so too does the state-friendly doctrine of *parens patriae*. American courts, including the Supreme Court, have long accepted the notion that government has a special interest in ensuring that its citizens receive a proper education so they can contribute to society rather than become a social burden (Wang 2011, 420; Dumas, Gates, and Schwarzer 2010, 65). Even while striking down Oregon's discriminatory public school requirement in *Society of Sisters*, the Supreme Court acknowledged the "power of the state" to place "reasonable regulations" on a child's education. In the 1944 *Prince* case, the Court upheld the conviction of a mother who violated state child labor laws by having her minor daughter distribute Jehovah's Witness religious pamphlets on the street. Rejecting the mother's appeal to parental rights and religious freedom, the Court looked to the *parens patriae* doctrine. It explained the State has authority to "restrict the parent's control" through compulsory education laws, and "a wide range of power for limiting parental freedom and authority in things affecting the child's welfare, [including] to some extent, matters of conscience and religious conviction."

In sum, both sides in the homeschooling rights debate can cite historical and legal support for their basic views. In reality, they both have legitimate positions. When they clash, therefore, courts must rely on a nuanced evaluation of each side's argument and the application of various technical legal principles to resolve the case. Most important in this analysis is the court's assessment of whether or not the parental right at stake is fundamental.

"Fundamental" Rights and Homeschooling

Given the near-universal recognition of the parental right, one might wonder why calling it "fundamental" has become such a controversial proposition when applied to homeschooling. The explanation partly lies in how modern courts review government regulation under the Constitution.

Why "fundamental" rights matter

As a general rule, courts apply a deferential test when reviewing laws that do *not* impact fundamental rights, merely inquiring whether a law is reasonable – a process known as "rational basis" review. This deference stems from the recognition that the United States is a constitutional republic, where its citizens vote for their political leaders and hold them accountable at the ballot box when they act against the will of the people. Every time a judge strikes down a law passed by a democratic government, one single individual has discarded the will of the entire majority. If courts do this often, they can endanger their legitimacy and overstep their proper role in government.

Modern courts use a very different analysis when evaluating laws that impact "fundamental" rights, especially after the legal and cultural revolutions of the last sixty years. In the presence of a recognized fundamental right (such as the right to sexual intimacy between married couples) courts will apply "strict scrutiny" to any state action that interferes with that right (such as a law banning contraceptives).

Strict scrutiny is a tough legal standard to overcome, requiring the State to articulate "compelling" interests to support its regulation, and to use the "least restrictive means" to further that compelling interest. To roughly visualize this hurdle, if a government's "rational" reason is satisfied at the 50% level, its "compelling" reason must reach the 90% level. The significance of the loaded term "fundamental" now becomes apparent: it could mean the difference between victory and defeat.

Applying this concept to the issue at hand, if homeschooling is a fundamental right under the Due Process Clause of the Fourteenth Amendment, then before the State can place substantial limits on it (such as a requirement that parents teach certain subjects), it must prove under strict scrutiny that requiring children to learn those subjects is an interest of the highest order and that lesser means to achieve that interest are unavailable. A state could overcome this legal hurdle by presenting the court with persuasive data that shows why certain subjects are necessary for children to succeed as a productive member of society, and that the best place to learn those subjects is in the childhood school setting. Obviously, government regulators do not want their every rule subjected to this level of scrutiny.

Is the parental right to homeschool "fundamental"?

In its broadest sense, the parental right surely includes the decision to educate children at home (perhaps subject to reasonable state regulation). The string of Supreme Court cases already discussed weighs in favor of the view that such a right is "fundamental" under the Constitution. Yet that is not clearly the case today. Why? Partly because *Meyer* and *Pierce* were both decided prior to the Court's development of key modern constitutional doctrines, such as the strict scrutiny test (Aleshire 2009; Witte 1996). There is disagreement whether, as used in those two cases, the word "fundamental" – now a legal term of art – should be taken literally (Good 2005, 647). These doubts were reinforced in the *Troxel* case in 2000. Despite the pro-parent language already quoted from that case, a majority of the Court resolved the issue without applying strict scrutiny. Only Justice Clarence Thomas suggested that the Court should apply strict scrutiny in every case involving parental rights. Still, if one adds up the votes of the Justices in *Troxel* it appears that a majority of them would apply some level of heightened judicial review, even if not strict scrutiny (Good 2005, 658–659).

So how do courts determine whether or not the parental right is fundamental, and whether to apply strict scrutiny or a mere rational basis review? It often depends on the facts of the case and the arguments of the parties. Several lower court cases, discussed below, have rejected homeschoolers' fundamental rights arguments and applied the deferential rational basis review instead. In other cases, lingering doubt about the modern usage of the term "fundamental" has led courts, in an abundance of caution, to default to strict scrutiny review when resolving parental rights claims.

Applying Rational Basis Review

At the beginning of the homeschool movement, most decisions approving or denying home education were made by local school boards, which often seemed to act arbitrarily (Gaither 2008, 182). Beginning in the 1970s, parents litigated a series of challenges to the regulation of homeschooling. The US Supreme Court never took any of these cases on appeal, and most of the challenges failed, with lower courts applying rational basis review and narrowing the scope of the parental right.

A hallmark of homeschool advocacy has been the belief that parents can teach their children without oversight by the State. By and large, this broad position has been rejected by judges who refuse to apply strict scrutiny to state regulations (Wang 2011, 421). For example, the Illinois federal judge who decided *Scoma v. Chicago Board of Education* (1974) believed that parents who sought to educate their children "as they see fit" – in that case, without having to teach the same classes taught to public school children – were attempting to create "new and wide-ranging 'fundamental' constitutional rights." The problem was not the parents' desire to homeschool, but to do so without regulation. The federal judge from Michigan who decided *Hanson v. Cushman* (1980) later used a similar analysis, noting the State had "concede[d] that parents have the right" to homeschool, but that the parents were seeking a much broader right: "to educate their children at home without complying with a state law requiring state certification of all persons who give instruction to children within the state." In 1993, the Supreme Court of Michigan found likewise in *People v. Bennett*, refusing to apply strict scrutiny and rejecting the Fourteenth Amendment claim of parents who homeschooled their children without receiving the required teacher certification under state law (Tocco 1994, 1060–1061). The court faulted the parents for seeking "to direct their children's secular education free of reasonable regulation." The Massachusetts Supreme Judicial Court has ruled similarly (Barnett 2013, 351–352).

In each of these cases, the court's stated problem with the homeschoolers' position was that the parents sought a "new" right beyond simply giving their children "education suitable to their station in life." None of the courts rejected the idea of a narrower fundamental parental right to homeschool (subject to reasonable regulation). Indeed, the *Hanson* court expressly presumed such a fundamental right existed. In short, the defect was the breadth of the parents' claimed right: not merely a right to homeschool, but a right to homeschool without government oversight. This "wide-ranging" right was not one the courts were willing to endorse as fundamental (Ross 2010, 999). With no fundamental rights at stake, courts were free to apply a mere rational basis review and uphold the laws.

Critics of the above cases fault the judges for erroneously defining the scope of the fundamental right by reference to the parents' desire not to be regulated. For instance, the First Amendment clearly protects the fundamental right of free speech. Imagine if that right were no longer deemed fundamental simply because a person wanted to speak in a public park without censorship. A court could not redefine the right as "a desire to speak without regulation" and then treat it as though the Constitution had nothing to say on the matter. In a similar way, the "circular" reasoning of the above courts contains "several doctrinal and analytical problems" that conflate two distinct doctrinal steps (Waddell 2010, 575). Unfortunately, the judges' analysis in these cases mirrored a line of reasoning used by the US Supreme Court in the context of private schools (Barnett 2013, 350; Ross 2010, 993). In *Runyon v. McCrary* (1976), the Supreme Court agreed that parents had a right under the Constitution "to send their children to private schools," but it found no right "to provide their children with private school education unfettered by reasonable government regulation." Importing this (faulty) reasoning from private schools to home schools was not a big stretch for the judges, especially because many homeschoolers use their states' private schooling laws as their basis to educate at home. A less problematic way for a modern court to reach a similar result would be to apply the "direct and substantial interference" test developed by the Supreme Court in *Zablocki v. Redhail* (1978), involving a state's regulation of the "fundamental" right to marry. In that case, the Court noted that the State could place "reasonable regulations" on the right to marry, as long as the State did not "interfere directly and substantially with the right...." A similar analysis could be applied to homeschooling regulations without a court resorting to the circular reasoning represented by the *Runyon* line of cases.

Right or wrong, after this losing string of cases, legal battles over homeschooling shifted more to the narrow question of whether the State had acted reasonably in regulating the right to homeschool (Hasson 2012, 2). When conducting these inquiries under rational basis review, courts should be careful to analyze the question properly. To be considered "reasonable," a regulation must actually further the interest put forward by the State (Dumas, Gates, and Schwarzer 2010, 65). Thus, courts must test the asserted state interests in these cases to ensure that the interest logically connects with the regulation the State has put into place. For instance, if a state requires that all homeschooling parents possess a college degree, a court should ask whether that requirement actually furthers some legitimate interest in educating children. Some studies have shown no correlation between the education level of the parent and the standardized test scores of the homeschooled student (Alarcon 2010, 413). If that is the case, a court should determine whether the degree requirement is rational – whether it actually furthers the state's interest in better teaching. If the requirement in no way improves the education of children, then how can such a requirement be reasonable even under a rational basis review?

Applying Strict Scrutiny

Though it rarely happens, if a court applies strict scrutiny in a homeschooling case, the chances of a parental win obviously increase. Even then, however, parents might not prevail, depending on the regulation under consideration and the asserted state interests supporting the rule. If the regulation is the least restrictive way to further a compelling government interest, then the State can still overcome strict scrutiny. States have asserted at least four distinct "compelling" interests in these cases.

First, the most commonly accepted state interest is the general *parens patriae* duty to ensure children receive an adequate education for the benefit of society

(Blokhuis 2010; Alarcon 2010, 403). Some courts find this interest sufficiently weighty to count as compelling. For instance, in *Murphy v. Arkansas* (1988), the US Court of Appeals for the Eighth Circuit rejected a religious homeschooling family's challenge to a law requiring their children to take a standardized test. The court applied strict scrutiny to the law but concluded the State had a "compelling interest in educating all of its citizens" and that education has always been a "preeminent goal of American society." The Court also agreed that Arkansas had used the "least restrictive means" because the State's "only safeguard to ensure adequate training of the home-schooled student is the standardized achievement test."

Second, the State may assert a more specific type of education interest on behalf of the children themselves. All state constitutions expressly grant their citizen-children the right to a free public education (Wang 2011, 420). In some of those jurisdictions, the state constitution goes further and recognizes the child's *own* fundamental right to education, giving the State an even stronger interest to ensure children get the education they deserve in a homeschooled environment (Hersher 2008, 28).

Third, states put forward a strong government interest in the protection of homeschooled children from emotional, physical, or sexual abuse (Barnett 2013, 343). For instance, in *Jonathan L. v. Superior Court* (2008), a California appellate court examined a dependency decision regarding a family's right to teach at home. The homeschooling father had previously committed sexual abuse against two of his daughters, and a dependency hearing had determined both parents to be unfit. The Court explained there is no "absolute" right to homeschool apart from valid state interests. Even so, in an abundance of caution the Court evaluated the case using strict scrutiny, as though a fundamental right were at stake. In light of the prior sexual abuse, the Court easily found that the State possessed a compelling interest to support a decision to disapprove homeschooling.

Fourth, in child custody cases where parents are deadlocked about the decision to homeschool, state courts will act in the "best interests of the child." In these situations courts are faced with a clash of fundamental rights, with dueling assertions of the parental right over the education decision. It is not unusual in these cases for state courts to prohibit homeschooling (Kolenc 2011). For example, in *In re Kurowski* (2011), the New Hampshire Supreme Court sided with a non-custodial father who wanted his daughter to attend public school, despite the wishes of the child and her custodial, homeschooling mother. The court applied the traditional "best interests of the child" standard because the parents – with equal legal rights – had deadlocked with opposite desires for their child's education. In the court's opinion, the child would be better served outside the homeschool setting.

Other Lines of Legal Attack

Not every homeschooling legal battle has centered on the fundamental parental right, or even on the substantial line of First Amendment cases under the freedom of religion, to be discussed below. In some situations, parents are simply able to take advantage of sloppy decision-making by school districts or poor statutory drafting by state legislatures. For instance, in *Perchemlides v. Frizzle* (1978), parents in Massachusetts avoided the absolutist position taken in *Scoma* and simply sought to teach their children at home under whatever reasonable conditions the State put in place. Finding in their favor, a state court judge agreed that homeschooling was a constitutionally protected parental right, with its origin in the Ninth Amendment and the Right of Privacy. The judge noted that the State could not "set standards that are so difficult to satisfy that they effectively eviscerate" the right to homeschool. In the end, however, he did not have to rule on any of the usual thorny constitutional issues in the case. The local school district had done such a poor job considering the parents' petition to homeschool that the judge noted the procedural defect and sent the case back for reconsideration. When the school district reevaluated the family's petition using proper procedures, it approved the parents' request to homeschool, ending any further litigation (Gaither 2008, 118–122).

Ironically, the most effective attacks against compulsory education statutes have had nothing to do with parental rights. In several states – Georgia, Iowa, Minnesota, Missouri, Pennsylvania, and Wisconsin – homeschoolers had success defending against compulsory education laws and regulations that were written in such nebulous terms that the courts had little choice but to strike them down as "unconstitutionally vague" (Gaither 2008, 183). Usually the offending terms were subjective words in the statute, such as "equivalent instruction" or "private school," that could be interpreted several ways. These victories were a short-term solution that bought homeschoolers time as states rewrote their laws more precisely. As the HSLDA and other home education advocates grew in effectiveness, this reprieve also gave them a chance to help shape the form of those laws as they were being rewritten.

Religion Cases and the First Amendment

Up to this point the discussion has focused primarily on parental rights under the Due Process Clause; however, another legal defense became increasingly popular over time – the First Amendment's protection of religious freedom. Not every family homeschools for spiritual reasons, but many view it as a parental duty to provide their children a "godly" education, or at least one uncorrupted by concepts "destructive to their beliefs" (Bach 2004, 1344). In 2012, a substantial majority of surveyed families considered religious instruction to be an important factor in their reason to homeschool (Noel et al. 2013). Such families often sought shelter from homeschooling regulations in the First Amendment's Free Exercise Clause or under a Religious Freedom Restoration Act (RFRA).

The Free Exercise Clause

When religion is a factor in home education, parents have often raised a claim under the First Amendment's Free Exercise Clause, which guarantees that government "shall make no law ... prohibiting the free exercise [of religion]." Parents sometimes contend that their exercise of religion is burdened by government regulation that restricts or prevents them from homeschooling because it impairs their ability to practice their religion and pass it on to their children.

As with the fundamental parental right, murky Supreme Court precedent makes it unclear just how much protection the Free Exercise Clause actually provides. The issue once again revolves around the level of scrutiny to which the courts will subject the law. If a court applies strict scrutiny, parents have a better chance of winning; however, if a court applies the deferential rational basis test, parents will likely lose. Prior to 1990 most legal scholars assumed that courts would apply strict scrutiny to laws that imposed a burden on the free exercise of religion. This was not surprising, considering the Supreme Court apparently had done just that in ten cases since 1963 (Good 2005, 653). The most famous example was *Wisconsin v. Yoder* (1972), where the Court applied strict scrutiny and exempted Amish families from portions of Wisconsin's compulsory education law due to the serious impact of the law on their way of life.

The situation changed, however, after the Supreme Court decided *Employment Division v. Smith* (1990), upholding an Oregon statute that criminalized the use of the drug peyote, even as part of a sacramental Native American religious ceremony. In *Smith*, the Court "clarified" that strict scrutiny was *not* the proper standard to use in Free Exercise Clause cases – at least not where the government had passed a "neutral, generally applicable law" that did not target religion. Without doubt, *Smith* had far-reaching effects and upended the vast majority of cases brought under the Free Exercise Clause (Kolenc 2007, 840–842). In the homeschooling context, neutral statutes regulating home education would now be subjected merely to rational basis review even if they burdened a family's religious practice under the First Amendment...unless homeschoolers could find an exception.

The "hybrid rights" exception

In the wake of *Smith*, homeschooling families bringing Free Exercise claims were left with only one potential loophole to convince courts to apply strict scrutiny. *Smith* had carved out a "hybrid rights" exception to its holding. While discussing the proper standard of judicial review, the *Smith* Court admitted it had sometimes applied strict scrutiny against neutral laws, but only where a case was a "hybrid" that triggered the Free Exercise Clause "in conjunction with other constitutional protections, such as ... the right of parents, acknowledged in *Pierce v. Society of Sisters*, to direct the education of their children." This language – which some scholars argue is mere surplus *dicta* (Ross 2010, 1001) – seems to provide homeschoolers a tailor-made "hybrid rights" argument for strict scrutiny (Good 2005, 655; Chaplin 1999, 683).

In perhaps the greatest homeschool legal victory of all time, the Michigan Supreme Court decided a "hybrid rights" case in favor of a homeschooling family in *People v. DeJonge* (1993) – handed down the same day the court rejected the Bennett family's secular Fourteenth Amendment claim (Gaither 2008, 178–179). The juxtaposition of *DeJonge* and *Bennett* provides a useful comparison of the difference that strict scrutiny can make in a case. Both cases dealt with Michigan's requirement that homeschooling parents possess a teacher's certification. Applying the rational basis test in *Bennett*, the court ruled against the family and upheld the certification. The Court reached the opposite conclusion in *DeJonge* by using the *Smith* hybrid rights theory, thus raising the level of review to strict scrutiny. The Court required Michigan to make an exception to its certification requirement, but only where religious freedom was burdened. Notably, the Court did not weigh Michigan's right to regulate education in general, but instead it weighed one particular regulation – the certification requirement – against the family's religious beliefs. Due to strict scrutiny, religion won the day.

Outside Michigan, the lower courts have applied the hybrid rights doctrine inconsistently and sporadically (Aleshire 2009, 622; Chaplin 1999, 683–686). For instance, in *Combs v. Homer-Center School District* (2008), the US Court of Appeals for the Third Circuit rejected a challenge to a Pennsylvania homeschooling law despite the parents' hybrid rights argument. Six Christian families objected on religious grounds to the requirement that homeschoolers report to their public school districts and submit education portfolios for review. The Court refused to apply strict scrutiny, however, because it did not see the case as a "hybrid": it recognized the validity of the Free Exercise right, but it did not recognize any right under the Constitution for "parents to educate their children 'unfettered by reasonable government regulation.'" This essentially followed the reasoning of *Scoma*, *Hanson*, and *Bennett*. Thus, the Court applied rational basis review and easily upheld the law (Martin 2010, 270–271).

The Religious Freedom Restoration Act (RFRA)

About twenty states offer an additional avenue for parents to raise religious freedom as a shield from homeschool regulation. Beginning in the 1990s, in reaction to *Smith*, the Federal Government and many states began passing Religious Freedom Restoration Acts (RFRAs). In essence, RFRA raises the level of judicial review to strict scrutiny in all cases where religious freedom is substantially burdened – essentially reversing the holding in *Smith* (Lagos 2011, 126). The Obama Administration felt the sting of the federal version of RFRA when the Supreme Court partially struck down the Obama contraceptive mandate under the Affordable Care Act in *Burwell v. Hobby Lobby Stores, Inc.* (2014) because the mandate substantially burdened Hobby Lobby's exercise of religion.

State-level RFRAs are the source of few cases each year and are by no means a surefire win for parents (Lund 2010, 479–482). Three problems can await those who look to RFRA for protection. First, RFRA is available in less than half the states. In those states without it, parents are left only with the Free Exercise Clause to protect them. Second, as discussed earlier, there are situations where the State can articulate a compelling interest in support of a reasonable regulation of home education. In those cases, parents are likely to lose even with strict scrutiny (Tocco 1994, 1064–1065). Finally, in order for most RFRAs to apply, parents must show how a homeschool regulation substantially burdens their exercise of religion. A similar requirement exists in Free Exercise Clause cases (Barnett 2013, 352–353). Proving this elusive fact may not be as difficult as it sounds. For instance, it may seem strained to argue that a teaching certification burdens one's religion; however, courts are hesitant to question the sincerity or logic of an individual's religious beliefs. In *DeJonge*, for example, the Michigan Supreme Court accepted the lower court's finding that the family "believe[s] that the word of God commands them to educate their children without state certification." This judicial hesitance to pass judgment on religious beliefs makes it achievable to prove a substantial burden.

The Triumph of Homeschool Laws

Parents possess a fundamental right to homeschool their children, subject to reasonable state regulation. The discussion thus far, however, has illustrated the difficulty parents encountered in the courts when fighting for an absolute, unfettered right to homeschool. For various reasons, most courts did not apply strict scrutiny under the Due Process Clause, making it much easier for states to support reasonable regulations on homeschooling. Cases under the Free Exercise Clause and RFRA fared little better, due to vagaries in the law. Even where courts applied strict scrutiny, there was no guarantee that parents would win. In short, the courts were a fickle field of battle for the homeschooling cause. A different strategy was needed to deal with the reality that homeschool laws were here to stay.

Shifting strategy from litigation to legislation

Leaders in the homeschool movement, such as John Holt, knew from early on that a major tactic in the war for homeschool rights needed to be political combat in legislatures across the nation (Gaither 2008, 184). In the fertile soil of the 1980s, with a burgeoning homeschool lobby led by the HSLDA, the movement focused much of its effort on passing legislation that provided homeschoolers a legal environment in which to educate, subject to as little regulation as possible. As power in state legislatures shifted to homeschool-friendly Republicans, the lobby made its move.

What parents could not win in the courtroom, they mostly achieved through the political process. Indeed, homeschoolers soon garnered a reputation as being "the most effective educational lobby" (Waddell 2010, 549). In the span of a decade, home education became officially legal in every jurisdiction, with most states passing "remarkably lenient" laws containing very little regulation (Waddell 2010, 547). From 1982 to 1991, thirty-two states enacted some type of homeschooling legislation, with four more states and the District of Columbia passing such laws by

2009 (Bhatt 2014). From 2010 to 2015, the lobby won more relaxed rules in states that had been known for stricter regulation, such as Iowa, Pennsylvania, and New Hampshire (Rich 2015).

Due to the political realities on the ground, all this lobbying has created "a patchwork of laws that vary widely between states" (Kunzman and Gaither 2013, 25–26). For instance, Maryland, New York, and Ohio allow their state-level agencies, such as the board of education or department of education, to pass homeschooling regulations (Lagos 2011, 101). Other states permit homeschoolers to qualify as a private or church school under existing law – an option popularized when the movement began to grow, before there was specific homeschool legislation (Bhatt 2014; Ross 2010, 994–995). Still others (Texas, Kansas, and Michigan) have passed "parental rights acts" to enshrine language that extolls the importance of parental decision-making in education and other areas (Lagos 2011, 127). And, of course, Oklahoma stayed homeschool-friendly, having passed a constitutional amendment in 1907 that required compulsory education in public school "unless other means of education are provided" – a clear reference to homeschooling. This is just a sampling of the diversity across the nation.

Summary of homeschooling laws

The HSLDA has categorized the current status of homeschooling across the nation by labeling states as either high, moderate, low, or no-regulation jurisdictions (HSLDA 2015). As the map in Figure 3.1 illustrates, a handful of states have passed no homeschool-specific rules – apparently content with general language in compulsory education laws that reference the existence of "other education" – or they have legislated options that do not require parents to give notice of their intent to homeschool (Lagos 2011, 106). Fourteen "low-regulation" states require mere notice to a school district, without imposing other requirements on parents. In the "moderate regulation" category, about twenty states and the District of Columbia require both notification and some method of assessing progress, such as standardized testing or a teacher evaluation. Finally, a handful of "high-regulation" states in the Northeast require not only notice or test scores, but also compliance with more onerous restrictions, such as curriculum approval, teacher certification, and required instruction times (Wang 2011, 428).

How Much Regulation?

In light of the political successes of the home education lobby, the legal struggle has shifted in recent decades from the courts to the legislatures, with homeschooling advocates seeking laws that essentially deregulate the practice – "a total hands-off policy," as one HSLDA attorney stated – while critics argue for more intrusive government rules and oversight (Rich 2015). Some advocates suggest that states should legislate only minimally intrusive regulations that are capable of "pass[ing]

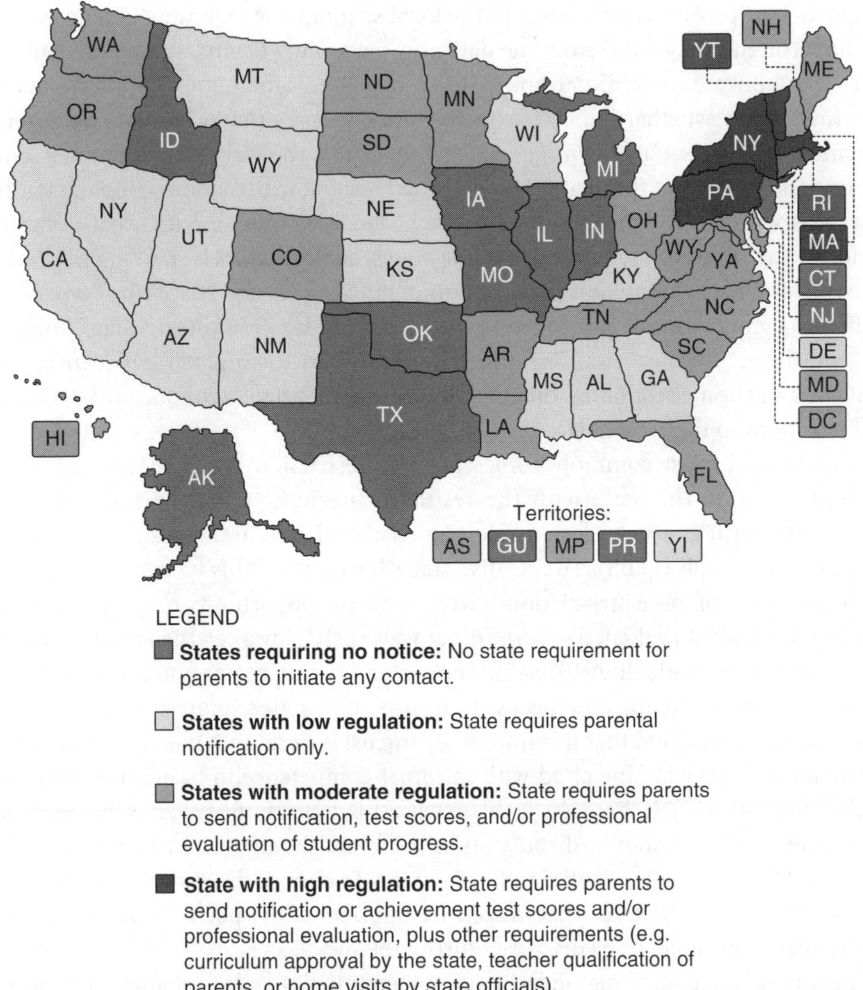

Figure 3.1 State laws on homeschooling as of January 13, 2015 (see hslda.org/laws for current map and details for each state). © HSLDA, used by permission.

the strict scrutiny test" (Alarcon 2010, 409). In contrast, a growing number of scholars have demanded more onerous restrictions on home education to further crucial state interests and "liberal" values (Lagos 2011, 134–141). This active area of the law warrants further comment.

Current homeschool regulations

The "notice" requirement – still the most prevalent homeschooling rule in the nation – has encountered the least amount of resistance from home educators due to its minimal intrusiveness. Although the details of this rule vary by state, it typically requires that parents send a letter to the local school board within a certain period of time (often thirty days) from the date homeschooling begins, stating the family's intent to educate the child at home. In some states, ambiguous laws have led to confusion over whether the notice must be filed before or after homeschooling has begun. For instance, in *Nebraska v. Thacker* (2013), the Nebraska Supreme Court struggled to interpret that state's law, eventually siding with a homeschooling family that was wrongfully prosecuted for truancy due to school absences that occurred prior to the filing of the notice. In some states, such as Florida, parents must also provide notice of their intent to cease homeschooling (Lagos 2011, 103–104). Most scholars rightly view the notice requirement as necessary to protect a state's interest in education "because it allows the government to distinguish between truant students and home schooling students," and because it provides important "statistical information" to the state (Alarcon 2010, 411).

The second most common homeschooling restriction is the requirement that parents provide the State with the results of periodic standardized testing of students – perhaps a State-designed test or a national measurement such as the Iowa Tests of Basic Skills (ITBS). Twenty-five states have passed this type of requirement, although some of these jurisdictions give parents the opportunity to avoid testing by having the student evaluated in some other way, such as by a certified teacher (Lagos 2011, 108–109; Waddell 2010, 548). Supporters of this requirement contend that annual testing is an absolute necessity to protect a state's interest in ensuring an educated citizenry, and that it is minimally intrusive because it merely requires that "parents must provide the child with minimal competence in basic, core subjects" (Alarcon 2010, 412). If there is a problem with this restriction at all, it is the potential that overly specific standardized tests will dictate the material to be covered by students, thus infringing on the right of parents to choose the topics of instruction. This concern is similar to that voiced by opponents of specific state-mandated curricular requirements, as discussed further below.

Less-used regulatory methods in certain jurisdictions also attempt to measure whether students are receiving an adequate education. Some states require an annual student evaluation by a certified teacher, school official, or psychologist; however, this requirement is sometimes optional if the student takes a standardized test. In about half the states that demand notice, parents must keep additional data in a student portfolio, including such details as daily attendance and records of academic progress. Those portfolios may be inspected at the request of school district officials in some jurisdictions (Lagos 2011, 103). Homeschooling advocates claim that these methods are too burdensome to pass strict scrutiny, if it were ever applied, and that they "unnecessarily trample parents' fundamental constitutional right to direct the education of their children" (Alarcon 2010, 410–413). Homeschoolers would like to see these restrictions die out, just as the now-rare practice of involuntary "home visits" died after *Brunelle v. Lynn Public Schools* (1998), when the Supreme Judicial Court of Massachusetts found them to be unconstitutional. Unlike home visits, however, the methods above do not involve the same level of intrusion into privacy, making it unlikely that they will fail in the courts.

A handful of states still place some type of teacher certification or competency requirement on parents who homeschool – perhaps the restriction most despised by homeschoolers because it has the potential to disqualify countless families. Modern variations of this requirement are not as severe as in the past. Seven states and the District of Columbia merely require a high school diploma or graduate equivalency degree to teach, while North Dakota requires parents to be monitored by a certified teacher for two years (Lagos 2011, 107; Alarcon 2010, 410). Homeschooling advocates contend that these restrictions do "not ensure that the parent will actually provide higher quality education" (Alarcon 2010, 413). Indeed, the "weight of available empirical evidence" challenges the foundation of this rule because the data reveals that "un-credentialed parents" are "turning out well-educated, well-adjusted children who are becoming productive citizens" – the very goal of a state's education system (Dumas, Gates, and Schwarzer 2010, 67–68, 83). Thus, advocates argue that the requirement of a teaching credential is unnecessary and does not further reasonable state interests.

Several states regulate the curriculum used for teaching homeschoolers (Lagos 2011). This is an area where states must be careful to legislate clearly, avoiding vague statutory language that has sometimes been struck down, such as the requirement for "equivalent instruction" to the public schools. Dictating curriculum coverage is most intensive in New York, Pennsylvania, and North Dakota, which require homeschoolers to complete various credits in specific subjects in order to graduate. Idaho is an example of a state that provides less guidance, requiring (a bit vaguely) that children be "comparably" instructed in subjects "commonly and usually taught in the public schools." These rules pale in comparison to the situation in Rhode Island and Massachusetts, which still require homeschoolers to have a public school official "approve" their plans in advance based on such subjective factors as the "thoroughness and efficiency" of the proposed instruction. If implemented in a reasonable manner, curriculum rules can further the valid state interest of ensuring a minimum level of general education for its citizenry. If done unreasonably, however, the far-reaching effect of these dictates could unconstitutionally infringe the freedom of parents to direct their children's education.

Finally, a handful of states dictate the amount of time homeschoolers must spend on their daily instruction. Approximately five states require that children spend an "equivalent" amount of time in class as students attending public school, and three states simply require that the teaching be "regular and thorough" (Lagos 2011, 111). The problem with time restrictions is that one of the major advantages of home education is to cut out the wastefulness and inefficiency of brick and mortar schools, which must expend time instructing large numbers of students, including the extra time it takes to repeat material for slower students who require additional in-depth explanations.

Despite the objection of homeschooling advocates, most of the restrictions in this section can, and have, survived legal challenges in the courts – when implemented reasonably. Homeschoolers now tackle these restrictions at the policy level, persuading state legislators to settle for less regulation instead of more and encouraging politicians to think carefully before creating a rule that does little or nothing to further a state's valid interest in an educated citizenry. In most states, this lobbying has been effective. Indeed, homeschoolers have been so successful that they now face criticism from those who believe states are improperly abdicating their *parens patriae* duties, as discussed further below.

The new debate

With lax regulation nationwide, critics of homeschooling have been warning that states are "relinquishing their supervisory role in education by affirmatively allowing home schooling parents to take complete control over their child's education" (Wang 2011, 430). Some scholars show particular concern for religious homeschoolers – "those who believe in an absolute truth [and] … that other belief systems are mistaken at best, and at worst, evil" (Ross 2010, 1008). These "liberal political theorists" seek rules to mitigate the perceived harm that "homeschooling instills 'illiberal' attitudes, produces children who are 'ethically servile' to their parents, or fails to produce children committed to the 'constitutional norm of tolerance'" (Hasson 2012, 11–12). They decry "intolerant" homeschoolers who "mistakenly believe" that their parental rights "entitle them to protect their children from exposure to ideas that conflict with the messages parents are inculcating at home" (Ross 2010, 1000). To cure these ills, these scholars argue the State should add "lessons on mutual respect for diverse populations and viewpoints as a mandatory curricular requirement" and force tolerance and other liberal virtues on homeschoolers – "at least during the portion of the day they claim to devote to satisfying the compulsory schooling requirement" (Ross 2010, 1005).

For obvious reasons, these recommendations by liberal scholars cause great concern to homeschooling advocates. The suggestions are "troubling" because the clamor for more regulation ignores the constitutional rights of parents and relies "on presumptions based on ideology rather than on empirical data." Not only is there "no data [to] suggest[] that homeschoolers educate their children in the reclusive silos imagined by critics," but to the contrary, these critiques "fail to consider existing research that casts doubt on the accuracy of their assumptions" (Hasson 2012, 13–15). Why add more restrictions and regulations to solve a problem that, by and large, is a non-issue?

The proposed "inculcation" of liberal values also raises serious First Amendment concerns, both with freedom of religion and speech. In essence, these scholars seek to force parents to teach their children objectionable content despite the parents' religious or philosophical beliefs. For instance (to use one of today's hot-button issues), these scholars would not be satisfied with parents merely "discussing" a topic with their children, such as the existence of same-sex marriage. Instead, they would expect parents – whether they like it or not – to proclaim as a societal good the diversity of sexual orientations and the equality of same-sex marriage, even where the parents' religious or philosophical beliefs might view such conduct or unions as "sinful" or harmful to society at large. This type of forced speech within the home to align children with government-sanctioned values might be acceptable in a totalitarian regime, but not in a democracy that values freedom.

Trending Legal Issues

Aside from the foundational concepts and discussions already presented, two other legal issues warrant comment below. The first topic analyzes how the privacy of the home under the Fourth Amendment interacts with the State's *parens patriae* duty with regard to the prevention of child abuse in homeschooled households. The second topic examines the demand by some parents to access public school benefits while at the same time choosing to educate their children at home without regulation.

Child abuse, homeschooling, and the Fourth Amendment

As discussed earlier, the State has a strong interest in protecting children from abuse or neglect, whether physical, sexual, emotional, or educational. Some worry that offenders will use the protective cloak of homeschooling to hide their abusive activities (Barnett 2013). When parents send their kids to school outside the home, they are entrusting the care of their children to teachers, counselors, and administrators, who can observe the children and ask questions about potentially abusive situations. This outside set of eyes provides the State with some expectation that it can prevent and catch child abuse at home. This is not the case with homeschooled children, whose parents may keep them away from the watchful gaze of social workers and school officials. One study of seventeen abused children found that 47% of them were allegedly being "homeschooled" (Knox et al. 2014).

To deal with this concern, some scholars have recommended that homeschoolers be forced into brick-and-mortar schools to teach their children, or that social workers employ a robust use of no-notice home visits where a child can be interviewed and the safety of the home inspected (McMullen 2002). The truth is that social workers are placed in a very difficult position in these cases. If an allegation of neglect is filed against a homeschooling family, the need to investigate increases exponentially and often triggers legal duties. As a typical example in Florida, when state officials are presented with allegations of child abuse, Florida Statutes § 39.301(7) requires them to conduct protective investigations, which include a mandatory "face-to-face interview with the child, other siblings, parents, and other adults in the household and an onsite assessment of the child's residence." This leads to an important inquiry, especially when it involves homeschooled children: must officials first obtain a search warrant before entering the house of a homeschooled child to check for compliance with educational standards or to investigate potential abuse? The answer lies with the Fourth Amendment of the US Constitution.

Since the US Supreme Court began expanding federal judicial power in the 1950s, the Fourth Amendment has increasingly restricted the actions of state and local government officials, to include truancy officers, social workers, and school administrators. It prohibits them from violating "[t]he right of the people to be secure in their persons, houses, papers, and effects, against unreasonable searches and seizures," and requires that "no warrants shall issue, but upon probable cause, supported by oath or affirmation, and particularly describing the place to be searched, and the persons or things to be seized." The Supreme Court has vigorously enforced these individual rights through the use of the "exclusionary rule," which prevents prosecutors from admitting trial evidence that has been improperly seized. Congress has also endeavored to protect these rights by authorizing citizens to sue the government for money damages when officials violate the Fourth Amendment.

State and local officials have argued that the Fourth Amendment should not apply to their actions, especially when it comes to their role in education, including investigations of truancy or child abuse. Although the Supreme Court has never ruled on this issue, lower courts almost unanimously have found that the Fourth Amendment applies to such officials, especially when investigating child abuse or neglect. In *Andrews v. Hickman County, Tennessee* (2012) – a case involving social workers who entered a family's home to inspect the premises and interview the children – the US Court of Appeals for the Sixth Circuit noted wide agreement among the federal courts and explained that the Fourth Amendment applies "to the activities of civil as well as criminal authorities," because "the individual's interest in privacy and personal security 'suffers whether the government's motivation is to investigate violations of criminal law or breaches of other … standards.'"

Therefore, assuming the Fourth Amendment applies, it places two conditions on government inspections of the home. First, there must be "probable cause" – a sufficient amount of information to convince a prudent person that evidence of a crime will be found in the home. In the context of a child neglect investigation, perhaps the home contains dangerous, unsanitary living conditions. This data must be supported by a person willing to swear under oath to the presence of these bad conditions – perhaps a neighbor who visited the home and witnessed the sickening conditions. Second, before officials can invade the sanctity of the home they must obtain a search warrant from a "neutral and detached magistrate" – an unbiased judge who can evaluate the evidence and decide whether to issue a warrant. In some jurisdictions, this streamlined process may take very little time, perhaps only an hour in a well-documented case. There are exceptions to the Fourth Amendment, also. For instance, a homeschooling parent might consent to a home inspection without a warrant. Likewise, state officials may become aware of an "exigent circumstance," such as hearing cries of terror from a child inside the home, which requires the officials to enter without a warrant to deal with an apparent emergency.

In addition to the Fourth Amendment, recent statutory changes also impact abuse investigations against parents. In the past, families complained that social workers were not respecting constitutional privacy rules when following up on complaints made against homeschoolers. Often, the suspected parent might have no idea what kind of allegation had been lodged against them. For example, was it a complaint of alleged sexual abuse, or merely a failure to mail the notice of intent to homeschool? In recent years, many states have passed "Child Abuse Prevention and Treatment Acts" that protect families during investigations by providing "clearly defined procedures" to help avoid the trampling of privacy rights (Logas 2011, 127–128). This rash of new legislation was sparked by a 2003 federal law – 42 U.S.C. § 5106a(b) – that placed certain obligations on states that accepted federal money to help fight child abuse. Notably, states agreed that their officials would advise individuals "at the initial time of contact" about "the complaints and allegations made against" them. In the context of a child neglect investigation, officials in many states are now required by law to tell families at the time of first contact the substance of any child neglect allegations.

The combined effect of the Fourth Amendment and these additional statutory procedures has been to provide homeschoolers with greater levels of protection from intrusive investigations based on mere suspicion or anti-homeschool prejudice. Those who educate at home have long complained of such harassment by those who do not approve of their lifestyle. If state officials have sufficient evidence to seek a warrant, they can proceed with an investigation. They will not be free, however, to show up and demand entry to a homeschooler's house based on speculations that are kept hidden from the family. Critics of home education will be quick to point out the flip side to this situation: these protections come at a dangerous price and provide yet more reasons to worry about home education. They fear that – in the largely unregulated frontier of homeschooling – parents will hide misconduct from state officials while at the same time invoking individual rights to thwart abuse inquiries. These concerns are quite understandable, and the abuse of even one child is an unspeakable tragedy; still, the reality is that investigators possessing sufficient levels of suspicion can overcome the fairly low threshold of probable cause and obtain the proper warrant to ensure that parents are not engaged in abuse. This will protect any children in jeopardy while at the same respecting the rights of the parents.

Accessing public school resources

A final area of interest involves a growing movement in many states to give homeschoolers access to public school sports programs, extracurricular activities, and even traditional courses in the curriculum. The position of some homeschooling families has been simple: they pay taxes to support the local public schools, so why are their children prohibited from receiving all benefit from the school district? Why must their decision to homeschool be an all-or-nothing choice? Some families have unsuccessfully attempted to force the State's hand by bringing litigation to secure access to these programs. Courts have found, however, that parents have no right to dictate how a school district allocates resources, especially where there are rational reasons to limit them to public school students.

In *Swanson v. Guthrie* (1998), parents in Oklahoma sought to supplement their daughter's religious homeschooling with select courses in public school, in violation of a policy that offered these resources only to children attending the school full-time. Arguing that the policy burdened their religious and parental rights to homeschool, the Swanson's hoped to fit their case into the *Smith* hybrid rights exception, thereby subjecting the policy to strict scrutiny. On appeal, the US Court of Appeals for the Tenth Circuit flatly rejected this argument, finding no parental right "that would force a local school board to allow parents to dictate that their children will attend public school for only part of the school day." Rejecting a similar argument in *Reid v. Kenowa Hills Public School* (2004), a Michigan appellate court brushed aside a group of parents' freedom of religion arguments by finding an inconsistency in their position. The religious parents in that case were asking that their children be permitted to participate in public school sports activities. The court, however, could not understand how secular extracurricular activities might benefit the family's religious curriculum. Finding no burden on their religion, the court applied rational basis review and easily dismissed the case.

Stymied by the courts, homeschooling advocates again found success in state legislatures. After much lobbying, almost thirty states have now stopped discriminating against homeschooled students in public school activities, especially in sports programs (HSLDA 2016). Yet this success has not come without much internal hand-wringing among homeschoolers themselves. Some in the movement are worried that other homeschoolers would return to the public schools looking for government support. They fear that asking legislators to allocate public school resources for homeschooling will only spell trouble in the end, inviting greater regulation of home education and breeding dependency among homeschoolers on a government bureaucracy that should be distrusted (Watt 2013).

This final issue proves that homeschooling has entered the mainstream of American legal life. The movement started as a countercultural backlash against an inept bureaucracy – a courageous stand by dedicated parents who risked fines and jail for their principles. It toiled through many difficult years, seeking out courts that would protect the fundamental rights of parents from the persecutions of big government. When political allies came to power, it grew from a tiny upstart to perhaps the most effective lobbying block in all of education. And now, with most of its goals achieved through the political process, it has set its sights on reengagement with that same public school bureaucracy from which it originally broke, hoping to receive the benefit of its tax dollars while still holding on to the astonishing degree of freedom it won in the struggle. Only time will tell whether this new strategy will backfire, striking at the core of homeschooling – the pure parental desire simply to be left alone to raise and educate their children as they see fit.

References

Alarcon, Paul A. 2010. "Recognizing and Regulating Home Schooling in California: Balancing Parental and State Interests in Education." *Chapman Law Review*, 13: 391–416.

Aleshire, Noah. 2009. "Defining the New 'Species': Recommendations for California Home school Legislation After *Jonathan L. v. Superior Court*." *West's Education Law Reporter*, 246: 607–635.

Bach, Laura J. 2004. "For God or Grades? States Imposing Fewer Requirements on Religious Home Schoolers and the Religion Clauses of the First Amendment." *Valparaiso University Law Review*, 38: 1337–1398.

Barnett, Tyler. 2013. "Pulling Back the Curtains: Undetected Child Abuse and the Need for Increased Regulation of Home Schools in Missouri." *Brigham Young University Education and Law Journal*, 2011, 2: 341–356.

Bartholomew, Khianna. 2007. "Avoiding Implicit Acceptance of Bigotry: An Argument for Standardized Testing of Home-Schooled Children." *Cornell Law Review*, 92: 1177–1199.

Bhatt, Rachana. 2014. "Home is Where the School Is: The Impact of Homeschool Legislation on School Choice." *Journal of School Choice: International Research and Reform*, 8:2: 192–212. DOI: 10.1080/15582159.2014.905394

Blokhuis, J.C. 2010. "Whose custody is it, anyway?: 'Homeschooling' from a *parens patriae* perspective." *Theory and Research in Education*, 8:2: 199–222. DOI: 10.1177/1477878510368628

Chaplin, Michael E. 1999. "*Peterson v. Minidoka County School*: Home Education, Free Exercise, and Parental Rights." *Notre Dame Law Review*, 75: 663–690.

Cloud, Robert C. 2008. "Balancing Parental Rights and State Interests in Home Schooling." *West's Education Law Reporter*, 235: 697–708.

Dumas, Tanya K., Sean Gates, and Deborah R. Schwarzer. 2010. "Evidence for Homeschooling: Constitutional Analysis in Light of Social Science Research." *Widener Law Review*, 16: 63–87.

Gaither, Milton. 2008. *Homeschool: An American History*. New York: Palgrave Macmillan.

Good, Heather M. 2005. "'The Forgotten Child of Our Constitution': The Parental Free Exercise Right to Direct the Education and Religious Upbringing of Children." *Emory Law Journal*, 54: 641– 679.

Hasson, Mary Rice. 2012. "The Changing Conversation Around Homeschooling: An Argument for More Data and Less Ideology." *University of St Thomas Journal of Law and Public Policy*, 7: 1–23.

Hersher, Michael E. 2008. "'Home schooling' in California." *Yale Law Journal Pocket Part*, 118: 27– 31.

Home School Legal Defense Association. 2013. "State Laws Concerning Participation of Homeschool Students in Public School Activities." Accessed January 13, 2015. http://www.hslda.org/docs/nche/Issues/E/Equal_Access.pdf

Home School Legal Defense Association. 2016. "State Laws." Accessed April 8, 2016. https://www.hslda.org/laws/

Kaestle, Carl F. 2010. "Victory of the Common School Movement: A Turning Point in American Educational History." In *Historians on America: Decisions That Made a Difference*, edited by George Clack, 52–68. dot1q Publishing.

Knox, Barbara L., et al. 2014. "Child Torture as a Form of Child Abuse." *Journal of Child & Adolescent Trauma*, 7: 37–49. DOI 10.1007/s40653-014-0009-9

Kolenc, Antony Barone. 2007. "'Mr. Scalia's Neighborhood': A Home for Minority Religions?" *St John's Law Review*, 81: 819–880.

Kolenc, Antony Barone. 2011. "When 'I Do' becomes 'You Won't!' – Preserving the Right to Homeschool After Divorce." *Ave Maria Law Review*, 9: 263–302.

Kunzman, R., and Milton Gaither. 2013. "Homeschooling: A Comprehensive Survey of the Research." *Other Education: The Journal of Education Alternatives*, 2: 4–59.

Lagos, Julio Alberto. 2011. "Parental Education Rights in the United States and Canada: Homeschooling and its Legal Protection." PhD diss., Pontificia Universitas Sanctae Crucis Facultas Iuris Canonici.

Lines, Patricia M. 2000. "Homeschooling Comes of Age." *The Public Interest*, 140: 74–85.

Lopez, Maria Pabon, and Diomedes J. Tsitouras. 2008. "From the Border to the Schoolhouse Gate: Alternative Arguments for Extending Primary Education to Undocumented Alien Children." *Hofstra Law Review*, 36: 1243–1270.

Lund, Christopher C. 2010. "Religious Liberty After *Gonzales*: A Look at State RFRAs." *South Dakota Law Review*, 55: 466–497.

Martin, Aaron T. 2010. "Homeschooling in Germany and the United States." *Arizona Journal of International and Comparative Law*, 27: 225–282.

McMullen, Judith G. 2002. "Behind Closed Doors: Should States Regulate Home schooling?" *South Carolina Law Review*, 54: 75–109.

Moran, Courtenay E. 2011. "How to Regulate Homeschooling: Why History Supports the Theory of Parental Choice." *University of Illinois Law Review*, 2011: 1061–1094.

Murphy, Joseph. 2012. *Homeschooling in America: Capturing and Assessing the Movement*. Thousand Oaks: Corwin.

Noel, Amber, and Patrick Stark, Jeremy Redford, and Andrew Zukerberg. 2012 (rev. May 2015). "Parent and Family Involvement in Education, from the National Household Education Surveys Program of 2012: First Look." *National Center for Education Statistics*. http://nces.ed.gov/pubs2013/2013028rev.pdf

Olsen, Chad. 2009. "Constitutionality of Home Education: How the Supreme Court and American History Endorse Parental Choice." *Brigham Young University Education and Law Journal*, 2: 399–423.

Page, Jr., Bruce D. 2002. "Changing Our Perspective: How Presumptive Invalidity of Home School Regulations Will Further the State's Interest in an Educated Citizenry." *Regent University Law Review*, 14: 181–214.

Provasnik, Stephen. 2006. "Judicial Activism and the Origins of Parental Choice: The Court's Role in the Institutionalization of Compulsory Education in the United States, 1891–1925." *History of Education Quarterly*, 46: 311–347.

Rich, Motoko. 2015. "Home Schooling: More Pupils, Less Regulation." *New York Times*, January 4, 2105. Accessed January 13, 2015. http://www.nytimes.com/2015/01/05/education/home-schooling-more-pupils-less-regulation.html?_r=0

Ross, Catherine J. 2010. "Fundamentalist Challenges to Core Democratic Values: Exit and Homeschooling." *William and Mary Bill of Rights Journal*, 18: 991–1014.

Ross, William G. 2000. "The Contemporary Significance of *Meyer* and *Pierce* for Parental Rights Issues Involving Education." *Akron Law Review*, 34: 177–207.

Schlueter, Linda L. 2001. "Parental Rights in the Twenty-First Century: Parents as Full Partners in Education." *Saint Mary's Law Journal*, 32: 611–77.

Steilen, Matthew. 2009. "Parental Rights and the State Regulation of Religious Schools." *Brigham Young University Education and Law Journal*, 2009: 269–339.

Tocco, Joseph P. 1994. "Home Schooling in Michigan: Is There a Fundamental Right to Teach Your Children at Home?" *Detroit Mercy Law Review*, 71: 1053–1079.

Waddell, Timothy Brandon. 2010. "Bringing It All Back Home: Establishing a Coherent Constitutional Framework for the Re-regulation of Homeschooling." *Vanderbilt Law Review*, 63: 541–97.

Wang, Linda. 2011. "Who Knows Best? The Appropriate Level of Judicial Scrutiny on Compulsory Education Laws Regarding Home Schooling." *Journal of Civil Rights & Economic Development*, 25: 413–448.

Watt, Fred. 2013. "What's Wrong with the Tebow Bill?: An Open Letter to Texas Homeschoolers." *Northside Falcons* website. Accessed March 22, 2015. http://www.northsidefalcons.com/tebow-bill.htm

Witte, Daniel E. 1996. "*People v. Bennett*: Analytic Approaches to Recognizing a Fundamental Parental Right Under the Ninth Amendment." *Brigham Young University Law Review*, 1996: 183–280.

Yuracko, Kimberly A. 2008. "Education Off the Grid: Constitutional Constraints on Homeschooling." *California Law Review*, 96: 123–184.

4

The Calculus of Departure
Parent Motivations for Homeschooling

Joseph Murphy, Milton Gaither,
and Christine E. Gleim

> Common to these parents is the belief that the traditional schools available to them are not meeting the needs of the total child (Gray 1993, 9).

> Home schoolers proceed from the insight that the institution of public education cannot adequately serve their children in the ways they want them served (Lubienski 2000, 211).

> The home school parents believed that the public schools were academically and, more importantly, spiritually bankrupt, and that placing their children there was to put them at great risk—spiritually, intellectually, socially, and all too often physically (Cochran 1995, 278).

Though we could employ a wide-angle lens to explore the larger social, cultural, political, and economic forces that have provided the context for the growth of homeschooling in the US, here we examine the causal universe with a narrower lens, the views of parents who have selected homeschooling for their children. In part one of the chapter, we provide a few general clarifying notes on parental motivations. We then investigate how context influences motivations. In the second part of the chapter, we forge and then employ a motivational scaffold to examine parental actuations. We begin by reviewing major frameworks provided by scholars from 1980 to 2015. We then deepen our analysis by exploring the four major motivations for homeschooling in detail: religious-grounded motivations, academic-anchored reasons, school environment-focused motivations, and family-based rationales.

The Wiley Handbook of Home Education, First Edition. Edited by Milton Gaither.

Motivational Dynamics

> Home education represents an exit from the formal educational system, an exit based on a complex set of needs, motivations, and expectations that are often idiosyncratic when examined individually but are united collectively into an organized and sophisticated sociopolitical movement (Marlow 1994, 440).

Prime motive

> The different rationales that parents have for home instruction are obvious. The underlying commonality between them, however, is less apparent. In each instance, homeschooling provides parents the opportunity to expand personal and family rights, regardless of their secular or religious orientations. Looked at in this way, the growth of the home school movement represents the attempt of a widely diverse group of parents to decide how their children will be educated, what values they will learn, and which socialization experiences they will encounter. (Mayberry et al. 1995, 39)

> The right of parents to raise and educate their children – and the complete lack of government authority in that regard – is perhaps *the* foundational conviction in homeschooling. (Kunzman 2009, 181)

Before we unpack actuational complexities, we need to be explicit about the universal, prime motive for homeschooling, one that is somewhat underemphasized (or assumed and skipped over) in much of the empirical literature on home-based education. At the core, parents homeschool for one overarching reason: they want control of their children and their education (Mayberry et al. 1995; Lines 1991). They do not want to give that authority away to the school (Caruana 1999; Colfax 1990). This is the foundation on which is built all other motives. It is the vehicle to meet other goals, for example to impart cherished values or to protect children from social harm.

Three sources of motives

> Parents' recollections of school and of learning environments thus figured prominently in their thinking about home education (Knowles1991, 219).

> Their rejection of the public school is often shaped by the experiences they have had while their children have been enrolled in public schools. (Mayberry 1989b, 177).

Researchers have helped us discern the wellsprings from which homeschooling motives flow. To begin with, as Knowles (1988; 1991; Knowles, Muchmore, and Spaulding 1994) was the first to systematically document, motives for homeschooling are nurtured by the schooling and family experiences parents had when they were children, especially unpleasant ones (Arai 2000; Wyatt 2007). These, Knowles maintains, are as important as present conditions in convincing parents to educate their children at home. Knowles and team, for example, document a need for some parents to protect their children from the type of unhealthy learning environments in play when they were students. Other scholars report on parents hoping to shield their children from the less-than-stellar academic regiment they experienced in school (Williams, Arnoldson, and Reynolds 1984). Second, motives grow from the challenges and problems freighted on children by today's schools (Groover and Endsley 1988). Third, reasons emanate from a ferocious critique of America's schools in general, independent of one's own experiences and the experiences of one's children (Van Galen and Pittman 1991; Vigilant, Tyler, and Trefethren 2013).

Push–pull dynamics

> Combined frequencies suggest that choices for homeschooling are made for both reactive and proactive reasons (Dahlquist, York-Barr, and Hendel 2006, 366).

We also learn from a rich trove of studies that there are both positive and negative reasons for homeschooling, with the former featuring the perceived benefits of educating at home (e.g., building a stronger family) and the latter underscoring the personal costs of public schooling (e.g., becoming peer-dependent) – what Hertzel (1997) calls pull and push factors. We have much to report on findings in each of these two domains in the sections that follow. Our only objective here is to confirm the dual nature of motives. We also note that positive motives are underemphasized in the general literature vis-à-vis their importance in the empirical studies.

Complexity and overlapping rationales

> The reasons to homeschool are as diverse as the methods employed (Lyman 2000, 14).

> The decision to educate at home involves a complex set of motivations (Marlow 1994, 441–442).

> Reasons which compel home education families to teach their children at home may not be mutually exclusive (Marshall and Valle 1996, 4).

Research consistently reveals that the attribution of uniformity in homeschooling motives often seen in popular literature is inaccurate. Studies generally confirm that the motives of homeschooling families are multidimensional (Ray 2009; Sutton and Bogan 2005; Lois 2013). They also document that there is considerable variety in the reasons parents supply for homeschooling their children (Apostoleris 1999; Nemer 2002; Kunzman 2009), what Mayberry and colleagues (1995) refer to as a myriad of perspectives and beliefs shaping homeschooling decisions. Motives also tend to be complex (Wartes 1987), making understanding more arduous than often assumed (Knowles 1988). Finally, there seems to be considerable overlap in motives (Dahlquist et al. 2006), and these can change over time (Safran 2010). Fixed boundaries between motives that defined the early modern era of homeschooling seem to be disintegrating (McKeon 2007; Muntes 2006) and motivational bundles seem to be more varied today (Isenberg 2007).

Shifts in motivations

There is some important empirical work that reveals that the motivational geography of homeschooling is changing. For example, one conclusion is that ideological rationales in general and religious-based motivations in particular, although still quite significant, are becoming less important (Noel, Stark, and Redford 2013; Bielick 2008; Green and Hoover-Dempsey 2007). Another finding is that as a new generation of middle grounders has moved onto the homeschooling stage, motivations are less polarized (Collom and Mitchell 2005; Gaither 2008). These findings must not lead us to conclude, however, that the classic division of motivation into a more secular pedagogically motivated group and a more religious ideologically motivated group (discussed at length below) has disappeared. Many families continue to fall into one or both of these two camps (Hanna 2011).

Investigators are also documenting that even in the same family motivations for homeschooling are not fixed and can change over time (Collom 2005; Safran 2010). Analysts have discovered that families sometimes begin homeschooling for one set of reasons but reference a different bundle of motivations for continuing the practice (Gray 1993; Nemer 2002; Safran 2010). Dobson (2001) and Ray (2004), for example, suggest that there may be movement from reactive to proactive rationales as parents settle into homeschooling. More specifically, the case has been made that involvement in the work and networks of homeschooling can transform motives and increase commitment (Collom 2005; Safran 2010). Relatedly, investigators document that parental motives vary by the age of the child (Isenberg 2002). For example, Muntes (2006) finds that parents place more weight on the importance of developing character and values for younger than for older children.

Three other insights merit note in any review of homeschooling motives. First, there is at least a hint in the literature that motivations follow from the decision to homeschool rather than drive the original choice (McKeon 2007), a finding not inconsistent with the larger stream of research on human motivation. Second, for many families motives for homeschooling are a piece of a larger perspective on life (Kunzman 2009); they are nested in a web of motivations that power particular lifestyles (Nemer 2002). Finally, almost no one has addressed the motivational quandary first surfaced by Mayberry and team (1995); that is, why do some roughly equivalent families in terms of demographics, values, and lifestyles vary in their selection of homeschooling as an educational option?

Context Considerations

> A parent's decision to homeschool is motivated not only by the parent's psychological beliefs but also by the parent's perception of contextual variables that influence the feasibility of homeschooling (Green and Hoover-Dempsey 2007, 272).

> The propensity to home school is not only responsive to observed characteristics of schools, but also to household characteristics (Isenberg 2002, 23).

One of the essential laws of social science is that context almost always matters. Nowhere is this conclusion more obvious than in the realm of homeschooling. Employing nomenclature such as environmental variables, economic determinants, and structural conditions, scholars identify four bundles of contextual conditions that can differentially shape motivations to homeschool: the school, the household, the student, and the community.

Schooling characteristics

> These results indicate that public school quality issues are important when a family considers the choice between public and home education. (Houston 1999, 101).

The leading economically grounded scholar in the area of homeschooling divides schooling conditions in two categories, those that relate directly to the quality of the public schools and those that measure environmental conditions in the school district in which a given school is located (Houston 1999). We also learn from other researchers that the state context plays a role in influencing decisions to homeschool (Isenberg 2007).

Turning first to *measures of school quality*, Houston (1999) in his path-breaking research concluded that when the quality of schools goes down homeschooling increases. Or, stated inversely, the availability of quality schools decreases homeschooling (Isenberg 2007). While acknowledging that identifying the best measure of public school quality is not an easy assignment, Houston (1999) identifies some proxies that are linked to home-based education. Examining one indicator, expenditure level per student, he affirms that lower investments of resources in a public school increase motivation to homeschool and, subsequently, home-based enrollment. Alternatively, higher levels of expenditures are associated with an increased likelihood of selecting public schooling (Houston and Toma 2003; Isenberg 2002). These scholars also demonstrate that school quality as measured in terms of low levels of student achievement has a small effect in pushing up homeschool enrollment. A parallel finding is reached when dropping out is the measure of school quality. When schools have difficulty holding youngsters in school, more families turn to homeschooling (Houston 1999). Finally, Isenberg (2007) has shown that when relationships among students are used as an indicator of quality, homeschooling increases as negative peer socialization in schools increases.

As noted above, Houston (1999) has investigated a second cluster of school characteristics that shapes parental motivation to engage in homeschooling, what might best be described as school *environmental conditions*. Collectively, the storyline runs as follows: "If schools are unable to deliver a product that is valued by the household because of the prevalence of negative environmental factors then the household will seek out alternative forms of education, including home education" (Houston 1999, 86).

One school environmental factor is level of income. The higher the poverty level in the district, the more push and pull there is toward home-based education.

More specifically, researchers affirm a positive correlation between the percentage of children in the free and reduced lunch program and the extent of homeschooling in a district (Thompson 1994), suggesting that this socioeconomic condition in a district "does influence parents to homeschool their children" (16). Houston (1999) arrives at a parallel conclusion employing the percentage of people living below the poverty line in the district as the measure of low income. An even stronger association has been drawn between heterogeneity of income in a school district and homeschooling (Houston 1999), with greater heterogeneity associated with expanded homeschool enrollment (Houston and Toma 2003). An empirical relationship has also been documented between race and homeschooling, at least for African Americans. Houston and Toma (2003) find, for example, that a higher percentage of African Americans in a district increases the probability of homeschooling.

Investigators have also established a connection between the robustness of state regulations and the motivation to homeschool. Analysts affirm that greater amounts of regulations in general will push homeschool enrollment downward (Houston and Toma 2003). More specifically, they find that states that mandate testing dampen enthusiasm for homeschooling (Houston 1999). Finally, there is evidence that a context rich in options for schooling, both public and private, will act as a brake on homeschooling (Houston 1999; Houston and Toma 2003).

Household characteristics

> The actual decision to homeschool is often triggered by unique circumstances that vary from family to family (Collom 2005, 309).

> Certain characteristics of the household may predispose a family to home education (Houston 1999, 105).

Analysts bundle a second group of context conditions into a category labeled "household characteristics." Generally included here are family income, education level of the parents, race/ethnicity, religious affiliation, and marital status. In regards to income, scholars document an interesting pattern. Up to a point on the income continuum, greater wealth is positively associated with additional homeschooling, most likely because higher income provides the opportunity for one parent to stay at home. But past some point on the continuum homeschooling turns downward as costs of foregone income by keeping one parent out of the labor force rise to unacceptable levels. At this point, paying private school tuition costs can become a more attractive option than homeschooling (Houston 1999; Isenberg 2002). Not surprisingly, the findings on education are similar to those on income. As Houston (1999) has documented, more highly educated women (those with a bachelor's degree or more) are less likely to homeschool because of reluctance to forgo returns from the labor market.

Race also appears as a variable in the household characteristics equation. McDowell and colleagues (2000) maintain that African American families that mirror white families in income and education often are motivated to homeschool for different reasons. Several studies have identified as a push factor the desire among African American parents to protect their children (especially their boys) from prejudice in public schools, and as a pull factor the desire to inculcate a positive racial identity through an Afrocentric curriculum (Mazama and Lundy 2012, 2014b; Fields-Smith and Kisura 2013).

Involvement in the labor force is another relevant household characteristic, with job holding by the mother pushing down homeschooling (Belfield 2004b). So too is marital status. Indeed it is the strongest household determinant of homeschooling (Houston 1999). Finally, there is evidence that another contextual condition, religious affiliation, influences the homeschooling decision of families. Membership in the Catholic faith has historically depressed homeschooling (Belfield 2004b; Houston 1999). On the other hand, affiliation with an evangelical community of faith enhances the likelihood of homeschooling (Houston 1999).

Student and community characteristics

> Households are more likely to choose public schools over home schools in more densely populated areas (Houston and Toma 2003, 930).

Surprisingly, little empirical work has been completed that examines how student characteristics beyond "special needs" status influence families to homeschool. There is a discernable line of argumentation in the literature that families with special education students, both gifted and learning disabled, may be attracted to homeschooling. But there is almost no systematic research on the issue (Kunzman 2009; Jolly, Matthews, and Nester 2013).

Conditions in communities, which overlap considerably with environmental conditions in districts, are also known to influence homeschooling (Houston and Toma 2003). Ruralness pulls families toward homeschooling while urban environments depress homeschooling (Thompson 1994). We also know that vis-à-vis rural families, urban parents have somewhat different reasons for homeschooling (Isenberg 2002). The density of schooling options in a community is also important in the homeschooling narrative. An absence of private school options, for example, will increase homeschooling (Isenberg 2007). The perceived ability of parents to influence local policy is a relevant contextual variable as well. For example, the greater the percentage of funding for education provided by the state (as opposed to the local community) the higher the level of homeschooling (Isenberg 2002).

Motivational Frameworks

> While reasons for homeschooling are wonderfully diverse…they tend to fall into roughly defined categories (Dobson 2001, 5).

> The idea of two distinctly motivated types of homeschoolers—the Ideologues (religiously motivated) and the Pedagogues (academic and methodology motivated)—is a recurring theme throughout the available literature (Taylor-Hough 2010, 4).

> There is a general consensus among researchers that the decision to home school is motivated by four broad categories of concern: (a) religious values, (b) dissatisfaction with the public schools, (c) academic and pedagogical concerns, and (d) family life. (Collom and Mitchell 2005, 277).

Prevalent typologies

Analysts over the last three decades have devoted considerable energy exploring the reasons that parents choose to educate their children at home. At one end of the workbench are investigators who present answers in unbundled form; that is, in lists of motives. At the other end of the workbench are researchers who aggregate rationales to create more comprehensive motivational categories. Collectively, these motivational detectives provide an especially rich understanding of the calculus of departure, that is, why families are turning to this historically unorthodox educational option. In this section, we review in historical sequence some of the most important frameworks that these scholars have provided. In the next section, we collapse all the findings on motivations into a four-dimensional framework: religious-based reasons, academic-grounded reasons, school socialization reasons, and family-based reasons.

One of the earliest motivational frameworks was provided by Holt (1981, 23) who answered the question of why parents choose homeschooling as follows:

> Mostly for three reasons: they think that raising their children is their business not the government's; they enjoy being with their children and watching and helping them learn, and don't want to give that up to others; they want to keep them from being hurt, mentally, physically, and spiritually.

In the first major study on homeschooling, Gustavsen (1981, 3) listed four major motivational categories:

> concern about the moral health and character development of their children; detrimental effect of rivalry and ridicule in conventional schools; parent-perceived poor quality of public school education; and the desire to extend parent–child contact.

In 1984, homeschool parents provided the rationales that allowed Taylor (1985, 29) to craft this motivational typology:

> (1) academic – children can learn better, (2) religious – it is a better way to foster religious beliefs and values, (3) social/moral – avoid negative influences and reinforce family values, (4) intuitive – the family offers a more natural and nurturing environment, and (5) philosophical – avoid undesired philosophies such as humanism and socialism.

Williams and colleagues (1984, 1) collapsed their case study findings on reasons for homeschooling as follows:

> unsuitability of children for school, desire of parents for control, socialization, conceptualization of the learning process, ideas about content, and personal interest.

Over the late 1980s and throughout the 1990s, Knowles and Mayberry added entire new chapters to the book on homeschooling motivations, and deepened existing sections of the book as well. In an early investigation, they uncovered:

> four groups of rationales for home school operations: family environments of the home school parents; parents' schooling and other learning experiences; contemporary problems children experienced in schools; and parents who believed they could provide a superior learning climate. (Knowles 1988, 73–74).

Based on their studies in Oregon and Utah, Mayberry and Knowles (1989, 214) discussed two overarching bundles of motivations, in order of priority: (1) religious, sociorelational, academic, or New Age reasons and (2) protection, control, self-actualization, and closeness.

Van Galen (1991) has provided the most cited and most well-regarded framework in the homeschooling literature, collapsing parent motivations into two broad orientations: ideologues, whose decision to homeschool is driven by opposition to perceived indoctrination and negative socialization in schools combined with a desire to strengthen the parent-child bond; and pedagogues, whose decision to homeschool is driven by concerns that formal classrooms and the broader school climate do not meet their child's needs.

In his dissertation, Parker (1992, 167–168) bundled rationales into four categories: religious convictions, parental concerns, the goal of academic excellence, and the goal of providing children with a healthy socialization experience. In his review, Jeub (1994, 50) distilled motivations into four containers: social, academic, family, and religious. Hertzel (1997, 68) has provided a seven-part motivational architecture:

1. Instructional and curricular issues
2. Safety issues
3. Social issues
4. Convenience issues
5. Health/handicap issues
6. Values issues
7. Self-esteem issues.

Lyman (1998, 6), based on an analysis of 300 magazine and newspaper articles, created four categories to house rationales for homeschooling: dissatisfaction with the public schools, the desire to freely impart religious values, academic excellence, and the building of stronger family bonds. At the end of the 1990s, Lange and Lui

(1999, 14–15) forged eighteen separate boards into five broad motivational beams: educational philosophy, special needs of the child, school climate, family lifestyle and parenting philosophy, and religion and ethics.

In an especially important historical analysis, Stevens (2001), in an effort to improve on Van Galen's typology, designated two motivational groupings, inclusives and believers. In his work for the National Home Education Research Institute, Ray has explored the issue of family motivation for homeschooling numerous times. His framework (2001, 1) is representative of his work. It includes four categories: "Teaching specific philosophical or religious values, controlling social interactions, developing close families, and high level academics." Boyer, (2002, 21), provides the following motivational categories: "psychological and emotional well being, relevant involvement of family, personal safety, and pedagogical needs." Collom (2005) and Collom and Mitchell (2005) have also explored the motivations of homeschooling families. They discuss four categories: "religious values, dissatisfaction with the public schools, academic and pedagogical concerns and family life" (Collom and Mitchell 2005, 277). Using the data from the National Household Education Survey, Isenberg (2007, 401) sorts motivations into three large bins: religion, education, and behavioral or special need. Using a psychologically grounded lens rather than economic and sociological lenses, Green and Hoover-Dempsey (2007, 266) weave together two bundles of motivations: psychological motivations and perceptions of personal life context variables.

Building from these frameworks and factoring in the balance of empirical work on homeschooling motivations, we employ the following four categories to capture a deep understanding of reasons why parents choose to school at home: (1) religion; (2) schooling: academics; (3) schooling: socialization; and (4) family. We unpack each of these four dimensions in detail below. Before we do so, however, we note a few of the lesser-noted reasons for homeschooling.

Lesser-noted motives

Perhaps most surprising, while not completely ignored in the literature (see Kunzman 2009; Ray 1997a) few of the lists of motives include parents moving toward homeschooling because of evidence that it works, i.e., "we homeschool our children because we are impressed with the evidence of its success." On the other hand, the belief that parents can do a better job than the school is ribboned throughout the literature (Mayberry et al. 1995; Perry and Perry 2000). Relatedly, there are indications that some parents are pulled toward homeschooling by learning about other families that have been successful in implementing this innovative approach to education (Mayberry et al. 1995). Support organizations often play an important role here (Safran 2010). There is some evidence that parents can be motivated to homeschool by interest in the concept expressed at the houses of faith they attend (Knowles 1991).

There is also some evidence that homeschooling occurs for some children because it ends up being easier to keep youngsters home than to battle with school authorities. This rationale is often linked to special needs children (Peterson 2009; Jolly, Matthews, and Nester 2012). Costs appear as a light thread in the motivational fabric as well (Wartes 1987). Specifically, it is argued that the high costs of private schools may direct parents to the homeschooling option (Taylor 1985; Marshall and Valle 1996). Finally, some analysts have uncovered evidence that some parents in the past chose homeschooling to avoid desegregation in general and busing in particular (Reinhaller and Thomas 1996; Taylor 1985). Others are less circumspect, suggesting that the data may implicate racism in the motivational algorithm of some homeschooling families (Cochran 1995; Kunzman 2009).

Religious-based motivations

> Participation in social movements such as the home education movement is often motivated by perceived threats to particular moral understandings and a desire to reinforce and protect the beliefs and values to provide a stable worldview and guide to life (Marlow 1994, 441).

> The extant body of research illustrating the motivations of home educators reveals that the goals are not mysterious or hidden. Repeatedly, consistently, unequivocally, the finding is reported that the primary motivation for most home educators reflects a moral, spiritual, or religious component (Cizek 1993, 1).

> Religiosity has long been associated with homeschooling (Clements 2002, 3).

In the material that follows, we discuss spiritual motivations in two sections: the significance of religion in the lives of many (most) homeschooling families and the secularization of public schooling.

The religious life

> Many families are motivated by their religious beliefs to begin home schooling. Their home school activity can only be understood within the context of their religious philosophy (Mayberry and Knowles 1989, 215).

> But even more central in the mindset of conservative Christian homeschoolers is the fundamental conviction that educating their children is a God-given right and responsibility, and one they can delegate only at great moral and spiritual peril (Kunzman 2009, 6).

While religious motivations did not fuel the initial phase of the modern homeschooling movement, within a decade religious convictions had become a critical variable in the homeschooling algorithm (Gaither 2008). For about twenty years beginning in the early 1980s, studies consistently documented that homeschooling families were motivated primarily by religious convictions and spiritual beliefs. On surveys and in interviews throughout this period, parents routinely told researchers that God was behind their decision to homeschool (Dahlquist, York-Barr, and Hendel 2006; Parker 1992). And because religious ideology is often intertwined with other choice options in these surveys and interviews (e.g., build strong families), religion is probably an even more potent motivational force than it appears.

More recent studies add to the spiritual motivational story in two ways. They confirm that religious convictions remain at or near the top of the list of reasons why families homeschool (Noel, Stark, and Redford 2013; Bielick 2008; Princiotta and Bielick 2006). At the same time, they reveal that there has been a narrowing of the gap between religious and other rationales for choosing home-based education (Noel, Stark, and Redford 2013; Bielick 2008; Muntes 2006).

The moral imperative One of the most interesting themes in the religious motivational chronicle is that a large number of homeschoolers believe they are commanded by God to keep their children at home (Gladin 1987; Van Galen 1991; Wilhelm and Firman 2009; Vigilant, Tyler, and Trefethren 2013). They often make this point with specific references to scripture (Nemer 2002; Schemmer 1985). They are apt to discuss homeschooling in terms of divine will (Guterson 1992; Stevens 2001).

In many instances, this scriptural obligation is linked to the belief that public schools morally harm children (Klicka 1995; Welner 2002), thus adding significance to the admonition. But this coupling is hardly universal. Some who homeschool from religious convictions do not anchor this work in the moral hazard of public education. It is sufficient to know that God has given parents sole responsibility for the education of their children, especially inculcation of moral values (Kunzman 2009; Parker 1992).

While most homeschool research cited thus far has focused on the motivation and feelings on mothers in homeschooling, Vigilant has begun a series of studies that look at the motivation of homeschool fathers. Stemming from the belief that public schools cannot be trusted, the Christian fathers in his sample see homeschooling as a way to create a protected environment where the parents can be the moral influence. These fathers tend to be the true "ideologues," viewing public versus homeschool as a spiritual battleground for the child (Vigilant, Tyler, and Trefethren 2013). The choice to homeschool is motivated by the father's belief that homeschooling is God's preferred method of education because it results in children maturing into godly adults (Vigilant, Tyler, and Trefethren 2014). These convictions, however, have not translated into significant fatherly contribution to the daily work of homeschooling itself (Lois 2013; Vigilant, Tyler, and Trefethren 2014).

To fulfill the call to integrate Christian doctrine into the lives of their children (Klicka 2004) and to bring unity to and to maintain the family (Knowles 1991), many parents believe that they must (1) form a wall between home and state, to take control; and (2) have their children with them for significant parts of the day (Gorder 1990; Kunzman 2009). In total then, for a large number of parents homeschooling has the potential to both protect children from the unacceptable values in play in public schools and society at large and to foster the Christian perspective that is the lifeblood of their families (Mayberry and Knowles 1989; Van Galen 1981; Anthony 2013).

The integrative principle It should be clear from the analysis above that religiously motivated homeschooling parents do not divide the world into discrete units – home, school, after-school activities, and so on. They see their faith as an animating force that places God at the center of their lives and pulls all dimensions of their lives into a principled whole (Klicka 2004; Wilhelm and Firman 2009), a force that organizes all dimensions of their existence. Homeschooling for many of these believers becomes an essential, if not the essential, vehicle for this integrative work (Mayberry et al. 1995; Van Galen 1991).

The centrality of values and evangelical beliefs Martin (1997) reminds us that as we move into the "content" at the heart of religiously motivated homeschooling two issues stand out. First, homeschooling is fundamentally about values (Kunzman 2009). As we discuss below, homeschooling happens for these families because first and foremost parents want to inculcate in their children the values they consider important for life and essential for salvation (Gorder 1990; Klicka 2004; Welner 2002). Second, homeschooling happens because parents want to integrate these values and beliefs into all dimensions of the curriculum; each subject is taught from the perspective of scripture (Gaither 2008).

On the first issue, researchers consistently demonstrate that religiously motivated parents have specific values they want their children to absorb (Aurini and Davies 2005; Basham, Merrifield, and Hepburn 2007). It is also clear to them that these values are not being directly taught or indirectly learned in public schools (Nemer 2002). Worse, they perceive that deviant values are being taught and absorbed by America's youngsters (Williams, Arnoldson, and Reynolds 1984; Vigilant, Tyler, and Trefethren 2013). Particularly salient here, and consistent with the integrative principle just analyzed, homeschooling permits parents to reproduce their spiritual way of life in their children (Apple 2000; Mayberry 1989a), to mold the life of their youngsters in significant and enduring ways (Kunzman 2009), in what advocates think of as a "protective cocoon" (Vigilant, Tyler, and Trefethren 2013, 208) and critics define as possible brainwashing (Apple 2000; Berliner 1997; Curren and Blokhuis 2011; Yuracko 2008).

The general storyline here is about the centrality of moral and ethical character development (Welner 2002). The particular narrative is about the induction of religious values (Collom 2005). These are most often conservative and fundamentalist frames of reference (Cochran 1995; McKeon 2007) – what Klicka (1995) describes as traditional Christian values and Taylor (1985) labels a Christian conception of God's laws.

On a second front, we also learn from the research that religious-based rationales for homeschooling grow from the desire by some parents to thread these critical spiritual values and beliefs throughout the curriculum and across the school day (Mirochnik and McIntire 1991; Parker 1992). According to Klicka (1995), the hallmark point here is that scriptural lessons should stretch across all aspects of life. Therefore, it is essential that all subjects be investigated through the prism of doctrine. Sacred ideology and subject content, according to these homeschoolers, should be inexorably intertwined (Hertzel 1997; Mayberry et al. 1995). Personal beliefs and values need to be integrated into each curricular domain (Romanowski 2001). Instruction should unfold from religious perspectives (Whitehead and Bird 1984). The Bible is the skeleton on which all learning is to be fleshed out (Kunzman 2009).

Faith and the divine become the reference point from which all subject area exploration occurs (Klicka 1995) in the service of guiding children into a comprehensive Christian worldview (Kunzman 2009).

This Biblicist approach to education has been shown to apply not only to White fundamentalists but also to the small percentage of Black homeschoolers who identify more with conservative religion than with racial categories (Mazama and Lundy 2014a; Ray 2015). Other equally religious African American homeschoolers, however, think of their Christian homeschooling more in the tradition of liberation theology (Fields-Smith and Kisura 2009).

The secularization of public schools

> Probably a majority of home schoolers are religious fundamentalists, unhappy with the failure of public schools to teach religious and spiritual tenets and with what they sometimes describe as the "secular humanism" that these schools allegedly espouse (Divoky 1983, 396).

> Religiously motivated parents tend to regard secular humanism and apparent student immorality as characteristics of public schools that they wish to counteract by operating home schools for their children (Knowles, Marlow, and Muchmore 1992, 196).

> Christian fundamentalists firmly believe that schools are battlegrounds in struggles between Christians and their opponents (Van Galen 1991, 69).

The meaning of secularization As we just reported, on one hand many families are being pulled to homeschool because of a deep commitment to their faith. At the same time, many of these families also feel pushed away from public schools by what they view as the growth of an educational system at odds with that faith (Apple 2007; Klicka 1995). This divergent moral system was arrived at, according to these parents and many faith-based support groups, by two paths. Path one comprises a series of actions that removed core religious planks that had been part of the foundation of public schools for over a century (Erickson 2005; Kirschner 1991), what Houston (1999) describes as a growing away from a Protestant-grounded to a non-denominational, non-religious system of public education. Central here is the separation of the sacred and secular into two distinct spheres (Holt 1981), with the former, according to many homeschoolers, being shown the schoolhouse exit door. Essential markers here were a series of Supreme Court decisions in the 1960s that (1) made prayer unconstitutional in schools, (2) prohibited school-sponsored Bible reading, and (3) outlawed the display of the Ten Commandments and other symbols of Christianity (Gaither 2008; Klicka 2004).

Path two toward the formation of a public school system at odds with faith was what religious-based homeschoolers and support groups see as the active secularization of education (Carper 2000; Lines 1991; Reich 2002). This idea is laced throughout the literature, although it is not especially well defined by homeschooling advocates. It is never used in a positive sense. It is seen as an insidious historical pattern, one defined both by the good ideas it precludes as well as the bad ideas it nourishes – "a destructive force that directly opposes their fundamental religious and moral principles" (Marlow 1994, 441 Secularism refers to what remains after faith and the divine are displaced, "a philosophy of the absence of a God" (Gorder 1990, 50). Still, at a high level of abstraction, it has been defined by Klicka (1995) and others as the belief that man is the center of all things. Moving a bit closer to the concrete end of the definitional yardstick, analysts define secular humanism in terms of the loss of traditional values and moral absolutes (Gray 1993; Van Galen 1991). Here some homeschoolers discern a dismantling of foundational moral pillars of society such as the traditional family, conservatism, and a melting-pot culture (Mayberry et al. 1995).

The impact of secularization A major outcome of the secularization movement for many families has been the loss of a well-defined and quite visible Christian culture in the public schools (Gaither 2008), and the removal of the divine and his commandments and guiding moral worldview (Klicka 1995). In turn, there has been a palpable sense of disenfranchisement among homeschoolers (Apple 2000; Klicka 2004). At the least harmful end of this disenfranchisement continuum, we find those who believe that (1) Christian values are insufficiently acknowledged in public schools (Jeub 1994), and (2) that religion is conspicuous by its absence (Basham, Merrifield, and Hepburn 2007; Mayberry 1992). They see a moral vacuum in school (Cai, Reeve, and Robinson 2002; Gray 1993). In the middle of the continuum are the many homeschooling families who discern not only the absence of attention to religion but the development of a hazy anti-religious perspective in public schools (Erickson 2005; Riegel 2001).

At the far end of the disenfranchisement continuum are homeschool parents who see secular humanists wielding their philosophical tools to actively strangle religion in education (Jeub 1994; Romanowski 2001). They discern a school system working assiduously against their convictions and perspectives (Isenberg 2007; Klicka 2004). They believe that their values and morals are being intentionally and aggressively undermined (Hadeed 1991; Parker 1992). Specifically, these parents point to collections of school programs and interventions that they believe subvert Christian values and honor humanistic worldviews. They observe school emphasizing what they hold to be immoral ideologies such as political correctness (Lyman 2002), socialist values (Welner 2002), moral relativism (Gorder 1990), consumerism/materialism (Apple 2005), careerism for women (Welner 2002), pluralistic values (Gray 1993), social liberalism (McKeon 2007), humanism (Klicka 2004), and statism (Glanzer 2008).

In the instructional program domain, religiously motivated homeschool parents often express an uneasiness about teachers, pedagogy, and curricula in public schools that they consider to be oppositional to doctrine and their deeply held beliefs (Klicka 1995; Mayberry 1989b; Nemer 2002). In particular, faith-based homeschoolers express considerable angst over subject matter such as evolution, sex education, and life adjustment (Gladin 1987; Gorder 1990; Taylor 1985). They also are troubled by frames such as "values clarification," a perspective that they believe undermines Christian commitment to moral absolutes (Wilhelm and Firman 2009).

The perceived amoral culture of schools is also of concern to many religiously motivated homeschooling parents (Klicka 1995).

Recent studies by Anthony (2013) and Vigilant, Tyler, and Trefethren (2013; 2014) have provided new vocabulary for some of these themes. Anthony's subjects are distrustful of mainstream American society. They are devoted "not to the common good" but to the particular good of raising godly children, which they view as a countercultural and subversive act (Anthony 2013, 6). Similarly, in the minds of Vigilant's subjects public education has experienced a "legitimation crisis" as Christians have lost the culture war and think the schools now promulgate "an atheist/anti-Christian worldview" (Vigilant, Tyler, and Trefethren 2013, 212) Homeschoolers stand against these trends as islands of faithfulness, preserving what they take to be a coherent Christian culture for future generations. This is why so many of them are drawn to classical education models and to long out-of-print 19th century textbooks (Hahn 2012; Pfitzer 2014).

School-based motivations: academic deficiencies

> One of the major reasons why people are turning to home schooling is because the state-run public school system has become academically bankrupt. (Klicka 1995, 19)

> Clearly, home schools are often an expression of intense dissatisfaction with public school outcomes (Knowles 1989, 393).

In the next two sections, we explore school-based motivations for homeschooling, looking first at academic reasons and then social rationales. Before we begin, however, it is instructive to remind ourselves of two caveats introduced earlier. First, almost all homeschoolers are motivated by multiple factors. Second, the four categories we highlight in this chapter are not mutually exclusive. For example, there is a good deal of faith-based ideology in the family-based motivational category.

Starting with academics, reviewers routinely find that parents are motivated to homeschool because of the poor quality of the public schools available for their children (Lines 2000; Webb 1989). Or alternatively, homeschooling provides an important condemnation of America's public schools (Colfax and Colfax 1988; Nemer 2002). The academic critique, reflected in parental disenchantment, discontent, dissatisfaction, and despair (Hadeed 1991; Moore 1982; Van Galen 1991), is constructed on thirty years of reports about the academic shortcomings of public schools (Basham, Merrifield, and Hepburn 2007; Isenberg 2002). Under an avalanche of negative news, some parents have become profoundly dispirited; they have lost faith in the public schools (Vigilant, Tyler, and Trefethren 2013). More join the carousel of despair every day. They have come to believe that schools will harm their children academically (Holt 1981; Riegel 2001). In reaction, many have elected to educate their children at home (Mayberry et al. 1995; Whitehead and Bird 1984; Mazama and Lundy 2013b). We examine academic motivations below in two sections, a more general critique of public schooling that informs homeschooling decisions and a more localized analysis that relies on the voices of homeschooling parents.

The general storyline Two tributaries of critique mix to form the larger river of academic discontent fueling homeschooling: the sense that the current system of public education is failing and the belief that it is incapable of reforming.

A sense of failure On the first matter, many homeschool parents have come to believe that public schools are broken academically. Moore (1982, 373) captured this angst at the outset of the homeschool movement when he reported that an increasing number of parents "are rising in anger and despair at the course the schools are taking." What analysts see as parental frustration over the continuing inadequacies of primary and secondary education in the United States is a multifaceted phenomenon. Or, stated in an alternate form, the perception that the level and quality of education in the United States is less than many desire is buttressed by data on a wide variety of outcomes. Specifically, according to many analysts, data assembled in each of the following performance dimensions provide a not-very-reassuring snapshot of the current academic performance of the American educational system: (1) academic achievement in basic subject areas (compared to student performance in other countries); (2) functional literacy; (3) preparation for employment; (4) the holding power of schools (dropout rates); (5) knowledge of specific subject areas such as geography and economics; and (6) mastery of higher-order skills (Committee for Economic Development 1994; Murnane and Levy 1996; Murphy 2010). Though the data may not be as dire as many believe (Lubienski 2013), at the level of public perception at least, "the experience of most Americans tells them that the nation's school system is in trouble and that the problems are getting worse" (Mathews 1996, 1).

Two issues in particular define analyses of academic outcomes: (1) the inability of the educational enterprise to enhance levels of productivity to meet the needs of the changing workforce, and (2) the failure of schools successfully to educate all of the nation's children, especially the poor (Fusarelli 1999; Murphy 2010). Analysts fault the education enterprise for its inability to keep pace with the increasing expectations from a changing economy.

One side of the problem these critics discuss is the belief that systems that hold steady in today's world are actually in decline (Murphy and Meyers 2008). They see "increasing obsolescence of the education provided by most U.S. schools" (Murnane and Levy 1996, 6). The other side of the productivity issue raised by these reviewers is the claim that because of the changing nature of the economy, the level of outcomes needed by students must be significantly increased. Critics find that the schools are not meeting this new standard for productivity. They argue that many students fail to graduate with the skills they need (Marshall and Tucker 1992), that "American schools are not providing students with the learning that they will need to function effectively in the 21st century" (Consortium on Productivity in the Schools 1995, 3).

An inability to reform Analysts also have a good deal to report about the second tributary feeding the river of discontent over academics in America's schools; that is, the failure of the system to heal itself (Taylor 2005), or growing skepticism about the effectiveness of various educational reforms (Luebke 1999). What has resulted from nearly forty years of unbroken efforts at reform, critics argue, has not been an increase in academic quality but rather a proliferation of professional and bureaucratic standards (Payne 2008), the creation of subsidies for bureaucracy (Beers and Ellig 1994), a deepening rift between professional educators and the public (Marshall and Tucker 1992), and the strengthening of a centralized educational system (Bulkley 1998; Tyack 1992) in which downside risks are passed onto parents and children (Payne 1995). The effect, analysts assert, is that reform has reinforced the very dynamics that are promoting the imploding of public schooling. The natural consequence, they maintain, is the emergence of new forms of education. And homeschool may end up as the most prominent of the new models (Collom 2005).

The localized storyline

> Home schooling parents are dissatisfied with the quality of education they see. Teachers and academic programs are held suspect in the minds of many of these parents (Gray 1993, 9).

> Most of the recent homeschoolers joining the ranks appear to be motivated primarily by academic reasons (Taylor-Hough 2010, 4).

While the analysis above featured the push and pull dynamics in the general critique of academics in public schools, here we examine academic motivation more specifically through the eyes of homeschooling parents. Case studies of homeschools and surveys of homeschooling parents consistently converge on a concern about academic quality (Dahlquist, York-Barr, and Hendel 2006; Ray 1997b). Previously when ranked in order of importance, academic motivations usually follow religious rationales and concerns about the social environment in schools (Princiotta, Bielick, and Chapman 2004; Princiotta and Bielick 2006). More recently, researchers have been discovering that academic concerns are rising in importance in the motivational hierarchy of homeschoolers. The 2013 NCES survey revealed a shift, bringing concerns about the school environment to the top, followed by religious and moral motives, and dissatisfaction with public school academics (Noel, Stark, and Redford 2013).

Pedagogy A variety of patterns are visible in the motivational tapestry of academic deficiencies that has been woven together from insights provided by homeschooling parents. One pattern highlights inadequate teachers (McKeon 2007; Stevens 2001). A second reveals poor quality instruction (Lange and Liu 1999; Van Galen 1991; Anthony and Burroughs 2012). A third pattern features teaching methods that are troublesome to some parents (Knowles 1988; Welner 2002; Jolly, Matthews, and

Nester 2012). For example, some homeschooling parents are opposed to whole language instruction or other "progressive" pedagogies (Lyman 2000; Anthony and Burroughs 2012). In general, however, it is safe to conclude that the counsel of despair among homeschoolers around pedagogy remains fairly abstract. Reviewers provide only an incomplete analysis of the geology of instructional problems.

African American homeschoolers especially see teachers as having a lack of commitment to African American students (Mazama and Lundy 2013b). Teachers have lower expectations for Black children and place a disproportionate number in special education. Boys are especially discriminated against. The school system has been come a pipeline for young African American men to the criminal justice system (Mazama and Lundy 2014b). This population of homeschoolers also faults public education's patronizing and shallow attention to Black history (Fields-Smith and Kisura 2009; Mazama and Lundy 2013a)

Content Concern is also expressed by homeschoolers about the inappropriately low academic standards they believe characterize the schools their children could be attending (Dobson 2001; Duvall et al. 1997). A general refrain is expressed that their children are not being asked to master ambitious learning targets, that they are insufficiently challenged academically (Muntes 2006; Ray and Weller 2003; Winstanley 2009).

Relatedly, concerns about the curriculum in their local public schools add fuel to the motivational fire for some homeschooling families (Pearson 1996; Schemmer 1985; Welner and Welner 1999). This includes worries about content that is featured as well as about content that is not covered. One codicil is that there is considerable entanglement here with religious-based motivations, many of which, as we saw, are rooted in disillusionment with the secular, humanistic underpinnings of the public school curriculum. A second codicil is that concerns about content vary a good deal depending on the perspective informing a homeschooling family. That is, curricular deficiencies that trouble homeschoolers from the more liberal wing of the movement are distinctly different than those that motivate more conservative families. For both wings of the movement, however, the heart of the issue is the same: a perceived incongruity between a preferred cultural identity and the one they see in the school curriculum (Glanzer 2008; Welner 2002).

One of the most commonly cited motivations for African American homeschoolers is what Mazama and Lundy have called "racial protectionism." While African American share in the general critiques that the public school curriculum is adult-centric, boring, narrowly focused on rote memorization and test preparation (Mazama and Lundy 2013b), they augment these common concerns with the belief that homeschooling is a way to rescue their children from the racist experiences found in schools. Institutional racism is especially prevalent. These parents feel that the curriculum perceives African American history as beginning with slavery and ending with Martin Luther King Jr. (Mazama and Lundy 2012), that the curriculum has an "add-ethics-and-stir" approach (Mazama and Lundy 2013b), and that it fails to provide a global perspective (Fields-Smith and Kisura 2013). Homeschooling allows such families to escape the Eurocentric public school curriculum (Mazama and Lundy 2013a) and to reclaim the legacy of self-education African Americans have practiced in the past (Mazama and Lundy 2012).

Structure The structure of the academic program also raises alarms among some families, thus pulling them into the orbit of homeschooling (Guterson 1992; Lange and Liu 1999). One element of the structural critique centers on schooling's regimentation of children, having all children in lockstep in an instructional dance that requires them to learn the same material at the same time (Arai 2000; Colfax 1990). For some parents, this regimentation is inexorably linked to an academic program defined by uninspiring routines and deadening, purposeless activities (Knowles 1991; Parker 1992).

The major structural problem for homeschoolers, and one that shares considerable space with the regimentation critique, is the belief that public schooling fails to provide needed individualization for children (Dalaimo 1996; McKeon 2007; Nemer 2002). Almost by necessity, it is held, teachers teach to the children "in the middle" (Kerman 1990; Holt 1981). Youngsters who are capable of moving more quickly are, it is argued, held back while students who are struggling are left behind (Aurini and Davies 2005; Gray 1993). And even for the children in the middle, the instructional match can be less than ideal. Unique individual academic needs and interests for many, therefore, it is argued, go unmet (Colfax 1990; Delahooke 1986; Welner 2002). The cardinal point is that clumping youngsters together by age for six or more hours per day makes desired individualization nearly impossible to achieve (Hanna 2011; Wartes 1987). Overcrowding or creating larger and larger clusters of children is seen as especially troublesome for homeschooling families (Hertzel 1997; Schemmer 1985).

Impact These pedagogical, curricular, and structural deficiencies in schools lead to a number of problems according to homeschooling parents. Learned passivity is often noted in this regard (Riegel 2001), as are its handmaidens, diminished interest in learning and withdrawal (Dobson 2001; Knowles 1991; Stevens 2001). Also noted are the stifling of independent thinking and the tamping down of creativity (Dalaimo 1996; Nemer 2002). Most importantly, academic failure, or at least what is seen as woefully insufficient academic progress, is found on the list of problems (Knowles 1989; Mayberry et al. 1995). Or as Holt (1981, 25) nicely put it near the inception of the modern era of homeschooling, "One reason people take their children out of school is that they aren't learning anything."

School-based motivations: social/environmental problems

> Home schooling is partly about saving children from multiple contaminants (Stevens 2001, 53).

> In spite of the diverse reasons that draw parents to home schooling, they share a profound belief that the public schools are not providing a healthy environment for their children (Divoky 1983, 397).

> A major category of reasons for homeschooling relates to the parents' perception that the public or private school environment is harmful to their child (Lange and Liu 1999, 5).

Deeply embedded in the studies that investigate parental motivations for homeschooling is the trenchant belief that public (and private) schools at a minimum expose children to harm and at worst actually damage them. According to parents and homeschool support groups, damage can stretch across five domains: spiritual, academic, physical, emotional (psychological), and social. In our earlier analysis, we explored spiritual and academic harm in some detail. Here we turn the spotlight on the last three domains, which aggregate into a bundle we label school social environment. The entry point into the analytic narrative is that assessments of school climate often lead parents to conclude that schools are bad places for their children, physically, emotionally, and socially (Fager and Brewster 2000; Ray and Weller 2003), and that the home can provide a much healthier environment for learning (Knowles 1989).

Over the last thirty years, studies have consistently documented that school social/environmental issues rank high on the motivational lists of homeschooling families (Dahlquist, York-Barr, and Hendel 2006; Gladin 1987; Lyman 1998). In the 2013 National Center for Educational Statistics study, fully 91% of homeschooling parents identified concerns with the school environment as important in their homeschool calculations, more so than the religious (77%) and academic (74%) rationales discussed previously. Social concerns also edged out religious motivation as the single most important motivation (25% compared with 17%) (Noel, Stark, and Redford 2013), a change from the turn of the century when religion was chosen as the most important reason for homeschooling (Bielick, Chandler, and Broughman 2001).

Protection from physical and emotional harm

> For an increasingly large number of parents, public schools are now seen as threatening in an even more powerful way. They are dangerous bodily; that is, they are seen as filled with physical dangers to the very life of one's children (Apple 2000, 70).

> The second strongest PULL factor was that parents believe it is "safer at home" (Hertzel 1997, 71).

One reason parents decide to homeschool is because they are worried about the physical wellbeing of their children when they are at school (Boyer 2002; Gray 1998; Wyatt 2007). While this concern has been on the motivational landscape for some time, it appears to be increasing in significance. Of particular importance here is the uneasiness that gnaws at parents because of perceived violence in schools (Mayberry et al. 1995; Ray 2004). Gang problems, drug use, bullying, and weapons are often singled out by homeschooling parents (Lyman 2000; McKeon 2007; Nemer 2002). Feelings run hot on this issue, and there is a sense among some in the homeschooling literature that crime is unfolding unchecked across America's public schools (Klicka 1995).

Parents are also motivated to homeschool to protect their children from emotional harm (Gordon and Gordon 1990; Moore 1982). They sometimes attempt to shield their children from what they view as an overly competitive environment, one that promotes unhealthy rivalry, ridicule, and meanness (Wyatt 2007; Williams, Arnoldson, and Reynolds 1984).

Protection from social harm

> Home school parents often claim that the current social environment of formal schools is actually a compelling argument for operating a home school (Mayberry et al. 1995, 3).

> Other studies that have surveyed parents' reasons for home-schooling commonly report that parents see socialization as a negative aspect of school (Rakestraw and Rakestraw 1990, 74).

> For some parents, this issue of socialization is at the head of their decision to homeschool (Moore and Moore 1994, 61).

The hallmark environmentally anchored motivation for homeschooling is the prevention of the dysfunctional socialization that many parents believe defines public schooling (Kitchen 1991; Winstanley 2009). Some parents see schools enveloped in a dark cloud of poor health (Collom 2005; Luke 2003), one that bodes ill for children (Cochran 1995; Medlin 2000). They judge the public school to be "a socially corrosive institution" (Riegel 2001, 91), little more than a chalice of social wretchedness (Klicka 1995). They maintain that homeschooling provides the only effective antidote to the public school socialization problem (Dalaimo 1996; Medlin 2000).

Analysts who study these matters inform us that socialization problems, according to some in the homeschooling community, are spawned in a hideous brew of peer pressure (Boone 2000; Marshall and Valle 1996), in a caldron which in turn is supported by an ill-framed scaffolding of age segregation (Milner 2006; Moore 1982; Tillman 1995) and the separation of youngsters from ongoing, meaningful interactions with adults (Erickson 2005; Lines 2000), a collective condition perhaps best defined as social stagnation (Gorder 1990; Riegel 2001). This, in turn, fosters the formation of a negative school climate (Holt 1981; Kitchen 1991), one that promotes peer dependency and drives wedges between children and their parents (Gaither 2008; Groover and Endsley 1988; Parker 1992).

The avoidance of this negative socialization is often cited by parents to explain their commitment to home-based education (Ray and Weller 2003; Saunders 2010). They see their children avoiding the grim harvest of bad habits and traits associated with peer pressure (Divoky 1983; Gatto 1992; Lyman 2000). And they believe that homeschooling will prevent accompanying and equally negative outcomes such as rejection of parental values, diminished self-worth, and reduced personal accountability (Glanzer 2008; Kelley 1991; Parker 1992). Some African American families add that joining homeschooling cooperatives allows their children to escape the hyper-segregation of urban schools (Fields-Smith and Kisura 2013).

Family-based motivation

> Several factors account for the home school movement, including a desire to strengthen the family (Cai, Reeve, and Robinson 2002, 372).

> Parental interest in participating in the education of their children is a primary reason for starting home schools (Mayberry 1989b, 178).

> Many parents report homeschooling to meet the individual needs of their child or children or to meet the needs of their family and their chosen lifestyles (Lange and Liu 1999, 14).

So far we have examined three of the four essential bundles of motivations for homeschooling: religious-based reasons, academic-grounded reasons, and school social/environmental reasons. While generally highlighted less than these rationales, there is considerable agreement that parents also homeschool to strengthen the family (Hertzel 1997; Mayberry 1989a; Wyatt 2008). And there is accompanying evidence that for some parents, family-based rationales are the central theme in the homeschooling motivational portrait. Based on the work of those who have preceded us, we cluster family-based motivations into five categories: parent responsibility for the education function; desire to be with one's children; special circumstances; meeting the requirements of special needs students; and promoting healthy families.

Responsibility for education

> Homeschool parents appear to decide to homeschool because they believe that they are personally responsible for their child's education (Green and Hoover-Dempsey 2007, 278).

> Home schooling was a part of their perceived parental duties. To them, putting their children in any educational environment without them (the parents) in direct control would have been like placing their children in foster homes (Parker 1992, 166).

In our discussion of religious motivations for homeschooling, we noted that some parents maintain that they, not the state, hold responsibility for the education of their children. We also reported that they believe that this obligation has been handed down from God. They find scriptural confirmation for this belief. This same sense of obligation is found among parents who homeschool for family reasons as well. For many of these families, the handiwork of the divine is evident. For others it is not. What is shared, however, is the idea that parents are responsible for the development of their children and this obligation extends into formal education (Kunzman 2009; Parker 1992; Riegel 2001).

Desire to be with one's children

> It was as though we had assumed that going to school was simply something children *did* – no questions asked, and when we finally learned to ask those questions, we felt somewhat cheated by the years our children had been away from us (Ressler 1997, 51).

> Some parents simply like to watch their children learn. They enjoy being parents and enjoy learning with their children (Williams, Arnoldson, and Reynolds 1984, 10).

A number of parents tell researchers that they are sensitive to the chill of separation. They homeschool because they want to be with their children, to be a part of their growth and learning to a much greater extent than is possible when children are away at school (Lois 2013; Lyman 2000). They enjoy being with their children and do not want to turn them over to the care of others no matter how well intended or competent those others may be (Hegener and Hegener 1997; McCurdy 1997). To do so, they maintain, would be to deny themselves critical aspects of satisfaction that accompany the parental role (Guterson 1992). For parents like this, it seems self-evident that homeschooling would be a family's "first choice," when it comes to education (Lois 2013, 47).

Special circumstances

> One group of homeschoolers is the conglomerate of children who engage in one form or another of intensive extracurricular activity (Gaither 2008, 223).

Although not a major theme in the overall motivational narrative, special circumstances do pull some families into home-based education. For example, the desire for a flexible lifestyle and schedule can lead some families toward homeschooling (Dahlquist, York-Barr, and Hendel 2006). Relatedly, irregular work patterns (e.g., intermittent work abroad) are sometimes noted as a motivation to homeschool (Blok 2004). Finally, intensive activity on the part of some children in careers (e.g., music, acting) or areas of interest (e.g., athletics) can nudge families toward homeschooling as a preferred option (Gaither 2008; Perry and Perry 2000).

Meeting the requirements of special needs children

> Although no comprehensive research exists, homeschool advocates contend that the customized, individual attention made possible in a homeschooling context can be of particular benefit to students with special needs (Kunzman 2009, 54).

> Homeschooling can be a last resort for frustrated families where gifted children are not having their complex needs met through mainstream schooling (Winstanley 2009, 347).

Some parents are motivated to homeschool because they conclude that their children have special needs that schools have not, will not, or cannot address appropriately (Collom 2005; Mayberry 1989a). Here we see considerable overlap with other themes in the larger motivational portrait, particularly with the academic deficiency rationale, i.e., schools failing to do their jobs well. Some parents believe that the additional time and attention that can be provided at home may be the only thing that can save their children. "Special needs" children usually fall into three overlapping categories: children who are simply lost and floundering in formal educational settings (Lines 1987; Taylor 1985); youngsters whose parents believe they need to learn in unique ways (Van Galen 1991); and traditionally defined special needs students such as learning disabled and gifted youngsters. This latter group occupies almost all the space in this sub area of the homeschooling literature (Hurlbutt 2011; Jolly, Matthews, and Nester 2012). There is also evidence that homeschooling of gifted and learning-disabled students has been increasing in recent years (Ensign 1997). We highlight each of these two groups below.

According to various studies, some families are turning to the homeschooling of their gifted children out of frustration with the education available in public schools (Knowles 1991; Nemer 2002; Winstanley 2009). These parents find that their children are not being sufficiently challenged by the curriculum or the pedagogy in schools (Arai 2000; Perry and Perry 2000). Parents also sense that their gifted children receive insufficient personal attention in school (Martin 1997; Pearson 1996). They discern less than luminous results. Overall then, these parents conclude that the special gifts of their children are not being recognized or nurtured sufficiently in public schools (Nemer 2002). Feeling trapped in a system that does not adequately address their child's needs, these parents turn, sometimes reluctantly, to homeschooling for relief (Ensign 1997; Knowles, Muchmore, and Spaulding 1994; Jolly, Matthews, and Nester 2012).

In a similar vein, frustration with public schooling leads some parents of children with learning disabilities to keep them at home to be educated (Gray 1993; Hanna 2011). Parents often fear that their children are being allowed to drop further and further behind age-appropriate standards. They believe that regular classroom teachers are often ill-prepared and ill-resourced to address the needs of their children and they question the appropriateness of special education programs (Hurlbutt 2011; Lange and Liu 1999). They worry about the social stigmatization that often rides shotgun with the special education driver (Henry 1997). Concern that their learning disabled children will be poorly prepared for life often looms large on the horizon for these parents. As a result, they often decide that their children need a warmer and more nurturing environment than a regular school can provide (Hurlbutt 2011; Pearson 1996). The result is that increasing numbers of parents are choosing homeschooling for their learning disabled children (Nemer 2002).

Promoting healthy families

> Most parents express the importance of family relationships and family unity in their decision to teach their children at home. These parents see teaching at home as an essential element in developing close family relationships (Mayberry and Knowles 1989, 214).

> Home school parents want to enhance family relationships between children and parents and among siblings, through more time spent with one another (Ray 2004, 4).

The most acknowledged and analyzed family-based motivation for homeschooling centers on the importance of supporting the development of individual families and maintaining the institution of the family (Erickson 2005; Kunzman 2009; Wyatt 2008). The starting point here is that many parents see the family as the most important institution in society, one that is superior to all others, including schools (Jeub 1994; Parker 1992; Tillman 1995). Concomitantly, many parents discern a pervasive weakening of the family unit in American life (Mayberry and Knowles 1989), especially the decline of the nuclear family (Gray 1993) and the growth of dysfunctional families (Knowles 1991). They maintain that it is in society's best interest to create policies to strengthen the family (Parker 1992). One way this can occur, some in the homeschooling community assert, is by consolidating child-rearing functions inside the family rather than encouraging them to be spread across a variety of locations. In particular, activities that nurture family relationships as opposed to peer connections are valued (Gatto 1992; Williams, Arnoldson, and Reynolds 1984). Fewer substitutes for parents are in order (Gaither 2008) and more time is to be spent by parents with their children (Mirochnik and McIntire 1991). The home is to be the core unit of the child's life (Taylor 1985). And if all this is to be realized, then the education function needs to be housed in the home under the auspices of parents, not in some distant venue under the control of external socialization agents, i.e., professional educators (Mayberry 1989a; Vigilant, Tyler, and Trefethren 2013).

Here, as Mayberry and colleagues (Mayberry 1989a; Mayberry and Knowles 1989) confirm, homeschooling is essential for more than its effects on individual children. It is a keystone element in the quest to restore and nurture the American family (Marlow 1994; Marshall and Valle 1996). It promotes family cohesion and integrity (Gray 1993; Lange and Liu 1999). It is the core strategy by which (1) bonds within the family are developed (McKeon 2007; Romanowski 2001), i.e., positive relations among family members are knitted (Dahlquist, York-Barr, and Hendel 2006; Ray and Weller 2003); (2) adult socialization cascades over children (Parker 1992); (3) parenthood, fatherhood, and motherhood are taught (Erickson 2005); and (4) family unity is realized (Aurini and Davies 2005; Mayberry and Knowles 1989).

All of the healthy family narrative crafted so far rests on the twin pillars of shared time and mutual activity. Better relationships develop because homeschooling parents and children spend more time together (Stevens 2001; Wyatt 2008) sharing work that conveys important family values to children (Dobson 2001; Marlow 1994; Parker 1992).

Conclusion

In this chapter, we examined the reasons parents cite for homeschooling. We began with a note on control as the keystone in the motivational arch. We outlined the three sources of parental motivations and presented a framework that emphasizes both positive (pull) and negative (push) forces. We discussed at some length how schooling, household, student, and community contexts shape homeschooling decisions. We provided a framework that pulled together all existing research on motivation to homeschool into four categories: religious-based reasons; schooling-based reasons, academic; schooling-based reasons, socialization; and family-based reasons. We unpacked each of these into its component elements, being cognizant however that overlapping and changing motivations give this topic a dynamism that cannot be fully captured by any taxonomy.

References

Anthony, K. 2013. "Declarations of Independence: Home School Families' Perspectives on Education, the Common Good, and Diversity." *Current Issues in Education*, 16: 1–15.

Anthony, K., and Burroughs, S. 2012. "Day to Day Operations of Home School Families: Selecting from a Menu of Educational Choices to Meet Students' Individual Instructional Needs." *International Education Studies*. 5: 1–17.

Apostoleris, N.H. 1999. The Development of Children's Motivation in the Homeschool Setting. Paper presented at the Biennial Meeting of the Society for Research in Child Development, Albuquerque, NM.

Apple, M. 2000. "The Cultural Politics of Home Schooling." *Peabody Journal of Education*, 75: 256–271.

Apple, Michael W. 2005. "Away with all the Teachers: The Cultural Politics of Homeschooling." *Home Schooling in Full View: A Reader*, edited by B.S. Cooper, 75–95. Greenwich, CT: Information Age Publishing.

Apple, M. 2007. "Who Needs Teacher Education? Gender, Technology, and the Work of Home Schooling." *Teacher Education Quarterly*, 34: 111–130.

Arai, B. 2000. "Reasons for Home Schooling in Canada." *Canadian Journal of Education*, 25: 204–217.

Aurini, J., and S. Davies 2005. "Choice Without Markets: Homeschooling in the Context of Private Education." *British Journal of Sociology of Education*, 26: 461–474.

Basham, P., Merrifield, J., and Hepburn, C. 2007. "Home Schooling: From the Extreme to the Mainstream." *Studies in Education Policy Series*. Vancouver, BC: Fraser Institute.

Beers, D., and Ellig, J. 1994. "An Economic View of the Effectiveness of Public and Private Schools." In *Privatizing Education and Educational Choice: Concepts, Plans, and Experiences*, edited by S. Hakim, P. Seidenstat, and G.W. Bowman, 19–38. Westport, CT: Praeger.

Belfield, C. 2004b. "Modeling School Choice: A Comparison of Public, Private-Independent, Private-Religious, and Home-Schooled Families." *Education Policy and Analysis Archives*, 12: 1–16.

Berliner, D. 1997. "Educational Psychology Meets the Christian Right: Differing Views of Children, Schooling, Teaching, and Learning." *Teachers College Record*, 98: 381–416.

Bielick, S. 2008. *1.5 Million Homeschooled Students in the United States in 2007*. Washington, DC: National Center for Education Statistics.

Bielick, S., Chandler, K., and Broughman, S. 2001. "Homeschooling in the United States: 1999." *Education Statistics Quarterly*, 3: 1–13.

Blok, H. 2004. "Performance in Home Schooling: An Argument Against Compulsory Schooling in the Netherlands." *International Review of Education*, 50: 39–52.

Boone, J. 2000. "Homeschool Alumni". *Paths of Learning: Options for Families & Communities*, 3: 25–30.

Boyer, W. 2002. "Exploring Home Schooling." *International Journal of Early Childhood*, 34: 19–29.

Bulkley, K.E. 1998. *Telling Stories: The Political Construction of Charter Schools*. Unpublished doctoral diss., School of Education, Stanford University, Palo Alto, CA.

Cai, Y., Reeve, J., and Robinson, D. 2002. "Home Schooling and Teaching Style: Comparing the Motivating Styles of Home School and Public School Teachers." *Journal of Educational Psychology*, 94: 372–380.

Carper, J. 2000. "Pluralism to Establishment to Dissent: The Religious and Educational Context of Home Schooling." *Peabody Journal of Education*, 75: 8–19.

Caruana, V. 1999. "Partnering with Homeschoolers." *Educational Leadership*, 57: 58–60.

Cizek, G. 1993. "The Mismeasure of Home Schooling Effectiveness (A Commentary)." *Home School Researcher*, 9: 1–4.

Clements, A. 2002. "Variety of Teaching Methodologies Used by Homeschoolers: Case Studies of Three Homeschooling Families." Paper presented at the annual meeting of the Eastern Educational Research Association, Sarasota, FL.

Cochran, C. 1995. "The Home School Movement in the U.S.: Georgia as a Test Case, 1979–1984." Doctoral diss., Emory University, Atlanta, GA.

Colfax, D. 1990. "Beyond the Classroom." In *Schooling at Home: Parents, Kids, and Learning*, edited by A. Pederson and P. O'Mara, 191–199. Santa Fe, NM: John Muir Publications.

Colfax, D., and Colfax, M. 1988. *Homeschooling for Excellence*. New York: Warner Books.

Collom, E. 2005. "The Ins and Outs of Homeschooling: The Determinants of Parental Motivations and Student Achievement." *Education and Urban Society*, 37: 307–335.

Collom, E., and Mitchell, D. 2005. "Home Schooling as a Social Movement: Identifying the Determinants of Homeschoolers' Perceptions." *Sociological Spectrum*, 25: 273–305.

Committee for Economic Development. 1994. *Putting Learning First: Governing and Managing the Schools for High Achievement*. New York: Author.

Consortium on Productivity in the Schools. 1995. *Using What We Have to Get the Schools We Need*. New York: The Institute on Education and the Economy, Teachers College, Columbia University.

Curren, R. and Blokhuis, J. "The *Prima Facie* Case Against Homeschooling." *Public Affairs Quarterly*. 25: 1–19.

Dahlquist, K., York-Barr, J. and Hendel, D.D. 2006. "The Choice to Homeschool: Home Educator Perspectives and School District Options." *Journal of School Leadership*, 16: 354–385.

Dalaimo, D. 1996. Community Home Education: A Case Study of a Public School-Based Home Schooling Program. *Educational Research Quarterly*, 19: 3–22.

Delahooke, M. 1986. "Home Educated Children's Social/Emotional Adjustment and Academic Achievement: A Comparative Study." Doctoral diss., California School of Professional Psychology, Los Angeles, CA.

Divoky, D. 1983. "The New Pioneers of the Home-Schooling Movement." *Phi Delta Kappan*, 64: 395–398.

Dobson, L. 2001. *The First Year Homeschooling Your Child: Your Complete Guide to Getting off to the Right Start*. Roseville, CA: Prima Publishing.

Duvall, S., Ward, D.L., Delquadri, J., and Greenwood, C. 1997. "An Exploratory Study of Home School Instructional Environments and Their Effects on the Basic Skills of Students with Learning Disabilities." *Education and Treatment of Children*, 20: 150–172.

Ensign, J. 1997. *Homeschooling Gifted Students: An Introductory Guide for Parents*. Reston, VA: Council for Exceptional Children, ERIC Clearinghouse on Disabilities and Gifted Education.

Erickson, D.A. 2005. "Homeschooling and the Common School Nightmare." In *Home Schooling in Full View*, edited by B.S. Cooper, 21–44. Greenwich, CT: Information Age Publishing.

Fager, J., and Brewster, C. 2000. *Making Positive Connections with Homeschoolers*. Washington, DC: Office of Educational Research and Improvement.

Fields-Smith, Cheryl, and Kisura, Monica Wells 2009. "Motivations, Sacrifices, and Challenges: Black Parents' Decision to Home School." *Urban Review* 41: 369–389.

Fields-Smith, Cheryl, and Kisura, Monica Wells 2013. "Resisting the Status Quo: The Narratives of Black Homeschoolers in Metro-Atlanta and Metro-DC." *Peabody Journal of Education* 88: 265–283.

Fusarelli, L.D. 1999. "Reinventing Urban Education in Texas: Charter Schools, Smaller Schools, and the New Institutionalism." *Education and Urban Society*, 31: 214–224.

Gaither, M. 2008. *Homeschool: An American history*. New York: Palgrave MacMillan.

Gatto, J.T. 1992. *Dumbing Us Down: The Hidden Curriculum of Compulsory Schooling*. Philadelphia, PA: New Society Publishers.

Gladin, E. 1987. "Home Education: Characteristics of its Families and Schools." Doctoral diss., Bob Jones University, Greenville, SC.

Glanzer, P. L. 2008. "Rethinking the Boundaries and Burdens of Parental Authority over Education: A Response to Rob Reich's Case Study of Homeschooling." *Educational Theory*, 58: 1–16.

Gorder, C. 1990. *Home Schools: An Alternative*. Tempe, AZ: Blue Bird Publishing.

Gordon, Edward E., and Elaine H. Gordon. *Centuries of Tutoring: A History of Alternative Education in America and Western Europe*. Lanham: University Press of America.

Gray, D.W. 1998. "A Study of the Academic Achievements of Home-Schooled Students Who Have Matriculated into Postsecondary Institutions." Doctoral diss., University of Sarasota, FL.

Gray, S. 1993. "Why Some Parents Choose to Home School." *Home School Researcher*, 9: 1–12.

Green, C., and Hoover-Dempsey, K. 2007. "Why do Parents Homeschool? A Systematic Examination of Parental Involvement." *Education and Urban Society*, 39: 264–285.

Groover, S., and Endsley, R. 1988. "Family Environment and Attitudes of Homeschoolers and Non-Homeschoolers." Unpublished master's thesis, University of Georgia.

Gustavsen, G. 1981 "Selected Characteristics of Home Schools and Parents Who Operate Them." Diss., Andrews University, Berrien Springs, MI.

Guterson, D. 1992. *Family Matters: Why Homeschooling Makes Sense*. New York: Harcourt Brace Jovanovich.

Hadeed, H. 1991. "Home Schooling Movement Participation: A Theoretical Framework." *Home School Researcher*, 7: 1–9.

Hahn, C. 2012. "Latin in the Homeschooling Community." *Teaching Classical Languages*. 4: 26–51.

Hanna, L.G. 2011. "Homeschooling Education: Longitudinal Study of Methods, Materials, and Curricula." *Education and Urban Society*, 43: 1–23.

Hegener, M., and Hegener, H. 1997. *The Homeschool Reader: Collected Articles from Home Education Magazine, 1984–1994*. Tonasket, WA: Home Education Press.

Henry, S. 1997. "Homeschooling is for Everyone." In *The Homeschool Reader: Collected Articles from Home Education Magazine, 1984–1994*, edited by M. Hegener and H. Hegener, 24–30. Tonasket, WA: Home Education Press.

Hertzel, J. 1997. "Literacy in the Homeschool Setting." In *Literacy: Building on What We Know*, edited by Philip H. Dreyer, 61–81. Claremont, CA: Claremont Reading Co.

Holt, J. 1981. *Teach Your Own: A Hopeful Path for Education*. New York, NY: Delacorte Press.

Houston, R. 1999. "The Economic Determinants of Home Education." Doctoral diss., University of Kentucky, Lexington, KY.

Houston, R., and Toma, E. 2003. "Home Schooling: An Alternative School Choice." *Southern Economic Journal*, 69: 920–935.

Hurlbutt, K. 2011. "Experiences of Parents who Homeschool their Children with Autism Spectrum Disorder." *Developmental Disabilities*, 26: 239–249.

Isenberg, E. 2002. "Home Schooling: School Choice and Women's Time Use." National Center for the Study of Privatization in Education, Teachers College, Columbia University, New York, NY.

Isenberg, E. 2007. "What Have We Learned about Homeschooling?" *Peabody Journal of Education*, 82: 387–409.

Jeub, C. 1994. "Why Parents Choose Home Schooling." *Educational Leadership*, 52: 50–52.

Jolly, J., Matthews, M., and Nester, J. 2012. "Homeschooling the Gifted: A Parent's Perspective." *Gifted Child Quarterly*, 57: 121–134.

Kelley, S. 1991. "Socialization of Home Schooled Children: A Self-Concept Study." *Home School Researcher*, 7: 1–12.

Kerman, K. 1990. "Home Schooling Day by Day." In *Schooling at Home: Parents, Kids, and Learning*, edited by A. Pederson and P. O'Mara, 17–18. Santa Fe, NM: John Muir Publications.

Kirschner, J. 1991. "The Shifting Roles of Family and School as Educator: A Historical Perspective." In *Homeschooling: Political, Historical, and Pedagogical Perspectives*, edited by J. Van Galen and M. Pittman, 137–158. Norwood, NJ: Ablex Publishing Corp.

Kitchen, P. 1991. "Socialization of Home School Children Versus Conventional School Children." *Home School Researcher*, 7.

Klicka, C. 1995. *The Right Choice: The Incredible Failure of Public Education and the Rising Hope of Home Schooling: An Academic, Historical, Practical, and Legal Perspective*. Gresham, OR: Noble Publishing Associates.

Klicka, A. 2004. *Academic Statistics on Homeschooling*. Purcelville, VA: Home School Legal Defense Association.

Knowles, J.G. 1988. "Parents' Rationales and Teaching Methods for Homeschooling: The Role of Biography." *Education and Urban Society*, 21: 69–84.

Knowles, J. Gary. 1989. "Cooperating with Home School Parents: A New Agenda for Public Schools?" *Urban Education*, 23(4): 392–411.

Knowles, J.G. 1991. "Parents' Rationales for Operating Home Schools." *Journal of Contemporary Ethnography*, 20: 203–230.

Knowles, G., Marlow, S., and Muchmore, J. 1992. "From Pedagogy to Ideology: Origins and Phases of Home Education in the United States." *American Journal of Education*, 100: 195–235.

Knowles, G., Muchmore, J., and Spaulding, H. 1994. "Home Education as an Alternative to Institutionalized Education." *The Education Forum*, 58: 238–243.

Kunzman, R. 2009. *Write These Laws on Your Children: Inside the World of Conservative Christian Homeschooling*. Boston: Beacon Press.

Lange, C., and Lui, K.K. 1999. *Homeschooling: Parents' Reasons for Transfer and the Implications for Educational Policy*. Minneapolis, MN: National Center on Educational Outcomes.

Lines, Patricia M. 1987. "An Overview of Home Instruction." *Phi Delta Kappan*, 68 (7): 510–517.

Lines, P.M. 1991. Home Instruction: The Size and Growth of the Movement. In *Homeschooling: Political, Historical, and Pedagogical Perspectives*, edited by J. Van Galen and M. Pittman, 9–42. Norwood, NJ: Ablex Publishing Corp.

Lines, Patricia M. 2000. "When Home Schoolers Go to School: A Partnership Between Families and Schools." *Peabody Journal of Education*, 75(1&2): 159–186.

Lois, J. 2013. *Home is Where the School Is: The Logic of Homeschooling and the Emotional Labor of Mothering*. New York: New York University Press.

Lubienski, C. 2000. "Whither the Common Good? A Critique of Home Schooling." *Peabody Journal of Education*, 75: 207–232.

Lubienski, C. 2013. *The Public School Advantage: Why Public Schools Outperform Private Schools*. Chicago: University of Chicago Press.

Luebke, R.V. 1999. *Homeschooling in Wisconsin: A Review of Current Issues and Trends*. Milwaukee, WI: Wisconsin Policy Research Institute.

Luke, C. 2003. "Home Schooling: Learning from Dissent." *Canadian Journal of Educational Administration and Policy*, 25. Accessed April 1, 2011. http://www.umanitoba.ca/publications/cjeap/articles/caluke.html

Lyman, L. 1998. "Homeschooling: Back to the Future?' *Policy Analysis*, 294: 1–15.

Lyman, I. 2000. *The Homeschooling Revolution*. Amherst, MA: Bench Press International.

Lyman, Isabel. 2002. "Generation Two." *American Enterprise*, 13(7): 48–49.

Marlow, S. 1994. "Educating Children at Home: Implications for Assessment and Accountability." *Education and Urban Society*, 26: 438–460.

Martin, M. 1997. "Homeschooling: Parents Reactions." Accessed March 5, 2011. http://www.eric.ed.gov/PDFS/ED415984.pdf

Marshall, D., and Valle, J. 1996. "Public School Reform: Potential Lessons from the Truly Departed." *Education Policy Analysis Archives*, 4: 1–15.

Marshall, R., and Tucker, M. 1992. *Thinking for a Living: Work, Skills, and the Future of the American Economy*. New York: Basic Books.

Mathews, D. 1996. *Is There a Public for Public Schools?* Dayton, OH: Kettering Foundation Press.

Mayberry, M. 1989a. "Characteristics and Attitudes of Families Who Home School." *Education and Urban Society*, 21: 32–41.

Mayberry, M. 1989b. "Home-Based Education in the United States: Demographics, Motivations, and Educational Implications." *Educational Review*, 41: 171–180.

Mayberry, M. 1992. "Home-Based Education: Parents as Teachers." *Continuing Higher Education Review*, 56: 48–58.

Mayberry, M., and Knowles, G. 1989. "Family Unity Objectives of Parents Who Teach Their Children: Ideological and Pedagogical Orientations to Homeschooling." *Urban Review*, 21: 209–225.

Mayberry, M., Knowles, G., Ray, B., and Marlow, S. 1995. *Home Schooling: Parents as Educators*. Thousand Oaks, CA: Corwin Press/Sage.

Mazama, Ama, and Lundy, Garvey 2012 "African American Homeschooling as Racial Protectionism." *Journal of Black Studies* 43: 723–748.

Mazama, Ama, and Lundy, Garvey 2013a. "African American Homeschooling and the Question of Curricular Cultural Relevance." *Journal of Negro Education* 82: 123–138.

Mazama, Ama, and Lundy, Garvey 2013b. "African American Homeschooling and the Quest for a Quality Education." *Education and Urban Society* 20: 1–22.

Mazama, Ama, and Lundy, Garvey 2014a. "African American Homeschoolers: The Force of Faith and the Reality of Race in the Homeschooling Experience." *Religion and Education* 41: 256–272.

Mazama, Ama, and Lundy, Garvey 2014b. "'I'm Keeping My Son Home': African American Males and the Motivation to Homeschool." *Journal of African American Males in Education* 5: 53–74.

McCurdy, K. 1997. "Why Homeschool?" In *The Homeschool Reader: Collected Articles from Home Education Magazine, 1984–1994*, edited by M. Hegener and H. Hegener, 15–16. Tonasket, WA: Home Education Press.

McDowell, S., Sanchez, A., and Jones, S. 2000. "Participation and Perception: Looking at Home Schooling through a Multicultural Lens." *Peabody Journal of Education*, 75: 124–146.

McKeon, C.C. 2007. "A Mixed Methods Nested Analysis of Homeschooling Styles, Instructional Practices, and Reading Methodologies." Doctoral diss., Capella University, MN. Accessed March 5, 2011. http://www.eric.ed.gov/PDFS/ED504128.pdf

Medlin, R.G. 2000. "Home Schooling and the Question of Socialization." *Peabody Journal of Education*, 75: 107–123.

Milner, M. 2006. *Freaks, Geeks, and Cool Kids*. New York: Routledge.

Mirochnik, D.A., and McIntire, W.G. 1991. *Homeschooling: Issues for Administrators. (Occasional Paper Series, No. 12)*. Orono, ME: University of Maine.

Moore, R. 1982. "Research and Common Sense: Therapies for our Homes and Schools." *Teachers College Record, 84*: 355–377.

Moore, R., and Moore, D. 1994. *The Successful Homeschool Family Handbook: A Creative and Stress-Free Approach to Homeschooling*. Camas, WA: Moore Foundation.

Muntes, G. 2006. "Do Parental Reasons to Homeschool Vary by Grade? Evidence from the National Household Educational Survey." *Home School Researcher*, 16: 11–17.

Murnane, R.J., and Levy, F. 1996. *Teaching the New Basic Skills: Principles for Educating Children to Thrive in a Changing Economy*. New York: The Free Press.

Murphy, J. 2010. *The Educator's Handbook for Understanding and Closing Achievement Gaps*. Thousand Oaks, CA: Corwin.

Murphy, J., and Meyers, C.V. 2008. *Turning Around Failing Schools: Lessons from the Organizational Sciences*. Thousand Oaks, CA: Corwin.

Nemer, K.M. 2002. *Understudied Education: Toward Building a Homeschooling Research Agenda (Occasional Paper)*. New York: National Center for the Study of Privatization in Education, Teachers College, Columbia University.

Noel, Amber, Stark, Patrick, and Redford, Jeremy. 2013 *Parent and Family Involvement in Education, from the National Household Education Survey Program of 2012.* Washington, DC: US Department of Education.

Parker, R.D. 1992. "Inside Home Schools: A Portrait of Eighty-Four Texas Families and the Schools in Their Homes." Master's thesis. Texas Tech University.

Payne, C. 2008. *So Much Reform, So Little Change: The Persistence of Failure in Urban Schools.* Cambridge: Harvard University Press.

Payne, J.L. 1995. *Profiting from Education: Incentive Issues in Contracting Out.* Washington, DC: Education Policy Institute.

Pearson, R.C. 1996. *Homeschooling: What Educators Should Know.* Accessed March 5, 2011. http://www.eric.ed.gov/PDFS/ED402135.pdf

Perry, J., and Perry, K. 2000. *The Complete Guide to Homeschooling.* Los Angeles, Lowell House.

Peterson, D. 2009. "You Can Homeschool Your Child with Special Needs." *Exceptional Parent*, 39: 38–39.

Pfitzer, G. 2014. *History Repeating Itself: the Republication of Children's Historical Literature and the Christian Right.* Amherst: University of Massachusetts Press.

Princiotta, D., and S. Bielick 2006. *Homeschooling in the United States: 2003.* Washington, DC: National Center for Education Statistics.

Princiotta, D., Bielick, S., and Chapman, C. 2004. *1.1 Million Homeschooled Students in the United States in 2003.* Washington, DC: National Center for Education Statistics.

Rakestraw, J., and Rakestraw, D. 1990. Home Schooling: A Question of Quality, an Issue of Rights. *Educational Forum*, 55: 67–77.

Ray, B. 1997a. *Home Education Across the United States: Family Characteristics, Student Achievement, and Longitudinal Traits.* Salem, OR: Home School National Defense Fund.

Ray, B. 1997b. *Strengths of Their Own: Home Schoolers Across America.* Salem, OR: NHERI Publications.

Ray, B. 2001. *Home Schooling Achievement.* Purcellville, VA: National Home Education Research Institute. Accessed March 5, 2011. http://www.hslda.org/docs/study/comp2001/HomeSchoolAchievement.pdf

Ray, B. 2004. *Home Educated and Now Adults: Their Community and Civic Involvement, Views About Homeschooling, and Other Traits.* Salem, OR: National Home Education Research Institute.

Ray, B. 2009. *Research Facts on Homeschooling: General Facts and Trends.* Salem, OR, National Home Education Research Institute.

Ray, B. 2015. "African American Homeschool Parents' Motivations for Homeschooling and Their Black Children's Academic Achievement." *Journal of School Choice*, 9: 71–96.

Ray, B. and Weller, N. 2003. "Homeschooling: An Overview and Financial Implications for Public Schools." *School Business Affairs*, 69: 22–26.

Reich, R. 2002. "The Civic Perils of Homeschooling." *Educational Leadership*, 59: 56–59.

Riegel, S. 2001. "The Home Schooling Movement and the Struggle for Democratic Education." *Studies in Political Economy*, 65: 91–116.

Reinhaller, N., and Thomas, G. 1996. "Special Education and Home Schooling: How Laws Interact with Practice." *Rural Special Education Quarterly*, 15: 11–17.

Ressler, C. 1997. "The Most Meaningful Lesson." In *The Homeschool Reader: Collected Articles from Home Education Magazine, 1984–1994*, edited by M. Hegener and H. Hegener, 49–55. Tonasket, WA: Home Education Press.

Romanowski, M. 2001. "Common Arguments About the Strengths and Limitations of Home Schooling." *The Clearing House*, 75: 79–83.

Safran, L. 2010. "Legitimate Peripheral Participation: How Commitment to Homeschooling Grows." *Teaching and Teacher Education*, 26: 107–112.

Saunders, M. 2010. "Previously Homeschooled College Freshmen: Their First Year Experiences and Persistence Rates." *Journal of College Student Retention*, 11: 77–100.

Schemmer, B.A.S. 1985. "Case Studies of Four Families Engaged in Home Education." EdD diss., Ball State University, IN.

Stevens, M. 2001. *Kingdom of Children: Culture and Controversy in the Homeschooling Movement*. Princeton, NJ, Princeton University Press.

Sutton, L., and Bogan, Y. 2005. "School Choice: The Fiscal Impact of Home Education in Florida." *AASA Journal of Scholarship & Practice*, 2: 5–9.

Taylor, J. 1985. "Self-Concept in Home-Schooling Children." Doctoral diss., Andrews University, MI: UMI Dissertation Services.

Taylor, V. 2005. "Behind the Trend: Increases in Homeschooling Among African American Families." In *Home Schooling in Full View*, edited by B.S. Cooper, 121–133. Greenwich, CT: Information Age Publishing.

Taylor-Hough, D. 2010. "Are All Homeschooling Methods Created Equal?" Accessed May 7, 2016. http://www.inreachinc.org/are_all_homeschooling_methods_created_equal.pdf

Tillman, V.D. 1995. "Home Schoolers, Self Esteem, and Socialization." *Home School Researcher*, 11: 1–6.

Thompson, J. 1994. "The Impact of Structural Costs on Home Schooling Decision in Rural and Non-Rural Districts." Paper presented at the annual meeting of the American Educational Finance Association, Nashville, TN, March 16–19.

Tyack, D. 1992. "Can We Build a System of Choice that is Not Just a 'Sorting Machine' or a Market-Based 'Free-for-All'?" *Equity and Choice*, 9: 13–17.

Van Galen, J. 1991. Idealogies and Pedagogues: Parents who Teach Their Children at Home. In *Homeschooling: Political, Historical, and Pedagogical Perspectives*, edited by J. Van Galen and M. Pittman, 63–76. Norwood, NJ: Ablex Publishing Corp.

Van Galen, J., and Pittman, M. 1991. "Introduction." In *Homeschooling: Political, Historical, and Pedagogical Perspectives*, edited by J. Van Galen and M. Pittman, 1–5. Norwood, NJ: Ablex Publishing Corp.

Vigilant, Lee Garth, Anderson, Tyler C., and Trefethren, Lauren Wold. 2014. "'I'm Sorry You Had a Bad Day, but Tomorrow will be Better': Stratagems of Interpersonal Emotional Management in Narratives of Fathers in Christian Homeschool Households." *Sociological Spectrum: Mid-South Sociological Association* 34: 293–313.

Vigilant, Lee Garth, Anderson, Tyler C., and Trefethren, Lauren Wold. 2013. "'You Can't Rely on Somebody Else': How Homeschooling Dad's Think." *Humanity and Society* 37: 201–224.

Wartes, J. 1987. *Report from the 1986 Homeschool Testing and other Descriptive Information about Washington's Homeschoolers*. WA: Washington Homeschool Research Project.

Webb, J. 1989. "The Outcomes of Home-Based Education: Employment and Other Issues." *Educational Review*, 41: 121–133.

Welner, K.M. 2002. *Exploring the Democratic Tensions within Parents' Decisions to Homeschool (Occasional Paper)*. New York: National Center for the Study of Privatization in Education, Teachers College, Columbia University.

Welner, Kariane Mari and Kevin G. Welner. 1999. "Contextualizing Homeschooling Data: A Response to Rudner." *Education Policy Analysis Archives*, 7(13).

Whitehead, J., and Bird, W. 1984. *Home Education and Constitutional Liberties: The Historical and Constitutional Arguments in Support of Home Instruction*. Westchester, IL: Crossway Books.

Wilhelm, G., and Firman, M. 2009. Historical and Contemporary Developments in Home School Education. *Journal of Research on Christian Education*, 18: 303–315.

Williams, D., Arnoldson, L.M., and Reynolds, P. 1984. "Understanding Home Education: Case Studies of Home Schools." Paper presented at the annual meeting of the American Educational Research Association, New Orleans, LA, April 23–37.

Winstanley, C. 2009. "Too Cool for School?: Gifted Children and Homeschooling." *Theory and Research in Education*, 7: 347–362.

Wyatt, G. 2008. *Family Ties: Relationships, Socialization, and Home Schooling*. Lanham, MD: University Press of America.

Yuracko, K. 2008. "Education Off the Grid: Constitutional Constraints on Homeschooling." *California Law Review*. 96: 123–184.

5

Academic Achievement
Making an Informed Choice about Homeschooling

Sandra Martin-Chang and Kyle Levesque

Parents are faced with endless decisions regarding the welfare of their children (e.g., breast milk vs. formula; co-sleeping vs. crib-sleeping; immunization vs. non-immunization; spanking vs. not spanking). Parents who wish to understand the impact of their choices often seek advice from researchers or pediatricians to help guide their decisions. This either takes place in the form of face-to-face meetings or via media correspondence (such as by reading books and listening to the news). Thankfully, many controversial topics have been the source of scientific inquiry; therefore, parents can access a wealth of unbiased information to help inform their opinions. However, unlike several topics related to child-rearing, the subject of homeschooling remains greatly understudied. The paucity of research on homeschooling poses a serious dilemma for parents who are considering home-based education as a means of fostering favorable and long-lasting academic achievements in their children. To illustrate, a scholarly search of "academic achievement of homeschooled students" results in only three published studies, whereas a Google search reveals over 85,000 hits. Therefore, what is "known" about the academic impact of homeschooling is based primarily on anecdotal information which is heavily subject to personal bias (Murphy 2014). How then are parents expected to make informed choices about homeschooling? In this chapter, we review what little scientific evidence has been collected regarding the academic achievements associated with homeschooling, and we supplement this relatively novel area of study by briefly reviewing two closely related fields.

Homeschooling, or home-based education, comprises a viable alternative form of education whereby parents/guardians assume the primary responsibility of educating their children at home rather than through more traditional public or private school institutions (Isenberg 2007; Rudner 1999). Parents who choose to homeschool their

The Wiley Handbook of Home Education, First Edition. Edited by Milton Gaither.

children do so for a myriad of reasons. While the breadth of this topic falls beyond the scope of the current chapter, parental reasons for homeschooling generally fall under recurring themes, such the desire to live in accordance with religion, discontentment with the public school system, or the desire to create strong family cohesion (for review, see Kunzman and Gaither 2013). It is not surprising, however, that the academic well-being of their children also falls among the top considerations for adopting home-based education (Bielick, Chandler, and Broughman 2001).

Given the large investment of time and effort, as well as the financial commitment associated with homeschooling, it is important for parents to know that their decision is in the best interest of their child's learning trajectory. Indeed, parents who are contemplating home-based education must seriously weigh the academic benefits of this teaching approach. Unfortunately, the scarcity of empirical research on this topic – in contrast to the abundance of anecdotal reports – makes is especially difficult for parents to discern the educational validity of homeschooling.

As such, the primary goal of this chapter is to review the scientific evidence that exists on the academic achievements of homeschoolers to date. We review the literature in a transparent and unbiased fashion with the goal of identifying the strengths of existing findings while also highlighting some of the important empirical shortcomings of prior research. In doing so, we hope to provide valuable information to homeschooling parents as well as call attention to gaps in the literature for future research endeavors.

Academic Achievement of Homeschooled Students

First and foremost, scientific research is best conducted by *non-stakeholders*. This sentiment was well expressed by Richard Muller with regard to his work on climate change:

> We are bringing the spirit of science back to a subject that has become too argumentative and too contentious. We are an independent, non-political, non-partisan group. We will gather the data, do the analysis, present the results, and make all of it available. There will be no spin, whatever we find. (Quoted in Sample 2011, par. 6)

In stark contrast to this model, the majority of the work investigating the academic impact of homeschooling has been commissioned by the homeschooling groups themselves. Several reports and unpublished dissertations have studied the effects of homeschooling on educational success (Ray and Wartes 1991) but because many of the studies have been conceived by homeschooling groups, it leaves their findings open to question. For example, Rudner (1999) sampled over 20,000 homeschooling families in the United States and found children in the homeschooling group were outperforming the children in the public-schooling group in several areas including reading, language arts, mathematics, social studies, science, and information services (Rudner 1999).

Over a decade later, Ray (2010) conducted another nationwide study on behalf of the National Home Education Research Institute. Ray's sample contained just over half as many students as Rudner's (1999) and drew similar conclusions, namely that children who had been homeschooled were more advanced than the public-schooled children with regards to reading, language, math, social science, and science. Ray went on to examine the environmental factors that were associated with the highest scores on the standardized tests in his sample. He found that children with the highest scores came from families who spent more time in structured learning activities, spent more money on learning materials, and had parents with more education themselves. Of all of these factors, parental education accounted for the most unique variance in the children's standardized scores.

Like all scientific studies, the reports listed above were not without flaws. The extent of the limitations in each of the reports have been discussed at length elsewhere (e.g., Kunzman and Gaither 2013; Lubienski, Puckett, and Brewer 2013; Martin-Chang, Gould, and Meuse 2011; Murphy 2014), and will only be summarized briefly here. To begin, both Rudner (1999) and Ray (2010) collected their data through educational testing companies that provided standardized testing to homeschooling families. Although this method of data collection resulted in large participant pools, both studies were limited to those families who (a) sought educational testing and (b) could afford to have it administered. These families may have differed systematically from other homeschooling families who put less emphasis on standardized tests, or who could not afford to pay for professional testing. It is perhaps no surprise, then, that both samples included an overrepresentation of parents who earned sizeable incomes and who were highly educated. In addition, even within these fairly homogenous samples, a large number of families who decided to have the standardized testing carried out still elected not to participate in the study. While acknowledging that parents agreed to participate *before* knowing their children's precise scores, it is nevertheless possible that the 11% to 19% of parents who agreed to share their children's results might also have been the parents who were most confident in their children's academic abilities.

In addition to non-randomized self-selected samples, some of the most influential homeschooling studies (e.g., Rudner 1999) have also lacked critical controls relating to family background (for review, see Kunzman and Gaither 2013). This is problematic because accounting for confounding factors such as socioeconomic status and parental education is critical when evaluating students' academic achievement (Belfield 2005). For instance, researchers have found clear links between a homeschooling mother's education background and (a) their child's achievement test scores (Medlin 1994) and (b) the quality of their instructional practices (Kunzman 2009). To illustrate, a comparison study of SAT scores between homeschooled vs. public- and private-schooled students revealed very little difference between the groups once family background was accounted for (Belfield 2005).

A final methodological limitation from Rudner (1999) and Ray's (2010) studies comes from the fact that neither included a similar group of publicly educated children to use as a comparison group. In each study, the scores of a specific group of self-selected homeschooled children (e.g., the homeschoolers were largely Caucasian and Christian, from two-parent families, with well-educated parents who held a high socioeconomic status) were compared to unselected, representative norms. This obstacle substantially limits the conclusions that can be drawn from such studies. Yet, summaries of these reports nevertheless conclude that "the home-educated [children] typically score 15 to 30 percentile points above public-school students on standardized academic achievement tests," without explicitly stating that the odds were in favor of the homeschooling groups from the onset (Ray 2015, "Academic Performance," par. 1).

In 2011, an independent group of researchers approached the study of homeschooling from a very different vantage point. Martin-Chang, Gould, and Meuse (2011) worked with a much smaller number of participants ($N=74$) under much more controlled circumstances. Like the studies conducted by Rudner (1999) and Ray (2010), Martin-Chang and colleagues also used standardized tests as a marker of academic achievement; however, unlike their predecessors, they conducted the tests themselves following the standardized procedures. This stands in stark contrast to Rudner (1999) and Ray's (2010) data, which was largely the result of tests administered by the children's parents and scored by an educational company. Martin-Chang, Gould, and Meuse (2011) also did the testing free of charge, making it more equitable for families from all social economic groups to participate.

Importantly, Martin-Chang, Gould, and Meuse (2011) followed a strict quasi-experimental design that included a comparison group of children who were attending public school. Each homeschooled child was matched with a public-schooled child from the same geographical area, who was similar in age, and had a mother with a similar level of education. The researchers also attempted to equate for family income between the two groups, however, an advantage remained for the public school group, most likely due to the fact that more of the public-schooled children came from families with two full-time income earners.

In addition to the demographic information listed above, Martin-Chang and colleagues also asked the homeschooling mothers questions about the amount of structure they provided during lessons (Martin-Chang, Gould, and Meuse 2011). Specifically, the homeschooling mothers were asked how often they used pre-made curricular or homemade structured lesson plans to teach their children. Responses to these questions were used to define two different subcategories of homeschoolers, which the authors referred to as *structured* ($n=25$) and *unstructured* ($n=12$) homeschoolers. The main difference between the two groups was that the structured homeschooling mothers conceptualized themselves as their children's teachers, whereas the unstructured homeschooling mothers embraced a child-directed learning philosophy; a number of mothers in the unstructured group also self-identified as being "unschoolers."

When Martin-Chang, Gould, and Meuse (2011) examined the scores between these two subgroups of homeschoolers, the results were striking. Namely, the structured homeschoolers were performing consistently above grade level, whereas the unstructured homeschoolers were performing at (or below) grade level in all subject areas tested. Indeed, statistical analyses revealed that the structured homeschoolers were significantly outperforming the unstructured homeschoolers in five out of the seven measures tested (letter-word identification, reading comprehension, science, social science, and calculation).

When the public school group was added into the equation, Martin-Chang, Gould, and Meuse (2011) found that the standardized test scores of children attending public school fell in between the two homeschooling groups. Structured homeschoolers achieved higher scores on all seven tests administered compared to the publicly schooled children, and the magnitude of the differences (i.e., effect sizes) between groups across all tests ranged from medium to large. In turn, the publicly schooled children achieved higher scores in all subjects tested compared to the children in the unstructured group and the differences between the groups were medium to large in four areas (word reading, reading comprehension, social science, and science).

To summarize, Martin-Chang and colleagues made an attempt to lessen the methodological limitations noted in the previous studies in two ways. First, they included a comparison group of public-schooled children in the investigation. Second, they had trained researchers administer the standardized tests, under controlled conditions (Martin-Chang, Gould, and Meuse 2011). However, this study had its own set of shortcomings – the primary one being the modest sample size. Indeed, the unstructured homeschooled group was comprised of only twelve students, which severely restricts the generalizations that can be drawn from this study.

Despite the small sample size, the paired-sampling approach utilized in the Martin-Chang, Gould, and Meuse (2011) study represents progress in homeschooling research. Moreover, their results are in accordance with a recurring trend associated with the academic achievements of homeschoolers, namely that children who are schooled at home tend to show superior achievements in the subject areas of language and literacy (e.g., Belfield 2005; Frost and Morris 1988; Ray and Wartes 1991; Rudner 1999). However, Martin-Chang and colleagues also found that structured homeschoolers were significantly advantaged in comparison to publicly schooled students on a standardized calculations subtest. These results stand in stark contrast to other studies that reported slightly below average performance in math (Belfield 2005; Qaqish 2007; Ray and Wartes 1991). For example, a recent exploration of unpublished data from a large network of homeschoolers ($N = 11007$) in the state of Alaska found that homeschooled students comparatively *overperformed* in reading but *underperformed* in math (Coleman 2013). However, it is difficult to draw direct comparisons between these studies because Martin-Chang and colleagues separated their homeschooling sample by structure (see also Ray 2010), whereas Coleman did not. Such conflicting findings further reiterate the pressing need for additional empirically based, peer-reviewed research on the academic outcomes of homeschoolers.

Given that very few studies on academic achievement in homeschooling have been conducted, and that each of those were methodologically flawed in their own ways, how are parents expected to make an informed choice about whether they should homeschool? One thing to look for is patterns in the research. For example, although the studies by Ray (2010) and Martin-Chang, Gould, and Meuse (2011) used very different methodologies, both noted the positive consequences associated with structured learning provided by the parents with regards to the level academic achievement attained by the children. This is particularly relevant in the discussion of homeschooling, because qualitative research (e.g., Arai 2000; Van Galen 1987, 1991) has established that many homeschooling parents differ drastically in how much they value structured learning.

In general, a distinction has been made between homeschooling parents who disagree with the school curriculum because it contradicts their personal beliefs and parents who disagree with the overarching structure of public education (Arai 2000; Mayberry and Knowles 1989; Van Galen 1987, 1991). Among the latter group, some parents have turned to an extreme form of home education referred to as "unschooling." John Holt, the *New York Times* bestselling author on educational reform, first coined the phrase to embody the notion of complete and natural self-directed learning on the part of the child – free from teachers, textbooks, and formal assessment. After spending several years observing the educational system, he concluded that "to a very great degree, school is a place where children learn to be stupid. [...] children come to school curious; within a few years most of that curiosity is dead [...]" (Holt 1964, 196).

Therefore, parents who are willing and have the means of implementing a home-based style of education must then decide *how* exactly they will educate their children. The decision to follow a more structured homeschooling approach and the decision to unschool both fall under the purview of parents exercising their rights to assume the primary responsibility of educating their children. However, the two groups deviate radically in their views of the parent-as-teacher, and in the use of pre-planned curriculum. Whereas many homeschooling parents teach their children from structured (either purchased or self-made) curriculum or lesson plans, parents who unschool focus to a greater degree on unstructured "experiential learning" or "learning by doing." For example, when Sandra Dodd, an author and spokesperson for the unschooling movement, was asked to give advice to parents on how to unschool she said:

> Try not to learn. Don't try to learn. Those two aren't the same thing but they're close enough for beginners. If you see something *educational* don't say a word. Practice letting exciting opportunities go by, or at least letting the kids get the first word about something interesting you're all seeing. If a family experimenting with unschooling can try to go some amount of time – a week, a month – without learning anything, but during that time they keep active, talkative, busy with life, maybe some art, some music, theatre or movies, walks to collect things (in the woods, in the dumpsters, it doesn't matter) – just being, but being busy – at the end of that time (or halfway through) I think it will become apparent that learning cannot be turned off, that given a rich environment, learning becomes like the air – it's in and around us. (Quoted in Subler 1998, "Since unschooling is a lifestyle", par. 2)

Although it was estimated that approximately 150,000 children in the United States were being unschooled in 2005 (Tamura and Gutierrez 2006), the academic effects of this practice are grossly understudied. However, there is a relevant literature from the field of psychology on "discovery learning" that touches on many of the core principles of unschooling.

Discovery Learning

Learning by discovery is a method of schooling in which students are encouraged to explore their surroundings and learn with little or no structure imposed by a teacher (Saulny 2006). This form of education relies on students to uncover for themselves higher-order concepts and procedures that would traditionally be the topic of direct instruction (Tuovinen and Sweller 1999). The advocates of unschooling posit that learning by discovery is a more fruitful form of education, where great student achievements are associated with less externally imposed direction. For example, Holt argued that:

> if a child is doing the kind of learning that most do in school, when they learn at all [the learning] will not be permanent, or relevant, or useful. But a child who is learning naturally, following his curiosity where it leads him, adding to his mental model of reality whatever he needs can find a place for, and rejecting without fear or guilt what he does not need, is growing in knowledge, in the love of learning and in the ability to learn. (Holt 1964, 220)

Yet even in Holt's time, the notion of discovery learning was not new. Almost a decade earlier, Craig (1956) had investigated the effectiveness of discovery learning by comparing the learning trajectories of two groups of college students. Participants were placed in either the *independent* group where they worked on word problems without assistance or they participated in the *directed* group where they were guided towards the most relevant cues to solving the problems (without being given the answers). Craig concluded that young adult learners made greater progress when they were given guidance towards solving the puzzles. In addition, the directed group remembered an equal number of principles and they were able to transfer their learning to new problems with similar accuracy as the independent group.

Converging evidence was presented by Kittell in 1957. He extended the research paradigm employed by Craig (1956) by including a *rote learning* condition in addition to the *independent* and *directed* conditions outlined above. Although it was anticipated that the rote learning condition would result in the worst learning outcomes, Kittell (1957) reported that the sixth grade students in his sample made the fewest gains when placed in the independent learning group. Kittell (1957) replicated Craig's (1956) pattern of results by finding once again that the directed discovery offered the most advantageous conditions for learning.

More recent work by Tuovinen and Sweller (1999) has suggested that the effectiveness of discovery learning may vary as a function of both the difficulty of the task and the expertise of the learner. They posit that material that can be learned as independent units (i.e., factual information, vocabulary knowledge) lends itself more to discovery learning than material that requires a high degree of integration, such as learning to read or computer programing. In their study, Tuovinen and Sweller (1999) divided participants into an *exploration* condition, where the undergraduates learned on their own, and a *guided* condition, where the participants were given examples to work from. The data showed that students who were unfamiliar with other similar databases learned significantly less under the exploration condition compared to the guided condition. However, students who were knowledgeable about other databases were equally successful under both learning conditions. Overall, then, it appears that Holt's philosophy of learning-by-discovery does not hold up under more rigorous experimental investigation (Anthony 1973; Craig 1956; Kittell 1957; Tuovinen and Sweller 1999; Wittrock 1963).

Children learning to read in a first language would be akin to novice participants (e.g., Tuovinen and Sweller, 1999). Therefore, unschooled children might be expected to experience particular difficulty learning how to read. This hypothesis is consistent with a large body of evidence highlighting the importance of direct instruction in learning to read; several distinct lines of evidence now suggest that explicitly teaching children the links between letters and sounds results in superior literacy skills (for review, see Ehri 2014). In contrast, requiring students to abstract the letter–sound correspondences themselves impedes success (Tunmer and Chapman 2002). This prediction was born out in Martin-Chang, Gould, and Meuse's (2011) sample where the discrepancy between the unstructured homeschoolers and the other two groups (structured homeschoolers and public school students) was most apparent in the reading subtasks.

In summary, the outcomes associated with self-directed/discovery learning do not appear optimal. And, these less-than-favorable learning outcomes are likely to be compounded for skills that naturally require more guidance and scaffolding from a knowledgeable teacher. Based on the literature reviewed above, it might seem prudent for parents who elect to homeschool to create a structured learning environment for their children.

Before endorsing a structured approach to homeschooling, however, it bears asking what influence "structure" plays in the homes of public-schooling families. For instance, in public-schooling families, helping with homework provides an opportunity for parents to influence their children's learning experience (Wingard and Fosberg 2009). In many ways, doing homework can be likened to "kitchen table schooling." Like the diverse approaches to homeschooling, public- schooling parents have various ways of structuring the homework setting.

Provision of Structure

Three dimensions have been associated with exemplary parenting. The first two: *supporting autonomy* and *supplying high degree of warmth*, are commonly associated with good parenting. However, it might come as a revelation that *providing structure* is also named as the third key component to successful child-rearing. With regards to the homework environment, Patall, Cooper, and Robinson (2008) conducted a meta-analysis of North American studies that estimated the relationship between parental structure during homework completion and student achievement. In keeping with the literature reviewed on discovery learning, Patall, Cooper, and Robinson (2008) found that parental involvement was most beneficial in the early years of schooling, and especially in skills that were complex in nature (such as language and literacy related activities). Moreover, the authors found that parents who were most focused on creating a structured environment were also the most likely to have children who excelled academically.

When contemplating Patall, Cooper, and Robinson's (2008) findings, it is important to note that "structure" was not equated with "control." Control, which is conceptualized as intrusive and accompanied by negative emotion, is distinct from structure. Simply put, parents provide structure when they help tailor the environment to promote children's competence (Farkas and Grolnick 2010). In fact, Patall and colleagues stated that highly controlling parental behavior in the form of monitoring during homework was associated with poorer student academic performance (Patall, Cooper, and Robinson 2008). In contrast, providing structure was associated with positive schooling outcomes. Moreover, Patall, Cooper, and Robinson (2008) demonstrated that when parents provided direct assistance to their children in the form of teaching/helping, the children were more likely to excel academically. The authors speculated that parental teaching might have resulted in better understanding of the material, whereas parental monitoring/control without assistance might have been experienced negatively by the children.

Several subcomponents have been identified within the overarching umbrella of "structure," including providing (1) clear rules and guidelines; (2) predictability; (3) task focused information and feedback; (4) opportunities to meet expectations/succeed; (5) rationales for rules and expectations; and (6) authority (Farkas and Grolnick 2010). Through semi-structured interviews with children in grades 7 and 8, Farkas and Grolnick (2010) studied how the components of structure listed above related to different student outcomes. Of particular interest here, they found that several dimensions of structure, including communicating clear rules and guidelines as well as providing predictability, were positively associated with perceived cognitive competence and higher grades for their children. Furthermore, providing the opportunities to succeed was "related to children's perceived control over academic success, perceived cognitive competence, engagement in academic behaviors, and grades" (Farkas and Grolnick 2010, 277). Remarkably, providing opportunities to succeed was the *only* component of structure that was also related to children's feelings of self-worth. Thus, the authors suggested that parents should provide their children with opportunities to succeed by setting aside the time and resources necessary for learning, and by helping/teaching their children as needed.

Grolnick et al. (2014) extended this work to examine how parental structure affected not only homework but also unsupervised time and responsibilities in grade 6 children. They conducted interviews and collected questionnaires from 160 families and concluded "when parents provided structure, children felt more in control of outcomes and less helpless with regard to success and failures" (Grolnick et al. 2014, 379). However, the authors acknowledged that their data was correlational and pointed out that longitudinal studies were needed to help elucidate the direction of the relationships they observed.

Fortunately, Dumont et al. (2014) were able to provide longitudinal data the following year. Using student questionnaires, they followed over 2800 students and their parents from grades 5 to 7. The authors gathered data in relation to perceived parental control, responsiveness, and structure as well as administering standardized tests at both time points. Results showed that more perceived parental control in grade 5 was *negatively* associated with academic functioning in grade 7. On the other hand, parental responsiveness and structure during homework sessions in grade 5 was associated with better reading skills and academic functioning in grade 7.

The positive influence of parental involvement seems to extend beyond grade school. A 2004 survey gathered from over 100 high school seniors asked students to categorize subjects by the degree to which their parents were involved in their learning. Students from the "high parent involvement" cohort scored significantly higher on a national college entrance exam (ACT) than students reporting low levels of involvement. Importantly, the scores of the students who reported high parent involvement in their schooling were on par with homeschoolers taking the same test (Barwegen et al. 2004).

Therefore, to summarize the work examining structure in relation to the homework setting in public-schooling families, its seems that positive outcomes are related to situations where parents organize their children's environment to encourage proficiency, without detracting from the child's sense of independence.

Points to Consider When Making an Informed Decision about Homeschooling

The increasingly diverse and expanding homeschooling movement creates a vital need for researchers, educators, and parents to better understand the academic outcomes associated with home-based education. There is no denying that the literature directly studying the impact of homeschooling on academic achievement is scarce. What is clearly needed is more scientific research, using carefully designed studies, conducted by independent groups of researchers in this area. However, due to the practical constraints of studying homeschooling (e.g., small dispersed populations, issues around self-selection, random sampling, etc.) it may take a long time for this research to reach the public. During that time, many parents will have to make life-defining choices for their children. So what, if anything, can we conclude from the research that has been conducted thus far?

Although the results of the studies should be interpreted with caution, the fact remains that in some cases, real differences seem to exist between the academic achievements of children who attend traditional school and children who are homeschooled (Martin-Chang, Gould, and Meuse 2011; Ray 2010, 2013; Rudner 1999). It has been stated that homeschooled children are outscoring their peers who attend schools (Ray 2015; Rothermel 2004; Van Galen and Pitman 1991; Wartes 1990) and so far, the research supports this position. However, preliminary evidence suggests a caveat to the positive academic achievements associated with homeschooling; namely, that these academic benefits may not extend to children who are being unschooled, or to other largely unstructured, discovery-learning experiences (Martin-Chang, Gould, and Meuse 2011).

There are theoretical reasons to expect that the achievements of homeschooled children will greatly depend on the amount of structure being provided in the home (Martin-Chang, Gould, and Meuse 2011; Ray 2010; Ray 2015). Drawing on previous work from the discovery learning literature (e.g., Tuovinen and Sweller 1999), it was noted that students experienced more success when given guidance during the learning tasks compared to when they were left to learn on their own. Discovery learning, on the other hand, did *not* result in accelerated acquisition of knowledge or in a knowledge base that was more flexible.

In terms of providing structure, the opposite patterns of findings have emerged, specifically, "parents who provide children with structure in the academic domain have children who feel better about and more competent in their school related actions and are more effective and successful in school" (Farkas and Grolnick 2010, 277). Indeed, this statement reflects the findings from a number of studies. It is also consistent with the observations made about the homeschooling populations studied by Martin-Chang, Gould, and Meuse (2011) and Ray (2010).

Therefore, at present, parents who seek advice from researchers or pediatricians might be told that although the academic achievement associated with homeschooling can be very positive, skepticism remains about the proposed merits of unschooling. While the unschooling movement has received considerable airtime through internet blogs and social media outlets, the benefits of this approach to students' academic achievements have not been supported by empirical research. This should not be taken to mean that academic success in homeschooling is only obtainable through rigid, formal styles of instruction. In fact, home-based education can take many forms and can vary greatly in how closely it resembles traditional classroom practices. Thus, even very informal, or less traditional, homeschool settings do not necessarily equate to "unschooling." However, what *does* appear to be crucial for fostering academic success in homeschoolers is a structured approach that intermixes a high level of parental input and interest along with guided instruction across meaningful learning experiences. In any case, whether parents elect to homeschool or send their children to school outside the home, research opinion recommends creating a learning environment that is warm and loving, autonomy affirming, and rich in the types of structure that inspires competence.

References

Anthony, W. S. 1973. "Learning to Discover Rules by Discovery." *Journal of Educational Psychology*, 64: 325–328. DOI:10.1037/h0034585

Arai, A. Bruce. 2000. "Reasons for Home Schooling in Canada." *Canadian Journal of Education*, 25: 204–217.

Barwegen, Laura M., Nancy K. Falciani, S. Junlah Putnam, Megan B. Reamer, and Esther E. Star. 2004. "Academic Achievement of Homeschool and Public School Students and Student Perception of Parent Involvement." *School Community Journal*, 14: 39–58.

Belfield, Clive R. 2005. "Home-Schoolers: How Well Do They Perform on the SAT for College Admissions?" In *Home Schooling in Full View: A Reader*, edited by Bruce S. Cooper, 167–178. Greenwich, CT: Information Age Publishing.

Bielick, Stacey, Kathryn Chandler, and Stephen Broughman. 2001. *Homeschooling in the United States: 1999* (NCES 2001–033). US Department of Education. Washington, DC: National Center for Education Statistics.

Coleman, Rachel. 2013. "Homeschoolers and Academics: The Alaska Data." *The Politics of Childhood*, November 19. Accessed April 26, 2015. http://politicsofchildhood.org/2013/11/19/homeschoolers-and-academics-the-alaska-data/#more-982

Craig, Robert C. 1956. "Directed Versus Independent Discovery of Established Relations." *Journal of Educational Psychology*, 47: 223–234. DOI:10.1037/h0046768

Dumont, Hanna, Ulrich Trautwein, Gabriel Nagy, and Benjamin Nagengast, B. 2014. "Quality of Parental Homework Involvement: Predictors and Reciprocal Relations with Academic Functioning in the Reading Domain." *Journal of Educational Psychology*, 106: 144–161. DOI:10.1037/a0034100

Ehri, Linnea. C. 2014. "Orthographic Mapping in the Acquisition of Sight Word Reading, Spelling Memory, and Vocabulary Learning." *Scientific Studies of Reading*, 18: 5–21. DOI:10.1080/10888438.2013.819356

Farkas, Melanie S., and Wendy S. Grolnick. 2010. "Examining the Components and Concomitants of Parental Structure in the Academic Domain." *Motivation and Emotion*, 34: 266–279. DOI:10.1007/s11031-010-9176-7

Frost, Eugene A., and Robert C. Morris. 1988. "Does Home-Schooling Work? Some Insights for Academic Success." *Contemporary Education*, 59: 223–227.

Grolnick, Wendy S., Jacquelyn N. Raftery-Helmer, Kristine N. Marbell, Elizabeth S. Flamm, Esteban V. Cardemil, and Monica Sanchez. 2014. "Parental Provision of Structure: Implementation and Correlates in Three Domains." *Merrill-Palmer Quarterly*, 60: 355–384.

Holt, John. 1964. *How Children Fail*. New York: Dell Publishing.

Isenberg, Eric J. 2007. "What Have we Learned about Homeschooling?" *Peabody Journal of Education*, 82: 387–409. DOI:10.1080/01619560701312996

Kittell, Jack E. 1957. "An Experimental Study of the Effect of External Direction during Learning on Transfer and Retention of Principles." *Journal of Educational Psychology*, 48: 391–405. DOI:10.1037/h0046792

Kunzman, Robert. 2009. *Write these Laws on your Children: Inside the World of Conservative Christian Homeschooling*. Boston: Beacon Press.

Kunzman, Robert, and Milton Gaither. 2013. "Homeschooling: A Comprehensive Survey of the Research." *Other Education: The Journal of Educational Alternatives*, 2: 4–59.

Lubienski, Christopher, Tiffany Puckett, and Jameson Brewer. 2013. "Does Homeschooling "Work"? A Critique of the Empirical Claims and Agenda of Advocacy Organizations." *Peabody Journal of Education*, 88: 378–392. DOI:10.1080/0161956X.2013.798516

Martin-Chang, Sandra, Odette N. Gould, and Reanne E. Meuse. 2011. "The Impact of Schooling on Academic Achievement: Evidence from Homeschooled and Traditionally Schooled Students." *Canadian Journal of Behavioural Science*, 43: 195–202. DOI:10.1037/a0022697

Mayberry, Maralee, and Gary J. Knowles. 1989. "Family Unity Objectives of Parents who Teach their Children: Ideological and Pedagogical Orientations to Home Schooling." *The Urban Review*, 21: 209–225.

Medlin, Richard G. 1994. "Predictors of Academic Achievement in Home Educated Children: Aptitude, Self-Concept, and Pedagogical Practices. *Home School Researcher*, 10: 1–7.

Murphy, Joseph. 2014. "The Social and Educational Outcomes of Homeschooling." *Sociological Spectrum: Mid-South Sociological Association*, 34: 244–272. DOI:10.1080/02732173.2014.895640

Patall, Erika A., Harris Cooper, and Jorgianne C. Robinson. 2008. "Parent Involvement in Homework: A Research Synthesis." *Review of Educational Research*, 78: 1039–1101. DOI:10.3102/0034654308325185

Qaqish, Basil. 2007. "An Analysis of Homeschooled and Non-Homeschooled Students' Performance on an ACT Mathematics Test." *Home School Researcher*, 17: 1–12.

Ray, Brian. D. 2010. "Academic Achievement and Demographic Traits of Homeschool Students: A Nationwide Study." *Academic Leadership Journal*, 8. Accessed September 30, 2014. http://contentcat.fhsu.edu/cdm/ref/collection/p15732coll4/id/835

Ray, Brian D. 2013. "Homeschooling Associated with Beneficial Learner and Societal Outcomes but Educators do not Promote it." *Peabody Journal of Education*, 88: 324–341. DOI:10.1080/0161956X.2013.798508

Ray, Brian D. 2015. "Research Facts on Homeschooling." Accessed April 26, 2015. http://www.nheri.org/research/research-facts-on-homeschooling.html

Ray, Brian D., and John Wartes. 1991. "The Academic Achievement and Affective Development of Home-Schooled Children." In *Homeschooling: Political, Historical, and Pedagogical Perspectives*, edited by Jane A. Van Galen and Mary Anne Pitman, 43–61. Norwood, NJ: Ablex Publishing Corp.

Rothermel, Paula. 2004. "Home-Education: Comparison of Home- and School-Educated Children on PIPS Baseline Assessments." *Journal of Early Childhood Research*, 2: 273–299. DOI:10.1177/1476718X04046650

Rudner, Lawrence M. 1999. "Scholastic Achievement and Demographic Characteristics of Home School Students in 1998." *Education Policy Analysis Archives*, 7: 1–38.

Sample, Ian. 2011. "Can a Group of Scientists in California End the War on Climate Change?" *The Guardian*, February 27. Accessed April 26, 2015. http://www.theguardian.com/science/2011/feb/27/can-these-scientists-end-climate-change-war.

Saulny, Susan. 2006. "Home Schoolers Content to Take Children's Lead." *The New York Times*, November 26. Accessed April 26, 2015. http://www.nytimes.com/2006/11/26/education/26unschool.html?pagewanted=all&_r=0

Subler, Emily. 1998. "An Interview with Sandra Dodd." Accessed January 12, 2015. http://sandradodd.com/interview

Tamura, Traci, and Thelma Gutierrez. 2006. "No School, No Books, No Teacher's Dirty Looks." *CNN*, February 3. Accessed April 26, 2015. http://www.cnn.com/2006/US/01/27/gutierrez.unschooing/index.html?section=cnn_us.

Tunmer, William E. and James W. Chapman. 2002. "The Relation of Beginning Readers' Reported Word Identification Strategies to Reading Achievement, Reading-Related Skills, and Academic Self-Perceptions." *Reading and Writing: An Interdisciplinary Journal*, 15: 341–358. DOI:10.1023/A:1015219229515

Tuovinen, Juhani E., and John Sweller. 1999. "A Comparison of Cognitive Load Associated with Discovery Learning and Worked Examples." *Journal of Educational Psychology*, 91: 334–341. DOI:10.1037/0022-0663.91.2.334

Van Galen, Jane A. 1987. "Explaining Home Education: Parents' Accounts of their Decisions to Teach their Own Children." *The Urban Review*, 19: 161–177.

Van Galen, Jane A. 1991. "Ideologues and Pedagogues: Parents who Teach their Children at Home." In *Homeschooling: Political, Historical, and Pedagogical Perspectives*, edited by Jane A. Van Galen and Marry Anne Pitman, 63–76. Norwood, NJ: Ablex Publishing Corp.

Van Galen, Jane A., and Mary Anne Pitman. 1991. Introduction to *Homeschooling: Political, Historical, and Pedagogical Perspectives*, edited by Jane A. Van Galen and Mary Anne Pitman, 1–5. Norwood, NJ: Ablex Publishing Corp.

Wartes, John .1990. "Recent Results from the Washington Homeschool Research Project." *Home School Researcher*, 6: 1–7.

Wingard, Leah, and Lucas Fosberg. 2009. "Parents' Involvement in Children's Homework in American and Swedish Dual-Earner Families." *Journal of Pragmatics*, 41: 1576–1595. DOI:10.1016/j.pragma.2007.09.010

Wittrock, M. C. 1963. "Verbal Stimuli in Concept Formation: Learning by Discovery." *Journal of Educational Psychology*, 54: 183–190. DOI:10.1037/h0043782

6

Homeschooler Socialization
Skills, Values, and Citizenship

Robert Kunzman

As this handbook emphasizes, research about homeschooling faces many methodological challenges. Insights and data about participants, approaches, and outcomes are partial at best. But when considering the topic of homeschooler socialization, it's not only the answers that are unclear, but the questions themselves. Perhaps the most emotionally charged and conceptually dense topic in the homeschooling research literature, socialization involves a range of normative – and highly contested – assumptions and claims. Media stereotypes and outside observers raise concerns about homeschoolers being socially isolated, lacking in sufficient exposure to peer groups and formative public interactions that institutional schooling typically provides. Defenders of homeschooling respond that the multitude of learning cooperatives and extracurricular group activities increasingly available to homeschoolers provide ample opportunity for social interaction beyond the family. But beneath the question of social exposure lies a more basic disagreement about what constitutes appropriate socialization in the first place. Homeschooling advocates often question the value of age-segregated school milieus, sometimes caricaturing schools as rampant with peer pressure, bullying, and violence.

Underlying these debates, then, are certain fundamental questions. What does it mean to be properly socialized? Which values are important to learn, and how should that occur? What role should parents, peers, and the broader society play in the process of socialization? To help organize this chapter and keep these normative questions in mind, the topic of homeschooler socialization will be divided into three related but distinct strands:

- personal interaction (learning how to interact effectively with others, including groups and broader society)

The Wiley Handbook of Home Education, First Edition. Edited by Milton Gaither.

- values and beliefs (navigating peer, parental, and societal influences in the formation of one's identity and commitments)
- civic identity and engagement (coming to see oneself as a citizen with rights, responsibilities, and the capacity to exercise them).

Despite the complexity of the topic, the "socialization question" has received significant (albeit unsystematic) attention among researchers and scholars. As well it should: in the United States, 46% of homeschool parents identified socialization-related concerns as *the* primary motivation for their decision to homeschool their children when surveyed by the National Center for Education Statistics (NCES). These socialization-related reasons – more specifically, concern about conventional school environments, a desire to provide moral instruction, and a desire to provide religious instruction – were three of the four most common reasons given overall by parents (Noel, Stark, and Redford, 2013).

While not offered as a choice in the NCES survey, a motivation that in some ways encompasses these other reasons is an emphasis on family as the center of daily life (Kunzman 2016; Murphy 2014). Many parents view homeschooling as both a protective and nurturing enclave, a personalized resistance against the broader culture. While some homeschool parents identify a tradeoff being made between family cohesion and wider social engagement, an abundance of studies reveal that homeschool parents generally think their children are receiving necessary – and often superior – socialization experiences through interactions with family, learning cooperatives, extracurricular activities, and broader community engagement (Medlin, 2000, 2013).

Socialization for Personal Interaction

In light of homeschool advocates' criticism of institutional schooling's socialization process, we should be clear that asking, "Do homeschooled children acquire the necessary social skills to function effectively in broader society?" does not presume that homeschoolers should necessarily mimic the behavior and customs of the wider culture. Instead, the relevant question is whether children gain the social fluency to *navigate* that context, learning how to develop relationships and work effectively with others who may be different from them.

When examining the range of studies on homeschoolers' social skills, three major methodological limitations become apparent. The first one is common across homeschooling research more generally: most study participants are drawn from small convenience samples, preventing any reliable generalizations about the "average homeschooler." The second weakness of research on homeschooler socialization is that it relies heavily on the perceptions of parents or students themselves.

The third methodological shortcoming deserves a bit more elaboration: most studies treat school attendance as a binary – students are either homeschoolers or not, with no distinction regarding the years they have spent homeschooled as compared to conventionally schooled. But given the apparently significant number of children who move between homeschooling and conventional schooling, it is important to take into consideration how long someone has been homeschooled when trying to evaluate its possible effect on socialization and other outcomes. Children who have been homeschooled their entire lives might conceivably have very different experiences and outcomes than those who did so for only a year or two.

Most empirical studies of homeschooler socialization consist of participants (children and/or their parents) being asked to complete a questionnaire such as the Social Skills Rating System (with subtopics of cooperation, assertiveness, empathy, and self-control) or the Piers-Harris Children's Self-Concept Scale; other surveys inquiring about peer friendships and loneliness have also been used. These studies generally find that homeschooled children (or their parents) view their social skills as at least as robust as the broader school-age population views their own. Participants describe themselves (or parents describe them) as generally possessing social confidence, contentment, and skills, and they report engagement in extracurricular activities at rates similar to students in institutional schools (Kunzman and Gaither 2013; Murphy, 2014).

A few studies, even while presenting largely positive analyses of homeschoolers' socialization, observe that homeschoolers occasionally express a greater sense of social isolation and appear less peer-oriented than public school students (Delahooke 1986; Seo 2009; Shirkey 1987). This perception is frequently echoed in concerns voiced by public school officials, who worry that homeschoolers do not receive adequate peer socialization (Abrom 2009; Fairchild 2002; Kunzman 2005). A different interpretation, however, is offered by other researchers who suggest that a lower dependence on peer relationships may have some positive benefits, such as less concern about social status and unreflective conformity (Medlin 2000). One small-scale study found that homeschoolers actually reported similar peer victimization as conventionally schooled children – but interestingly, the homeschoolers expressed less distress about it (Reavis and Zakriski 2005). The researchers speculate that perhaps such peer conflicts may be less of a threat to social status in the homeschool context.

Most of the studies mentioned, however, suffer from all three methodological limitations noted above: they rely on small convenience samples, depend entirely on the perceptions of parents or the children themselves, and fail to include "years of homeschooling" as a variable. The results of these surveys are then often compared to national US samples of the broader school-age population, a misleading exercise at best.

A handful of studies have pushed beyond the limits of self- and parent-evaluation to consider social behaviors and outcomes for homeschoolers cataloged by either disinterested observers or more objective measures. Shyers (1992) employed a double-blind protocol of behavioral observations of seventy homeschoolers and seventy public school students which revealed significantly fewer "problem behaviors" among homeschooled children ages 8 to 10. Chatham-Carpenter (1994) asked children to track all substantial (longer than two minutes) social interactions over a timeframe of one month; homeschoolers reported no statistically significant differences in the number of social contacts they had compared with public school students, although public school students had more frequent interactions with those contacts. Homeschoolers, however, reported interactions with a wider range of ages than their public school counterparts. Haugen (2004) asked children's teachers to rate their social behavior and skills (in the case of homeschoolers, their parents selected teachers from church, learning co-ops, or other classes available in the community). Homeschoolers' teachers rated them significantly higher on social skills and significantly lower on problem behaviors than the ratings provided by teachers of conventionally schooled students. All of these studies, however, still used convenience samples, so results cannot be reliably extrapolated across the broader population.

A few large-scale surveys have also been conducted of homeschool graduates. The most highly publicized of these have been conducted by Ray (1997, 2004). These paint an extremely rosy portrait of homeschooler socialization outcomes but suffer from the same methodological shortcomings of non-random sampling and self-reporting. A more recent large-scale survey of homeschool graduates shared a similar methodology but yielded a decidedly more mixed picture of satisfaction with the homeschooling experience and healthy outcomes as adults (Coalition for Responsible Home Education 2014). In both cases, the clearly non-random respondent pool seems likely to have shaped the findings in ways that tell us little about homeschooler socialization more broadly.

In studying long-term outcomes, Knowles and Muchmore (1995) offered a richer methodology than the Ray (1997, 2004) and Coalition (2014) studies. Their research, while far less expansive in number, probed more deeply by conducting life history interviews with ten adults who had been homeschooled (culled from a pool of forty-six volunteers to represent a range of demographic diversity). The authors found little indication that the homeschooling experience had produced significant social disadvantage; rather, they suggested that it may have in fact contributed to a strong sense of independence and self-determination.

This latter observation is echoed by research examining the social integration of homeschoolers in the college setting, which finds that homeschoolers compare favorably to their institutionally educated peers in social behavior and leadership (Galloway and Sutton 1995; Sutton and Galloway 2000). As Medlin (2000) notes, however, the college setting for this research may have been especially well-suited for homeschoolers, since so many of them enrolled there.

One of the few studies that has actually employed random samples of homeschoolers from the broader population offers a decidedly mixed evaluation of homeschooler socialization over the long term. The Cardus Education Survey explored the perspectives of high school graduates from the United States and Canada, and found that religious homeschoolers expressed higher rates of "lack of clarity of goals and sense of direction" and "feelings of helplessness in dealing with life's problems," although the Canadian differences were attributed to demographic variables rather than homeschooling itself (Pennings et al. 2011, p. 24; 2012, 40). Further complicating the picture are some other results from the US survey: for example, religious homeschoolers felt strongly (relative to the other subgroups) that their schooling had prepared them for personal relationships, friendships, and family relations, especially marriage. In addition, they scored highest on the question that asked whether high school prepared them for a vibrant religious and spiritual life. How these findings relate to religious homeschoolers reporting higher divorce rates, lack of clarity and sense of direction, and greater feelings of helplessness in dealing with life's problems merits further investigation. It is also worth noting that the survey represents the views and experiences of those who, in some cases, were homeschooled more than two decades ago. Between 1999 and 2007, it's estimated that homeschooling grew nearly 75% in the United States, so the Cardus survey data reflects only some of that growth. Finally, while the actual number of homeschoolers who participated in the surveys was relatively small (82 in the United States, 58 in Canada), the fact that they were obtained via random sampling makes them more statistically reliable than the Ray (1997, 2004) and Coalition (2014) research mentioned above.

Another study that combined a large randomized dataset with control variables was not explicitly focused on social skills, but used data on more than 180 000 students from the National Survey on Drug Use and Health to examine homeschoolers' rate of drug abuse and extracurricular participation relative to the broader school population (Green-Hennessey 2014). Controlling for key demographic variables, the analysis revealed that only 3% of homeschoolers with strong religious ties reported having a substance disorder, compared with 6% of religious, conventionally schooled students. More than 15% of homeschoolers with weak or no religious ties, however, reported substance abuse. Regarding extracurricular participation, less-religious homeschoolers were two and a half times more likely to report no extracurricular engagement than their less-religious counterparts in conventional schools. Religious homeschoolers were 60% *less likely* to report no extracurricular participation than religious conventionally schooled students. Interestingly, 20% of religious homeschoolers reported that church-based activities were their only kind of extracurricular activity; less than 4% of religious conventionally schooled students reported church-based activities as their sole social outlet.

As is evident from this brief summary of research, both critics and advocates can find data in the empirical record to support their stances on homeschoolers' development of social skills, but the methodological weaknesses of most studies renders any comprehensive judgments elusive. Not surprisingly, this empirical uncertainty leaves room for a range of normative arguments about social skills and group interactions in the scholarly literature as well, with a frequent emphasis by homeschool proponents on the ways in which the very culture of institutional schooling inhibits creative thinking and the cultivation of a rich and cohesive family life (Meighan 1984; Ray 2013). These arguments challenge the "common-sense" narrative that institutional schooling is necessary for normal social development and a stable society. The vision of institutional schooling as serving the best interests of the child, they assert, instead actually privileges perpetuation of the system itself, over and against children's individual needs and interests (Monk, 2004). Wyatt

(2008) contrasts this dynamic with a thoughtful case for homeschooling as an appropriate and effective means of socialization for many families. He surveys the literature on the social context of public schools and theorizes that many choose homeschooling in pursuit of an alternative conception of the family and in resistance to broader culture and its values. Merry and Howell (2009) affirm this idea, arguing that homeschooling enables attentive parents to develop more intimate, supportive family relationships that foster healthy social and personal development in their children.

The health care community occasionally weighs in on the topic of homeschooler socialization as well, offering practitioners a variety of perspectives. The few homeschooling-related articles published in medical journals reveal some concern among health care providers as it relates to homeschooled children's socialization, including their exposure to cultural and value diversity, as well as children's eventual capacity to navigate mainstream society (Klugewicz and Carraccio 1999; Murray 1996). Pediatricians are urged to exercise extra vigilance with homeschooled children due to the absence of health care screening (formal and informal, mental and physical) that is typically conducted in school settings. This vigilance would include directing parents of children with special needs to resources otherwise provided in schools, as well as encouraging parents to provide group socialization opportunities outside the family context (Abbott and Miller 2006; Johnson 2004; Wallace 2000). Despite these various cautions and recommendations, however, the professional medical literature suggests a growing acceptance of homeschooling as a legitimate educational option, much in the way that some alternative medicine has slowly gained legitimacy among practitioners (Abbott and Miller, 2006). Medical professionals do note the need for long-term outcome data, however, to help better inform their understanding and interactions with homeschool families (Murray 1996).

Socialization for Values and Beliefs

Developing the interpersonal skills necessary to navigate day-to-day interactions is only part of the socialization process, of course. As they grow up, children acquire values and beliefs that help shape their social and ethical identities. Parents are typically the first and most significant factor in this identity formation process, but numerous other influences – peers, local community, and broader culture – emerge as the child grows and begins to engage more fully with the world.

The role of education in the formation of children's values and beliefs is certainly not a topic unique to the homeschooling literature. There exists a rich scholarly discourse exploring both the process of self-determination and the degree to which core value commitments can be arrived at independently; psychologists typically speak of *agency*, while philosophers use the term *autonomy*. These are vigorously contested concepts, however: given the complex array of influences that shape us, what does it mean to think and act for oneself, and how important is such self-determination in leading a good life?

Answers to these questions run the gamut, from the stance that free will is ultimately illusory, to the assertion that autonomy requires boundless choice and self-creation (Feinberg 1980; Skinner 1971). Neither extreme, however, is useful in illuminating the process of identity formation or the role of education in cultivating certain values and beliefs. Even if sharp distinctions cannot always be drawn between education and indoctrination, certainly a meaningful difference exists between an environment marked by opportunities to question, reflect, and judge, and one demanding unreflective adherence to received tradition (Snook 1972). At the same time, however, a moderate version of autonomy doesn't require radical independence – one can still draw from the wisdom of community, culture, and tradition, and willingly rely on others; such interdependencies, in fact, often support the development of further autonomy (Chirkov et al. 2003; Ryan and Deci 2001, 2006).

As homeschooling has grown in popularity and opportunities for diverse learning experiences have multiplied, the stereotype of children huddled around a kitchen table secluded from the broader world has become increasingly inaccurate (Green-Hennessey 2014). Nevertheless, the flexibility that homeschool parents have to shape their children's education in ways that adhere closely to their own values and priorities raises questions about the development of homeschooled children's autonomy: how much influence should parents have on the identity and beliefs of their child, particularly as they transition toward young adulthood?

Few would dispute the notion that a central responsibility of parenting is to instill certain values and commitments in one's children, and certainly when children are very young this often is accomplished through direct inculcation. Even as children begin to differentiate from their parents during adolescence, the process is not simply about separation, but rather identification with and integration into a broader community and its values (Bar-Yam Hassan and Bar-Yam 1987; Helwig 2006; Lewis 2013; Schachter and Venture, 2008). Furthermore, differentiation need not entail ideological and relational rupture – parents and other influential adults can serve as pivotal "identity agents" who co-participate in adolescents' identity formation, even while leaving them ample room for choice and self-determination (Freeman and Almond 2012; Koepkie and Denissen 2012; Schachter and Venture 2008).

One avenue of potential insight into homeschooling learning contexts is through analysis of parenting styles. A significant body of research exists on the relationship between parenting styles and the cultivation of autonomy in children, irrespective of schooling choice. Research on parenting styles typically identifies four distinct categories: authoritarian (strict demands on children with little room for questioning or dissent, and a lack of emotional warmth); authoritative (clear expectations and consequences but room for dialog and perhaps compromise, with abundant emotional warmth); permissive (minimal expectations or control but abundant emotional warmth); and disengaged (offering neither behavioral expectations nor emotional warmth) (Collins and Laursen, 2004; Maccobby and Martin1983). Some parenting styles, however – especially those from non-Western cultures – don't fit as easily within this framework, such as parents who combine strict demands and little room for negotiation with abundant emotional warmth and connectedness (Baumrind 1987). Furthermore, parents rarely fall into just one of these categories exclusively in terms of their interactions with their children, and oftentimes their parenting style differs across the children in their own family (East 2009). This appears to be the case in terms of gender expectations in some conservative religious homeschool families (MacFarquhar 2008; McDannell 1995; Joyce 2009; Talbot 2000).

Those qualifications notwithstanding, research on adolescents generally supports the idea that authoritative parenting produces outcomes more strongly associated with autonomy – providing a balance between clear expectations for adolescents and room to develop their own values and decision making as they continue to grow in judgment and responsibility (Steinberg 2000). This is not to suggest, however, a direct correspondence between parental styles and actions and any adolescent's emerging sense of identity and autonomy. Many other factors, including a range of social influences and the responses of adolescents themselves create a complex web of outcomes (Arnett 2013).

A few empirical studies of homeschoolers suggest that conservative religious parents adopt a more authoritarian stance in their homeschooling (Cai, Reeve, and Robinson 2002; Manuel 2000; Vaughn 2003). Batterbee (1992), on the other hand, found that homeschoolers tested higher for intrinsic motivation and autonomy. McEntire (2005) found homeschoolers to be more settled in their personal values and commitments than a comparison group of public school students – but whether this serves as evidence of thoughtful personal reflection or inflexible adherence to dogma remains unclear. In a study of 30 children and their parents from two Christian homeschool support groups, Kingston and Medlin (2006) found no statistical difference in their response to the statement, "I want my child to decide for him/herself what values to believe in," as compared with the responses of fifty public school parents from the same geographical area. Of course, what parents say they want for their children, and the actions they take in that regard, do not necessarily align. In addition, all these studies were relatively small convenience samples, so the usual caveats about broader applicability apply.

The role of schooling in fostering personal autonomy has received ample attention in philosophical scholarship as well (Brighouse and Swift 2006; Callan 1997; Galston 2002; Spinner-Halev 2000), and recent years have seen theorists turn their attention more squarely on homeschooling in this regard. Reich (2002, 2008) contends that parents, children, and the state all have legitimate interests in the educational process – sometimes these converge, but other times they exist in tension with one another. Children, he argues, have an interest in "minimalist autonomy": they should develop the capacity to reflect critically on their values and commitments, and they should have a range of meaningful life options to select and pursue. Reich and similarly minded scholars (Blokhuis 2010; West 2009; Yuracko 2008) worry that some forms of homeschooling will inhibit the development of such autonomy in children, since parents can serve as sole instructors and ostensibly restrict exposure to a variety of ideas and perspectives.

Other theorists disagree with Reich's emphasis on autonomy, or dispute his contention that the homeschooling milieu poses a particular risk to its development, often questioning whether public schools are any more likely to foster minimalist autonomy (Glanzer 2008; Merry and Karsten 2010). Even among those who find the value of autonomy conceptually compelling, it appears destined to remain an ideal whose inherent imprecision prevents reliable measurement. In this respect, it seems highly doubtful that the state, in the role of guarantor of children's rights (Brighouse 2002), possesses either the wisdom or capacity to evaluate whether anyone has met some minimum threshold for autonomy (Conroy 2010; Kunzman 2012).

A homeschool environment emphasizing the inculcation of values and commitments that run counter to the broader culture would not necessarily inhibit the development of autonomy, of course. As noted previously, homeschooling is a countercultural endeavor for many families, and an ethos of resisting authority and questioning professional expertise is not uncommon (Meighan 1984). Consider the efforts toward "educational protectionism" identified by Mazama and Lundy (2012, 2013) in their study involving 74 African American homeschooling families. The reasons these parents gave for homeschooling were not simply about protection but also empowerment – they sought to help their children develop a positive self-image by providing cultural role models (both racial and religious) and a supportive community that would provide a powerful ideological counterweight to a broader society and promote the development of their children's autonomy in ways that institutional schooling could not (see also Fields-Smith and Kisura 2013; Fields-Smith and Williams 2009; Lundy and Mazama 2014).

This goal of protectionism is certainly at play in the motivations of many religious homeschooling parents. Their often passionate commitment to instilling religiously informed values and beliefs in their children adds another layer of complexity to the project of values formation and the question of children's autonomy. Buss (2000) contends that adolescents need exposure to ideologically diverse peers to help facilitate the process of identity development, and she argues that religiously inspired homeschooling may inhibit such development, especially in adolescents (see also Blokhuis 2010; West 2009, Yuracko 2008). But there may also be a way in which religious homeschooling promotes independent thinking and offers alternative life options to consider.

For at least some religiously motivated homeschoolers, the very act of homeschooling serves as an assertion of their religious identity (Liao 2006), and this countercultural ethos may in turn foster the kind of mindset that characterizes autonomous thinking. One can imagine learning contexts where children are encouraged to interrogate "conventional wisdom" in ways that actually foster critical thinking and alternative viewpoints. Much depends, of course, on whether such cultural resistance is informed by a range of alternative perspectives, or merely the unreflective acceptance of a single competing narrative (Kunzman 2010).

Some studies have attempted to explore the socialization effects of homeschooling contexts that are motivated in large part by parental desire to instill religious values and commitments in their children. Hoelzle (2013) interviewed four young adult Christians, exploring how they viewed the impact of their homeschooling experiences in shaping their values and beliefs, as well as they ways in which these now align with or diverge from their parents. Hoelzle asserts that Reich's (2002) concerns about lack of exposure to diverse ways of life are overstated, pointing to participants' acknowledgment that they had encountered ideas and people not scripted by their parents as well as their assertions that they felt free to shape their own lives. Even while retaining generally close relationships with their parents, participants revealed not insignificant divergence from their parents' religious views in ways that suggest autonomous functioning. Kunzman's (2009) study of six conservative Christian homeschooling families also found indications that – despite some parents' concerted efforts to the contrary – children were exposed to outside social and ethical influences in ways that appeared to moderate religious ideology. Whether such moderation was sustained into adulthood remains an open question, however.

Of course, it is possible that participants in retrospective studies such as this are not always able to recognize the ways in which their supposed perceptions and choices were actually narrowly channeled by powerful parental influence. Self-deception or lack of awareness seems an unavoidable possibility with survey or interview research; to the extent that childhood memories and adult self-appraisal could be triangulated by other participant perspectives, a richer and more compelling picture of socialization might emerge.

The most empirically compelling data regarding religious value formation suggests that parents' religious commitments are far more significant in shaping the religiosity of their children than the method of schooling their children experience. In his analysis of the National Survey of Youth and Religion database, Uecker (2008) found that, for children with deeply religious parents, whether or not they were homeschooled made no statistical difference in their religious behavior and commitments. The parents' influence was the same regardless, a counterintuitive finding that calls into question the assumption by many theorists that the homeschool milieu increases the ideological influence of parents.

As noted at the outset of this chapter, one parental motivation for homeschooling that cuts across several listed in the NCES survey is the desire to make family the center of daily life. Often this motive has religious impetus (Carper 2000; McDannell 1995; Sun 2007), but certainly the desire of parents to retain deeper influence and involvement in their children's daily lives resonates well beyond religious affiliation. For many homeschool parents, schooling is seen as naturally embedded in the broader project of education, which is in turn embedded in the even broader project of parenting. Homeschooling becomes a means to strengthen the bonds among family members, to provide a context that honors individual needs and interests, and to create a source of social and ethical support that parents may find lacking in the conventional school setting (Brabant, Bourdon, and Jutras

2003; Dahlquist, York-Barr, and Hendel 2006; Mayberry and Knowles 1989; Morton 2010; Wyatt 2008).

Does homeschooling contribute significantly to these goals of making family the centerpiece of daily life, a bulwark against the wider culture? Butler and others (2015) explored this question by comparing 35 homeschool with 38 public-school families, all of whom were rated as having a strong "family-centric orientation" – the parents highly valued family cohesion and desired to create an environment in which members encouraged, supported, and collaborated with one another. The researchers found that the homeschoolers did experience somewhat greater family cohesion than their public school counterparts, but not to an extent that would suggest inherent superiority of the homeschooling model. As the authors conclude, "Family-centric families appear to find ways and means to achieve reasonably comparable family cohesion and positive interaction outcomes irrespective of the type of schooling they choose" (Butler et al. 105).

Here we may arrive at a central finding for the educational process of values formation. Both Uecker's (2008) large dataset and Butler et al.'s (2015) smaller sample offer intriguing comparisons between the effects of schooling type on children's socialization experiences, particularly in relation to the formation of core values and beliefs. In both cases, it appears that parents who are committed to a particular ethical vision of values formation in their children do not need homeschooling to accomplish this. There may be a range of other benefits (and tradeoffs) to homeschooling, but viewing it as either reliable protection against social influence or an indispensable lever for ethical maturity is likely misguided.

Nevertheless, any conclusions about the relative influence of homeschooling as an educational choice on the formation of students' values and beliefs remain tentative at best. The transmission of values from parent to child is hardly a straightforward matter, regardless of schooling context. Continued exploration of these complex questions, combining the bird's eye view of survey research with the nuanced texture of narrative inquiry – particularly when long-term perspectives and outcomes are included – remains a rich field of study.

Socialization for Civic Identity and Engagement

Liberal democracies depend on the cultivation of citizens who can participate in the political process and engage respectfully with diverse viewpoints informed by a multitude of values and commitments. Some scholars view homeschooling as an extreme form of educational privatization that threatens the mutual civic obligation and tolerance vital for a democratic public (Apple 2000; Lubienski 2000, 2003; Nemer 2004; Ross 2010). Homeschoolers, they worry, may lack sufficient exposure to a range of cultural and ethical diversity and thus may be ill-equipped for a citizenship that requires critical self-awareness and respectful engagement with pluralism (Blokhuis 2010; Reich 2008). But homeschoolers typically do not see their avoidance of public schools and their resistance to contemporary culture as a rejection of community; some view homeschooling as a way to reestablish local communities in a modern society where such associations have withered (Moss 1995).

Before turning to the research on civic formation of homeschoolers, however, a review of the broader literature on civic identity and engagement identifies several key influences in cultivating engaged democratic citizenship in youth. Not surprisingly, participation in voluntary groups focused on community service, public speaking, and fostering communal identity all appear to make future political activity more likely (Hart et al. 2007; McFarland and Thomas 2006). The orientation toward political discourse as experienced in the family context plays a critical role as well. Parents serve as important models for civic volunteerism, but also as influential dialogical partners: adolescents who talk about politics with their parents score higher on measures of civic skills and behavior (Andolina et al. 2003; McIntosh, Hart, and Youniss 2007). Significantly, alignment of parental and adolescent political viewpoints is not a pivotal factor in cultivating a commitment to democratic citizenship; rather, it is the modeling by parents of a dialogical process wherein they genuinely listen to their children's perspectives and honor their prerogative to hold their own opinions that matters. When parents genuinely engage with adolescents' viewpoints and arguments, their children come to see themselves as viable participants in the civic realm. In this way, families serve as "mini-polities where the civic dispositions and identities of younger generations are being formed" (Flanagan 2013, 93).

Dinas (2014) also explores the civic effects of parent–child interactions, employing data from surveys spanning multiple generations to show that highly politicized parents produce initially like-minded children – but then these children are more likely to shift away from their parents' view in young adulthood. Dinas' analysis of the reasons behind this dynamic deserve additional scrutiny, however. He asserts that active political talk helps children become more attuned to alternative viewpoints – and thus sets the stage for a future change of heart – but one could easily imagine political talk occurring instead within an echo chamber of consistently one-sided arguments offered by parents. If additional perspectives are not presented by other sources outside the home, it seems less likely that children will change their political beliefs. In fact, Dinas identifies two necessary conditions for such a shift: adolescents "must be attentive to the political cues and messages that others are providing" and they "must develop accurate beliefs about others' opinions" (5). It is certainly possible that eventual college and/or employment contexts will eventually expose young adults to alternative viewpoints – in which case disillusionment with and rejection of parental political views may follow as Dinas contends – but simply the presence of political talk at home seems unlikely to suffice.

So what does the research say about participation in civic life by homeschoolers specifically, and their development of key liberal virtues such as tolerance? Empirical data regarding the civic outcomes for adults who were homeschooled provide some insights but leave many questions unanswered. Ray's (2004) well-publicized study of adults who were homeschooled shows them voting more often than national averages, and volunteering for civic organizations at a much higher rate, but he neither employed random sampling nor controlled for income, education, or other key demographics. By contrast, studies employing rigorous methodology paint a more complex and uneven picture.

At least some research suggests that homeschoolers contribute significantly to their communities. Drawing on data from the National Household Education Survey, Smith and Sikkink (1999) found that homeschool families are consistently more involved in civic activities than public school families, even when controlling for key variables such as parental income and education levels. Most homeschoolers, they assert, are "embedded in dense relational networks" (20) of other families, support organizations, and community activities. Of course, the value of local community for the broader civic good depends mightily on the nature of those associations and the willingness of its members to engage beyond its boundaries with those who may not share the same values and beliefs. As noted previously, some scholars raise concerns that homeschooling allows parents to ensconce their children in social cocoons that limit exposure to the wide range of values, beliefs, and ways of life found in broader society (Ross 2010). So one unanswered question is how cross-cutting these networks are – do they help create bridges across diverse social groups, or simply reinforce bonds among like-minded citizens (Putnam 2000)?

While Smith and Sikkink's research focused on homeschooling families, Hill and den Dulk (2013) explored whether the type of schooling (public, Catholic, Protestant, or homeschooling) has any impact on whether civic engagement persists among those graduates during adulthood. Given that schools often provide a site and social network for volunteerism, the question of whether homeschooling affords the same opportunity and encouragement seems a reasonable one. Hill and den Dulk found that homeschoolers were about half as likely to volunteer as public school students (and even less compared with Catholic or Protestant school students). This disparity held true even when controlling for a wide range of family background variables and even school-related characteristics such as the cultivation of social networks, volunteer opportunities, or motivational encouragement. The authors speculate that perhaps students unknowingly internalize certain "social scripts" about adult civic responsibility, or perhaps certain kinds of schools connect adolescents to volunteer organizations that retain their commitment into adulthood. This latter dynamic might be especially relevant for religiously related service.

The strong influence of religion in the lives of many homeschoolers creates additional complexities when considering questions of civic identity and engagement. Weithman (2002) presents an array of empirical data to argue that churches, mosques, and synagogues provide settings and resources in which citizens develop an identification with and capacity to enact their democratic citizenship. They see themselves as having the rights and duties of citizens as well as the skills and opportunities to exercise them. Churches, mosques, and synagogues provide political information, opportunities for discussion, an emphasis on individual empowerment, and a vision of the public good (Verba, Schlozman, and Brady 1995).

Data from the Cardus Education Surveys, the large randomized samples of the US and Canadian populations mentioned earlier, offer some insights into the political activity of religious homeschool graduates (Pennings et al. 2011, 2012). In general, they were less involved in politics and public affairs, although Canadian (non-Quebecois) graduates reported volunteering frequently in their religious congregations. The study authors note that their data appear to counter the perception that graduates of religious schools and homeschools are highly politicized.

Another common perception that recent research calls into question relates to the political tolerance of homeschoolers. Cheng (2014) compared the political tolerance of college students who had been homeschooled with those who had not. He first asked 304 students at a private Christian university to identify the social or political group whose beliefs were most strongly antithetical to their own. Defining political tolerance as "the willingness to extend basic civil liberties to political or social groups that hold views with which one disagrees" (49), Cheng then posed a series of questions to measure how politically tolerant students were of the group each had chosen. Results showed that study participants who had been homeschooled prior to college were more politically tolerant that those who had attended public schools, and the more years students had been homeschooled, the more politically tolerant they were – although the school effects were significantly less than demographic effects of race, gender, parent education, and family income. It is also worth pointing out that Cheng's survey questions set quite a low bar for political tolerance, asking whether the least-liked group should be allowed to exercise basic rights such as making a public speech, running for elected office, and holding public demonstrations. While such attitudes are obviously to be encouraged – and offer a counterpoint to misperceptions of homeschoolers as intolerant – they fall well short of the kinds of virtues necessary for a healthy democracy undergirded by mutual understanding.

Much of the research exploring the civic impacts of homeschooling focuses on what might be lacking among homeschoolers, but it seems important to keep in mind the ways that opportunities might look quite different in the homeschool context. As educational options proliferate, and shifts in policy and advances in technology blur the boundaries between formal schooling and alternative learning, the possibilities for new forms of civic engagement will undoubtedly emerge. Local homeschool cooperatives and support communities pose some of the same challenges – and opportunities for civic navigation – as more public institutions such as schools. Certainly many home educators who help organize and run learning cooperatives know that such "institutions" (however informal) require collaboration and compromises among participants if their organizations are going to sustain themselves over time. Newcomers are initiated into these "communities of practice" through the sharing of group history and norms and even, at times, peer monitoring that encourages quality practice (Kunzman 2009; Safran 2010). These communities must negotiate their internal shapes, striving to cultivate a collective sense of purpose while also providing flexibility in response to members' individual learning goals and needs. It may also be that the political advocacy sometimes engendered among home educators – through their efforts to communicate with local education authorities and advocate for the legitimacy of home education practice – can serve as a model of civic engagement for their children (Brabant and Bourdon 2012).

In this respect, perhaps these homeschool learning communities and support organizations can serve as incubators of democracy in ways similar to Dewey's (1938/1997) vision of the common school. Yet one could also imagine some such communities remaining decidedly insular, navigating only low-stakes logistical matters, rather than providing a vital training ground for citizens of a globally connected world marked by profoundly different visions of how we ought to live together. Much depends on the particulars of the context, of course. But this holds true not only for homeschoolers, but citizens prepared in public and private schools as well. The common school vision – no matter where it is enacted – remains largely an aspiration rather than achievement.

Opportunities for Further Study

As noted, much of the empirical work on homeschooler socialization has drawn from convenience samples and relies on self-reports of students and their parents. Research into homeschoolers' development of social skills would benefit from structured behavioral observations of random sample pools, in order to paint a fuller picture of homeschoolers more generally and offer more revealing comparisons with the broader school-age population. Such a methodology would also provide a more consistent view unmediated by self-report or potential biases of parents or other familiar adults.

Another methodological weakness deserving attention is the lack of information and analysis relative to the number of years that children are homeschooled in comparison to other schooling contexts they may have experienced. It appears that a significant number of students move back and forth between homeschooling and institutional schooling, so binary categories of schooling type almost certainly compromise data analysis. This variable will become even more complicated and pertinent with the proliferation of online schooling; it may even become difficult to define whether someone is homeschooling or "attending" an institution at any single given point in time.

An even more complex challenge is exploring the formation of homeschoolers' values and commitments, and how these manifest in graduates' roles as citizens. Most extant studies aimed on homeschoolers' values formation employ surveys that offer a broad view of homeschoolers' (or their parents') perceptions of their socialization experiences – but these instruments cannot capture the nuances of what that process means for their values and beliefs as adults. Gaining insight into how young people (homeschoolers or not) navigate the influences of parents, peers, and society in shaping their lives requires deeply textured, qualitative research. That sort of inquiry likely involves some sort of narrative approach, more akin to the studies conducted by Hoelzle (2013) and Knowles and Muchmore (1995) – although a larger pool of participants than those studies would also be helpful.

Some intriguing evidence does suggest that homeschooling, for all its structural flexibility and opportunities to customize content and experiences to emphasize certain values and beliefs, may not be the powerful influence that its advocates claim and its critics fear. Further qualitative inquiry that explores the stories of homeschoolers might help clarify the relative influence of parental values and the homeschooling context itself, both during homeschooling and in the years of adulthood that follow.

This latter need points to the broader lacuna for homeschooling research more generally – randomized, longitudinal studies where important variables (family income, parental education, years spent homeschooling) can be accounted for. To the extent that education is best understood as a long-term process, one that extends well beyond formal schooling, then the most fulsome insights into the challenges and opportunities of homeschooling will be uncovered by research that takes stock of what it means for participants long after they leave their educational home.

References

Abbott, Myles B., and Jennifer A. Miller. 2006. "What You Need to Learn about Homeschooling." *Contemporary Pediatrics*, 23(11): 48–58.

Abrom, Arthur W.C. 2009. *Pennsylvania's Superintendents: Current Thoughts on the State of Homeschooling*. Unpublished doctoral dissertation, Widener University, Chester, PA.

Andolina, Molly W., Krista Jenkins, Cliff Zukin, and Scott Keeter. 2003. "Habits from Home, Lessons from School: Influences on Youth Civic Development." *PS: Political Science and Politics*, 36(2): 275–280.

Apple, Michael W. 2000. "The Cultural Politics of Homeschooling." *Peabody Journal of Education*, 75(1–2): 256–271.

Arnett, Jeffrey J. 2013. *Adolescence and Emerging Adulthood: A Cultural Approach*, 5th ed. Boston: Pearson Education.

Bar-Yam Hassan, Aureet, and Miriam Bar-Yam. 1987. "Interpersonal Development across the Life Span: Communion and Its Interaction with Agency in Psychosocial Development." In *Contributions to Human Development, Vol. 18: Interpersonal Relations: Family, Peers, Friends*, edited by J.A. Meacham, 102–128. Berkeley, CA: Karger.

Batterbee, Dennis J. 1992. *The Relationship between Parent-Child Interactive Systems and Creativity in Home Schooled Children*. Unpublished doctoral dissertation, United States International University, Nairobi, Kenya.

Baumrind, Diana. 1987. "A Developmental Perspective on Adolescent Risk Taking in Contemporary America." In *Adolescent Social Behavior and Health, New Directions for Child Development*, 37, edited by Charles E. Irwin, 93–125. San Francisco: Jossey-Bass.

Blokhuis, Jason C. 2010. "Whose Custody Is It Anyway?: 'Homeschooling' from a *Parens Patriae* Perspective." *Theory and Research in Education*, 8: 199–222.

Brabant, Christine, Sylvain Bourdon, and France Jutras. 2003. "Home Education in Quebec: Family First." *Evaluation & Research in Education*, 17(2/3): 112–131.

Brabant, Christine, and Sylvain Bourdon. 2012. "Educational Change and Reflexive Governance: Experimentation of an Appropriation of Change Model by Quebec Home Educators Group." *Education et Francophonie*, 40(1): 32–55.

Brighouse, Harry. 2002. "What Rights (if Any) Do Children Have?" In *The Moral and Political Status of Children*, edited by David Archard and Colin M. Macleod, 31–52. Oxford: Oxford University Press.

Brighouse, Harry, and Adam Swift. 2006. "Parents' Rights and the Value of the Family." *Ethics*, 117: 80–108.

Buss, Emily. 2000. "The Adolescent's Stake in the Allocation of Educational Control between Parent and State." *University of Chicago Law Review*, 67: 1233–1289.

Butler, Mark H., James M. Harper, Matthew L. Call, and Mark H. Bird. 2015. "Examining Claims of Family Process Differences Ensuing from the Choice to Home-School." *Education and Urban Society*, 47(1): 86–108.

Cai, Yi., Johnmarshall Reeve, and Dawn T. Robinson,2002. "Home Schooling and Teaching Style: Comparing the Motivating Styles of Home School and Public School Teachers." *Journal of Educational Psychology*, 94: 372–380.

Callan, Eamonn. 1997. *Creating Citizens: Political Education and Liberal Democracy*. Oxford: Oxford University Press.

Carper, James C. 2000. "Pluralism to Establishment to Dissent: The Religious and Educational Context of Home Schooling." *Peabody Journal of Education*, 75(1–2): 8–19.

Chatham-Carpenter, April. 1994. "Home vs. Public Schoolers' Relationships: Differences in Social Networks." *Home School Researcher*, 10(1): 15–24.

Cheng, Albert. 2014. "Does Homeschooling or Private Schooling Promote Political Intolerance? Evidence from a Christian University." *Journal of School Choice*, 8(1): 49–68.

Chirkov, Valery, Richard M. Ryan, Youngmee Kim, and Ulas Kaplan. 2003. "Differentiating Autonomy from Individualism and Independence: A Self-Determination Theory Perspective on Internalization of Cultural Orientations and Well-Being." *Journal of Personality and Social Psychology*, 84(1): 97–110.

Coalition for Responsible Home Education. 2014. "A Complex Picture: Results of the 2014 Survey of Adult Alumni of the Modern Christian Homeschooling Movement." *Homeschool Alumni Reaching Out*, December 2.

Collins, W. Andrew, and Brett Laursen. 2006. "Parent–Adolescent Relationships. In *Close Relationships: Functions, Forms and Processes*, edited by Patricia Noller and Judith A. Feeney, 111–125. Hove, England: Psychology Press/Taylor & Francis.

Conroy, James C. 2010. "The State, Parenting, and the Populist Energies of Anxiety." *Educational Theory*, 60: 325–340.

Dahlquist, Kari L., Jennifer York-Barr, and Darwin D. Hendel. 2006. "The Choice to Homeschool: Home Educator Perspectives and School District Options." *Journal of School Leadership*, 16(4): 354–385.

Delahooke, Mona Maarse. 1986. *Home Educated Children's Social/Emotional Adjustment and Academic Achievement: A Comparative Study*. Unpublished doctoral dissertation, California School of Professional Psychology, Los Angeles.

Dewey, John. 1935/1997. *Experience and Education*. New York: Free Press.

Dinas, Elias. 2014. "Why Does the Apple Fall Far From the Tree? How Early Political Socialization Prompts Parent–Child Dissimilarity." *British Journal of Political Science*, April: 1–26.

East, Patricia L. 2009. "Adolescents' Relationships with Siblings." In *Handbook of Adolescent Psychology, Contextual Influences of Adolescent Development*, Vol. 2, edited by Richard M. Lerner and Laurence Steinberg, 43–73. Hoboken, NJ: John Wiley & Sons, Inc.

Fairchild, Ellen Elizabeth. 2002. *Home Schooling and Public Education in Iowa: The Views of Rural Superintendents*. Unpublished Doctoral dissertation, University of Iowa, Iowa City, IA.

Feinberg, Joel. 1980. "The Child's Right to an Open Future." In *Whose Child? Children's Rights, Parental Authority, and State Power*, edited by William Aiken and Hugh LaFollette, 124–153. Totowa, NJ: Rowman & Littlefield.

Fields-Smith, Cheryl, and Meca Williams. 2009. "Motivations, Sacrifices, and Challenges: Black Parents' Decisions to Home School." *Urban Review*, 41: 369–389.

Fields-Smith, Cheryl, and Monica Wells Kisura. 2013. "Resisting the Status Quo: The Narratives of Black Homeschoolers in Metro-Atlanta and Metro-DC." *Peabody Journal of Education*, 88(3): 265–283.

Flanagan, Constance A. 2013. *Teenage Citizens: The Political Theories of the Young*. Cambridge, MA: Harvard University Press.

Freeman, Harry, and Tasha Almond. 2009. "Predicting Adolescent Self Differentiation from Relationships with Parents and Romantic Partners." *International Journal of Adolescence and Youth*, 15: 121–143.

Galloway, Rhonda A., and Joe P. Sutton. 1995. "Home Schooled and Conventionally Schooled High School Graduates: A Comparison of Aptitude for and Achievement in College English." *Home School Researcher*, 11(1): 1–9.

Galston, William A. 2002. *Liberal Pluralism: The Implications of Pluralism for Political Theory and Practice*. Cambridge, MA: Cambridge University Press.

Glanzer, Perry L. 2008. "Rethinking the Boundaries and Burdens of Parental Authority over Education: A Response to Rob Reich's Case Study of Homeschooling." *Educational Theory*, 58(1): 1–16.

Green-Hennessy, Sharon. 2014. "Homeschooled Adolescents in the United States: Developmental Outcomes." *Journal of Adolescence*, 37: 441–449.

Hart, Daniel, Thomas M. Donnelly, James Youniss, and Robert Arkins. 2007. "High School Community Service as Predictor of Adult Voting and Volunteering." *American Educational Research Journal*, 44(1): 197–219.

Haugen, Denise Lopez. 2004. *The Social Competence of Homeschooled and Conventionally Schooled Adolescents*. Unpublished doctoral dissertation, George Fox University, Newberg, OR.

Helwig, Charles C. 2006. "The Development of Personal Autonomy throughout Cultures." *Cognitive Development*, 21: 458–473.

Hill, Jonathan P., and Kevin R. den Dulk. 2013. "Religion, Volunteering, and Educational Setting: The Effect of Youth Schooling Type on Civic Engagement." *Journal for the Scientific Study of Religion*, 52(1): 179–197.

Hoelzle, Braden Ryan. 2013. "The Transmission of Values and the Transition into Adulthood within the Context of Home Education." *Journal of Research on Christian Education*, 22(3): 244–263.

Johnson, Deborah. 2004. "Making the Grade: Home-school Movement Puts Onus on Pediatricians to Ensure Immunizations are Current, Developmental Issues Are Addressed." *AAP News*, 25(4): 178.

Joyce, Kathryn. 2009. *Quiverfull: Inside the Christian Patriarchy Movement*. Boston: Beacon Press.

Kingston, Skyler T., and Richard G. Medlin. 2006. "Empathy, Altruism, and Moral Development in Home Schooled Children." *Home School Researcher*, 16(4): 1–10.

Klugewicz, Susan. L., and Carol L. Carraccio. 1999. "Home Schooled Children: A Pediatric Perspective." *Clinical Pediatrics*, 38: 407.

Knowles, J. Gary, and James A. Muchmore. 1995. "Yep! We're Grown up, Home-Schooled Kids – and We're Doing Just Fine,Thank You!" *Journal of Research on Christian Education*, 4(1): 35–56.

Koepke, Sabrina, and Jaap J. A. Denissen. 2012. "Dynamics of Identity Development and Separation-Individuation in Parent–Child Relationships During Adolescence and Emerging Adulthood – A Conceptual Integration." *Developmental Review*, 32: 67–88.

Kunzman, Robert. 2005. "Homeschooling in Indiana: A Closer Look." *CEEP Policy Brief Series*. Bloomington, IN: Indiana University.

Kunzman, Robert. 2009. *Write These Laws on Your Children: Inside the World of Conservative Christian Homeschooling*. Boston: Beacon Press.

Kunzman, Robert. 2010. "Homeschooling and Religious Fundamentalism." *International Electronic Journal of Elementary Education*, 3(1): 17–28.

Kunzman, Robert. 2012. "Education, Schooling, and Children's Rights: The Complexity of Homeschooling." *Educational Theory*, 62(1): 75–89.

Kunzman, Robert. 2016. "Home Education: Practices, Purposes, and Possibilities." In *Palgrave Handbook of International Education*, edited by Helen Lees and Nel Noddings. New York: Palgrave Macmillan.

Kunzman, Robert, and Milton Gaither. 2013. "Homeschooling: A Comprehensive Survey of the Research." *Other Education*, 2(1): 4–59.

Lewis, Rowan D. 2013. "Individuation and Faith Development in Adolescence and Emerging Adulthood." *St Mark's Review*, 224: 42–61.

Liao, Monica Smatlak. 2006. *Keeping Home: Home Schooling and the Practice of Conservative Protestant Identity*. Unpublished doctoral dissertation, Vanderbilt University, Nashville, TN.

Lubienski, Chris. 2000. "Whither the Common Good? A Critique of Homeschooling." *Peabody Journal of Education*, 75(1–2): 207–232.

Lubienski, Chris. 2003. "A Critical View of Home Education." *Evaluation and Research in Education*, 17: 167–178.

Lundy, Garvey, and Ama Mazama. 2014. "'I'm Keeping My Son Home': African American Males and the Motivation to Homeschool." *Journal of African American Males in Education*, 5(1): 53–74.

Maccobby, Eleanor E., and J. Martin. 1983. "Socialization in the Context of the Family: Parent–Child Interaction." In *Handbook of Child Psychology, Socialization, Personality and Social Development* (Vol. 4), 1–101. New York: Wiley.

MacFarquhar, Neil. 2008. "Resolute or Fearful, Many Muslims Turn to Homeschooling." *New York Times*, 26 March, A14.

Manuel, Laura Lucille. 2000. *The Moral Development of Home Schooled and Public Schooled Adolescents*. Unpublished doctoral dissertation, University of Northern Colorado, Greeley, CO.

Mayberry, Maralee, and J. Gary Knowles. 1989. "Family Unit Objectives of Parents Who Teach Their Children: Ideological and Pedagogical Orientations to Home Schooling." *Urban Review*, 21(4): 209–225.

Mazama, Ama, and Garvey Lundy. 2012. "African American Homeschooling as Racial Protectionism." *Journal of Black Studies*, 43(7): 723–748.

Mazama, Ama, and Garvey Lundy. 2013. "African American Homeschooling and the Quest for a Quality Education." *Education and Urban Society*, 20(10): 1–22.

McDannell, Colleen. 1995. "Creating the Christian Home: Home Schooling in Contemporary America." *American Sacred Space*, edited by David Chidester and Edward Tabor Linenthal, 187–219. Bloomington, IN: Indiana University Press.

McEntire, T. Wayne. 2005. "Religious Outcomes in Conventionally Schooled and Home Schooled Youth." *Home School Researcher*, 16(2): 13–18.

McFarland, Daniel, and R. Jack Thomas. 2006. "Bowling Young: How Youth Voluntary Associations Influence Adult Political Participation." *American Sociological Review*, 71: 401–425.

McIntosh, Hugh, Daniel Hart, and James Youniss. 2007. "The Influence of Family Political Discussion on Youth Civic Development: Which Parent Qualities Matter?" *PS: Political Science and Politics*, 40(3): 495–499.

Medlin, Richard G. 2000. "Home Schooling and the Question of Socialization." *Peabody Journal of Education*, 75(1–2): 107–123.

Medlin, Richard G. 2013. "Homeschooling and the Question of Socialization Revisited." *Peabody Journal of Education*, 88(3): 284–297.

Meighan, Roland. 1984. "Home-Based Educators and Education Authorities: The Attempt to Maintain a Mythology." *Educational Studies*, 10: 273–286.

Merry, Michael S., and Charles Howell. 2009. "Can Intimacy Justify Home Education?" *Theory and Research in Education*, 7(3): 363–381.

Merry, Michael S., and Sjoerd Karsten. 2010. "Restricted Liberty, Parental Choice, and Homeschooling." *Journal of Philosophy of Education*, 44: 497–514.

Monk, Daniel. 2004. "Problematising Home Education: Challenging 'Parental Rights' and Socialisation.'" *Legal Studies*, 24: 568–598.

Morton, Ruth. 2010. "Home Education: Constructions of Choice." *International Electronic Journal of Elementary Education*, 3(1): 45–56.

Moss, P. A. (1995). *Benedictines without Monasteries*. Unpublished doctoral dissertation, Cornell University, Utica, NY.

Murphy, Joseph. 2014. "The Social and Educational Outcomes of Homeschooling." *Sociological Spectrum*, 34(3): 244–272.

Murray, Bridget. 1996. "Home Schools: How Do They Affect Children?" *APA Monitor*, 1: 43.

Nemer, Kariane Mari. 2004. *Schooling Alone: Homeschoolers, Individualism, and the Public Schools*. Unpublished doctoral dissertation, University of California, Los Angeles.

Noel, Amber, Patrick Stark, and Jeremy Redford. 2013. *Parent and Family Involvement in Education, From the National Household Education Surveys Program of 2012* (NCES 2013-028). Washington, DC: National Center for Education Statistics, Institute of Education Sciences, US Department of Education.

Pennings, Ray, and John Seel, Deani A. Neven Van Pelt, David Sikkink, and Kathryn L. Wiens. 2011. *Cardus Education Survey: Do the Motivations for Private Religious Catholic and Protestant Schooling in North America Align with Graduate Outcomes?* Cardus: Hamilton, Ontario.

Pennings, Ray, and David Sikkink, Deani Van Pelt, Harro Van Brummelen, and Amy Von Heyking. 2012. *Cardus Education Survey: A Rising Tide Lifts All Boats: Measuring Non-Government School Effects in Service of the Canadian Public Good*. Cardus: Hamilton, Ontario.

Putnam, Robert D. 2000. *Bowling Alone: The Collapse and Revival of American Community*. New York: Simon & Schuster.

Ray, Brian D. 1997. *Home Education across the United States: Family Characteristics, Student Achievement, and Other Topics*. Purcellville, VA: HSLDA Publications.

Ray, Brian D. 2004. *Home Educated and Now Adults: Their Community and Civic Involvement, Views about Homeschooling, and Other Traits*. Salem, OR: NHERI Publications.

Ray, Brian D. 2013. "Homeschooling Associated with Beneficial Learner and Societal Outcomes but Educators Do Not Promote It." *Peabody Journal of Education*, 88(3): 324–341.

Reavis, Rachael, and Audrey Zakriski. 2005. "Are Home-Schooled Children Socially At-Risk or Socially Protected?" *The Brown University Child and Adolescent Behavior Letter*, 21(9).

Reich, Rob. 2002. "Testing the Boundaries of Parental Authority over Education: The Case of Homeschooling." In *Moral and Political Education*, edited by Stephen Macedo and Yael Tamir, 275–313. New York: NYU Press.

Reich, Rob. 2008. "On Regulating Homeschooling: A Reply to Glanzer." *Educational Theory*, 58(1): 17–23.

Ross, Catherine J. 2010. "Fundamentalist Challenges to Core Democratic Values: Exit and Homeschooling." *William and Mary Bill of Rights Journal*, 18: 991–1014.

Ryan, Richard M., and Edward L. Deci. 2001. "On Happiness and Human Potentials: A Review of Research on Hedonic and Eudaimonic Well-Being." In *Annual Review of Psychology* (Vol. 52), edited by S. Fiske, 141–166. Palo Alto, CA: Annual Reviews, Inc.

Ryan, Richard M., and Edward L. Deci. 2006. "Self-Regulation and the Problem of Human Autonomy: Does Psychology Need Choice, Self-Determination, and Will?" *Journal of Personality*, 74(6): 1557–1585.

Safran, Leslie. 2010. "Legitimate Peripheral Participation and Home Education." *Teaching and Teacher Education*, 26(1): 107–112.

Schachter, Elli P. and Jonathan J. Ventura. 2008. "Identity Agents: Parents as Active and Reflective Participants in Their Children's Identity Formation." *Journal of Research on Adolescence*, 18(3): 449–476.

Seo, Deok-Hee. 2009. "The Profitable Adventure of Threatened Middle-Class Families: An Ethnographic Study on Homeschooling in South Korea." *Asia Pacific Education Review*, 10: 409–422.

Shirkey, Brenda Tetrick. 1987. *Students' Perspective of Home Schools: A Descriptive Study*. Unpublished doctoral dissertation, University of Florida, Gainesville, FL.

Shyers, Larry E. 1992. *Comparison of Social Adjustment between Home and Traditionally Schooled Students*. Unpublished doctoral dissertation, University of Florida, Gainesville, FL.

Skinner, B. F. 1971. *Beyond Freedom and Dignity*. New York: Knopf.

Smith, Christian, and David Sikkink. 1999. "Is Private School Privatizing?" *First Things*, 92: 16–20.

Snook, I. A. 1972. *Indoctrination and Education*. New York: Routledge and K. Paul.

Spinner-Halev, Jeff. 2000. *Surviving Diversity: Religion and Democratic Citizenship*. Baltimore, MD: Johns Hopkins University Press.

Steinberg, Laurence. 2000, April. *We Know Some Things: Parent–Adolescent Relations in Retrospect and Prospect*. Presidential Address at the biennial meeting of the Society for Research on Adolescence, Chicago, IL.

Sun, Laura Li-Hua. 2007. *Dare to Home School: Faith and Cultural Experiences of Chinese Christian Mothers*. Unpublished doctoral dissertation, Biola University, Los Angeles.

Sutton, Joe P., and Rhonda S. Galloway. 2000. "College Success of Students from Three High School Settings." *Journal of Research and Development in Education*, 33: 137–146.

Talbot, Margaret. 2000. "A Mighty Fortress." *New York Times Magazine*, 27 February, 34–41.

Uecker, Jeremy. E. 2008. Alternative Schooling Strategies and the Religious Lives of American Adolescents. *Journal for the Scientific Study of Religion*, 47: 563–584.

Vaughn, Pamela A. 2003. *Case Studies of Homeschool Cooperatives in Southern New Jersey*. Unpublished doctoral dissertation, Widener University, Chester, PA.

Verba, Sydney, Kay Lehman Schlozman, and Henry Brady. 1995. *Voice and Equality: Civic Volunteerism in American Politics*. Cambridge, MA: Harvard University Press.

Wallace, Sue. 2000. "Home-Schooled Population Requires Additional Vigilance." *AAP News*, 17(2): 62.

Weithman, Paul. 2002. *Religion and the Obligations of Citizenship*. New York: Cambridge University Press.

West, Robin L. 2009. "The Harms of Homeschooling." *Philosophy and Public Policy Quarterly*, 29: 7–11.

Wyatt, Gary. 2008. *Family Ties: Relationships, Socialization, and Home Schooling*. Lanham, MD: University Press of America.

Yuracko, Kimberly A. 2008. "Education off the Grid: Constitutional Constraints on Home Schooling." *California Law Review*, 96: 123–184.

7

Homeschoolers and Higher Education

Marc Snyder

Introduction

A survey of the research landscape on homeschooling and higher education is generally found wanting. The International Center for Home Education Research (ICHER) reveals only 126 articles under the topic college/postsecondary; moreover, not all articles are empirically based studies. According to Kunzman and Gaither (2013), for the research that is available, most studies are quantitative in nature that use convenience samples, a handful of studies are qualitative that lack generalizability (for obvious reasons), and still other studies – notably those by Brian Ray – seem biased towards advancing the political agenda in favor of homeschooling (Ray studies). Scattered among this literature are a handful of well-done studies. Despite what one thinks about the quality of research, one thing is certain: more research needs to be done to determine decisively the impact of homeschooling on higher education. The following chapter seeks to accomplish three things: (1) it reviews and synthesizes all available literature on homeschooling and higher education; (2) it offers an in-depth conclusion and critical analysis; and (3) it suggests opportunities for further study in the field.

Collecting reliable data on the number of homeschooled students is often a difficult task. This is due to the fact that many states do not require reporting of homeschooled students (Coalition for Responsible Homeschooling 2013). The most reliable data present on the number of homeschooled students is offered by the National Center for Education Statistics (NCES). Based on its most recent survey in 2011, the number of homeschooled students was reported to be 1.77 million (Noel, Stark, and Redford 2013). Given the trend that the number of homeschooled students has been steadily increasing over the years (850 000 in 1999; 1.096 million

The Wiley Handbook of Home Education, First Edition. Edited by Milton Gaither.

in 2003; 1.508 million in 2007), it seems safe to say that the number is now over 2 million (Ray 2011). Such high numbers of homeschooled students in K–12 education can only mean that a large number of homeschooled students have entered college and graduated, in addition to the many more that will be entering college in the near future (Klicka 2007a). The growing number of homeschoolers attending institutions of higher learning has led many researchers to ask how successful the social phenomenon of homeschooling is at preparing students for college and adulthood when compared to traditional schooling.

Literature Review on Homeschooling and Higher Education

A thorough review of the literature on homeschooling and higher education reveals four major themes. These themes, in one way or another, address the question of "success" as it relates to homeschooling. The following literature review will be centered on these four themes, which include: (1) academic preparedness for and achievement in college; (2) socialization and transitional experiences into college; (3) college friendliness and admission officers' attitudes towards and perceptions of homeschoolers; and (4) homeschoolers as adults and participation in civic life.

Academic preparedness and achievement

Much of the scholarly literature has been concerned with the academic preparedness of homeschooled children for college. The answer to the "college preparedness" question can be determined by looking at ACT and SAT scores, both of which are reliable predictors of college success (Kim et al. 2010). Kim et al. (2010) noted a strong, positive correlation between ACT/SAT and academic achievement (as measured by first-year, college grade point average (GPA)), which has been validated by other studies (Cornwell, Mustard, and Parys 2008; DeBerard, Spielmans, and Julka 2004; Kobrin et al. 2008). However, ACT and SAT scores alone are not sufficient for determining "academic achievement" once students begin to progress through college. Therefore, colleges use GPA as the standard continual measure of academic achievement (as measured by various types of formative and summative assessments) (Horn 2006). Yet, GPA alone can sometimes be misleading due to the fact that students often take courses that are more or less rigorous than others (Hsu and Schombert 2010). Nevertheless, when taken together, ACT/SAT and GPA (and class rank) can serve as powerful predictors in determining college preparedness and academic achievement.

Studies 2004–2014 A number of studies have been done that compare the ACT and/or SAT scores, as well as GPA, of homeschooled students to their traditionally schooled counterparts. Jones and Gloeckner (2004a) compared the ACT Composite and subtest (English, Mathematics, Reading, and Science Reasoning) scores of fify-five homeschooled students attending Colorado colleges and universities to fifty-three traditionally schooled students (public, private, and parochial) at similar institutions. Results indicated that homeschooled students outperformed their traditionally schooled peers on the ACT Composite and all subtests, approaching statistical significance in the Composite, Mathematics and Science subtests. Despite the small sample size, Jones and Gloeckner make it a point to state that the test results match the national average of homeschooled students. In addition, Jones and Gloeckner compared first-year college GPA of homeschooled students to traditionally schooled students and found that homeschooled students came out on top (2.78 compared to 2.59). Correlation tests were run and a positive correlation was found between ACT Composite scores, retention, cumulative GPA, and cumulative credits earned with ACT Composite scores generally predicting the other three.

Instead of looking at ACT scores as a determinant of academic preparedness for college, Clemente (2006) compared the SAT scores of 2959 high school seniors who had matriculated to seven Christian colleges and universities. The population included three intact groups unequal in size: 1792 public-schooled students, 945 private-schooled students, and 222 homeschooled students. Results indicated that homeschooled students outperformed their traditionally schooled counterparts with a mean SAT score of 1123 compared to 1054 (private-schooled) and 1039 (public-schooled). Non-parametric tests revealed a statistically significant difference in favor of homeschooled students when compared separately to private-schooled and public-school students. However, Clemente made it clear that the study cannot prove scientifically that homeschooling causes students to be better prepared for academic success in college. No study has been able to able to accomplish this task (Ray 2000). Yet, this causal-comparative study, and others like it, can help one draw conclusions that homeschooling parents are able to adequately prepare their children – at least academically – for college success.

Advocates of increased homeschooling regulations fear that the lack of regulations could potentially harm students (Reich 2008; Waddell 2010; Yuracko 2008). The argument goes something like this: if there is more state regulation of homeschooling, then parents are ultimately kept "in check" by the state and the academic outcomes are generally more positive. Less state regulation means more unpredictable academic outcomes. Ray and Eagleson (2008) attempted to test this hypothesis by looking at the relationship between state regulation of homeschooling and academic preparedness for college as measured by the SAT. In their study, Ray and Eagleson collected state average SAT scores from 6170 homeschooled students in states that are considered to have low, moderate, and high regulation laws for homeschooling. After comparing scores, the results indicated that no significant difference existed between homeschooled students' SAT scores in states that have low, moderate, or high regulation. In fact, students in states with the lowest regulation did better than students in more highly regulated states (and vice versa). An important limitation, however, included not knowing how long students were homeschooled in specific states. And while it is difficult to draw definitive conclusions about the relationship between homeschooled students' SAT scores and state regulation, it seems safe to say that, at least, more regulation does not make them do any better.

Additional comprehensive studies have looked at not only the academic preparedness of homeschooled students for college (ACT/SAT scores), but also their academic achievement (and persistence) once enrolled. Cogan (2010), for example, explored first-year GPA, four-year GPA, fall-to-fall retention, and four-year graduation rates of a small group of homeschooled students (76; only 1.0% of the population) compared to traditionally schooled students (public, Catholic, private non-Catholic) attending a single, upper Midwest (presumably Catholic) college. Bivariate and multivariate tests were used to determine outcomes. Bivariate test (ANOVA and Chi-Square) results indicated that homeschooled students had a higher first-year GPA compared to the other students (3.41 vs. 3.12) and a statistically significant higher four-year GPA (3.46 vs. 3.16). Multivariate analyses revealed that the homeschool variable had a positive impact on GPAs (when taking into account other factors measured), but did not have a positive impact on fall-to-fall retention and four-year graduation rates. Nevertheless, homeschooled students did achieve higher retention (88.6%) and graduation (66.7%) rates when compared to their traditionally schooled counterparts (87.6% and 57.5%, respectively). Despite the positive results in favor of homeschooled students, Cogan admits the limitation of a small sample size.

Most studies on homeschooling and their academic preparedness and achievement in college have been done at selective colleges and universities. Bagwell (2010) conducted a mixed methods study to determine the academic success of homeschooled students attending South Carolina Technical College with an open-door admissions policy. For this study, Bagwell compared 273 homeschooled students and a random sample of 273 traditionally schooled students enrolled in the college between 2001 and 2008. In the quantitative portion of the study, independent samples t-tests were used to determine statistical significance in the COMPASS placement test (writing, algebra, and reading scores) and collegiate, first-semester GPA, math GPA, science GPA, English composition GPA, and overall GPA. Results indicated that homeschooled students outperformed traditionally schooled students in all measured areas except COMPASS college algebra, with a statistically significant difference in all areas except COMPASS algebra and college algebra. In the follow-up qualitative portion of the study, all eight participants (four homeschooled and four traditionally schooled) agreed to being well-prepared for college, generally speaking, with a feeling of inadequate math preparation.

To corroborate Cogan's findings (above), Snyder (2011, 2013) conducted a similar quantitative study at Ave Maria University, a private, Catholic university located in Ave Maria, Florida. Instead of using a small sample size (like Cogan), Snyder looked at the entire population of students (408) attending the university. Of these, 129 students were homeschooled, 137 were public-schooled, and 142 were Catholic-schooled. ACT/SAT scores, overall GPA, core GPA, and major GPA were compared using independent samples t-tests to see if any statistically significant differences existed between these students. Results indicated that homeschooled students outperformed their conventionally schooled peers on all measures of academic aptitude and achievement, with Catholic-schooled students scoring at the mean, public-schooled students scoring below the mean, and homeschooled students scoring above the mean. Statistically significant differences were found in ACT/SAT scores and overall GPA only. Since 95% of the students attending the university were Catholic, Snyder was able to draw an interesting comparison of Catholic homeschoolers in particular. At the very least, results indicate that homeschooling does not, in and of itself, impede success for the kind of dedicated homeschooling families who send their children to colleges like Ave Maria.

Earlier studies (1994–2003) Earlier studies on the academic preparedness and achievement of homeschooled students in college seem to yield similar results when compared to studies done in the last decade. Galloway (1995), for example, examined the English college aptitude and achievement of all homeschooled students ($N = 60$) compared to a random sampling of conventional public- ($N = 60$) and private-schooled students ($N = 60$) attending a large, liberal arts, Christian university in the Southeast. Success in English was used to infer students' general college aptitude and achievement. Aptitude measures included students' ACT English subtest and ACT Composite scores; achievement was measured by English writing and usage skills as further measured by tests, quizzes, and a library research paper for a required, college-level English course. Statistical testing revealed comparable ACT Composite scores, with a statistically significant difference between homeschooled and private-schooled students in the ACT English subtest. No statistically significant difference was found between students in English writing and usage, yet they all displayed similar abilities. Based on the results, Galloway concluded similar academic preparedness amongst all three schooling types.

In a similar study to Galloway, Gray (1998) conducted a quantitative study looking at the SAT scores, English grades, and overall GPA of homeschooled students ($N = 56$) compared to traditionally schooled students ($N = 44$) attending public and private colleges and universities in Georgia. In addition, Gray explored the perceptions of homeschooled students and parents ($N = 38$) in regards to their homeschooling program and socialization (to be examined later). Once again, the study was designed to determine how well homeschooled students are prepared for college and how well they succeed academically once enrolled. Independent samples t-tests were used to determine statistical significance on SAT scores, English grades, and overall GPA. Results indicated that no significant difference existed in any of the three, above-mentioned measures (although homeschooled students outperformed their traditionally schooled peers in all three). In regards to homeschool students and parents' perceptions about their homeschooling program, 100% of the students believed that homeschooling had prepared them for college and 100% of the parents believed that homeschooling had built their child's confidence level. Once again, results seem to look favorably on homeschooling.

What about homeschool students who are not 18, yet seek admission to a community college to supplement their homeschool experience? How well are they prepared to succeed academically when compared to other students? Such was the focus of a quantitative study conducted by Jenkins (1998). In this study, Jenkins focused on the academic performance of students in community colleges in Texas. The study analyzed 101 transcripts to determine if any statically significant differences existed between first-time, part-time homeschooled students and first-time, full-time homeschooled students compared to their conventionally schooled counterparts as measured by GPA; additional analyses were done on the impact of student age (under 16, 16–17, and 18 and over) as measured by GPA. Texas Academic Skills Program (TASP) tests (reading, math, and writing scores) were also compared between all groups. Statistically significant differences were found in favor of homeschooled students in all measures except for TASP writing scores. Most impressive was how much better young (under 18), part-time homeschooled students did GPA-wise when compared to their non-homeschooled peers.

Up to this point, all of the studies surveyed looked at the academic preparedness and achievement of homeschooled students in college as measured by ACT/SAT scores, GPA, and grades in particular subjects. In a study conducted by Sutton and Galloway (2000), a much broader view of college success was examined. The final sample for this study included twenty-one homeschooled, twenty-six private-schooled, and seventeen public-schooled students who attended a 67-year-old liberal arts university in the Southeast and had graduated with a baccalaureate degree. Forty indicators of college success were examined which centered on the following five domains: (a) achievement; (b) leadership; (c) professional aptitude; (d) social behavior; and (e) physical ability. Multivariate analysis of variance (MANOVA) tests, followed up by univariate and Bonferroni statistics, were used to determine statistical significance. Results indicated that thirty-three of the forty indicators of college success revealed no statistical significance. Interestingly enough, statistical significance was found in the leadership domain with homeschooled students holding more types of offices (religious, appointed, high, and total) and for a longer period of time than their private-schooled counterparts.

Sutton and Galloway (2000) concluded that no statistical significance means that homeschooled students are performing on par with traditionally schooled students. However, they make two important observations that must be pointed out. These observations continue to hold true for most studies done on the academic achievement of students in college even to this day. First, the samples of such studies are generally small, convenience samples rather than randomized (samples). Moreover, the studies are typically done on homeschooled students attending religiously affiliated institutions (e.g., Bob Jones University, Wheaton College, and Ave Maria University) where many homeschooled students typically congregate. As a result, it becomes difficult to be sure if the success of homeschooled students attending these schools is the result of thc high school setting per se or because such students hold similar educational philosophies as to their respective universities. Second, most studies use class rank, GPA, and/or ACT/SAT scores as predictors of college success. More longitudinal studies would be helpful to see the long-term effects of the quality and intensity of high school curriculum on college success. These conclusions will be further developed later on. For now, it is only important to note, at this point, such limitations of homeschooling studies.

One final study will be mentioned before moving on to socialization and the transitional experiences of homeschooled students. This study, conducted by Holder (2001), sought to solve the "small sample size problem" by conducting a qualitative study on the academic achievement (and socialization) of homeschooled students in college. Seventeen homeschooled students and seventeen traditionally schooled students from a private, Christian, four-year institution in the Southeast were interviewed with the express intention of learning more about their homeschooling experiences. When asked how they felt about homeschooling, in general, all but one reported positive feelings. In regards to the kind of high school curriculum exposed to, the students' responses consisted of a variety of curricula and methodologies used by their parents. The aspect of the homeschool curriculum that best prepared them for college was their ability to learn and study independently. They felt least prepared in writing research papers, taking notes, coping with deadlines, and performance in math and science. Mixed feelings existed amongst the homeschooled students when asked to compare their level of academic preparation for college to their traditionally schooled peers.

Socialization and transitional experiences

Based on the above-mentioned studies done in the last twenty years (Bagwell 2010; Clemente 2006; Cogan 2010; Galloway 1995; Gray 1998; Holder 2001; Jenkins 1998; Jones and Gloeckner 2004a; Ray and Eagleson 2008; Snyder 2013; Sutton and Galloway 2000), despite their limitations, it seems safe to say that there is nothing to fear about a parent's ability to academically prepare their child(ren) for success in college. And while the academic achievement of homeschooled students in college is not really in question, their socialization, for many, still is (Luebke 1999; Saunders 2006; 2009). Nevertheless, the majority of studies conducted on homeschooling and socialization find them comparable to their traditionally schooled peers (Klicka 2007b; Smith 2009). As stated in Romanowski (2006), research findings indicate that homeschooled students are exposed to a wide variety of socialization opportunities compared to those in a traditional classroom setting and have a similar self-concept. Moreover, every indication is given in favor of the kind of socialization experienced by homeschooled students; which, in fact, may be even more favorable than the kind of socialization experienced by students attending traditional schools (Medlin, 2013).

Before continuing with a review of the literature on homeschooling and socialization, it is important to define the term "socialization." According to Medlin (2000) this is no easy task since many people define socialization differently. For some people, socialization means "social activity" – which means, providing children with the chance of interacting with their friends and being involved in extra-curricular activities, such as sports and drama. For others, it means "social influence" – that is, teaching students to behave in a way acceptable by most people in society. And still for others, it means "social exposure" – exposing children to the values and cultures of different groups of people. While all of these may be part of socialization, socialization can be defined simply as "the process whereby people acquire the rules of behavior and systems of beliefs and attitudes that equip a person to function effectively as a member of a particular society" (Durkin 1995, 614). This definition leads to the following question: how do homeschooled students fare in regards to socialization when compared to traditionally schooled students, especially as it applies to college life?

Too few studies have been done on homeschooled students in regards to their social adjustments in college (Medlin, 2013). Some of the studies mentioned above on academic achievement also address socialization. These studies indicate that homeschooled students are involved in a number of extracurricular activities, are socially integrated into their college campus, are less influenced by peer pressure, and have a high self-concept (Holder 2001; Sutton and Galloway 2000). In a qualitative study conducted by Lattibeaudiere (2000), twenty-five homeschooled students in public and private colleges were interviewed in regards to their social adaptation to college. Faculty and staff were also asked their opinions about students' social transitions. Results indicated that homeschooled students had an overall positive experience in adjusting to college life. In fact, there seemed to be a positive correlation between the number of years homeschooled and their ease in transitioning. Students who lived on campus were better adjusted than those who did not. And from the perspective of faculty, even though homeschooled students seemed a bit shy at first and took more time in socializing, they interacted well with people of all ages.

Kranzow (2004) also conducted a qualitative study on the social adaptations of homeschooled students in college. It is important to note, parenthetically, that qualitative studies are not meant to provide statistical generalizability but to probe more deeply into a particular phenomenon. For Kranzow's study, eighteen homeschooled students and six administrators from two, private, Christian institutions in the Midwest were interviewed about their social transitions into college. Interestingly, three of the six administrators, identified as student development professionals, said that homeschooled students were less socially prepared. This same feeling, however, was not felt by admissions personnel, who generally had a more positive view. Out of the eighteen homeschooled students interviewed, all but one felt they were socially prepared for college. Students said they had challenges balancing social activities with the amount of time needed for academics. A common theme to emerge was that students respected and felt very comfortable approaching their professors for help, which was attributed to the level of comfort they had with mom (or dad) who functioned as their teacher(s) in homeschool.

In a similar study to Jenkins, Lavoie (2006) sought to describe young homeschoolers' (under 17) developmental experiences in a community college environment. Providing part of the conceptual framework for this study was Chickering's Theory of Student Development (Chickering and Reisser 1993). Chickering's theory states that students must move through seven "vectors" of development. Only the first three were pertinent to this study since it applies to freshmen and sophomore students. These include: (1) developing academic, physical, and interpersonal competence; (2) managing emotions; and (3) moving through autonomy towards interdependence. Six early-entrant homeschoolers (aged 16 and under) attending a community college in Connecticut were interviewed about these vectors, as were their parents and faculty. In regards to student perceptions, all six said they had academic competence, none reported gaining physical competence, half reported making friends, two mentioned they had grown in handling their emotions, and most (five) said they were moving towards greater autonomy and interdependence. Parents had similar perceptions to students. However, only one parent felt their child made significant growth socially. None of the faculty perceived social growth and were, in general, more reticent to admit student development in the first three vectors.

The above-mentioned studies reveal somewhat mixed feelings about the socialization question of homeschooled students in college. Depending on who is answering the question, responses range from "no problem" with social adjustments to having difficulties (at least at first). Following up on the socialization question, Saunders (2006; 2009) looked at the social integration and first-year persistence rates of various schooling types (including homeschooled students) attending Wheaton College in Chicago. Tinto's (1975) interactionalist theory served as a model for this study; the instrument for this study was a 36 question, closed-ended survey. Findings showed that schooling type did not have a significant effect on social integration. However, further analysis showed that homeschooled students had higher rates of both communal potential and institutional integrity, which are antecedents to, and therefore affect, social integration. Moreover, a correlation was found between homeschooled students and institutional commitment, which was shown to have an impact on student persistence. Saunders concluded that similar colleges (to Wheaton) need not worry about schooling type (e.g., homeschooled students) in regards to their social integration and persistence in college.

Using a similar interview-based instrument as Lattibeaudiere (2000), and using Tinto's theory of transition (1988; 1993) as a conceptual framework, Bolle, Wessel, and Mulvihill (2007), sought to explain the transitional experiences of first-year college students who were homeschooled. For this qualitative study, six homeschooled students were interviewed from a mid-sized, public, doctoral granting university in the Midwest. The following three questions served as the basis for the interview: (a) what transitional issues were encountered in adjusting to college; (b) how were these issues related to Tinto's transitional theory model; and (c) what interventions by the university helped (or hindered) in the transition? In response to these questions, several themes emerged. Students spoke about loneliness after leaving home, positive effects of independence, challenges in meeting students with different values and worldviews, developing their own identity, involvement in co-curricular activities, and growing in self-confidence. Most students were able to make friends with relative ease; however, one student mentioned having difficulty in making friends, which he attributed to homeschooling. Institutional interventions cited as being helpful included orientations, having resident assistants, and student organizations. Transitional issues experienced by homeschooled students were closely related to Tinto's (1993) theory.

While the above-mentioned study by Bolle, Wessel, and Mulvihill examined the transitional experiences of homeschooled students in their first year of college, Wood (2011) conducted a qualitative study looking at the lived experiences of homeschooled students beyond their first year. For this study, six homeschooled students attending a large, public university in the Southeast were interviewed; Bronfenbrenner's (1993) ecological model helped form the theoretical framework. After performing in-depth interviews, several themes emerged that linked together the students' transitional experiences. The first theme to emerge centered on the importance of parents in preparing the students for college, especially in the academic realm. Moreover, students had a wide range of expectations before entering, mostly centered on the amount of work they would be required to do. They were a bit surprised that the campus was less diverse than expected and were surprised by the amount of gossiping and cheating taking place. Being in a classroom environment did not seem to pose any real challenges to the students, although some academic adjustments were necessary. All of the students made it a point to connect socially with their peers outside the classroom, yet many felt the need for independence.

One of the participants from Wood's study summed up the socialization and transitional experiences of homeschooled students well when he expressed that college "levels the playing field" for everyone, despite their schooling background. Bolle and Wessel (2012), in a follow-up study of the same students five years later, after looking at the college experiences, including social and academic integration, and environmental pull factors, such as family commitments, finances, and work, concluded that homeschooled students experienced college in a similar way to non-homeschooled students. They were found to be, in every respect, "normal college students." Confirming these sentiments was the research done by Drenovsky and Cohen (2012). They surveyed 185 college students who had been homeschooled and traditionally schooled to determine their campus engagement and social adjustments as measured by self-esteem and depression surveys. Results indicated no statistically significant difference between schooling type and self-esteem. Homeschooled students had significantly lower levels of depression than those who had never been homeschooled, reported higher levels of academic achievement, and claimed an excellent college experience overall.

College friendliness and admission officers' attitudes and perceptions

As homeschooling has gone from essentially a fringe movement to a mainstream educational phenomenon that has gained widespread acceptance (Gaither 2009), it is not uncommon for colleges to boast of their open and friendly attitude towards homeschooler admissions. Media headlines often read: "Public universities, private colleges, and Ivy League schools – homeschoolers are everywhere" (Remmerde 1997, 12). Homeschooled students now attend over 900 colleges and universities, including some of the nation's most prestigious (Davis 2005; Klicka 2007a). And yet, despite the seeming openness of colleges towards homeschoolers, this same attitude is not always felt by homeschoolers. Not only do few homeschoolers find this friendly and open attitude assimilated into the college application process, many homeschoolers are met with quite the opposite. Some report resistance in the financial aid and application processes; others find little help from colleges in general (Walker 2010). This leads to another important question with which the literature has been concerned: how friendly are colleges towards homeschoolers?

At the turn of the twenty-first century, the National Center for Home Education Research (NCHER) (2000), a division of the Home School Legal Defense Association (HSLDA), conducted a survey of 913 colleges and universities, with a response rate of 56% (511 colleges), for the purposes of determining what colleges require of homeschooled applicants, comparing these requirements with recommendations made by the HSLDA, and creating a rating-system of various institutions' homeschooling friendliness. The NCHER's rating-system consisted of the following tiers: Tier 1 means that colleges have admissions policies similar to those recommended by the HSLDA (parent's transcript, generalized standardized achievement test, and student portfolio in place of an accredited diploma); Tier 2 means that in place of, or in addition to, Tier 1 requirements, the General Educational Development (GED) is also required; Tier 3 means that standardized achievement tests (SAT II) are required for homeschooled students, but not traditionally schooled students, and that higher SAT scores are required of homeschooled students. Tier 1 was thus classified as the most homeschooling friendly and Tier 3 as the least. Results of the survey revealed that 349 colleges (or 68%) fell in the Tier 1 category, 144 colleges (28.1%) fell in Tier 2, and only 18 colleges (3.5%) fell in Tier 3. The high percentage of colleges classified as Tier 1 indicate that many schools are aligned with NCHER guidelines and can thus be considered homeschool friendly.

In a more recent descriptive study conducted by Duggan (2010), homeschooler friendliness was determined by looking at the websites of 105 community colleges in an eleven-state accreditation region. Homeschooler friendliness was defined by creating a twenty-item checklist, including some of the following criteria: (a) flexible transcripts; (b) clear admissions policies; (c) alternative admissions criteria, such as essays, letters, and interviews; (d) a clearly defined homeschooled student section, including the number of clicks needed to access it, and; (e) the ability to chat with an admissions officer live. Results indicated that 65% of websites did not have a section for homeschooled students. For the ones that did, an average of three clicks was necessary to access the information. In regards to admissions policies, some college websites required homeschooled students to follow the same procedures for a placement exam as those without a high school transcript, other websites required homeschooled students to fill out a special packet, 50% of the websites said that students must have their GED, and 30% of the websites did not offer assistance to homeschooled students in regards to official high school transcripts. Based on this information, while showing some "friendliness," college websites are not clearly as homeschooling friendly as they could be.

Jones and Gloeckner (2004b) conducted a study with the purpose of gaining a deeper understanding of college admission officer's perceptions and attitudes towards homeschooled students. Moreover, Jones and Gloeckner examined college admission policies. Fifty-five admission officers were surveyed from four-year institutions belonging to four regional college associations. In regards to admission policies, 74.5% said they had an official admission policy for homeschoolers. Some of the required documents for admission, listed in order of importance, included: ACT or SAT score, essay, GED, letters of recommendation, SAT II subject tests, personal interview, and portfolio. When asked about homeschooled students' overall success compared to traditionally schooled students, 78% expected them to be as successful or more successful. Approximately 76% of admission officers said they expect homeschooled students to have a first-year GPA as high as or higher than traditionally schooled students. When asked about first-year retention rate, 65.5% of admission officers expected homeschooled students to be about the same or higher compared to traditionally schooled students. Finally, only 43.6% admission officers thought homeschooled students would cope socially as well as traditionally schooled students.

Following up on Jones and Gloeckner, Sorey and Duggan (2008) surveyed twelve admission officers from twelve different community colleges in a mid-Atlantic state. The first part of the survey was open-ended and asked admission officers to describe their admission policies; the second part of the survey asked for admission officers' attitudes and perceptions using a Likert scale. Regarding admission policies for homeschooled students, 50% said they had an official policy. In place of high school transcripts, various documents for admission were reported as being acceptable, including ACT/SAT scores, GED, and letters of recommendation. When asked about their perceptions of 18-year-old or older homeschooled students in college, 100% strongly agreed and agreed they would be successful. Sixty-four percent strongly agreed and agreed that homeschooled students were academically prepared and 55% strongly agreed and agreed that they were socially prepared for college. One admission officer reported, "Homeschooled students are as prepared or even better prepared for college academics as their high school graduate counterparts. Occasionally, socialization might be a concern but not very often" (Sorey and Duggan 2008, 26). Responses were not as favorable when asked about the academic and social preparedness of homeschooled students for college under the age of 18.

Homeschoolers as adults and participation in civic life

While the academic preparedness and achievement of homeschooled students in college, and perhaps to a lesser extent their socialization skills, seem to get a pass from the opponents to homeschooling (although not entirely, see Lubienski,, Puckett, and Brewer 2013), the effects of homeschooling, in particular, deregulated homeschooling, on adult life, especially as it relates to civic engagement, is more debated (Apple 2005; Lubienski 2000; Reich 2002). According to Ray (2013), all of the negativity towards homeschooling can be categorized into one of four classes. The first criticism is that homeschooling is bad for the common good of society.

Second, since homeschooling tends to keep students socially isolated from those who are different and do not share their same religious or political point of view, the "social glue" that schools provide will, in effect, be loosened. The third criticism is that parents may actually harm their children, be it either physical or psychological harm. Finally, more state regulation of homeschooling is needed for the following reasons: (a) a balance needs to exist between the rights of parents and the rights of the state in bringing up children; (b) this balance must include the rights of children; and (c) only state-run schools can provide children with certain goods.

Additional claims, as cited by Ray (2013), include those who say that homeschooled students will grow up to be more selfish as a result of being the constant center of attention. Others say that certified teachers are most properly qualified to decide what should be taught and how to best prepare children for adult civic life. And still others say that homeschooled students are less likely to become self-determining adults than those in state-run schools. Despite all the claims on the perils of homeschooling on adulthood, few empirical studies have been done to justify or argue against such claims (Ray 2004b). Knowles and Muchmore (1995) were amongst the first scholars to look at the effects of homeschooling on adulthood. Extensive data was collected on a group of adults who had been homeschooled for at least six years prior to turning 17. Results indicated that these adults held professional and entrepreneurial occupations, were self-reliant and focused, and had strong family values. Moreover, they were found to be happy with homeschooling and had no ill feelings towards homeschooling or negative views about living in a diverse and democratic society. Homeschooled adults were found to be no less socially and politically engaged than adults who were traditionally schooled.

In 2003, Ray (2004a) conducted the largest research study of its kind on homeschooled adults. For this study, over 7300 home-educated adults were surveyed (over 5000 adults were homeschooled for over seven years). The data collected was compared to US Census data with a sample size of over 27 000 000 people. Ray found that approximately 75% of homeschooled adults have taken college courses compared to less than 50% of the general US population. In addition, homeschooled adults had no problems finding jobs. Regarding involvement in the community, 71% said they participated in various types of service activities (such as volunteering at a local church or school) compared to 37% of the US adult population. Moreover, 88% of homeschooled adults belonged to an organization compared to 50% (of US adults). Only a small percentage of homeschooled adults (4.2%) said government and politics was too complex for them to understand compared to a much higher percentage of US adults (35%). Seventy-six percent of homeschooled adults (ages 18–24) said they voted in the past five years compared to a much lower 29% of US adults the same age. The number of older homeschooled adults who voted (ages 25–39 and 40–54) was even greater, 95% and 96%, respectively, compared to their US adult peers (40% and 53%). Finally, 59% of homeschooled adults said they were very happy with life and 95% said they were glad they homeschooled.

Despite the seeming positive results above, in favor of homeschooling, it is important to point out some of the limitations of this study. The main methodological problems include the following: (1) bias – Ray sent this survey to HSLDA online networks, and publicized it via homeschooling organizations' newsletters and via word-of-mouth, thus ensuring that respondents would already have positive views on homeschooling and likely be involved in the community; (2) non-representative sample – most of the respondents in his sample were White, Protestant college students between the ages of 18 and 24; moreover, the sample size of homeschooled students (approximately 5000) was much smaller than the general US sample size, and therefore cannot be considered representative of the homeschooling population (Coalition for Responsible Homeschooling 2013; Lubienski, Puckett, and Brewer 2013); (3) unfair comparison – Ray's study compared survey data from adults who were homeschooled in 2003 to survey data from the national survey, which was conducted six years before (Nolin, Chapman, and Chandler 1997). Based on what has been said, it is clear that much caution needs to be taken when interpreting the results of Ray's above-mentioned study.

Investigating similar civic outcomes, Smith and Sikkink (1999) sought to answer the following question: "Are families that choose…home education for their children more likely than families involved in public schools to be socially isolated and withdrawn from participation in civic life?" (par. 1). To answer this question, data from the 1996 National Household Education Survey (NHES) was collected and analyzed. A sample of 9393 parents of school-age children was used. These children reported attending the following schooling types: public school, Catholic school, private (non-Catholic), and home school. In addition to schooling-based questions, parents were asked to respond to nine forms of civic engagement: whether they belonged to a community organization; their participation level in community service activities; whether they attended a public library; if they participated in state and national elections in the past five years; if they had contacted a public official; if they had attended a public meeting; if they contributed financially to a candidate or campaign; whether they worked in support of a political cause; and if they participated in a boycott or protest. The results indicated that private-schooled families, including those homeschooled, were significantly more engaged in seven out of nine forms of civic participation, even when potentially influential variables were controlled for, such as differences in education level, age, and race.

Painting quite the opposite picture of homeschooled adults was the Cardus Education Survey conducted by Pennings et al. (2011). The main purpose of this survey was to obtain evidence from both Catholic and Protestant-schooled adults, in the US, on their educational outcomes, spiritual, and cultural engagement. Incidentally, evidence from religious (and non-religious) homeschoolers was also collected. For this study, a random sample of American adults (age 24–39) was surveyed. Out of the 1471 survey respondents, 61 were categorized as religious homeschoolers and 20 as non-religious homeschoolers (as defined by whether or not their mother attended religious services). Results indicated that religious homeschoolers scored lower on the SAT, were more likely to attend an open admissions college, less likely to attend a research university, and less likely to attend college and receive an advanced degree; like conservative Protestants, religious homeschoolers said they had a legalistic, moral outlook, and reported high church attendance; they rated themselves lower than public-schooled students in terms of their political interests, were less likely to be involved in a political campaign or public demonstration; religious homeschoolers reported a greater sense of helplessness and lack of direction in life (compared to public school students); finally, religious homeschoolers reported having fewer children, more divorces, giving less to charity, and volunteering less. In a follow-up study, Canadian (religious) homeschoolers had a more positive outlook (Pennings et al. 2012).

In 2013, Hill and Den Dulk conducted a study for the purpose of seeing how the schooling type a child receives impacts their voluntarism in young adulthood. Data was taken from the National Study of Youth and Religion (NSYR), a longitudinal study that used a representative sample of the American population. It is worth noting, as an aside, that such studies are rare in homeschooling research and provide quite valuable information. While controlling for background variables and using multivariate regression analysis, Hill and Den Dulk found that students who attended Protestant schools were three times as likely to volunteer in adulthood as students who attended public schools. Catholic-schooled students were a little bit more likely to volunteer in adulthood than public-schooled students. And most interestingly, homeschooled students were least likely to volunteer in adulthood – almost half as likely when compared to public-schooled students. What accounts for this? Hill and Den Dulk suggest that different types of schools may be better at socializing students in the importance of volunteering, which later transfers on to adulthood; they also suggest that different types of schools may be better at facilitating volunteer activities for adolescents with particular institutions that also transfer over to adulthood. Regardless of the explanation, this study, once again, like the Cardus Education Survey, paints quite the opposite picture of homeschooled adults and civic engagement (e.g., when compared to Ray's study 2004a).

Since many homeschooling families choose to homeschool their children for religious and moral reasons (National Center for Education Statistics 2009), an important question that must be asked is: does it transmit into adulthood? Do they keep their faith as adults? In a qualitative, exploratory design, Hoelzle (2013) looked to address the following: (1) how do homeschooled adults perceive the effects of homeschooling on the development of their own beliefs and values; (2) in what ways do homeschooled adults see their values aligned with, or different from, their parents; and (3) how do these same adults view their transitioning into adulthood in regards to establishing their own values and beliefs? For this study, four participants were interviewed in a semi-structured format. Two participants were male, two female, a broad range of ages was represented (18–32), and all four were homeschooled for at least eight years; moreover, a broad range of parental and personal education was represented. Findings proved interesting. Two of the participants expressed that their values were aligned with their parents' Christian beliefs. The two other participants acknowledged having similar values, but gave examples that showed more dissimilarity. One participant did not seem to display any faith connection with that of her parents. The reason given for similarities with their parents was the time spent with them due to homeschooling. Finally, in transitioning into adulthood, the participants expressed experiencing transitional bumps, realizing it was time to move on, a lack of rebellion, and having an overall positive relationship with their parents.

Most recently, Cheng (2014) conducted a study to determine the relationship between schooling type (public schools vs. private schools and homeschooling) and political tolerance. This study was done in response to reports that public schools are better than private schools (including homeschooling) at bringing about political tolerance in its students. For this study, 304 students attending a Christian university in the Western US were surveyed using a well-known valid and reliable instrument called the content-controlled political tolerance scale. Schooling type and the number of years each students attended a particular school was determined. Political tolerance was determined by asking students to identify their least-liked group and then measuring the participant's willingness to extend civil liberties to members of that group. Unsurprisingly, the least-liked groups were identified as atheists, pro-choice people, and gay-rights activists. Regression analyses were used to determine results. Findings indicated that increased private schooling does not decrease political tolerance levels. Interestingly, increased exposure to homeschooling revealed higher levels of political tolerance when compared to public schooling. These findings go against beliefs that public schooling is necessary for students to acquire political tolerance.

In another recent study, Uecker and Hill (2014) examined the effect of schooling type (Catholic, Evangelical, homeschool, and public school) on first marriage and first birth. Using data from the Cardus Education Survey (above; $N = 1{,}496$), regression models were used to show that Catholic-schooled students married later and had their first child later than students who attended public schools. Graduates of Evangelical schools were most likely to be married in their early 20s and have their first child by their mid to late 20s. Interestingly, homeschoolers looked a lot like the graduates of public schools with some marrying and having their first child very young; however, the majority of homeschoolers, like public-schooled students, did not marry or have their first child until much later in life (age 39). Religiosity of parents seemed to have a positive effect on the early age of homeschoolers getting married. This same effect was not felt by Evangelicals. Following along the lines of religiosity, Uecker (2008) sought to explain what effect the religiosity of parents would have on the religious commitment of their children. Using the NSYR data (mentioned above), and performing regression analysis, results indicated that parent religiosity had a powerful influence. However, when controlling for this variable, and looking only at schooling type, most interestingly, religious homeschoolers were no different in their religious commitment than religious public schoolers.

This literature review has both surveyed and synthesized the academic preparedness and achievement of homeschooled students in college, their socialization and transitional experiences into college, college friendliness and perceptional attitudes of college admission officers, and how homeschooled adults fare in the "real world" with particular emphasis placed on their participation in adult civic life. The results reveal the following general conclusion about homeschooled students: "no problem here" (Ray 2004a). However, in order to give just treatment to the homeschooling movement, in particular, as it relates to its impact on college, a more in-depth conclusion and analysis is necessary. The following sections will include a robust and balanced analysis and conclusion, as well as future directions for the field of homeschooling research and higher education.

Conclusion: A Balanced Approach

Much of the research on homeschooling, including the studies mentioned in this chapter, suffer from methodological problems that often render their findings inclusive. According to the Coalition for Responsible Home Education (2013), the following major problems can be found, in one way or another, in the existing body of home education research: "1) confusing correlation with causation; 2) lack of external validity and random sampling; and 3) failure to correct for background factors" (par. 4–7). These problems are either glossed over in the research, mentioned somewhere at the end of the study, or not mentioned at all. Proponents of homeschooling (Ray), people trying to advance their political agenda (HSLDA), or simple laymen with an untrained scientific mind are quick to draw broad generalizations about homeschooling from these studies when such generalizations should be made rather cautiously. On the other hand, opponents of homeschooling (e.g., Apple, Lubienski, and Reich) are quick to point out these problems and give little to no recognition to counterbalance the over-generalizations. What is needed is an unbiased, balanced approach that points out problems, but also gives recognition when there is something worthy of merit in such studies.

Methodological problems

Confusing correlation with causation To start off with, it is important to note that none of the research done on homeschooling has used a true experimental design (controlled experiment) to prove causation; most have used a correlational design (non-controlled experiment) in which variables are simply compared (Lips and Feinberg 2009). In a controlled experiment, there is an experimental group and a control group. The experimental group is manipulated and used to measure the effects of a given treatment; the results can thus be used to suggest a cause. In a non-controlled experiment, intact groups are observed and used without any attempt at changing them; therefore, the results can only be used to suggest a correlation (Galvan 2006). Despite the stated differences between correlation and causation, it is not uncommon to confuse the two. For example, in a study cited by Bracey (1998), the College Board demonstrated that there was a high, positive correlation between students who took algebra in eighth-grade and those who went on to college. The results were interpreted by the Secretary of Education, who consequently promoted taking algebra in eighth-grade as the "gateway" to college. Hence, correlation was confused with causation; which might have led to an influx of students taking algebra in eighth-grade, even those not developmentally ready.

In a similar vein, it is possible to confuse schooling type, such as homeschooling, as the cause for greater academic preparedness and achievement in college. This could lead to an even greater exit of students from public and private schools; which could lead to unintended and detrimental consequences. Nevertheless, no study could ever prove that one schooling type causes improved academic performance. In fact, trying to perform such an experiment would be almost impossible to do, if not, unethical (Ray 1999). To conduct such an experiment, one would have to create a randomized homeschooling (experimental) group and a public- or private-school (control) group, let them learn in their respective setting for at least five to ten years, and then measure their academic (or social) performance afterwards. And at the same time that no research on homeschooling has been done to prove that it is the cause of increased academic achievement, it does not mean that the correlational studies done are without merit (Devroop 2000; Jaffe 2010). In many cases, these are the only studies that can be done. Is one to say that smoking does not cause cancer because one cannot, ethically speaking, set up a controlled experiment to prove it? Certainly not. The more correlational studies done between variables that prove positive, the more one can say with assurance that one is the cause of the other (Clemente 2006). Such could be said to be the case with homeschooling and the impact results discussed in this chapter.

Lack of external validity and random sampling According to Steckler and McElroy, external validity can be defined as "whether causal relationships can be generalized to different measures, persons, settings, and times" (2008, 1). In layman's terms, external validity is the degree to which conclusions are said to hold regardless of the people used, where the study was done, or when it was it was done (Trochim 2006). High external validity is often the result of good, random sampling. The opposite is also true: low external validity is often the result of non-random, or convenience, sampling. In regards to the homeschooling research mentioned above, there is a lack of random sampling and – as a result –external validity (this is not the case, however, with the Cardus Education Survey by Pennings et al. 2011 already mentioned). Such is the case with Ray's studies. In a critical review of Ray's study on the "Academic Achievement and Demographic Traits of Homeschool Students: A Nationwide Study (2010)," where Ray attempts to prove that homeschooled students have higher standardized test scores than their conventionally schooled peers, McCracken (2014) points out Ray's sample of homeschooled students is non-random, non-representative, and self-selected, and thus lacks any type of external validity. The only people that the results can be said to hold true for is the people who took the survey – i.e., conservative, White, Christians, whose parents are married, have high-paying jobs, and are well-educated.

Despite individual homeschooling studies lacking external validity, one can make the following argument: the target population of homeschooled students can never be known. The only two sources of homeschooling information come from state-administrative data sets and national cross-sectional surveys (e.g., NHES), both of which are considerably flawed and not necessarily representative of the target homeschooling population (Isenberg 2007). Therefore, true random sampling (from the target) in not possible. The only solution is to use accessible populations and to randomly select from them (Bracht and Glass 1968). As Ray (2013) has commented, the accessible homeschool populations that are available consistently show that these students do better (academically) than traditionally schooled students. Data from the Oregon Department of Education show that homeschooled students score above average on standardized tests. The same can be said about Washington data on homeschooled students, as well as Alaskan and Alabaman homeschooled students (Ray 2013). The more accessible populations that are examined, the more one can generalize with greater external validity. Another way of justifying external validity is by using Campbell's proximal similarity model (as cited in Trochim and Donnelly 2008). When true random sampling is not possible, as it has already been established that it is not, study contexts (persons, places, and times) are compared for similarities to draw conclusions; however, one is not able to generalize with absolute certainty.

Failure to correct for background factors Another problem with many of the studies reviewed in this chapter is the failure to correct for background factors. For example, many of the studies that compare homeschooled students to their traditionally schooled peers do not take into account differences in both socioeconomic and motivational predispositions – both of which are known to be highly influential in effecting (academic) results (Coleman et al. 1966; Sacks 2007; Wrigley 2011). Homeschooled students who come from families with high family income, high parental educational attainment, and parents who have a high interest in their child's education – characteristics which are common to homeschooling families (Ray 2010) – cannot be reasonably compared to the national averages of students in traditional schools who come from a background with oftentimes opposing characteristics without controlling for these variables (Lubienski, Puckett, and Brewer 2013). In Saunders' (2006; 2009) study that compared schooling type, social integration, and first-year persistence rates, the greater levels of social integration and higher first-year persistence rates of homeschooled students are as likely to be attributed to the fact that the students attending Wheaton College, a conservative Christian institution, have parents who are more educated and more vested in their child's education, and who serve as good role models, as being attributed to the actual schooling type itself.

In an attempt to rectify biases that result from the failure to control for background factors, Martin-Chang, Gould, and Meuse (2011) conducted a study of thirty-seven homeschooled and thirty-seven public-schooled students living in Canada. While this study does not fall within the realm of higher education, it is a good example of a study that controls for potentially influential variables and avoids the pitfalls of comparing more advantaged homeschoolers to national averages. For this study, several variables were controlled for including: geographical area of students, testing administration, maternal educational level, marital status, household size, parental employment, and family income. The demographics survey revealed that homeschooled students could be divided into two subgroups based on the structuring of their schooling: structured ($N=25$) and unstructured ($N=12$). Students were administered the Woodcock-Johnson Test (a standardized test), which consisted of the following seven subtests: Letter-Word Identification, Passage Comprehension, Calculation, Science, Social Science, Humanities, and a Word Attack. Using MANOVA and follow up t-tests, results revealed that structured homeschooled students did far better than public-schooled students across all seven subtests and public-schooled students outperformed unstructured homeschoolers in all seven areas. Martin-Chang, Gould, and Meuse concluded that structured homeschooling may offer opportunities for increased academic performance and that such benefits cannot be accounted for by differences in the variables controlled for (family income, parental educational level, and so on).

The verdict is in

Based on the above-mentioned methodological problems, much caution is needed before drawing any sweeping conclusions. In regards to both the quantitative and qualitative studies done on homeschooling and its impact on higher education, one can conclude the following: not a lot is empirically known. What is known is that homeschooled students are now commonly accepted into the most prestigious colleges in the US (Davis 2005; Klicka 2007a), many colleges now actively recruit homeschooled students as viable candidates (Mason 2004), standardized achievement tests for admissions (e.g., ACT/SAT) are at least comparable to, if not better than, traditionally schooled students (Clemente 2006; Galloway 1995; Gray 1998; Jones and Gloeckner 2004a; Ray and Eagleson 2008; Snyder 2013), even when background variables are corrected for (Belfield, 2004); college admissions policies for homeschooled students are quite flexible and resemble those for any other student (Jones and Gloeckner 2013), college admissions officers believe that homeschooled students, especially those 18 and over, are as prepared (academically and socially) for college as traditionally schooled students (Jones and Gloeckner 2004b; Sorrey and Duggan 2008), and many college admissions officers are quite impressed with homeschooled students' varied experiences and purposeful approach to learning (Basko 2012).

Once admitted into college, homeschooled students do as well academically, if not better than, traditionally schooled students. The most common measure of academic success in college is GPA, and homeschooled students clearly show no deficit in regards to this (Bagwell 2010; Cogan 2010; Gray 1998; Jenkins 1998; Jones and Gloeckner 2004a; Snyder 2013; Sutton and Galloway 2000). GPA levels for homeschooled students remain high through college, while first-and fourth-year GPA is at least comparable to traditionally schooled students (Cogan 2010; Snyder 2013). Despite their self-proclaimed weaknesses in math and science (Bagwell 2010; Holder 2001) homeschooled students demonstrate comparable GPA levels to their traditionally schooled peers in both areas; the same can be said for English GPA (Bagwell 2010; Gray 1998). In regards to staying in college through graduation, homeschooled students show similar persistence (Cogan 2010). It would seem fair to say that homeschooled students need to make some initial adjustments to the academic life of college (e.g., keeping to deadlines, adjusting to different professors' teaching styles, expectations, and so on) (Holder 2001); however, this does not hinder their ability to ultimately adjust well and find success. While some parents are less successful at preparing their children to do well academically in college, this is likely to be the exception rather than the rule (Clemmitt 2014).

In regards to the "s" question, socialization, homeschooled students seem to do fine integrating into the social life of their college campus, getting involved in extracurricular activities, and even taking on leadership roles, despite, perhaps, being shy at first and taking some time to "open up" (Holder 2001; Lattibeaudiere 2000; Saunders 2006, 2009; Sutton and Galloway 2000). Moreover, homeschooled students seem to have an easier time integrating into certain types of colleges, especially where there is a high degree of "institutional fit" (Saunders 2006, 2009). For example, homeschooled students brought up in a conservative, Christian household would have an easier time integrating into colleges like Patrick Henry or Ave Maria as opposed to some other secular school. Homeschooled students have also shown, in many circumstances, to have an easier time relating to their college professors, which is most likely the result of spending time socializing with people from older age groups (Kranzow 2004). When personally asked about their socialization in college, most homeschoolers say, "No problem"; nevertheless, mixed feelings exist amongst faculty and student development professionals (Lavoie 2006). Overall, homeschooled students seem to transition into college with relative ease, while experiencing some challenges in encountering students with different world views and values (Bolle, Wessel and Mulvihill 2007). At the end day, college levels the playing field for all students (Wood 2011).

The one area that has garnered even more criticism than homeschooling and the "socialization question" is homeschooling and its impact on adult life, especially unregulated homeschooling and its perceived negative effect on adult participation in civic life (Apple 2005; Lubienski 2000; Reich 2002). Research has shown mixed results in regards to homeschooled adults. Some homeschooled adults are less willing to participate in volunteer activities (Hill and Den Dulk 2013; Pennings et al. 2011) while others are more engaged citizens: volunteering in local schools, churches, and organizations, participating in state and national elections, as well as contributing financially to political campaigns (Ray 2013; Smith and Sikkink 1999). Moreover, some have suggested that homeschooling inculcates students to become politically intolerant adults (Reich 2002; West 2009) and less engaged (Pennings et al. 2011). Other have found quite the opposite is true (Cheng 2014; Kunzman 2009; Ray 2004a). Homeschooled adults have been found to range in their own religious commitment (Hoelzle 2013; Uecker 2008). Some homeschooled adults are found to be just as happy and satisfied in life as students from other educational backgrounds (Van Pelt 2003); while others reported a greater sense of unhappiness, helplessness, and lack of direction in life (Pennings et al. 2011). Finally, homeschool adults are said to be very similar to public-schooled students in regards to when they first get married and have their first child (Uecker and Hill 2014). As a matter of fact, all in all, homeschooled adults seem to be, in many respects, very similar to adults having attended other schooling types.

A final word (or two)

After surveying the research on homeschooling and its impact on higher education, the writer feels comfortable in concluding the following: homeschooling works. It can help prepare students to get into the college of their choice and do well academically once accepted, it helps to form students who are socially capable of engaging with their college peers or persons of any age group, and it can help to form adults who are responsible and civically engaged in a liberal democracy. Nevertheless, saying that homeschooling works is like saying that public and private schooling works to accomplish the same things. And, yet, intuitively this is known to be true. Who would argue that some of the brightest and most capable adults in the US are products of all three schooling types? What is not known, however, is why it works. According to the Coalition for Responsible Home Education (2013), there are several possible reasons: (1) students who are homeschooled have involved parents who are well educated, have greater access to resources, and are better able to provide their children with ample social experiences; (2) homeschooling is especially suited to the educational achievement and development of some students; and (3) homeschooling provides students with rich and varied learning opportunities that instill in them positive habits towards learning and make many of them into lifelong learners.

Finally, despite all the methodological limitations of the above-mentioned studies, such as the use of self-reporting (of students who are already motivated and do well academically), the use of convenience samples (especially homeschooling populations attending Christian colleges and universities), the inability to generalize to the wider homeschooling population at large (especially homeschooling students attending public colleges and universities), and the failure to correct for background variables (even if entire college populations are used); and although homeschooling cannot be proven to be the cause of greater levels of collegiate academic achievement, nor can it be proven to be the superior educational schooling type, what is known is that homeschooled students who go on to college and adulthood do quite well.

Future Directions of Homeschooling Research

On a final note, much more research needs to be done on homeschooling before any definitive conclusions can be made about its impact on higher education. As has already been said, causal studies are not practical (or even ethical) in homeschooling research. Therefore, more correlational studies need to be done. Such studies are needed to help determine if homeschooled students are prepared for the academic challenges of college and are able to navigate its complex social landscape. Since many of the studies on homeschooling have been done at Christian colleges, more correlational studies need to be done to include homeschoolers from different religions (Jewish, Muslim, etc.), and non-religious homeschoolers, attending public and private (non-Christian) colleges. This would help determine the degree to which the literature summarized above applies to others beyond the motivated Christians attending select Christian institutions. While broadening the base of homeschooling studies to include secular institutions, additional correlational studies need to be done that involve homeschoolers from both genders (male and female), different races (White, Black, Asian, etc.), ethnicities (Anglo-Saxon, Hispanic/Latino, Han-Chinese, etc.), political persuasions (liberal democratic, conservative republican, etc.), and socioeconomic status (low, middle, high) – also attending a wide array of colleges and universities. This would further help to eliminate the stereotype of homeschooling applying only to wealthy, White, Christian conservatives.

In addition to performing more correlational studies to include a much wider demographic of homeschoolers, careful studies need to be done that correct for background variables. Since homeschoolers come from such wide and varying backgrounds, it is important that these variables are matched against traditionally schooled students when comparisons are being made. What are not needed are more studies that take homeschooled students with wide-ranging demographics and then compare them to national averages without correcting for background variables. When variables are not corrected for, it becomes very difficult, if not impossible, to ascertain the actual cause of superior academic performance. Ray's studies regularly fall victim to this, but then so do many studies performed by other researchers, especially doctoral dissertations concerned with homeschoolers and higher education.

Homeschooling research also needs more quantitative studies utilizing random sampling. Random sampling allows for one to generalize to the larger population of homeschooled students. In random sampling, some type of procedure is used to ensure that each member of the population has an equal chance at being selected. Nearly all of the homeschooling research done so far has used convenience samples, which do not allow for such randomization and thus generalizability. For example, as already mentioned, Ray's studies are widely known for using volunteers or recruits. In such studies, a large number of homeschooled students who belong to homeschooling advocacy groups are recruited to take part in a study, or homeschooled families who are highly committed and dedicated volunteer for the same purpose. This produces biased results invariably in favor of homeschooling. Only with random sampling can one hope to get an authentic picture of the real effects of homeschooling on all families, not just the ones who are doing it particularly well and want to promote it. The problem with random sampling, however, is getting enough homeschoolers to participate given their small percentage in the overall population. Even large randomized studies like the Cardus Education Survey or the data collected by the National Center for Education Statistics must base their generalizations on a small number of identified homeschoolers. Nevertheless, if it is a true random sample, without any kind of sampling error, small size does not undermine validity.

Finally, in order to get the most complete picture of homeschooling, more longitudinal studies need to be done. Nowadays, since many people homeschool their child(ren) for several years, then send them to a traditional school for a few years, and sometimes homeschool them again for several years, it's difficult to know exactly how long students have been homeschooled. When studying homeschooled students who have gone off to college, it's often only possible to account for their high school experience. But how many of these students were homeschooled for their first eight years of schooling and then attended a traditional school, or vice versa? The schooling-type variable thus becomes very difficult to completely isolate. What is needed are longitudinal studies that look at students who have been homeschooled for their entire schooling years (K–12), examine family dynamics, what methodology-type was used (traditional textbook, unschooling, eclectic), curricula used, and then follow these students through college and adult life. The only problem with conducting such studies is the amount of time, energy, and resources they take to complete. An interesting avenue of future research would be to focus specifically on unstructured homeschoolers (unschooling) and compare them to structured homeschoolers (traditional textbook). The writer is inclined to believe, based on limited research and anecdotal evidence, that there is a definite difference between the two in regards to college outcomes.

References

Apple, Michael. 2005. "Away with All Teachers: The Cultural Politics of Homeschooling." In *Homeschooling in Full View: A Reader*, edited by Bruce S. Cooper, 75–95. Greenwich, CT: Information Age.

Bagwell, Jack. 2010. "The Academic Success of Homeschooled Students in a South Carolina Technical College." PhD diss., University of Nebraska.

Basko, Aaron. 2012. "Homeschooling Comes of Age in College Admission." *The Old Schoolhouse*. Accessed June 8, 2014. http://thehomeschoolmagazine.com/articles/highschool/homeschooling-comes-of-age/

Belfield, Clive. R. 2004. "Homeschooling in the U.S." Occasional Paper No. 48, National Center for the Study of Privatization in Education, Teachers College, Columbia University.

Bolle, Mary B., Roger D. Wessel, and Thalia M. Mulvihill. 2007. "Transitional Experiences of First Year College Students who were Homeschooled." *Journal of College Student Development*, 48: 637–654.

Bolle-Brummond, Mary B., and Roger D. Wessel. 2012. "Homeschooled Students in College: Background Influences, College Integration, and Environmental Pull Factors." *Journal of Research in Education*, 22: 223–249.

Bracht, Glenn H., and Gene V. Glass. 1968. "The External Validity of Experiments." *American Educational Research Journal*, 5: 437–474.

Bracey, Gerald W. 1998. "Tips for Readers of Research – No Causation from Correlation." *Phi Delta Kappan*, 79: 711–712.

Bronfenbrenner, Urie. 1993. The Ecology of Cognitive Development: Research Models and Fugitive Findings. In *Development in Context: Acting and Thinking in Specific*

Environments, edited by Robert H. Wozniak and Kurt W. Fischer, 3–44. Hillsdale, NJ: Lawrence Erlbaum Associates.

Cheng, Albert. 2014. "Does Homeschooling or Private Schooling Promote Political Intolerance? Evidence from a Christian University." *Journal of School Choice*, 8: 49–68.

Chickering, Arthur W., and Linda Reisser. 1993. *Education and Identity*, 2nd ed. San Francisco, CA: Jossey-Bass.

Clemente, Dale F. 2006. "Academic Achievement and College Aptitude in Homeschooled High School Students Compared to their Private-Schooled and Public-Schooled Counterparts." EdD diss., Regent University.

Clemmitt, Marcia. 2014. "Homes Schooling: Do Parents Give their Children a Good Education?" *CQ Researcher*, 24: 217–240.

Coalition for Responsible Home Education. 2013. Accessed June 8, 2014. http://www.rcsponsiblehomeschooling.org

Cogan, Michael F. 2010. "Exploring Academic Outcomes of Homeschooled Students." *Journal of College Admission*, 208: 18–25.

Coleman, James S., Ernest Q. Campbell, Carol J. Hobson, James McPartland, Alexander M. Mood, Frederic D. Weinfeld, and Robert L. York. 1966. *Equality of Educational Opportunity*. Washington, DC: US Department of Health, Education, and Welfare.

Cornwell, Christopher M., David B. Mustard, and Jessica V. Parys. 2008. "How Does the New SAT Predict Academic Achievement in College?" Accessed April 13, 2016. https://www.researchgate.net/profile/Christopher_Cornwell/publication/228871851_How_Does_the_New_SAT_Predict_Academic_Achievement_in_College/links/0deec527d515b12c74000000.pdf

Davis, Aislin. 2005. "Evolution of Homeschooling." *Distance Learning* 8: 29–35.

DeBerard, M. Scott, Glen I. Spielmans, and Deana L. Julka, D. 2004. "Predictors of Academic Achievement and Retention Among College Freshman: A Longitudinal Study." *College Student Journal*, 38: 66–80.

Devroop, Karendra, 2000. "Correlation Versus Causation: Another Look at a Common Misinterpretation." Paper presented at the annual meeting of the Southwest Educational Research Association, Dallas, TX, January 27–29.

Drenovsky, Cynthia K., and Isaiah Cohen. 2012. "The Impact of Homeschooling on the Adjustment of College Students." *International Social Science Review*, 87: 19–34.

Duggan, Molly H. 2010. "Are Community Colleges Home-School Friendly?: An Exploration of Community College Web Sites as an Indicator of Friendliness." *Community College Journal of Research and Practice*, 34: 55–63.

Durkin, Keven. 1995. "Socialization." In *The Blackwell Encyclopedia of Social Psychology*, edited by Anthony S.R. Manstead and Miles Hewstone, 614–618. Cambridge, MA: Basil Blackwell.

Gaither, Milton. 2009. "Home Schooling Goes Mainstream." *Education Next*, 9: 10–18.

Galloway, Rhonda A. Scott. 1995. "Home Schooled Adults: Are they Ready for College?" Paper presented at the annual meeting of the American Educational Research Association, San Francisco, CA, April 18–22.

Galvan, Jose L. 2006. *Writing Literature Reviews: A Guide for Students of the Social and Behavioral Science*, 3rd ed. Glendale, CA: Pyrczak.

Gray, Dovie W. 1998. "A Study of the Academic Achievements of Homeschooled Students who have Matriculated into Post-Secondary Institutions." EdD diss., University of Sarasota.

Hill, Jonathon P. and Kevin R. Den Dulk. 2013. "Religion, Volunteering, and Educational Setting: The Effect of Youth Schooling Type on Civic Engagement." *Journal for the Scientific Study of Religion*, 52: 179–197.

Hoelzle, Braden. R. 2013. "The Transmission of Values and the Transition into Adulthood Within the Context of Home Education." *Journal of Research on Christian Education*, 22: 244–263.

Holder, Melvin A. 2001. "Academic Achievement and Socialization of College Students who were Homeschooled." EdD diss., University of Memphis.

Horn, Brian. 2006. "GPA as a Measure of UNT Student Learning in the Teacher Candidate Program." Paper submitted in partial fulfillment of the requirements for EDCI 6030, University of North Texas.

Hsu, Stephen. D.H., and James Schombert. 2010. "The Value of Hard Work: College GPA Predictions from SAT Scores." Unpublished work, University of Oregon.

Isenberg, Eric J. 2007. "What Have We Learned About Homeschooling?" *Peabody Journal of Education*, 82: 387–409.

Jaffe, Adi. 2010. "Correlation, Causation, and Association – What Does it All Mean?" *Psychology Today*. Accessed June 8, 2014. http://www.psychologytoday.com/blog/all-about-addiction/201003/correlation-causation-and-association-what-does-it-all-mean

Jenkins, Toni. 1998. "The Performance of Home Schooled Students in Community Colleges." EdD diss., Texas A&M University.

Jones, Paul, and Gene Gloeckner. 2004a. "First-Year College Performance: A Study of Home School Graduates and Traditional School Graduates." *The Journal of College Admission*, 183: 17–20.

Jones, Paul, and Gene Gloeckner. 2004b. "Perceptions of and Attitudes Toward Homeschool Students." *The Journal of College Admission*, 185: 12–21.

Jones, Paul and Gene Gloeckner. 2013. "Reflections on a Decade of Changes in Homeschooling and the Homeschooled into Higher Education." *Peabody Journal of Education*, 88: 309–323.

Kim, Eunhee, Fred B. Newton, Ronald G. Downey, and Stephen L. Benton. 2010. "Personal Factors Impacting College Student Success: Constructing College Learning Effectiveness Inventory." *College Student Journal*, 44: 112–125.

Klicka, Chris J. 2007a. *Homeschooled Students Excel in College*. Purcellville, VA: Home School Legal Defense Association.

Klicka, Chris J. 2007b. *Socialization: Homeschoolers in the Real World*. Purcellville, VA: Home School Legal Defense Association.

Knowles, J. Gary, and James A. Muchmore. 1995. "Yep! We're Grown-Up Home-School Kids – and We're Doing Just Fine, Thank You." *Journal of Research on Christian Education*, 4: 35–56.

Kobrin, Jennifer L., et al. 2008. *Validity of the SAT for Predicting First-Year Grade-Point Average* (College Board Research Report No. 2008–5). Accessed April 13, 2016. https://research.collegeboard.org/sites/default/files/publications/2012/7/researchreport-2008-5-validity-sat predicting-first-year-college-grade-point-average.pdf

Kranzow, Jeannine. 2004. "Taking a Different Path: The College Experiences of Homeschooled Students." PhD diss., Indiana University.

Kunzman, Robert. 2009. *Write These Laws on Your Children: Inside the World of Conservative Christian Homeschooling*. Boston, MA: Beacon Press.

Kunzman, Robert, and Milton Gaither. 2013. "Homeschooling: A Comprehensive Survey of the Research." *Other Education: The Journal of Educational Alternatives*, 2: 4–59.

Lattibeaudiere, Vivien H. 2000. "An Exploratory Study of the Transition and Adjustment of Former Homeschooled Students to College Life." PhD diss., University of Tennessee.

Lavoie, Lisa D. 2006. "Examining the Perceived Academic and Social Development of Six Early Entrant Home-Schooled Students in a Connecticut Community College: A Practical Action Research Study." EdD diss., University of Hartford.

Lips, Dan, and Evan Feinberg. 2009, September. "Homeschooling: The Sleeping Giant of American Education." *USA Today*, 138: 22.

Lubienski, Christopher. 2000. "Whither the Common Good: A Critique of Homeschooling." *Peabody Journal of Education*, 75: 207–232.

Lubienski, Christopher, Tiffany Puckett, and T. Jameson Brewer. 2013. "Does Homeschooling 'Work'? A Critique of the Empirical Claims and Agenda of Advocacy Organizations." *Peabody Journal of Education*, 88: 378–392.

Luebke, Robert V. 1999. "Homeschooling in Wisconsin: A Review of Current Issues and Trends." *Wisconsin Policy Research Report*, 12: 1–29.

Martin-Chang, Sandra, Odette N. Gould, and Reanne E. Meuse. 2011. "The Impact of Schooling on Academic Achievement: Evidence from Homeschooled and Traditionally Schooled Students." *Canadian Journal of Behavioral Science*, 43: 195–202.

Mason, Gary. 2004. "Homeschool Recruiting: Lessons Learned on the Journey." *Journal of College Admission*, 185: 2–3.

McCracken, Chelsea. 2014. *How to Mislead with Data: A Critical Review of Ray's "Academic Achievement and Demographic Traits of Homeschool Students: A Nationwide Study" (2010).* Canton, MA: Coalition for Responsible Home Education.

Medlin, Richard G. 2000. "Homeschooling and the Question of Socialization." *Peabody Journal of Education*, 75: 107–123.

Medlin, Richard G. 2013. "Homeschooling and the Question of Socialization Revisited." *Peabody Journal of Education*, 88: 284–297.

National Center for Education Statistics. 2009. *1.5 Million Homeschooled Students in the United States in 2007* (NCES 2009–030). Washington, DC: US Department of Education.

National Center for Home Education. 2000. *1999 College Survey: College Admission Policies Opening to Homeschoolers*. Purcellville, VA: Homeschool Legal Defense Association.

Noel, Amber, Patrick Stark, and Jeremy Redford. 2013. *Parent and Family Involvement in Education, from the National Household Education Survey Program of 2012* (NCES 2013–028). Washington, DC: US Department of Education.

Nolin, M.C., C. Chapman, and K. Chandler. 1997. *Adult Civic Involvement in the United States: National Household Education* Survey (NCES 97–906). Washington, DC: US Department of Education.

Pennings, Ray, et al. 2011. *Do the Motivations for Private Religious Catholic and Protestant Schooling in North America Align with Graduate Outcomes*. Hamilton, Ontario: Cardus.

Pennings, Ray, David Sikkink, Deani Van Pelt, Harro Van Brummelen, and Amy von Heyking, A. 2012. *A rising tide lifts all boats: Measuring non-government school effects in service of the Canadian public good*. Hamilton, Ontario: Cardus.

Ray, Brian D. 1999. *Homeschooling on the Threshold: A Survey of Research at the Dawn of the New Millennium*. Salem, OR: National Home Education Research Institute.

Ray, Brian D. 2000. "Homeschooling: The Ameliorator of Negative Influences on Learning?" *Peabody Journal of Education*, 75: 71–106.

Ray, Brian D. 2004a. *Home Educated and Now Adults: Their Community and Civic Involvement, Views About Homeschooling, and Other Traits*. Salem, OR: National Home Education Research Institute.

Ray, Brian D. 2004b. "Homeschoolers on to College: What Research Shows Us." *Journal of College Admission*, 185: 5–11.

Ray, Brian D. 2010, Winter. "Academic Achievement and Demographic Traits of Homeschool Students: A Nationwide Study." *Academic Leadership*, 8.

Ray, Brian D. 2011. *2.04 Million Homeschooled Students in the United States in 2010*. Salem, OR: National Home Education Research Institute.

Ray, Brian D. 2013. "Homeschooling Associated with Beneficial Learner and Socictal Outcomes But Educators Do Not Promote It." *Peabody Journal of Education*, 88: 324–341.

Ray, Brian D, and Bruce Eagleson. 2008. "State Regulation of Homeschooling and Homeschoolers' SAT Scores." *Academic Leadership: The Online Journal*, 6.

Reich, Rob. 2002. "The Civic Perils of Homeschooling." *Educational Leadership*, 59: 6–59.

Reich, Rob. 2008. "On Regulating Homeschooling: A Reply to Glanzer." *Educational Theory*, 58: 17–23.

Remmerde, Juniper. 1997, October 6. "How Homeschoolers Move from Family Room to College Campus." *Christian Science Monitor*, 12.

Romanowski, Michael H. 2006. "Revisiting the Common Myths About Homeschooling." *The Clearing House*, 79: 125–129.

Sacks, Peter. 2007. *Tearing Down the Gates: Confronting the Class Divide in American Education*. Los Angeles, CA: University of California Press.

Saunders, Mary K. 2006. "Comparing the First Year Experiences and Persistence Rates of Previously Homeschooled College Freshmen to College Freshmen Who Were Not Homeschooled." EdD diss., Vanderbilt University.

Saunders, Mary K. 2009. "Previously Homeschooled College Freshmen: Their First Year Experiences and Persistence Rates." *Journal of College Student Retention*, 11: 77–100.

Smith, Michael. 2009. "Homeschooling: Socialization Not a Problem." Accessed June 8, 2014. http://www.washingtontimes.com/news/2009/dec/13/home-schooling-socialization-not-problem/

Smith, Christian, and David Sikkink. 1999, April. "Is Private School Privatizing?" *First Things*. Accessed June 8, 2014. http://www.firstthings.com/article/1999/04/001-is-private-schooling-privatizing

Snyder, Marc. 2011. "An Evaluative Study of the Academic Achievement of Homeschooled Students Versus Traditionally Schooled Students Attending a Catholic University." EdD diss., Nova Southeastern University.

Snyder, Marc. 2013. "An Evaluative Study of the Academic Achievement of Homeschooled Students Versus Traditionally Schooled Students Attending a Catholic University." *Catholic Education: A Journal of Inquiry and Practice* 16: 288–308.

Sorey, Kellie, and Molly Duggan. 2008. "Homeschoolers Entering Community Colleges: Perceptions of Admission Officers." *Journal of College Admission*, 200: 22–28.

Steckler, Allan, and Kenneth R. McLeroy. 2008. "The Importance of External Validity." *American Journal of Public Health*, 98: 9–10.

Sutton, Joe P., and Rhonda S. Galloway. 2000. "College Success of Students from Three High School Settings." *Journal of Research and Development in Education*, 33: 137–146.

Tinto, Vincent. 1975. "Dropouts from Higher Education: A Theoretical Synthesis of Recent Research." *Review of Educational Research*, 45: 89–125.

Tinto, Vincent. 1988. "Stages of Student Departure: Reflections on the Longitudinal Character of Student Leaving." *Journal of Higher Education*, 59: 438–455.

Tinto, Vincent. 1993. *Leaving college*. Chicago, IL: University of Chicago Press.

Trochim, William M. K. 2006. "External Validity." Last modified October 20, 2006. http://www.socialresearchmethods.net/kb/external.php

Trochim, William M. K., and James P. Donnelly. 2008. *The research methods knowledge base*, 3rd ed. Mason, OH: Cengage Learning.

Uecker, Jeremy E. 2008. "Alternative Schooling Strategies and the Religious Lives of American Adolescents." *Journal for the Scientific Study of Religion*, 47: 563–584.

Uecker, Jeremy E. and Jonathan P. Hill. 2014. "Religious Schools, Home Schools, and the Timing of First Marriage and First Birth." *Review of Religious Research*, 56: 189–218.

Van Pelt, Deani A.N. 2003. *Home Education in Canada*. London, Ontario, Canada: Canadian Centre for Home Education.

Waddell, Timothy B. 2010. "Bringing it all Back Home: Establishing a Coherent Constitutional Framework for the Re-Regulation of Homeschooling." *Vanderbilt Law Review* 63: 541–598.

Walker, Veronica. 2010. "Attending College When You've Never been to High School: Integrating Homeschoolers into the College System." *Student Pulse: The International Student Journal*, 2: 1.

West, Robin L. 2009. "The Harms of Homeschooling." *Philosophy and Public Policy Quarterly*, 29: 7–12.

Wood, Alexa L. 2011. "From the Kitchen Table to the Lecture Hall: Reaching an Understanding of the Lived Experiences of Home-School Students in Institutions of Higher Learning." Master's thesis, North Carolina State University.

Wrigley, Terry. 2011. "Culture, Class, and Curriculum: A Reflective Essay." In *Marxism and Education: Renewing the Dialogue, Pedagogy, and Culture*, edited by Peter E. Jones, 11–38. New York, NY: Palgrave Macmillan.Yuracko, Kimberly A. 2008. "Education off the Grid: Constitutional Constraints on Homeschooling." *California Law Review*, 96: 123–184.

8

Homeschooling Motherhood

Jennifer Lois

Homeschooling is an ever-growing alternative to conventional schooling. Research suggests that 1.77 million American children were homeschooled in 2012, an estimated 3.4% of the school-age population in the United States. This percentage has seen a steady increase, up from 1.7% in 1999 (National Center for Education Statistics 2015). Though we know numbers are rising, studies have been unable to capture very detailed demographics of the homeschooling population as a whole because of the difficulty in obtaining a representative sample. The research that comes closest, however, clearly shows that homeschooling is not a monolithic movement. Homeschoolers are from all races, though are typically white; are from all socioeconomic statuses, though are usually middle class and above; hold a variety of religious orientations, though most often are Evangelical or mainstream Protestant; and have larger-than-average families (Bauman 2002; Mayberry et al. 1995; National Household Education Surveys Program 2008; Ray 2000; Wagenaar 1997).

The one area with the least demographic variation among homeschoolers, however, is in gendered family structure. The vast majority of homeschooled children are taught by stay-at-home mothers in two-parent, heterosexual families with a father supporting the family in the paid labor force (Aurini and Davies 2005; Bauman 2002; Mayberry et al. 1995; Stevens 2001; Wagenaar 1997). That is not to say that homeschooling is impossible when a mother works, when a father is in charge of the children's education, or in single-parent families – indeed, homeschooling happens in all types of family configurations – but because homeschooling takes an extraordinary amount of time and attention, it is much easier to accomplish when the labor is divided so that one parent can be devoted to it full time. Since mothers are much more likely than fathers to leave the paid labor force to care for young children (see Bianchi, Robinson, and Milkie 2006), this gendered family arrangement is extremely

The Wiley Handbook of Home Education, First Edition. Edited by Milton Gaither.

common among homeschooling families. For example, Bauman found that the presence of a "non-working adult" in the home is "one of the strongest" and "highly [statistically] significant" influences on homeschooling (2002, 10; see also Lois 2012; Mayberry et al. 1995; Stevens 2001).

Despite the disproportionate involvement of mothers in homeschooling, very little research has examined their experiences in depth. This chapter will review the ways mothers' experiences have been addressed in the scholarly literature on homeschooling, present the main findings that have arisen from it, and suggest avenues for future research.

Maternal Motivations for Homeschooling

Though the research on homeschooling is scant, parents' reasons for choosing it is easily the most commonly investigated topic. Most of these studies do not differentiate between mothers' and fathers' motivations; however, when they do make gender a central feature of analysis, a more nuanced picture of homeschooling emerges.

"Parents'" motivations: obscuring gender

Van Galen (1988) was the first to typologize homeschooling parents by their motivations, dichotomizing them into "ideologues" and "pedagogues." Basing her research mainly on in-depth interviews with "23 parents from 16 homeschooling families" who had withdrawn their children from conventional schools, she highlighted some broad-brush differences between these two groups (1988, 54). The "ideologues" homeschooled for religious reasons: they opposed the public schools' secular orientation and believed it was their family's right, not the state's, to take charge of their children's education. The "pedagogues" homeschooled for academic reasons, though some portion was highly religious as well. They believed the public schools were too inept to teach their children, in some cases, but certainly not all, because their children had special needs or gifts. Pedagogues had "exhausted the schools' resources for solving the problem" their children were experiencing (1988, 56).

In subsequent research based on fifteen in-depth interviews and a large survey of homeschooling parents, Mayberry (1988; with Knowles 1989) confirmed Van Galen's two categories. She also elaborated on the typology, describing some of the homeschooling parents she studied as motivated by "socio-relational" reasons because they feared the negative peer influence in public schools and wanted to increase their family's unity (these homeschoolers were also highly likely to be religious). Mayberry also identified "New Age" homeschooling parents, the smallest proportion, who wanted the right to teach their children a globally focused worldview that emphasized the interrelatedness of all life. Both Mayberry and Van Galen's works were instrumental in beginning to uncover the homeschooling motivations of "parents" and "families" (see also Knowles 1991). Although these early works did reveal that most of the day-to-day homeschooling work is done by mothers, most of the research that followed has continued on a gender-neutral trajectory, consistently referring to "parents" and "families" despite acknowledging that "the parent/teachers are overwhelmingly the mothers of the children" (Collom 2005, 316). This scholarly trend of degendering homeschoolers' motivations may be masking the potentially important ways gender plays a role in parents' decisions to homeschool.

For example, in the survey phase of their study, Klein and Poplin (2008) mailed out 1422 surveys to members of a virtual charter school (in effect, homeschoolers) and received responses from 143 mothers and 3 fathers. Setting aside the 10% response rate, these numbers are interesting in that 98% of respondents were mothers and 2% were fathers, which raises the question of how gender may matter in deciding to homeschool one's children – or at least how it may matter in relating those decisions via survey responses. However, when discussing their sample, Klein and Poplin state, "it would appear that the parent-teacher tends to be more educated, more religious, and more likely to be married than the general population" (2008, 379). Given that 98% their respondents were mothers, it might make sense to add that homeschooling "parent-teachers" are also more likely to be women "than the general population." Not only do Klein and Poplin fail to comment on the highly gendered nature of their sample, they actually eclipse gender by continually referring to their respondents – 98% of whom are mothers – as "parents" (e.g., "parents were impressed with..." and "parents were dissatisfied with...." [2008, 384]). Had they acknowledged that their sample was so unbalanced, they may have been able to compare mothers' responses against the few from fathers to get a cursory read on any glaring gender differences. At the very least, the highly skewed sample provided an opening to speculate about how homeschooling mothers' motivations may depart from fathers', a topic worthy of discussion as research shows robust differences between mothers' and fathers' parenting ideologies (see Blair-Loy 2003; Hays 1996; Stone 2007). By degendering their analysis, however, Klein and Poplin preclude any insight they could have contributed to the gendering of parents' homeschooling motivations.

Other research on homeschoolers' motivations has similarly neutralized the gendered nature of the samples. For example, Arai (2000) conducted an interview-based study of twenty-three homeschooling families' "reasons for homeschooling" in Ontario and British Columbia. He refers to his subjects as "parents" and "families," but does not state if he interviewed mothers, fathers, or some combination. Arai further obscures parents' gender by attributing numbers to his interviewees' quotations (i.e., "interview #11") instead of using gender-marked pseudonyms or labeling interviewees as "mother" or "father." There are a few places Arai tangentially identifies respondents' gender in the text (e.g., one "parent" who "described herself as..." or "talked about the change she saw..." or "two mothers explicitly said..."), but neglecting gender so often does a disservice to the literature on "parents'" motivations by collapsing categories and blinding the reader to the significance of gendered parental motivations. Arai, however, does acknowledge that "home schooling is usually possible only when an adult stays at home with the children," then notes that in Canada, "the proportion of dual-income families is increasing" (2000, 214). Since, as mentioned earlier, women are far more likely than men to leave paid work to stay home with young children, Arai's degendered analysis simultaneously implies that gender is an important factor in understanding the decision of "parents" to homeschool.

Given that almost every study on homeschooling finds that (a) most homeschooling occurs in two-parent, heterosexual families with a stay-at-home mother and a wage-earning father, and (b) that mothers are by far the more likely partner to be the primary homeschooling parent (Aurini and Davies 2005; Bauman 2002; Lundy and Mazama 2014; Mayberry et al. 1995; Sherfinski 2014; Sherfinski and Chesanko 2014; Stevens 2001; Wagenaar 1997), it is a curious circumstance that the research on homeschoolers' motivations so often masks parents' gender and fails to consider how motherhood (and fatherhood) impact individuals' and families' reasons for deciding to homeschool their children.

To make the matter more complicated, studying motivations is tricky because people often have multiple reasons for their behavior, which may not always be fully represented by the predetermined choices they are offered on a survey. Furthermore, the reasons people begin things are not always the reasons they continue to do them. When researchers ask subjects about the reasons they began an activity, it is likely that their current motivations to continue the activity will influence how they retrospectively report their original reasons to begin. Just as retrospection in and of itself may filter responses about past events, so too may identity. Research shows that our self-narratives about the past are heavily influenced by who we understand ourselves to be in the present (e.g., Irvine 1999). Thus when analyzing people's motivations, the best that social scientists can do is to understand that they are capturing people's present understanding about their past behavior. By this logic, it seems imperative that research on homeschoolers' motivations makes demographic and identity-related categories indispensable features of analyses. These disproportionate representations in the homeschooling population – mostly white, middle- and upper-middle class, Evangelical stay-at-home mothers in heterosexual families – require full exploration to reveal how each of these factors, alone and in tandem, influences the decision to homeschool.

There are a few studies that give more explicit attention to parents' identities when analyzing their motivations to homeschool their children. In my own research (Lois 2012) based on in-depth interviews with twenty-four homeschooling mothers, I found that mothers' identities significantly factored into their homeschooling motivations. For instance, when I asked mothers about their decision to homeschool, they always framed their answers primarily in terms of how they thought of themselves as mothers, rather than as Christians or New-Agers, for example, and more than anything else, tied their decision in some way to their status as *stay-at-home mothers*. In the process, they frequently discussed whether homeschooling was their preferred educational choice or an acceptable alternative to some other unavailable option. I called these groups "first-choice" and "second-choice" homeschoolers respectively. Nineteen of the twenty-four mothers in my sample were first-choicers because they believed that homeschooling was a logical extension of their commitment to stay at home with their young children, one that fell into place easily because it "felt right," even as their children aged. The remaining five mothers were second-choicers because they struggled with the pros and cons of extending this stay-at-home commitment beyond their children's preschool years and frequently wished for an acceptable alternative to homeschooling.

When I sorted mothers by first- and second-choice motivations, I found that these groupings disrupted the previous categories that researchers have identified. For example, many first-choice homeschoolers were ideologues, but I also found ideologues among the second-choicers, who would have preferred to send their children to private Christian school but could not afford the tuition. Likewise, I found some pedagogues who were first-choicers, and others who were second-choicers because they thought their children's educational needs would be better served in the right school setting. Thus, the distinction between ideologues and pedagogues (or other categories, for that matter) did not hold across my first-choice/second-choice dichotomy. My conceptualization does not invalidate previous categories, but rather demonstrates the importance of preserving a gendered analytic lens to ferret out the complexity of homeschoolers' experiences.

Another study that has made strides in understanding homeschoolers' motivations is Fields-Smith and Williams' (2009) interview-based study of Black homeschoolers. They found that the majority of mothers in their study did not have a predisposition to stay-at-home motherhood. In fact, leaving the workforce was very difficult, especially for those who had earned college degrees, because older relatives disapprovingly viewed it as sacrificing their financial independence. This perspective was highly salient to these homeschoolers' identities as Black women; they felt that leaving their careers was betraying the Black community because it represented an "abandonment of hopes and dreams of two generations…[and] of the rewards obtained from a long struggle toward equality in the workplace" (2009, 381). Despite this significant conflict, these mothers chose to homeschool for "ethnological" reasons: because they were concerned about the negative racial environment their children – especially their sons – experienced in conventional schools (see also Lundy and Mazama 2014). Focusing on gender- and race-identities in their analysis allowed Fields-Smith and Williams to show how complex homeschoolers' motivations are and the degree to which parents' gender- and race-identities are important determinants in their homeschooling decisions.

The complications of gendered faith motivations

While gender tends to be overlooked in the parental motivation literature on homeschooling, faith is not; it is the most commonly investigated factor in the research on parents' motivations. But this is not without its challenges. For example, one survey listed parents' possible reasons for homeschooling as "dissatisfaction with traditional schools," "religious motives," "protection from unwanted influences," and "maintenance of the family unit," (Chapman and O'Donoghue 2000, 24), and another asked parents to rank such motivations as "better socialization through family and community life," "Godly prescription," "parents in a better position to educate," "parental responsibility," "peer dependence," "negative experiences in school," and "curriculum enrichment" (Brabant, Bourdon, and Jutras 2003, 117–118). However, the highly complex nature of faith and its role in people's lives makes studying faith-related motivation impossible to assess through survey research, as evidenced by the widely disparate statistics that exist on the topic. For example, in 2007 the National Household Education Surveys Program (2008) collected data from a small number of homeschoolers as part of a larger, representative sample of Americans. Of these homeschooling respondents, 83% reported that they did so "to provide religious or moral instruction" (up from 72% in 2003), but only 36% gave this as their "most important" reason. With such inconsistent phrasing of faith-motivation indicators, it's no wonder there are such vastly different conclusions drawn about how "religious" homeschoolers are. Given this ambiguity, it becomes nearly impossible for survey research to accurately assess how religion influences parents' decision to homeschool.

The problem with measuring motivations in these ways, especially when trying to draw conclusions about the role of religion, is that many of the motivations provided in fixed-choice survey questions may be measuring some aspect of faith they do not intend. For example, parents may be concerned about "peer dependence" for reasons that are specifically faith-based – or not. Yet researchers often decide which of these measures reflect parents' religious motivations and which do not (see Brabant, Bourdon, and Jutras (2003) for an example of how such motivations are sorted into categories), and then make claims such as "motivations directly related to God and religion rank at the lowest level of importance" (Brabant, Bourdon, and Jutras 2003, 126), contradicting findings such as those I reported above, which suggest the polar opposite. Apple (2004) has discussed how religion may underlie many of the motives that other researchers assume are distinct from faith, such as parents wanting a closer relationship with their children, their dissatisfaction with schools, and their desire to instill "morality" and "character" in their children. The most credible studies do indicate that Evangelical Christian homeschoolers constitute a disproportionately large portion of the homeschooling population, so examining faith-based motivations is essential to understanding homeschoolers' motivations overall.

However, since traditional gender roles are such a large part of most conservative religions (the most common faiths among the homeschooling population – see Kunzman 2009), it seems that any discussion of faith as a motivator should include a gendered analysis since the prescriptions for Godly motherhood are distinctly different than those for Godly fatherhood. Thus, because fundamentalist Christian beliefs are so prevalent in the homeschooling population, and because they interact so strongly with gender, the most complete picture of homeschoolers' motivations must include in-depth qualitative analysis of both gender and faith.

To that end, some research does address the role of faith in mothers' decisions to homeschool. For instance, several studies have revealed that Evangelical Christian mothers report being "called by God" to homeschool their children (Fields-Smith and Williams 2009; Lois 2012; Sherfinski 2014; Stevens 2001), which they understand as a spiritual imperative to live up to their duties as "Godly women" (Stevens 2001). Stevens' (2001) work most deeply explores this gender–faith intersection, and in the process, reveals that this is indeed an important factor in understanding some mothers' motivation to homeschool. Through in-depth interviews with homeschooling parents, field notes of homeschooling events, and a content analysis of homeschooling magazines and other printed material, Stevens shows that Christian mothers understood their role as being "in service" to their children whereas fathers saw themselves as "benevolent leaders," overseeing the family more broadly (see also Joyce's 2009 journalistic account of the Quiverfull movement). The anti-feminist rhetoric of some vocal Christian proponents of homeschooling help Stevens make a convincing case that many homeschooling mothers decide to homeschool for reasons that are intricately tied to both gender and faith. Though other research has given in-depth attention to the role of evangelical Christianity in parents' motivations to homeschool (e.g., Kunzman 2009; Sherfinski 2014; Sherfinski and Chesanko 2014), Stevens' work makes the largest contribution to the complex interplay of faith and gender as important motivational factors.

Gender Role Ideology in the Family as Facilitator

Since homeschooling takes a great deal of resources and work on parents' part, even those who are "motivated" to homeschool do not always have the ability to do it, thus research should also examine how families implement (or fail to implement) homeschooling. Given that mothers are more likely to be the primary parent-teachers, it stands to reason that gender takes an even more pronounced role in conquering the logistics required to homeschool than can be captured in attitudinal survey research examining parents' motivations only. Yet in the research that investigates the factors that facilitate families' ability to homeschool, the discussion again tends to be degendered, which limits our understanding of how gender ideology may influence who homeschools and why.

According to Bauman's (2002) analysis of several national household surveys from the late 1990s, one of the strongest predictors of homeschooling, as I mentioned earlier in this chapter, is the presence of a "non-working adult in the household" (2002, 10). This was the situation for 60% of the homeschooled children in Bauman's data set, compared to 30% of non-homeschooled children. Of course substantial research shows that these "non-working" adults are much more likely to be mothers than fathers, not just among homeschooling families (Aurini and Davies 2005; Bauman 2002; Lundy and Mazama 2014; Mayberry et al. 1995; Sherfinski 2014; Sherfinski and Chesanko 2014; Stevens 2001; Wagenaar 1997) but also US families in general (e.g., Bianchi, Robinson, and Milkie 2006; Stone 2007). This demographic pattern justifies the importance of understanding how gender ideology in families – for instance the "choice" some women make to stay out of the paid labor force – affects homeschoolers. Yet, as with the studies of parents' motivations, the research on the factors that facilitate families' entry into homeschooling also tends to degender the discussion, particularly with respect to family ideologies, which tend to be highly gendered and reverberate through many areas of family life.

For example, in the interview phase of their study, Klein and Poplin (2008) interviewed ten "parents," all of whom were mothers, even though in one of those households the primary parent-teacher was a father. As the female interviewees talked about the challenges of homeschooling, some mentioned sacrificing "career opportunities." Klein and Poplin's analysis, however, neutralizes the gendered nature of these data by continually attributing mothers' comments to "parents," despite the great potential that mothers' and fathers' gender ideologies significantly shape what it means to sacrifice "career opportunities" to prioritize family.

Similarly, in noting that homeschooling is becoming less stigmatized in Canada, Aurini and Davies (2005) cite several sources of this growing acceptance, from neoliberal ideologies to human capital theory. They argue, however, that these previous explanations are incomplete because they do not take into account the "expressive motives of homeschoolers" (2005, 469). Aurini and Davies' argument therefore debunks the market logic of previous explanations and replaces it with "expressive logic" because North American parents increasingly perceive children as "too precious to be entrusted to the care of others" (2005, 469; see also Stevens 2001). The researchers support the significance of this expressive logic by noting that "many homeschooling families make enormous financial and career sacrifices," and explain that some of their interviewees "left secure, well-paying jobs and risked their financial status to enter a highly uncertain venture" (2005, 470). They go on to cite Bauman's (2002) finding that "the strongest predictor of home schooling is having a non-working adult in the household" (Aurini and Davies 2005, 470).

Yet Aurini and Davies continue to refer to "parents" and the "intensive parenting" that has come to dominate scholarly analyses of child-rearing, even though the "expressive logic" of parenting derives directly from the ideology of intensive *mothering*, a gender-specific theory developed by Hays (1996), whom Aurini and Davies cite. More curious still, in describing their interview data with seventy-five "key actors" in the homeschooling movement (parents among them), they do not provide any numerical breakdown of their sample demographics, particularly the gender of the parents they interviewed. The data they use in their article do seem to suggest, however, that Aurini and Davies' sample is highly gendered. For example, in the seven snippets of qualitative data they provide, respondents' gender is identifiable in six of them – and all are mothers.

Thus, gender ideology is not only a puzzling omission in some of this homeschooling research; its absence almost certainly obscures some of the realities for homeschooling families and the expressive logic they employ in making these sacrifices for their children. In fact, Stambach and David (2005) observe a similar degendering trend in their research. They note that the resource guides and trade books marketed toward the homeschooling community often include gender in the title ("mother" or "father") but then treat the reader as "parents." They "use *parent* for both mothers and fathers, even when they are not interchangeable" (2005, 1645). Stambach and David see this as an oversight because of mothers' key role in family and education decisions, citing the "ideology of intensive mothering" as an analytical tool that can help us understand homeschooling "parents'" experiences. I concur, particularly with respect to examining homeschooling mothers' willingness to stay home.

A great deal of previous research (including Hays' on intensive mothering) has shown that gender ideology is an extremely salient factor in parents' decision to leave the workforce for family-related reasons. We know that, compared to men, women are more likely to interrupt or abandon careers to stay home with young children (Bianchi, Robinson, and Milkie 2006), more likely to take low-paying, part-time, flexible jobs outside of their career expertise for family- and child-related reasons (Webber and Williams 2008), experience more strain between the identities of "mother" and "worker" (Hays 1996), and are much more likely to absorb the conflict between the institutions of work and family by sacrificing their career identities (Blair-Loy 2003; Stone 2007). The question of how homeschooling families are able to arrange their roles such that one "parent" is able to stay home is an inherently gendered one, and gender ideology must certainly be a part of this discussion.

When homeschooling research has made gender and gender ideology salient in the analysis, we see more nuanced discussions of the factors that facilitate taking on the substantial commitment of educating one's children. Primarily these analyses revolve around women's identities and negotiating the dual pressures of family and career (or lack thereof). Indeed, the growth of the homeschooling movement is best understood in relation to women's developing social roles and subsequent identities. In his historical analysis, Gaither (2008) links the rise of homeschooling, in part, to the changes in women's roles and gender ideologies in the 20th century. Gaither discusses how postwar family- and gender ideologies set the stage for the cultural revolution, and once it began, second-wave feminism pushed ideas about women's roles further than before. As a result, two significant branches of gender-ideology emerged for women: the hippie left and the (largely) religious right. Both of these movements "refused to show deference to established leaders and institutions," which led some mothers to reject public schooling (2008, 113). Those gendered ideological roots of homeschooling, Gaither shows, are crucial to understanding not only the realities of the movement today, but also the way some perceive it as feminist and others as entirely anti-feminist (2008, 224). In focusing on how the meaning of family has changed over time, Gaither clearly illustrates that gender ideology has been an integral part of homeschooling from the beginning.

In contemporary analyses, Stevens' (2001) ethnography paved the way for understanding homeschooling in terms of gender, particularly the chapter in which he delves into the gender ideologies of the mothers he interviewed. One aspect of this analysis is the detailed comparison between his liberal subjects (the "inclusives") and his religious subjects (the "believers") in terms of their maternal ideologies. He found that the inclusives' understanding of themselves as "natural" mothers helped them see homeschooling as an obvious fit for them and their families because it meshed well with their other natural mothering ideologies, such as homebirthing, extended breastfeeding, and vegetarianism. Stevens' religious subjects, on the other hand, often realized it was not God's plan for them to work as well as to raise children, which prompted those mothers who had been working in the paid labor force to quit, despite financial hardship. Their decision to dedicate themselves to homeschooling their children, which they saw as "divine intervention" (2001, 95), helped them embrace God's vision for "Godly Womanhood," a distinct gender ideology that was clearly important in facilitating their entry into homeschooling.

Despite these differences between the inclusives and the believers, Stevens devotes quite a bit of analysis to their common goal of trying to reconcile the contradictory demands of contemporary motherhood (see Hays 1996) and the cultural "choice" foisted upon them between self (career) and children (stay-at-home motherhood). Stevens finds that both sets of mothers may use homeschooling to resolve some of these tensions:

> Homeschooling women may appear to make their peace with the [work-family] dilemma by coming down squarely on the side of motherhood. But a closer look reveals that their choice is more nuanced than that….While it may look traditional at first blush, home schooling's dramatically expanded motherhood is also subtly in keeping with liberal feminist demands that contemporary women be more than "just" housewives (2001, 76).

In this sense, both groups of homeschooling mothers have much in common, yet Stevens gives such detailed attention to their gender- and faith-ideologies that he is able to draw out even finer distinctions to show exactly how they reconciled these tensions. The believers used homeschooling to integrate their traditional gender ideologies with more contemporary definitions of "ideal womanhood," whereas the inclusives used homeschooling to come to terms with staying out of the workforce. Homeschooling allowed both groups a "renovated domesticity – a full-time motherhood made richer by the tasks of teaching, and some of the status that goes along with those tasks" (2001, 83; see also Sherfinski 2014).

My own research (Lois 2012) also examines how gender ideology facilitates mothers' entry into homeschooling, particularly when comparing first-choice and second-choice homeschoolers. First-choice homeschoolers, who rarely, if ever, sought other educational options, talked a great deal about how their powerful feelings for their children pulled them to stay at home full time, rather than enter or return to the paid labor force. They loved being stay-at-home mothers and considered homeschooling the perfect way to continue being home with their children. However, first-choicers tied their homeschooling decision to stay-at-home motherhood in two different ways. Some had emotional epiphanies upon becoming mothers, which made their decision to stay at home full time a monumental one; after that, the choice to homeschool was trivial. For other first-choicers, staying at home was a given part of their gender ideology; the difficult decision came later, when they considered homeschooling.

Homeschooling was second choice for five of the twenty-four mothers in my sample, all of whom expressed real difficulty – ideologically and practically – in staying at home with their school-age children. Four women in this group had chosen to be stay-at-home mothers for at least one child's preschool years, but all had planned to send their children to conventional schools at age five (some did so) and return to the workforce. However, at some point their conventional-school choice became unavailable, and they chose homeschooling as an alternative, which meant extending their commitment to stay at home with their children. The adjustment was hard on them, and they often talked about it at length. In contrast to first-choicers, who fully embraced stay-at-home motherhood, second-choice homeschoolers struggled with equating the intense love they had for their children with their commitment to stay at home indefinitely. Therefore, second-choicers' maternal ideologies made it harder for them to come to grips with extending the stay-at-home commitment for one of two reasons: either their children were not thriving in their conventional schools and the alternatives were not feasible, or their husbands' own gender- and family-ideologies pressured them to embrace the extended, homeschooling version of stay-at-home motherhood. I found that mothers' satisfaction with their homeschooling roles were tightly bound to their gender and mothering ideologies. Together Stevens' and my own work illustrate some of the intricately gendered family dynamics at play for homeschooling parents.

Though I have argued that gender ideology is essential in analyzing the factors that facilitate families' ability to homeschool, we know from feminist research that gender intersects with other identity categories that significantly influence how people see and experience the world. For this reason, Fields-Smith and Williams' (2009) study of Black homeschoolers provides important insight into how gender and race intersect for Black women in terms of adopting a more traditional gender ideology to stay out of the workforce. Although the researchers do not explicitly describe the gender breakdown of the "parents" they studied, it appears as though twenty-three of the twenty-four parents were mothers. Interestingly, unlike the few studies that examine the influence of conservative Christianity on gender ideology and show it is a factor in women's predisposition to stay out of the workforce (Lois 2012; Stevens 2001), Fields-Smith and Williams' study illuminates the opposite dynamic. Despite the highly religious nature of their sample (twenty-one out of twenty-four reported that faith played a role in their decision to homeschool; six of those twenty-one said God led them to homeschool), these educated Black women were loath to leave the workforce because, as I mentioned earlier, some in the Black community would view it as "abandonment of the hopes and dreams of two generations" and as a disregard for "the rewards obtained from a long struggle toward equality in the workplace" (2009, 381). Though most of the study does not focus on parents' gender per se, this analytical nugget about Black homeschoolers' (96% of whom were mothers) ideologies reveals the complexity with which gender, race, and social class impinge on women's decisions and ability to homeschool.

Thus the question of how homeschooling families are able to arrange their roles such that one "parent" is able to stay home is an inherently gendered one, though very little of the homeschooling research has approached the question from this angle. Gender ideology matters because there are extensive implications for what parents give up to stay home, depending on their gender, and it's clear that overwhelmingly in the homeschooling community, these stay-at-home parents are mothers. What are the consequences for homeschooling mothers in terms of career and wage sacrifice? On their share of the household labor? On their sense of maternal identity? Degendering the discussion of these questions as well as the factors that facilitate "parents'" entry into homeschooling does a disservice to the social-scientific understanding of homeschoolers' experiences.

Challenges in the Homeschooling Experience

A minority of homeschooling studies deal with families' and mothers' day-to-day experiences. A review of this literature reveals that the three main challenges – workload stress, time sacrifice, and being judged – are all gender-related, yet some research attends to the gendered elements more than others.

Workload stress

Research shows that homeschoolers often feel stress and over-commitment because of what Mayberry et al. (1995, 49) call the immense "physical and psychological workloads." There are two aspects to this problem: one is the unequal burden of household labor placed on the parent doing the homeschooling, and the second is the emotional strain and burnout that result.

Some of the homeschooling research in this vein does focus specifically on mothers, showing that part of this psychological workload arises from their insecurity about covering specific subjects they do not feel prepared to teach, such as math and science (Mayberry 1992), or from a generalized fear that they will miss crucial elements of their children's education (Fields-Smith and Williams 2009; Lois 2006; Sherfinski 2014; Stevens 2001). Some studies suggest that these fears are more common among beginning homeschoolers, but attenuate with increased experience and support from veteran homeschoolers (Lois 2006; Stevens 2001). A second source of the psychological workload stems from the physical workload Mayberry et al. refer to. Many homeschooling parents are full-time homemakers, parents to other children, and spouses. The challenge of juggling all of these role responsibilities is overwhelming enough, but when educating children is added to the workload, it can significantly stress the primary homeschooling parent, which in most cases, as we have seen, is the mother (Fields-Smith and Williams 2009; Lois 2006; Mayberry et al. 1995; Sherfinski 2014; Stevens 2001). Since this gendered pattern is so salient, it makes sense that the research on workload gives dedicated attention to gender. However, when studies do not, several significant features of the homeschooling experience are lost.

For example, as discussed previously, Klein and Poplin's (2008) survey- and interview-samples were highly gendered: of 146 surveys returned, 98% were from mothers, and of their subsequent ten in-depth interviews, 100% were with mothers. Their research revealed the significant stress associated with the complexities of managing a homeschooling household:

> The juggling of children at various levels, organization and timing of different activities, independent and directed work, and integration of faith activities and other outside activities reveal a highly complex, delicately balanced day that requires extensive coordination and direction by parents (2008, 392).

Klein and Poplin's choice to use "parents" in lieu of "mothers" severely limits our understanding of these dynamics. In degendering their analysis, they erase women's immense contributions to this family project and obscure the gendered realities most homeschooling families face.

This is notable because a great deal of sociological research on families has demonstrated that how much time mothers have, along with the ways they use it, significantly impacts their experiences and identities as mothers. Much of this literature has focused on the gendered division of labor in the home, quantitatively examining the "second shift" (Hochschild 1989) of household work that women perform relative to their male partners. Studies find that in general, women perform two to three times more housework and childcare than their male partners, who, since the 1960s, have been very reluctant to increase their contributions to this work (Coltrane 2000). The result is that married mothers – both those who work in the paid labor force and those who don't – feel strapped for time and become emotionally exhausted from trying to juggle all of their domestic responsibilities with very little husband support (Bianchi, Robinson, and Milkie 2006; Blair-Loy 2003; Hochschild 1989; Stone 2007; Webber and Williams 2008). These dynamics are exacerbated in families with significantly more household labor, which is why examining how this work is accomplished along gendered lines is crucial to understanding the experiences of homeschooling families.

When homeschooling research does focus on the gendered division of labor, it finds that indeed women do the lion's share of the daily work (e.g., Mayberry et al. 1995; Sherfinski 2014; Stevens 2001), and whereas some fathers do contribute and thus decrease mothers' stress (Lois 2006), most fathers tend to be in support roles, if they are involved at all. Stevens (2001) found that fathers tended to talk about how homeschooling is great in theory; mothers talked about how it is hard in practice. His and other research has shown that when homeschooling parents explain the gendered division of labor, typically mothers plan and execute the daily lesson plans, organize schedules, and keep children motivated. When we compare this work with fathers' homeschooling contributions, we see power and status emerge: fathers "help" mothers by doing impromptu activities that both parents consider to be an occasionally important, but mostly unreliable, part of the homeschooling (Lois 2012; Stevens 2001); by serving as "principal" of the homeschool to discipline the children if needed (Kunzman 2009); and by "bankroll[ing] the whole thing" so their wives can stay out of the workforce and homeschool the children (Kunzman 2009, 29).

Some studies even show that fathers may occasionally pose an additional challenge that adds to the mother's workload. Kunzman provides a poignant example in his qualitative study when he describes a father who believed that his role was "backing up Mom," because she was the one doing the bulk of the homeschooling work. However, this very father, because of his seasonal work schedule, was home for long stretches in the day and "spen[t] his time watching TV and playing video games, disrupting the homeschool routine" (2009, 55). Rich gendered data like these demonstrate that it is imperative to examine homeschooling through a gendered lens, as the labor it adds so often threatens to deepen gender inequality at home.

My own work (Lois 2006) has found that mothers' anxiety, both from fear of failure and increased workload, initially prompted them to intensify their curricular structure, which only increased their labor and stress and often led to emotional burnout (see also McDonald and Lopes 2014; Sherfinski 2014; Sherfinski and Chesanko 2014). As they gained experience homeschooling and learned from seasoned homeschoolers, most mothers eventually adjusted in two ways. First, they relaxed their high standards for housework, which they understood as prioritizing their children (see also Stevens 2001). This shift was both logistical in that it opened up more time in mothers' schedules, as well as ideological in that it freed them from the identity "failure" of having a messy house. Meanwhile, prioritizing homeschooling their children rooted their identities more firmly in their mothering roles. The second type of adjustment mothers made was developing confidence that their children would learn without a highly structured curriculum. Indeed, the move from a structured to unstructured curriculum is one of the most common findings in the homeschooling literature (Charvoz 1988; Knowles 1988; Mayberry et al. 1995; Stevens 2001; Van Galen 1988). Some of these studies have delved deeper to reveal that de-structuring the curriculum accompanies mothers' shift from compartmentalizing education and family to thinking about the two more "holistically" and as an "integral and ongoing part of family life" (Mayberry et al. 1995, 50). This change in perspective significantly eases the workload stress for mothers, though it does not eradicate it entirely (see Kunzman 2009; Lois 2006; Stevens 2001). From the little research that does exist on the challenges of conquering the labor of homeschooling, we can see that gender matters and has significant, lasting impacts on *mothers'* ability to juggle household responsibilities over the years it takes to educate children at home.

Time sacrifice

There are additional challenges for homeschooling mothers, however, beyond their lack of time to bear the disproportionate burden of household labor. Two studies examine this time issue more subjectively and ask how homeschooling mothers willingly sustain this level of sacrifice for their children over time. This question is intricately entwined with the social construction of good mothering, which is yet another reason homeschooling must be examined with a gendered lens.

Stevens' (2001) qualitative study of the homeschooling movement gives particular attention to mothers' understanding of sacrifice. The mothers in his study homeschooled despite the immense domestic burden because it resonated with how they defined good mothering. They thought about their maternal roles in terms of "delayed gratification," where they put their own wants aside to meet their children's "needs" (2001, 86). Mothers in my own qualitative longitudinal study understood time sacrifice similarly, making statements such as "there will be time for me later to pursue anything that interests me" (Lois 2010, 434). These rationales for maternal sacrifice are interesting in that they suggest a subjugation of the self for one's children, and in this sense align closely with the mainstream definition of good mothering (see Hays 1996). Yet embracing this mainstream definition in and of itself infrequently leads mothers into homeschooling. Therefore, both Stevens and I dig deeper into homeschooling mothers' rationales and uncover different but complementary facets of the phenomenon.

Stevens' research reveals that the secular homeschooling mothers he studied (the inclusives) "make sense of their extraordinary commitment by rendering it invisible" (2001, 87). These mothers embraced child-centered pedagogies and reaffirmed their "natural" role to prioritize their children's potential. Because "natural mothers" understood their homeschooling in this way, they tended to overlook the gendered costs for homeschooling mothers such as increased household labor and decreased time and career opportunities relative to their husbands, as well as relative to non-homeschooling mothers. In contrast, the "believers" Stevens studied made their maternal roles quite visible because they viewed their homeschooling as part of women's domestic role in God's "divine plan" (2001, 87). These gendered rationalizations were crucial to these women's prolonged commitment to educating their children.

My own qualitative study (Lois 2010) of homeschooling mothers also raises some questions about mothers' extended commitment to their children. Though some of the time-related challenges homeschoolers discussed seemed related to the household division of labor (as I have mentioned earlier), some of the temporal issues mothers raised were not easily quelled by doing less housework, de-structuring their curriculum, and asking their husbands to contribute more. It seemed that these other responsibilities – childcare, housework, and homeschooling – trumped mothers' personal time, which consistently got pushed to the bottom of their priority lists. I heard countless mothers say that they had put their "own life on hold" to homeschool their children (see also McDonald and Lopes 2014; Stevens 2001). They had "absolutely no time for myself," because they were with their kids "twenty-four hours a day, seven days a week," and were "devoting every particle" of themselves to their children.

The homeschooling mothers I studied had mixed feelings about having no discretionary time to pursue their own interests. Though they were happy to live up to the ideals of good mothering by devoting an enormous amount of time to their children, they also wished for what they called "me-time." The lack of personal time created a great deal of stress, which mothers tried to alleviate by managing their time – reserving a small quantity for themselves every week. This strategy inevitably failed, however, and I saw that mothers resorted to "temporal emotion work": managing their feelings by manipulating their subjective experiences of time. Homeschooling mothers performed temporal emotion work in two ways. First, they learned to compartmentalize phases of their lives according to their children's development, a strategy Garey (1999) and Bobel (2002) have called "sequencing" in their research on other (non-homeschooling) mothers. Sequencing helped homeschooling mothers justify the disproportionate amount of time they devoted to their children while they were young. They feared looking back someday and regretting not having spent enough time with them. Second, mothers in my study also focused intently on the present and "savored" their time with their children to get the most out of their moment-to-moment relationships. These two temporal-emotional strategies helped mothers assuage any resentment over their lack of discretionary time and continue their extraordinary commitment to homeschooling their children. When qualitative research explores homeschooling "parents'" experiences in depth, we see many more ways gender matters and runs deep in homeschooling families' experiences.

Being judged

A third significant challenge for homeschoolers is being judged negatively for not enrolling their children in conventional schools. The unconventional educational choice prompts many people outside homeschooling circles to question homeschooling parents' decisions and to insist they justify their choice (Fields-Smith and Williams 2009; Lois 2009; Mayberry et al. 1995; Stevens 2001). Most of the practical literature on homeschooling acknowledges the stigma parents experience for their choice – indeed much of it goes to great lengths to explain why homeschooling might be a *better* educational route (see for example Holt's *Teach Your Own* (1981), Moore and Moore's *Home Grown Kids* (1984), and Gatto's *Dumbing Us Down* (1991)) and thereby provides ready rationales for parents to defend themselves. Yet despite the frequency with which homeschooling advocates discuss outsiders' misperceptions, relatively little of the scholarly literature has given detailed attention to this aspect of homeschooling parents' experience.

Homeschooling scholars do recognize and report the stigma of homeschooling. Via parents' extended narratives, Mayberry et al.'s (1995) research included detailed descriptions of how family members, school personnel, and friends negatively judged their homeschooling choice. Fields-Smith and Williams' work gives slightly more analytical attention to the impact of "negative comments from family members, friends or strangers" on parents' decision to homeschool (2009, 384). The Black homeschoolers they studied struggled with elder family members' beliefs that homeschooling mothers "sacrifice" their education and "waste" it at home with their children (and thereby negate the hard-won gains of the Civil Rights movement, as I discussed earlier in this chapter). The Black mothers in this study, however, saw their homeschooling instead as a noble pursuit – a sign they were dedicated to their children – who in conventional schools experienced "limited possibilities and opportunities" because of interpersonal stereotyping and institutional racism (see also Lundy and Mazama 2014). Though Fields-Smith and Williams gloss over some of the gendered implications of mothers being far more likely than fathers to stay out of the workforce, they do draw attention to the ways racial and ethnic ideologies may impede mothers from embracing the culturally dominant standards of good (white, middle-class) mothering.

Homeschoolers in Stevens' (2001) study also discussed feeling negatively judged for their decision to homeschool. He showed how the "natural mothers" and "Godly women" he studied similarly justified their homeschooling choice to outsiders by drawing on the "ideology of intensive mothering" (Hays 1996), by recasting it as "good" mothering because it "requires careful attention to the minute idiosyncrasies that make children individuals[,] constant nurturing of a child's physical and cognitive development[,] and the consistent elevation of children's needs above virtually all other of life's demands" (2001, 75). They do this, Stevens argues, because outsiders cannot dispute homeschoolers' choice when they frame their endeavors in terms of good mothering.

My own research (Lois 2009) similarly reveals that a large part of parents' homeschooling burden is defending their decision to outsiders. Although my data show that some homeschooling fathers had to defend their decision to outsiders, mothers received the brunt of the criticism, not only because they were with children more often and were primarily in charge of the homeschooling, but also because proving good parenting disproportionately falls to mothers over fathers (see Blair-Loy 2003; Hays 1996; and Stone 2007). In addition, when outsiders did criticize fathers, they rarely attacked their paternal responsibilities, whereas when they criticized mothers, they clearly questioned their maternal identities. Therefore, mothers quickly learned to defend themselves by invoking particular justifications to neutralize the stigma of irresponsible mothering – a significant way gender matters in examining homeschooling parents' experiences.

My data further showed that although on the surface, outsiders wanted mothers to explain the deviant behavior of homeschooling, each accusation underneath targeted mothers' deviant *emotions* – specifically their excess emotional intensity – which outsiders assumed underlay mothers' motivation to homeschool. Mothers were cast as deviant not for homeschooling per se, but for allegedly letting their maternal emotions spin out of control, which led to the irresponsible behavior of homeschooling.

The homeschooling mothers I studied defended themselves in four specific ways, aiming each of their justifications at a particular charge of excessive maternal emotional intensity. First, to counter non-homeschoolers' accusations that they felt arrogant about the academic demands of homeschooling, homeschooling mothers cast themselves as appropriately confident because they knew their children better than a teacher could. Second, when they were accused of homeschooling because they were "overprotective," a maternal feeling that would prevent children from developing the skills to function in society, mothers argued that homeschooling appropriately shielded their children from the real dangers present in conventional schools. The third type of stigma homeschoolers bore was that they were self-righteous and morally extreme, feelings that allegedly led them to teach their children values that would forever position them at the margins of society. Homeschooling mothers neutralized these charges of extremism by emphasizing the mainstream view that responsible mothers cultivate their children's moral development and raise upstanding, productive citizens. And fourth, the homeschooling mothers I studied were accused of being hyperengaged with their children – a charge implying that their abnormally strong desire to be emotionally and physically close to their children caused them to be excessively involved with every aspect of their lives. Critics claimed that these intense feelings were a sign of mothers' own psychological "issues" (usually cast as codependency or something similar), and would lead to an unhealthy mother–child bond that would prevent children from developing independence. Homeschooling mothers justified their high level of engagement by avowing the close bond with their children while denying it was unhealthy. They explained that homeschooling fostered these close family relationships, which were in their children's best interests, and this neutralized the stigma of irresponsible mothering. Analyzing the clash between critics' and homeschoolers' definitions of appropriate maternal emotions helps us see not only the extensive challenges of homeschooling, but also the significant gendered impact it may have on homeschooling mothers' identities.

Conclusion

In this chapter, I have contended that the research on homeschooling parents has neglected to flesh out the full extent to which gender impacts families' experiences. We know that mothers are a great deal more likely than fathers to be the primary parent-teachers, and for this reason experience homeschooling differently than their male partners who are overwhelmingly serving as the family's sole wage-earner in the paid labor force. As I have shown, the areas most significantly affected by gender are parents' motivations, their faith, the factors that facilitate their entry into homeschooling, and the challenges they face in the role, such as time-stress and stigmatization from those who disapprove of their choice to homeschool. While some research has attended to the gendered nature of mothers' (and to a lesser extent, fathers') experiences in these areas, other research has disregarded gender entirely, effectively masking the nuances of homeschooling families' experiences. Given these shortcomings in the existing literature, there are several directions scholars may take to bridge this gap in our understanding.

First, research on homeschooling families must take gender into account theoretically and conceptually. Not only will this illuminate some of the subtleties in mothers' experiences within the most common homeschooling family-configuration (stay-at-home, married, heterosexual), it will also allow researchers to give more attention to the experience of fathers, single parents, and LGBTQ-identified parents. These identity categories will prove to be important variables to investigate. Along similar lines, researchers should also attend more intentionally to parents' other identity-relevant categories, particularly race, ethnicity, and socioeconomic status. Crucial insights into homeschooling parents' experiences exist at these points of intersection.

Second, scholars must avoid obscuring gender in their research designs and analyses. For example, surveys should be sure to ask which parent is the primary homeschooling parent, and if at all possible, solicit data from that parent. When the non-teaching parent fills out a questionnaire speaking for the teaching parent's experiences, the validity of those data may be compromised. There are many studies that seemingly do not attend to this issue; at the very least, researchers must be cognizant of who they are receiving data from and be proactive in discussing the implications in their work. We have much to learn from every parent in all types of homeschooling families, but if we do not capture the gendered specifics, our understanding will not progress.

References

Apple, Michael W. 2004. "Away with All Teachers: The Cultural Politics of Home Schooling." In *Pedagogy of Place: Seeing Space as Cultural Education*, edited by David M. Callejo Perez, Stephen M. Fain, and Judith J. Slater, 149–173. New York: Peter Lang.

Arai, A. Bruce. 2000. "Reasons for Home Schooling in Canada." *Canadian Journal of Education* 25: 204–217. DOI:10.2307/1585954

Aurini, Janice, and Scott Davies. 2005. "Choice without Markets: Homeschooling in the Context of Private Education." *British Journal of Sociology of Education*, 26: 461–474. DOI:10.1080/01425690500199834

Bauman, Kurt J. 2002. "Homeschooling in the United States: Trends and Characteristics." *Education Policy Analysis Archives* 10(26): 1–21. Accessed March 31, 2015. http://epaa.asu.edu/ojs/article/view/305/431

Bianchi, Suzanne M., John P. Robinson, and Melissa A. Milkie. 2006. *Changing Rhythms of American Family Life*. New York: Russell Sage.

Blair-Loy, Mary. 2003. *Competing Devotions: Career and Family among Women Executives*. Cambridge, MA: Harvard University Press.

Bobel, Chris. 2002. *The Paradox of Natural Mothering*. Philadelphia, PA: Temple University.

Brabant, Christine, Sylvain Bourdon, and France Jutras. 2003. "Home Education in Quebec: Family First." *Evaluation and Research in Education* 17: 112–131. DOI:10.1080/09500790308668296

Chapman, Anne, and Tom A. O'Donoghue. 2000. "Home Schooling: An Emerging Research Agenda." *Educational Research and Perspectives*, 27: 19–36.

Charvoz, Adrienne. 1988. "Reactions to the Home School Research: Dialogues with Practitioners." *Education and Urban Society*, 21: 85–95. DOI:10.1177/0013124588021001008

Collom, Ed. 2005. "The Ins and Outs of Homeschooling: The Determinants of Parental Motivations and Student Achievement." *Education and Urban Society*, 37: 307–335. DOI:10.1177/0013124504274190

Coltrane, Scott. 2000. "Research on Household Labor: Modeling and Measuring the Social Embeddedness of Routine Family Work." *Journal of Marriage and the Family*, 62: 1208–1233. DOI:10.1111/j.1741-3737.2000.01208.x

Fields-Smith, Cheryl, and Meca Williams. 2009. "Motivations, Sacrifices, and Challenges: Black Parents' Decisions to Home School." *Urban Review*, 41: 369–389. DOI:10.1007/s11256-008-0114-x

Gaither, Milton. 2008. *Homeschool: An American History*. New York: Palgrave Macmillan.

Garey, Anita Ilta. 1999. *Weaving Work and Motherhood*. Philadelphia, PA: Temple University Press.

Gatto, John Taylor. 1991. *Dumbing Us Down: The Hidden Curriculum of Compulsory Schooling*. Gabriola Island, BC: New Society Publishers.

Hays, Sharon. 1996. *The Cultural Contradictions of Motherhood*. New Haven: Yale University Press.

Hochschild, Arlie R. 1989. *The Second Shift*. New York: Avon.

Holt, John. 1981. *Teach Your Own*. New York: Delacorte Press.

Irvine, Leslie. 1999. *Codependent Forevermore: The Invention of Self in a Twelve-Step Group*. Chicago: University of Chicago Press.

Joyce, Kathryn. 2009. *Quiverfull: Inside the Christian Patriarchy Movement*. Boston: Beacon Press.

Klein, Carol, and Mary Poplin. 2008. "Families Home Schooling in a Virtual Charter School System." *Marriage and Family Review*, 43: 369–395. DOI:10.1080/01494920802073221

Knowles, J. Gary. 1988. "Parents' Rationales and Teaching Methods for Home Schooling: The Role of Biography." *Education and Urban Society*, 21: 69–84. DOI:10.1177/0013124588021001007

Knowles, J. Gary. 1991. "Parents' Rationales for Operating Home Schools." *Journal of Contemporary Ethnography* 20: 203–230. DOI:10.1177/089124191020002004

Kunzman, Robert. 2009. *Write These Laws on Your Children: Inside the World of Conservative Christian Homeschooling*. Boston, MA: Beacon Press.

Lois, Jennifer. 2006. "Role Strain, Emotion Management, and Burnout: Homeschooling Mothers' Adjustment to the Teacher Role." *Symbolic Interaction*, 29: 507–530. DOI:10.1525/si.2006.29.4.507

Lois, Jennifer. 2009. "Emotionally Layered Accounts: Homeschoolers' Justifications for Maternal Deviance." *Deviant Behavior*, 30: 201–34. DOI:10.1080/01639620802069783

Lois, Jennifer. 2010. "The Temporal Emotion Work of Motherhood: Homeschoolers' Strategies for Managing Time Shortage." *Gender & Society*, 24: 421–446. DOI:10.1177/0891243210377762

Lois, Jennifer. 2012. *Home Is where the School Is: The Logic of Homeschooling and the Emotional Labor of Mothering*. New York: New York University Press.

Lundy, Garvey, and Ama Mazama. 2014. "'I'm Keeping My Son Home': African American Males and the Motivation to Homeschool." *Journal of African American Males in Education*, 5: 53–73.

Mayberry, Maralee. 1988. "Characteristics and Attitudes of Families Who Home School." *Education and Urban Society*, 21: 32–41. DOI:10.1177/0013124588021001004

Mayberry, Maralee. 1992. "Home-Based Education: Parents as Teachers." *Continuing Higher Education Review*, 56: 48–58.

Mayberry, Maralee, and J. Gary Knowles. 1989. "Family Unity Objectives of Parents Who Teach Their Children: Ideological and Pedagogical Orientations to Home Schooling." *The Urban Review*, 21: 209–225. DOI:10.1007/BF01112403

Mayberry, Maralee, J. Gary Knowles, Brian Ray, and Stacey Marlow. 1995. *Home Schooling: Parents as Educators*. Thousand Oaks, CA: Corwin.

McDonald, Jasmine, and Elaine Lopes. 2014. "How Parents Home Educate Their Children with an Autism Spectrum Disorder with the Support of the Schools of Isolated and Distance Education." *International Journal of Inclusive Education*, 18: 1–17. DOI:10.1080/13603116.2012.751634

Moore, Raymond, and Dorothy Moore. 1984. *Home Grown Kids: A Practical Handbook for Teaching Your Children at Home*. Nashville, TN: W Publishing Group.

National Center for Education Statistics. 2015. "Table 206.20. Percentage Distribution of Students Ages 5 through 17 Attending Kindergarten through 12th Grade, by School Type or Participation in Homeschooling and Selected Child, Parent, and Household Characteristics: 1999, 2003, and 2007." Accessed March 11, 2015. http://nces.ed.gov/programs/digest/d13/tables/dt13_206.20.asp

National Household Education Surveys Program. 2008. "Issue Brief: 1.5 Million Homeschooled Students in the United States in 2007." National Center for Education Statistics. Accessed June 20, 2010. http://nces.ed.gov/pubs2009/2009030.pdf

Ray, Brian D. 2000. "Home Schooling: The Ameliorator of Negative Influences on Learning?" *Peabody Journal of Education*, 75: 71–106. DOI:10.1080/0161956X.2000.9681936

Sherfinski, Melissa. 2014. "Contextualizing the Tools of a Classical and Christian Homeschooling Mother-Teacher." *Curriculum Inquiry*, 44: 169–203. DOI:10.1111/curi.12046

Sherfinski, Melissa, and Melissa Chesanko. 2014. "Disturbing the Data: Looking into Gender and Family Size Matters with US Evangelical Homeschoolers." *Gender, Place, and Culture* (no volume): 1–18. DOI:10.1080/0966369X.2014.991703

Stambach, Amy, and Miriam David. 2005. "Feminist theory and Educational Policy: How Gender Has Been 'Involved' in Family School Choice Debates." *Signs*, 30: 1633–1658. DOI:10.1086/382633

Stevens, Mitchell L. 2001. *Kingdom of Children: Culture and Controversy in the Homeschooling Movement*. Princeton, NJ: Princeton University Press.

Stone, Pamela. 2007. *Opting Out? Why Women Really Quit Careers and Head Home*. Berkeley: University of California Press.

Van Galen, Jane A. 1988. "Ideology, Curriculum, and Pedagogy in Home Education." *Education and Urban Society*, 21: 52–68. DOI:10.1177/0013124588021001006

Wagenaar, Theodore C. 1997. "What Characterizes Home Schoolers? A National Study." *Education* 117: 440–444.

Webber, Gretchen, and Christine Williams. 2008. "Mothers in 'Good' and 'Bad' Part-Time Jobs: Different Problems, Same Results." *Gender & Society*, 22: 752–777. DOI:10.1177/0891243208325698

9

Homeschooling among Ethnic-Minority Populations

Cheryl Fields-Smith

Introduction

Education in the US began with parents holding full responsibility for their children's learning, among indigenous groups and also during colonial times (Gaither 2014; Hiatt-Michael 2000). However, the push for a centralized, public schooling system shifted the responsibility for educating children away from families to formalized, compulsory schooling. Kunzman and Gaither (2013) inform, "From the establishment of large-scale public and private education systems in the United States in the 19th century through the late 1970s, nearly all American children received their formal education in schools. But, beginning in the late 1970s, and increasing steadily since then, the home has become a popular educational locus for an ever expanding number of families across an ever widening swath of the U.S. population" (4). Obtaining accurate homeschool population counts can be challenging due to several factors. Homeschool reporting mandates vary from state to state such that some states require homeschool families to provide notice of their intent to homeschool while other states do not. There are also some states that do not monitor the number of students who are homeschooled. Additionally, some homeschool families may opt to enroll their children in virtual, public charter schools, or even face-to-face classes offered at public schools on a part-time basis, which could include them in the public school count rather than the homeschool population within a state. The National Household Education Survey has been documenting the rising homeschool population since 1999. The most recent report indicates that 1.77 million children were homeschooled for the 2011–2012 school year, representing a more than double increased since 1999 (Noel, Stark, and Redford 2013). Other estimates have suggested that the homeschool population has grown to over two million students (Ray 2014;

The Wiley Handbook of Home Education, First Edition. Edited by Milton Gaither.

Economist 2012). Despite the issues related to accuracy of such reports, all support a trend toward families increasingly choosing to homeschool their children in the US.

Typically, homeschooling has been characterized as a White, middle-class, and conservative phenomenon. In addition, homeschool has frequently been associated with religious fundamentalism. However, demographic data suggests that diversity among the homeschool population has also increased in terms of ethnic or racial background, social class, and religious affiliation. For example, some Muslim immigrants have turned to homeschooling as a way to pass on their religious and cultural traditions, especially to their daughters (MacFarquhar 2008; Economist 2012). Noel, Stark, and Redford (2013) reported US homeschool population demographics as follows: White families (68%), Black families (8%), Hispanic families (15%), and Asian or Pacific Islander families (4%). This chapter will focus on ethnic and racial diversity among homeschooled students in the US.

Homeschool families vary in their motivations to homeschool. Van Galen's (1991) seminal research on homeschooling yielded two categories of homeschool motivations, ideologues and pedagogues, the former representing families who homeschooled because they believed parents should serve as the primary educators for children and the latter representing families who disagreed with the instructional methods found within conventional schools. Fields-Smith and Williams-Johnson's (2009) study of African American home educators found ethnological, or race-based factors that led families to homeschool.

This chapter explores the extent to which Latino and Asian American families' decisions to homeschool represent similar or dissimilar ethnological motivations to Black families. Currently, empirical literature on non-White ethnic groups focuses primarily on African Americans. Research on homeschool families representing other racial and ethnic groups remains scarce. Therefore, this chapter utilizes periodicals, blogs, and organizational reports to extend the scant empirical knowledge and to infer knowledge of Latino homeschool families. A synthesis of the African American research on African American families will be presented first, followed by a synthesis of available literature on Latino homeschool families.

What We Know About African American Homeschool Families

In his inspiring treatise, The Complexities of Black Homeschooling, Apple (2006) acknowledges the significance of African Americans, who have traditionally been oppressed in the US, moving toward home education. Empathizing with the condition of Black education, Apple stated:

> Their reasons are varied and understandable: the tragic rates at which black children are miseducated in or pushed out of public schools; the stereotyping that goes on; the loss of one's cultural and political heritage; and yes, for some, religious motivations are also there. Let us be honest. For all too many children of color in this nation, their own

> schooling experience has been anything but effective and their parents are consistently marginalized by the bureaucratic and often racializing structures that pervade schools and the larger society (2006).

In this section, I demonstrate how the literature on family engagement has undeniably documented the racialized experiences of Black children in traditional schools and the subsequent disenfranchisement of Black parents' advocacy on behalf of their children. In addition, this section will demonstrate the corroboration between family engagement literature and Black parents' motivations to homeschool as documented in the emerging Black homeschool literature.

Relevant Family Engagement Literature

Presumably, children achieve success when the adults in the home, school, and community share responsibility for children's learning (Epstein 2010). While this decades-old conceptual perspective may be true, in reality, differences in cultural beliefs and practices, discriminatory policy and practices, reliance on cultural stereotypes, and an overall belief in the intellectual inferiority of Black children prevent the mutual trust needed to embody shared responsibility among teachers, parents, and administrators, particularly given the sociohistorical legacy of conflict Black families have experienced in US public schools.

Governmental reports and research have documented the plight of many Black children in public schools. For example, the disproportionality in discipline of Black children begins as early as pre-Kindergarten (pre-K), where although Black children made up 18% of the student enrollment across the US, they represented 48% of the children who were suspended from school (USDOE 2014). In comparison, White students made up 43% of the pre-K population, but only 26% of the children suspended from pre-K classrooms. Educational scholars have documented the condition of Black boys labeled as problem children within their classrooms, which has led to disproportionality in discipline referrals for Black children and again, Black males in particular (e.g., Howard 2008; Monroe 2005). Hatt's (2011) yearlong ethnography provided a peek into a kindergarten classroom to understand how the concept of smartness became associated with the ubiquitous "stoplight" variety of disciplinary practice, where students have to move a clip from green to yellow and then to red to indicate "bad" behavior, and shaped students' self-identity and perceptions of their peers along ethnic and social class lines. The scholar documents ways in which a Black male kindergartner named Jackson was negatively positioned within the classroom as result. Hatt reported:

> For many poor students and students of color such as Jackson, they learn early on school is not where they belong or worth investing in, so they begin to disengage. These students may not perceive themselves as "dumb" but may have figured out that

> regardless of talent or effort they will never be identified as smart within the institution of schooling. I maintain this relation is what led Jackson to state he hated school before he had even finished kindergarten (2011, 456).

Interactions such as these are younger versions of the microaggressions described by Howard's (2008) study featuring the narratives of ten Black male middle and high school students in which one student stated, "I watch it all the time. One of us (Black males) do something, and we get suspended or expelled. A White kid does the exact same thing, and he gets a warning, or an after school referral. Sometimes it's so obvious that they treat us different than them" (Howard 2008). Microaggressions occur in the inequitable implementation of policy and interactions among school staff and Black students, such as a male high school senior from Howard's study retelling his experience of not being recognized for being accepted to Morehouse College because the school administrator explained to him, "They were only calling up the kids who were going to 'good colleges,' and they didn't think that Morehouse was a really good college" (973). From pre-k to 12th grade, regardless of achievements and ability, Black children can experience school in ways quite different from their White peers. If school faculty and administrators adhere to inequitable application of school policies, what recourse do Black parents have in advocating for resolution and elimination of such treatment in schools?

Black family engagement literature has documented the marginalization of Black parents' advocacy on behalf of their children; whether they are of middle or low income (e.g., Abrams and Gibbs 2002; Lareau and Horvat 1999). Lareau and Horvat's (1999) and Lareau's (2000) seminal work demonstrates that parents' engagement deemed acceptable by teachers, and therefore most effective, can be characterized as White, middle-class ways of approaching parental involvement. Teachers described acceptable behaviors as supportive of school goals and approaches (Lareau and Horvat 1999). However, when Black middle-class parents questioned a teacher's decision to not allow their daughter to be included in an advanced reading group they had to push harder to advocate, and the teacher perceived them as loud and aggressive. In fact, Black parents' engagement has often been characterized as combative in comparison to White, middle-class perspectives of parental engagement (Cooper 2007; Chapman and Bhopal 2013). These stereotypical characterizations of Black parental engagement have contributed to the disfranchisement of Black parents' ability to serve as agents on behalf of their children in public schools. In their study, Abrams and Gibbs (2002) found that parent-to-parent relationships could break down along racial lines due to negative perspectives of Black parents' engagement style, as when two African American moms complained to a school parent group about a new policy that appeared to exclude them from participating in an after-school program. A White mother interviewed for the study focused on the anger of the two Black moms instead of the validity of their complaints. She dismissed the episode as causing "damage done to a collaborative process because of the time taken up in dealing with two angry women" (401). As Abram and Gibbs explained, "… in many instances the school still possesses the power to practice exclusion or to impede parents' utilization of their cultural capital or their voice. All parents, then, bring some bargaining chips to the table, but the school maintains the power to include or exclude their presence or input" (386). Given these racialized experiences of Black children and their parents' challenges in eradicating them, Black parents' decisions to homeschool represent a form of resistance to avoid these types of destructive experiences and to overcome the marginalization of Black families' engagement in their children's schooling experiences.

Relevant Black Homeschooling Literature

The emerging literature on African American homeschooling reveals several key race-based factors, which correlate with findings from the family engagement literature and effectively push Black families out of conventional schools (public and private). Authors who have contributed to this literature usually highlight the persistent achievement gap between Black students and their White counterparts, high dropout rates, and overall school failure, which contributes to educators' perceptions that Black students are academically inferior (e.g., Fields-Smith and Wells Kisura 2013; Mazama and Lundy 2012; Taylor 2005). However, Black parents' motivations to homeschool become more evident in descriptions of their children's schooling experiences and of their attempts to advocate for their children as told poignantly in their own self-reports, empirical or otherwise.

Introducing her book, which consisted of a collection of essays written by Black home educators and their children, Llewellyn (1996) stated, "…many black people homeschool to save themselves from a system which limits and destroys them, to reclaim their own lives, families, and culture, *to create for themselves something very different from conventional schooling*" (13). Indeed, the empirically based data presented in the scant literature available corroborates many aspects of this statement.

The published research literature on Black homeschooling has focused primarily on understanding Black parents' motivations to educate their children at home rather than at school. These articles represent three different databases of Black homeschool participants. Fields-Smith and Williams-Johnson (2009) present findings from a Metro-Atlanta-based study, Fields-Smith and Wells Kisura (2013) compare findings from the Metro-Atlanta study and a Metro-D.C. dissertation study, and Mazama and Lundy (2012; 2013a; 2014) present data on the largest sample of Black educators across multiple metropolitan areas in the US.

As described by Llewellyn (1996), Fields-Smith and Williams-Johnson (2009) found that Black home educators framed their motivations as a way of protecting their children from "limited possibilities and opportunities" available to their children within conventional schools, public or private. Home educators perceived that their children experienced racism in school in the form of low expectations. As one father explained, by homeschooling, "There isn't any preconceived notion of them [their children] not being able to achieve, and everyone around them has been affirming them"(376). Parents in this study perceived that low expectations could be attributed to school staff's beliefs in an academic inferiority of Black people, males in particular. Black parents also related their decisions to homeschool to the resegregation of their public schools. One mother explained:

> We moved from the suburbs of New Jersey to Georgia, and realized that the school system here was very segregated so where race is concerned home schooling was one of the decisions we had to make because of the segregation. In our neighborhood, many children are bussed north where the schooling is better, but they travel over an hour just to get to school. That wasn't an option for us. (378).

This Metro-Atlanta school district, like many other urban school districts, had become resegregated under the loosening of desegregation mandates. Residents in the southern portion of the school district consisted of predominantly Black and Hispanic families, and therefore the racial composition of the schools had similar patterns. But the northern portion of the school district had a predominantly White composition. Parents perceived that schools located in the northern portion of the school district had better resources, but their access to enrolling in those schools was limited by district policies. The twenty-four Metro-Atlanta home educators represented in Fields-Smith and Williams-Johnson (2009) did not prioritize religion as a primary motivating factor in their decision to homeschool. Instead, religion or spirituality supported their decision to homeschool, and their homeschool practice became a way to integrate academic learning and faith-based learning.

Similarly, Fields-Smith and Wells Kisura's (2013) comparative study of Black home educators in Metro-Atlanta and the Metro-D.C. area found similar beliefs related to the role of race in parents' home schooling decisions. The findings expand our understanding of the context of schooling for Black males in both metropolitan areas. Home educators in both cities and surrounding areas reported experiences where their boys had been labeled troublemakers in their classrooms similar to the experiences of Black males in the conventional school literature.

Using a conceptual framework of Afrocentricity, Mazama and Lundy (2012, 2013a, 2014) have published a collection of articles based on their study of seventy-four Black home school families in three different US geographic regions (Mid-Atlantic, South Atlantic and Midwest). Data sources for this study included interviews, participant observation, surveys, and focus group sessions. Participants resided in major metropolitan areas including Philadelphia, Washington DC, New York, Atlanta, and cities located in South Carolina and Delaware as well. Combined, the findings from each of these publications conceptualize Black homeschooling as necessary to guard Black children's positive cultural identity. The authors further explained, "African American parents' inspiration to homeschool their children was often couched as a desire to protect one's child from possible racist actions or, as is often the case, as a reaction to an egregious racist incident when their children attended school" (Mazama and Lundy 2012, 728). In short, Black families choose to homeschool to counter the need to fight against institutional and individual racism experienced in schools.

Throughout Llewellyn's (1996) text, Black families frame their homeschool motivations in terms of the freedoms from constraints found in conventional schooling. Similarly, across each of the studies conducted on Black homeschooling, whether using Afrocentricity, Critical Race Theory, or Black Feminist Theory, researchers have found that Black parents also decide to homeschool their children in order to provide them with a culturally compatible learning experience. Homeschooling enables Black home educators to infuse an African American perspective as they learn about history, science, or any other subject by teaching children the contributions of Black innovators within their field of study. Making culturally relevant connections has long been held as critical in multicultural education (e.g., Irvine 1991), yet mandates such as No Child Left Behind and Race to the Top, which touted greater educational accountability through high stakes test scores and merit pay for teachers, have led to a tendency to focus on teaching to tests instead of teaching to student interests, including cultural relevance. This narrowing of the curriculum can leave African American children believing that their history begins with slavery and ends with Martin Luther King (Mazama and Lundy 2012). By authentically embedding a culturally relevant focus in their practice, Black homeschool parents enhance their children's self-identity and naturally maintain their children's motivation to learn.

Cultural relevance in instruction supports Black families' desire to have their children experience learning that facilitates transmission of their cultural values, which is important to families of all cultural backgrounds. Black home educator and creator of homeschool magazine *The Drinking Gourd* Nichols-White (1996) wrote, "I have been contacted by people of different races, ethnic groups, and religions throughout the world. The most constant message I receive from these people is that they want to be able to maintain their culture, history and identity. It seems that schools are designed to destroy what is most important to the people they supposedly serve" (72).

In the same way, Black families report that their decisions to homeschool enable them to imbue their religious beliefs into their children's learning. The available studies of Black education suggest diversity among the intensity and role of religion in parents' decisions to homeschool, with minimal representation of the "God made me do it" type of motivation. Fields-Smith and Williams-Johnson (2009) found that parents' religion or spirituality supported their decisions to homeschool rather than serving as the impetus of their homeschooling. Mazama and Lundy (2014) found that within their sample of seventy-four Black homeschool families, 15% or 11 families prioritized their religious beliefs over race when describing their rationale for homeschooling. The authors likened these Black home educators' views to the White Christian fundamentalist perspective. Unlike the majority of other Black homeschoolers represented in the research, these fundamentalist Christian Black parents do not necessarily name racial discrimination in schools as a factor in their homeschool decision. In fact, it could be inferred that Black families who homeschool from birth may be highly represented by this Black Christian fundamentalist perspective.

The incipient literature focused on Black homeschooling accentuates the issue of racism in public schools and at the same time demonstrates that African American families are not monolithic. This body of literature as a whole also provides a counter-narrative to the discourse suggesting Black families do not care about their children's education. Apple's (2006) empathy for Black parents who choose to homeschool ends with his devotion to the purposes of public schools and the ideology of democracy. But when Black families decide to homeschool, they do so in contrast to their longstanding legacy of looking to public schools for cultural uplift and mobility. Moving away from this critical heritage signals Black families' growing lack of confidence in the ability of public schools to fulfill this dream for their children. In the context of school choice, it is their right to choose the educational alternative they believe will be the right fit for their children, not just academically, but also socially, spiritually, and psychologically. For a growing number of Black families, schooling at home addresses these concerns more effectively than public school.

What We Know About Latino/Hispanic American Homeschool Families

Latino families represent 15% of the homeschool families in the United States (Noel, Stark, and Redford 2013). Yet literature searches in multiple databases (e.g., ERIC, PsycINFO, Education Research Complete) within the GALILEO search system yielded no publications, or even unpublished dissertations, focused on homeschooling of Latino or Hispanic families. Using Google Scholar resulted in several studies of homeschooling that included Hispanic or Latino families, but they tended not to specifically report findings for them. Instead, authors lumped Latino, African American, and other non-White groups into a category of "ethnic-minority". For example, Collom (2005) conducted a quantitative study of homeschool parents' motivations and student achievement among 235 families. 16.6% of the 235 participants identified as ethnic-minorities, attended a homeschool school in California, that is, a school formed by a homeschool parent who assumes responsibility for the education of other homeschooled children as well. A majority of the ethnic-minority families (61.3%) identified themselves as Latino American families, while African Americans consisted of 22.6% of the ethnic-minority participants and 16.1% identified as Asian American. Collom found that ethnic-minority home educators were more likely to be motivated to homeschool due to criticism of public schools than their White counterparts. Unfortunately, the author does not disaggregate the data by ethnic group, which allows the issues of perceived racism to remain uncovered.

However, like African American families, Latino families have definitely experienced marginalization within the schooling process as demonstrated in the research literature. For example, Harris and Kiyama (2015) describe the perilous context of Latino/a education. In the forward of their book, Antrop-Gonzalez conceptualizes Latino/a dropouts as "pushouts" because "Referring to a youth as a high school **dropout** implies that this young person has decided on her own accord to leave school. Hence, suggesting that such a student has voluntarily chosen to cease her studies makes it easy to place the blame for this student's greatly reduced life changes squarely on her own shoulders" (Harris and Kiyama 2015, vii). The authors provide a richly detailed explanation of the factors in Latino/a schooling experiences contributing to Latino/a pushout. These factors include the resegregation of schools, particularly in urban districts, language barriers, and a lack of sociocultural synchronization between home and school.

Very similar to African Americans, Latino/a families have formed advocacy groups (local and national in focus) and turned to the legal system in search of justice in the form of equality, equity, and excellence in education. One advocacy group in Arizona determined that informing Latino/a families about School Choice would be an effective way to overcome the Latino achievement gap (Nevarez 2015). Yet, the author did not mention homeschooling as one of the available options for Latino families, focusing instead solely on charter vs. non-charter schools. This suggests that the advocacy groups may not consider homeschooling as a viable option for Latino/a families.

Easterday (2011) conducted a study as part of his undergraduate experience. While his work has never been published, much can be discerned from the abstract available. This young scholar's work demonstrates that similar to African American families, Hispanic families choose to homeschool in order to "pass on their cultural heritage." This most likely includes familial historical legacy and cultural traditions. Like African American homeschool families, passing on a cultural heritage may also include identifying Hispanic perspectives within the subject area content.

According to Easterday's work, Hispanic families also decided to homeschool in order to participate more directly in their children's learning. As stated in Easterday's abstract, many Hispanic families are unable to fully engage in their children's learning due to a conflict between their work schedule and the school schedule. This suggests that like the African American families in Fields-Smith and Williams-Johnson (2009), Hispanic families forgo one income in order to homeschool their children, which represents a significant economic sacrifice.

Language concerns presented a clear departure from African American families' motivations to homeschool. Easterday stated, "By homeschooling, Hispanic parents are able to focus on the education of their children without being hindered by a lack of effective cross-cultural communication" (2011, abstract). Indeed, his study also found that Hispanic families seek a bilingual education for their children. A statement on a Latino homeschool blog called Mommy Maestra, which when translated means Mommy Teacher, supports Hispanic families' motivation to homeschool to obtain bilingual education for their children. On the home page of the blog the author writes:

> I want to know numbers. To give encouragement to other Latino families who are considering homeschooling. To show publishers and other education companies that they need to be thinking about us when they are creating their education materials. To show publishers that they need to create Spanish and bilingual curricula to help bilingual families successfully raise bilingual children without having to sacrifice academic achievement (Mommy Maestra 2012).

The strong connection between language and culture makes this parental desire quite understandable and even to be expected. The primary purpose of bilingual education is to provide students some instruction in their native language. Thus, bilingual education would provide a method for retaining one's heritage while learning new skills and concepts.

However, bilingual education has had a rocky history in the US, and it continues to divide communities (Nieto 2009). In 1968, The Bilingual Education Act acknowledged the rights of non-English speaking students, but "The law did not force school districts to offer bilingual programs, but it encouraged them to experiment with new pedagogical approaches by funding programs that targeted principally low-income and non-English speaking populations" (as cited in Nieto 2009, 63). In 1974 the Bilingual Education Act was changed to reflect more specific definitions and to eliminate the low-income requirement for bilingual education. At the same time, the *Lau vs. Nichols* Supreme Court case determined that school districts were responsible for providing modifications and special programs for non-English speaking students. However, this mandate stopped short of provided explicit remedies and more specifically did not require bilingual education. Today, bilingual education is less common than in our educational past. Instead, bilingual students tend to be integrated into regular education classes with an English as a Second Language (ESOL) instructor in the classroom or students being pulled out during the school day for ESOL instruction. Further, ESOL today does not necessarily mean that children will receive instruction in their native language. Instead, ESOL instruction tends to focus on enhancing non-English-speaking children's ability to learn English. Understandably, today's Spanish-speaking families who are seeking to have their children retain their native language would not see the benefits of ESOL instruction.

Directions for Future Research

Parker (2003) argued that democracy happens when the voices of the majority have been heard. When it comes to homeschooling research, the voices of ethnic-minority and religious minority families have not been documented well. Research on the homeschooling decisions and practices among families of color and other minorities (ethnic and religious) remains scarce. Research on the motivations and practices of ethnic and other minority homeschool families provides authentic understanding to issues related to family engagement, home–school partnerships, and learning achievement experienced by these families' children. Given the lingering educational attainment disparities faced by these families, such knowledge would appear to be valuable toward reaching sustainable and effective relationships with non-White families and the academic success of their children.

Though an emerging literature exists on Black home education, additional research on African Americans would be beneficial. Most of the existing literature on Black homeschooling has focused on parents' motivations. A significant portion of the literature remains in the format of unpublished dissertations or home educators' biographies, which might be ignored in the typical review of the literature. An increase in empirically based, peer-reviewed scholarship would provide a stronger foundational understanding of Black home education. To date the published, empirically based literature consists of just two studies: Mazama and Lundy's study of seventy-four families representing northern and Midwest cities (2012, 2013a, 2013b, 2014) and Fields-Smith and Williams-Johnson's (2009) study of forty-six families in the Metro Atlanta area. This leaves much of the southern and western regions of the US completely unexamined. Future research could provide comparative knowledge of Black families who homeschool in regions where the previous studies already exist as well.

In addition to greater regional representation, research on Black homeschool families could be disaggregated by year of entry to enhance our understanding of their motivations to homeschool. This research would query the differences and similarities between Black parents' decisions to homeschool when they begin from birth compared to those who leave public schools during early years (K–2) or families who begin to homeschool later in the elementary school experience (3rd–5th grade). Such studies may more specifically identify the school-related factors that push families out of public schools into homeschooling as described by (Fields-Smith and Wells Kisura 2013).

Research on Black home education needs longitudinal studies. Such studies would provide understanding of factors that influence homeschool practice over time. Longitudinal studies would also provide data regarding Black homeschool student outcomes in terms of academics, self-efficacy civic engagement, and career choices. Longitudinal studies could also trace Black families' overall engagement in homeschooling in reverse. During Fields-Smith and Williams-Johnson's (2009) study, Black homeschool mothers reported that Black women served as their mentors in the early 2000s. These veteran Black home educators reportedly began homeschooling their children in the 1990s or earlier, which means that Black families chose to homeschool in the South long before the implementation of the No Child Left Behind (NCLB) Act in 2000. Given that many of the motivations to homeschool tend to be aimed at public schools' emphasis on high stakes testing, investigation of Black homeschooling prior to NCLB could result in new motivations to homeschool. Depending on how far back Black home education could be documented, one may find that Black families chose to homeschool in the 1970s–1990s to avoid the racial tension caused by integration policy and practices, which were not fully implemented until the 1970s (Morris 2009).

Given that Latino/a families have experienced similar marginalization of their engagement and disparities in their children's academic and behavioral experiences within public schools, each of the calls for additional research presented for Black homeschooling above would also apply to Latino/a homeschooling. The fact that there is currently no published data representing homeschooling among Latino families is unacceptable. Trends suggest that the population of Spanish speaking families has been and will continue to be on the rise for years to come (Harris and Kiyama 2015).

Therefore, understanding the educational beliefs, values, and practices of Latino/a families who choose to homeschool provides critical knowledge regarding the education of their children. As found in Black home education research, research on Latino/a American families' experiences in schools contributes to our understanding of what works, and what does not work, in home–school partnerships.

Moreover, studies of Latino/a American family homeschooling should consider focusing on subgroups of Hispanic cultures (e.g., Mexican American, Puerto Rican American, or Dominican American families) as research has demonstrated that each group can have different experiences. For example, Harris and Kiyama inform us, "Educational disparities also exist among Latino/a subgroups, with 49% of Mexicans and 33% of Puerto Ricans obtaining less than a high school diploma, and Cubans attaining the highest high school completion rate, at almost 39%" (2015, 2). Therefore, Latino American homeschool families' motivations and practices may vary by subgroup as well.

Homeschooling has become quite diverse beyond ethnic and racial lines (Gaither 2008). The existing research agenda appears to have ignored this fact completely by focusing only on White and Black homeschooling experiences. Future homeschool research should seek understanding of home education as experienced by families of other cultures such as Jewish and Muslim home educators or Native American families. The current research lacks a thorough acknowledgment of Asian American homeschooling as well. As with Latin American families, researchers should privilege the voices of families who represent the various subgroups among Asian American families (e.g., Japanese, Chinese, Korean, or Hmong) and distinctions between Southeast Asian groups and those representing the South Pacific region. A homeschool research agenda should also include the voices of immigrant or migrant families located in the US.

Conclusion

Latino/a and African American families choose to homeschool for similar and unique reasons compared to the predominantly White homeschool population. More research is needed to fully understand the ethnically unique motivations of Latino/a and African American families. One motivation to homeschool common to both groups includes a desire to provide their children an educational experience fully integrated with their ethnic or cultural heritage. This includes, for example, teaching their children about history from a multicultural perspective with particular attention to their cultural heritage and learning about the contributions of inventors and other societal leaders representing their ethnic background. This motivation stands in stark contrast to the relatively monocultural approach to teaching history and most other subjects in public schools. By infusing instruction with a cultural perspective, ethnic-minority home educators effectively do what multicultural education scholars have urged public schools to do for decades (Gay 2000; Irvine 1991; Ladson-Billings 1995).

Language desires may represent one difference between Black and Hispanic homeschool family motivations. Latin American families who favor a bilingual approach to teaching and learning may choose to homeschool because bilingual education programs have tapered off in conventional schools in favor of ESOL programs, which do not typically provide instruction in one's native language. In this way, Latin American families' decisions to homeschool represent resistance to a lack of access to the type of education they desire for their children.

Ethnic-minority families' alternative schooling decisions matter. More research on ethnic-minority families' homeschool motives and practice is needed. Frequently, ethnic-minority families and children experience marginalization in conventional schools because of the school's adherence to spoken and unspoken White middle-class cultural beliefs and values. Homeschooling research focused on Latino/a and African American families contributes to understanding of the schooling of Latino and African American children from the perspective of their parents.

References

Abrams, L., and J. Gibbs. 2002. "Disrupting the Logic of Home-schooling Relations: Parent Involvement Strategies and Practices of Inclusion and Exclusion." *Urban Education*, 37(3): 384–407.

Apple, Michael. 2006. "The Complexities of Black Homeschooling," December 21. *Teachers College Record*. Accessed March 10, 2008. http://www.tcrecord.org/Content.asp?ContentID=12903

Chapman, Thandekea, and Kalwant Bhopal. 2013. "Countering Common-sense Understandings of 'Good Parenting': Women of Color Advocating for their Children." *Race Ethnicity and Education*, 16(4): 562–586. doi.org/10.1080/13613324.2013.817773

Collom, Ed. 2005. "The Ins and Outs of Homeschooling: The Determinants of Parental Motivation and Student Achievement." *Education and Urban Society* 37(3): 307–335.

Cooper, Camille. 2007. "School Choice as 'Motherwork': Valuing African-American Women's Educational Advocacy and Resistance." *International Journal of Qualitative Studies in Education*, 20(5): 491–512.

Easterday, Luke. 2011. "Cross-Cultural Educational Fallbacks: A Study of Homeschooling in the Hispanic Community and the Reasons for Its Utilization." *Celebration of Undergraduate Scholarship*. Paper 5. Accessed March 20, 2015. http://scholar.valpo.edu/cus/5

Economist 2012. "Keep it in the Family: Home Schooling is Growing even Faster," December 22. Accessed June 2013. http://www.economist.com/news/united-states/21568763-home-schooling-growing-ever-faster-keep-it-family?zid=316&ah=2f6fb672faf113fdd3b11cd1b1bf8a77

Epstein, Joyce. 2010. "School/Family/Community Partnerships: Caring for the Children We Share." *Phi Delta Kappan*, 92(3): 81–96.

Fields-Smith, Cheryl, and Meca Williams-Johnson. 2009. "Motivations, Sacrifices, and Challenges: Black Parents' Decisions to Homeschool." *Urban Review*, 41: 369–389.

Fields-Smith, Cheryl, and Kisura Wells. 2013. "Resisting the Status Quo: The Narratives of Black Homeschoolers in Metro-Atlanta and Metro-D.C." *Peabody Journal of Education*, 88(3): 265–283.

Gaither, Milton. 2008. *Homeschool: An American History*. New York: Palgrave Macmillan.

Gaither, Milton. 2014. "The History of North American Education, 15000 BCE to 1491." *History of Education Quarterly*, 54(3): 323–348.

Gay, Geneva. 2000. *Culturally Responsive Teaching: Theory, Research, and Practice*. New York: Teacher College Press.

Harris, Donna Marie, and Judy Marquez Kiyama. 2015. *The Plight of Invisibility: A Community-Based Approach to Understanding the Education Experiences of Urban Latina/os*. New York: Peter Lang Publishers.

Hatt, Beth. 2011. "Smartness as a Cultural Practice in Schools." *American Educational Research Journal*, 49(3): 438–460.

Hiatt-Michael, Diana. 2000. "Parent Involvement in American Public Schools: A Historical Perspective." *School Community Journal* (4)2: 247–258.

Howard, Tyrone. 2008. "Who Really Cares? The Disenfranchisement of African American Males in PreK-12 schools: A Critical Race Theory Perspective." *Teachers College Record*, 110(5): 954–985.

Irvine, Jacqueline Jordan. 1991. *Black Students and School Failure: Policies, Practices, and Prescriptions*. Westport, CT: Praeger Publishers.

Ladson-Billings, Gloria. 1995. "But That's Just Good Teaching! The Case for Culturally Relevant Pedagogy." *Theory Into Practice*, 34(3): 159–165.

Lareau, Annette. 2000. *Home Advantage: Social Class and Parental Intervention in Elementary Education*. Lanham, MD: Rowan and Littlefield Publishing Group, Inc.

Lareau, Annette, and Horvat, Erin. 1999. "Moments of Social Inclusions and Exclusion Race, Class, and Cultural Capital in Family-School Relationships." *Sociology of Education* 72(1): 37–53.

Llewellyn, Grace. ed. 1996. *Freedom Challenge: African American Homeschoolers*. Eugene, OR: Lowry House.

MacFarquhar, Neil. 2008. "Resolute or Fearful, Many Muslims Turn to Home Schooling," March 26. *New York Times*, 157(54261): 14.

Mazama, Ama, and Lundy, Garvey. 2012. "African American Homeschooling as Racial Protectionism." *Journal of Black Studies*, 43(7): 723–748.

Mazama, Ama, and Garvey Lundy. 2013a. "African American Homeschooling and the Quest for Quality Education." *Education and Urban Society*, 20 (10): 1–22.

Mazama, Ama, and Garvey Lundy. 2013b. "African American Homeschooling and the Question of Curricular Cultural Relevance." *Journal of Negro Education*, 82(2): 123–138.

Mazama, Ama, and Garvey Lundy. 2014. "African American Homeschoolers: The Force of Faith and the Reality of Race in the Homeschooling Experience." *Religion and Education*, (41)3: 256–272.

Mommy Maestra. March 5, 2012. *Where Are All the Latino Homeschoolers?* Accessed March 20, 2015. http://www.mommymaestra.com/2012/03/where-are-all-latino-homeschoolers.html

Monroe, Carla. 2005, September/October. "Why are 'Bad Boys' Always Black?: Causes of Disproportionality in School Discipline and Recommendations for Change." *The Clearing House*, 79(1): 45–50.

Morris, Jerome. 2009. *Troubling the Waters: Fulfilling the Promise of Quality Public Schooling for Black Children*. New York: Teachers College Press.

Nevarez, Griselda. March 12, 2015. "Could School Choice Help Close the Latino Education Gap? *El Diario*. Accessed March 20, 2015. http://www.eldiariony.com/2015/03/12/could-school-choice-help-close-the-latino-education-gap/

Nichols-White, Donna. 1996. "Free at Last." In *Freedom Challenge: African American Homeschoolers*, edited by G. Llewellyn. Eugene, OR: Lowry House.

Nieto, David. Spring, 2009. "A Brief History of Bilingual Education in the United States." *Perspectives on Urban Education*, 61–70. Accessed March 20, 2015. http://www.urbanedjournal.org/sites/urbanedjournal.org/files/pdf_archive/61-72--Nieto.pdf

Noel, Amber, Stark, Patrick, and Redford, Jeremy. 2013. *Parent and Family Involvement in Education*. National Household Education Survey Program of 2012 (NCES 2013–028). Washington, DC: National Center for Education Statistics. Institute of Education Sciences, US Department of Education.

Parker, Walter. 2003. *Teaching Democracy: Unity and Diversity in Public Life*. New York: Teachers College Press.

Taylor, Venus. 2005. "Behind the Trend: Increases in African American Homeschooling." In *Homeschooling in Full View: A Reader*, edited by B. Cooper. Charlotte, NC: Information Age Publishing.

US Department of Education Office for Civil Rights. 2014, March. Civil Rights Data Collection: Data Snapshot. (School Discipline).

Van Galen, Jane A. 1991. "Ideologues and Pedagogues: Parents who Teach their Children at Home." In *Homeschooling: Political, Historical, and Pedagogical Perspectives*, edited by Jane A. Van Galen and Marry Anne Pitman, 63–76. Norwood, NJ: Ablex Publishing Corp.

10

Teaching the Child with Exceptional Needs at Home

Karen Hurlbutt-Eastman

Introduction

In 1975, President Ford signed Public Law (PL) 94-142 into effect, which was referred to as the Education for all Handicapped Children Act. This law was intended to ensure a free, appropriate, public education for all children with disabilities. At that time, through Child Find activities funded by the federal government, personnel from local schools and state education departments were challenged to identify children with disabilities who were not being served by local education agencies (i.e., public schools). Through these efforts, over one million students with disabilities were found at home, excluded from being educated in the public schools (An Act 1975; OSERS 2010). Additionally, the results of each state's Child Find activities indicated that there were at least another 8 million students with disabilities nationwide already in the public school system who were being ineffectively educated (Boyer 1979). In many cases, parents were paying for institutional care or specialized programs for their children out of their own pockets.

Prior to this law being passed, it was the parents who were the most important advocates for their children with disabilities. They fought diligently to have their children obtain the right to be educated in the public schools, which paved the way for future laws regarding the education of students with disabilities. In 1971, in *Pennsylvania Association for Retarded Children (PARC) v. Commonwealth of Pennsylvania*, several parents of children with intellectual disabilities challenged a state law regarding the required ability age level of students to be enrolled in the first grade, and won. In 1972, in *Mills v. Board of Education of the District of Columbia*, several parents sued the school district for excluding their children from receiving an education, and won. The court declared that insufficient funding was not an

The Wiley Handbook of Home Education, First Edition. Edited by Milton Gaither.

allowable excuse for not providing educational opportunities for children with disabilities (Education Law 2012).

By 1975, the Education for all Handicapped Children Act was in effect, and schools had three years to create programs for students with disabilities, hire and train additional special educators, and identify the money and space to serve these students in their schools. At that time, the federal government promised payment of 40% of each state's excess costs in order to provide educational services to students with disabilities. This percentage of funding has never been close to being awarded, as funding was only at 17% in 2008, and dropped to 16% in 2014 (Federal Education Budget Project 2014). School systems to this day struggle with having enough funding to serve their students with disabilities in the best way possible.

During the 1980s, informed parents challenged the law, trying to clarify what a free, appropriate, public education meant for their children with special needs. The relationship between these parents and the schools was often fraught as a result of these disputes. Ever since PL 94-142 was enacted, parents maintained the right to challenge educational decisions made by the schools, which was meant to ensure accountability on the part of the schools. These parents filed complaints with the schools and state education departments, some of which made it all the way to the Supreme Court level. As a result, a number of components of PL 94-142 were clarified and so ordered by the Supreme Court. In some cases, the parents won, and in others, the school districts won.

In 1990, the Education for all Handicapped Children Act was renamed to the Individuals with Disabilities Education Act (IDEA). During the 1990s, local and state education agencies (i.e., public schools and state education departments) as well as federal government agencies emphasized inclusive practices in the schools, and not a mainstreaming philosophy. Mainstreaming was defined as moving a child with special needs out of a self-contained special education classroom for parts of the day, and placing him or her in a general education classroom for certain subjects or activities. Inclusion focuses on having students with special needs included in the general education setting from the start and receiving supportive or individualized services as needed. Ideally, this would reduce the number of segregated special education classrooms and help students with disabilities be educated with their typical peers.

Amendments to IDEA occurred in both 1997 and 2004, and issues such as references to participation and progress in the general education curriculum became required. States were also required to begin offering mediation services to help resolve disputes before formal due process hearings occurred. It appeared as though parents had made a great deal of progress, for they led the push toward having their children with disabilities appropriately served in their local public schools with their siblings and neighborhood peers. This history could be read as a series of victories for the parents of children with special needs.

Nevertheless, after all of the disagreements, complaints, court cases and rulings, it started becoming clear to many parents of children with exceptionalities that schools may not be the very best option for their children after all. Increasingly, more parents are homeschooling their children with special needs. Perhaps we have come full circle. But for different reasons? And with different concerns?

Homeschooling in general has been on the rise in the past thirty years. The number of homeschooled children has risen from approximately 93000 in the early 1980s to 1000000 in the mid to late 1990s, to approximately 2000000 currently, which is about 3% of the school aged population (National Center for Education Statistics 2013). Many of these students have exceptionalities, ranging from those with disabilities to those who are gifted/talented. Much of the professional research available regarding homeschooling students with special needs is unique in that, unlike homeschooling in general, most has been published internationally, specifically in the UK and Australia. Discussions of several issues and topics that have been identified in the literature follow. These include a discussion of why more and more parents of children with special needs choose to homeschool, some of challenges that parents encounter when homeschooling, some of the problems faced by students with special needs in the schools, as well as a discussion of evidence-based strategies that are recommended in teaching students with exceptionalities. Recommendations for future research are identified at the end of this chapter.

Why Homeschool?: Parental Motivation

The National Center for Education Statistics (2013) reported that for the 2011–2012 school year, the main reason (91%) that parents reported for homeschooling their children was because of concern about school environment, and close behind that were the desire to provide religious and moral instruction and a dissatisfaction with the academic instruction in the schools. This report also noted that 17% of the parents identified having a child with special needs as their reason for homeschooling. This is up considerably from 2007 when the National Center for Education Statistics (2008) reported that approximately 4% of parents surveyed indicated that the most important reason they were homeschooling was because their children had special needs.

While the numbers of children with exceptionalities who are homeschooled has increased, the reasons for the choice may be different for parents of these children than for other homeschoolers. In a review of the literature, these parents do not homeschool for religious reasons (Hurlbutt 2011; Jolly, Masters, and Nester 2012; Lundy and Mazama 2014; Parsons and Lewis 2010; Winstanley 2009). In one study, however, religion was an influence in the decision made to homeschool and as a part of the curriculum (Fields-Smith and Williams 2009). The research base does indicate several reasons parents gave for why they do homeschool their children. The main reason was that parents believe that what their child needs differs significantly from what the public schools are doing (Hanna 2012; Hurlbutt 2011; Jolly, Masters, and Nester 2012; Kidd and Kaczmerak 2010; McDonald and Lopes 2014; Parsons and Lewis 2010; Winstanley 2009). These parents have felt they were forced into this decision, that it was their only choice, due to the schools' inability to provide the education the parents felt their children needed. These parents had chosen to homeschool not because they preferred the lifestyle, but rather out of necessity.

Many parents of students with disabilities have found themselves needing to educate school staff yearly, and have believed that the school setting was not the best fit for their child, and that their goal of preparing their child for the real world differed from the schools' goals and practices (Boyd et al. 2008; Fields-Smith and Wells Kisura 2013; Hurlbutt 2011; Pyles 2004; Samuels 2008). Most of the parents in one study expressed their concerns over what appeared to be a cookie cutter approach they believed exists in the schools (Hurlbutt 2011).

Additionally, parents of children with exceptionalities have reported other reasons for homeschooling their child. Some cited the fact that they did not want their children inappropriately placed in classes with students with severe disabilities (Hurlbutt 2011; Starr, Foy, and Cramer 2001). Others believed that children with milder disabilities were more likely to be educated in the general education environment, but that general education teachers were not equipped to provide the differentiated instruction students with disabilities need (Hurlbutt 2011; Starr, Foy, and Cramer 2001). Some parents were more concerned with their children being able to participate in educational programs that met their unique needs rather than being served in the general education setting (Hurlbutt 2011; Parsons and Lewis 2010; McDonald and Lopes 2014) while other parents felt that the traditional school system in general was not the appropriate setting for their child (Jolly, Masters, and Nester 2012; Lundy and Mazama 2014). In many cases, parents decided to pull their child from the school system because the child experienced a great deal of stress, unhappiness or depression, physical symptoms, and bullying (Hurlbutt 2011; Lawrence, 2012; Parsons and Lewis 2010; Winstanley 2009).

Another motivating factor in the decision to homeschool is the overrepresentation of diverse students who qualify for special education. This is especially the case for African American male students. Fields-Smith and Wells Kisura (2013) found that more Black boys are homeschooled than Black girls, and that Black and White teachers alike held low expectations regarding educational performance for Black children. Lundy and Mazama (2014, 56) discussed the "biased teacher expectations" regarding the academic ability of African American students, particularly boys, which often has a negative impact on academic performance. African American parents often choose to homeschool their boys to keep them from being inaccurately diagnosed as having special needs (most often intellectual disabilities). Lundy and Mazama (2014, 56) referenced a long history of the overrepresentation of Black students, mostly boys, in special education, dating back to 1968. Fields-Smith and Wells Kisura (2013) noted that parents believe that homeschooling gives Black children the opportunity to learn more about their own culture as well as being exposed to different cultures. Additionally, Lundy and Mazama (2014) discussed the connection between the criminal justice system and African American males, many of whom were school dropouts. Because of the unsafe and often violent conditions in public schools and the reasons discussed above, some parents of Black children have chosen to homeschool their children.

Reasons why parents homeschool their gifted children are similar, and for the most part, they, too, want individualized programs for their children who may not be challenged enough or whose educational programming does not fit their varied and individual needs (Jolly, Masters, and Nester 2012; Winstanley 2009). Many of these parents are already supplementing their gifted child's schoolwork and can make the transition to fulltime homeschooling. Gifted children can become bored in school and may not feel challenged, and parents may feel their children are not being supported to reach their full potential (Winstanley 2009).

Challenges in the Schools

According to the law (IDEA), the least restrictive environment for every child with disabilities must be determined by the child's Individual Education Program plan team at school. For most students, this has meant being placed in general education classrooms with their peers. While this push for inclusion has resulted in the opportunity for both typical students and their peers with disabilities to interact with each other, it has also resulted in a great variety of ability levels found in the classrooms, with general education teachers not properly trained, ignorant about, or not having the time to differentiate for each student (Duffey 2002; Hurlbutt 2011; McDonald and Lopes 2014; Myles, Simpson, and deBoer 2008; Starr et al. 2006). Often, students are grouped according to disability category and not by individual needs. This practice has again resulted in some children being placed in the same classroom with students with incompatible needs. Being inappropriately grouped with students who are vastly different is also the case for gifted students, who may feel self-conscious about their abilities when not placed with other gifted children, and may act out, tune out, or give up in this situation (Winstanley 2009).

Because the schools are attempting to meet the unique needs of so many students, the flexibility needed for students with exceptionalities is generally not an option. Medical issues, medications and side effects, sleep problems, illnesses, and aggressive or self-injurious behaviors often interfere with a student's ability to perform well. Research has shown that many parents believe the school system not to be set up to accommodate those issues on a daily basis (Hanna 2012; Hurlbutt 2011; Parsons and Lewis 2010). In one longitudinal study, two families who homeschool their children with disabilities did so because they felt the school could not meet their child's medical needs, and that the public school environment was not an "acceptable environment for their children" (Hanna 2012, 624). Thus, many parents believe that the schools are not meeting the needs of students with disabilities and are not able to effectively individualize or provide an appropriate public education (Hanna 2012; Hurlbutt 2011; Kidd and Kaczmerak 2010; McDonald and Lopes 2014; Parsons and Lewis 2010).

IDEA requires that both general education and special education teachers understand the need to provide evidence-based instruction and to provide adaptations and accommodations that are appropriate for each student; however, many parents believe that teachers are not equipped to do so (Blok 2004; Gargiulo 2015; Hurlbutt 2011; Samuels 2008; Starr et al. 2006). Many teachers have found themselves without the knowledge to appropriately teach and support students with exceptionalities in the classroom (Myles, Simpson, and deBoer 2008; Taylor, Smiley, and Richards 2014). With a wide range of ability levels and challenges in the classrooms today, it is difficult to meet the needs of each student. Problems can develop for students with disabilities in school when their unique and challenging needs are not met. For example, requiring a student with ADHD (attention deficit hyperactivity disorder) to sit still in a desk in rows, while the teacher stands at the front of the room and lectures for a 50 minute class period, can lead to disaster (Taylor, Smiley, and Richards 2014). Requiring a student with a writing disability to take copious notes from the board also lends itself to failure because of the extra time required to do so (Hallahan et al. 2005). Holding timed tests in reading and math can create great stress for students with learning disabilities (Beech 2010). Calling on students to read out loud in front of the class often results in embarrassment and frustration for students with speech disorders (Taylor, Smiley, and Richards 2014). Requiring group work, or having noisy group interactions, can be very challenging for a student on the autism spectrum. Evaluating a student's knowledge on a topic by requiring significant amounts of writing can be a laborious task for a student with autism who has sensory issues and dislikes the feel of paper and pencil (Simpson and Myles 2008). For many students with exceptionalities, schools can be stressful and overstimulating. There are many sounds, smells, and changes in schedules, routines, and teachers which can cause a great deal of strain and stress on a child's coping ability (Parsons and Lewis 2010). Any of these situations can easily result in outbursts, temper tantrums, and other negative behaviors that can embarrass the student and result in loss of learning time.

Benefits of Homeschooling

Given such challenges, many parents come to believe that they know their child better than anyone and can truly understand and best teach their child with learning challenges. In a homeschooling situation, children can learn at their own pace, have more flexibility in their day, and show improvement in motivation and coping, especially because the daily routine can be adjusted when necessary (Duffey 2002; Hurlbutt 2011; Kidd and Kaczmarek 2010; Starr et al. 2006). There is less distraction, little to no competition, and opportunity to explore subjects and topics that are of interest to the child. Sometimes, especially for children on the autism spectrum, these interest areas are unique and unusual, and there is usually not enough time in the school day for a classroom teacher to allow these students to pursue their individual interests (Lawrence 2012). Winstanley (2009), too, describes how the curriculum in the schools does not provide the opportunity for gifted students to spend time engaging in, and learning more about, their unique interests.

Research has shown that many students with disabilities and/or exceptionalities demonstrated a significant improvement in their moods, emotions, and coping after being removed from the schools and being homeschooled (Hurlbutt 2011; Kidd and Kaczmerak 2010; McDonald and Lopes 2014). They are away from the stresses of their daily life in school and do not have to face the isolation, exclusion, challenges, bullying, anxiety, emotional issues, teacher bias, and the worry about potential involvement in the criminal justice system that they did previously (Hurlbutt 2011; Lundy and Mazama 2014; Parsons and Lewis 2010; Reed, Osborne, and Corness 2007).

Other benefits to homeschooling children with exceptionalities have been noted in the literature. Children are able to learn at their own pace, are free from bullying and other negative social aspects in the schools, have their individualized needs met, and benefit from flexible scheduling when bad days occur and when the learning needs of the student warrants (Hurlbutt 2011; Jolly, Masters, and Nester 2012; Kidd and Kaczmerak 2010; Lundy and Mazama 2014; McDonald and Lopes 2014; Parsons and Lewis 2010).

Demands on Parents who Homeschool their Children with Special Needs

Even though the benefits of homeschooling children with exceptionalities are compelling, the demands on homeschooling parents are just as significant. Parents have reported feeling isolated and tired, and have identified other issues, such as the cost for materials, loss of free time, and increased strain on the mother (Hurlbutt 2011; Jolly, Masters, and Nester 2012; Kidd and Kaczmerak 2010; McDonald and Lopes 2014; Parsons and Lewis 2010). Sometimes this can lead to isolation for those parents who face the challenge of organizing and carrying out the schedule for their child with special needs. Jolly, Matthews, and Nester (2012) described this as being difficult for the (mostly) mothers who may have given up professional careers to stay at home as a full-time homeschooling parent. This difficult transition can have an impact on everyone in the family. The role responsibilities will most likely change, as will the rhythm of the day. Research literature has indicated a need for parents to take care of themselves, as they often find themselves exhausted, isolated, and with no break (Hurlbutt 2011; McDonald and Lopes 2014; Parsons and Lewis 2010). Research has also noted a strain on financial and personal resources, and the need to balance the needs of the other children in the family, make decisions as a couple, share the workload, and utilize their own strengths and interest areas (Fields-Smith and Williams 2009; Hurlbutt 2011; Jolly, Masters, and Nester 2012; Parsons and Lewis 2010).

The strain on financial resources can be significant. In most cases, one parent has to stay home, having quit his or her job to do so. Couples need to weigh the options regarding employment, impact on loss of salary, which parent has the better insurance, and which parent is most able to take on the primary role of homeschooling (Hurlbutt 2011). In most cases, the mother was found to assume the bigger role in organizing and carrying out the homeschooling responsibilities (Fields-Smith and Williams 2008; Hurlbutt 2011; Jolly, Masters, and Nester 2012). In Fields-Smith and Williams (2009), the fact that the African American mothers gave up their careers to stay home to homeschool, was a significant issue because of the fight for workplace equity, but parents felt that the sacrifice was worth it in order to provide an effective education for their children.

The cost of educational and curriculum materials has been another financial issue for many parents (Hurlbutt 2011; Jolly, Masters, and Nester 2012). Even with the benefit of finding materials and resources online, parents spent money for materials and enrichment activities, and even involved their children in the decision-making process for deciding which activities to participate in due to cost. For the most part, schools do not share materials or resources with parents who homeschool, so parents often experiment with different curriculum options, and need to pay for different textbooks, workbooks, and other materials (Hurlbutt 2011; Jolly, Masters, and Nester 2012; Parsons and Lewis 2010).

Another financial issue that was a concern in Hurlbutt (2011) was the cost of therapeutic services, such as speech therapy. What was once offered in the schools when the child was a student may now need to be pursued outside of the school system. Not all insurance companies pay for therapies such as speech therapy, occupational or physical therapy, or behavioral therapy, and many of the parents were paying for these costs out of pocket (Hurlbutt 2011). This situation is improving considerably, as currently, thirty-eight states have enacted autism insurance reform laws, while another six states have endorsed insurance reform bills, one state is currently pursuing insurance reform, and only five states are not currently pursuing it (Autism Speaks 2015). In Hurlbutt (2011), some parents' private insurance companies did pay for therapies, while a couple of other parents sent their child to school for therapeutic services, paid for by the school.

Involvement from the schools in addition to providing therapeutic services has been a concern to many parents. About half of the parents in Parsons and Lewis (2010) indicated that the local school agency was involved in monitoring their child's performance and progress. Many of the parents in that study wished for a collaborative relationship with the schools to work on effectively teaching their children; however, only about a quarter of the parents felt the need for some type of state funding. In Hurlbutt (2011), the local school districts did not provide any kind of monitoring, which was a concern to most of the parents. Most of them felt that it was easier to be left alone but did believe that some kind of monitoring system should occur either at the local or state level. The special education teachers in Hurlbutt (2012) were split in their opinions of whether the schools should have to or be willing to provide support, materials, and advice. Some teachers felt that if the parents chose to remove their child, then the parents probably felt confident enough to be able to home educate without support from the school. Some teachers felt that it was important to offer support to the parents if they were interested, while others felt that if the child was pulled, then the schools should not feel obligated to provide support or resources.

Review of the literature indicates that parents often have a difficult time finding the support they need to homeschool. Parents have found support by reaching out to homeschool organizations and co-ops, by talking with other homeschooling parents, and by researching information on the internet, either in general or by researching homeschooling websites (Hurlbutt 2011; Kidd and Kaczmerak 2010; Parsons and Lewis 2010). The research base indicates a need for parents to learn about state requirements on their own for issues such as monitoring, grade reporting, and participation in testing (either state-wide testing or providing evidence of testing having been completed) (Fields-Smith and Williams 2009; Hurlbutt 2011; McDonald and Lopes 2014; Parsons and Lewis 2010). One parent in Fields-Smith and Williams (2009, 382) had a homeschool liaison officer who gave her a "hard time," while parents in other studies indicated that the school was the least helpful source of support and indicated a need for outside support (Hurlbutt 2011; Lundy and Mazama 2014; McDonald and Lopes 2014; Parsons and Lewis 2010). Parents of gifted children who were homeschooled had a difficult time being accepted into either homeschooling groups or parent groups for gifted children (Jolly, Masters, and Nester 2012). As indicated in Jolly, Masters, and Nester, without sufficient support for homeschooling parents, home education could become ineffective. It appears as though a best practice may be that the schools should at least offer support and resources, and it should be up to the parents to decide if they want to accept that support.

Areas of Disability and Exceptionality

Children with exceptionalities who are homeschooled are no different than students with special needs who are served in the public school system. They all are subject to the same evaluative and diagnostic criteria required for eligibility for instructional and supportive special education services provided under IDEA. The following section contains a brief summary of the categories of disability under IDEA, including gifted/talented, as well as a discussion of some recommended evidence-based strategies.

Learning disabilities

Individuals who have learning disabilities demonstrate difficulties in areas such as oral expression, listening comprehension, written expression, information-processing problems, memory difficulties, metacognition, reading disorders, quantitative or mathematics skills, and social emotional behavior (Gargiulo 2015). Previously, students were identified using the discrepancy model, where it was determined there was a "severe discrepancy between achievement and intellectual ability" (US Office of Education 1977, 65083). However, even though this provision was removed from IDEA in 2004, schools may still use this process, or a procedure referred to as Response to Intervention (RTI). This is when a student is exposed to increasing levels of empirically validated interventions, and his or her responsiveness to the interventions is measured. Generally, a lack of progress leads to a referral to special education for possible services. Lerner and Johns (2012) estimated that more than half of students with learning disabilities experience reading challenges, and about one-fourth of students with learning disabilities struggle with mathematics. Reading challenges range from reading comprehension to word recognition errors to oral reading errors. Math challenges include calculations, word problems, writing numbers and shapes, fractions, and computations. Individuals with learning disabilities also demonstrate problems in written language, which include penmanship, handwriting, spelling, and composition (Vaughn, Bos, and Schumm 2014).

Some of the more common accommodations used with these individuals include additional time for tests or having tests read, allowing frequent breaks, breaking tasks down into smaller segments, providing use of a study carrel, and allowing individuals to respond orally to tests or other assignments or to dictate to a scribe or into a recorder, and providing an alternative or quiet test site. Because of the wide variation and types of learning challenges for individuals with learning disabilities, the number of strategies are as varied. Table 10.1 discusses evidence- based approaches commonly used when teaching children and youths with learning disabilities.

Intellectual disabilities

Individuals with intellectual disabilities have sub-average intellectual ability and deficits in adaptive behaviors such as communication, social, self-help and daily living skills, and these limitations must be present during the developmental period, prior to age 18 (AAIDD 2012). Children and youths with intellectual disabilities generally perform significantly below grade level in all academic areas, and low achievement is noted across all content and skill areas. There is a significant range in ability levels, from a mild impairment to more severe impairment, and from limited intensity levels of support required to more extensive intensity levels of support. Overall, there are some common areas of concern in individuals with intellectual disabilities. These include difficulty with receptive and expressive language, articulation problems, poor use of logic and organization, lower level metacognition skills (self-regulation, memory, reasoning, self-awareness, etc.), motor difficulties, attention, memory, motivation, discrimination, generalization of skills, and as mentioned above, difficulty with academic activity and social skills (Snell and Brown 2010).

Research-based instructional programming for these individuals emphasizes communication (making requests, initiating greetings, interactions with others, gaining attention, etc); academic activity (sight words and phonics, functional math and reading skills, problem-solving strategies); and social skills (basic skills of

Table 10.1 Evidence-based approaches commonly used when teaching children and youths with learning disabilities.

Interventions	*Description*
Cognitive training (for example, self-instruction and mnemonic strategies)	Strategies to modify a person's thought patterns to result in observable changes in performance.
Direct or explicit instruction	Adult-directed, scripted, fast-paced lessons, elicit student response (choral response), correct answers are praised, incorrect answers receive corrective feedback. Teacher models, provides guided practice, and then allows time for independent practice.
Learning strategies (most common include the Strategic Instruction Model developed at the University of Kansas)	Students taught how to help themselves to learn and recall new material. There are strategies for reading, writing, math, motivation, studying and remembering information, improving assignment and test performance, and effectively interacting with others.[1]
Scaffolding	Support given that is tailored to the needs of the child. Instructional information is modeled, constructive feedback and guidance are provided while the child learns new material.
Graphic organizers	Organized visual display of information with words or concepts related to the content to help students understand the hierarchical and sequential relationships of the material.
Guided notes	An outline of the lecture content where students write in important facts and concepts during the lecture/lesson.

Sources: Archer and Hughes 2010; Dawson and Guare 2009; Gargiulo 2015; Reid, Lienemann, and Hagaman 2013; Swanson, Harris, and Graham 2013.

greeting others, manners, turn-taking), making friends, dealing with feelings, alternatives to aggression, and sexuality (Snell and Brown 2010).

Table 10.2 shows evidence-based methods that are commonly used when working with individuals with intellectual disabilities.

Autism spectrum disorders

Individuals with autism spectrum disorders (ASD) have difficulty with social-communication skills, such as echolalia, which involves repetition of words and phrases, delayed or lack of language, apparent lack of interest in others, difficulty with nonverbal body language, eye contact, and interactions with others, and they often exhibit repetitive and restrictive behaviors such as strict adherence to routines, preoccupation with parts of objects, sensitivity to sensory stimuli, and repeated body movements such as hand flapping, rocking, and spinning (Wheeler, Mayton, and Carter 2015). Areas to focus on for instructional purposes include developing

Table 10.2 Evidence-based methods commonly used when working with individuals with intellectual disabilities.

Interventions	*Description*
Task analysis	Breaking a task down into small steps, as small as necessary.
Chaining	Forward chaining – learner learns and performs the first step in the chain (task analysis), then the first and second steps and links them together, then the third step, and so on. Backward chaining – learner learns and performs the last step in the chain (task analysis), then learns the last step with the next-to-last step and links them together, then the third-to-last, and so on.
Prompts and fading	Assistance or support given to the learner along with the task being taught; can be verbal, gestural, symbols/pictures, or physical assistance. Fading is the gradual removal of prompts and reinforcers.
Shaping	The development of a new behavior by successive reinforcement of closer approximations until skill is learned.
Direct instruction	Adult-led explicit instruction of specific skills.
Mand modeling	Establish attention, present mand (direction).Correct student response receives praise; incorrect response – give another direction or model, corrective feedback, access to praise/reinforce.
Augmentative and alternative communication systems	Nonverbal communication systems – gestures, pictures, computer voice output systems.

Sources: Gargiulo 2015; Hunt and Marshall 2012; Snell and Brown 2010; Taylor, Smiley, and Richards 2014.

communication (receptive and expressive language, appropriate topics of conversation, spontaneous conversation skills, and nonverbal body language) and social skills (interactions with others, preparing for transitions and changes in routine, and decreasing negative behaviors (Simpson and Myles 2008).

Research has not identified one strategy determined to be effective for all individuals with ASD; however, the development of functional communication skills and social skills, and skills of independence is recommended (Heflin and Alaimo 2007; Wilkinson 2010). Table 10.3 describes evidence-based interventions that are commonly used with children with ASD.

Emotional behavioral disorders

Individuals with emotional and/or behavioral disorders are generally identified as having a chronic condition of behaviors that differ from typical same-age peers and

Table 10.3 Evidence-based interventions commonly used with children with ASD.

Interventions	*Description*
TEACCH – Treatment and Education of Autistic and related Communication Handicapped CHildren	Organizing the physical environment, developing schedules and work systems, making expectations clear and explicit, and using visual materials.
Discrete Trial Training/Applied Behavior Analysis (DTT/ABA)	ABA is an approach involves systematic manipulation of antecedents and consequences to affect an individual's behavior. Discrete Trial Training includes gaining student attention, presentation of the stimulus, student response and feedback, and presentation of reinforcer.
Picture Exchange Communication System (PECS)	A system designed to help children learn to communicate with the use of pictures, to initiate requests, make comments, and answer questions.
Social stories	Individualized stories written to describe a situation, event, or activity, and address the child's behavior or response using cues and typical, acceptable responses.
Pivotal Response Training (PRT) Joint Action Routines (JARS) Incidental Teaching	Interventions that are rooted in ABA principles but are designed to maximize independence, promote generalization, and facilitate social initiations; can be incorporated into daily home and community routines.

Sources: Gargiulo 2015; Heflin and Alaimo 2007; Simpson and Myles 2008; Taylor, Smiley, and Richards 2014; Wheeler, Mayton, and Carter 2015.

accepted standards, and that have an adverse effect on their academic and other work performance. These behaviors can include not only aggression, self-injury, non-compliance, acting out, and disruption, but also conditions of mental health disorders such as depression, anxiety, schizophrenia, affective disorders, and conduct disorders (Council for Children with Behavioral Disorders 2015).

Children and youths often display significant academic deficits and school failure. These students are at risk for academic failure and poor academic performance, low rates of grade retention and high school graduation, as well as increased tendency toward delinquency and incarceration (Gargiulo 2015). Current research has noted that many students with emotional or behavioral disorders earn scores that are in the low range of intellectual ability (Kauffman and Landrum 2013). Also common are language and communication deficits, including difficulty with using language that is inappropriate to the social situation, using less elaboration when speaking, and having difficulty with staying on topic. Socially, individuals with emotional and/or behavioral disorders struggle with developing and maintaining interpersonal relationships with peers and others (Taylor, Smiley, and Richards 2014).

Table 10.4 contains strategies and interventions that are commonly used when working with individuals with emotional and/or behavioral disorders.

Table 10.4 Strategies and interventions commonly used when working with individuals with emotional and/or behavioral disorders.

Interventions	*Description*
Management of time, transition, classroom	Strategies designed to maximize student engagement time and teaching time management skills; improving transition times between assignments, activities, and class periods; setting up a learning environment that is clear of distractions, and seating students close to teacher/adult for successful monitoring.
Instructional interventions (academic curriculum and instructional delivery)	General education curriculum that is modified to ability level, is relevant and motivating. Mnemonic devices to remember material; self-monitoring strategies to record their efforts and progress; content enhancement (e.g., graphic organizers, diagrams, semantic maps, guided notes, and study guides) to help students understand material and link to learned concepts.
Behavioral and cognitive-behavioral interventions	Sources of external and internal control including praise, ignoring, contingencies, peer- and self-management, overcorrection, punishment, and exclusion.
Social skills training, interpersonal problem solving, and conflict resolution	Teaching of such skills as body language, asking for help, following rules and routines, avoiding and resolving conflicts, coping with stress, and utilizing problem-solving strategies.

Sources: Gargiulo 2015; Shepherd 2009; Yell et al. 2013.

Attention disorders

This category includes attention deficit disorder (ADD) and attention deficit hyperactivity disorder (ADHD). These disorders are not currently recognized as a separate category under IDEA; however, these students may be determined to be eligible for special education under the category of Other Health Impairments (Gargiulo 2015). Approximately 5% of school-age children have been diagnosed with ADHD (American Psychiatric Association 2013). ADHD is one of the most common disorders in childhood and may continue into adulthood. According to the American Psychiatric Association (2013), common traits include difficulty with focusing on tasks, inattention, difficulty controlling behavior, and hyperactivity. Children with ADHD can be either disruptive when exhibiting hyperactivity behaviors or quiet and overlooked when they are sitting at their desks, appearing to be paying attention when they may not be. These children may be easily distracted or bored within a few minutes, may have difficulty processing information, may fidget or squirm, may struggle with completing quiet activities, and may interrupt conversations or blurt out inappropriate comments (American Psychiatric Association 2013). Attention and impulse control are important for school and academic success, which is where children and youths with ADHD struggle. Table 10.5 shows recommended strategies and approaches for use with children and youths with attention difficulties.

Table 10.5 Recommended strategies and approaches for use with children and youths with attention difficulties.

Interventions	*Description*
Instructional adaptations and modifications	Utilize adaptations and modifications, such as seat away from distractions, low student–teacher ratio, repeat instructions, use visual and tactile cues, use checklists and schedules, adapt worksheets for content and quantity, use activities that encourage active participation.
Behavioral (self-regulation) strategies	Designed to help a student become aware of his or her behaviors, and how to monitor, regulate, and reinforce them.
Medications	Recommend use in combination of instructional and behavioral interventions. Common psychostimulants (to arouse central nervous system that allow individuals to concentrate better and control impulsivity, and increase attention span) include Ritalin, Dexedrine, Adderall, Strattera.
Counseling and psychotherapy	To develop strategies to work on anger management, relationship skills, coping with stress, social skills (for example, turn-taking, responding to teasing, praising oneself, and recognizing facial expressions).

Sources: Barkley 2013; Boring 2006; Gargiulo 2015; Taylor, Smiley, and Richards 2014.

Physical and health disabilities, and traumatic brain injury

This is a very diverse group of children and youths. Those with physical disabilities have a physical condition that may prevent them from easily walking, talking, or moving, and these conditions can range from mild to severe (Best, Heller, and Bigge 2009). Some of the more common physical disabilities include cerebral palsy, muscular dystrophy, amputations, burns, spina bifida, and juvenile arthritis (Gargiulo 2105). Those with health disabilities have medical diagnoses that also can range from mild to severe and that can affect stamina and overall functioning throughout the day. Some of the most common health impairments include epilepsy or seizure disorders, asthma, and serious, life-threatening infectious diseases (Gargiulo 2015). And last, because of similar needs, those with a traumatic brain injury (TBI) are being included in this section of this chapter, although TBI is considered to be a separate category under IDEA.

The impact on learning can be significant for children and youths with any of the above disabilities or conditions, and those, too, can range from a mild impact to a more severe impact. Some students may just need to be monitored for specific symptoms while others need support and accommodations throughout the day. Many of these children require frequent trips to the hospital or to clinics for treatment, while some may be homebound at times. The effects of their condition may result in communication impairments, fatigue, motor abilities, and possible cognitive or intellectual impairments, some of which can be addressed in individualized healthcare plans (Taylor, Smiley, and Richards 2014). Psychosocial issues are also a concern for these students and they often experience difficulty with motivation, self-esteem, and social interactions with others (Best, Heller, and Bigge 2009).

Learners with any of the above conditions may require physical or health monitoring, academic modifications and adaptations (such as extended time), environmental adaptations (room arrangement or schedule adjustment), and computer access and/or assistive technology, such as communication devices, voice recognition software, and self-care support (adaptations for eating, dressing, positioning and seating, using the bathroom, etc) (Best, Heller, and Bigge 2009; Canales and Lytle 2011; Feldman 2013; Gargiulo 2015).

Visual and hearing impairments

Individuals in this group have either visual impairments (have some vision or are blind) or hearing impairments (have some hearing or are deaf). There is a small group of individuals who are considered to be deaf-blind that results in the need for unique programming to address both impairments. Someone is considered to have legal blindness if visual acuity is 20/200 or less in the better eye after correction, or if the visual field is no greater than 20 degrees (Gargiulo 2015). Low vision usually means that the visual impairment has an impact on the person's ability to perform daily activities. Orientation and mobility training is generally a necessary component to educational programming for students who have a visual impairment, as is other assistive technology to meet their needs including Braille, magnified reading devices, speech readers, large print, oral presentation of materials, and talking watches and calculators (Taylor, Smiley, and Richards 2014).

Hearing losses can be a result of structural damage, blockages in or disorders of the inner, middle, and outer ear, or from accidents or illnesses. Degree of hearing loss ranges from 16 dB to more than 90 dB (Herer, Knightly, and Steinberg 2002). Students may require amplification such as a hearing aid or a personal FM system, speechreading, sign language, or any combination of these supports (Fiedler 2001; Gargiulo 2015; Taylor, Smiley, and Richards 2014).

Gifted and talented

The National Association for Gifted Children (2013) estimated there to be approximately 3 million children and youths considered to be gifted and/or talented, or 6% of the school-age population. States have established their own definition of gifted and talented, and some states have included it as a category of special education, so all of the special education laws regarding supports and services applies to these students. Renzulli and Reis (2003) described students considered to be gifted as having high levels of intelligence and ability (abstract thought, problem-solving ability, specific area of knowledge, leadership), commitment to task (hard work and determination, setting high standards for own work), and creativity (taking risks, curious, and originality of thought). Piirto (2007) identified talent areas to include verbal, academic, musical, creative, mechanical, spiritual, performing, and relationship talents.

Children and youths who are gifted/talented often work well independently, are curious and highly motivated, have exceptional problem-solving skills, enjoy learning, are self-starters, learn rapidly, and are intrinsically motivated (Taylor, Smiley, and Richards 2014). Some of these traits can also be problematic for these children. As a result, they may be very critical of themselves, may be perfectionists, may burn out from the pressure to perform, and may not be able to distinguish between work and play. They may also be very inquisitive and ask many questions, which can be misinterpreted by others as being distractible or arrogant (Piirto 2007). Because many teachers do not have adequate understanding of techniques for working with these students and do not take the time necessary for curriculum adaptations, gifted students can become bored and frustrated, which can lead to underachievement (King 2005).

There is also a group of students/children who are considered to be twice-exceptional. They have a diagnosed disability and also are gifted/talented (Taylor, Smiley, and Richards 2014). For example, a student may have a large vocabulary and excellent verbal skills, but have a writing disability. Or a student may have a reading disability but exceptional talents in leadership skills. And another student may have extremely sophisticated computer and technology skills but have a significant math disability. Too often, the students' exceptional abilities and talents are overshadowed by the disability, and attention is focused on remediating their struggles instead of

Table 10.6 Recommended instructional interventions and modifications for working with gifted/talented children and youths.

Intervention	*Description*
Curriculum compacting	Streamlining academic activities to allow for replacement time for more challenging and interesting work. Instructional outcomes are identified, a system for determining mastery of outcomes is utilized. Children can move quickly through the curriculum when mastered which leaves time to work on enrichment activities.
Problem-based learning	Requires critical-thinking skills and problem-solving abilities, which are common traits in gifted children. Real-world problems/situations are presented, and students are asked to solve the problem. Teacher serves as facilitator and may model problem-solving strategies. Very motivating.
Independent study	Exploring topics and areas that are of interest,. Child can pose questions and outcomes for research; need to learn how to work independently first and take responsibility for own learning.

Sources: Gargiulo 2015; Stanley 2011; Trail 2010.

developing their abilities and talents (King 2005). This can be very frustrating and discouraging for these children and can lead to low self-esteem, a lack of motivation, and depression (King 2005). These children have very unique needs in that they need a combination of supports and services to address both their disability as well as their areas of giftedness or talent. Recommended practices to use when teaching students who are gifted/talented include helping them understand both their gifts and, where relevant, their disabilities and developing realistic goals and coping strategies for when feeling frustrated, and providing structured learning environments and opportunities to interact with peers, especially in their area of exceptional abilities (King 2005).

Table 10.6 shows recommended instructional interventions and modifications for working with gifted/talented children and youths.

Treatments, Strategies, and Programming in Homeschooling

Parents who homeschool their children with special needs identify unique and highly individualized goals they have for their children. The parents in Hurlbutt (2011) discussed a variety of goals they focused on with their children, ranging from providing specialized diets, increasing positive behaviors and decreasing aggressive behaviors, providing more structure than the school was able to do, stabilizing health concerns, providing academic instruction at the child's ability level, facilitating independence, and learning self-advocacy. Some parents had a goal of having their child return to the school setting while others do not consider that to be a viable option (Hurlbutt 2011; Parsons and Lewis 2010).

The treatment methods and programs that homeschooling parents use are as varied as the reasons why they homeschool and what their specific goals are for their children (Fields-Smith and Williams 2009; Hurlbutt 2011; Parsons and Lewis 2010; Winstanley 2009). These parents have made significant commitments to researching and trying a wide variety of treatment methods and options to find something that works, that benefits their children, and that helps their children succeed. In Hurlbutt (2011, 247), parents reported having found "a treatment plan that works," and did not have plans to change what they had been doing. The treatment plans varied greatly as illustrated below.

One model was full-time homeschooling, where the child was served only by the parents at home and in the community, and was the most common in the study by Hurlbutt (2011). In this model, the parents utilized no services from the school. Another model was where the child received training in academics and other topic areas at home, but attended school for activities such as social skills groups or specific therapies. A third model was where a tutor or specialist was hired to work with the child in the home during the day. In one situation, the specialist was a behavior therapist contracted to conduct ABA (Applied Behavior Therapy) sessions. Another model involved utilizing a program that the school considered to be controversial and non-evidence based.

In Parsons and Lewis (2010, 81), most parents felt that the problem was not the subject material that needed to be taught, but rather the way the children were taught it. They preferred a "more child-centred, flexible and personalised approach," which they believed could only happen if their child was educated at home. In Jolly, Masters, and Nester (2012, 127), just about all parents utilized an "eclectic approach," incorporating a "variety of strategies" when setting up a curricular approach for their children that was "closely tailored to the ability and interest profile of their children." And in Lundy and Mazama (2014, 65), the goal of the parents was to provide a safe place for their children (mostly males) to learn away from biased teachers, to embrace their culture, and to "construct a positive image of Black masculinity."

While different parents set up the daily routine in different ways and have different reasons for focusing on what they do, many parents who homeschool their children with exceptionalities report that they generally spend a specific amount of time on instruction and independent academic work per day, in addition to regular field trips, socialization opportunities, computer time, self-directed activities, and therapy sessions (Fields-Smith and Williams 2009; Hurlbutt 2011, Jolly, Masters, and Nester 2012; Parsons and Lewis 2010). The parents listed a vast number of socialization opportunities they purposely set up for their children to provide opportunities for interaction with their peers. However, in Hurlbutt (2012), special education teachers were surveyed about their perceptions and beliefs about homeschooling students with autism spectrum disorders, and a significant concern the teachers had was their belief that these students were missing out on social opportunities, which they believed could not be solely met through homeschooling. Interestingly, while just about all of the parents of children with disabilities had no concerns about a lack of socialization opportunities for their children, parents of the gifted children in one study commented that some of their children continued to feel isolated, having no other students to interact with throughout the day. For a couple of those students, the feelings of isolation that the gifted students felt while being in school only intensified when they were homeschooled (Jolly, Matthews, and Nester 2012). In Parsons and Lewis (2010), only two out of twenty-seven parents identified a lack of social opportunities as being an issue. All other parents in the above studies actively scheduled opportunities for socialization.

Current research shows that the majority of parents who homeschool their children with exceptionalities felt that homeschooling was their only option and would have preferred their children to stay in the schools. However, they believe that homeschooling provides them the opportunity to meet the individual needs of their child, allows for needed flexibility, creates an environment where the child does not experience the stress he or she did in the public school setting, lends itself to meeting the needs of the family, and provides rich, stimulating opportunities for success that prepare the child to live well in the real world (Hurlbutt 2011; Jolly, Masters, and Nester 2012; Kidd and Kaczmerak 2010; Lundy and Mazama 2014; McDonald and Lopes 2014; Parsons and Lewis 2010).

Future Research

The home education of students with special needs has historically been, and remains, a woefully understudied topic. Recent years have seen a small but growing number of publications regarding homeschooling students with special needs, many of them directed toward parents and other interested individuals, and some of these practical manuals offer advice grounded in the empirical scholarship on special education. However, academic study of homeschooling among children with exceptionalities remains very minimal, especially in the United States. A number of issues exist that require further study and attention. Several are explained below:

1. There is a need to conduct more qualitative studies with a large number of parents to learn about their experiences and advice that they have. The qualitative studies that have been published have very small samples. These findings cannot be generalized to all families who homeschool their children with special needs, so interviewing more parents, and perhaps observing in the homes, would add substantially to the literature available.
2. In addition to qualitative studies, there is a need for large quantitative studies to determine demographic-type information such as education level of parents, age of parents, race, ethnicity, as well as those in rural vs. urban vs. suburban vs. small town settings. How do all of these statistics compare to each other? Are there differences in the numbers of parents who homeschool or in the challenges they face when taking these variables into consideration?
3. In much of the literature that is available, it appears as though most parents who are included in these studies and books are well-educated professionals who enjoy a higher socioeconomic status. It would be beneficial to hear from parents who are less educated and/or in a lower socioeconomic bracket. What are their needs, perceptions, challenges, and successes? How are things going for those families?
4. In many studies, the mothers were the ones who completed the surveys or interviews. It would be interesting to hear from the fathers to learn about their understanding, perceptions, and experiences.
5. Frequently enough, students who were pulled from the school system do return to school, and those who didn't start do in time attend. What is the average length of time spent in homeschooling? Are there differences for those who never attended school vs those who did but were pulled because of any number of possible reasons? What changes may occur that influence the decision to continue homeschooling children with special needs or send them to, or back to, the public school system?
6. It would be interesting to hear from the children themselves, both children with disabilities and those who are gifted/talented. What are their perceptions and preferences? What are the advantages and disadvantages from the child's point of view? Would this information be helpful to parents?

7. Longitudinal studies are needed to investigate life outcomes, including job situations, living arrangements, social skills, and finances of young adults with disabilities who were homeschooled as opposed to those who attended the public school system. Are there significant differences? Is either group more successful? What are the specific situations for either group of young adults?

Note

1. (Center for Research on Learning (http://kucrl.org/index.shtml)

References

American Association on Intellectual and Developmental Disabilities (AAIDD). 2012. *User's Guide to Accompany the 11th Edition of Intellectual Disability: Definition, Classification, and Systems of Supports*, 11th ed. US: AAIDD.

American Psychiatric Association. 2013. *Diagnostic and Statistical Manual of Mental Disorders*, 5th ed. Arlington, VA: Author.

An Act. 1975. US Government Publishing Office. Accessed June 2014. http://www.gpo.gov/fdsys/pkg/STATUTE-89/pdf/STATUTE-89-Pg773.pdf

Archer, Anita, and Charles Hughes. 2010. *Explicit Instruction: Effective and Efficient Teaching*. New York, NY: Guilford Press.

Autism Speaks. 2015. *Advocacy in Action: 10 Great Accomplishments*. Accessed March 2015. https://www.autismspeaks.org/blog/2015/02/23/advocacy-action-10-great-accomplishments

Barkley, Russell. 2013. *Taking Charge of ADHD: The Complete, Authoritative Guide for Parents*, 3rd ed. New York, NY: Guilford Press.

Beech, Marty. 2010. *Accommodations: Assisting Students with Disabilities*, 3rd ed. Tallahassee, FL: Florida Department of Education, Bureau of Exceptional Education and Student Services.

Best, Sherwood, Kathryn Heller, and June Bigge. 2009. *Teaching Individuals with Physical or Multiple Disabilities*, 6th ed. Upper Saddle River, NJ: Pearson.

Blok, Henk. 2004. "Performance in Home-schooling: An Argument Against Compulsory Schooling in the Netherlands." *International Review of Education*, 50: 39-52.

Boring, Melinda. 2006. *Heads Up Helping!! Teaching Tips and Techniques for Working with ADD, ADHD, and Other Children with Challenges*. Bloomington IN: Trafford Publishing.

Boyd, Brian, et al. 2008. "Descriptive Analysis of Classroom Setting Events on the Social Behaviors of Children with Autism Spectrum Disorder." *Education and Training in Developmental Disabilities*, 43: 186–197.

Boyer, Ernest. 1979. "Public law 94-142: A Promising Start?" *Educational Leadership*, 36: 298 –301.

Canales, Lindsay, and Rebecca Lytle. 2011. *Physical Activities for Young People with Severe Disabilities*. Champaign, IL: Human Kinetics.

Council for Children with Behavioral Disorders. 2015. "Definitions, Characteristics and Related Information." Accessed March 2015. http://www.ccbd.net/about/ebddefintion

Dawson, Peg, and Richard Guare. 2009. *Smart but Scattered: The Revolutionary "Executive Skills" Approach to Helping Kids Reach Their Potential.* New York, NY: Guilford Press.

Duffey, Jane. 2002. "Home Schooling Children with Special Needs: A Descriptive Study." *Home School Researcher*, 15: 1–13.

Education Law. 2012. "Mills v. Board of Education of the District of Columbia: The Court's Ruling." Accessed May 6 2016. http://www.specialeducationadvisor.com/special-education-laws/brief-history-of-special-education-court-cases/

Federal Education Budget Project. 2014. "IDEA – Funding Distribution." Accessed November 2014.http://febp.newamerica.net/background-analysis/individuals-disabilities-education-act-funding-distribution

Feldman, Heidi. 2013. *Redesigning Health Care for Children with Disabilities: Strengthening Inclusion, Contribution, and Health.* Baltimore, MD: Paul H. Brookes Publishing Company.

Fiedler, Barbara. 2001. "Considering Placement and Educational Approaches for Students who are Deaf and Hard of Hearing." *Teaching Exceptional Children* 34: 54–59.

Fields-Smith, Cheryl, and Meca Williams. 2009. "Motivations, Sacrifices, and Challenges: Black Parents' Decisions to Home School." *The Urban Review* 41: 369–389.

Fields-Smith Cheryl, and Monica Wells Kisura. 2013. "Resisting the Status Quo: The Narratives of Black Homeschoolers in Metro-Atlanta and Metro-DC. *Peabody Journal of Education* 88: 265–283.

Gargiulo, Richard. 2015. *Special Education in Contemporary Society*, 5th ed. Thousand Oaks, CA: Sage Publications, Inc.

Hallahan, Daniel, John Lloyd, James Kauffman, Margaret Weiss, and Elizabeth Martinez. 2005. *Learning Disabilities: Foundations, Characteristics, and Effective Teaching*, 3rd ed. Boston, MA: Allyn & Bacon.

Hanna, Linda. 2012. "Homeschooling Education: Longitudinal Study of Methods, Material, and Curricula." *Education and Urban Society* 44: 609–631.

Heflin, Juane, and Donna Alaimo. 2007. *Students with Autism Spectrum Disorders: Effective Instructional Practices.* Upper Saddle River, NJ: Pearson Education.

Herer, Gilbert, Carol Knightly, and Annie Steinberg. 2002. ""Hearing, Sounds, and Silences." In *Children with Disabilities*, edited by M. L. Batshaw, 5th ed., 193–227. Baltimore, MD: Paul H. Brookes.

Hunt, Nancy, and Kathleen Marshall. 2012. *Exceptional Children and Youth*, 5th ed. Independence, KY: Cengage Learning, Inc.

Hurlbutt, Karen. 2011. "Experiences of Parents who Homeschool their Children with Autism Spectrum Disorders." *Focus on Autism and Other Developmental Disabilities*, 26: 239–249.

Hurlbutt, Karen. 2012. "Special Education Teachers' Perceptions and Beliefs Regarding Homeschooling Children with Autism Spectrum Disorders." *Home School Researcher*, 27: 1–9.

Jolly, Jennifer, Michael Matthews, and Jonathan Nester. 2012. "Homeschooling the Gifted: A Parent's Perspective." *Gifted Child Quarterly*, 57: 121–134.

Kauffman, James, and Timothy Landrum. 2013. *Characteristics of Emotional and Behavioral Disorders of Children and Youth*, 10th ed. Upper Saddle River, NJ: Pearson Education.

Kidd, Theresa, and Elizabeth Kaczmerak. 2010. "The Experiences of Mothers Home Educating Their Children with Autism Spectrum Disorder." *Issues in Educational Research*, 20: 257–275.

King, Emily. 2005. "Addressing the Social and Emotional Needs of Twice-Exceptional Students." *Teaching Exceptional Children*, 38: 16–20.

Lawrence, Clare. 2012. *Autism and Flexischooling: A Shared Classroom and Homeschooling Approach*. London, England: Jessica Kingsley.

Lerner, Janet, and Beverley Johns. 2012. *Learning Disabilities and Related Mild Disabilities*, 12th ed. Belmont, CA: Wadsworth/Cengage Learning.

Lundy, Garvey, and Ama Mazama. 2014. "I'm Keeping my Son Home: African American Males and the Motivation to Homeschool." *Journal of African American Males in Education*, 5: 53–74.

McDonald, Jasmine, and Elaine Lopes. 2014. "How Parents Home Educate their Children with an Autism Spectrum Disorder with the Support of the Schools of Isolated and Distance Education." *International Journal of Inclusive Education*, 18: 1–17.

Myles, Brenda, Richard Simpson, and Sonya de Boer. 2008. "Inclusion of Students with Autism Spectrum Disorders in General Education Settings." In *Educating Children and Youth with Autism*, 2nd ed., edited by Richard Simpson and Brenda Myles, 357–382. Austin, TX: Pro-Ed.

National Association for Gifted Children. 2013. "What is Gifted?" Accessed October 2014. http://www.nagc.org/.

National Center for Education Statistics. 2008. "1.5 Million Homeschooled Students in the United States in 2007." Accessed March 2015. http://nces.ed.gov/pubs2009/2009030.pdf

National Center for Education Statistics. 2013. "Parent and Family Involvement in Education from the National Household Education Surveys Program of 2012." Accessed May 6, 2016. https://nces.ed.gov/pubsearch/pubsinfo.asp?pubid=2013028rev

OSERS. 2010. "Thirty-Five Years of Progress in Educating Children with Disabilities Through IDEA." Accessed August 2014. http://www2.ed.gov/about/offices/list/osers/idea35/history/index_pg10.html

Parsons, Sarah, and Ann Lewis. 2010. "The Home-Education of Children with Special Needs or Disabilities in the UK: Views of Parents from an Online Survey." *International Journal of Inclusive Education*, 14: 67–86.

Piirto, Jane. 2007. *Talented Children and Adults: Their Development and Education*, 3rd ed. Waco, TX: Prufrock Press.

Pyles, Lisa. 2004. *Homeschooling the Child with Asperger Syndrome*. London, England: Jessica Kingsley.

Reed, Phil, Lisa Osborne, and Mark Corness. 2007. "The Real World Effectiveness of Early Teaching Interventions for Children with Autism Spectrum Disorders." *Exceptional Children*, 73: 417–433.

Reid, Robert, Torri Lienemann, and Jessica Hagaman. 2013. *Strategy Instruction for Students with Learning Disabilities*, 2nd ed. New York, NY: Guilford Press.

Renzulli, Joseph, and Sally Reis. 2003. "The School-Wide Enrichment Model: Developing Creative and Productive Giftedness." In *Handbook of Gifted Education*, 3rd ed, edited by Nicholas Colangelo, and Gary Davis, 184–203. Boston, MA: Allyn & Bacon.

Samuels, Christina. 2008. *Parents of Children With Autism Pessimistic, Survey Says*. Accessed August 2014. http://www.edweek.org/ew/articles/2008/12/16/16autism.h28.html

Shepherd, Terry. 2009. *Working with Students with Emotional and Behavior Disorders: Characteristics and Teaching Strategies*. Upper Saddle River, NJ: Pearson.

Simpson, Richard, and Brenda Myles. 2008. *Educating Children and Youth*, 2nd ed. Austin, TX: Pro-Ed.

Snell, Martha, and Fredda Brown. 2010. *Instruction of Students with Severe Disabilities*, 7th ed. Upper Saddle River, NJ: Pearson.

Stanley, Todd, 2011. *Project-Based Learning for Gifted Students: A Handbook for the 21st-Century Classroom*. Waco, TX: Profrock Press.

Starr, Elizabeth, Janice Foy, and Kenneth Cramer. 2001. "Parental Perceptions of the Education of Children with Pervasive Developmental Disorders." *Education and Training in Developmental Disabilities*, 36: 55–68.

Starr, Elizabeth, Janice Foy, Kenneth Cramer, and Henareet Sigh. 2006. "How are Schools Doing? Parental Perceptions of Children with Autism Spectrum Disorders." *Education and Training in Developmental Disabilities*, 41: 315–332.

Swanson, H. Lee, Karen Harris, and Steve Graham. 2013. *Handbook of Learning Disabilities*, 2nd ed. New York, NY: Guilford Press.

Taylor, Ronald, Lydia Smiley, and Stephen Richards. 2014. *Exceptional Students: Preparing Teachers for the 21st Century*, 2nd ed. New York, NY: McGraw-Hill Education.

Trail, Beverly. 2010. *Twice-Exceptional Gifted Children: Understanding, Teaching, and Counseling Gifted Students*. Waco, TX: Profrock Press.

US Office of Education. 1977. "Assistance to States for Education of Handicapped Children: Procedures for Evaluating Specific Learning Disabilities." *Federal Register*, 42: 65082– 65085.

Vaughn, Sharon, Candace Bos, and Jeanne Schumm. 2014. *Teaching Students Who are Exceptional, Diverse, and At Risk*, 6th ed. Upper Saddle River, NJ: Pearson Education.

Wheeler, John, Michael Mayton, and Stacy Carter. 2015. *Methods for Teaching Students with Autism Spectrum Disorders*. Boston, MA: Pearson.

Wilkinson, Lee. 2010. *Autism and Asperger Syndrome in Schools: A Best Practice Guide to Assessment and Intervention*. London, England: Jessica Kingsley.

Winstanley, Carrie. 2009. "Too Cool for School? Gifted Children and Homeschooling." *Theory and Research in Education*, 7: 347–362.

Yell, Mitchell, Nancy Meadows, Erik Drasgow, and James Shriner. 2013. *Evidence Based Practice for Educating Students with Emotional and Behavioral Disorders*, 2nd ed. Upper Saddle River, NJ: Pearson.

11

Homeschooling 2.0

An Overview of Online Learning in K–12 Education across the United States

Bryan Mann

Introduction

Homeschooling, like many other aspects of modern society, has gone online. Students and parents can remotely access schooling content from their home via the internet, providing the opportunity to receive the same curricula as any student in a traditional school. In a sense, online learning is "homeschooling 2.0" because it uses online instruction, resources, and curricula in unison with parental support to allow for student learning at a location that is not a school building. However, this form of schooling differs from traditional homeschooling not only because of its use of web technologies but also because the majority of online programs are primarily connected to publicly and privately run schools. In other words, parents have a role in supporting their children in online learning, but they are not the sole instructors in an online setting.

Over the last decade, states and local governments in the United States have increasingly supported this online version of homeschooling as part of the choice-based public school movement. Through this movement online charter schools (identified in this chapter as "cyber charter schools"), district-based online schools, online private schools, and even statewide virtual schools have developed. This development has occurred rather sporadically with no uniform model across the United States. Various types and patterns of online learning and online schools have emerged haphazardly around the country. Scholarly research on kindergarten through 12th grade (K–12) online learning has struggled to keep pace with this uneven growth. With these considerations, this chapter has two main purposes. The first is to provide an overview of the various, albeit scattered, types of K–12 online

The Wiley Handbook of Home Education, First Edition. Edited by Milton Gaither.

learning that have developed in the United States. The second is to describe the current state of research and make suggestions for future research directions.

This chapter is therefore divided into four sections. The first is a brief history of online learning in the United States. The second provides a basic typography of the forms of K–12 online learning, describing enrollment trends and basic research related to each, and concluding with recommendations for research at the end of each subsection. The third gives an overview of research about K–12 online learning across a few major topics, including funding and policy debates, teacher quality, school leadership, and learning outcomes and, again, concluding with recommendations for research at the end of each subsection. The fourth section summarizes and concludes the chapter.

A Brief History of Online Learning in the United States

Learning from a distance with technology is not new. The roots of using technology for distance learning in K–12 schooling started with distance education programs paired with radio broadcasting in the 1920s. The focus of this chapter is on trends and developments specifically related to online learning, whose origins lie in the web-based platforms that developed in the 1990s (Clark and Barbour 2015). This chapter uses Watson and Kalmon's (2005) definition of online learning: a form of schooling where "instruction and content are delivered primarily over the internet" (127). This type of learning can happen part-time where a student formally receives instruction and content on a specific course topic from a public or private virtual school, full-time where a student receives the entirety of his or her schooling experience online, or even in a supplemental capacity where a student uses popular online learning tools such as Massive Open Online Courses (MOOCs) or the Khan Academy to enrich whatever schooling type they experience full-time, be it homeschooling, private schooling, or traditional schooling.

The first K–12 online schools began in the 1990s as internet access and use grew. One of the first documented US online schools is the Laurel Springs School, which is a private online school that started as a text-based distance education program in 1991 and developed its online curriculum in 1994 (Watson et al. 2014). From this point, there were two major developments that catalyzed K–12 online learning on a larger scale. The first was the launching of the Florida Virtual School (FVS) in 1996. This event was critical because the school is a large-scale, state-sponsored program that offered online courses to students across the entire state, eventually growing to provide courses to students in other states. The second development was the emergence of "cyber" versions of charter schools in the late 1990s and early 2000s (Clark and Barbour 2015). These are typically full-time schools that, in some states, enroll several thousand students. Now, while only making up a small proportion of nationwide students, online learning is the fastest growing school choice option in the United States (Miron and Welner 2012). Supplemental online learning programs developed more recently, with the Khan Academy starting in 2006 and the current form of MOOCs emerging around 2012 (Khan Academy; Emanuel 2013).

While there are many forms of online learning, this chapter will focus on programs that provide learning capabilities primarily to a student's home (or other non-school location). In doing so, this chapter will describe three models frequently used: full-time, part-time and supplementary online learning options. The rationale for focusing on these is that they align most closely with traditional homeschooling where a student does not go to a school building for instruction. This chapter does not focus on another highly popular version of online learning called "blended learning." Blended learning is a formal schooling practice where traditional schools mix place-based, face-to-face learning with online learning. Some predict blended learning will "disrupt" traditional schooling practices entirely (Horn and Staker 2015). This chapter does not focus on blended learning because it occurs at least partially in a school building and thus does not fall squarely within the homeschooling conversation.

Types of Online Schools and Enrollment

The providers of K–12 online learning come in several forms that are typically identified by the organizational type with which the student is affiliated; some of these are full-time, while others are part-time or supplemental. The organizational types of online learning include cyber charter schools (often full-time), district online schools (sometimes full-time), private online schools (often full-time), statewide virtual schools (typically part-time), and Massive Open Online Courses (MOOCs), which began in a post-secondary context but have started to enroll younger students (supplementary and not usually for credit, but some for-credit options are developing). There are additional supplementary options available that are not affiliated with any school; the most popular version of this type is the Khan Academy. The cyber charter schools, district online schools, private online schools, and statewide virtual schools are formalized in that they are linked to state or private schools and their courses are counted as credit for graduation requirements. MOOCs and the Khan Academy can be used as tools to supplement homeschooling instruction conducted entirely by the family.

Formal online schools also differ within the types listed above because they have multiple ways they create and offer content. Some online schools create and offer their own content, while others sometimes outsource curriculum and even instruction to providers. The schools that outsource content provision to others can include cyber charter, district online, and private online schools that purchase content from companies such as K^{12} Inc. or Connections Academy. When these companies run the entire operation of a cyber charter school they are called educational management organizations (EMOs) (Clark and Barbour 2015). For-profit EMOs are the most popular providers of formal online learning, operating in several US states (Miron, Horvitz, and Gulosino 2013). Further details of the mechanisms that create and offer content will not be expanded upon in this chapter, but they are an important part of the online learning ecology. In the 2013–2014 school year, for-profit EMOs ran 40% of online schools nationwide and accounted for 71% of enrollments in full-time online schools (Molnar 2015, iii). The state-sponsored virtual schools, like FVS, enrolled the majority of supplemental online students.

Informal platforms like MOOCs and the Khan Academy are different because they do not typically count toward an educational credential (some universities are starting to provide for-credit MOOC options). MOOCs are college-level courses created by universities offered to the public for free. The Khan Academy started as a non-profit venture to deliver tutoring services to individual students. MOOCs and the Khan Academy are not affiliated with K–12 educational agencies, but they have the capability of assisting homeschooling parents in the delivery of content. However, some states are now beginning to incorporate these platforms with public school classrooms, often in informal ways (Curtis 2013; Watson et al. 2014, 65).

The enrollment statistics presented in this section for each organizational type are largely drawn from the series *Keeping Pace with K–12 Digital Learning* by the Evergreen Education group. This series of annual reports explains the most current state of enrollment in K–12 online schools in the United States (Watson et al. 2014). The recent report shows that thirty states offer a form of full-time online school with an enrollment of more than 315 000 students across the US, while more than 740 000 students enroll in supplementary online courses (5). These numbers are likely underestimates because they consider mainly state virtual schools and cyber charter schools as it has been difficult to quantify the scale of online learning in the other settings.

Cyber charter schools

Cyber charter schools have the word "charter" in their name because they are linked to the charter school organizational type. This organizational type is unique in that the founding of a charter school happens through receiving a "charter" from authorizers who are decided by state law, and charter schools are managed by outside organizations that are either local or national and either for-profit or nonprofit (Ravitch 2010). In other words, charter schools are publicly funded but managed and funded through different structures than typically found in traditional public schools. Cyber charter schools are an online version of charter schools and thus operate independently from school districts while still receiving public monies to operate. Cyber charter schools vary by type in that some use hybrid delivery content models, where students might do some work at home and go to a resource center during the week, while others teach students entirely online (Ahn 2011). Cyber charter schooling is typically different than homeschooling because teachers using the online platform are the sole instructors of students. Parents can assist students, but the students are formally linked to the school, meaning they receive grades, credits, and eventually a diploma.

Cyber charter schools are widely known because of politically contentious debates about their operation. The critics of cyber charter schools tend to be local and national media outlets that have reported stories about cyber charter schools, ranging from embezzlement scandals to poor learning outcomes on traditional school evaluation metrics (Saul 2011; Niederberger 2012, 2013). Advocates argue these indicators are not representative of the true value of cyber charter school programs because cyber charter schools tend to attract the most struggling students and should therefore be judged based on student growth instead of aggregate metrics (Hanak 2015). Mann and Barkauskas (2014) synthesize these arguments and explain cyber charter schools have the potential to produce either positive or negative opportunities for the educational system as a whole depending on how the programs are constructed and funded, but these authors raise questions about the capability of current structures.

Despite these debates surrounding cyber charter schools, they are the most popular version of full-time online education. In the 2013–2014 school year, cyber charter schools operated in twenty-six states and served about 200 000 students (Watson et al. 2014, 18). The states with the highest enrollment include Arizona, California, Ohio, and Pennsylvania, all of which enroll more than 30 000 students, or between 2% and 4% of their statewide student populations. This shows that clearly there is uneven development of cyber charter schools across the United States because in some states the option is growing, while in other states cyber charter schools do not exist.

The link between cyber charter schools and traditional homeschooling is unclear. It is difficult to capture the number of enrolled students who originally came from homeschooling before joining cyber charter school programs, but cyber charter schools are the likely candidate as being the most popular option for homeschoolers. This is because cyber charter schools have the highest enrollment of full-time online students nationwide and these programs are paid with tax dollars (there is no tuition fee for families). While the precise number of homeschooled students now enrolled in cyber charters is unclear, a report from the largest EMO indicates that more than a fourth of their students were either homeschooled, not in school, or from a private schools (K[12] Inc. 2013).

While it is not clear if the primary reason for the growth of the cyber charter schools is due to enrolling many homeschooling students, there is research about the motivation as well as the demographic types of all students enrolled. One study explores what causes parents to choose specific types of cyber charter schools: the ability to customize for a child's needs, the lack of financial risk involved with the decision to join given that they are free, and parental hope that this new option of schooling type will finally be the right choice for their children that they lack in traditional brick-and-mortar settings (Marsh, Carr-Chellman, and Sockman 2009). Other studies on cyber charter school enrollment show that cyber charter schools nationally enroll a lower than average percentage of students who are eligible for free and reduced lunch (35.1% compared to 45.4% nationally), lower than average English language learners (0.1% compared to 9.6% nationally), and higher than average percentage of White students (69.6% compared to 53.9% nationally), indicating that the schools tend to be wealthier and less diverse than traditional public schools (Miron and Gulosino 2015).

Additional research relating to cyber charter schools is largely critical of cyber charter school funding and practice. For example, DeJarnatt (2013) and Wagner (2012) look at the Pennsylvania cyber charter schools and argue that there is a lack of financial accountability in the schools, showing that funding formulas unfairly give more money to cyber charter schools than they actually need to operate. Rapp, Eckes, and Plucker (2006) collated early literature to offer policy recommendations while claiming that cyber charters pose major questions about their sponsorship, funding, enrollment, accountability, and special education practices. Meanwhile, Huerta, González, and d'Entremont (2006) as well as Brady, Umpstead, and Eckes (2010) describe a lack of legal oversight and the need for updated policy that holds stricter accountability standards. Others raise concern with the seemingly large influence of privatization in the cyber charter school sector (Meyn-Rogeness 2010). More recently, Hasler Waters, Barbour, and Menchaca (2014) conducted a comprehensive literature review of cyber charter schools and restated these earlier concerns, summarizing that in the literature there are still concerns about a lack of accountability, funding structures, and questionable performance.

Taken together the research on cyber charter schools leaves many unanswered questions across several research topics, and there is a two-sided debate related to these schools: one that argues that the platform is filled with potential and promise, allowing a new version of homeschooling that can provide unprecedented levels of access to educational content in an emerging type of learning modality; the other questions the current quality, funding structures, and fairness of cyber charter schools, seeking reform to try to either improve or eliminate the programs. This indicates that there is interest in cyber charter schools and that conversations are typically devoid of enough knowledge to resolve the debates. For one, there needs to be more research on cyber charter school quality. Scholars need to look closer at student learning metrics and consider the types of students best served by cyber charter schools.

There is also a research need related to cyber charter schools and homeschooling. Specifically, there is a lack of understanding about the number of homeschooling families who enroll their children in cyber charter schools and if this option is something that does serve these homeschooling families better. While there is some knowledge that exists that shows that the cyber charter schools option has enticed some homeschooling families away from independent homeschooling, the extent to which this has happened is not clear. There is also little research on ways cyber charter schools can specifically improve their programs to meet the needs of these families.

District and private cyber schools

More traditional formal schooling providers, school districts and private schools, have also developed supplementary and even full-time online programs. They do this by creating content and curricula similar to what is seen in cyber charter schools, so again this is different than typical homeschooling because students are linked to formal schools to receive content and instruction, although, as with cyber charter schools, they receive this content and instruction from a distance through the internet. These versions of online schools offer sometimes full-time and sometimes part-time courses that students take in addition to enrolling in a brick-and-mortar school full- or part-time.

Quantifying the scale of these practices has proven to be challenging because districts often merge online programs into their own school district system and attach the programs to brick-and-mortar schools that already exist. This means that in the current setup, state enrollment data often identifies full-time online students as being enrolled within a brick-and-mortar school. Similar patterns and difficult quantification abilities occur in the private sector, as private school data is not always readily available to researchers (Watson et al. 2014, 25). This creates a research gap where there is a need to quantify activity within these organizational types.

There is also limited knowledge about the particular versions of online learning that school districts use and the rationale for these uses. Waters (2011) explains that in California traditional public schools compete for students with virtual schools. The author shows that due to this competition, districts responded with three options: full-time, supplementary, and blended modes of online learning. Watson et al. (2014) argue that they believe the vast majority of traditional school districts use some form of digital learning. However, their report called for more precise quantification of trends because a lack of data exists. This lack of data leads to a potential substantial underestimation of online learning activity overall because 84% of all US students attend public schools. It is not clear how many of these millions of students are participating in online learning. Thus, tracking of online learning trends in K–12 districts has relied mostly on observational data, which shows that online learning is used mostly at the high school level for credit recovery, alternative education, and advanced placement courses (Watson et al. 2014, 10).

The understanding of online learning trends within the private school sector is equally murky. Brick-and-mortar private schools are usually tuition based, and less than 9% of K–12 students in the United States attend private schools. Despite the fact that the first online school in the US started in the traditional private school format (where parents pay tuition or get vouchers to pay tuition, as opposed to the charter school model where school districts pay tuition directly), private schools tend to "lag behind" public schools in their use of digital and online learning (Watson et al. 2014, 23). The little research that has been done on the small number of full-time online private schools that exist suggests that they tend to enroll fewer students than the cyber charter schools, that they are tuition based, and that some enroll students from both inside and outside of the United States (25).

A primary understanding from the knowledge related to school district and privately run online schools is that there are different types of programs growing, though the scale and compositions of these programs is unclear. It appears that in some areas there are school districts that have online learning, sometimes mixing it with classroom practices and sometimes offering full-time online programs of their own. Use of online learning in the private school sector seems less extensive, as the practice within brick-and-mortar private schools and the existence of full-time online private school does not appear to have the same scale as cyber charters or even traditional public school districts. More research is needed in determining how accurate these preliminary understandings are.

The lack of substantial data in this domain of academic literature leaves an obvious need for research: scholars need to understand the scale of online learning in traditional public school districts and private schools and, in turn, how these developments impact homeschoolers. There is the potential that these online learning models are ways in which traditional public schools can appeal to a homeschooling audience that obviously opted out of the public schooling system. However, it is not clear if homeschooling families use, or even want to use, traditional public school and private online learning programs. Research on the relationship between homeschooling and these versions of online learning, as well as the potential for this relationship, would serve as a viable next step.

State virtual schools

The type of online learning with the highest enrollment is the state offerings of online courses. Watson et al. (2014) define this type of schooling as "programs created by legislation or by a state level agency, and/or administered by a state education agency, and/or funded by a state appropriation or grant for the purpose of providing online learning opportunities across the state" and show that twenty-six state virtual schools collectively enrolled 741 516 students in 2013–2014. The Florida Virtual School enrolled the most students, accounting for more than 370 000 (27). The report also notes that aggregate enrollments stalled in 2013–2014, which was the first time in at least a decade where there was not overall growth. Like the other types of online schools already discussed, this form of online schooling relies on a formal agency to instruct and provide the content for its students. This means that homeschooling families can use this option, but it would be linked to a formal affiliation with a state-run public schooling agency.

Research on state virtual schools explains that there is not one consistent model across the states and learning performance varies. To depict the lack of consistency across models, Thomas (2002) shows that state virtual schools were created for a variety of reasons depending on state context, and a key diverging point for states is if they purchase the content or create it themselves. However, this research is becoming outdated, and it would be interesting to see if there is now more consistency across models as more states are beginning to develop statewide online courses. What is clear, though, is that like the other models of online learning, some states have popular versions of these programs, while other states do not use them.

Overall, state virtual schools provide an opportunity for homeschooling parents to provide supplementary material for their children, but depending on how they are funded across different state contexts, they may charge enrollment fees

(Watson et al. 2014, 27). Like the other modes of online learning, models and availability differ depending on the state in which the homeschooling family resides. This state virtual schooling option has enrolled the most students nationwide and grew consistently for a decade until 2014 (the most recent year for which data were collected at the time of writing).

The most pressing homeschooling research needed for scholars studying state virtual schools is examining policy across state contexts to determine the models that allow access to homeschooling families. Supplementary online courses are theoretically an intriguing option for homeschoolers because they allow students to take specific courses at home while not having to opt into learning a school's entire curriculum. This allows for an option of choosing specific content; however, the accessibility of this option for homeschooling families is not clear. Scholars should research the extent to which homeschooling families take advantage of this option and how well the courses serve this population.

Massive Open Online Courses (MOOCs) and the Khan Academy

There are other online learning options available to homeschooling students that are not affiliated to K–12 schools or state education programs whatsoever. These tools allow parents to decide on the curriculum (to whatever extent they are legally allowed) and use the online learning tools in a capacity that assists them with instruction. The most high profile online models that allow this option for parents are MOOCs and the Khan Academy.

MOOCs are college-level courses that universities create and offer to the public for no charge. These courses cover the entire spectrum of university material. Despite starting as a way to serve adult audiences, MOOC providers allow for anyone (including K–12 students) to enroll in their courses for free. A few have even begun tailoring content to K–12 students. In September of 2014 two of the major university sponsors, Harvard and MIT, partnered to create MOOCs for high schoolers. The purpose of this collaboration was both to prepare high schoolers for Advanced Placement (AP) exams and to expand their academic knowledge (Atkeson 2014). The University of Houston System also launched two MOOCs to help prepare students for AP exams. Coursera, a popular MOOC platform provider, enrolled more than 3000 K–12 students, and other providers are starting to follow (Watson et al. 2014, 65). However, initial enrollment data about MOOCs suggests that the typical student is a highly educated, while high schooler and that K–12 students in general do not make up a sizable portion of enrollees (Emanuel 2013). Adams and Yin (2015) explain that MOOCs have started to enroll children and youth who participate in MOOCs with their parents (or independently) from both inside and outside the K–12 school system, but they could not deduce exactly how many. As MOOCs start to include K–12 students, some states, like Florida and Ohio, have adopted a strategy to include MOOC courses into the traditional classroom (Watson et al. 2014).

Other research on MOOC participation and enrollment shows that in the first wave of MOOC courses the typical MOOC enrolled more than 43 000 students, but participation, and thus enrollment, decreased with each additional week added to the course, leaving completion rates to fall to about 6.5% of the original enrolled population (Jordan 2014). To understand exactly what students are doing in the MOOC setting and why they do not complete, one study shows that 76% of participants only browsed course offerings, accounting only for 8% of time spent in the course; however, the 7% of certificate-earning participants averaged 100 hours each and accounted for 60% of total time spent by all participants (Seaton et al. 2014). Greene, Oswald, and Pomerantz (2015) show that the strongest predictor of retention in a MOOC course is a student's expected time they will spend in the course. What this means is that the vast majority of students in a MOOC course do not really intend to finish it or take it seriously, but those whose goal is to finish it spend a great deal of time in the course and have a higher likelihood of completion.

The Khan Academy is an online learning platform created by former hedge fund manager Salman Khan in 2009 as a way to tutor one of his family members. He eventually received sponsorship from major foundations such as the Bill and Melinda Gates Foundation to grow the platform, allowing for students around the world to use the free lecture videos and exercises. Khan has started to pilot his online lecture materials within brick-and-mortar school locations (Thompson 2011).

Research on how the Khan Academy is used in educational settings is much less clear than for other types of online learning used in formal educational settings. The platform is typically used for tutoring services and has piloted programs in educational settings, but most writing about the program is in the popular press (e.g., Thompson 2011). The program is one that has promise because it uses highly effective gamification principles in improving student learning (Barata et al. 2013). However, there is not a strong thread of academic research showing success or efficacy of the Khan Academy. For homeschoolers, this platform gives parents access to supplemental lectures for use with their children, but it does not serve as a formal credential or diploma granting school. While the videos have been downloaded tens of millions of times, it is unclear how many of these videos are used specifically for homeschooling purposes (Khan Academy).

Taken together, the state of current research about both MOOCs and the Khan Academy suggests that scholars need to focus on a number of topics. These include understanding the types of students who are drawn to these platforms and how best to serve these student populations. Additionally, scholars should focus on examining implementations of these programs and how they relate to student learning. Research about MOOCs and the Khan Academy is also needed for scholars interested in homeschooling. There is little to no research about enrollment trends of homeschooling students using these programs. It could very well be that due to the free nature of these platforms, as well as their lack of ties to traditional schooling settings, homeschooling families may be drawn to these types of online learning platforms. However, with limited research evidence on enrollment trends, as well as on how to serve the platorms' students, it is difficult to understand and guide the directions of homeschoolers in these online learning environments.

General Online Learning Research

As shown, there are a variety of types of online learning that have developed in different contexts across the United States. The general research related to K–12 online learning practice and policy is limited but has grown in the last decade. Technical reports, meta-analyses, and literature reviews repeatedly state that more empirical analysis about several topics in K–12 online education is needed (e.g., Barbour and Reeves 2009; Glass and Welner 2011; Huerta, González, and d'Entremont 2006; Means et al. 2010; Miron, Horvitz, and Gulosino 2013). One of the most comprehensive collections of online learning literature comes in annual policy briefs released by the National Educational Policy Center (NEPC). The most recent NEPC brief (Molnar 2015) suggests that general research in the current landscape of K–12 online learning research should continue to focus around topics such as funding of formal online programs, teacher quality and leadership in online schools, and K–12 online learning outcomes. This section will therefore consider these issues and present current research related to each.

Funding and policy debates about formal online programs

Debates about the funding of online learning usually concern the formal online programs (cyber charter schools, district online schools, private online schools, and statewide virtual schools), and partisans tend to fall into two camps. One group believes that online schools should receive the same amount of funding as brick-and-mortar schools, while the other holds that such schools should receive funding in keeping with their actual proven cost of operation. Hausner (2004), in one of the first studies on online schooling cost, explains that costs do not tend to be "enormously higher than for in class students" and suggests that the longer an online school is open the more cost efficient it becomes. Shortly after Hausner, Anderson et al. (2006) conducted an analysis in which they argue that the costs to operate an online school are about the same as brick-and-mortar schools. More recently scholars Baker and Bathon (2013) and Barbour (2012) have argued that online learning may actually cost less and should be evaluated on a program-by-program basis. They argue that costs should be derived from the structure and nature of the courses provided, while advocacy groups tend to indicate that current funding formulas, however they are derived, tend to be rooted in traditional schooling metrics and thus are not sophisticated enough to provide the funds the schools need (Watson and Gemin 2009).

Funding arguments usually focus specifically on cyber charter schools, as these tend to be the most controversial version of the programs because they typically are funded through a formula that sees school districts financing the cyber charter school operation. In one state context, Pennsylvania, cyber charter school policy from 2002 to 2014 has largely been shaped by controversies over how to fund cyber charter schools and whether or not the schools should exist at all. These arguments have even led to a federal investigation into the practices of one of the largest cyber charter school providers in the state. As funding arguments tend to focus on the cyber charter form of online learning and since these conversations have been so politically contentious, there has not been a space for public dialog about the non-cyber charter school versions of online learning, such as district, state, and private providers

Thus, the funding and political debates come in the cyber charter sector due to their funding structure that counts on enrollment payments from local school districts. Outside of funding fairness, additional debates stem from arguments that cyber charter schools tend to have lower Adequate Yearly Progress (AYP) performance indicators than the district from which their enrolled students originated (Schafft et al. 2014). The NEPC reports, as well as work from advocacy groups and additional education scholars, outline this issue and discuss legal and financial concerns about cyber charter schools (Glass and Welner 2011; DeJarnatt 2013; Wagner 2012). The authors of the reports argue that cyber charter schools need to be better controlled and that government officials need to create formulas that rely less on tuition payment funds coming directly from traditional public schools.

Advocates suggest that despite performance indicators, parents should be able to choose the schooling option they believe best fits their child. Based on this, some suggest that the very presence of online learning – which seemingly arose from the choice movement – indicates that these programs emerged to fill a need (Moe and Chubb 2009). Mann and Barkauskas (2014) explain that choice-based arguments, such as those described by Moe and Chubb (2009) have become key selling points for cyber charter school providers. If one believes that the option of allowing parental school choice is something that should be made available to all, then one is likely to fall on the side of the debate of allowing and deregulating cyber charter schools and online learning. Advocacy groups for online learning in general tend to echo these types of models, declaring statements like policy should "enable funding to follow the student to the program and course level" (International Association for K–12 Online Learning 2012).

Based on these debates on cyber charter schools and online learning in general, scholars should continue to conduct research on identifying the fairest possible funding mechanisms for online schools. However, the debates on cyber charter school funding and policy seem more to be rooted in philosophical differences rather than empirical evidence. If it is indeed true that cyber charter schools promote qualitatively worse educational outcomes than traditional schools, then research should focus on promoting the types of schools and policies surrounding these schools that lead to better outcomes. If for some reason these programs are inherently worse, then the divisions are still unlikely to be solved, as advocates suggest choice should be a fundamental provision that all parents should be afforded.

Funding and policy research related to homeschoolers and online learning should seek to understand the ways in which these mechanisms impact homeschooling enrollment in online learning. Do certain funding structures entice homeschoolers to join an online school? Do certain policies and course requirements better promote learning for homeschooling students? What are the fairest funding and policy structures that are advantageous for all students, homeschooling and traditional, in terms of online learning? Research at this point in time on policy and funding reflects the fact that online learning is still a relatively recent development, but this research has improved and should continue to do so. The annual reports from the NEPC as well as activity from other scholars are encouraging starting points.

Teacher quality and school leadership in online schools

Conversations about teacher quality and school leadership might not typically find their way into homeschooling conversations due to the role of parents as teachers (and leaders) in traditional homeschooling settings. However, if homeschooling families wish to use formal online schools for part or all of their homeschooling experience then issues about teacher quality and online school leadership become important. This is because online schools instruct students with online teachers who are led by online principals and administrators.

Research about teacher quality in online learning tends to show that there is a lack of preparation for online teaching. Many teachers from the start of their careers are not trained in online instruction or enter their employment unprepared (Barbour et al. 2012; Compton, Davis, and Mackey 2009). The reason for this trend is that university teacher training programs have limited courses (and sections of courses) about online learning, and only 1.3% of pre-service teacher training programs provide field practice in online teaching (Kennedy and Archambault 2013). Out of the skills needed to teach in an online school, K–12 online teachers felt they were most deficient in their ability to navigate issues related to technology (Archambault and Crippen 2009). Not only were new teachers unprepared, but veteran teachers who moved from teaching in traditional to online settings also were not prepared and required professional development (Pape, Adams, and Ribeiro 2005; Dawley, Rice, and Hinck 2010; Barbour et al. 2010)

These findings indicate that as the online education movement grows, teacher-training programs will have to incorporate new curricula in order to meet the needs of a changing educational landscape that includes an increasing number of students who learn online. Researchers have identified this need and are starting to fill in the gaps. DiPietro et al. (2008) interviewed sixteen teachers who were considered the best practitioners in the Michigan Virtual School program and identified indicators of best practice, which include, but are not limited to: understanding and being able to adapt to new technology, having a flexible time schedule, using online data in learning and assessment, diversifying practices through both technology and pedagogy, understanding specific components of course-pacing unique to an online environment, finding ways to manage online behavior from a distance, and delivering effective online assessments.

Additional research shows that there is great importance in fostering student interaction with their online instructors. Hawkins et al. (2013) found a high correlation between teacher–student interactions and student performance and completion rates in a virtual high school. They show that these interactions, as well as the perceptions of the quality of these interactions, also make a substantive difference in student achievement in online schools (79). Borup, West, and Graham (2012) show that teachers can use certain features of technology to be the caring and present teachers that students may miss in an online setting, explaining that targeted use of asynchronous video tools can increase instructor presence in online courses. This use of video can also help students feel teachers are capable of cultivating caring relationships with them (Borup, Graham, and Velasquez 2013). A main takeaway from these studies is that teachers can discover strategies to engage better with their students. Online teachers should consider these practices as they attempt to create an effective classroom, and families should look for these traits in the teachers to which their children are assigned.

To ensure these best practices get implemented into teacher training and professional development programs, online schooling advocates have proposed national online teaching standards (Southern Regional Education Board 2003; International Association for K–12 Online Learning 2011) and have conducted studies not only about best practices but also about how to implement these best practices in training programs (Kennedy and Archambault 2013; Ferdig et al. 2009). Most recently, Archambault, DeBruler, and Freidhoff (2014) analyzed the training and policy landscape across the United States and offered the following recommendations: align online curriculum to standards, require online field training, forge partnerships between educators and online course providers to enhance training, and begin to integrate online and virtual teacher training into teacher preparation programs.

Like the research on teacher quality, research on school leadership in virtual school settings is in the early stages. The most recent work points more to the challenges that leaders have rather than to the solutions that exist in solving them. As with the teacher preparation programs, very few leadership programs provide preparation for dealing with issues in an online learning setting, and many of the leaders are inexperienced in leadership settings in general (LaFrance and Beck 2014). The issues that do arise relate to the amount of time needed to run an online school, the sporadic nature of always being on call, and a general need for virtual school leaders to be very adaptable in their use of resources, including personnel, because often the online school settings are in a state of flux (Beck, LaFrance, and Richardson 2014).

The general takeaway from research about online teachers and leaders is that research is developing but sparse. A key future direction for this work is to analyze the effectiveness of teacher and leader training programs if and when they start to become more popular with universities and professional development programs. At this point in the formal online learning movement, it seems clear that little time and money has been spent on ensuring high quality teaching and leadership (i.e., the inputs).

With these literature domains in mind, it is difficult really to predict the influence that online teachers and leaders will have on homeschooling students. Homeschooling parents did not originally have to concern themselves with the actions of teachers and leaders in the school setting prior to online learning, because they themselves acted as the teacher and leader in their homeschool. Understanding the challenges and strengths of these officials is important for a homeschooling parent who opts into an online learning environment because these may be a facet of the schooling life of which they previously had limited experience. Instructional quality is never guaranteed, even in public schools, so parents should evaluate online learning programs and resources carefully, especially since there is little that has been done to prepare teachers to teach or lead in an online setting.

Learning outcomes

As with the rest of the research about online learning, the literature related to the outcomes is still developing but has grown substantially during the last decade. Studies about online schools that depict aggregate student outcomes tend to show that formal online schools have lower traditional achievement ratings than traditional public schools. Studies specifically about individual student learning and individual growth outcomes in K–12 online schools tend to show more mixed results. The overall impression from research on learning outcomes tends to support the notion that there is potential in online learning through positive outcomes in some circumstances; however, more research and support from government agencies is needed in determining actual student outcomes and where improvements are needed (Molnar 2015).

The largest meta-analyses of the studies about online learning report mixed findings, with two showing positive effect sizes of online learning and one showing a negative effect size (Cavanaugh 2001; Cavanaugh et al. 2004; Means et al. 2010). Other outcome-based studies show that when comparing performance between students studying face-to-face and those studying online, there is often not much of a difference (Barbour and Mulcahy 2008; Cavanaugh et al. 2008; O'Dwyer, Carey, and Kleiman 2007). A study done by the Center for Research on Education Outcomes (CREDO 2011), focusing on cyber charter schools specifically in Pennsylvania, shows that student achievement in cyber charter schools is significantly lower than that of traditional public schools. Smith, Clark, and Blomeyer (2005) report on eight studies conducted about online learning in North Carolina, and their evidence shows that online schools seem to promote positive academic achievement.

Meanwhile, Miron, Horvitz, and Gulosino (2013) looked at the traditional performance metrics that the US government uses to evaluate schools – Adequate Yearly Progress (AYP) scores and high school graduations rates – and found less encouraging results. Their report shows lower graduation rates for cyber charter schools compared to all schools in the US (37.6% compared to 79.4%) in 2011–2012. It also shows that the cyber charter schools had 71.9% academically unacceptable programs in 2011–2012, with only 30% of schools meeting AYP. This study was conducted at the school level and not the student level, so there may be a negative selection bias at play. This means there is a possibility that the schools are doing better with lower performing students and are evaluated on a population of students that typically perform poorly from the outset. The authors of the study refute these claims by showing enrollment trends indicate this may not be the case, but it still is a question because the scores are not at the student level.

Chingos and Schwerdt (2014) explain in their article that while there is a smattering of studies in isolated environments there seems to be a lack of literature about how students in full-time online schools achieve when measured within the confines of a large-scale data set. To address these concerns, the authors show that students in the Florida Virtual School perform equal to or better than their brick-and-mortar peers in the same high school age range.

Other studies tend to take more qualitative approaches to determine student perceptions in understanding the quality of online schools. This includes Barbour, McLaren, and Zhang (2014) who show that students interviewed in a Canadian context did not view their experience of learning online as being very challenging. Meanwhile, additional work points to the potential of online learning as being a useful tool to meet a variety of educational needs, including meeting the needs of students who require a different learning environment or schedule, and suggests that online learning can even change traditional practices in teaching and learning (Patrick and Powell 2009; Patrick, Wicks, and Watson 2012).

The most pressing need for research about online learning is to continue to determine the contexts in which online schools promote effective student learning and to identify the characteristics these schools possess. These characteristics may include both the types of programs that work best and the types of students who stand to benefit from enrolling in an online program as opposed to a traditional program. This has often proven difficult because much of the popular (and sometimes even academic) discussion focuses on types of studies that ask how online programs compare to traditional programs. Instead, the questions should focus on examining the conditions in which online learning proves to be an effective learning tool and the conditions in which it does not. This may also include a variety of definitions for the word "effective" because the needs of the students are likely not going to be determined by single test scores and metrics that only provide a singular market for student success.

What this research conversation means for a homeschooling audience is that learning outcomes range in online schools and that there is not absolute agreement on the state of this research. There is not definitive proof that online learning is inherently better or worse than traditional public schools. That being said, this line of research might matter less to a homeschooling audience because there is no research to date that compares traditional homeschooling practices with online learning. It could very well be that homeschooling with the assistance of online learning promotes better learning outcomes for students, but there is no research to support or refute this in any capacity.

Conclusions

One theme that emerges across the research about online learning and how these programs relate to homeschooling families is that there is a great need for further inquiry. Research in general about K–12 online learning is still in the early stages but has grown during the last decade. This knowledge includes the understandings that there are policy debates and unsettled questions over fair funding formulas; teachers and school leaders need more training and resources; learning outcomes seem to be generally on par with traditional brick-and-mortar schools while school-level quality raises questions about overall quality; and MOOCs and the Khan Academy are interesting and encouraging platforms that have started to draw in students from a variety of backgrounds.

The next steps for research more or less reflect next steps often considered in a variety of other educational research. Scholars need to identify the types of online learning that are most appropriate for different types of students. They need to continue to develop appropriate policies that guide these understandings and promote funding mechanisms that are fair to online and traditional students alike. The research and policy implementation should consider the needs of online teachers and learners and set up training programs to ensure these needs are met. In short, as online learning has grown and while research and policy have developed during the last decade, there is clearly much more work to do for scholars and policymakers alike.

These difficulties in mind, the state of online education as related to homeschooling is in the early stages but certainly becoming of interest to academics and policymakers. There are students who were once homeschooled in a traditional sense who are now enrolled online, but the scale of this trend, as is the case with many trends related to online learning, is unclear.

Overall, as different types of online programs have emerged in various places throughout the United States, scholars have started to develop knowledge about online learning practices, learning outcomes, policy debates, and teaching and leadership in an online setting. However, it is difficult to consider how to conceptualize this body of research within the homeschooling paradigm. On one hand all students who learn from home in an online setting can be classified as homeschooled students because they are receiving instruction at home. On the other hand, the specific details related to these classifications can be unclear. For example, some students learn part-time at home and part-time in a school building. Other students receive their instruction from a schooling institution while getting this instruction in their home on the internet. Another example would be traditional homeschooled students logging into the Khan Academy to learn content that their parents may not have knowledge about. Are these three types of students the same, all considered homeschooling students? It is questions like these that make classifying homeschool research within the online education platform difficult. But it is also questions like these that will help push forward both the homeschooling and the online learning literature.

References

Ahn, June. 2011. "Policy, Technology, and Practice in Cyber Charter Schools: Framing the Issues." *Teachers College Record*, 113(1): 1–26.

Adams, Catherine, and Yin Yin. 2015. "The World of MOOCs for a Child: The Case of Dino 101." *Global Learn*, 2015(1): 694–698.

Anderson, Amy, John Augenblick, Dale DeCesare, and Jill Conrad. 2006. *20/20 Costs and Funding of Virtual Schools*. Atlanta, GA: BellSouth Foundation. Accessed September 21, 2015. https://www.heartland.org/sites/all/modules/custom/heartland_migration/files/pdfs/28390.pdf

Archambault, Leanna, and Kent Crippen. 2009. "Examining TPACK among K–12 Online Distance Educators in the United States." *Contemporary Issues in Technology and Teacher Education*, 9(1): 71–88.

Archambault, Leanna, Kristen DeBruler, and Joseph Freidhoff. 2014. "K–12 Online and Blended Teacher Licensure: Striking a Balance between Policy and Preparedness." *Journal of Technology and Teacher Education*, 22: 83–106.

Atkeson, Sam. 2014. "Harvard–MIT Partnership Opens MOOCs for High Schoolers." *EdWeek*. September 23, 2014. Accessed September 29, 2015. http://www.edweek.org/ew/articles/2014/09/24/05moocs.h34.html

Baker, Bruce. D., and Justin Bathon. 2013. *Financing Online Education and Virtual Schooling: A Guide for Policymakers and Advocates*. Boulder, CO: National Education Policy Center. Accessed September 21, 2015. http://nepc.colorado.edu/publication/financing-online-education

Barata, Gabriel, Sandra Gama, Joaquim Jorge, and Daniel Gonçalves. 2013. "Improving Participation and Learning with Gamification." Paper presented at the First International Conference on Gameful Design, Research, and Applications, New York, NY. DOI: 10.1145/2583008.2583010

Barbour, Michael. K. 2012. "Point: Virtual Schools are more Cost-Effective Compared to Traditional, Brick-and-Mortar Schools." In *Technology in Schools: Debating Issues in American Education*, edited by Kevin P. Brady, 84–90. Thousand Oaks, CA: Sage.

Barbour, Michael, Jim Kinsella, Matthew Wicks, and Sacip Toker. 2010. "Continuum of Change in a Virtual World: Training and Retaining Instructors." *Journal of Technology and Teacher Education*, 17(4): 437–457.

Barbour, Michael K., Angelene McLaren, and Lin Zhang. 2012. "It's Not That Tough: Students Speak about Their Online Learning Experiences." *Turkish Online Journal of Distance Education*, 13(2), 12: 226–241.

Barbour, Michael K., and Dennis Mulcahy. 2008. "How are They Doing? Examining Student Achievement in Virtual Schooling." *Education in Rural Australia*, 18(2): 63–74.

Barbour, Michael. K., and Thomas C. Reeves. 2009. "The Reality of Virtual Schools: A Review of the Literature." *Computers & Education*, 52(2): 402–416. DOI:10.1016/j.compedu.2008.09.009

Barbour, Michael. K., Jason Siko, Elizabeth Gross, and Kecia Waddell. 2012. "Virtually Unprepared: Examining the Preparation of K–12 Online Teachers." *Teacher Education Programs and Online Learning Tools: Innovations in Teacher Preparation*, edited by Richard Hartshorne, Tina L. Heafner, and Teresa M. Petty, 60–81. Hershey, PA: IGI Global.

Beck, Dennis, Jason LaFrance, and Jayson W. Richardson. "Voices of Virtual School Leaders; Challenges and Advice." 2014. April. Paper presented at the American Educational Research Association Conference, Philadelphia, PA.

Borup, Jered, Charles Graham, and Andrea Velasquez. 2013. "Technology-Mediated Caring: Building Relationships between Students and Instructors in Online K–12 Learning Environments." *Advances in Research on Teaching*, 18: 183–202.

Borup, Jered, Richard E. West, and Charles R. Graham. 2012. "Improving Online Social Presence through Asynchronous Video." *The Internet and Higher Education*, 15(3):195–203. DOI: 10.1016/j.iheduc.2011.11.001

Brady, Kevin. P., Regina R. Umpstead, and Suzanne E. Eckes .2010. "Unchartered Territory: The Current Legal Landscape of Public Cyber Charter Schools." *Brigham Young University Education and Law Journal*, 2:191.

Cavanaugh, Cathy. 2001. "The Effectiveness of Interactive Distance Education Technologies in K–12 Learning: A Meta-Analysis." *International Journal of Educational Telecommunications*, 7(1): 73–88.

Cavanaugh, Cathy, et al. 2004. *The Effects of Distance Education on K–12 Student Outcomes: A Meta-Analysis*. Naperville, IL: Learning Point Associates. Accessed October 2, 2015. http://files.eric.ed.gov/fulltext/ED489533.pdf

Cavanaugh, Cathy, Kathy Gillan, Jan Bosnick, and Melinda Hess. 2008. "Effectiveness of Online Algebra Learning: Implications for Teacher Preparation." *Journal of Educational Computing Research*, 38(1): 67–95.

Center for Research on Education Outcomes. 2011. *Charter School Performance in Pennsylvania*. Stanford, CA. Accessed October 11, 2015. http://credo.stanford.edu/reports/PA%20State%20Report_20110404_FINAL.pdf

Chingos, Matthew M., and Guido Schwerdt. 2014. "Virtual Schooling and Student Learning: Evidence from the Florida Virtual School." *Program on Education Policy and Governance Working Papers Series*. Cambridge, MA: Harvard Kennedy School. Accessed October 2, 2015. http://www.hks.harvard.edu/pepg/PDF/FLVS%20PEPG%20working%20paper%20(3).pdf

Clark, Tom, and Michael Barbour. 2015. "Introduction." In *Online, Blended and Distance Education in Schools: Building Successful Programs*, edited by Tom Clark and Michael Barbour, 3–9. Sterling, VA: Stylus Publishing.

Compton, Lily K.L., Niki Davis, and Julie Mackey. 2009. "Virtual Field Experience in Virtual Schooling." *Journal of Technology and Teacher Education*, 17(4): 459–477.

Curtis, Will. 2013. "Alternatives to Mainstream Schooling." In *Education Studies: An Issue Based Approach*, edited by Will Curtis, Stephen Ward, John Sharp, and Les Hankin, 106–119. Thousand Oaks, CA: Sage.

Dawley, Lisa, Kerry Rice, and Glori Hinck. 2010. *Going Virtual! The Status of Professional Development for K–12 Online Teachers*. Boise, ID: Boise State University. Accessed September 30, 2015. http://edtech.boisestate.edu/goingvirtual/goingvirtual3.pdf

DeJarnatt, Susan. 2013. "Keep Following the Money: Financial Accountability and Governance of Cyber Charter Schools." *Urban Lawyer*, 45: 915–951.

DiPietro, Meredith, Richard E. Ferdig, Erik W. Black, and Megan Preston. 2008. "Best Practices in Teaching K–12 Online: Lessons Learned from Michigan Virtual School Teachers." *Journal of Interactive Online Learning*, 7(1): 10–35.

Emanuel, Ezekiel J. 2013. "Online education: MOOCs Taken by Educated Few. *Nature*, *503* (7476): 342. DOI: 10.1038/503342a

Ferdig, Richard E., et al. 2009. "Virtual Schooling Standards and Best Practices for Teacher Education." *Journal of Technology and Teacher Education*, 17(4): 479–503.

Glass, Gene V., and Kevin G. Welner. 2011. *Online K–12 Schooling in the U.S. Uncertain Private Ventures in Need of Public Regulation*, 1–21. Boulder, CO: National Education

Policy Center. Accessed September 21, 2015. http://nepc.colorado.edu/files/NEPC-VirtSchool-1-PB-Glass-Welner.pdf

Greene, Jeffrey A., Christopher A. Oswald, and Jeffrey Pomerantz. 2015. "Predictors of Retention and Achievement in a Massive Open Online Course." *American Educational Research Journal*. DOI: 10.3102/0002831215584621

Hanak, James. 2015. "Another View: Defending Cyber Charter Schools." *Daily Local News*, February 26. Accessed September 15, 2015. http://www.dailylocal.com/opinion/20150226/another-view-defending-cyber-charter-schools

Hasler Waters, Lisa, Michael K. Barbour, and Michael P. Menchaca. 2014. "The Nature of Online Charter Schools: Evolution and Emerging Concerns." *Journal of Educational Technology & Society*, 17(4): 379–389.

Hausner, Lucy. 2004. *Estimated Cost of Operating a Cyberschool in Colorado*. Denver, CO: Donnell-Kay Foundation. Accessed. September 21, 2015. http://www.dkfoundation.org/sites/default/files/files/CyberschoolCostReportFeb2004CCA.pdf.

Hawkins, Abigail, Charles R. Graham, Richard R. Sudweeks, and Michael K. Barbour. 2013. "Academic Performance, Course Completion Rates, and Student Perception of the Quality and Frequency of Interaction in a Virtual High School." *Distance Education*, 34: 64–83. DOI:10.1080/01587919.2013.770430

Horn, Michael B. and Heather Staker. 2015. *Blended: Using Disruptive Innovation to Improve Schools*. San Francisco, CA: Jossey-Bass.

Huerta, Luis. A., María-Fernanda González, and Chad d'Entremont. 2006. "Cyber and Home School Charter Schools: Adopting Policy to New Forms of Public Schooling." *Peabody Journal of Education*, 81(1): 103–139.

International Association for K–12 Online Learning. 2011. *National Standards for Quality Online Teaching*. Vienna, VA. Accessed September 25, 2015. http://www.inacol.org/wp-content/uploads/2015/02/national-standards-for-quality-online-teaching-v2.pdf

International Association for K–12 Online Learning. 2012. *Statement of Principles for Model Legislation in States*. Vienna, VA. Accessed September 25, 2015. http://www.inacol.org/wp-content/uploads/2015/02/Principles-For-Model-Legislation-2012.pdf

Jordan, Katy. 2014. "Initial Trends in Enrolment and Completion of Massive Open Online Courses." *The International Review Of Research In Open And Distributed Learning*, 15(1).

K[12] Inc. 2013. *2013 K[12] Academic Report*. Accessed September 23, 2015. http://www.k12.com/sites/default/files/pdf/2013-K12-Academic-Report-Feb6-2013.pdf

Kennedy, Kathryn and Leanna Archambault. 2013. *Partnering for Success: A 21st Century Model for Teacher Preparation*. Vienna, VA: International Association for K–12 Online Learning. Accessed September 5, 2015. http://www.inacol.org/wp-content/uploads/2015/02/partnering-for-success.pdf

Khan Academy. "About." Accessed September 24, 2015. https://www.khanacademy.org/about

LaFrance, Jason. A. and Dennis Beck. 2014. "Mapping the Terrain: Educational Leadership Field Experiences in K–12 Virtual Schools." *Educational Administration Quarterly*, 50(1): 160–189. DOI: 10.1177/0013161X13484037

Mann, Bryan and Nik Barkauskas. 2014. "Connecting Learners or Isolating Individuals?: The Social Justice Frames in the Cyber Charter Schools in Pennsylvania." *International Journal of Cyber Ethics in Education*, 3(2): 39–50. DOI: 10.4018/ijcee.2014040104

Marsh, Rose. M., Alison A. Carr-Chellman, and Beth R. Sockman. 2009. "Selecting Silicon: Why Parents Choose Cybercharter Schools." *TechTrends*, 53(4): 32–36. DOI: 10.1007/s11528-009-0303-9

Means, Barbara, et al. 2010. *Evaluation of Evidence Based Practices in Online Learning: A Meta-Analysis and Review of Online Learning Studies*, 1–66. Washington, DC: US Department of Education Office of Planning, Evaluation, and Policy Development Policy and Program Studies Service. Accessed September 1, 2015. https://www2.ed.gov/rschstat/eval/tech/evidence-based-practices/finalreport.pdf

Meyn-Rogeness, Tammy. 2010. "Privatization and Cyber Charter Schools." PhD diss., DePaul University. Accessed April 14, 2016. http://via.library.depaul.edu/soe_etd/6

Miron, Gary, Brian Horvitz, and Charisse Gulosino. 2013. "Full-Time Virtual Schools: Enrollment, Student Characteristics, and Performance." In *Virtual Schools in the US 2013: Politics, Performance, Policy, and Research Evidence*, edited by Alex Molnar, 22–36. Boulder, CO: National Education Policy Center. Accessed September 21, 2015. http://nepc.colorado.edu/publication/virtual-schools-annual-2013

Miron, Gary, and Kevin G. Welner. 2012. "Introduction." In *Exploring the School Choice Universe: Evidence and Recommendations*, edited by Gary Miron, Kevin G. Welner, Patricia H. Hinchey, and William J. Mathis. Charlotte, NC: Information Age Publishing.

Miron, Gary, and Charisse Gulosino. 2015. "Full-Time Virtual Schools: Enrollment, Student Characteristics, and Performance." In *Virtual Schools in the US 2015: Politics, Performance, Policy, and Research Evidence*, edited by Alex Molnar, 59–84. Boulder, CO: National Education Policy Center. Accessed October 16, 2015. http://nepc.colorado.edu/files/rb-virt-2015-all.pdf

Moe, Terry. M., and John E. Chubb. 2009. *Liberating Learning: Technology, Politics, and the Future of American Education*. New York: John Wiley and Sons.

Molnar, Alex. 2015. "Executive Summary." In *Virtual Schools in the US 2015: Politics, Performance, Policy, and Research Evidence*, edited by Alex Molnar, i–iii. Boulder, CO: National Education Policy Center. Accessed September 21, 2015. http://nepc.colorado.edu/files/rb-virt-2015-all.pdf

Niederberger, Mary. 2012. "Franklin Park Home is a Cyber Schoolhouse." *Pittsburgh Post-Gazette*, September 3. Accessed September 15, 2015. http://www.post-gazette.com/news/education/2012/09/03/Franklin-Park-home-is-a-cyber-schoolhouse/stories/201209030162

Niederberger, Mary. 2013. "No Cyber Charter School in Pennsylvania made Adequate Yearly Progress." *Pittsburgh Post-Gazette*, January 23, 2013. Accessed September 15, 2015. http://www.post-gazette.com/news/education/2013/01/23/No-cyber-charter-school-in-Pennsylvania-made-Adequate-Yearly-Progress/stories/201301230245

O'Dwyer, Laura M., Rebecca Carey, and Glenn Kleiman. 2007. "A Study of the Effectiveness of the Louisiana Algebra I Online Course." *Journal of Research on Technology in Education*, 39(3): 289–306. DOI:10.1080/15391523.2007.10782484

Pape, Liz, Ruth Adams, and Carol Ribeiro. 2005. "The Virtual High School: Collaboration and Online Professional Development." In *Virtual Schools: Planning for Success*, edited by Zane L. Berge and Thomas A. Clark, 118–132. New York, NY: Teachers College Press.

Patrick, Susan, David Edwards, Matthew Wicks, and John Watson. 2012. *Measuring Quality from Inputs to Outcomes: Creating Student Learning Performance Metrics and Quality Assurance for Online Schools*. Vienna, VA: International Association for K–12 Online Learning. Accessed September 25, 2015. http://www.inacol.org/wp-content/uploads/2015/02/iNACOL_Quality_Metrics.pdf

Patrick, Susan, and Allison Powell. 2009. *A Summary of Research on the Effectiveness of K–12 Online Learning*. Vienna, VA: International Association for K–12 Online Learning. Accessed October 8, 2015. http://files.eric.ed.gov/fulltext/ED509626.pdf

Rapp, Kelly, Suzanne E Eckes, and Jonathan A. Plucker. 2006. *Cyber Charter Schools in Indiana: Policy Implications of the Current Statutory Language*. Bloomington, IN: Center for Evaluation & Education Policy. Accessed October 11, 2015. http://files.eric.ed.gov/fulltext/ED490889.pdf

Ravitch, Diane. 2010. *The Death and Life of the Great American School System: How Testing and Choice are Undermining Education*. New York, NY: Basic Books.

Saul, Stephanie. 2011."Profits and Questions at Online Charter Schools." *New York Times*, December 12. Accessed September 15, 2015. http://www.nytimes.com/2011/12/13/education/online-schools-score-better-on-wall-street-than-in-classrooms.html?_r=0

Schafft, Kai. A., et al. 2014. *Assessing the Enrollment Trends and Financial Impacts of Charter Schools on Rural and Non-Rural School Districts in Pennsylvania*. Harrisburg, PA: The Center for Rural Pennsylvania. Accessed September 23, 2015. http://www.rural.palegislature.us/documents/reports/Charter_School_2014.pdf

Seaton, Daniel T., et al. 2014. "Who Does What in a Massive Open Online Course?" *Communications of the ACM*, 57(4): 58–65. DOI: 10.1145/2500876

Southern Regional Education Board. 2003. *Essential Principles of High-quality Online Teaching*. Atlanta, GA: Southern Regional Education Board. Accessed October 1, 2015. http://info.sreb.org/programs/edtech/pubs/PDF/Essential_Principles.pdf

Smith, Rosina, Thomas Clark, and Robert L. Blomeyer. 2005. *A Synthesis of New Research on K–12 Online Learning*. Naperville, IL: Learning Point Associates. Accessed October 3, 2015. https://www.heartland.org/sites/all/modules/custom/heartland_migration/files/pdfs/28155.pdf

Thomas, William R. 2002. *Considerations for Planning a State Virtual School: Providing Web-based Courses for K–12 Students*. Atlanta, GA: Southern Regional Education Board. Accessed October 1, 2015. http://info.sreb.org/programs/EdTech/pubs/PDF/State_Virtual_School.pdf

Thompson, Clive. 2011. "How Khan Academy is changing the Rules of Education." *Wired Magazine*, July 15. Accessed September 18, 2015. http://www.wired.com/2011/07/ff_khan/

Wagner, Jack. 2012. *Charter and Cyber Charter Education Funding Reform Should Save Taxpayers $365 Million Annually*. Harrisburg, PA: Pennsylvania Department of the Auditor General. Accessed September 18, 2015. http://www.paauditor.gov/Media/Default/Reports/CyberCharterSpecialReport201206.pdf

Waters, John. K. 2011. "Competing for the Virtual Student." *THE Journal (Technological Horizons In Education)*, 38(7): 28.

Watson, John, and Butch Gemin. 2009. Promising Practices in Online Learning: Policy and Funding Frameworks for Online Learning. Vienna, VA: International Association for K–12 Online Learning. Accessed September 21, 2015. http://www.inacol.org/wp-content/uploads/2015/02/funding-and-policy-frameworks-for-online-learning.pdf

Watson, John F., and Stevan Kalmon. 2005. *Keeping Pace with K–12 Online Learning: A Review of State-Level Policy and Practice*. Naperville, IL: Learning Point Associates. Accessed September 20, 2015. http://files.eric.ed.gov/fulltext/ED489514.pdf

Watson, John, et al. 2014. *Keeping Pace with K–12 Digital Learning: An Annual Review of Policy and Practice, Eleventh Edition*. Mountain West, CA: Evergreen Education Group. Accessed September 20, 2015. http://www.kpk12.com/wp-content/uploads/EEG_KP2014-fnl-lr.pdf

Part II
Home Education Worldwide

12

Home Education in Canada

Christine Brabant and Marine Dumond
Translated by Kaitlin Wingert

Introduction

This portrait of home education (a term we use interchangeably with homeschooling in this chapter) in Canada reflects the presence of two colonizing nations in the country. Indeed, the distinct French and English traditions lead to differences in homeschooling parents' motivational profiles and political actions and to two rather mutually exclusive research corpuses. This portrait also reflects Canada's proximity to and interaction with the United States, in that it has facilitated and influenced the home education movement's development and that the two countries have in common a North American scientific culture. Hence, although Canadian scientific studies on home education are scarce, some are worth noting for their wide-ranging or sound empirical methodologies. Still, Canadian homeschooling has its particularities and its researchers have their originality, which the following chapter will reveal. Another interesting advantage of this literature overview is its inclusion of Francophone publications.

This chapter begins with a brief orientation to the basic home education situation in the Canadian provinces and territories, for the benefit of non-Canadian readers and newcomers to this area of research. Then, it provides a synthesis of current scholarship and scholarly debates on "Home education in Canada," through the presentation of a literature review pursued with this title's largest possible interpretation in mind, that is: studies on Canadian homeschooling and homeschoolers, whether conducted by Canadian or foreign researchers, as well as studies on homeschooling conducted by Canadian researchers, even when they did not collect data in Canada per se. Thus, this chapter presents a double panorama: that of home education in Canada and that of the research done on this subject from Canada.

The Wiley Handbook of Home Education, First Edition. Edited by Milton Gaither.

Within this "home education research in Canada" scope, our literature review focused on presenting only the most serious and reliable scholarly work, according to the international scientific community's strictest standards. Thus, firstly, we retained all sound research articles published in scholarly journals satisfying usual academic standards: academic editorial board, peer-reviewed selection of articles upon scholarly criteria, aims, and scope oriented towards knowledge production and open discussion, without defending or promoting a specific political or ideological option. Secondly, we retained books presenting research results and published by academic publishing houses. As for graduate students research, we only considered masters and doctoral theses when their scientific value had been sanctioned by having their results published in at least one of the two previous categories. When this was the case, we sometimes consulted the original theses to further our understanding of the research. Thirdly, we included research from government agencies, private research centers and homeschooling associations when the work demonstrated the same methodological and writing criteria as the previous categories, according to our evaluation. Finally, we retained only work published in the last fifteen years or so, previous work being used to compose the brief historical synthesis in the chapter's first section. Needless to say, this strict selection process left behind many writings and conferences from researchers and advocacy groups who, although sometimes prolific and influential among Canadian homeschoolers, do not meet the scientific standards expected for this handbook's scholarly objectives.

After this thorough review and rigorous selection, few studies remained, which we categorized by theme. Thus, a first part of the chapter will discuss studies about homeschooling parents, including a description of them, their motivations for this educational choice, the parental culture that it reveals, and their opinions on education at home and in schools. The second part of the chapter looks at the studies pertaining to home education practices and outcomes. In the third part, we present a sociopolitical analysis of homeschooling parents' political discourse followed by studies offering legal perspectives. Finally, the fourth and last part introduces studies on the participation of parental and institutional actors in the governance of home education. When a study covers more than one theme, it will be divided and presented along with others covering the same theme.

Context

Because of a lack of historical research on the Canadian home education movement, it is hard to develop a reliable account of it. However, traces and earlier studies help us sketch its evolution. The surfacing of a movement promoting home learning as an alternative to schooling is generally recognized as starting at the end of the 1960s. According to Common and MacMullen (1986), the movement follows a similar evolution to that of the United States, only a few years behind. Thus, in 1976, Wendy Priesnitz launched the *Natural Life* magazine, including homeschooling as part of its "alternative lifestyle" back-to-the-land focus. Then, in 1979, she created the Canadian

Alliance of Home Schoolers. The Supreme Court of Canada looked into homeschooling in the *Jones v. the Queen* case in 1987. A Canadian affiliate of the Home School Legal Defense Association was founded in 1991, similar to the one that existed in the United States since 1983. Other facts demonstrate the American movement's influence in Canada. For example, Anglophone homeschooling publications (including Holt's) were frequently distributed on both sides of the United States–Canada border. Yet, Priesnitz nuances the role of the United States' home education movement among the sources of the Canadian movement:

> Although there inevitably would have been some influence from the U.S., due to the close alignment of culture, media, etc. between Canada and the U.S., I believe that the modern home education movement erupted somewhat spontaneously in a number of countries around the same time. The 60s were a time of massive social change and Canada experienced its own rich brew of university ferment, questioning of authority, the women's movement, free schools, etc (W. Priesnitz, personal correspondence with first author, October 22, 2005).

Priesnitz also states that "one of the big differences between how the movement in general developed in Canada and in the US is that it's always been legal in the various Canadian provinces (or at least not explicitly illegal), while homeschoolers in many American states had to fight for the right."

Indeed, concerning the legislative aspect, it should be pointed out that education in Canada has been exclusively under provincial jurisdiction since the 1867 Constitutional Act. There is no federal jurisdiction in education. Consequently, as the country is divided into ten provinces and three territories, coast to coast there are thirteen different legal frameworks for homeschooling. Canada-wide portraits of these regulations (Lagos 2011, 2012; Luffman, 1997; Smith, 1996) show that each provides an exception from compulsory school attendance or an option allowing homeschooling, as long as the parents fulfill conditions stated in the law, be it "efficient," "equivalent," "satisfactory" or "adequate" education, as verified through diverse evaluations. Nonetheless, these terms' lack of precision results in differing interpretations and enforcements. In addition, most provinces require that parent-educators obtain a formal authorization recognizing their decision to homeschool their children. Also, they generally require curriculum approval and monitoring of the child's progression according to provincial standards. Although these practices generally converge, there is greater divergence among evaluation strategies and services offered by the public education system. Hence, only a few provinces provide part-time schooling options for children or financial and material support to parent-educators in order to help them with their educational project.

Some studies have begun with limited success to document the growth of this practice in Canada. The official numbers for registered home-educated children are 1000 in 1986 (Common and MacMullen 1986), 9344 in 1993 (Smith 1993), 17 500 during the 1995–1996 school year and 19 114 during the following school year (Luffman 1997), that is about 0.5% of the school-aged population. In the latter study, the author explains that this percentage is higher only in Alberta, reaching over 1% of the school-aged population, where subsidies offered by the provincial government to parent-educators could have encouraged them to register with their local school boards (Luffman 1997). Yet, it should be noted that this data does not include home-educated children in Quebec. In effect, the Ministry of Education of the Francophone province, which accounts for nearly a quarter of the Canadian population, was not gathering data on homeschooling before the 2002–2003 school year. Homeschooling associations and supporters have estimated much higher numbers: 30 000 Canadian children in 1993 (Smith 1993) and between 60 000 and 95 000 at the turn of the century (Fraser Institute 2001; Ray 2001), corresponding to "about 1.5% of Canada's public and private school enrollment combined" (Ray 2001, 1).

Today, the Canadian official statistics and school enrollment indicators merge homeschooled children with private school enrollment (Statistics Canada, 2013), thus interfering with the possibility of getting national data on homeschooling. For this reason, in order to offer readers an approximation, we asked three provincial ministries of Education about their homeschooling enrollment during the school year 2013–2014. We chose the provinces as being important in terms of population and of home education tradition: Alberta (11% of the Canadian population), British Columbia (13%) and Quebec (24%) (Statistics Canada, 2014). Alberta has the highest figures with 11,693 homeschooled students (Alberta 2015). Among them, 1859 children are enrolled in the "Blended Programs" option, which corresponds to mixed schooling, part-time schooling or courses on demand. Calculation is slightly different in British Columbia. In that province a growing number of previously independent home educators have enrolled in distance learning programs under British Columbia's distributed learning initiative. Thus, for the 2013–2014 school year, only 2033 children are accounted for as homeschooled (British Columbia 2015), whereas there were already over twice as many (4776) eighteen years earlier (Luffman 1997). Finally, in Quebec, where there is neither a distance learning option for children nor a mixed schooling alternative, 1180 children are officially reported as homeschooled.

If a total of 13 047 children are exclusively home educated in these provinces, which together amount to 48% of the Canadian population, and supposing that the registered homeschoolers are spread out proportionally in the rest of Canada, we could sketch a rough estimate of 27 181 registered homeschooled children in the country, representing 0.5% of all school-aged children, according to the last available data of 5032183 school-age children in 2011–2012 (Statistics Canada, 2013). In addition, it is no surprise that the President of the Quebec Association for Home-Based Education considers that, in fact, the numbers could be quadrupled to take into account unregistered children (Martel 2015). If he is right, and if this is the case in other provinces and territories as well, keeping in mind that some provinces offer financial incentives to registration, one could extrapolate tentatively that homeschooling could encompass as many as 1.5% or even 2% of school-aged children, though in reality no one knows if the number is closer to official data counts or estimates.

Finally, it should be mentioned, to complete this section on context, that Canada is sometimes described as hosting "two solitudes," meaning that its composition of French and English colonizing nations still defines two distinct population subgroups. While the First Peoples inhabited North America, the French colonized Canada (then called "Nouvelle-France") and ruled it for a little over two centuries in the name of France. They lost their dominion to the British in 1763, but French-Canadians' linguistic, political, and religious rights were preserved. Their descendants remain for the most part in the province of Quebec, and welcome mostly French-speaking immigrants. Quebec society, already recognized as "distinct" in the 1987 Canadian Constitution and hosting independentist aspirations, gained "distinct nation" status in recent federal politics. It still reflects the cultural and social aspects of its history, with a vast majority of Francophone citizens, a civil law system and traces of Catholic traditions, although the "Révolution tranquille" in the 1960s brought about a major decline in religious practice and in the importance of the Catholic Church in Quebec society. Its educational system also has its particularities when compared to that of "English-Canada," like its totally secularized public school system and the important public subsidizing of a large (semi-)private secondary schools sector. In particular, the differences between the two populations in language, culture, political, and educational orientations will be evoked throughout this chapter on homeschooling, for explanatory purposes.

After this brief overview of the Canadian home education context through a few elements of historical, regulatory, and administrative information, we will now introduce the first research theme addressed in our literature review: home-educating parents.

Understanding Parents

As in other countries, research on home education in Canada first addressed the "who" and the "why" questions. This section presents recent research on Canadian homeschooling parents and families. It offers a couple of family sociodemographic profiles, then presents studies on parents' motivations, deepened by research on their educational culture and their conceptions of education, at home and in schools.

Family profiles

The most recent pan-Canadian study aiming to describe Canadian homeschooling families is Ray's, published in 1994. Brian D. Ray is president of the National Home Education Research Institute (NHERI), a private research center on homeschooling. He sent a questionnaire to homeschooling parents through the Home School Legal Defense Association of Canada, which 808 homeschooling families filled out. In the households of participating parents, the level of education was somewhat superior to that of the general population, and family revenue was slightly inferior to that of average Canadian households. About 14% of mothers worked outside the home for an average of 11.9 hours per week. The families had significantly more children (3.5) than the national average. Mothers provided children with 88% of formal instruction, while fathers provided 9%. They utilized a broad variety of educational resources, and their children engaged in multiple activities and social outlets. While this study offered a portrait of participating Canadian parents, it also described children, their academic success, and the correlations between these two studied variables. However, we will present more recent studies on these themes.

It should be noted that only 4.9% (40) of this sample are Quebec families, of which less than a half are French-speaking, while this province represents close to 25% of the Canadian population and has French as its only official language. As seen in the previous section, following Ray, the pan-Canadian governmental study offering numbers of registered homeschoolers (Luffman 1997), did not include Quebec homeschoolers or French-speaking families.

Therefore, aiming at drawing the first sociodemographic profile of Quebec homeschooling families, Christine Brabant, professor in educational foundations and administration at University of Montreal in Quebec, in 2003 conducted a study by questionnaire (Brabant 2004; Brabant, Bourdon and Jutras 2003, 2004). Paper and online questionnaires, in French and in English, were distributed through homeschooling publications, a symposium, a provincial association, local support groups, online discussion forums, and a curriculum producer. They reached a wide, diverse range within the target group, as demonstrated by the results, which surveyed 203 families (among which 47 responded to a questionnaire in English, while 156 responded in French) who represented 505 school-aged children. Knowing that the total number of registered homeschooled children in 2002–2003 was revealed the next year by the government as being 388 children (Quebec 2013) and that two contemporary surveys found a registration rate of 40% (Brabant's 2003 study) and 50% (Quebec Association of Home Based Education, 2005), this group of parents of 505 homeschooled children constitutes, in sum, a very large sample. This remains true even when comparing it to the generous estimate of 2500 to 5000 homeschooled children (six to thirteen times the number of registered children), made by the Quebec Association for Home-Based Education's president (Tremblay 2002). Despite the researcher's efficiency in reaching all subgroups of the movement (religious and not religious; rural and urban; English-speaking and French-speaking; experienced and newcomers; registered and not registered, etc.), this sample is considered a convenience sample and its representativity is limited. Therefore, the results are to be read as exploratory. Still, the number of respondents is large enough to allow for complex statistical operations like factor analysis, as presented in later sections in this chapter covering motivations and conceptions on education.

The questionnaire stipulated that the parent who "best" knew the family and its reasons for choosing home education was to fill out the questionnaire. Among those 203 respondents, 192 were women. Concerning the parents' level of education, 20% reported that at least one parent in the household has obtained a master's or a doctoral degree; 38% reported that at least one parent in the household has obtained a bachelor's degree or a university certificate; 16% reported a college diploma (in Quebec, it should be noted, college level studies are the beginning of postsecondary studies, where both technical and pre-university programs are offered); and 24% reported a secondary school diploma. These data, within the limits of the sample's representativity, indicate an overrepresentation of parents who have obtained university diplomas, especially at the master's and doctoral levels, among home educators. On the other hand, no remarkable overrepresentation or underrepresentation was noticed for the factors of family income or place of residence. Families from almost every region of Quebec participated in the study. Participants were almost equally distributed between cities (29%), suburbs (22%), small towns and villages (22%), and rural areas (26%).

As said earlier, 40% of respondents in this sample stated that educational authorities were not aware of their decision to educate their children at home. The remaining respondents had an agreement with their local school board (20%), were in conflict with their local school board (3%), or informed the school board of their decision but had neither an agreement nor a conflict with them (36%). The language of instruction was French for 73% of families. As 87% of all children registered in Quebec schools study in French (Ministère de l'Éducation du Québec, 2003), the sample's figures could indicate that a larger number of home-educating families are offering instruction in English or in both languages, or that more English-speaking families participated in the survey. As for religious or spiritual commitment, 27% answered that religion or spirituality was fundamental to their family lives; 15% said it had "some influence" on their family lives; 43% indicated that they value some type of spiritual belief but have no specific organized religious affiliation or practice, and 13% indicated that they have no religious or spiritual commitment at all. Finally, 44% of parents responsible for their children's education had some training or work experience in education.

Motivations

The results of the first Canadian studies on parental motivations (Common and MacMullen 1986; Priesnitz 1990) echoed the educational ideology conveyed by the leaders of the United States movement, John Holt and Raymond and Dorothy Moore. In order to find traces of motivations unique to Canadian parents, one must await the turn of the century and researchers' interest in the population of Quebec.

One initial study attempted to analyze the motives that could incite Canadian parents to opt for homeschooling, comparing the results of leading studies on the same subject in the United States. Bruce Arai (2000), presently Dean of the Faculty of Human and Social Sciences at Wilfrid Laurier University in Ontario, carried out interviews with eighteen families from Ontario and five families from British Columbia. The results suggest that the Canadian parents did not have exactly the same reasons for choosing homeschooling as American parents. In effect, religious beliefs were not a principal motivation for homeschooling; several parents had made the choice after a bad experience with the school system. Moreover, the poverty of the environment offered by schools, weak academic standards levied on students, and the moral and religious conflicts motivated their choice to differing degrees. Additionally, the perceived positive changes in their children after withdrawing them from school and the strengthening of the family bonds that followed were supplementary motivations a posteriori. Finally, the style of living that accompanies homeschooling was in accord with other alternative values often cultivated by parent-educators, such as alternative medicine, vegetarianism, environmentalism, and other preoccupations with social justice. The main conclusion of this research was that the dichotomy of classification proposed in American research, separating parents according to either ideological or pedagogical motivations, does not apply to the parents Arai met, who instead express an amalgamation of motives.

Brabant (2004; Brabant, Bourdon and Jutras 2003, 2004) also investigated the motivations of Quebec parents in her previously mentioned questionnaire. A list of fifty statements about the motivations for homeschooling was developed by compiling reasons invoked in the specialized and scientific literature on the subject, and from an analysis of discussions over a Quebec web-based discussion forum on home education. The results showed that the motivations are many and heterogeneous, demonstrating great diversity among families. A statistical analysis (principal component analysis with varimax rotation) of this unrepresentative sample reveals an internal logic structured as seven motivational factors for home education (in order of importance): (1) a desire to engage in a family educational project; (2) an objection to the social or pedagogical organization of school; (3) a desire to offer academic enrichment; (4) a preoccupation with a child's socio-affective development; (5) the transmission of religious, moral or spiritual values; (6) a child's negative schooling experience, and (7) a dissatisfaction with the discrepancy between what the school can offer and the child's particular characteristics. The rationale grounding the family decision to home educate consisted on average of four factors. These results, like Arai's (2000), corroborate those of studies that demonstrate the complexity of decision-making rationales instead of looking to associate categories of families with categories of motivations. Even though 25% of participants mention religious association and beliefs, religious motivations per se rank among the lowest in importance (14%), unlike results in American and English Canadian studies. Besides, motivations related to home educating as a family project are clearly dominant. Finally, particular to these results is that no philosophical, political or religious voice appears to dominate, or even take up much room in Quebec home educators' discourse. The same observation can be made about the categorical rejection of state intervention in education. The authors suggest that the relatively recent implementation of compulsory schooling in Quebec (1943), in conjunction with an appreciation of the importance of interconnected relationship between family and State in family matters and a caring for the protection of children, might have generated this home education movement mainly founded on a new vision of family life and on a criticism of education being delivered in schools, rather than on religious or anti-state discourses.

Educational culture

Janice Aurini, assistant professor in the Sociology and Legal Studies Department at the University of Waterloo (Ontario) and Scott Davies, professor in the Sociology and Offord Center for Child Studies at McMaster University (Ontario), examined the rapid development of the homeschooling phenomenon in Canada in the greater context of the growth of the private education movement (Aurini and Davies 2005). The authors adopt a critical sociological posture in order to analyze the decision-making rationale at the root of the choice of private education (including homeschooling) by parents in the province of Ontario. This analysis relies on the analysis of secondary sources, as well as an empirical portion conducted over two years by visiting places and events and by interviews (*n*=75) carried out with a variety of different key players in Ontarian private education, including those of home education. Rather than proposing categories of reasons, the authors' interpretation of the parental choices suggests the idea of a particular parent culture, that of "intensive childrearing":

> We situate homeschooling within a framework that distinguishes the logics by which different forms of private education appeal to their clients. Comparing market-consumer, class reproduction, human capital and "expressive" logics, we argue that homeschooling is the most expressive segment of private schooling, and trace this to a burgeoning culture of "intensive childrearing" (462).

In effect, the researchers found that neither the rational criteria associated with the rise of neoliberal ideology, nor those of social class reproduction, nor the demands of increased valuation of human resources summarize the motives of the educational choice of home-educators well. Unlike certain parents who choose private school, several parent-educators look to withdraw their children from the hold of market logic reproduced at school. Additionally, they consider that their children are too precious to be entrusted into the care of others, preferring to give them personal attention and a form of custom-tailored pedagogy. Homeschooling also attracts parents because of the cultural advantages it brings, in terms of instilling parent values, reinforcing family unity or protecting children from certain dangers. Also, despite representing a risk from an economic point of view, homeschooling can match the educational ideal of parents. In the end, the authors understand that Canadian homeschoolers aim for educational gains other than those advantages that often motivate the choice of private school. Thus, they do not appear to be guided by a motivation to reproduce their social class membership, to improve their social capital or to better prepare their offspring for the competitive ferocity of the economic market. According to the authors, the combination of important investments of time and effort required by homeschooling with the more or less uncertain educational results that can result from homeschooling – a "counter-productive" strategy from an economic point of view – renders this form of alternative education the most "expressive" (as in expressive logic) of types of private education, the participant of a booming culture dubbed "intensive parenting."

Opinions on education and schools

One last part of the previously mentioned study on homeschooling in Quebec, conducted in 2003 by Brabant, was published in her book in 2013. It aims to define parents' attitudes towards education, as well as their perceptions on schools' attitudes towards education, and to explore possible relations with family or parents' characteristics (Brabant 2013). Opinions on education were collected through the Dutch Educational Attitudes Questionnaire (Denessen, Michels, and Felling 2000), situating respondents' positions according to two independent ideological orientations in education, using Dewey's categories (*The Child and the Curriculum*, 1902). Category A refers to a traditional/content-oriented ideology, and category B refers to a progressive/student-oriented one. The questionnaire categorized each subject as A or B in three different educational domains: (1) educational goals, (2) pedagogical relation, and (3) instructional emphasis. Content-oriented attitudes (category A) tend to emphasize career-development as an educational goal, discipline and order within the learning environment as pedagogical relations, and core subjects, achievement, and the attainment of the highest diploma possible as instructional emphases. The accent for category A is thus on the educational *product*. Student-oriented attitudes (category B) emphasize personal and social development as educational goals, active participation and involvement of students within the learning environment as pedagogical relations, and the social and creative subjects taught through both independent and cooperative learning as instructional emphases. The accent is thus on the educational *process*. The two orientations are conceptualized as perpendicular axes, where one's ideological orientation can be situated in any of the four quadrants, thus possibly expressing their agreement with attitudes from both ideologies or from neither. In the questionnaire, agreement with each statement is expressed on a five-point Likert-type scale.

Following Brabant's strategy, in an initial phase the parents indicated their degree of agreement or disagreement with each statement. In a second phase, they again filled out the questionnaire, indicating this time the degree of agreement or disagreement of the school system with each statement, according to them.

The results of the survey demonstrate that, in a general manner, parent-educators agree with both ideologies (progressive and traditional), but more highly value the progressive/student-oriented one. Additionally, the group of respondents expressed an accord, to different degrees, with all six studied attitudes except one: the emphasis on the educational product. The participants generally disagree with this attitude and prefer the more progressive attitude where the emphasis is on the learning process.

In crossing these results with the variables described within the families, Brabant notes that the parents who show more accord with the progressive ideology are those who attained a higher level of schooling, those who adopt a less structured educational approach, and those who express less spiritual or religious engagement. In contrast, interestingly, the tendency toward progressive ideology decreases when a man is the principal parent-facilitator of children's learning.

On the other hand, parents who demonstrate more accord with traditional ideology are those that benefit from a higher family revenue, those that adopt a more structured educational approach, and those who express greater spiritual or religious engagement. These last group members, however, are less numerous than the parent-educators of the progressive ideology in this Quebec sample, since the group average was definitely more progressive than traditional.

In regard to homeschooling parents' perceptions of the schools' attitudes towards education, the survey reveals that, as a group, they perceive that the school system adopts both ideologies (traditional and progressive), just like them, although it values the traditional ideology more than they do. On the level of attitudes, according to them, schools adopt five out of six possible attitudes, excluding the progressive attitude on pedagogical relation, which would encourage the child's involvement and active participation.

Crossing these responses with family characteristics again reveals some significant correlations. For example, the more structured the educational approach of parents, the less they attribute a traditional, content-oriented ideology to the school system, and, in all logic, the less their educational approach is structured, the more they consider the educational vision of the school system to be traditional. Likewise, the parents attribute more of a traditional orientation to the school system when their choice of homeschooling relies on the concern of the social-emotional development of their child, and they attribute less to a traditional orientation when their choice relies on the transmission of religious, moral, or spiritual values.

The data provided few explanations for the characteristics of some families who consider the school to be of a progressive orientation, apart from the fact that these parents are more likely to withdraw their children from school because of the inadequacy of the school's ability to cater to the particular characteristics of a child.

With these statistical analyses, Brabant contributed to understanding educational conceptions of parents and to establishing some correlations between these conceptions and their sociodemographic, motivational characteristics as well as their educational practices. For example, the parent-educators who affirm some strong religious values generally demonstrate more traditionalist educational values and adopt a more scholarly approach in the home, in the traditional sense of the term (structured with an emphasis on curriculum). Those who completed university studies, especially a master's degree or doctorate, which are characterized by a more personal and autonomous study plan, adopt a more flexible educational approach and encourage engaging the child in his or her learning progression. Moreover, parents' general disagreement with an emphasis on educational product will contribute to better understanding of the resistance of several parents to interact with school authorities who are uniquely mandated to evaluate the learning of the child, including on standardized test performance. Finally, Brabant concludes that the choice to homeschool, whether according to a progressive or traditionalist orientation, allows parents to feel that they are doing a better job of realizing their ideals for their children's education than would happen in conventional schools. However, she also notes that, ironically, the conceptions of parents, the ones that they attribute to the school system and the ones that the Quebec Ministry of Education itself expresses in official documents, all adopt attitudes centered on the child and on the curriculum. Thus, the conceptions of the two groups are not so distant from one another after all, which could facilitate an eventual collaboration between parents and the school in researching the way to achieve these conceptions.

The research commonalities of authors cited in this section allow a nuanced and quite in-depth understanding of homeschooling parents. On the one hand, the research contradicts certain prejudices, to the effect that families might descend from elite economic and social status and might be attempting to reproduce that status by educational strategy; on the contrary, families have diverse sociodemographic profiles and motivational rationale. On the other hand, statistical analysis reveal links between family characteristics and the conception of education that makes them homeschooling parents. Finally, some distinctions appear between families from the United State, English Canada, and Quebec, notably the lesser importance of religious and anti-government attitudes among Canadian homeschoolers, especially among Quebec homeschoolers, and, when they exist, the weaker importance that they hold in their educational decisions. The next section will be about the materialization of motivations and conceptions in the parents' educational practices, then about their outcomes.

Educational Practices and Outcomes

This section first presents Canadian research about certain aspects of homeschoolers' educational practices, namely citizenship education and homeschooling as a religious community of practice, and then presents some research about its outcomes in childhood and adulthood.

Citizenship education

Arai (1999) is interested in the practice of citizenship education within home education, wondering whether a homeschooled child can become a "good citizen," since it is often believed that school attendance is the only means by which one absorbs the common values necessary for future participation in civic life. In order to explore this question, he reviews research literature on home education, as well as the major objections to it, and analyzes it with regards to different issues of citizenship and citizenship education.

Arai suggests that homeschooling families implicitly elaborate an alternative vision of citizenship. According to his analysis, parent-educators do not wish to withdraw from society; rather, they are operating under a different understanding of citizenship than that assumed by much of the modern world. In effect, according to parent-educators, the school is not a primary agent in the formation of good citizens, and the credit that is attributed to it should instead be given back to parents who are engaging in this sense with their children. Despite certain methodological limitations in the studies he reviews, Arai does not doubt that the homeschooled children are very involved in extracurricular activities outside the house. Additionally, he reports that parent-educators believe that intense, solid family bonds are more favorable to the civic development of children than is school attendance. Arai believes that homeschooling benefits them twice: developing their self-esteem as much as it does their social and interpersonal skills. Furthermore, their alternate living style permits homeschooled children to have a capacity for exploring the world in a less conventional, sometimes critical manner, developing more independent and creative minds.

Following his analysis, Arai (1999) concludes that parent-educators' vision of citizenship corresponds to the concept of "multidimensional citizenship," as discussed by Kubow, Grossman and Ninoyama, as well as Cogan and Derricott (quoted in Arai1999). Parent-educators stress different dimensions of this concept with the means at their disposal, notably in the application of citizenship principles in the familial structure and daily participation in community life, while the school essentially puts the accent on the civic content delivered by history, geography, and human science courses. Thus, parent-educators engage in a different, though also valuable, citizenship education process than that existing in the school system.

Arai recommends that the educational politics related to citizenship education emphasize the importance of the active participation involved in living together, which, in his eyes, would have the impact to reduce the gap between the dissonant visions of citizenship cast by the school and the home. Beyond that, he recommends recognizing that it is possible to define different visions of what it means to be a citizen, and that the educational choice of parents will affect the way children will shape their understanding of what it means to become a member of society.

Religious communities of practice

In this study, Richard Rymarz (2011), an Australian scholar now teaching Catholic Religious Education at the University of Alberta, Canada, was interested in the Catholic homeschooling families in Alberta, and, more specifically, in the transmission of beliefs and Catholic religious practices from one generation to the next, in a society where, according to him, the diversification of worldviews calls into question some religious structures. He thus explored the possibilities homeschooling presents to parents desirous of establishing a familial and educational structure as the primary agent of transmission of religious practice.

Rymarz conducted in-depth interviews with twenty Albertan Catholic homeschooling families (with the two parents, in most cases), recruited using a snowballing technique, which were completed by emails and follow-up interviews. He analyzed their practice with the aid of the concept of "design for living" (Linton 1969, in Rymarz 2011), where life designs represent certain patterns of life embraced by particular sociological groups, especially in terms of organization of time. Rymarz found that families gained more time for engaging in pursuits connected to their ideals by foregoing the transport time most families spend getting their children to and from school. Rymarz also found that networks of like-minded homeschoolers tended to form practical communities, or what he called "domestic churches" that act as surrogates for and in some cases replacements to Catholic schools and parishes (Rymarz 2011).

Framed in a grounded theory paradigm, a content analysis revealed three main categories: intentional parenting, networked individuals, and the role of women in homeschooling. The theme of intentional parenting has to do with the practices and educational choices of parents. The participants emphasized their intention to engender a religious sensibility and culture among their children. They explained this unconventional life choice by a desire to develop a familial culture, in living a different educational and relational experience. Homeschooling brings them more liberty: no imposed daily planning, no summative exam of learning, various learning contexts adapted to the needs of children, and the possibility of developing critical thinking among their children. The "networked individuals" category involves four levels: association with other families through common school boards; socialization activities with other Catholic homeschooling families; peer support; and involvement in their local parish. The last category refers to the role of mothers, who occupy a position of leader in daily family logistics and who guide children in the religious domain, with practices like prayers and catechism. Mothers also become educational visionaries, adapting their practices to the educational needs and character of their children. The mothers play a key role in the socialization activities of children as well.

Finally, according to the interpretation of Rymarz, the participating families effectively constitute some practical communities because their beliefs and their practices permit the creation of formal and informal processes, in part, and also because their members share some intentions, beliefs, and practices. Thus, parents have a predominant and deliberate role in the general and religious education of their children, whose principal socialization is a result of interactions with family members.

Arai's and Rymarz's respective studies followed particular educational practices current among Canadian homeschooling families. Both emphasized the social aspects of the children's principally familial and communal lifestyle, rather than the academic aspect. Arai valorized the citizenship education that takes place there, while Rymarz depicted the practical religious community among Catholic families and their networks. The studies that follow are interested in the outcomes of this form of education among children who are now adult-age.

Academic performance

A study by Sandra Martin-Chang, Odette N. Gould, and Reanne E. Meuse (2011) compares the academic success of children educated at regular public school and those at home. Their methodological approach is exceptionally robust. Although the first author is a professor at a university in Quebec (Concordia University, Department of Education), the researchers recruited the participating children from two Atlantic Provinces (Nova Scotia and New Brunswick). Participants were between 5 and 10 years of age, from different school boards, and with divergent academic backgrounds and heterogeneous social origins. In total, seventy-four children participated in the study, half of which ($n = 37$) did not attend school. The children were selected with the goal of being paired with similar profiles, the aim being to achieve direct comparison between the homeschoolers and the children who attend public school. This pairing was carried out while taking into account marital status of parents as well as number of children in the family. Among the homeschoolers, a first subgroup ($n = 25$) was characterized by some learning methods deemed "structured" and a second ($n = 12$) by non-structured methods, more commonly called unschooling. This distinction was established by interrogating the parent-educators on their educational program. Because of its small size, the group of unschoolers was not included in the main analysis, only in subsequent exploratory analyses.

The academic level of children was measured by the Woodcock–Johnson Test of Achievement A Revised, administered by a trained experimenter in controlled conditions. Finally, the study was conducted by a team of independent, impartial researchers that had no link with any homeschooling organizations. The Woodcock–Johnson Test consists of eight subtests that measure the following competencies: (1) Letter-Word Identification test (real word reading); (2) Passage Comprehension test (comprehension); (3) Word Attack test (pure decoding); (4) Science test (scientific knowledge pertaining to biology, physics, and chemistry); (5) Social Science test (vocations, geography, history, and politics); (6) Humanities test (literature, music, art, and popular culture); (7) Calculation test (simple number identification to complex algebra).

Following MANOVA and follow up t-tests, results show that children who are homeschooled in a structured fashion attain better results in standardized tests than children schooled in public schools on all subjects tested, with results ranging from a little more than a half-grade advantage in math to 3.3 grade levels in reading. Moreover, after statistical verification, such benefits cannot be accounted for by differences in the variables controlled for: geographical area of students, testing administration, maternal educational level, marital status, household size, parental employment, and family income. Also, since both structured homeschoolers and public schoolers performed above their age group, possibly as a result of a self-selection of children and parents, the relative differences between their scores remain significant and in favor of homeschooling. According to the researchers, this advantage may be explained by several factors like smaller class sizes, more individualized instruction or more academic time spent on core subjects such as reading and writing.

The unschoolers (unstructured homeschooling), in smaller number as they are often harder to access, could only be studied for exploratory analyses. They performed less well than the two other groups in all subjects, and even below their age group in calculation, social science, humanities and comprehension.

The results show an academic advantage in homeschooling, possibly limited to situations where the parents create structured learning environments. That at least appears true in regard to academic achievement tests.

Graduates' lives and social contribution

Two studies on home-educated adults were conducted and published by Cardus, a non-profit organization presenting itself as a

> think tank dedicated to the renewal of North American social architecture. Drawing on more than 2000 years of Christian social thought, (…) to enrich and challenge public debate through research, events, and publications, for the common good (Cardus).

Cardus has three offices in Canada and one in Los Angeles. Funded by Christian institutions on both sides of the border, its surveys study private education in Canada and the US. Although the studies are clearly ideologically oriented, their research methodologies are rigorous enough for their results to be presented here, bearing in mind some caution about the interpretations offered. In particular, the random sampling methods grant the results an interesting representativity, often absent from studies on home education. However, in the writing of the reports, the studies' authors tend to overgeneralize the results to populations larger than what the samples allow for. For example, the 2012 report discusses results for Canadian homeschooling graduates in general, even though non-religious homeschoolers and Quebec participants were excluded from the sample. Comparisons between Canadian and US graduates are also hazardous, since the sample composition in each country is quite different.

The objective of the first study is to study "alignment between the motivations and outcomes of Christian education, to better understand the role of Christian schools in students' lives, in families, and in larger society" (Pennings et al. 2011, 5) by measuring three outcomes of Christian education: spiritual formation, cultural engagement, and academic development. In order to do so, it combines multiple methods designs which were conducted by different research teams over five years. The first component of the research design, a quantitative study, assembles two web-based surveys conducted by an internet survey firm, Knowledge Networks. One survey accessed a representative random sample of US high school graduates, aged 23–49 years, while the second one used an oversample of 1000 US private schools graduates (including Catholic, conservative Protestant or "Christian school," other type of Christian school, non-Christian religious school, nonreligious school, and home school) and 500 public schools graduates, all aged 23–40. This first report (2011) describes the eighty-one US homeschool graduates from these two surveys (Gaither 2011). Regression analyses were operated to isolate demographic variables in order to predict the "type-of-schooling effect." Presented results are preliminary:

tables of results are not always commented on, and the rare comments about homeschooling graduates do not include all of the three studied outcomes. The following results are partial, and sometimes they are our reading of the tables, selected for their interest.

Analyses show that, regarding spiritual formation, US homeschool graduates attend "church with greater regularity than their public, Catholic, and non-religious school peers" (Pennings et al., 16) and encourage reverence for church's authority. They believe that "morality is unchanging and absolute" (17) and consider that "premarital sex, living together before marriage, and divorce are morally wrong" (17). Also, homeschooling seems to influence spiritual practices within couples without children (talking about God and reading the Bible with the partner). However, US homeschool graduates appear to spend similar time as public school graduates reading the Bible and praying alone.

Under the cultural engagement category, some results are much more negative for homeschoolers than for other Christian school graduates. Tables of results show that US homeschool graduates express feeling "helpless in dealing with life's problems" and feeling a "lack of clarity of goals and sense of direction" a lot more than other Christian education graduates (24). They appear to get married younger, to have fewer children, and to get divorced in larger proportion. Also, they describe themselves as less politically engaged, namely having less "interest in politics and publics affairs" and not having "actively campaigned for a political party" or participated "in a political protest, march or demonstration" (28).

Finally, as with academic achievement, some of the other results reported by Cardus were less flattering to homeschooling than those of previous studies using a less rigorous methodology. US homeschool graduates are more likely than their peers in Catholic, non-religious private and public schools to attend an open-admission college (which is less competitive) and they attend "prestigious universities significantly less often than their peers" (33).

The objective of the second study (Pennings et al. 2012), a survey conducted in March 2012, is to measure non-government school effects on cultural, economic, and social engagement, academic achievement, spiritual formation, and religious engagement of graduates from "English-speaking Canada" or "English Canada," defined by the authors as Canada excluding Quebec. It should be noted, then, that this division is more cultural than linguistic, since there are Francophone minority groups in all officially unilingual Anglophone provinces, there is an Anglophone minority in Quebec, and the province of New Brunswick is officially bilingual. Therefore, the terms "English" and "French" refer to the traces of the founding nations' traditions and not to languages. Thus, all results for Quebec participants are analyzed separately, a decision that the report's authors justify because of the cultural gap between this province and others. It can be inferred that they expect the results in Quebec to be quite different, so that their inclusion would alter the national results which would no longer represent the "English Canada" which the researchers seem primarily interested in. The results should then be presented rigorously as those of "Canada excluding Quebec." Given that, as mentioned earlier in this chapter,

Quebecers represent nearly a quarter of the Canadian population, the sample cannot be considered as representative of Canadians.

This survey includes a large oversample of non-government high school graduates aged 23–40, selected from a Vision Critical internet panel. When the numbers allow it, subgroups are formed among the 2054 respondents to study them distinctly: public school, separate Catholic school, independent Catholic school, non-religious independent school, conservative Protestant school, and religious homeschooling. Concerning homeschooling, the sample contains forty-one religious homeschoolers which are included in the analysis, while the seventeen non-religious homeschoolers subgroup is insufficient and therefore excluded. The religious/non-religious distinction refers to the graduate's mother attending religious services regularly or not. After the exclusion of participants from Quebec, the religious homeschooling sample of forty-one comes down to thirty-four participants. Data about the seven Quebec homeschooling graduates are not treated. Therefore, the results presented here concern a sample of thirty-four "English Canadian religious homeschooling graduates" (ECRHG). Nested regression analyses reveal the main tendencies on each theme, compared to other graduates, while demographic and family background variables are controlled. Yet, the researchers point out a limitation of the results about homeschoolers in their study:

> Finding statistically significant results is more difficult with the religious home schooling sector. Some of the estimated differences between this group and public schoolers are very large, even though the small sample size makes it difficult to conclude that these differences are not due to sampling fluctuations (Pennings et al., 63).

Keeping this warning in mind, the results of the subgroup ECRHG show that, in relation to participants who received a governmental education, adults who have been homeschooled are more prone to being married and having more children and less prone to being divorced or separated. It is also more probable that they have carried out some volunteer work in a religious congregation rather than, for example, in a school or cultural organization, or for a political cause. The civic participation of ECRHG in neighborhood or community groups was positively placed in the forefront by the results, just as their propensity to participate and contribute financially to their congregation and to other religious causes. However, it appears less frequent that they contribute to other types of organizations, with the exception of community groups and youth groups.

Concerning employment, there is no significant statistical difference from public school diplomas for occupation of higher-level posts but the ECRHG are more susceptible to being employed part-time or being unemployed. In terms of expectations, they expect a job to allow for creativity but not friendship. They have a strong sense of vocational calling and expect a job to fulfill that calling. They also expect their job to be an important financial support as well as a possibility for establishing ties with the community. While they are concerned about justice in employer policies, they are more strongly oriented towards hard work and efficiency.

ECRHG feel a high sense of obligation to political involvement; however, their actual involvement is about as much as that of government school graduates. Also, while ECRHG are notably more likely to feel obligated to care for the environment, they are no more politically active on this or other issues than their government school peers. They show more confidence in corporations and the federal government, but less in the institutions of the federal government, the Supreme Court, the media, and the scientific community. This confidence in government could be explained by the fact that, at the time of survey, the Canadian government and Prime Minister were from the Conservative Party.

Concerning academic success, the ECRHG complete, in general, equal or fewer years of study than public school graduates. Nevertheless, when they attend a university, they more often obtain the highest degree, a PhD, rather than an intermediate degree.

As for spiritual and religious facets, all of the indicators show that their training on this theme seems more significant compared to that of other groups, and equal to that of Christian school graduates.

Pennings et al. conclude optimistically that English Canadian religious homeschool graduates are "grounded, contributing, faithful, diligent, conservative, and dependable" (51) and that, like other forms of non-governmental education, homeschooling contributes in an important manner to education provided in Canada, and, consequently, to the greater public.

The studies presented in this section have solid methodologies that offer revealing results about the outcomes of homeschooling in English Canada and the United States. They use random sampling and comparative designs. Martin-Chang, Gould, and Meuse (2011) produced a rigorous comparison between home educated and school educated children, aged 5 to 10, on academic learning. The results are strongly positive for home education, although exploratory analyses point towards a serious difference in the specific case of unstructured home education. The participants in Cardus' studies (2011, 2012) being 23 to 40 or 49 years old at the time of their participation, the surveys measured how children who were religiously home educated between 1966 and 2005 feel about their education and how their adult lives demonstrate cultural, economic, and social engagement, academic achievement, spiritual formation, and religious engagement. The results are mixed and do not allow for a totally positive conclusion. Generally, religious and conservative values seem transmitted well, but the comparison with public school or private school graduates on academic attainment and on cultural and social engagement in non-religious settings are not always favorable to homeschoolers, religious or not, from English Canada or the US.

These outcomes echo the conclusions of the studies on home education practices presented at the beginning of this section, namely Arai's documentary study on citizenship education (1999) and Rymarz's empirical study on religious communities of practice (2011). Indeed, Arai might well be right when he says: "Homeschooling is not just about where kids will learn their ABCs, it affects the very definition of what it means to be a member of society" (10) and makes a recommendation about emphasizing the "importance of participation as a crucial element" (9) in "multi-dimensional citizenship." Besides, Rymarz's "intentional parenting" and "networked individuals" categories (2011) are reflected in Cardus' study results about the home-school graduates' religious practice and engagement in church related activities. As for the homeschooled young children's competitive academic results found by Martin-Chang, Gould, and Meuse (2011), they are not extended into the academic and professional attainment of the homeschool graduates represented in the Cardus studies. Many explanations could be suggested, but clearer answers should come from more studies, hopefully as methodologically robust.

Political and Legal Aspects

This third section presents a discussion about the political and legal rights aspects involved in home education. The first study presented constructs a sociopolitical analysis of the growing legitimacy and size of the homeschooling movement, and this is followed by two works that offer legal analyses of home education in Canada.

Political culture

Davies and Aurini (2003) examine the elements of homeschooling political culture, suggesting that what began as a marginal pedagogical movement has grown into a powerful political player. To arrive at this conclusion the authors use the same data as that showcased in their 2005 work, described earlier in this chapter (Aurini and Davies 2005).

According to their study, firstly, the greater legitimacy of homeschooling results from a growing educational pluralism demanded by more and more actors (charter schools, voucher experiments, new private schools or homeschooling):

> Rather than framing homeschooling as a radical departure, new advocates conceive homeschooling as simply another alternative to public schooling. As such, it is viewed as an option among many, rather than as a wholesale rejection of public education (2003, 65).

Secondly, rather than framing their demands in terms of social critique against "technocracy" or "secular humanism," most homeschooling advocates express their views using a new and more mainstream language of individual rights, notably the rights of parents to choose their children's education. Hence, Davies and Aurini notice the growing gap between these parents and those still overtly criticizing and even looking down on the educational system as the source of all problems. Thirdly, a rising conception of pedagogical individualism concurs in making homeschooling more popular, valuing the tailoring of education to each child's learning specificities.

Thus, these three characteristic aspects of present educational policies (pluralism, rights and freedoms, and individualism) contribute to homeschooling's growing popularity and legitimacy in Canada. Davies and Aurini suggest that its continued growth will depend on whether governments will not only allow homeschooling, but encourage its existence by way of subsidies or tax measures. They conclude that, in this respect, homeschoolers would benefit from developing further their "rights talk" (71) in order to convince authorities and the public that they are entailed to more support, while attracting newcomers who will be reassured by a wider acceptance and tolerate more regulation on their practice. The following legal analyses further elaborate on the matter of rights.

Legal analyses

Two recent studies offer complementary legal analyses of home education, both using theoretical perspectives and documentary analyses of Canadian sources. Blokhuis examines the *parens patriae* doctrine with regards to home education and includes a comparison with the United States. Lagos compares Catholic canon law to Canada's civil laws and jurisprudence.

Jason C. Blokhuis (2009, 2010), professor of Social Science Studies at the University of Waterloo, in Ontario, and his colleague Curren (Curren and Blokhuis 2011) offer a comparative legal study of how courts in the Province of Ontario, Canada, and the State of New York, US, have interpreted and applied the common law doctrine of *parens patriae* (literally: parent of the nation, in Latin), the mechanism by which the state exercises plenary custodial authority in the welfare and developmental interests of children. Indeed, from its position as *parens patriae*, the State requires all custodians to subordinate their own interests to the independent interests of their children when they conflict. According to Blokhuis, compulsory schooling laws derived from the *parens patriae* doctrine and required all parents to share their day-to-day custody with publicly certified teachers for limited periods of time, in order to expose every child to formative influences other than those of their parents, to instruction, and to opportunities for social, economic, and civic participation beyond what their parents alone could provide.

Yet, say Curren and Blokhuis, in the United States, the obligation to safeguard the welfare and developmental interests of children under the doctrine of *parens patriae* has been interpreted as a duty arising only upon parental default or failure, particularly in circumstances when the life or health of a specific child is endangered by unreasonable parental decisions. For example, in the State of New York, the state supervenes when individual custodians demonstrate unwillingness or manifest inability to prioritize the independent welfare and developmental interests of a child. The 1972 *Yoder* decision, where Amish families were exempted from some of Wisconsin's compulsory education law because of the serious impact of the law on their way of life, further undermined the *parens patriae* doctrine. Blokhuis argues that "when the state accedes to parents seeking to exempt their children from compulsory schooling laws on religious grounds, the state violates its *parens patriae* duty to prioritize the welfare and developmental interests of all children" (206). Moreover, he writes that "Homeschoolers who repudiate any public role in childrearing and seek to isolate their children from public formative influences deny their children the non-exclusive custodial authority to which they are entitled at common law" (2009, 203).

As for Canada, Blokhuis' analysis reveals that American constitutional jurisprudence has played an influential, but not decisive role when cited by the Supreme Court of Canada since the advent of the Canadian Charter of Rights and Freedoms in 1982.

> Indeed, Canadian courts have sought to reconcile constitutional rights for children and the fundamental values underlying the Charter with the priority traditionally given to the welfare and developmental interests of children under the doctrine of *parens patriae* (208).

> Where reasons are given, the courts have tended to emphasize the desirability of diverse formative influences or the undesirability of exclusive or potentially indoctrinative parental authority (210).

After this historical overview of the development of *parens patriae* up to its connection to to compulsory schooling legislation and a comparative jurisprudential history of custody and home education cases in New York and in Ontario, Blokhuis moves on to policy implications with regards to homeschooling. In particular, considering that the *parens patriae* doctrine is the primary legal basis for the judicial regulation of custody and compulsory schooling laws for the benefit of all children, he insists that in New York and Ontario, where homeschooling is not statutorily prohibited, the State through its legislative and judicial organs continues to limit the custodial authority of homeschooling parents on the grounds that children's independent welfare and developmental interests include exposure to public formative influences.

Lagos' work (2011, 2012) adds to Blokhuis' analysis. Julio Lagos, presently Chaplain at an Opus Dei prelature in British Columbia, presented a doctoral thesis at Pontificia Universitas Sanctae Crucis, in Rome (Lagos 2011), where he analyzed parental education rights in Canada with regards to canon and civil law approaches to homeschooling. Relying on a documentary analysis method and a historical critique of sources, Lagos demonstrates that the normative framework noted within the Code of Canon Law is favorable to homeschooling and that Canadian legislation also permits it, which assures a degree of supervision that keeps things in line with the spirit of compromise between parental rights and the best interest of the child (according to the *parens patraie* doctrine).

The study by Lagos was carried out in four stages. It first examined parental educational rights in light of international public rights regulations: the principal agreements and conventions related to human rights, as well as the Convention on the Rights of the Child. According to Lagos, these regulations, inspired by natural rights principles and founded in recognition of human dignity, acknowledge that parental educational rights have a very vast range that gives parents, in fact, considerable discretionary ability in the matter of choosing the type of education that they will offer their children. This universally recognized right and duty that parents have to educate their children implies that they actively invest in them, but also that they have the power to decide the direction of their children's educational program. In addition, considering that parents really contribute a public service when they undertake to educate their children themselves, Lagos judges that the State should be appreciative of the parent-educators' exercising of this natural right and should thus be obligated to furnish them with material and the financial framework to permit alternative education methods – support without which parents would find themselves disadvantaged. However, the State nonetheless reserves the right to regulate the content of these alternative educational programs. International legal instruments acknowledge that home education is a form of expression of the educational choice that parents can make, unprejudiced by legal principle, and in the best interest of the child, which Lagos assumes to be a naturally present motive in parents.

In a second stage, Lagos analyzes the founding principles of parental educational rights according to the canonic right, which stipulates that parents have the right to choose the most appropriate methods to guarantee an education that conforms to their faith. These magisterial principles, based on natural law and the provisions of the Code of Canon Law, still give a very large amount of power to parents who want to promote and support private educational enterprises and alternatives like homeschooling. Thus, according to Lagos, the public administration should ensure the availability of a range of educational options and should guarantee the natural liberty of parents to educate their children with minimal interference.

In a third stage, analyzing the legal framework of homeschooling in Canada, Lagos summarizes the pan-Canadian setting, as our earlier section on context explains. On this matter, Lagos' account of the Quebec context and regulations is questionable. First, he states that home education is rarer in this province than in the rest of Canada, although no data is available to support this statement. This supposed rarity would be directly caused, according to him, by a recent change in Quebec legislation aimed at a reorganization of its newly secular school system, making religious education the responsibility of the parent, which should provide it in a way that seeks to respect the interest of the child. Lagos then decries this protection of children by the State as a threat to homeschooling parents, thus discouraging homeschooling in Quebec. However, the research literature on Quebec homeschoolers points to a lesser importance of religious motivations within this population, thus challenging the alleged causal relation between this legal change and a supposed scarcity of home educators in Quebec. This slightly skewed analysis of the Quebec situation is in keeping with the thesis's posture in favor of parental rights, religious ones in particular. Nonetheless, the author notes that the different provincial and territorial laws on education all acknowledge the right of parents to homeschool their children within the limits of their duties and responsibilities towards the best interest of their children.

In the fourth and final stage, Lagos analyzes Canadian jurisprudence relative to the phenomenon of homeschooling, affirming that the Canadian Constitution protects parents' educational rights that ensue from the freedom of conscience and religion guaranteed by the Canadian Charter of Rights and Freedoms. Parents can thus choose the education that is most suitable for their children, pursuing their ideological and religious convictions.

The author finally draws five statements from this analysis: (1) The Canadian Constitution protects parents' liberty interests in their relationship with their children, including recognition of the natural law principle of parents as first educators; (2) the provincial and territorial Canadian legislation recognizes the right of the State to regulate homeschooling; (3) the Supreme Court has upheld that provinces can require application for approval of homeschool plans and teacher certification (though no province requires certification); (4) the Court recognized religious protection for homeschooling; (5) in the case where absence of regulation could result in a threat to the interest of the child, the Court gave precedence to the interest of the State over the rights of parents.

In sum, the Canadian Constitution with the Charter of Rights and Freedoms of 1982 facilitates the recognition of homeschooling as an alternative education option, finding a balance between the rights of the state and those of parents, in a spirit of compromise which is, according to Lagos, recognized as a Canadian virtue. Finally, Lagos suggests that parents' and children's rights should not be seen as mutually opposed, just as parental and State rights should operate in harmony, as the State's interest rests in enabling parents to provide for their children's education. Hence, periodic formal assessment of homeschooled children or qualitative evaluations may be the most reasonable compromise between State and parents.

Davies and Aurini (2003) have suggested that some homeschooling parents in English Canada put forward a discourse based on parental and individual rights to legitimate their educational choice for their children. But as Blokhuis' and Lagos' studies have shown, parental rights remain limited by regulations imposed by states having in mind the best interests of the children and of society.

However, doctrine and jurisprudence neither give us clear indications as to this necessary balance or compromise and its concrete normative application, nor do they provide the social means to instigate the desired adherence to such norms. To fill in this void, the next section introduces research conducted in the field of governance.

Governance and Democratic Learning

Christine Brabant's research on the governance of home education (Brabant 2010, 2013, accepted; Brabant and Bourdon 2012) is in keeping with an ethical perspective on public interest governance. She highlights: (1) the limits of the present judicial instruments for regulating a new social practice like homeschooling; (2) the gap between official norms and applied norms, a symptom of both parents' and school administrators' lack of agreement with these norms; and (3) the often substantive or formal procedural nature of discourse on the pros and cons of homeschooling and their oppositional argumentative dynamics. These observations call for a mutual understanding between opposing parties about the educational stakes that are their shared interest as well as the necessity of co-constructing a normative framework supporting institutional change in the face of this new educational movement. In order to do that, Brabant relies on the theory of reflexive governance developed by Belgian philosophers of law Jacques Lenoble and Marc Maesschalck (2010). Looking to get past the shortcomings of the legalistic, market-based, or hierarchical (command-and-control) social regulation models, they approach regulation of questions of public interest, such as education, in a practical manner, like a joint problem-solving process. This pragmatic approach necessitates democratic learning from all players (individual, collective, and institutional) in order to generate a systemic reflexivity, of the manner described by Schön and colleagues (1971, 1978, 1994, 1996), for creating institutional renewal and social creativity. Thus, they aim for the attainment of Dewey's (1916, 1927, 1938) democratic ideal through democratic participation, collective action and social inquiry.

The theory of reflexive governance suggests that key players in home education have the opportunity to collectively establish the rules of coexistence, which will motivate their adherence to those norms more than educational authorities imposing a legalistic or administrative model of regulation; letting the rules of school markets dominate; or parent-educators resorting to strategies of ideological legitimization. For that to occur, it appears essential to support and better understand these key players' social learning process. That is the intention of the two pieces of research presented in this section.

Parents as collective actors

According to Brabant, the participation of parent-educators in the homeschooling movement can be described as collective action in search of solutions to similar problems encountered in their parenting practice with regard to their children's education and the private and public education offer. Thus, parent-educators try new experiences, evolving in an evaluative and sometimes concerted manner; questioning, by their practice, different foundations of education and structural variables of the education system. They thus operate the fundamental shift, described by Lenoble and Maesschalck (2010), from reflexive practice to an inferential reflexivity, eventually bringing about institutional learning.

In her first piece of research on governance, Brabant (2010, 2013; Brabant and Bourdon, 2012) accompanied three Quebec homeschooling support groups from different regions over a sixteen-month period in a "training–research" project. This dual process had a double objective: (1) the research objective was to better understand the democratic learning process at play when collective actors engage in participating in the reflexive governance of a domain of public interest they care about;

(2) the training objective was for the participants to work towards the production of governance propositions for the regulation and evolution of homeschooling in their area. About twelve volunteer homeschooling parents in each of the three groups participated in the study because they wanted to act upon their expressed desire for things to "change" or "improve" in the way homeschooling is regulated. Some also mentioned they wanted to develop their social or political abilities or set an example for their children in terms of civic participation.

An "accompanied auto-training" framework was offered, where the starting plan, consisting of a basic problem-solving process (from problem description to solution exploration to action plan), was to be appropriated by the groups and eventually re-invented by them, according to each group's progress and goals. Thus, the groups had total control over their learning process, and they launched their own inquiries (e.g., guest speakers, documentation, discussions, interactions with other actors) while receiving financial, methodological, and practical support from the researcher (e.g., childcare, meeting reports). At the end of the project, the groups reflected on their experience and on their learning process and validated the researcher's related observations.

Brabant carried out a multiple case study of the three groups' learning paths. The learning process data was collected by means of meeting recordings, participant observation, the taking of notes during and after meetings, observation checklists, clarification interviews, official documents, and work documents. Discursive data were summarized and then were validated by the participants. The analysis of the learning paths was carried out with the aid of collective skills grids inspired by the theoretical framework and lists of discussion stakes drawn out from the literature. The instruments evolved during the data collection in order to take new elements into account.

In addition to generating innovative solutions related to the governance of homeschooling, this research was able to describe and model the process of democratic learning of a collective actor in view of participation in reflexive governance. The results concern the types of learning carried out by the groups, their conditions of success as well as the governance propositions elaborated upon in the course of the process. According to Brabant, two types of learning were carried out by the participants. First and foremost, pragmatic learning relates to "the organization of practical conditions favorable to learning" (2013, 46). This type of learning refers to the necessary management of meetings by a steering committee, to the self-management of the group concerning the logistics of meetings, to the mobilization of members, and to the appropriation and participation of members in the collective project. Next, genetic learning is that which refers to "terms of auto-transformation of the group, of the upgrading to a level of proper capacity of engagement in governance" (47). This type of learning occurs when a group voluntarily interacts with a helping semi-outsider - the researcher, in this case; develops collective skills of reflexive thinking and action; assumes collectively the responsibility of desiring change; and finally, gives itself collective identity as a formalized group.

Brabant also identified four main conditions for succeeding in this type of democratic learning process, putting into contrast the advances and difficulties experienced by the different groups. Thus, it appeared necessary that this process take place in the long-term and that it could benefit from a certain quantity of financial, material, human, and methodological resources. The notion of trust is equally central. It has to exist between individuals, toward their group capacities, and with regard to the democracy – that is, the opening of the educational institution to take into account their propositions. Finally, the presence of exterior factors (in the form of accompaniment by a semi-outsider, some destabilizations caused by the learning process, the opinion of others toward which had to be developed a sentiment of legitimacy of their desire for change, and some interactions with exterior figures) was determinant for the progress of different groups.

Finally, Brabant presents a few propositions devised by the groups. As a whole, "the groups hoped for development and normalization of the option of homeschooling, so that it could be included in society and that their autonomy would be recognized" (2013, 49). For that to happen, the creation of a social organization for the education of children, specifically for home education (49) was proposed as well as a regional regulation system, stemming from consolidation of regional groups of parent-educators rather than being based on the local division of school boards or being based on individual relationships between each family and school authorities.

Brabant concludes that the parent groups evolved through a more trusting and open attitude towards the institution. They were invested in researching solutions stemming from their knowledge and their particular contexts, all taking into consideration some larger interests or interests other than their own.

School officials as agents of change

A second research–training project was led by Brabant (2013, accepted) with some school professionals responsible for supervising homeschooling families. This study had a dual objective: first, a training objective, to support these homeschool supervisors in their desire to improve their interactions with parent-educators; second, a research objective, to describe and model the process of learning how to participate in institutional reflexivity on the part of homeschooling supervisors. The nine participants came from four different school boards and occupied diverse functions: administrator, director of educational services, special needs teacher, principal or educational advisor. They each had to monitor one to thirty homeschooled children. All participants knew that there were other children in their area who were not registered for school but they viewed themselves as powerless and not responsible for the education of these children. In the monitoring of registered students, all participants reported having observed a gap between written policies and their application.

The research–training with homeschool supervisors took place partly in an individual manner. A first interview served to establish an initial portrait of the actual situation of governance of supervising home education, to clarify what the desired situation was and to identify the reasons for the gap between the two. Next, the participants accepted the sharing of interview reports between them. Additionally, different informative documents were furnished, as well as a presentation on the international homeschooling situation and a discussion meeting between all participants. One final interview allowed the researcher to collect the evolution of reflections and practices of participants, creating an assessment of the learning process and establishing a plan of action for each participant in his or her school board. Support, principally methodological, informative, and reflexive, was furnished by Brabant in the course of the process.

The results were presented in the same form as in the preceding piece of research, considering pragmatic and genetic learning as well as the governance propositions of the participants. The pragmatic learning, relative to creating "practical conditions favorable to the success of training" (Brabant 2013, 224), demanded homeschool supervisors to develop engagement in the process, project management, autonomous training and that of their work environment. As for the genetic learning process, it was relative to "transformation of the actor, to the passage to a superior level of capacity for action, likely to engagement in participation in reflexive governance" (225). Just as for parent-educators, opening to the researcher-trainer and to destabilization generated a higher level of reflexivity for homeschool supervisors. In addition, taking responsibility of change and innovation in their milieu allowed them to develop their professional identity toward that of sympathetic agent of change to the positive evolution of governance of homeschooling.

Their governance propositions were conceived in respect for plans of parent-educators, without intention of coercion but rather of collaboration, the whole assuring equality of opportunity for all children. Their wish for change made them focus on the improvement of practices of their school board, while aiming at an internal reorganization (type of intervention, procedures, and roles of leaders), although among them some also imagined a collaboration of a larger scale with other school boards or external actors.

Brabant concludes that these school leaders developed their attitude to depart "from uncertainty, ignorance and discomfort in their role of intervention and in their position between the school board and the parents" toward an attitude that was "more proactive, open and trusting agents of change in their school board territory and in their region" (223). Open to improving their practices of intervention and using their contextual knowledge to shed light on their organization, they learned how to feed the reflexivity of the institution and its capacity to adapt to change.

At the end of her research with parent-educators and then with school figures, Brabant stresses that the two categories of actors have demonstrated a capacity for social learning that could be fruitful for homeschooling in Quebec. In effect, the groups of parents evolved from the informal structure of a group of solidarity, to a collective actor who could eventually, suggests Brabant, obtain the status of political figure capable of participating in the governance of public education. On their side, the homeschool supervisors passed from the uncomfortable position of isolated, proxy intervening party to that of an agent of change who, with the institution, shares developed ideas and collaborations with parent-educators, opening the door to the creation of a new innovative figure in response to expressed needs. Finally, Brabant (2013, accepted) announced her next piece of research, which reunites experienced homeschooling parents and experienced homeschooling monitoring officials to pursue jointly this exploration of normative co-construction.

These original qualitative research designs, not only support parents' and school authorities' learning about stakes at play in home education, but participate in a concrete and contextualized problem-solving process, informed by a better understanding of relationships between citizens and institutions when democratic governance is challenged by emergent movements like homeschooling.

Suggestions for Further Research

This chapter has offered a review of research on Canadian home education and of research conducted by Canadian researchers on home education. The following themes created a varied reflection on diverse aspects of this phenomenon: (1) understanding parents; (2) educational practices and outcomes; (3) political and legal aspects; and (4) governance and democratic learning.

As written in our introduction, this portrait was sketched with the help of the few recent and sound studies available. In sum, only eight researchers or research teams were cited, cumulating some fifteen studies between them, about half of which are graduate work. Therefore, the first need to be mentioned in terms of further research on home education in Canada is simply more quality research as well as the furthering and diversification of research questions. Of course, since home education is not taught in education faculties, universities are less likely to hire and support scholars focusing on this research field. Yet, there is a clear need for sound knowledge, reflection, and practical expertise in local educational authorities, social services, parent associations, considering the growth of home education and of similar educational movements and the important stakes at play for families, children and society.

This chapter also presented a research overview where the French and English traditions in Canada seem to lead to differences in homeschooling parents' motivational profiles and political actions, and to rather mutually exclusive research corpuses. In terms of motivations, research indicate that English Canadian parents might be less religiously motivated than US homeschooling parents, but still closer to them on that matter than Quebec parents, who mainly express a desire to pursue a family educational project. In terms of political actions, English Canadian parents seem more inclined to rely on a parental rights discourse, legitimating their educational venture as an individual choice, while Quebec support groups participated in a collective action learning process, aiming at contributing to the governance of public education. Because of Quebec's distinct cultural context, on the one hand, English Canadian studies on home education tend to seek generalization but they exclude Quebecers, before or after recruiting participants, and they depict Quebec's situation as an anomaly within Canada; on the other hand, Quebec studies focus on Quebec homeschooling, seldom including English-speaking participants. Nonetheless, this duality is among the most interesting attributes of home education development and of home education research in Canada, when considering the large picture. In effect, the cohabitation and the possible comparisons between two such different homeschooling movements, in relation to their different sociopolitical contexts, could lead to a better understanding of (1) the relationship between sociopolitical contexts and parental profiles, motivations, home education practices, and political action; (2) the evolution and making of home education regulation in different societies and educational institutions; and (3) the deeper ideological foundations and educational needs that could be found to cross or transcend cultures and structures, finding their expression in the international home education movement. In a different measure, comparative studies between Canada and her neighbor, the United States, with regards to different aspects of home education, would be of interest too. In other respects, if specific subpopulations of Canadian homeschoolers are described as representative of the whole movement, administrators and legislators could react in a way that might be unfair to or inadequate for other subgroups. Therefore, for a better understanding of the movement, not only should the Canadian research corpus develop, but attention should be paid to the sampling methods and the results interpretation.

Finally, although Canadian scientific studies on home education are scarce, some are worth noting for their wide-ranging or sound empirical methodologies and their original perspectives or research designs. Further Canadian research should take over and continue to contribute to international knowledge and discussion about home education.

References

Alberta Ministry of Education. 2015, February. Data provided to authors.

Arai, B.A. 1999. "Homeschooling and the Redefinition of Citizenship." *Education Policy Analysis Archives*, 7 (27).

Arai, B.A. 2000. "Reasons for Home Schooling in Canada." *Canadian Journal of Education*, 25(3): 204–217.

Aurini, J., and Davies, S. 2005. "Choice Without Markets: Homeschooling in the Context of Private Education." *British Journal of Sociology of Education*, 26(4): 461–474.

Blokhuis, J.C. 2009. *Parens Patriae: A Comparative Legal Study of Sovereign Authority and Public Education Policy in the Province of Ontario and the State of New York*. Doctoral Thesis, University of Rochester, NY.

Blokhuis, J.C. 2010. "Whose Custody Is It, Anyway?: 'Homeschooling' from a Parens Patriae Perspective." *Theory and Research in Education*, 8(2): 199–222.

Brabant, C. 2004. *L'éducation à domicile au Québec : les raisons du choix des parents et les principales caractéristiques sociodémographiques des familles*. Master thesis, Faculté d'éducation, Université de Sherbrooke, QC. Accessed April 30, 2016. http://goo.gl/gJzP6a

Brabant, C. 2010. *Pour une gouvernance réflexive de l'«apprentissage en famille». Étude des processus d'apprentissage de trois groupes de parents-éducateurs au Québec*. Doctoral thesis, Faculté d'éducation, Université de Sherbrooke, QC. Accessed May 7, 2016. https://docs.google.com/file/d/0B0mcj_60xzVJdm56VWE1UVV3WlU/edit?pref=2&pli=1

Brabant, C. 2013. *L'école à la maison au Québec: un projet familial, social et démocratique*. Québec: Presses de l'Université du Québec.

Brabant, C., and Bourdon, S. 2012. "Le changement en éducation et la gouvernance réflexive. Expérimentation d'un modèle d'appropriation du changement par des groupes de parents-éducateurs au Québec." *Éducation et Francophonie*, XL(1) : 32–55. Accessed April 30, 2016. http://www.acelf.ca/c/revue/pdf/EF-40-1-032_BRABANT.pdf

Brabant, C., Bourdon, S., and Jutras, F. 2003. "Home Education in Quebec: Family First." *Evaluation and Research in Education*, 17(2–3): 112–131.

Brabant, C., Bourdon, S., and Jutras, F. 2004. "L'école à la maison au Québec: l'expression d'un choix familial marginal." *Enfances, Familles, Générations*, 1(1) : 59–83. Accessed April 30, 2016. http://www.erudit.org/revue/efg/2004/v/n1/008894ar.html

Brabant, C. (accepted). L'apprentissage de la participation à la réflexivité institutionnelle chez des intervenants en scolarisation à la maison. *Revue des sciences de l'éducation*.

British Columbia Ministry of Education. 2015, February. Data provided to authors.

Cardus. 2016. Accessed April 29, 2016. https://www.cardus.ca/organization/about/

Common, R.W., and Macmullen, M. 1986. "Home schooling… A Growing Movement." *Education Canada*, 26(2): 4–7.

Curren, R., and Blokhuis, J. 2011. "The Prima Facie Case Against Homeschooling." *Public Affairs Quarterly*, 25(1): 1–19.

Davies, S., and Aurini, J. 2003. "Homeschooling and Canadian Educational Politics: Rights, Pluralism and Pedagogical Individualism." *Evaluation & Research in Education*, 17(2–3): 63–73.

Denessen, E., Michels, C., and Felling, A. 2000. "Opvattingen over onderwijs: een onderzoek naar de validiteit en betrouwbaarheid van een meetinstrument." *Pedagogische Studiën*, 77(4): 193–205.

Dewey, J. 1916. *Democracy and Education: An Introduction to the Philosophy of Education*. New York: Macmillan.

Dewey, J. 1927. *The Public and its Problems*. New York: H. Holt and Company.

Dewey, J. 1938. *Logic: The Theory of Inquiry*. New York: H. Holt and Company.

Fraser Institute. 2001, October 9. *Home Schooling is an Effective Alternative to the Public School System*. News Releases. Vancouver Canada): Fraser Institute. Accessed May 7, 2016. http://oldfraser.lexi.net/media/media_releases/2001/20011009.html

Gaither, M. 2011, September 23. *The Cardus Education Survey and Homeschooling*. Home schooling research notes. Accessed April 30, 2016. https://gaither.wordpress.com/2011/09/23/the-cardus-education-survey-and-homeschooling/

Lagos, A.J. 2011. *Parental Education Rights in United States and Canada: Homeschooling and its Legal Protection*. Doctoral thesis, Pontificia Universitas Sanctae Crucis, Rome.

Lagos, A.J. 2012. "Parental Education Rights in Canada: Canon and Civil Law Approaches to Homeschooling." *Studia Canonica*, 46(2): 401–469.

Lenoble, J., and Maesschalck, M. 2010. *Democracy, Law and Governance*, Aldershot, UK: Ashgate.

Luffman, J. 1997. "Profil de l'enseignement à domicile au Canada." *Revue trimestrielle de l'éducation*, 4(4): 30–47.

Martel, T. 2015, February 4. "L'école à la maison vue de l'intérieur." *Québec Hebdo*. Accessed April 30, 2016. http://www.quebechebdo.com/Actualites/Societe/2015-02-04/article-4031645/Lecole-a-la-maison-vue-de-linterieur/1

Martin-Chang, S., Gould, O. N., and Meuse, R.E. 2011. "The Impact of Schooling on Academic Achievement: Evidence from Homeschooled and Traditionally Schooled

Students." *Canadian Journal of Behavioural Science/Revue canadienne des sciences du comportement*, 43(3): 195.

Ministère de l'Éducation du Québec. 2003. *Regards statistiques sur l'éducation, Sommaire 1997–1998 à 2001–2002*. Québec: Gouvernement du Québec.

Pennings, R., et al. 2012. *A Rising Tide Lifts All Boats: Measuring Non-Government School Effects in Service of the Canadian Public Good*. Hamilton, ON: Cardus.

Pennings, R., et al. 2011. *Do the Motivations for Private Religious Catholic and Protestant Schooling in North America Align with Graduate Outcomes?* Hamilton, ON: Cardus.

Priesnitz, W. 1990. *Home-Based Education in Canada: An Investigation and Profile*. Canadian Alliance of Home Schoolers.

Quebec Association for Home-Based Education. 2005. "Des nouvelles du comité légal." *Portfolio*, 8(2): 18–19.

Quebec Ministry of Education, Leisure and Sport. 2013, January. Data provided to authors.

Quebec Ministry of Education, Leisure and Sport 2015,.February. Data provided to authors.

Ray, B.D. 1994. *A Nationwide Study of Home Education in Canada : Family Caracteristics, Student Achievement, and Other Topics*. Salem, OR: National Home Education Research Institute.

Ray, B.D. 2001. "The Modern Homeschooling Movement." *Catholic Education: A Journal of Inquiry and Practice*, 4(3): 405–421.

Rymarz, R. (2011. A Study of Albertan Catholic Homeschoolers. *INTAMS review*, 17(1): 48–60.

Schön, D.A. 1971. *Beyond the Stable State*. New York: Norton.

Schön, D.A., and Argyris, C. 1978. *Organizational Learning: A Theory of Action Perspective*. Don Mills, ON: Addison-Wesley.

Schön, D.A., and Rein, M. 1994. *Frame Reflection: Toward the Resolution of Intractable Policy Controversies*. New York: Basic Books.

Schön, D.A., and Argyris, C. 1996. *Organizational Learning II: Theory, Method and Practice*. Wokingham, UK: Addison-Wesley.

Smith, D.S., 1993. *Parent-Generated Home Study in Canada: The National Outlook 1993*. Westfield, NB: The Francombe Place/Research Associates.

Smith, D.S., 1996. "Parent-generated Home Study in Canada." *The Canadian School Executive*, 15(8).

Statistics Canada. 2013, December 4. Summary elementary and secondary school indicators for Canada, the provinces and territories, 2006/2007 to 2010/2011. *The Daily*. Statistics Canada catalogue no. 11-001-X. Accessed May 7, 2016. http://www.statcan.gc.ca/pub/81-595-m/81-595-m2013099-eng.htm

Statistics Canada. 2014. "Age (131) and Sex (3) for the Population of Canada, Provinces, Territories and Federal Electoral Districts (2013 Representation Order), 2011 Census." *2011 Census of Canada: Topic-based Tabulations*. Accessed April 30, 2016. http://www12.statcan.gc.ca/census-recensement/2011/dp-pd/tbt-tt/Rp-eng.cfm?TABID=1&LANG=E&A=R&APATH=3&DETAIL=0&DIM=0&FL=A&FREE=0&GC=0&GID=0&GK=0&GRP=1&O=D&PID=108266&PRID=0&PTYPE=101955&S=0&SHOWALL=0&SUB=0&Temporal=2011&THEME=88&VID=0&VNAMEE=&VNAMEF=&D1=0&D2=0&D3=0&D4=0&D5=0&D6=0

Tremblay, M.2002, November. Personal communication with first author.

13

Home Education in the United Kingdom

Helen E. Lees and Fiona Nicholson

Introduction

Home education in the four countries – England, Wales, Northern Ireland and Scotland – of the UK flourishes. Numbers appear stable or rising, and we see reports of satisfaction from "proud and loud" practising families and of their educational success (see e.g., Thomas and Pattison 2010). Communities are forged with relative ease at the local and national levels with intricate networks of parents and children connecting up via social media to report, support, and encourage each other. Interest in this educational form increases on the part of academic researchers, each with their own understandings and visions of practice. Who has the duty then in regard to home education? What is this duty? A few politicians in England strongly support home educators and ask questions in parliament or take initiatives to ensure best possible circumstances are maintained or developed. In the 2015 general election one political party – the Green Party – even included open and active support of home education (and flexi-schooling) in its manifesto. Home education in the UK enjoys a legal position difficult to challenge at a fundamental level, allowing considerable freedoms to follow this pathway without undue interference from the state.

Parents in most of the UK do not need permission to home educate unless the child is a registered pupil at a special school. There is no legal duty to monitor parents' home education provision. However, in England and Wales there is a duty to make arrangements to identify children outside school who are not receiving suitable education, and, where it appears that a child is not being educated, a duty to begin the legal process which may culminate in a school attendance order. The crucial part of this is "if it appears." In other words, further information is only required in order to make a judgment after there appears to be a problem or failure in some way.

The Wiley Handbook of Home Education, First Edition. Edited by Milton Gaither.

In 2015, the Office for Standards in Education, Children's Services and Skills (Ofsted) which inspects local government children's services in England, said, in an email communication, "we have reminded inspectors that local authorities do not have a duty to evaluate the quality of the education provided for home educated children – for example, through routine visits – although they may intervene if it appears that the education is unsuitable"(Nicholson 2015a). This new stance taken in 2015 set in place a powerful guidance regarding "no duty" to evaluate; a duty which previously was subject to numerous misinterpretations. Potentially this clear statement against evaluation could have a significant impact across the home education scene in the UK, although it is too early to tell at present.

So, from the outside it might seem as though parts of the UK – England in particular – are among the best places in the world to practice this particular educational form. Whilst this would indeed be true for many reasons, it is however, not the whole story. That is a more complex and strife-riven picture. Moreover it is undoubtedly a picture where the threat of changes to this relaxed and permissive status quo always hovers over home educating families. Those with insight into the past, present, and future of home education in the UK keep watch warily on developments in government whilst they enjoy the current permissive legal climate. They also note a systematic lack of active state support for this option (Lees 2014).

This chapter will consider the situation in the UK regarding the legal status of home educating at the point of writing in 2015. It will also focus in on some specific local characteristics of the UK scene, born as they are of our peculiar national histories, particularly that of England, which has the largest home educator population among the four nations of the UK.

The chapter is co-written by an academic researcher and a long-time home educator, home education consultant and activist. This is a deliberate partnership with a view to democratically portraying the UK home education scene. Due to the nature of home education in the UK and the culture surrounding its practices and related academic research, it is likely that the best and most ethically underpinned research comes from such collaborations and cooperative endeavors.

On Not Knowing Your Options

Whereas in the US the concept of home education as an educational option seems fairly well established, publicized, and socially known, surprisingly perhaps, this is not the case in the UK. Far from it, indeed. Home educating is not well known and is badly understood within and across the four nations of the United Kingdom. For some people, it is not even known to exist at all. The concept is not an easy one to "get" for many in the UK, possibly due to a longstanding equation of schooling with education itself. Eddis highlights a background for this in referring to Watts:

> Watts' (2003) comparisons [a comparison between US and UK government and politics] suggested historical and cultural differences (namely acquiescence to the status quo of

state education, and a lack of conviction in ownership of a child's education), which play a limiting role in the development of the home education movement in England and Wales (Eddis 2015, 101).

Why so little parental ownership of their child's education? Apart from the UK's internal national politics and governance influences (i.e., not supplying or promoting the supply of information about alternatives away from the idea of the school; not collecting data on numbers to inform cross-national comparisons), the UK's history as a colonizing power with an agenda of aggressive and racist domination may play a part in its current lack of curiosity about educational difference. As imperial conquerors the British worked to subordinate local populations and then report home on their success as rulers of, for example, India or Australia and Canada and its people. These days, with the continuing dominance of a Eurocentric and western vision of being-in-the-world, those who "stubbornly insist on maintaining their own vision of 'progress' or 'reason' face the danger of being isolated, impoverished and discriminated against" (Canagarajah 2002, 245 in Andreotti 2011, 385). The long history of British colonialism lives on in the reservations many British people have about new and different forms of education bringing isolation from a given norm.

Not only then is a lack of ownership of a child's education at play, but a fear of being different persists with all the vulnerability that this entails: "The melancholia of the English remains trapped in a period before cultural complexity and multiculturalism, while nostalgically clinging to the presumed greatness of Empire" (Stevenson 2015, 6). Certainly the idea of normalcy brings with it influencing factors when it comes to home education (Stevens 2003b). For most UK parents involved with a colonial past via "English island dominion" and its concomitant normalizing forces for such dominion to hold sway, might it be that being educationally "normal" makes some kind of deeper sense among this population than in other places?

British colonial power was spread through systemized schooling attendance. This then has led to a significant legacy of British expertise inflicted not only on the conquered nations but also domestically among UK educationists (Sweeting and Vickers 2007). Pride and the reality that what the British do educationally continues to be copied abroad (Baker 2010) or has been seen in high esteem (Mukherjee 2010, 29) could incline British citizens to assume that the school is the first and last port of call when it comes to excellent education. Does the British population maintain belief in schooling because others abroad seem to believe in the British model, despite its imposition through power, as "good for people"? Is idolatry of the school as education a manifestation of an "an unashamed sense of cultural superiority" (Stevenson 2015, 7) that curtails the British educational imagination? Such speculations perhaps help explain why few British citizens express much interest in and enthusiasm for alternatives like home education.

Any or all of these hypotheses could go some way towards explaining why when a home education focused researcher went out onto the streets of England and asked residents "Did you know children don't have to go to school?" the reaction was often one of incredulity and resistance (Lees 2011a). They simply thought the question ridiculous (Lees 2013b). Yet legally speaking British people freely and, relative to other countries, easily are allowed to home educate. It is an option and has been clearly affirmed, through statute applying to all four nations, for at least seventy years. We have the wealth of technological, social and cultural resources to know this, but the UK seemingly remains conceptually and practically in the dark about the very possibility, even if taking up the option is not wanted.

It is not just ideological programming at play. *Confusion* abounds about the legal position regarding "compulsory" school attendance, despite, as mentioned above, it always having been a legal option in the UK not to attend a school. The threat of being fined or sent to prison on account of merely having a limited knowledge of education law is a reality. People in the UK think school attendance is compulsory because they do not know the real legal situation outlined here as it appeared in 1944 and which has not changed since:

> Duty of parents to secure the education of their children: It shall be the duty of the parent of every child of compulsory school age to cause him to receive efficient full-time education suitable to his age, ability, and aptitude, either by regular attendance at school or otherwise (Butler Education Act 1944, part 2, section 36).

Thus, home education in the UK is marginal and marginalized by ignorance. This is not just ignorance of possibility to practice, although that plays a significant part (Lees 2014) but also via what Eddis calls "mistaken identity" (Eddis 2015). Ignorance of this kind is a product of different cohorts of people (home education related state officials, home educators or non-home educating parents) calling home education elements and aspects by different names or the same name, but meaning different things. In the UK terms, symbols, identifiers, and vocabulary for education that is not school-based remains imprecise and confused (Thomas and Pattison 2013; Lees 2014; Eddis 2015). Developing a common vocabulary is not such an easy task, as identified below, due to the often incommensurable assumptions about education functioning between advocates of home education on one hand and a schooling mentality of set tasks and concomitant assessing on the other:

> A large part of the difficulty in discussing informal learning is the lack of accurate and meaningful vocabulary. Whilst preferring to eschew such terms as "teaching", "the learner", "curriculum", "engagement", advocates, nevertheless, often find themselves forced into using them for lack of alternatives. The moment is perhaps ripe to develop a new vocabulary based on a new epistemology of learning; one able to outline the terms of debate on how children learn, encompassing a much wider understanding of learning that does not rest on what is formally imposed, nor on the matrix of time and goals as its sole form of assessment (Thomas and Pattison 2013: 152).

Because home education is alternative practice and is unusual within a hegemonic school-based attendance society it may be incommensurable with mental conceptions of education for people in the UK. British national consciousness is indeed deeply imbued with the means and mechanisms for the school as a given for children's lives: what Flint and Peim identify as an "ontotheological" imperative of education (Flint and Peim 2012). British society seems so little open to educational difference embracing alternative pathways away from the school that the word "conservative" is used by ministers when they speak of the education system. Teaching staff are seen as agents resistant to education done differently from their preconceived notions of what education is and of its functions (Children Schools and Families Committee 2010). Difference in education is hard to swallow for the UK.

All of this means that few parents question the inevitability of schooling. In England, children are expected to start to school before their fifth birthday; indeed some will have only just turned four. Many home educators think this is rather young to begin school. In preparation for this early school start, local councils in England send out brochures to parents offering advice about which school to choose. They do not include in these brochures information about home education as an option (Lees 2011a). In other words, in general, if you want to know in the UK about the home educating pathway, the state will not be the one to inform you. Home education discovery here is a do-it-yourself or bricolage affair, and you are unlikely to know your options as a given.

Elective Home Education in the UK

All of this means then that in the UK the home education scene is a small one. Around 1% of all school aged children do not attend a school for their education, although this figure – based on some degree of guesswork as we explain below – is a fluid one. The Department for Education in England does not require local authorities to return data on the number of home educated children. In the absence of any such requirement, there is no standard way of collecting data on children out of school and in what is often called in England "elective home education" to differentiate it from state organized tuition at home for the medically ill. Instead, it is necessary to ask each of the English 152 local authorities individually (see Nicholson 2014a for just such collection data gathered through freedom of information requests since 2005).

With local authority figures in hand in July 2014, the number of home educated children in England sat at 27 292. The figure for July 2013 was 23 243. Thus, overall, the number of home educated children increased across England by 17% between July 2013 and July 2014. Over 15 000 children entered home education across the country during the academic year 2013–2014, but by the end of the year the total was only 4000 higher than the previous year. Therefore, it must be the case that many thousands of children also ceased to be home educated (Nicholson 2014b).

Keeping up-to-date records of home educated children, which can travel across local authorities when parents move, is not a priority in the UK. Some councils take snapshots but they don't keep a running total. Other councils do the opposite and add each new name to their list as the year progresses. Here are some comparisons found in 2012, illustrating the difference between the snapshot and the running total as part of a larger project to attain numbers (Nicholson 2014b):

Brighton 144 snapshot/275 annual total;
Devon 387 snapshot/644 annual total;
Doncaster 166 snapshot/264 annual total;
Essex 645 snapshot/1050 annual total.

Country-specific numbers in Wales, Northern Ireland, and Scotland are much smaller than in England. A headcount of children in Wales known to be home educated is carried out each January by local authorities and published by the Welsh Government in July/August. The figures for 2014 showed that 1225 children were home educated in Wales, meaning 3.4 out of every 1000 pupils in Wales were reported to be electively home educated (Welsh Government 2015a). The last official figures for home education in Northern Ireland date from 2012 when the Education Minister said that the total from the five Education and Library Boards in the province was 179 (Northern Ireland Assembly 2012). In Scotland numbers are hazy and range from official figures through the years at well under 1000 (see Lees 2013a) to much higher figures estimated by the Scottish home education organization Schoolhouse (Schoolhouse 2015).

Throughout the UK this reckoning does not take account of home educated children who are not known to local authorities. One estimate put the actual total of all home educated children in England alone, not taking into account the other three nations, at around 80 000 (Badman 2009). The present authors strongly doubt the veracity of this estimate even if other guesswork by deduction and analysis of figures of children in and out of school comes to a similar conclusion of roughly two thirds of home educated children being unregistered with the state (Boswell 2014; Rothermel 2002). The reason for our skepticism is that if schools do their job properly and notify the local council of any children taken off roll for home education, the only children not known are those who have never been to school or who are from highly mobile families. The likelihood that there is any meaningful correlation between these families and numbers of children who are taken out of school has never been demonstrated. Moreover, the figure of 80 000 was based on a steep projected rise in numbers of children taken out of school, which we know now did not take place. We consider the likely total number of home educated children in the UK at the time of writing to be less than 50 000. The extra numbers beyond the official figures in the 20 000s are from parents who have never chosen and registered for a nursery or school for their children and are thus not listed by the local authority.

It is notable in the UK that home educating families are not chased by officials – unless harm of some kind including educational negligence is feared – although they may come into contact with them. Doctors, for example, do not routinely check with the local authority when they encounter a home educated child to see if the child is registered with them. When this does happen it can be seen as "Big Brother" style communicating by home educating parents, who guard their independence zealously. Numbers then are perhaps fluid in the UK because there is significant freedom for them so to be. English local authorities have commented that the number of home educated children changes all the time "with pupils being added and taken off the register." Several authorities have commented that children might only be home educated for a matter of days. One officer remarked to Nicholson that the home educated population is "in constant flux," while another said it was "relatively turbulent over the year with a large number home educated for a relatively short time as many return to school or move away." Furthermore, local authority officials believe that "parents may find the reality of home education more difficult than they had anticipated, or they were only planning to home educate for a short time anyway" (personal correspondence with Fiona Nicholson, Autumn 2014).

Why the flux? Morton has suggested that it may be because home education is hard work (Morton 2010b). Safran Barson, however, challenges the notion that lack of time for oneself and over-laboring is a common reality of UK home education. On the contrary, she found parents along the full spectrum of possible responses to the issue of time for oneself, concluding most could "work out unique adjustments which enabled them to feel broadly satisfied with the home educating experience" (2015, 28).

A recurring theme in this chapter – as no doubt in other chapters in this handbook – is the difficulty in finding out more about the quantitative patterns of take up and rejection of home education in the UK. This is partly due to the flux of the scene, the individuality of localized authority approaches to data collection, families' desire for privacy, and in recent years a lack of finances or desire on the part of the State to pay home education more attention than it deserves in their eyes as a situation that doesn't need fixing because it isn't broken:

> In this structure we have at the moment, whilst it may look imperfect and it may not look as logical and structured as one might think it ought to be, it is, broadly speaking, working. We have to be careful not to upset that balance… (comment by Elizabeth Truss, Under Secretary of State for Education and Childcare, House of Commons Education Committee, 2012a).

This is a situation of leaving well alone that seems to have emerged from the State infamously getting its fingers burnt after an ill-conceived and ill-managed (see Children Schools and Families Select Committee 2009) commissioned independent review of home education (Badman 2009; Stafford 2012).

Why Choose Home Education in the UK at All?

Home education is often an exit from schooling as a fight–flight mechanism to shelter from educational, personal or social storms (Lees 2014; Meighan 1997; Morton 2010a; Parsons and Lewis 2010; Rothermel 2003; Wray and Thomas 2013).

This requires a different approach to understanding the community of home education in the UK than that of the school-based population. "Serendipity" and aimless happening in terms of engagement with this practice and pathway is a feature of the UK scene, as captured in a number of projects over the past ten years (e.g., Lees 2011a; Parsons and Lewis 2010; Thomas and Pattison 2007). This serendipity, however, typically leads parents into deep thoughtfulness, as the following illustrates:

> *Hannah spoke of how discovering that EHE [elective home education] was a possibility had a profound effect on her and required deep thought:*
>
> Hannah: "I talked and talked and talked to these people at the home ed group and they all said it isn't easy not a bed of roses and think really hard about it and so I did think really hard. It was such a big step to take and it didn't seem like one you could go back on all that easy so obviously you could send them back but once you'd started along that route you're committing yourself to a whole new way of life and a whole new belief in the fact that school wasn't the be all and end all, there was another way to do it. So I thought it was a huge choice to make…It was as big a change to reject that [schooling] as to reject the faith of your family. It feels that way to me" [Hannah, July 2009] (Lees 2011a, 154).

A second factor in the extensive deliberations associated with home education choice relates to underlying rationales for the practice. In a classic work Van Galen described two sorts of home educators: "Ideologues" and "pedagogues," meaning parents who either object to school content and deliberately avoid schools' curricula as anti-religious or who actively seek out home education for reasons of child development and flourishing (Van Galen 1991). Morton (2010a) found a similar dichotomy in the UK, and also described a third group who home educate only as a last resort after trying without success to make school work for their children. But the ambiguities of identity pointed to by Isenberg (2007) in knowing for sure how a diverse "group" of home educators in any country is formulated functions here also. It is an incredibly diverse community, to which the large number of UK created Facebook and Yahoo groups catering for a wide and sometimes incommensurable variety of home educating special interests and local networks gives testimony.

Issues of fight–flight from schooling and active choosing are not the only ones pertaining to the UK home education scene. Some children are home educated while parents wait for a place at their preferred school or because they cannot get the school of their choice and fear other options offered. With a crush on growing numbers for limited school places, this phenomenon of "home education without a school place" is taking on greater weight in more recent times, especially in England. There is a significant and pressing need identified for more school places in England: "According to Ofsted's 2014 annual report, England's schools are going to have to provide places for an extra 880 000 pupils by 2023" (Weale 2015). This equates to the need for roughly 1000 newly built secondary level schools on multi-acre brown- or green-field sites, within seven years.

That either involves a lot of quick planning and spending in times of economic austerity (McCormack 2009) or perhaps a revised policy about the ways in which government and media handling of home education as vilified or ignored keeps it marginal (Thomas and Pattison 2010). Some suggest an alternative, more positive, vision and understanding of what home education could provide as part of the solution for these missing school places (e.g., Summers 2014). However, another yet negative and backdoor approach to home educating has been identified by the UK Parliamentary Education Select Committee, which condemned a few school headteachers for pushing troublesome school children out of their remit into home education through suggestions to parents, thereby relieving the headteachers and the school of the supposed burden of these children (Children Schools and Families Select Committee 2009). A culture where home education develops into an excuse not to provide school places to those families whose preference would be for schooling is to be watched for with vigilance.

Anecdotal evidence suggests that a relatively higher proportion of young people are home educated in their last years of compulsory schooling, i.e., close to age 16. Many local authority officers in England have told Nicholson that schools push parents to take their children out of school where their attendance is low and/or poor exam results are predicted. Exit from schools may also be linked to the substantial exam pressures placed on UK children around this age and their impact on mental health in particular (Grass-Orkin 2013; Staff Writer 2011). Whatever the case, home education should be, we suggest, always elected for positive reasons as an educational choice on its own terms.

Historical Political Background

Despite mention in the introduction to this chapter of legal entitlements and freedoms for UK home education, there is in fact in England (as one example) no explicit right in law for either the parent to home educate or the child to be home educated. This is a part of why the situation has been a fragile one ever since the 1944 Butler Education Act first introduced the idea that education could be done "otherwise" than at school. Parents theoretically cannot *demand* home education, despite it seeming as though they have a right to do so based on legal statute.

This is because there is no positive right to education enshrined in English law (as one example within the four nations) at all. The European Convention on Human Rights' "right to education," as given effect in English law by virtue of the Human Rights Act 1998 (valid at the time of writing), is currently phrased negatively, in not being denied a right:

> No person shall be denied the right to education. In the exercise of any functions which it assumes in relation to education and to teaching, the State shall respect the right of parents to ensure such education and teaching is in conformity with their own religious and philosophical convictions (Article 2 Protocol 1 ECHR).

It is no accident that English law lacks any positive declaration of the child's right to education. A government minister explained to a parliamentary colleague that a positive right to education enshrined in law "might be interpreted as imposing an obligation on local authorities to ensure that children could receive education of a particular type or standard which the authorities were unable to provide (or which they considered undesirable to provide)" (Nicholson 2006). Instead of a right to education, education is the parents' responsibility or duty, which the parent discharges either by sending the child to school or "otherwise," through making alternative arrangements that can include home-based education. Section seven of the most up-to-date Education Act for England and Wales to which we can currently refer (1996) states:

> The parent of every child of compulsory school age shall cause him to receive efficient full-time education suitable –
>
> 1 to his age, ability and aptitude, and
> 2 to any special educational needs he may have, either by regular attendance at school or otherwise.

Given that there is nothing definitive or incontrovertible to which UK home educators can point and state with unwavering conviction "it says here I'm allowed to do this and here are the freedoms I have," home education operates in the UK by virtue of agreements rather than rights. As outlined below, the four nations each function in relation to home education with their own regulations – their own agreements – although a common theme is the agreed entitlement to pursue the practice.

A corollary to the above fragile scenario is that there are no minimum standards for education delivered at home by parents. A child – once grown up – cannot sue the government and claim she did not receive educationally all she was entitled to at home.

No rights does not mean that the kinds of political lobbying and protests which we have seen in the US (Stevens 2003a) do not take place in the UK. A robust, effective rebuttal and stance for the right to home education without undue interference was seen as recently as 2009 in the reaction by home educating families to the disastrous Badman Review for England mentioned above and discussed below (Select Committee Evidence 2009; Stafford 2012; Thomas and Pattison, 2010). Government civil servants and representatives from Ofsted – the inspectorate for local authorities – have made reference to highly effective lobbying on the part of home educators: "home educators are a well-organised lobby group" (Nicholson 2015b). New fights for rights to not be interfered with at the level of state interventions and protocols – for instance a stance in Scotland against a government scheme "Getting it right for every child (GIRFEC)" to track data on children there (mentioned later in this chapter) – emerge with regularity whenever home educators perceive a threat to their freedoms. This is especially the case when home educated children are wrongly included within the writing up of government initiatives aimed at children missing education or at risk of harm (Symons 2015; The Scottish Government 2014).

Politically, historically and educationally, viewing the UK as separate countries each with its own government and parliament, rather than one amalgam, is increasingly the politically correct line to take. Due to significant local and national features in each country, as it relates to home education, we now split the picture into England, Wales, Northern Ireland and Scotland to explain each more fully.

The Home Education Politics of England

On a day-to-day level, it is local government in England, not the central Westminster, London-based government, which has oversight of home educating families. The first thing a seasoned home educator always asks when someone new to the practice is seeking advice or support – and remember state support is patchy or missing – is "Where do you live?" It is rare for there to be no local intelligence about a particular area within parental-led home education circles. Charitable or privately run websites such as www.educationotherwise.org, www.heas.org.uk or www.edyourself.org, attempt to offer local advice links. Apart from this, a picture can usually be built up from internet searches, anecdotal evidence, and quite frequently from personal experience as the home education pathway is trodden. A home education family will not be that far away: the network is extensive, with families scattered around as outlined earlier this chapter in the section "Elective home education in the UK." Parents might possibly decide where to live based on the reputation of the local authority for dealing with home educators.

The individual attention to getting it right with regard to families being left free to practice is one element of the decision-making involved which could be called devotional, although by this "religious" is not meant. In the UK, Christian home educator communities exist but there is little in the way of a noticeable tradition of fundamentalist approaches such as can be found in the US (Kunzman 2009). Home education in England is instead often seen by "discoverees" as a secular lifestyle choice of great significance (Lees 2011a; Neuman and Avriam 2003) as the following parent outlines:

> Sorena: "…it was just the idea of her going to school and being changed in any way and I had to learn to accept that, and I just thought there was something very, very wrong about having to be made to feel like that so, and when I realised that there was a choice and I didn't have to send her then I suppose it just – just everything changed!" [Sorena, July 2009] (Lees 2011a, 155).

Often the key to a successful transition to home education is found to be a form of letting go of middle England expectations to keep up standards rather typical at least of the English middle classes (Dowty 2000; Khimasia 2015). In this sense the pedagogy of home education as freely constructed within any given family – and as allowed to thus be free in England – offers, for some, a chance for class-based cultural norms to be circumvented and perhaps forgotten. Although this is unlikely to be hegemonic as experience, in theory the significantly class-ridden nature of English society is not perpetuated within and through home education by organized shifting and sorting as in schools (Willis 1981). This freedom could become a kind of equalizing force for some children. That an educational option can offer this possibility to go against the social norms and their exclusionary factors is an opportunity here, even if the reality of tribal classism in England means few feel totally able to embrace it fully (for work on the heavy hand of class-based issues through education in England see Reay 2012).

For some families, home education in England tends towards an interest in autonomous and deschooled approaches, as research by Thomas and Pattison discovered (2007). But there is also within this a great interest in the curriculum and a more structured approach as well. It is understood, looking at the wide variety of UK community organized Facebook groups catering for differing styles, as a very mixed picture. This includes, it seems, an interest amongst home educators for communicating through online forums about how to "go autonomous" after starting with curricula structure. Part of this may be on account of recent UK-based research pointing to the educational success of such an approach (Thomas and Pattison 2007), where spontaneous conversation rather than deliberate instruction matters for learning and is shown as effective.

One might think that such tendencies would cause alarm in official educational circles where the emphasis is definitely on assessment and standards, levels, and tests. One might imagine that an English mentality towards home education could be to check and inspect it with regularity in line with our colonial history of supposed educational excellence and a need to maintain "standards." To an extent this is true because home education in the UK is seen negatively in this way by many and perhaps by teachers especially. However, the government guidelines in England say that the authority should only act officially if no "suitable and efficient" education is in place (DCSF 2007). Rothermel, in speaking about the tendency of authorities to be overly demanding in this regard, including asking inappropriately for a timetable of lessons, suggests that a reasonable request would be to ask for triangulation data such as tickets and photos from events out or diary entries about what activities have been pursued (Rothermel 2010). However, some home educators disagree vehemently that any proof or evidence is required at the outset, irrespective of the form it might take. The Welsh home education guidelines refer to "an indication that parents have thought through their reasons for home educating and what they hope to achieve; signs of commitment and enthusiasm…" (Welsh Government 2008, 7). Lees (2014) suggests this stance is useful – that home education is most likely taking place positively where there is an ability on the part of parents to talk at some length about what is occurring and of their education philosophy, a task which is hard to fake. In other words, an English satisfaction for standards could be meaningfully found by focusing on parental chatter. Given how home educators tend to deny that home education should be judged at all, any of this is a possible compromise for some.

On the issue of inspection or monitoring in England the situation among the 150 plus local authorities is very mixed: some local authorities have now, on account of austerity measures, disbanded their home education officer units – in the counties of Essex (Nicholson 2015b) and Somerset (Nicholson 2014c) for instance – as an unnecessary expense. They are instead focusing only on their statutory child safeguarding obligations and the duty to start the school attendance order process only if it appears a child is not being educated.

Home educators themselves largely vehemently disagree with any need for measurement. The people dealing with home education at the local council will most likely not be specialists in home education. They may grow to understand the practice better in time, but to start, they are teacher-trained for schools, as was noted during the review of the Badman (2009) reporting (Children Schools and Families Select Committee 2009). Having a schoolteacher background affects their perception of whether measurability and standards in relation to home education are appropriate or not. In the UK trained teachers are drilled in levels, ability grades, and comparative analyses of where a child is at according to age and related expectations of achievement. None of this really operates as a valid yardstick within the freedoms of home education. Thus politically, at the local level, home education suffers from a common incommensurability with expectations about how education operates "normally." A large part of this problem goes back to the ignorance around home education mentioned at the start of this chapter: an ignorance rife also in school settings, with headteachers and teachers often biased and negative about the practice. In recent times, on teacher training and other university education-related courses in England, home education more often focuses in curricula for the formation of students via textbooks including it with new prominence (e.g., Curtis et al. 2014) or through home education specialist lectures. This is likely an addition to curricula due to the influence of increased media coverage of home education in the UK since 2004 (Lees 2011a). Despite this, coverage in universities is superficial as much education for the formation of teachers is, naturally, highly focused on school experience rather than education more broadly conceived.

Misguided schooling oriented perceptions of home education practices was again a subject of debate in a 2012 UK parliamentary select committee enquiry on support for home educators (House of Commons Education Committee 2012a, 2012b). The issue of labeling home education in a category where Education Welfare, School Improvement, Inclusion, Alternative Provision (for those removed from schools), Special Needs or Traveller Education all sit as "other provision" brings concerns to bear on home education that many home educators in England feel are unhelpful. Prejudice about and against Traveller, Gypsy, and Roma appreciation for the freedoms and cultural appropriateness of home education for their chosen lifestyle and upbringing of their children is a particularly strong problem in the UK (D'Arcy 2014). At play too often is the powerful difficulty of suspicion linked to safeguarding concerns as we discuss in more detail below.

When speaking of home education in England it is tempting to discuss "the community." However this idea is often refuted by home educators who see themselves as disparate and un-networked in any grand way. Jane Lowe from the Home Education Advisory Service warned the Education Committee in 2012 that "you cannot systematize home education. It is not a community. It is 20 000 little schools, if you like. It is not a unity, and we cannot make it so and we should not try." Ian Mearns, Member of Parliament for Gateshead, summed this up in the same Select Committee Enquiry as: "having exerted fierce independence [from the state education system], independence from each other is equally important, I would think." (House of Commons Education Committee 2012b, Q64)

Thus, home education in England happens "in parallel" to the state. This is not to say it is forming a parallel community, as has been claimed as a concern about home education in Germany due to that nation's history with the rise of separatist ideologies (Spiegler 2003). Yet it is siloed by a lack of common understandings of it as practice and lifestyle and also perhaps by a government wish to "leave well alone" (Nicholson 2015b). Despite this, a look at any of the English home education Facebook groups gives the impression at least of a vibrant scene, communicating and sharing knowledge and exchanging advice as well as using social media to connect for play dates, joint learning, and so on. Home education in England and elsewhere in the UK proves that the state and its schools can be *theoretically* rendered redundant for education, at least for a small segment of the population. Despite this theoretical possibility, in reality many re-enter the education system (in England participation in education has been "raised" to encourage full-time education until age 18 at school, college or otherwise) at about age 16 to pursue examinations towards further and higher education or working careers. We know this trend from the relative silence in home education peer support groups for inquiries about 16+ education issues continuing in home education and taking exams privately, in contrast to massive online traffic in enquiries for pre-16 education and exams taken through home.

The Home Education Politics of Wales

In 2006 – the year before Guidelines were published in England – the Welsh Assembly Government published Elective Home Education Guidelines as part of a much larger document covering Inclusion and Pupil Support (Welsh Government 2008). There are a number of significant differences between the Government Guidelines for England and for Wales. Welsh guidelines specifically state that the authority should *assume* efficient educational provision is taking place, which is suitable for the child, unless there is direct evidence to the contrary. In addition, Welsh guidelines say that the law doesn't specifically require the authority to investigate home education. It is noteworthy that this explicit interpretation is not present in the English guidelines. However, Welsh guidelines do go on to say that the authority should make annual contact with the home educating family, which is not specifically mentioned in the English guidelines. Both English and Welsh guidelines derive substantially from the slightly earlier published Scottish Guidance (2004, mentioned below), perhaps most obviously in the "expected characteristics" of provision, namely:

> consistent involvement of parents or other significant carers – it is expected that parents or significant carers would play a substantial role, although not necessarily

constantly or actively involved in providing education recognition of the child's needs, attitudes and aspirations, opportunities for the child to be stimulated by their learning experiences access to resources/materials required to provide home education for the child – such as paper and pens, books and libraries, arts and crafts materials, physical activity, ICT and the opportunity for appropriate interaction with other children and other adults (Welsh Government 2008, 7).

As soon as the Welsh Government obtained powers in 2011 to make its own laws for education via its devolution settlement with the UK parliament, it was keen to flex its legislative muscles and to distance and differentiate itself from Westminster's education policies. A raft of changes regarding education was swiftly announced, the majority of which subsequently failed to materialize. One of the proposed new laws concerned the registration and monitoring proposals for home education. After a massive backlash from home educators the Welsh government quickly dropped these plans. Nothing more was heard for eighteen months until the new Education Minister Huw Lewis announced as a compromise, that there was to be new non-statutory guidance (Welsh Government 2014). At the time of writing there is draft guidance (Welsh Government 2015b), with periodic announcements of further delays to publication. New guidance is most likely an attempt to carve out some middle ground between those who are worried about "safeguarding" and those who are concerned that home education freedoms may be eroded. The Minister made reference to "good practice and good engagement by some local authorities with the home-educating community" which was also examined in a report (Mitchell 2011) for the Welsh Government.

The Home Education Politics of Northern Ireland

There are no Government Guidelines for Home Education in Northern Ireland. Nor is there legislation equivalent to "Children Missing Education" which prevails in both England and Wales.

In England and Wales, parents can fulfill their legal duty via "education otherwise" as outlined in Section 7 of the Education Act 1996. The comparable law in Northern Ireland is Article 45 of the Education and Libraries Order 1986 (Legislation.Gov.UK 1986) which says exactly the same.

Parents in Northern Ireland do not have to seek permission to home educate. Where a child is a registered pupil at a school and parents notify the school that they wish to take the child out in order to home educate the school must delete the child's name from the school register.

Before April 1, 2015 home education was dealt with by Education and Library Boards which are the local government for Northern Ireland. These were disbanded and replaced by the "Education Authority (EA)," a single organization with responsibility for delivering education services across Northern Ireland. Previously, if it appeared to a board that a parent of a child of compulsory school age in its area was failing to perform the duty imposed on him or her by Article 45, a notice in writing was served on the parent requiring them to satisfy the board, within fourteen days that the child was, by regular attendance at school or otherwise, receiving suitable education. In 2014 each of the five Education and Library Boards put forward radical proposals for a new settlement on home education (Nicholson 2015d). A petition protesting the changes attracted over 3000 signatures and many questions were asked in the Northern Ireland Parliament. The proposed policy included plans for the child to continue to attend school until an approved program of education was in place, together with an assessment of the child's learning environment at home. Annual monitoring assessments were to be introduced, covering "minimum standards" regarding physical, social, emotional health and wellbeing, and as part of the annual monitoring a designated officer would visit the family home to talk to the child. This was seen by local home educators as an attempt to "seize control of home education" (Dickinson 2014).

Bringing together the five boards into one organization will only happen very gradually over a number of years, and meanwhile the boards continue to operate as five subregions of the Education Authority and current board policies continue to apply. In March 2016 the Education Authority said it would develop new procedures and arrangements within the existing legislative framework.

The Home Education Politics of Scotland

Originally published in 2004, Revised Statutory Guidance on Home Education was issued three years later (The Scottish Government 2007). Home education in Scotland, like elsewhere, comprises many styles and occurs for a number of reasons, from a reaction to severe peer bullying and/or school-based teaching failures, to philosophical aspirations relating to lifestyle. Scotland, like England and Wales, has seen its share of home educated children cases linked to safeguarding (discussed further below). Such conflations of safeguarding with home education (see Lees 2014) have caused bias and suspicion of home education from politicians (Schoolhouse 2010). Incredulously toned media portrayals (e.g., Arkell 2013), as in English media (see below and Lees 2014) mean that for Scotland, home education remains a marginalized and marginal pursuit, a general pattern replicated elsewhere in the UK.

Little academic attention has been paid to home education in Scotland. One seminar presentation and one book chapter alone so far represent the only extant academic attention (Lees 2011b, 2013).

A difference between Scotland and the other nations of the UK is that, in law, parents in Scotland have to obtain approval for the educational program before children can be withdrawn if they are already registered with a school.

Also differentiating the nations is the present fight within Scotland alone against a Scottish legislative framework expected to be operational from August 2016 known as GIRFEC (Getting Information Recorded For Every Citizen): a system for giving every child "a named person" (e.g., health worker) to oversee their well-being and monitor their connections and social and personal behaviors. The Scottish home education organization Schoolhouse – www.schoolhouse.org – along with others fearful of the GIRFEC implications, has campaigned vociferously to counter the possibility that Scottish education law might permit new protocols dealing with home educated children and their parents, including a potential change in the law to align current freedoms with what seems to be astonishingly intrusive powers on the part of the state.

Interpersonal Exchanges in UK Home Education

Home education in the UK may be "under the radar" according to official perspectives, but due to use of Facebook and other social media for the sake of finding child and parent socialization contacts and peer support, many home educators are seemingly highly visible to each other. While each family has its own unique identity and is not simply part of a community or movement, private decisions relating to one's own family may still be subject to scrutiny in terms of their impact on others. For example, parents who meet with the local authority at home – which is referred to as "accepting home visits" – may find themselves reproached by other parents who say that this makes it more difficult for anyone else to refuse (see Home Education Forums 2011).

Home educators will say that they don't want anyone speaking on their behalf and that any individual can only speak for themselves and not represent anyone else. However, this fiercely independent attitude is also edged with fear that encouraging people to speak up for themselves might backfire, since some – from lack of political awareness of past struggles – may be dazzled by promises of support. In other words, judgments and approaches within any home educator community are sharp and, indeed, can be sharply articulated (e.g., Various Home Educators 2010).

Evidence is sometimes put forward for the claim that there is a fundamental difference in attitude between those who choose to home educate in full knowledge that they will have to provide for themselves without any help from the Government, and those who have been forced into home education because of the failings of the school system, and who might reasonably argue that they pay their taxes but get nothing in return. Parsons and Lewis, in their study of parents of children with special needs forced into home education because of bad schooling experiences, call the difference that of "substantial unhappiness" versus free choice (2010, 83). Winstanley noted the special needs of gifted and talented students as being often unfulfilled by schools, with home education as the best, but not always chosen, option (2009).

Families' attitudes towards the local authority are extremely diverse and as late as 2007 there was no consensus from central government about how local authority officers in England should deal with home educating families. When national guidelines finally did appear (DCSF 2007), the foreword – signed by government ministers – explained that "these guidelines have been prepared to help local authorities manage their relationships with home educating parents." Although the Guidelines were given a cautious welcome by home educators, the feeling amongst activists at the time was that they wouldn't be in existence for long, and that publishing guidelines was primarily a diversion or delaying tactic while the government paused to regroup and consider its next move. However, national guidelines have always been regarded in some quarters – and not without cause – as an aberration.

Conversations with local government officers at this time (Nicholson, private correspondence, 2007) revealed that this new conciliatory approach was completely unexpected. The guidelines were seen to be heavily weighted in favor of parents, for example paragraph 3.13 which contains a long list of what parents don't have to do:

> Home educating parents are not required to:
>
> - teach the National Curriculum
> - provide a broad and balanced education
> - have a timetable
> - have premises equipped to any particular standard
> - set hours during which education will take place
> - have any specific qualifications
> - make detailed plans in advance
> - observe school hours, days or terms
> - give formal lessons
> - mark work done by their child
> - formally assess progress or set development objectives
> - reproduce school type peer group socialization
> - match school-based, age-specific standards (DCSF, 2007, paragraph 3.13).

Dissatisfaction on the part of some local authority officers was still apparent in a document presented to the Department for Education in 2014 which admonished that it was "better to say what parents do have to do rather than not i.e., what is an efficient education" (Nicholson 2014e).

Safeguarding and Home Education in the UK

The home education scene in the UK has been, most notably since 2009, beset by the issue of safeguarding, an issue some home educators regard with fear and suspicion. Home education is seen by many unconnected to home education practice as a child abuse risk. Indicative of this are local exchanges between those interested in home education and those in positions of safeguarding responsibility. An example is an exchange in 2015 between Lees and a university- based social worker colleague who said: "Better all of them [home educators] get checked out than one child dies." Social services in the UK tend to hold a deep suspicion of home education. A couple being screened for suitability to adopt in 2010 who mentioned their interest in potentially home educating a prospective adoptive child were rejected and vilified for their "alternative views," forcing them to formally appeal the bias (Lees 2014). Despite the fact home education is allowed and viable in the UK, parents far too often must fight and hold their ground should they deal with social services.

An indication of this problem was seen with the independent Review of Home Education (Badman 2009), commissioned by the English government to assess the situation of home education in England and Wales. It began with a press announcement that: "The Elective Home Education Review will … consider what evidence there is to support claims that home education could be used as a 'cover' for child abuse such as neglect, forced marriage, sexual exploitation or domestic servitude" (Bates 2009).

Subsequent recommendations for sight of the child and interviews with the child alone as well as registration for monitoring purposes of home educating families and their children were welcomed by the incumbent government at the time (Balls 2009). The proposed changes were however dropped in the face both of fierce opposition by the home education community and of a review of the conduct of the Badman Review, which found the review wanting in its approach of suspicion as well as for other reasons linked to poor data analysis (Children Schools and Families Select Committee 2009; Stafford 2012). The 2007 Government Guidelines were retained instead.

Change on the Horizon?

From the moment that national Guidelines for England were published, local government officers consistently have come up with reasons for ignoring them. One argument is that the Guidelines are not legally binding, since they are non-statutory, and can be disregarded where they are deemed to be inadequate, inconvenient, ambiguous or vague. However, some home educators in Scotland, where the guidance is statutory, say this doesn't prevent its being disregarded. Home educators live in fear of changes. Rumours circulate from time to time that the Guidelines are about to be revised or dropped. However, a government official told the inaugural meeting of the Association of Elective Home Education Professionals in early 2015 that the fact that government guidelines dating from the past administration are still current "tells its own tale" i.e., that nobody is willing to touch them (Nicholson 2015c).

In 2012 Graham Stuart MP as the Chair of the Government Education Committee – who is also the Chair of the UK All Party Parliamentary Group on Home Education – asked whether central Government should issue new guidance (House of Commons Education Committee 2012). This was rejected by the Minister interviewed by the committee, who said that the situation wasn't broken so why fix it (House of Commons Education Committee 2012a; Lees 2014). Home educators at the same Committee meeting were unanimous in agreeing that changes were not required.

Unsurprisingly, people who want to help may conclude that the solution lies in something new and improved, rather than trying to fix something that is broken. This view is hotly contested by home educators, who believe that however bad things are now, tinkering will cause unforeseen problems, and is to be resisted at all costs. In this regard home educators are agreeing it seems with government.

In a sense then there are always guns at dawn on the horizon. Whether home educators appreciate the drama and tension in a tacit agreement to leave well alone is unknown, but their commitment to what could be called a "faith" in an educational pathway (Lees 2011a; Neuman and Avriam 2003) is not in doubt.

The situation then is a precarious one. In 2014, a survey was carried out (Nicholson 2014d) of local authority website information on home education across England. It highlighted various areas where the law was being misinterpreted or where councils were simply doing their own thing, thereby flouting government guidelines. If matters of "malpractice" on the part of officials are drawn to their attention, central government officials in England will write to local government officers to remind them what the national guidelines say and to reproach them for any breaches, but there are no sanctions. Recent positive changes to the way the national education inspectorate Ofsted is viewing home education may have some impact, although this remains to be seen.

Whatever the perception, it is clear that threats to the current home education legal and social situation do not go away. A 2015 media article mentioned opinions of the laws around home education as "scandalous" quoting influential MP, Barry Sheerman, former chair of the parliamentary education select committee and self-confessed supporter of home education: "'If we do not take action, there will be tragic consequences that we will regret" (Hill 2015).

Further Research? Postscript by Helen Lees

With only a few university-affiliated and paid, permanently employed researchers of home education in the UK, the majority of new academic knowledge about home education here, over the years, has been from PhD theses. Researchers specializing in home education for their PhD rarely want or find a university job where academically styled home education research can be carried out. Home educationists would find it hard to get a foothold in a university education department because: (a) they don't speak "education" on institutionalized terms, immersed as they are in other approaches than those of a school mentality, and (b) the work would rarely require home education expertise and would largely demand instead wide knowledge of schooling. It would be possible for a project on home education to occur, but such projects tend to be rare and short-lived and who would care to fund it?

A lack of researchers with time, funds, and support for new and cutting edge research aside, a list of wished for research can be compiled. It would, for example, be helpful to understand the extent of home education with reliable figures through an historical period of, say, ten years. It would be interesting to know more about autonomous educational readiness or the demographics of families. So far we have work emerging on reading learning readiness (Thomas and Pattison 2016), but work on writing learning readiness would be of benefit. Greater philosophical understanding of the theory underpinning the practices of the autonomous style in particular would be interesting and could usefully inform school education as it attempts to fit itself for the fluid, unpredictable times (Bauman 2000) in which we live. An investigation into the (controversial) idea of minimal standards for quality in home education could prove interesting, including considering the pedagogical importance of the structures and natures of family life, as Davies (2015a, 2015b) has begun to do.

Conclusion

The picture for home education in the UK is a localized, national, complex and good one with some challenging features coming from those who do not "get" what home education is as education. The major issues for home education coalesce around the law, linked to a UK obsession with safeguarding. By association with the idea of "not knowing," an unfortunate national history rife with historically tragic cases of silenced child abuse has set this land on edge to protect against further problems. Home education is seen – largely due to its difference and an encroaching State apparatus into family life – as an appropriate target to "safeguard" against further problems of this kind. There is potential to drag home education down if an overweening approach to avoid child abuse focuses on settings beyond the school. This is a real danger because schooling attendance is hegemonically seen as the simple solution to the problem of keeping daily tabs on children. The complexities of this position have been rehearsed above and do not need reiterating here.

Despite the tendency for some in media and government to associate home education with the potential for child abuse, the laws of the UK, unlikely to be fundamentally changed, mean trusting parents is also the only option we have or are likely to have.

In the UK, as elsewhere, home education is consistently proving itself to be an exciting, beneficial and vibrant field of educational practice, well suited to the idea of the flourishing, competent child fit for a productive and appropriately contributory social, democratic future. Given this track record and the organized and vocal advocacy of home educators for their rights, home education in the UK is very likely to continue to experience freedom.

Acknowledgments

This article was written with the support of the Czech Science Foundation through a project entitled "Home Education – Facts, Analyses, Diagnostics" registration number: 16-17708S.

References

Andreotti, Vanessa. 2011. "Towards Decoloniality and Diversality in Global Citizenship Education." *Globalisation, Societies and Education*, 9(3–4): 381–397.

Arkell, Harriet. 2013. "The Stay-at-home Children Who are Being 'Unschooled': Mother Lets Her Kids 'Teach' Themselves – By Playing Computer Games and Having 'Life Experiences'." *Daily Mail*, December 9. Accessed May 19, 2015. http://www.dailymail.co.uk/news/article-2520667/Unschooling-children-teach-games-life-experiences.html

Badman, Graham. 2009. *Review of Elective Home Education in England*. London: DCSF.

Baker, Mike. 2010. "UK and American School Reforms: Who is Copying Whom?" *The Guardian*, September 20. Accessed May 19, 2015. http://www.theguardian.com/education/2010/sep/20/school-reforms-usa-uk

Balls, Edward. 2009. "*Letter to Graham Badman From Ed Balls, Accepting the Badman Review's Recommendations*." Accessed April 15, 2016. http://daretoknowblog.blogspot.co.uk/2009/06/ed-balls-letter-to-graham-badman.html

Bates, D. 2009. "Home Schooling 'Could be a Cover for Child Abuse and Sexual Exploitation.'". Daily Mail Online, January 20. Accessed 22 April 2016 http://www.dailymail.co.uk/news/article-1123182/Home-schooling-cover-child-abuse-sexual-exploitation.html

Bauman, Z. 2000. *Liquid Modernity*. London: Polity Books.

Boswell, Josh. 2014. "87,000 'Invisible' Children at Risk of Abuse." *The Sunday Times*, December 7. Accessed 19 May 2015. http://www.thesundaytimes.co.uk/sto/news/uk_news/article1492826.ece

Butler Education Act. 1944. London: UK Government.

Children Schools and Families Committee. 2010. *From Baker to Balls: The Foundations of the Education System, Ninth Report of Session 2009–10*. London: House of Commons.

Children Schools and Families Select Committee. 2009. *The Review of Elective Home Education: Second Report of Session 2009-10*. London: House of Commons.

Curtis, W., S. Ward, J. Sharp, and L. Hankin, eds. 2014. *Education Studies: An Issue Based Approach*. London: Learning Matters.

D'Arcy, K. 2014. *Travellers and Home Education: Safe spaces and inequality*. London: Trentham Books.

Davies, R. 2015a. "A Suitable Education?" *Other Education*, 4(1): 16–32.

Davies, R. 2015b. "Home Education: Then and Now." *Oxford Review of Education*, online first.

DCSF. 2007. *Elective Home Education – Guidelines for Local Authorities*. London: Department for Children Schools and Families.

Dickinson, Sarah. 2014. "Danger Sign: Authorities Act Outside the Law to Seize Control of Home Education in Northern Ireland?" *Other Education*, 3(2) 95–97.

Dowty, Terri. 2000. *Free Range Education: How Home Education Works*. Stroud: Hawthorn Press.

Eddis, Sam. 2015. "A Case of Mistaken Identity: Perspectives of Home Educators and State Officials in England and Wales, and Florida, USA." In *International Perspectives on Home Education: Do we still need schools?* edited by Paula Rothermel. Basingstoke: Palgrave MacMillan.

Flint, Kevin. J., and Peim, Nick. 2012. *Rethinking the Education Improvement Agenda: A Critical Philosophical Approach*. London: Continuum.

Grass-Orkin, Chloe. 2013. "The Damage of An 'Exam Factory' Schooling Approach." *Young Minds*, August 23. Accessed March 11, 2015. http://www.youngminds.org.uk/news/blog/1579_the_damage_of_an_exam_factory_schooling_approach

Hill, Amelia. 2015. "State Must Raise its Game to Protect Home-Educated Children, Judge Insists". *The Guardian,* April 23. Accessed May 19, 2015. http://www.theguardian.com/society/2015/apr/23/state-must-raise-its-game-to-protect-home-educated-children-judge-insists

Home Education Forums. 2011. "Home Education and Home Visits: Yes, No or Maybe?" Accessed July 27, 2015. http://www.home-education.biz/forum/general-discussion/14044-home-education-and-home-visits-yes-no-or-maybe.html

House of Commons Education Committee. 2012a. *Select Committee Oral Evidence Session: Enquiry into Support for Home Education.* October 17, 2102. Accessed March 11, 2015. http://www.parliamentlive.tv/Main/Player.aspx?meetingId=11520

House of Commons Education Committee. 2012b. *Support for Home Education.* Accessed April 22, 2015. http://www.publications.parliament.uk/pa/cm201213/cmselect/cmeduc/559/120905.htm

Isenberg, Eric. J. 2007. "What Have We Learned About Homeschooling?" *Peabody Journal of Education,* 82(2–3): 387–409.

Khimasia, Alice. 2015. "Caesurae in Home Education: Losing Control, Gaining Perspective…" *Other Education,* 4(1): 57–60.

Kunzman, Robert. 2009. *Write These Laws on Your Children: Inside the World of Conservative Christian Homeschooling.* Boston, MA: Beacon Press.

Lees, Helen E. 2011a. "*The Gateless Gate of Home Education Discovery: What Happens to the Self of Adults Upon Discovery of the Possibility and Possibilities of an Educational Alternative?*" PhD diss., University of Birmingham.

Lees, Helen E. 2011b. "A History of (Elective) Home Education in Scotland?" *Historical Perspectives on Scottish Education Conference.* Edinburgh: Royal Society of Edinburgh.

Lees, Helen E. 2013a. "Alternative Education in Scotland." In *Scottish Education,* 4th ed, edited by Walter Humes and Tom Bryce. Edinburgh: University of Edinburgh Press.

Lees, Helen E. 2013b. "Is the Idea of Compulsory Schooling Ridiculous?" In *Philosophical Perspectives on Compulsory Education,* edited by Marianna Papastephanou, 143–156. Dortrecht: Springer.

Lees, Helen E. 2014. *Education Without Schools: Discovering Alternatives.* Bristol: Policy Press.

Legislation.Gov.UK. 1986. *The Education and Libraries (Northern Ireland) Order 1986, No. 594 (N.I. 3) PART V, General Article 45.* Accessed April 23, 2015. http://www.legislation.gov.uk/nisi/1986/594/article/45

McCormack, Steve. 2009. "Last Resort: When Schools are Forced into Makeshift Classrooms." *The Independent,* September 24. Accessed May 19, 2015. http://www.independent.co.uk/news/education/schools/last-resort-when-schools-are-forced-into-makeshift-classrooms-1792046.html

Meighan, Roland. 1997. *The Next Learning System: And Why Home-Schoolers are Trailblazers.* Nottingham: Educational Heretics Press.

Mitchell, Sue. 2011. *A Report and Recommendations from Initial Scoping Research of Elective Home Education in the Bridgend, Vale of Glamorgen and Neath Port Talbot Area.* Welsh Government, September 27, 2012. Accessed April 20, 2016. http://gov.wales/topics/educationandskills/schoolshome/pupilsupport/homeeducation/?lang=en

Morton, Ruth. 2010a. "Home Education: Constructions of Choice." *International Electronic Journal of Elementary Education* 3(1). Accessed April 22, 2016. http://files.eric.ed.gov/fulltext/EJ1052483.pdf

Morton, Ruth. 2010b. "Walking the Line: Home Education as a Fine Balance between Parental Fulfilment and Hard Labour." Paper presented at the annual meeting for the British Sociological Conference, Glasgow, April 7.

Mukherjee, Sumita. 2010. *Nationalism, Education and Migrant Identities: The England-returned.* Abingdon, Oxon: Routledge.

Neuman, Ari, and Avriam, Aharon. 2003. "Homeschooling as a Fundamental Change in Lifestyle." *Evaluation and Research in Education*, 17(2&3): 132–143.

Nicholson, Fiona. 2006. "Do Children in England have a Legal Right to Education?" Accessed May 19, 2015. http://edyourself.org/articles/childsrighteducation.php#alivslordgrey

Nicholson, Fiona. 2014a. "2014 Numbers Article Bar Charts Prevalence Map." Accessed May 19, 2015. http://edyourself.org/articles/lalinegraph.php

Nicholson, Fiona. 2014b. "Home Education Numbers 2013–14." Accessed May 19, 2015. http://edyourself.org/articles/numbers.php

Nicholson, Fiona. 2014c. "Somerset 2014." Accessed 22 April, 2015. http://edyourself.org/articles/somersetconsult.php

Nicholson, Fiona. 2014d. "Spreadsheet Local Authority Websites." Accessed April 23, 2015. http://edyourself.org/articles/councilwebpages.php#spreadsheet

Nicholson, F. 2014e. "47 Midlands Forum - DfE Guidance: Anomalies for Stephen Bishop 2014 compiled by West Midlands Forum working group on behalf of the members of the West Midlands Elective Home Education Forum." Accessed 24/04/2016. http://edyourself.org/articles/LAletters.php#47

Nicholson, Fiona. 2015a. "Matthew Brazier, Ofsted's National Adviser for Looked After Children in the social care policy team emails information about EHE and reporting." Accessed April 15, 2015. https://edyourself.wordpress.com/2015/04/02/ofsted-new-guidance-about-home-education-to-inspectors/

Nicholson, Fiona. 2015b. "Essex 2014–15." Accessed April 22, 2015. http://edyourself.org/articles/essex2014.php

Nicholson, F. 2015c. "Launch of the Association of Elective Home Education Professionals Part 2." Accessed May 19, 2015. https://edyourself.wordpress.com/2015/02/27/aehep-launch-post-2/

Nicholson, Fiona. 2015d. "Northern Ireland Consultation." Accessed April 23, 2015. http://edyourself.org/articles/NI2014.php

Northern Ireland Assembly. 2012. *AQW 9311/11-15 (Question on how many school-age children are currently not attending school).* Accessed April 9, 2015. http://aims.niassembly.gov.uk/terms/printquestionsummary.aspx?docid=128564

Parsons, Sarah and Lewis, Ann. 2010. "The Home Education of Children with Special Needs or Disabilities in the UK: Views of Parents from an Online Survey." *International Journal of Inclusive Education*, 14(1): 67–86.

Reay, D. 2012. "What Would a Socially Just Education System Look Like?: Saving the Minnows From the Pike." *Journal of Education Policy*, 27(5): 587–599.

Rothermel, Paula. 2002. "Home Education: Rationales, Practices and Outcomes." PhD diss., University of Durham.

Rothermel, Paula. 2003. "Can We Classify Motives for Home Education?" *Evaluation and Research in Education*, 17(2&3): 74–89.

Rothermel, Paula. 2010. "Home Education: Practising Without Prejudice?" *Every Child Journal* 1(5): 48–53.

Rothermel, Paula, ed. 2015. *International Perspectives on Home Education: Do We Still Need Schools?* Basingstoke: Palgrave MacMillan.

Safran Barson, Leslie. 2015. Home Educating Parents: Martyrs or Pathmakers? In *International Perspectives on Home Education: Do we still need schools?*, edited by Paula Rothermel. Basingstoke: Palgrave MacMillan.

Schoolhouse. 2010. *Schoolhouse Slams "Grave Robber" MSP over Riggi Remarks*. Accessed April 22, 2016. http://www.schoolhouse.org.uk/schoolhouse-slams-grave-robber-msp-over-riggi-remarks/

Schoolhouse. 2015. *Media FAQs*. Schoolhouse. Accessed March 11, 2015. http://www.schoolhouse.org.uk/media/media-faqs

Select Committee Evidence. 2009. *Elective Home Education: Minutes of Evidence Taken Before the Children, Schools and Families Committee, Uncorrected Transcript of Oral Evidence, Graham Badman, Ms Diana R. Johnson and Penny Jones*. October 12. London: House of Commons.

Spiegler, Thomas. 2003. Home Education in Germany: An Overview of the Contemporary Situation. *Evaluation and Research in Education*, 17(2&3): 179–190.

Stafford, B. 2012. "Bad Evidence: The Curious Case of the Government-Commissioned Review of Elective Home Education in England and How Parents Exposed its Weaknesses." *Evidence & Policy: A Journal of Research, Debate and Practice*, 8(3): 361–381.

Staff Writer. 2011. "GCSE's: Pressure of Exams Leaves Teens Suffering from Mental Illness." *The Telegraph,* August 25. Accessed May 19, 2015. http://www.telegraph.co.uk/education/educationnews/8720513/GCSEs-Pressure-of-exams-leaves-teens-suffering-from-mental-illness.html

Stevens, Mitchell. 2003a. *Kingdom of Children: Culture and Controversy in the Homeschooling Movement*. Princeton: Princeton University Press.

Stevens, Mitchell. L. 2003b. The Normalisation of Homeschooling in the USA. *Evaluation and Research in Education*, 17(2&3).

Stevenson, N. 2015. "Revolution from Above in English Schools: Neoliberalism, the Democratic Commons and Education." *Cultural Sociology* online first, 1–16.

Summers, Lily. 2014. "Rather than Focusing on Free Schools, Labour Should Consider Supporting Home Education." *Labour List*, August 29. Accessed March 11, 2015. http://labourlist.org/2014/08/rather-than-focusing-on-free-schools-labour-should-consider-supporting-home-education/

Sweeting, Anthony, and Vickers, Edward. 2007. "Language and the History of Colonial Education: The Case of Hong Kong." *Modern Asian Studies*, 41(1): 1–40.

Symons, Greg. 2015. *Children Missing from Education (Scotland) Service: Service Guidance*. Accessed April 22, 2016. http://www.gov.scot/Topics/Education/Schools/cmescotland/resources/serviceguidance

The Scottish Government. 2007. *Home Education Guidance*. Edinburgh: The Scottish Government.

The Scottish Government. 2014. *National Guidance for Child Protection in Scotland*. Edinburgh: The Scottish Government.

Thomas, Alan and Pattison, Harriet. 2007. *How Children Learn at Home*. London: Continuum.

Thomas, Alan and Pattison, Harriet. 2010. Home Education: Precious, Not Dangerous. *The Guardian*, July 28. Accessed March 11, 2015. http://www.theguardian.com/commentisfree/2010/jul/28/home-education-khyra-ishaq-naive

Thomas, A., and Pattison, H. 2013. "Informal Home Education: Philosophical Aspirations put into Practice". *Studies in Philosophy and Education*, 32(2): 141–154.

Thomas, Alan and Pattison, Harriet. 2016, in press. *Rethinking Learning to Read*. Shrewsbury: Educational Heretics Press.

Van Galen, Jane. 1991. "Ideologues and Pedagogues: Parents Who Teach Their Children at Home." In *Home Schooling: Political, Historical, and Pedagogical Perspectives*, edited by Jane Van Galen and Mary Anne Pitman, 63–76. Norwood: Greenwood Publishing Group.

Various Home Educators. 2010. Comments on Lord Lucas Blog "Home Education Under a Coalition Government." Accessed July 27, 2015. https://www.blogger.com/comment.g?blogID=34227922&postID=9000075735414763971&bpli=1

Watts, D. 2003. *Understanding US/UK government and Politics: A Comparative Guide*. Manchester: Manchester University Press.

Weale, S. 2015. "Thousands Miss First Secondary School Choice as Demand Rises across UK Cities. *The Guardian*, March 2.

Welsh Government. 2008. "Inclusion and Pupil Support - Section 6 - Elective Home Education; Summary of guidance for schools." Accessed April 22, 2016. http://gov.wales/topics/educationandskills/schoolshome/pupilsupport/elective-home-education-guidance/?lang=en

Welsh Government. 2014. "Huw Lewis: Written Statement – Elective Home Education – Analysis of Responses to the Welsh Government Consultation on Proposals to Introduce a Compulsory Registration and Monitoring Scheme for Those who Elect to Educate their Children at Home." Accessed July 27, 2015. http://gov.wales/about/cabinet/cabinetstatements/2014/electivehomeeducation/?lang=en

Welsh Government. 2015a. "Statistics: Pupils Educated other than at School." Accessed April 9, 2015. http://gov.wales/statistics-and-research/pupils-educated-other-than-school/?lang=en

Welsh Government. 2015b. "Consultation: Draft Non-statutory Guidance for Local Authorities on Elective Home Education." Accessed July 27, 2015. http://gov.wales/consultations/education/elective-home-education/?skip=1&lang=en

Willis, Paul E. 1981. *Learning to Labour: How Working Class Kids Get Working Class Jobs*. New York: Columbia University Press.

Winstanley, C. 2009. "Too Cool for School? Gifted Children and Homeschooling." *Theory and Research in Education*, 7(3): 347–362.

Wray, Alison and Thomas, Alan. 2013. "School Refusal and Home Education." *Journal of Unschooling and Alternative Learning*, 7(13): 64–85.

14

Common Themes in Australian and New Zealand Home Education Research

Glenda M. Jackson

Introduction

In 2014, home educators in New South Wales (NSW) succeeded in their request to the Legislative Council of the NSW Parliament to establish an inquiry into home education (Sansom 2014; Select Committee on Home Schooling, Legislative Council of the NSW Parliament 2014). They specifically wanted the Home Schooling Inquiry to address their concerns about the practices and increasingly more stringent requirements of the Board of Studies in NSW in relation to home educators. Many NSW home educators thought the Tasmanian system of monitoring home education was preferable to the more inflexible demands many of them experienced in NSW. Later in the year, the Tasmanian Minister of Education (Rockcliff and Department of Education, Tasmania 2014) made an unexpected announcement that he would review the supervision of home education in his state. In 2015, because of changes to the structures of TAFEs (Technical and Further Education colleges) in NSW as in other states, home-educated students' access to TAFEs was restricted and concerns from home educators were included in an inquiry into the restructured TAFE system by the Legislative Council of NSW (Jackson 2015c; Ross 2015).

Tensions between home educators, legislatures, and regulators are not new in Australia. In 2006 Victorian home educators were belatedly and very briefly introduced to changes to legislation on home education. Neither as a group nor as individuals were Victorian home educators able to contribute anything meaningful to the legislation (Townsend 2012, Whitehead 2006, Wight 2006). There are currently home educators in Queensland who would like to see the regulatory system established in 2004 relaxed, while a few members of the Victoria public seek increased regulation and others think home educators should receive government

The Wiley Handbook of Home Education, First Edition. Edited by Milton Gaither.

funding (Gannon 2015a, 2015b; Osmak 2013; Tomazin 2015). In mid- December 2015, the Victorian Registration and Qualifications Authority (VRQA) notified the Victorian Home Education Network (HEN) that there would be a review of the current legislation on home education due by 2017. Legislative changes were also introduced in the Northern Territory at the beginning of 2016 with little input from home educators (Department of Education, Northern Territory, 2016a, 2016b).

Since home education became part of the Australian educational landscape in the late 1970s and has become a growing phenomenon, tensions between legislatures and, more particularly, regulators and home educators have been evident. Leaders of organized home educator networks around Australia are aware of significant non-compliance, particularly in those states with tighter controls. Legislators and regulators have been known to comment that there is little information about the success or otherwise of home education practices and that involving home educators in meaningful community consultation is difficult because they are not easily visible in the community. Lack of community consultation and scarce use of available Australian research have contributed to these tensions. This overview of Australian research literature on home education seeks to make visible this research and its implications.

Home education in this setting is defined as education provided or directed by parents who use their home as a base to organize their children's learning, but which may include the services of tutors or attendance at specialist classes run by outside professionals (Education and Community Services, ACT 2001). These programs may include use of community resources.

In contrast to home education, conventional schooling in this context is used to define education as it is offered in formally registered institutions: primary and secondary schools whether owned by the state or by private institutions and including distance education as offered by state departments of education.

Australian Research

In Australia, there have been a number of academic research projects on various aspects of home education. One postgraduate study has been completed (Thomas 1998), while the rest of the academic research has been undertaken by research students at various levels. Four doctoral studies have been completed (Barratt-Peacock 1997; Harding 2011; Jackson 2009; Reilly 2007), while others have completed more comprehensive topics that include home education Masters or Honors level projects.

A number of conference papers, journal articles, and published and unpublished government departmental, parliamentary research and inquiry papers also contribute to the growing body of Australian research literature on home education. Several topics have been investigated in these studies, including the following:

- Numbers of home-educating families and students. These numbers are difficult to establish because of known non-compliance; however in 2014, registered home-educated students across Australia were about 13 000 (Chapman 2015; Townsend 2012).

- Demographic features of homeschooling families (Drabsch 2013; Harding 1997, 2003c, 2006a, 2006b; Office of the Board of Studies, NSW (OBOS) 2000, 2004; Patrick 1999; Education Queensland' 2003; Select Committee on Home Schooling, Legislative Council, NSW Parliament 2014).
- Parent reasons for home-educating their children (Barratt-Peacock 1997; Drabsch 2013; Chapman and O'Donoghue 2000; Habibullah 2004; Harding 1997, 2003a, 2011; Harding et al. 2003b; Harp 1998; Honeybone 2000; Hunter 1994; Jackson 2009; Jacob et al. 1991; Jeffrey and Giskes 2004; Kidd and Kaczmarek 2010; Maeder 1995; OBOS 2004; Patrick 1999; Select Committee on Home Schooling, Legislative Council, NSW Parliament 2014; Simich 1998; Thomas 1998).
- Parent management of home education (Barratt-Peacock 1997; Croft 2013; Habibullah 2004; Harding 2011; Honeybone 2000; Kidd and Kaczmarek 2010; Lampe 1988; McDonald 2010; Mc Donald and Lopes 2014; McHugh 2007; Reilly, Chapman, and O'Donoghue 2002; Reilly 2004, 2007; Simich 1998; Thomas 1998).
- Home educating families dealing with special needs (Jackson 2009; Kidd and Kaczmarek 2010; McDonald 2010; McDonald and Lopes 2014; Reilly 2001, 2004; Reilly, Chapman, and O'Donoghue 2002; Trevaskis 2005)
- The process of learning in home-educating (Barratt-Peacock 1997; Burke 2013; Honeybone 2000; Krivanek 1985; Reilly 2007; Simich 1998; Thomas 1998).
- Student competencies and social development (Brosnan 1991; Krivanek 1988), student perceptions of their home education experience (Broadhurst 1999, Carins 2002; Clery 1998; Honeybone 2000; Jackson 2007, 2009; McColl 2005),
- The legislative and legal situation in all states of Australia (Allan and Jackson 2010; Carins 1997; Drabsch 2013; Harding 2006a; Harding and Farrell 2003; Jackson 1999; Jackson and Allan 2010; Jacob et al. 1991; Jeffrey and Giskes 2004; Liberto 2015; Lindsay 2003; OBOS 2004; Education Queensland 2003; Select Committee on Home Schooling, Legislative Council, NSW Parliament 2014; Varnham and Squelch 2008).
- Examination of the works of John Holt (Adams 1982; Lipscombe 1980; Thornton-Smith 1989).
- Home education as an alternative form of education in rural New South Wales, (Ennis 1978).
- An action research project exploring ways to support home-educating parents encourage art (Burke 2013).

Sample sizes in these studies varied from 515 (Harding 2003a) to a family of one (McHugh 2007; Trevaskis 2005) to two students (Clery 1998). The studies which looked at the largest numbers of participants included:

Barratt-Peacock (1997) – 205 interviews;
Jeffrey and Giskes (2004) – 351 respondents;

Education Queensland (2003) – 351 respondents;
Harding (1997) – 165 Australian Christian Academy (ACA) parents;
Harding (2003a) – 515 ACA students;
Harding (2003c) – 151 ACA families;
Harding (2006a) – 301 responses.

Studies with smaller samples included:

Burke (2013) – 14 parents;
Croft (2013) – 55 teacher trained mothers including 7 in depth interviews;
Harding (2011) – 27 parents;
Harp (1998) – 78 survey responses;
Jackson (2009) – 85 participants of 40 students, 28 parents and 17 educational professionals;
Kidd and Kaczmarek (2010) – 10 mothers of ASD children;
Lampe (1988) – 78 participants of 42 parents and 36 students;
McColl (2005) – 70 former ACA students;
Mullalay 1993 (referred to in Hunter 1994) – 147 Accelerated Christian Education (ACE) families;
OBOS (2000, 2004) – 337 registered home educator questionnaire responses and 6 in depth interviews;
Patrick (1999) – 68 families;
Reilly (2007) – 9 families;
Thomas (1998) – 58 Tasmanian families (and 42 English families).

A few other studies focused on qualitative research with much smaller numbers of parents and home-educated students.

There are significant major themes that have consistently emerged from this literature. The relatively insignificant differences between studies appear to be a reflection of the different populations that have been explored, the different methods used by researchers, and their various theoretical frameworks and perspectives. These strong common themes and insignificant differences give credibility to the overall findings.

The People Who Home Educate – Demographic Information of Home Educating Families in Australia

Demographic information profiling home-educating families (Chapman 2015; Harding1997, 2003b, 2006a; Jackson 2009; Jacobs et al. 1991; OBOS 2000, 2004; Patrick 1999; Queensland Parliament 2003) usually appears to have been conducted without the knowledge or acknowledgment of any of other researcher's work. In spite of this, the findings in these studies, while having individual variations due to the different populations targeted and information sought, showed many common threads.

Key themes

Home educators were randomly located in capital and regional cities and rural locations. Distance from formal education facilities was not the main reason for home education. Families who engaged in home education came from a wide variety of education and income levels and various occupation types. In a few studies (Harding 1997; Jackson 2009; Patrick 1999) average family size was usually three or more children. The main home educator was most commonly the mother, some parents shared the role while only a very small number of fathers took on the role of main educator. Students were home educated between the ages of 4 and 18; however, about two thirds of home-educated students were of primary school age. In some studies (Harp 1998; OBOS 2000, 2004; Patrick 1999) many parents had made the commitment to home educate for the long term. Their concern for their children's best interests was a significant factor in the decision to home educate and to remain home educating. Family cohesiveness, parenting roles, religious beliefs, and academic success were all mentioned as significant reasons for home educating children. After practicing home education, families enjoyed greater family cohesiveness, and this developed into a reason for continuing home education. The negative aspects of traditional schools revolved around parent dissatisfaction with a number of features of the school system. These included unsatisfactory professional practice, large class sizes, lower academic status, poor discipline, social pressures, and religious reasons. While Barratt-Peacock (personal communication, 2006) found bullying to be a significant reason for leaving traditional schools in his research, other studies found bullying and student welfare were not always the most obvious factors for leaving the traditional school system.

Harding (1997) noted in his study that 79% of students had attended traditional schools, and a number of other studies noted that significant numbers of children were withdrawn from school to be home educated. Many students have moved in and out of conventional schools for a wide variety of reasons at various points in their education (Jackson 2007, 2009).

Many studies (most notably Barratt-Peacock 1997; Croft 2013; Jackson 2009; Jacob et al. 1991; Patrick 1999;OBOS 2004; Harding 2006a, 2008, 2011) found there were varying degrees of structure used by different families, with some referring to natural, unstructured learning or unschooling. Nearly half of the participants in Patrick's (1999) study of sixty-eight families used some form of semi-structured or unstructured learning. Most families moved from more formal to less formal structures as parental confidence grew over time (Croft 2013; OBOS 2004; Jackson 2009). It was also consistently noted that children had access to a wide range of social activities in their communities including many with same age peers.

Education levels of parents varied from year ten to tertiary qualifications. Few parents who had primary responsibility for the children's education had formal teaching qualifications (Harding 1997, 2006a; Jackson 2009; Krivanek 1988, Patrick 1999). This lack or teaching qualification appeared to make no difference to the learning outcomes of students (Carins 2002; Lampe 1988; Harding 1997, 2011;

Jackson 2009; Reilly 2007). Most mothers spent their time in the home, while a few had part-time work. The primary income earners came from a variety of professional, self-employed or trade positions. A few studies (Barratt-Peacock 1997; Harding 2003c, 2006a; Jackson 2009; Lampe 1988) found there were very few single parents involved with home education.

Parent reasons for choosing home education

Parent reasons for choosing home education were examined in a number of Australian studies (Barratt-Peacock 1997; Croft 2013; English 2013; 2015a, 2015b; Jeffrey and Giskes 2004; Harding 1997, 2003a, 2003c, 2011; Harp 1998; Honeybone 2000; Hunter 1994; Jackson 2009; Jacob et al. 1991; Kidd and Kaczmarek 2010; Krivanek 1985; Maeder 1995; OBOS 2000, 2004, Patrick 1999; Queensland Parliament 2003; Reilly, Chapman, and O'Donoghue 2002, Reilly 2004, 2007; Simich 1998; Thomas 1998). The reasons given for Australian parents' choice to home educate varied in different research and reflected the diverse population samples of each individual study, but there were two major characteristics of parent decisions. Patrick (1999) described this as "the push and pull" qualities created by interactions between the two main types of education – home education and conventional schooling (factors also observed by Thomas 1998). Parents listed negative aspects of traditional schools and positive features of home education.

The negative aspects of conventional schools included such things as lower academic achievement, learning difficulties not catered for (including gifted and special needs children), perceived weaknesses in the curriculum, social problems such as bullying, negative peer pressure and low self-worth, values expected by parents not upheld by conventional schools, and their own children's unhappiness with traditional schooling.

Home education was seen to offer positive benefits such as academic rigor, broader curriculum, flexible learning to cater for individual needs, one-on-one teacher/student ratios, holistic learning connected to the "real" world, meaningful social experiences and growth because of mixing with wide age ranges of people unlike the same age socialization that occurred in traditional schools, values teaching, and stronger family relationships.

Academic outcomes

While there were no major studies on the academic status of home-educated students in Australia, there was information available which found home-educated students were equal to, if not above average to their formally educated peers in academic status. Jackson (2007, 2009) and Thomas (1998) found that home-educated children had no difficulty entering conventional schools. This also supported the notion that academic achievement for these students was at least equal to the average achievement of conventionally educated students. In two studies, (Lampe 1988; Simich 1998) it was noted that those home-educated students who did sit standardized tests on occasions, usually scored above average. Harding (2003a) used competency based tests on students of ACA. They were tested at three different year levels (Years 3, 5, and 7) in families who were both regulated and unregulated in Queensland and from a third unregulated group in Victoria. Student competency levels were equivalent whether regulated or not. In 2005, a study of home-educated students who had used the ACA curriculum, revealed that students generally achieved very high academic results and that many had entered tertiary institutions with ease (McColl 2005). Many parents expected their children to achieve higher academic results through home education, and this was one of the common reasons given for choosing to home educate children. The fact that Australian researchers have not considered this an important area of research would indicate that the academic success of Australian home-educated students has not been a significant matter of concern or interest. However, any attempts to find representative samples were bound to fail because of the hidden nature of the home-educating population.

Socialization

While there was no large Australian research project on socialization, nearly all available studies addressed it, pointing out that socialization for most Australian home-educated students was a positive experience. Many home-educated children appreciated their social experiences at home, as opposed to negative experiences that some experienced when in schools (Broadhurst 1999; Chapman and O'Donoghue 2000; Clery 1998; Croft 2013; Harp 1998; Honeybone 2000; Hunter 1994; Jackson 2007, 2009; Krivanek 1985, 1988; Thomas 1998; Trevaskis 2005).

In one study (Brosnan 1991), home-educated children generally rated their families higher than traditionally educated students. Parental support provided by both mothers and fathers indicated that responsibilities were shared and there were low levels of physical punishment or the withdrawal of privileges used by mothers in particular. Sibling relationships were usually healthy and supportive. Self-esteem and mother support were significant while father support was also thought to lead to improved self-esteem in students. Housework was shared, democratic practices were evident, and there was notable use of conversation, discussion, and expression of opinions. Family cohesiveness was a significant feature noticed with homeschooling families. Findings on parents' and students' views of socialization in many subsequent studies concur with Brosnan's assessment (Barratt-Peacock 1997; Broadhurst 1999; Chapman and O'Donoghue 2000; Clery 1998; Harding 1997, 2006a; Honeybone 2000; Hunter 1994; Jackson 2009; Jeffrey and Giskes 2004; Kidd and Kaczmarek 2010, Lampe 1988; Maeder 1995; Patrick 1999; Simich 1998; Thomas 1998).

The definition of socialization as understood by home educators appeared to differ from the more commonly understood meaning of conventional school socialization, where students were rated for their ability to socialize with their peers and follow classroom protocols. Thomas (1998) found many parents thought the socialization provided in school only catered for same age interaction en masse, and as far as these parents were concerned this same age integration had no out of school relevance or equal in any other part of society. Honeybone (2000) explained home-educating parents' views on home education as providing vertical socialization as opposed to the horizontal socialization offered by traditional schools. Parents made the effort to ensure children had varied social experiences through home education networks, special interest groups or clubs, music groups, volunteer service opportunities of every kind, and church associations. They were often adamant that school socialization was unhealthy and damaged their children. With experience, parents became more confident that their children were becoming more competent and developing healthy self-concepts (Jackson 2009; Thomas 1998). One study found children's social experiences and autonomy were directly related to parental attitudes and practices (Krivanek 1988).

Student views of socialization were very similar. A few children who were withdrawn from traditional schools, found the social change too great and often returned to school (Thomas 1998). However, many more students found the many avenues to meet a wide range of people of all ages fulfilling and worthwhile (Broadhurst 1999; Clery 1998; Jackson 2007, 2009; McColl 2005; Reilly et al. 2002; Reilly 2004, 2007; Thomas 1998). The quiet times on their own were not usually viewed as a significant disadvantage. Socialization as experienced by home-educated students was particularly beneficial to students who had experienced social problems at school (Jackson 2007, 2009; Reilly et al. 2002; Reilly 2004, 2007).

On the other hand, parents and students regularly explained that they wished the general population were more informed about home education and socialization in particular (Croft 2013; Jackson 2009; OBOS 2000, 2004; Patrick 1999; Reilly et al. 2002; Reilly 2004, 2007; Simich 1998).

The practice of home education

A few studies investigated the process of home education in Australia. The two largest studies (Barratt-Peacock 1997; Thomas 1998) were particularly interested in this aspect of home education. Several smaller studies (Clery 1998; Croft 2013; Habibullah 2004; Honeybone 2000; Jackson 2007, 2009; Lampe 1988; Patrick 1999; Reilly et al. 2002; Reilly 2004, 2007; Simich 1998; Trevaskis 2005) found similar themes supporting the findings described in the larger studies. Families used three basic approaches to home education: structured, semi-structured, or unstructured or natural learning (also known as informal or incidental learning and unschooling) or various blends of these approaches. Any disparities between studies were the result of the different sample sizes and researcher perspectives. In many studies, parents began home educating using school timetables, structures, and classroom type environments to guide their programs. A few of these families maintained these structured programs, but research consistently found that the majority of families moved to various blends of informality (Barratt-Peacock 1997, 2008; Clery 1998; Croft 2013; Habibullah 2004; Jackson 2007, 2009; Jacob et al. 1991; Lampe 1988; Kidd and Kaczmarek 2010; McDonald and Lopes 2014; OBOS 2000, 2004; Patrick 1999; Reilly 2004, 2007; Simich 1998; Thomas 1998; Trevaskis 2005). Many families using a semi-structured approach used basic curriculum for math, English, comprehension, and writing in the mornings and then allowed students to direct their own learning for the rest of the day.

Barratt-Peacock (1997) and Thomas (1998) found that all families in their studies engaged in a lot of conversational learning and both came to the conclusion that family conversation was one of the more significant aspects of home education. Earlier, Brosnan (1991) had also found that conversation and family discussion were part of the everyday experiences, but he did not draw any particular attention to its importance. Conversational learning was also noted but not strongly identified as a significant aspect in other studies, notably Broadhurst (1999), Brosnan (1991), Clery (1998), Habibullah (2004), Honeybone (2000), Krivanek (1988), and Lampe (1988).

Student Views and Experience

Demography

Several studies explored the views and experiences of home-educated students (Broadhurst 1999, Carins 2002; Clery 1998; Honeybone 2000; Jackson 2007, 2009; Lampe 1988; McColl 2005). The age range of the students involved fell between 6 and 16, apart from the young adults in two studies (Carins 2002; McColl 2005). The average size of most studies was seven students, apart from four larger studies: Lampe's interviews of thirty-six students, (1988) Jackson's (2009) interviews of forty students, Carins'(2002) survey of twenty-six students and McColl's (2005) questionnaire covering fifty students. The latter two studies were based on former ACE and ACA students, which limits the degree of generalization one can make to the larger home education population. However, there were common threads even though the studies were conducted in different States (South Australia, Queensland, Victoria and Western Australia) and at different times and some of the researchers were unaware of other related Australian research.

Students' opinions of their home education experience

Students valued a number of aspects of home education: flexibility, personal decision making and responsibility, receiving prompt attention when needed, lack of classroom pressure, more personal time and space, opportunity to finish work promptly, ability to pursue interests over lengthy periods of time, casual home learning environment and strong healthy family relationships. The majority of students thought they would home educate their own children.

Several students thought there were no disadvantages of home education, and a number thought that although they missed friendship at school this was not a reason to return to school, and neither was occasional boredom. Senior students felt the need to connect with subject experts and engage in classroom discussions. In spite of the general public's persistently expressed concerns about the socialization of home-educated students, only one fifth of McColl's (2005) students thought they had missed out on social interaction opportunities.

Student attitudes to school attendance were dependent on their age of contact with formal school. Younger students who started their education in school all had negative perceptions of traditional school, and comments revolved around school workloads, poor social interactions, and victimization as a result of institutional practices that interfered with their ability to work and learn (Broadhurst 1999; Honeybone 2000; Jackson 2009). Uncomfortable institutional practices included time wasted waiting for help from teachers, boring work, and lack of time to learn concepts.

Older students who entered or re-entered conventional schools at the secondary school level found they easily fitted in to their year levels and achieved academically (Clery 1998; Jackson 2007, 2009). Students appreciated friendly and helpful teachers, interactions with specialist teachers, classroom discussions, contact with peers and "muck around" time. Areas students recognized were less than ideal were lengthy queues for teacher assistance, noisy and distracting classrooms, inflexible timetables, and time restraints on personally interesting topics, especially those not covered in typical school programs.

The vast majority of students appreciated their social opportunities at home. Although students recognized they could interact with more of their peers at school, they did not see social needs as a reason to return to conventional schools. Those students who had experienced negative social situations first at school, found that home education allowed them the opportunity to discover real friends in different environments. Being at home also allowed personal time and space to heal and develop healthier social interactions in more manageable social settings (Jackson 2007, 2009; Reilly 2007; Thomas 1998).

The development or presence of autonomy, student identity, and self-awareness were noted by four researchers (Brosnan 1991; Clery 1998; Jackson 2007, 2009; Krivanek 1988). Autonomy was the most valued aspect of students' home education experience. Personal time away from peers gave students the opportunity to better understand themselves. However, this is an area needing further research on larger populations in Australia.

Students wanted professionals to understand that home education provided an effective educational pathway containing many qualities unavailable in conventional education. These included qualities recognized as beneficial for successful learning such as student control over curriculum, relevance of material to personal needs and interests, and flexibility in use of time (Jackson 2007, 2009). Australian research on home-educated students' views and experiences should open the door to productive professional discussions about learning in different environments.

Special Needs and Home Education

A number of studies have referred to students with special learning and disability needs (Drabsch 2013; Harding 2003b; Jackson 2007, 2009; OBOS 2004; Patrick 1999; Queensland Parliament 2003; Rowntree 2012; Simich 1998) particularly in New South Wales, Queensland, Victoria and Western Australia. However, a few studies conducted in Western Australia have specifically focused on families dealing with special needs children (Kidd 2008; Kidd and Kaczmarek 2010; McDonald 2010; McDonald and Lopes 2014; Reilly 2001, 2004, 2007; Reilly, Chapman, and O'Donoghue 2002; Trevaskis 2005). In the homeschooling population sampled by Queensland Parliament (2003), 15% of the families cited special or medical needs as the primary reason for homeschooling. Research projects have explored autism spectrum disorders, language learning disabilities, and other significant diagnosed learning disorders.

There were a number of reasons these parents of children with special needs chose to home educate. Dissatisfaction with educational opportunities in conventional schools for children with disabilities was the main factor and included negative inclusion experiences into conventional schools, poor social growth opportunities, lack of academic progress, and a lack of professional understanding of the children's disabilities. Parents found they could better cover these aspects at home. Positive features of home education included flexibility to work with individual needs, one-on-one teaching, and the academic and social growth children were able to experience through home education.

A key feature of parental programs has been the way in which parents have continually altered programs, "progressively modifiying" them (to use the term coined by Reilly 2004, 2007 and noted by others – Kidd 2008, Kidd and Kaczmarek 2010, McDonald and Lopes 2014) to fit the constantly changing needs of these children. This aspect of parent programs reflects the way most home educators develop their educational programs (Barratt-Peacock 1997; Croft 2013; Jackson 2009; Thomas 1998).

These families in the studies mentioned frequently sought assistance from local schools, departments of education, distance education facilities, and other educational professionals. They often felt their needs were misunderstood and that advice and support given was inadequate, insufficient, and uninformed. A significant need was for educational professionals and government departments at all levels to be better informed about the benefits of home education and how they could better support parents and children using this educational approach. Home education networks were usually a useful connection and source of support and socialization for these special needs families.

Gifted children have been reported to thrive on home education (Jackson 2007, 2009; Williams 2004) and it is known that gifted children are using home education as an alternative educational option. However, the special needs of gifted children as met by home education is an area needing further research in Australia.

Challenging Aspects of Home Education

Two significant challenges to home educators were highlighted by a number of researchers. These were mother stress when organizing home education programs and parental dealings with bureaucracy.

Several studies noted that a few mothers experienced a certain degree of overload and stress (Clery 1998, Habibullah 2004, Honeybone 2000, Jackson 2009, Kidd 2008, Kidd and Kaczmarek 2010; Nicholls 1997; Patrick 1999; Simich 1998; Thomas 1998; Trevaskis 2005). Some of these studies found that mothers who more closely followed the conventional school model tended to experience more stress than mothers who used a less structured approach. A small number of mothers, especially those dealing with some form of special need, and/or were homeschooling because they felt that there was no other option, felt stress and disquiet about the homeschooling experience (Croft 2013; Kidd and Kaczmarek 2010; McDonald and Lopes 2014; Reilly 2004, 2007; Reilly et al. 2002; Trevaskis 2005). These parents would have appreciated greater support and encouragement, especially from relevant government agencies. One study listed concerns about keeping up with routine work, keeping children motivated, managing home and school work, and having little time for self (Jeffrey and Giskes 2004). Because distance education was included in this sample it is probable that these problems were specifically related to distance education rather than home education in general (Jackson 2009).

Significant levels of non-compliance to regulation and registration across Australia, strongly suggest parents do not find working with regulatory authorities easy or satisfactory (Carins 1997; Chapman 2015; Harding 2003c, 2006a; Harding and Farrell 2003; Jackson 1999; Jeffrey and Giskes 2004; Kidd and Kaczmarek 2010; McDonald and Lopes 2014; Patrick 1999). The recent 8% drop in registered numbers in NSW would tend to indicate greater non-compliance rather than a reduction in numbers (Chapman 2015). For example, parents who were more experienced in home education found the guidelines provided by the New South Wales OBOS (2004) did not reflect an understanding of home education. Other parents found that contact or the lack of appropriate contact with departments of education staff or distance education exacerbated felt needs (McDonald and Lopes 2014; Patrick 1999; Reilly 2004, 2007; Trevaskis 2005).

Home Education in Australia is not a Replica of Practices in the United States

While some Australian researchers of home education have relied significantly on data from the United States, others have noted differences in the practice and experience of home education between the two countries. The problems of this reliance on research material from overseas, and particularly from the United States, become evident when researchers contribute to discussions about legislation and regulation for government departments and state parliaments and rely on figures from the United States while providing little or no reference to Australian research (Drabsch 2013; Jeffrey and Giskes 2004; Queensland Parliament 2003; Varnham and Squelch 2008).

As Barratt-Peacock (1997) noted, there are historical and cultural differences between conventional education as found in the United States and that found in Australia. There are also differences in our legal and regulatory systems. He and others have found there are some similarities in home education practices and data between the two countries. However our "cultural and historical differences precluded the naïve transfer of US results to the Australian situation" (228). Differences can be seen in the way parents become aware of home education and take it up even though many of the reasons for home educating in the United States are similar to those of parents in Australia, especially concerns about the negative influences of conventional schools (Princiotta, Bielick and Chapman 2006; Queensland Parliament 2003). Some differences have included the plethora of guides and kits in the United States in contrast to Australia where parents have tended to develop their own resources. In the United States, there are prominent citizens who have been home educated, something lacking in Australia (Patrick 1999). The influence of right-wing politics and religion evident in the United States is not so obvious in Australia. Australians also appear to have clear beliefs that homeschooling caters for their children's best interests by providing better one-on-one education opportunities and strengthens family interactions and bonding (Honeybone 2000; Hunter 1990, 1994; Jackson 2009).

There is a definite need for the use of current Australian research to inform Australian educational professionals, the general public, legislatures, regulators, and home educators.

Home Education, Legislation, and Regulations

There was and is significant variation between the legislation and regulations of different state governments for home education and home educator response to this (Allan and Jackson 2010, Carins 1997; Chapman 2015; Drabsch 2013; Harding 2003c, 2006a; Harding and Farrell 2003; Gustafson 1989; Hobson and Cresswell 1993; Hopkins 1993; Hunter 1989, 1990, 1994; Jackson 1999, 2014, 2015c; Jackson and Allan 2010; Jacob et al. 1991; Jeffrey and Giskes 2004; Liberto 2015; Lindsay 2003; OBOS 2004; Mulford and Grady 2001; Queensland Parliament 2003; Select Committee on Home Schooling, Legislative Council, NSW Parliament 2014). However, every State and Territory recognizes home education as a viable education alternative and most have reviewed their home education legislation since 1990. Two reviews in 2014, one in NSW (Home Schooling Inquiry in NSW, Parliament of NSW) and the other in Tasmania (Rockliff and Department of Education, Government of Tasmania) illustrate the ongoing disparities between legislatures, regulators, and home educators. In 2006 in Victoria new legislation requiring formal registration was passed without any consultation with home educators – the interest group concerned. Home education networks have been vocal about these reviews and sought inclusion to the review process with varying degrees of success. Conflict between parent views and state views over responsibility of children were documented as far back as 1989 (Carrick 1989; Hunter 1990).

The earliest government sponsored study of home educators was conducted in Tasmania by a Ministerial Working Party of interested persons to provide a detailed state-wide examination of home education (Carins 1997; Barratt-Peacock, personal communication 2006; Jacob et al. 1991). The results of this investigation led the Tasmanian government to establish an authority – Tasmanian Home Education Advisory Council (THEAC) – to work with home educators and be answerable directly to the Minister for Education and Training.

The most obvious complicating feature of Australian home education has been the unavailability of a census of home educator numbers in any state, whether or not legislation required registration or notification. Any attempt at a census or accurate estimate has been impossible as there has been, and continues to be, high non-compliance to registration or notification around Australia. An illustration of the difficulties of completing an accurate census of home educator numbers can be found in the "Home Schooling Review" (Queensland Parliament 2003). The possible range of unregistered home-educated students was found to be between 3000 and over 11 000. Although the numbers could be explained in different ways it did indicate the possibility of a high level of civil protest and non-compliance to Queensland regulations. Other researchers have noted the complexities of determining accurate estimates of home educators and the existence of non-compliance (Harp 1998; Hunter 1994; Jackson 2009; Jacob et al. 1991; Lampe 1988; Lindsay 2003).

The balance between parental rights and the state's duty of care is at the center of arguments for and against regulation. All have agreed that parents had the right to determine the education of their children but also acknowledged the state's need to be assured that the children's right to an education was upheld through family practice. Determining the balance between these two positions has been, and is continuing to be, a difficult political process. After all, it is a child's right to receive an effective education. One suggestion has been for home education to become part of the Commonwealth's agenda (Lindsay 2003).

Legislation and regulation of home education in Australia is not uniform and is an ongoing process as it seems to irregularly come into the spotlight in the different states at various times. There needs to be further discussion and negotiation in light of available Australian research which should give direction as to what is in the "best interests of the child" (Allan and Jackson 2010; Jackson 2014).

Distance Education, Collaboration, and Student Transitions

The variety of definitions of home education or homeschooling have meant some researchers have included government or private school provision of distance learning in their definitions of home education, with or without reference to home education that is initiated and organized by parents (Carins 2002; Crump and Boylan 2010; Danaher 1998, 2001; Danaher, Moriarty and Danaher 2004; Danaher, Wyer and Bartlett 1994; Green 2006; Harding 1997, 2011, 2012; Harp 1998; Jefferson 2010; Jeffrey and Giskes 2004; McDonald and Lopes 2014; O'Sullivan 1997; Queensland Parliament 2003; Reilly 2004, 2007; Symes 2012; Trevaskis 2005). The benefits, difficulties and need for greater access of distance material have been noted in more recent years (Jackson 2009; McDonald and Lopes 2014; Reilly 2004, 2007). Access to the use of government provided distance education has become progressively easier to access across Australia (Barratt-Peacock 1997; Department of Education and Training, Victoria 2006a, 2006b; Jeffrey and Giskes 2004; Queensland Parliament 2003).

It has been recognized in most research that students have successfully moved in both directions between conventional education and home education and at any level (Barratt-Peacock 1997; Habibullah 2004; Harding 1997, 2003c, 2006a; Harp 1998; Honeybone 2000; Jackson 2007, 2009, 2010; Jacob et al. 1991; McDonald and Lopes 2014; Lampe 1988; OBOS 2004; Patrick 1999; Queensland Parliament 2003; Reilly et al. 2002; Reilly 2004, 2007; Thomas 1998; Trevaskis 2005). Student, parent, and educational professional experiences of this movement were the focus in Jackson's research (2007, 2009, 2010). Most movements into conventional schools occurred with ease, and children made the transitions to home education with even greater ease.

More recent researchers have commented on the existence and/or need for some form of collaboration between conventional education and home educators. There has always been a recognized need for the practice of home education to be better understood by professionals and the general public (Jackson 2007, 2009; McDonald and Lopes 2014; Reilly 2004, 2007).

Towards a Theory of Australian Home Education

The development of a theory of home education appears to have been a strong feature of Australian home education research. The main contributors to theoretical development have been Barratt-Peacock (1997, 2008), Jackson (2008, 2015a), Reilly (2004, 2007) and Thomas (1998). The findings of others support the core concepts of this theoretical framework (Croft 2013; Habibullah 2004; Honeybone 2000; Jacob et al. 1991; McDonald and Lopes 2014; Simich 1998).

There are two significant features to this theoretical framework. Firstly, there appear to be a gradation in the types of curriculum or family program styles and structures used by home educators. A simple analysis divides these into three basic types although families may use a combination of more than one style and/or be found anywhere on a continuum between these three program types: structured, eclectic and informal – also referred to as unschooling or natural learning (Barratt-Peacock 1997; Broadhurst 1999; Clery 1998; Croft 2013; Honeybone 2000; Hunter 1994; Jackson 2007; Jacob 1991; Jeffrey and Giskes 2004; Patrick 1999; Reilly et al. 2002; Reilly 2004; Thomas 1998).

The second feature is that no matter where family program styles start they mostly move to a less formal approach over time as parents gain confidence in their own and in their children's abilities to learn (Barratt-Peacock 1997; Croft 2013; Jackson 2009; McDonald and Lopes 2014; OBOS 2000, 2004; Thomas 1998). Very few families maintained a program using formal school model approaches. In NSW, the OBOS (2000, 2004) found that it was the more experienced home educators who had the most difficulty accepting regulations calling for tightly controlled and state directed curriculum. As mentioned earlier in this chapter, those researchers who focused on families with special needs children referred to this as progressive modification of learning programs (Kidd and Kaczmarek 2010; McDonald and Lopes 2014; Reilly 2004, 2007).

The implications of these two features are significant as they impact the way legislation and regulation is both administered to and received by home educators. In 2004, Jeffrey and Giskes noted there appeared to be high levels of home educator resistance to compliance with Education Queensland's regulation of home education because of the problems this created for parents who developed their own programs and which were rejected by departmental officers (see also Queensland Parliament 2003). This has also been a leading cause for the call in 2014 by home educators to have legislation and regulation changed in NSW (Home Schooling Inquiry, NSW Parliament 2014). The failure of the Office of the Board of Studies and Education Queensland (OBOS 2004; Queensland Parliament 2003) to understand the basic elements in Australian "theory of home education" significantly contributed to tensions between home educators and officialdom. It would appear that a more informed understanding of the theory of Australian home education practice should inform legislation and regulation of home education to achieve a more satisfactory result for all parties (Allan and Jackson 2010; Jackson and Allan 2010).

Other aspects of Australian theoretical analysis of home education include a recognition of home education as a "community of learning practice" or as a "supermodel of a community of practice" (Barratt-Peacock 1997, 2003, 2008). Exposure to the real world of adults through family conversation and informal learning opportunities has been identified as an efficient and effective learning mechanism in home education (Thomas 1998). Thomas' findings that home-educated children generally did not appear to learn sequentially and incrementally, but in leaps and bounds challenges the expectations of educators trained in conventional education methods. Mediated learning by more informed peers (parents in this case) and other best preferred learning experiences as understood through a Vygotskian sociocultural perspective were also found to be part of Australian home education practices (Jackson 2008). Work-based learning (Trevaskis 2005), parental roles as educators (Harding 2011), connections to the Pestalozzi method (Croft 2013) and progressive modification or fit (McDonald and Lopes 2014; Reilly 2004, 2007) are other theoretical frameworks developed to explain the effectiveness of home educator practice in Australia.

From the theoretical understandings developed to date, it becomes clear that home educators use effective but different approaches to education than those generally practiced in conventional schools. This helps to explain why legislation and regulation that attempts to impose traditional school models of curriculum, assessment and regulation have been difficult to enforce on home-educating families. Home education is distinctly different from traditional schooling. Any attempts to regulate home education need to carefully consider these defining holistic educational and learning qualities of Australian home education (Allan and Jackson 2010; Jackson and Allan 2010).

Problems of Home Education Research in Australia

Any interpretation of research on home education in Australia must consider the significance of the findings in light of the fact that all the research to date has been conducted with willing participants. There have been no quantitative studies with control groups or with randomly selected participants. This problem was also noted as one of the most significant weaknesses of overseas research (Jeffrey and Giskes 2004; Kunzman and Gaither 2013; Reich 2005; Welner and Welner 1999). However, the suggestion by a member of the Select Committee on Home Schooling during hearings that the National Assessment Program – Literacy and Numeracy (NAPLAN) be used to provide quantitative data on the academic outcomes of home-educated students has its own inherent problems. Because we know that at least 25% of current home educators have withdrawn children from school because of learning difficulties, data from the NAPLAN would be inherently skewed and need careful interpretation.

Another factor impacting home education research around Australia and New Zealand has been the poor access for Australian researchers to the works of other Australian and New Zealand researchers on home education. Distance, lost reports or research projects (Mullaly 1993 referred to in Barratt-Peacock 1997; Harding 2004; Howison, 1994, Hunter 1994; Reilly 2007; Wallace 1999), lack of publication and poor search engines have made it very difficult for researchers to locate the work of others. For example, Hunter (1994) who wrote on the development of home education in the Christian community made no mention of Ennis (1978), Krivanek (1988), or Brosnan (1991) who worked with more alternative groups, while Maeder (1995), only referred to Hunter (1990, 1991, 1994) and Krivanek (1988). Hunter's (1985) own doctoral thesis was completed in the United States and not listed in the Australian Education Index (AEI, see also Box 2014) as Australia's most common relevant academic search engine. Chapman and O'Donoghue (2000) in Western Australia posed research questions that had already been addressed by Barratt-Peacock (1997), Broadhurst (1999), Clery (1998), Harding (1997), Jacob et al. (1991), Krivanek (1988) and Thomas (1998). Reilly et al. (2002), and Reilly (2004) made reference to Jacob et al. (1991), a web page in the United States mentioning Harding in (2003), Hunter (1994), Nicholls (1997) and Simich (1998), but made no reference to the larger research projects of Barratt-Peacock (1997), Harding (1997) or Thomas (1998) in particular. A few academics when writing about home education

(Athanasou 2014, Box 2014, Nicholls 1997; Follett 2003) have made no reference to any Australian research literature.

Policymakers and parliamentary researchers have relied on figures and research in the United States and made little use of Australian research (Drabsch 2013; Queensland Parliament 2003; Jeffrey and Giskes 2004). The lack of public knowledge of available Australian research on home education has contributed to a lack of appropriateness and relevance in Australian legislative and regulatory decisions. It is no wonder that the Department of Education and Early Childhood of Victoria in 2006 told home educators upset at the lack of consultation and reference to Australian research when preparing new legislation and regulation that there was no Australian research to use (Trevaskis 2006, personnel communication). The Summary of Australian and New Zealand Home Education Research (Jackson 2015b) was initially constructed to provide the then Victorian Education Minister with a comprehensive list of Australian Research at that time. Very recently, the NSW Board of Studies Teaching and Educational Standards internally conducted a study of home-educated students who had completed NAPLAN tests. These results were accessed by home educators through the Freedom of Information Act and indicate that home-educated students are performing on par with their conventionally schooled peers in mathematics and are generally achieving above average in reading and writing (BOSTES 2014; Smith 2016).

Because the home-educating community has been so varied and segmented, and because much of the home education research literature has not been published and not promptly listed on the AEI research engine, access to valuable work has been limited. This difficulty of locating research information was also compounded by the control of information and network membership by some of the early home education proponents (Lampe 1988; Smith 2003). Very recently better listing of documents and speedy access through improved technologies on Australian research engines such as AEI have allowed wider access to this material. In spite of this, however, it seems that researchers from disciplines other than education may not have been aware of AEI as a suitable source of Australian research literature, as a few researchers from other subject disciplines appeared to be unaware of much if any of the listed Australian research, even in their specific interest area and from within their own state (Box 2014; English 2013; Kidd and Kaczmarek 2010; Varnham and Squelch 2008).

Locating Australian research has also been difficult because of the various definitions and labels that have been given to home education, as can be seen in the AEI classification of one thesis about homeschooling being about after-school hours care in the home (Simpson 1999). While the vast majority of researchers around Australia have referred to the practice of families educating their children at home as homeschooling, a few mostly Victorian researchers have consistently referred to this practice as home education and a couple of researchers (Krivanek 1988; Trevaskis 2005), as well as the Western Australian support network have until recently referred to it as home based learning. Other terms used by the home-educating community include "unschooling" and "natural learning" (Box 2014; Paine 2015). For many researchers these distinctions have not been significant. However, Tasmanian and Victorian researchers have generally referred to this practice as home education. They have insisted this form of education was not just about the practice of "school" in the home. Home education was viewed as a different form of education – more holistically embedded in the real world. Victorian network groups were also very particular to call their "education in the home" home education to clarify their legal position with state legislation which controlled schools but allowed parents to "educate otherwise" in their homes but not as schools (Jackson 1999). An appreciation of these differences in labels is useful when conducting literature searches. It is of interest to notice in New South Wales, that Carrick's (1989) and the recent Legislative Council Select Committee in the Home Schooling Inquiry in NSW (2014) government report made reference to "home schooling" while the Office of the Board of Studies (2001, 2004) researched "home education."

The New Zealand Research

Homeschooling has also been researched in New Zealand by postgraduate students at the doctoral, masters or honors level from the 1990s, by government agencies, private research, and one of the home education networks (Arthur 2005; Baldwin 1993; Barkley 2013; Campbell 1993; Donald 1998; Education Review Office 1998, 2001; Hendy-Harris 1983, 1996, 2004; Home Schooling Federation of New Zealand 1996, 2000; McAlevey 1995; Ministry of Education 1998, 2001, 2008, 2014; National Council of Home Educators New Zealand 2013, 2015; Nolan and Nolan 1992; Roache 2009; Roberts 1999; Shim 2000; Smith 2003; Stroobant 2006; Stroobant and Jones 2006; Varnham 2008; Wallace 1999). The topics included reasons for parent choice of home education, a case study of two families homeschooling, homeschooler use of public libraries and use of technology, school refusers and their use of homeschooling, legal analysis, as well as a sociological analysis of homeschooling, and government reviews of "The Quality of Homeschooling." To illustrate the difficulty of locating New Zealand research, one has to search each individual New Zealand university library to find these theses. Apart from the government reviews, Hendy-Harris (1983, 1996, 2004), Smith (2003), and Stroobant and Jones (2006), most of these research projects have not been published, while a number of tertiary institutions have amalgamated and changed names making the various theses difficult to locate.

A Brief History of Australian and New Zealand Home Education Research

A brief look at the history of Australian home education research is revealing. In the 1980s, it was recognized that home education had been practiced from the earliest days of European settlement of Australia, (Amies 1982, 1985, 1986, 1988;

Barcan 1980, 1988). The first research to include home education more recently was a study of alternative educational pathways that ended up becoming a home education program because of disagreements with educational authorities (Ennis 1978). During the 1980s, research projects and academic comment explored the practice of home education, particularly as alternative education (Knowles 1987; Krivanek 1988;Lampe 1988; Brosnan 1991) and this continued into the 1990s (Maeder 1995). During this time, research in both Australia and New Zealand looked at the impact of John Holt who visited here in the early 1980s (Adams 1982; Lipscombe 1980; Thornton-Smith 1989). Although Hunter (1985) completed his doctorate in the United States during the mid 1980s, it was not until the early 1990s that the Christian focus and interest in home education in both Australia and more particularly in New Zealand (Baldwin 1993; Campbell 1993; McAlevey 1995; Nolan and Nolan 1992; Wallace 1999) became more apparent, and other researchers have continued this line of inquiry (Beirne 1994; Box 2014; Carins 2002; Hunter 1989, 1990, 1991, 1993, 1994; Harding 1997, 2011; McColl 2005). From the mid 1990s through to 2015, research has examined the practice of home education more generally (Barratt-Peacock 1997; Honeybone 2000; Patrick 1999; Roache 2009; Simich 1998; Thomas 1998. There are also overviews of home education in New Zealand (Barkley 2013; Smith 2003). Research since 2000 has shown a shift from more pedagogical or religious type reasons for home educating to parental interest in best supporting the interests of children. (Aurini and Scott 2005; Croft 2013; Jackson 2009).

Since 2000, interest in particular aspects of home education practice have become more evident in both Australia and New Zealand. Three Western Australian researchers projects have conducted research in the area of special needs (Kidd and Kaczmarek 2010; McDonald 2010; McDonald and Lopes 2014; Reilly 2001, 2202, 2004, 2007). Other topics have included teachers who home educate (Croft 2013) and an action research project supporting parents encouraging the arts in the home (Burke 2013). In New Zealand, research has included school refusal (Stroobant 2006, Stroobant and Jones 2006), library use and information technology (Arthur 2005, Donald 1998) and early childhood learning experiences (Ellis 2005, Layland 2010, 2012, Roberts 1999, White 2003).

As early as 1989, the NSW government conducted a comprehensive look at its education policies, including homeschooling (Carrick et al.). In 1991, the Tasmanian government reviewed home education and conducted the first comprehensive look at home education practice in Australia (Jacobs et al. 1991). There were also submissions and legal representations to the Queensland government during that time (Gustafson 1989, Hobson and Cresswell 1993, Hopkins 1993, Hunter 1989). In 2003, the Queensland government again looked at home education (Harding and Farrell 2003, Harding et al., 2003a,b, 2004, Jeffrey and Giskes 2004, Lindsay 2003, Education Queensland 2003). In 2006, the Victorian government changed its legislation on home education without meaningful consultation with home educators. However, key Australian researchers (Barratt-Peacock, Harding, Jackson and Thomas) presented papers to parliamentarians on the day legislation was being presented. It was during 2006 that the Home School Legal Defense Association (HSLDA) announced that Australia had its own legal defense association for home educators (Harding and Whitrow 2006). There have been other papers looking at the legal issues relating to home education in Australia (Allan and Jackson 2010; Jackson 1999; Jackson and Allan 2010; Varnham 2008; Varnham and Squelch 2008). The topic of home education has continued to be a source of contention between legislators, regulators, and home educators, as was evident in 2014. In that year, the NSW parliament conducted an inquiry of homeschooling (Drabsch 2013; Home Schooling Inquiry, NSW Parliament 2014) and included submissions by five published academics – Barratt-Peacock 2014, English 2014, Harding 2014, Jackson 2014, Thomas 2014. The Tasmanian Minister for education announced his state would review home education as well (Rockliff et al. 2014).

Australian and New Zealand home education research began with an alternative education focus and was then taken up by Christians and other religious groups (Habibullah 2004). Home education has since been practiced by a broad range of people looking out for the best interests of their children (Croft 2013; Jackson 2009; Reilly 2007). Recent researchers have specialized in particular aspects of home educator practice, while discussions about suitable legislative and regulatory frameworks are still very relevant.

The Future of Australian Home Education?

Over the years, there have been Australian academics who have explored the educational possibilities of home education and its impact on the delivery of conventional education in the future (Athanasou 2014; Nicholls 1997; Reader 2009; White 1983). A common theme between these academics has been the recognition of the growing out-of-touch nature of conventional education with the direction society is heading. These academics felt home education practices were more suited to the directions society seems to be heading.

These scholars have identified aspects of the current schooling system that limit learning strategies, that are costly and limited in their ability to support children with special needs, and that foster negative behavior and other problems, including the growing problem of student disengagement with learning. Current educational practices have been established for and suit the industrial age, although we are now moving into a more fluid technological era. In favor of home education, these scholars have noted the greater room for flexibility regarding individual learning strategies, increased connection with mentors and situations embedded in the real world, vertical age groupings, core subjects with room for subjects of interest to students, and learning in communities, especially with the use of new technologies.

Perhaps a greater appreciation and respect for the learning possibilities and potentials available through the practice of home education by educators in conventional education could improve educational outcomes for all.

Areas for Further Research of Australian and New Zealand Home Education

Significant research has already assessed "how and why" Australian home-educating parents manage the process of educating their children at home. Areas Australian researchers have yet to address in meaningful ways are manifold, including:

- any area of meaningful quantitative analysis of home education in Australia, particularly of numbers of home educators, student academic achievements and life outcomes
- management of mother stress in the home education process
- subsets of home education populations such as home-educating single parents, various special interest and ethnic groups
- relationships between legislatures, regulators, and home educators
- the meaning and significance of socialization experiences to home-educated students
- student self-concepts
- further work on special needs, particularly for gifted students
- the movement of students between home education and conventional schooling and/or post school institutions such as TAFE, university, and employment
- an examination of inclusive or collaborative arrangements between home and conventional education
- professional opinion and experience with home educators
- further development of the theory of home education
- the history of home education in Australia
- investigation into the sociological reasons for non-compliance with legislation
- the dynamics of home educator networks
- specific topics or subject use within the home
- the use of technology and online learning options
- influence and workings of organizations and groups promoting home education and ongoing changes in the way people are introduced to and supported in home education, particularly through the use of social media
- perhaps most importantly, continuing research into and theorizing of the how and why of learning experiences in home education settings through different participant voices.

Answers to these types of questions will provide valuable directions to conventional educators, legislators and regulators, and home educators, especially when the new generation of researchers includes previously home-educated students (Bickers 2014, Collin 2013, Croft 2013).

Conclusion

Home education in Australia and New Zealand is a healthy and growing sector of the current educational landscape. In spite of the lack of quantitative research and poor access of researchers to the work of others, the findings of all researchers show consistencies. Topics covered have included home educator demography, parent reasons for choosing home education, instructional methods used in families, and student views and experiences. Two areas of concern include the need to support mothers experiencing stress, and the tensions between home educators and government legislators and regulators. Because the educational and life outcomes for many students have been positive, home education research and theory development needs greater attention and should inform legislation and regulation to achieve more collaborative and equitable results. Future research directions into home education and its practice have many unexplored doorways. This overview reveals that Australian and New Zealand home education is successful and that its research has a valuable contribution to make to educational professionals, legislators, regulators, and home educators.

References

Adams, Marin. 1982. *Home Schooling: an Evaluation of John Holt's Concept of Home Schooling with Special Reference to the Situation in New Zealand*. DipEdPsych: 180, University of Auckland, New Zealand.

Allan, Sonia, and Glenda Jackson. 2010. "The What, Whys and Wherefores of Home Education and Its Regulation in Australia." *International Journal of Law and Education*, 15(1): 55–77.

Amies, Marion. 1982. "Schooling at Home in Nineteenth Century Australian Fiction." *Discourse: Studies in the Ccultural Politics of Education*, 3(1): 40–56. DOI: 10.1080/0159630820030103

Amies, Marion. 1985. "Amusing and Instructive Conversations: The Literary Genre and its Relevance to Home Education." *History of Education* 14(2): 87–99. DOI: 10.1080/0046760850140201

Amies, Marion. 1986. "Home Education and Colonial Ideals of Womanhood." PhD: 381, Faculty of Education, Monash University, Clayton, Victoria.

Amies, Marion. 1988. "The Victorian Governess and Colonial Ideals of Womanhood." *Victorian Studies*, 31(4): 537–565.

Arthur, Erika J. 2005. "Analysis of the Information Needs and Information Seeking Behaviour of New Zealand Home Educators." MLibrary and InformationSt, partial fulfillment, Victoria University of Wellington, New Zealand.

Aurini, Janice and Scott Davies. 2005. "Choice Without Markets: Homeschooling in Context of Private Education." *British Journal of Sociology of Education*, 26(4): 461–474.

Athanasou, James. 2014. "Home Schooling is a Perfect Alternative to Schools Stuck in a Time-Warp." *The Sydney Morning Herald*, September 10. Accessed September 10, 2014. http://www.smh.com.au/comment/home-schooling-is-a-perfect-alternative-to-schools-stuck-in-a-timewarp-20140909-10e9co.html

Baldwin, Christina I. 1993. "Christian Home Schooling in New Zealand." In *Godly Schools?: Some Approaches to Christian Education in New Zealand*, edited by B. Gilling, 4. Hamilton, New Zealand: University of Waikato in conjunction with Colcom Press.

Barcan, Alan. 1980. *A History of Australian Education*. Melbourne: Oxford University Press.

Barcan, Alan. 1988. *Two Centuries of Education in NSW: A history and Practical Perspective*. Kensington, NSW: University of New South Wales Press.

Barkley, Jenny. 2013. *Beyond Homeschooling New Zealand*. Unpublished manuscript, North Canterbury.

Barratt-Peacock, John. 1997. *The Why and How of Australian Home Education*. PhD, Faculty of Education, La Trobe University, Bundoora, Victoria.

Barratt-Peacock, John. 2008 [2003]. "Australian Home Education: A Model." *Evaluation and Research in Education*, 17(2–3): 101–111. DOI: 10.1080/09500790308668295

Barratt-Peacock, John. 2014. "Home Education in New South Wales." *Select Committee on Home Schooling*,54.24. Legislative Council of New South Wales. Parliament House, Sydney, NSW. http://www.parliament.nsw.gov.au/prod/parlment/committee.nsf/0/2e3cee18fe7eeb50ca257d330077a75d/$FILE/0054 Mr John Barratt-Peacock.pdf

Beirne, Jo-Anne. 1994. "Home Schooling in Australia." *Annual Home Schooling Conference*. Sydney, Australia: Annual Home Schooling Conference.

Bickers, Claire. 2014. "Home School Genius." *Sunday Times (Perth, Australia)*, November 2: 30.

BOSTES (Board of Studies Teaching & Educational Standards NSW). 2014. *Academic Outcomes of Home Schooling – Review of Research and Analysis of Statewide Tests*. Sydney: BOSTES. (Obtained under Freedom of Information Act).

Box, Lance. A. 2014. "A Proposal to Deschool, then Unschool Australian Biblical Christian Education." PhD: 226, School of Christian Education, Appomattox, VA: The New Geneva Christian Leadership Academy.

Broadhurst, Donna.1999. "Investigating Young Children's Perceptions of Home Schooling." *AARE Annual Conference*, 12, Melbourne.

Brosnan, Peter. 1991. "Child Competencies and Family Processes in Homeschool Families." MEd, The University of Melbourne, Victoria.

Burke, Kate. (2013). "Exploring Arts Practices in Australian Home Education: Understanding and Improving Practice Through Action Research." MEd, partial fulfillment: 95, University of Southern Queensland, Toowoomba.

Campbell, Carolyn I. 1993. "An Examination of the Religious Dimensions of Some Home Schoolers in Canterbury." Research Essay, Department of Religions Studies, 63. University of Canterbury, Christchurch, New Zealand.

Carins, Kathleen. 1997. "Home Education in Tasmania." *Open, Flexible and Distance Learning: Education and Training in the 21st Century*. 13th Biennial Forum of the Open and Distance Learning Association of Australia (ODLAA), Launceston, Tasmania.

Carins, Kathleen. 2002. "Graduates' Perceptions of the ACE Program as Preparation for Life Long Learning." BEd (Honours): 100 University of Tasmania, Hobart.

Carrick, John and Committee of Review of NSW Schools. 1989. *Report of the Committee of Review of New South Wales Schools*. Sydney: Committee of Review of New South Wales Schools.

Chapman, Anne and Thomas A. O'Donoghue. 2000. "Home Schooling: An Emerging Research Agenda." *Education Research and Perspectives*, 27(1): 19–36.

Chapman, Stuart. 2015. "Principal's Address" *School Newsletter*. Accessed February 9, 2016. https://drive.google.com/file/d/0B6yr-d-aI2gPX2tUWml2NWplX1k/view?pli=1

Clery, Erica. 1998. "Homeschooling: The Meaning that the Homeschooled Child Assigns to This Experience." *Issues in Educational Research*, 8(1): 1–13.

Collin, Ben. 2013. "Home is Where the Class is – the Rise of Homeschooling." *ABC Press Release*. Accessed April 28, 2015. http://www.abc.net.au/local/stories/2013/11/04/3883619.htm

Croft, Kathryn E. 2013. "So You're a Teacher, and You Home Educate? Why Would You, and How Does That Work for You? Exploring Motivations For, and Implementation Of,

Home Education by Qualified Teachers in Australia." MA: 155, Faculty of Education, Avondale College, Cooranbong, NSW.

Crump, Stephen and Colin Boylan. 2010. "Open our Eyes: Interactive Distance Learning for Isolated Communities." *ARCL Project*. University of Newcastle and Charles Sturt University, NSW.

Danaher, Patrick A E. 1998. *Beyond the Ferris Wheel: Educating Queensland Show Children*. Rockhampton, Queensland: Central Queensland University Press.

Danaher, Patrick. A. 2001. "Learning on the Run: Traveller Education for Itinerant Show Children in Coastal and Western Queensland." PhD, Central Queensland University, Rockhampton, Queensland.

Danaher, Patrick. A., Beverly Moriarty and Geoff Danaher. 2004. "Three Pedagogies of Mobility for Australian Show People: Teaching About, Through and Towards the Questioning of Sedentarism." *Melbourne Studies in Education*, 45(2): 47–66.

Danaher, Patrick A., Doug Wyer, and V.L. Bartlett. 1994. "Distance Education, Itinerant Education, and Home Schooling: Theorising Open Learning. *Open Learning '94: Proceedings of the 1st International Conference on Open Learning*. Brisbane: Queensland Open Learning Network.

Department of Education, Northern Territory (2016a). *Policy, Home Education*. Darwin: Department of Education, Northern Territory Government Accessed April 20, 2016 from https://www.nt.gov.au/__data/assets/pdf_file/0008/257975/Home-Education-Policy-2015.pdf.

Department of Education, N. T. (2016b). *Guidelines. Home Education*. Darwin: Department of Education, Northern Territory. Accessed April 20, 2016 from https://www.nt.gov.au/__data/assets/pdf_file/0006/257973/Home-Education-Guidelines-2015.pdf.

Department of Education and Training, Victoria. 2006a. "Frequently Asked Questions." *Education and Training Reform Bill – Home Schooling Consultation*.

Department of Education and Training, Victoria. 2006b. *Education and Training Reform Bill – Home Schooling Consultation*. Accessed August 14, 2006..

Donald, Donna-Marie. 1998. "Home Schoolers and the Public Library." MLibrary and InformationSt, partial fulfillment, Victoria University of Wellington, New Zealand.

Drabsch, Talina. 2013. "Home Education in NSW." *NSW Parliamentary Research Service*, e-brief 15. Sydney: NSW Parliamentary Research Service. Accessed April 28, 2015. http://www.parliament.nsw.gov.au/prod/parlment/publications.nsf/key/HomeEducationinNSW/$File/Home%20schooling%20GG%203.pdf

Education and Community Services Department (Australian Capital Territory (ACT)). 2001. *Registration of Home Schooling in the ACT (Policy Document). Education and Community Services Department*. Canberra: Education and Community Services Department.

Education Queensland, Queensland Parliament, Leigh Tabrett, and Bob McHugh. 2003. Home Schooling Review. *Home Schooling Review*, 30. Brisbane: Queensland Parliament.

Education Review Office. 1998. "The Quality of Homeschooling." *Education Review Office*. Wellington: New Zealand Ministry of Education.

Education Review Office. 2001. "Education Review Office Reviews of Homeschooled Students." *Education Review Office*. Wellington New Zealand Ministry of Education.

Ellis, Fiona 2005. "Learning in Home Based Early Childhood Settings: Parent Perspectives." MEdTeaching: *62*, Dunedin College of Education, New Zealand.

English, Rebecca 2013. "The Most Private Private Education: Home Education in Australia." *Home School Researcher*, 29(4): 1–7.

English, Rebecca. 2014. Submission into Home Education in NSW. *Select Committee on Home Schooling,* 9.7. Legislative Council of New South Wales. Parliament House, Sydney, NSW.http://www.parliament.nsw.gov.au/Prod/parlment/committee.nsf/0/78c3e8a93a4093e3ca257d2c000fe084/$FILE/0009%20Dr%20Rebecca%20English.pdf

English, Rebecca. 2015a. "Use Your Freedom of Choice: Reasons for Choosing Homeschool in Australia." *Journal of Unschooling and Alternative Learning,* 9(17): 1–18.

English, Rebecca. 2015b. "Too Cool for Home School? Accessing Underground Unschoolers with Web 2.0." In *Mainstreams, Margins and the Spaces In-between,* edited by K. Trimmer, A. Black, and S. Riddle, 112–124. London, New York: Routledge, Taylor & Francis Group.

Ennis, Rex. 1978. "A Case Study of Attempts to Change the Range of Educational Alternatives in a Provincial City". MEd, University of Canberra, ACT.

Follett, Jeffrey. 2003. "When Home and School Become One: Home Schooling and the Adolescent." Paper presented at *Our Adolescents: Issues for Teachers, Schools and Communities Conference*: Flaxton, Queensland.

Gannon, Ed. 2015a. "Government Must Monitor Home School Students to Ensure Children Don't Fall Through Cracks." *Weekly Times,* January 28 (16).

Gannon, Ed. 2015b. "Time for the Victorian Government to Get Strict on Home Schooling, Editorial." *Weekly Times,* January 28 (16). Accessed March,25, 2015. http://www.weeklytimesnow.com.au/news/opinion/time-for-the-victorian-government-to-get-strict-o-n-home-schooling/story-fnkerdb0-1227198099980

Green, Nicole C. 2006. "Everyday Life in Distance Education: One Family's Home Schooling Experience." *Distance Education,* 27(1): 27–44.

Gustafson, Robert S. 1989. "A Rationale for Home Education in Queensland with Recommended Model Legislation." *Submission to the Minister of Education.* Ashmore, Queensland: Queensland Parliament.

Habibullah, Aaleyah. 2004. "'Mum, When's Recess?' A Glimpse into Two Contexts of Home Schooling." BEd (Hons), Faculty of Education, Monash University, Clayton, Victoria.

Harding, Terrence J.A. 1997. "Why Australian Christian Academy Families in Queensland Choose to Home School: Implications for Policy Development." MEd, partial fulfillment, Queensland University of Technology, Brisbane.

Harding, Terrence J.A. 2003a. "A Comparison of the Academic Results of Students Monitored by the State, with the Academic Results of Students Not Monitored by the State." *Home Schooling Review,* 6. Queensland Parliament, Brisbane: Australian Christian Academy.

Harding, Terrence J.A. 2003b. A Submission for the Home Schooling Review. *Home Schooling Review.* Queensland Parliament, Brisbane: Australian Christian Academy.

Harding, Terrence J.A. 2003c. The Study – Home School Law Reform – The Parents Speak. *Home Schooling Review,* 18. Queensland Parliament, Brisbane: Australian Christian Academy.

Harding, Terry. 2004. *The Growing Home Education Phenomenon,* 10. Queensland: Australian Christian Academy.

Harding, Terry. 2006a. "A Study of Victorian Home Educator – Home School Law Reforms." Paper presented at *the Home Education Symposium,* Camberwell Civic Centre and Victorian Parliamentary Presentation, Melbourne.

Harding, Terry. 2006b. "Don't 'Fix' What Isn't Broken." Paper presented at the *Home Education Symposium,* Camberwell Civic Centre and Victorian Parliamentary Presentation, Melbourne.

Harding, Terrence J.A. 2008. "Parent Home Educators: Teaching Children at Home. A Phenomenographic Study." Paper presented at the *Changing Climates: Education for Sustainable Futures*, Australian Association for Research in Education Conference, Queensland University of Technology. Accessed April 28, 2015. http://www.aare.edu.au/publications-database.php/5656/Parent-home-educators–teaching-children-at-home

Harding, Terrence. J.A. 2011. "A Study Of Parents' Conceptions Of Their Roles As Home Educators Of Their Children." PhD: 295, Centre for Learning Innovation, Faculty of Education, Queensland University of Technology, Brisbane.

Harding, Terry. 2012. "Non-government Distance Education Funding: The Need for Equity in Australian Schooling." *Distance Education*, 33(2).

Harding, Terry. 2014. Submission to the Select Committee on Home Schooling Inquiry into Home Schooling. *Select Committee on Home Schooling*, 163.34. Legislative Council of New South Wales. Parliament House, Sydney, NSW. Accessed March 28, 2015. http://www.parliament.nsw.gov.au/prod/parlment/committee.nsf/0/2458bdec01efdea4ca257d39001cca78/$FILE/0163%20Dr%20Terry%20Harding.pdf

Harding, Terry and Ann Farrell. 2003. "Home Schooling and Legislated Education." *Australia and New Zealand Journal of Law and Education*, 8(1): 125–133.

Harding, Terry and Michael Whitrow. 2006. "Australia Has Its Own Homeschool Legal Defense Association."

Harding, Terry, Bruce McNeice, Robert Osmak, and Eleanor Sparks. 2003a. CHLQ Policy Statements and Recommendations. Unpublished manuscript, Brisbane.

Harding, Terry Bruce McNeice, Robert Osmak, and Eleanor Sparks. 2003b. CHLQ Survey: Preliminary Result. Unpublished manuscript, Brisbane.

Harding, Terry Bruce McNeice, Robert Osmak, and Eleanor Sparks. 2004. CHLQ Response to – Home Schooling Review – 1 October 2003. Unpublished manuscript, Brisbane.

Harp, Blair. 1998. "A Study of Reasons Why Some Central Queensland Parents Choose the Home Schooling Alternative for Their Children." MEd, partial fulfillment, Central Queensland University, Rockhampton, Queensland.

Hendy-Harris, Jean. 1983. *Putting the Joy Back into Egypt: An Experiment in Education.* Auckland, New Zealand: Hodder and Stoughton.

Hendy-Harris, Jean. 1996. Home Schooling. In *Gifted and Talented: New Zealand Perspectives*, edited by D. McAlpine and R. Moltzen, 455–465. Palmerston North, New Zealand: Education Research and Development Committee Press, Massey University.

Hendy-Harris, Jean. 2004. "Home Schooling." In *Gifted and Talented: New Zealand Perspectives*, edited by D. McAlpine and R. Moltzen, 2nd ed. Palmerston North, New Zealand: Kanuka Grove Press.

Hobson, Peter, and Cresswell, Roger. 1993. "Parental Rights, Education and Liberal Tolerance." *Discourse*, 14(1), 44–51.

Home Schooling Inquiry, NSW. Parliament. 2014. "Home Schooling in NSW." *Select Committee on Home Schooling.* Legislative Council of New South Wales. Parliament House, Sydney, NSW. Accessed April 28, 2015. http://www.parliament.nsw.gov.au/Prod/Parlment/committee.nsf/0/3a5b892ff6c728b6ca257da50019b2d0/$FILE/141203%20Final%20Report.pdf

Homeschooling Federation of New Zealand. 1996. "Homeschooling in New Zealand: Some Public Policy Issues." *Homeschooling Federation of New Zealand.* Auckland, New Zealand.

Homeschooling Federation of New Zealand. 2000. Working Party on Homeschooling. *Homeschooling Federation of New Zealand.* Auckland, New Zealand.

Honeybone, Ruth. 2000. "A South Australian Case Study Examining the Home-Schooling Experiences of Eight Primary School Aged Children and Their Families." BEd (Hons)., University of South Australia, Adelaide.

Hopkins, Drew. 1993. "Regulating Home Education: Parents' Rights, Children's Rights and the Role of the State." *Second National Conference of the Australian and New Zealand Education Law Association. Australian and New Zealand Education Law Association.* Adelaide: Australian and New Zealand Education Law Association.

Howison, Kelli. 1994. *Teaching a Second Language at Home.* BEd diss,. Dunedin College of Education, New Zealand.

Hunter, Roger. S. 1985. "Accelerated Christian Education and Church State Relationships in Education: A Case Study Analysis." EdD: 341. Southern Illinois University at Edwardsville, IL,

Hunter, Roger. 1989. "Home, School and Education." *Education, Equity and National Interests,* Australian and New Zealand Comparative and International Education Society, University College, University of Melbourne.

Hunter, Roger. 1990. Homeschooling. *Unicorn,* 16(3): 194–196.

Hunter, Roger. 1991. "Home, School and Education." ANZCIES, 182–191, Macquarie University, NSW.

Hunter, Roger. 1993. "Christian Fundamentalist Education: A Twentieth Anniversary." In *Godly Schools?: Some Approaches to Christian Education in New Zealand,* edited by Bryan Gilling, 4. Hamilton, New Zealand: University of Waikato in conjunction with Colcom Press.

Hunter, Roger. 1994. The Home School Phenomenon. *Unicorn,* 20(3): 28–37.

Jackson, Glenda. 1999. "Home Education: Legal Issues in Australia." MEdSt: 139, Monash University, Clayton, Victoria.

Jackson, Glenda. 2007. "Home Education Transitions with Formal Schooling: Student Perspectives." *Issues in Educational Research,* 17(1): 62–84. Accessed April 28, 2015. http://www.iier.org.au/iier17/jackson.html

Jackson, Glenda. 2008. "Australian Home Education and Vygotskian Learning Theory." *Journal of Australian Research in Early Childhood Education,* 15(1): 39–48. Accessed April 28, 2015. https://www.academia.edu/209223/Australian_Home_Education_and_Vygotskian_Learning_Theory

Jackson, Glenda M. 2009. "'More Than One Way to Learn': Home Educated Students' Transitions Between Home and School." PhD: 350, Faculty of Education. Monash University, Clayton. Victoria. Accessed April 28, 2015. http://arrow.monash.edu.au/hdl/1959.1/83110

Jackson, Glenda M. 2010. "Home Educated Students Transitions Into Mainstream Institutions: Professional Considerations." *International Education Research Conference,* 18. Canberra: AARE. Accessed April, 28, 2015. http://www.aare.edu.au/publications-database.php/5902/Home-educated-students-transitions-into-mainstream-institutions–Professional-considerations

Jackson, Glenda. 2014. "Australian Research on Home Education: And How It Can Inform Legislation and Regulation." Invited submission (0412) to the *Select Committee on Home Schooling,* 142.16. Legislative Council of New South Wales. Parliament House, Sydney, NSW. Accessed April 28, 2015. http://www.parliament.nsw.gov.au/prod/parlment/committee.nsf/0/d98a8fff92635cb5ca257d39001beaa5/$FILE/0142%20Ms%20Glenda%20Jackson%20(PHD).pdf

Jackson, G. 2015a. "Reflections on Australian Home Education Research and Vygotskian Learning Theory." In *International Perspectives on Home Education: Do we still need schools?* edited by P. Rothermel, 30–43. Houndsmill, England: Palgrave McMillan.

Jackson, Glenda. 2015b. *Summary of Australian and New Zealand Home Education Research*, 29. Melbourne: AHEAS.

Jackson Glenda. 2015c. "Home Educated Students and TAFE Accessibility." Invited submission to the Legislative Council of NSW, General Purpose Standing Committee No 6 Sess. 16 (2015), Doc 0204. Accessed February 9, 2016. http://www.parliament.nsw.gov.au/Prod/parlment/committee.nsf/0/fba0751c8cf4bd35ca257eb30076ca08/$FILE/0204%20Australian%20Home%20Education%20Advisory%20Service.pdf

Jackson, Glenda and Sonia Allan. 2010. "Fundamental Elements in Examining a Child's Right to Education: A Study of Home Education Research and Regulation in Australia." *International Electronic Journal of Elementary Education*, 2(3): 349–364. Accessed April 28, 2015. http://eric.ed.gov/?q=source%3a%22International+Electronic+Journal+of+Elementary+Education%22&id=EJ1052038

Jacob, Alison, John Barratt-Peacock, Kathleen Carins, Georgie Holderness-Roddam, Alistair Home, and Kate. Shipway. 1991. *Home Education in Tasmania: Report of Ministerial Working Party*, October (1991). Hobart, Tasmania: Government Printer.

Jefferson, S. 2010. "The Show Must Go On… and the School Shall Follow…"*Inside Teaching*, *1*(3): 6–8, 10–11.

Jeffrey, Deborah and Renee Giskes. 2004. "Home Schooling." *Research Publications and Resources Section of Queensland Parliament*, 62. Brisbane: Queensland Parliamentary Library.

Kidd, Theresa. 2008. "Cognitive Theories of Autism Spectrum Disorders: How do They Impact Children's Ability to Learn in Education Settings?: Coming Home: Exploring the Experiences of Mothers Home Educating Their Children with Autism Spectrum Disorder. BA(Hons): 74, Faculty of Computing, Health and Science, Curtin, Edith Cowan University, Western Australia.

Kidd, Theresa and Elizabeth Kaczmarek. 2010. "The Experiences of Mothers Home Educating Their Children with Autism Spectrum Disorder." *Issues in Educational Research*, 20(3): 257–275. Accessed April 28, 2015. http://www.iier.org.au/iier20/kidd.pdf

Knowles, J. Gary. 1987. "Understanding Parents Who Teach Their Children at Home: The Value of a Life History Approach." *Educational Research: Scientific or Political?* Conference for Australian Association for Research in Education, University of Canterbury, Christchurch, New Zealand.

Krivanek, Rosamnund. 1985. *Children Learn At Home: The Experience of Home Education.* Melbourne: Alternative Education Resource Group.

Krivanek, Rosamnund. 1988. "Social Development in Home Based Education." MA, University of Melbourne, Victoria.

Kunzman, Robert and Milton Gaither. 2013. "Homeschooling: A Comprehensive Survey of the Research." *Other Education: The Journal of Educational Alternatives*, 2(1): 4–59.

Layland, Judy. 2010. "Affordance of Participation Rights for Children in Home-based Education and Care: An Interactive Process Model of Participation – 2007." *Children & Society*, 24(5): 386–399. DOI: 10.1111/j.1099-0860.2009.00254.x

Layland, Judy. 2012. "Applying a Model of Participation Rights in Home-Based Early Childhood Settings: A Case Study." *Early Childhood Folio*, 16(2): 26–32.

Lampe, Suzanne. 1988. "Home Education: A Survey of Practices and Attitudes. MEdSt, partial fulfillment, Faculty of Education, Monash University, Clayton, Victoria.

Liberto, Giuliana. D. 2015. "Fringe Dweller in the Heart: An Autoethnographic Study of the Effects of Non-Consultative Regulatory Change on Home-Education in NSW." Unpublished thesis, BSocSc (Hons), Western Sydney University, Bankstown, NSW, Australia.

Lindsay, Katherine. 2003. "The Law of Home Schooling in Australia." *Brigham Young University Education and Law Journal*, (1): 83–93.

Lipscombe, Neil R. 1980. "John Holt – Reformer to Deschooler." MEd, University of New England, Armidale, NSW.

Maeder, Gerda. 1995. "Parents' Reasons in the Hunter Area for Choosing a Montessori School, Steiner School or Home Schooling for the Early Schooling of Their Children." MEd, University of Newcastle, NSW.

McAlevey, Fiona. 1995. "Why Home School?: An Exploration into the Perspectives on Education of Parents who Home School in Otago and Canterbury." MA (Ed), partial fulfillment, University of Canterbury, Christchurch, New Zealand.

McColl, Andrew. 2005. "ACE Homeschooling: The Graduates Speak." MEd, partial fulfillment Christian Heritage College, Brisbane.

McDonald, Jasmine. 2010. "Seeking Progressive Fit: A Constructivist Grounded Theory and Autoethnographic Study Investigating How Parents Deal with the Education of Their Child with an Autism Spectrum Disorder (ASD) Over Time." PhD, Graduate School of Education, University of Western Australia, Perth.

McDonald, Jasmine and Elaine Lopes. 2014. "How Parents Home Educate Their Children with an Autism Spectrum Disorder with the Support of the Schools of Isolated and Distance Education." *International Journal of Inclusive Education*, 18(1): 1–17.

McHugh, Winsome G. 2007. "Meeting the Davis Family: A Case Study Examination of Values Education and Home Schooling." BA/BTeaching (Hons) diss., Avondale College, Cooranbong, NSW.

Ministry of Education. 1998. *Research Unit Survey of Homeschooling Families*. Wellington: New Zealand Ministry of Education.

Ministry of Education. 2001. *Statistics on Homeschooling*. Wellington: New Zealand Ministry of Education.

Ministry of Education. 2008. *Homeschooling*. Wellington: New Zealand Ministry of Education.

Ministry of Education. 2014. Home Schooling. *Education Counts*.

Mulford, Bill, and Neville Grady. 2001. "Perceptions of Victorians and Tasmanians of Australian Government (State) Schools." *Leading and Managing*, 7(1): 93–108.

Mullaly, Allan. 1993. *Christian Home School Families: A Selective Study*. Griffith University. Queensland.

National Council of Home Educators New Zealand (NCHENZ). 2013. *NCHENZ*, Wellington, *Statistical Survey 2013*. Accessed April 20, 2015. http://www.nchenz.org.nz/wp-content/uploads/2014/09/Statistical-Survey-2013.pdf

National Council of Home Educators New Zealand (NCHENZ). 2015. *NCHENZ*, Wellington, *Statistical Survey 2015 Results*. Accessed April 20, 2015. http://www.nchenz.org.nz/wp-content/uploads/2015/03/NCHENZ-Statistical-Survey-2015-Results.pdf

Nicholls, Sandra H. 1997. "Home Schooling: A View of Future Education?" *Education in Rural Australia*, 7(1): 17–24.

Nolan, Catherine. A., and C. J. Patrick Nolan. 1992. "Home Schooling in New Zealand: An Alternative to Mainstream Education?" *AARE/NZARE Joint Conference*. Geelong: AARE.

Office of the Board of Studies (OBOS, New South Wales). 2000. *Home Education Study: Report of Findings*. Sydney: New South Wales Board of Studies.

Office of the Board of Studies (OBOS, New South Wales). 2004. *Home Education Study: Report of Findings*. Sydney: New South Wales Board of Studies.

Osmak, Robert. 2013. Education Queensland – The Sledge-Hammer Approach to Education. *PLATO QLD – Queensland School Syllabus Commentary*, May 20. Accessed April 28, 2015. http://www.platoqld.com/?p=1683

O'Sullivan, Gail. 1997. "Still a Challenge – Educating Children in the Bush." *Education Links*, (54): 27–28.

Paine, Beverly. (2015). "The Educating Parent." Accessed April 28, 2015. http://homeschoolaustralia.com/articles/unschoolingindex.html

Patrick, Kate. 1999. "Enhancing Community Awareness of Home-schooling as a Viable Educational Option. BEd (Primary) (Hons), Faculty of Education, Avondale College, Cooranbong, NSW.

Princiotta, Daniel, Stacey Bielick, and Christopher Chapman. 2006. *Home Schooling in the United States: 2003* (NCES 2006–042). Washington, DC: Institute of Education Science, US Department of Education.

Reader, Paul. 2009. " 'Learning in Community'. Making Sense of Home Education and the Changing Context of Schooling." *Entering the Age of an Educational Renaissance: Ideas for Unity of Purpose or Further Discord*, University of New England, NSW.

Reich, Robert. 2005. "Why Home Schooling Should Be Regulated." *Home Schooling in Full View*, edited by Bruce S. Cooper 109–129. Greenwich, CT: Information Age Publishing.

Reilly, Lucy. 2001. "How Western Australian Parents Manage the Home Schooling of their Children with Disabilities." BA (Hons), University of Western Australia, Perth.

Reilly, Lucy. 2004. "How Western Australian Parents Manage the Home Schooling of Their Children with Disabilities." *Doing the Public Good: Positioning Education Research*, 18. Melbourne: Australian Association for Research in Education. Accessed April 28, 2015. http://www.aare.edu.au/data/publications/2004/rei04240.pdf

Reilly, Lucy. 2007. "Progressive Modification: How Parents Deal with Home Schooling Their Children with Intellectual Disabilities." Unpublished PhD, University of Western Australia, Perth. Accessed April 20, 2016. http://www.aare.edu.au/data/publications/2004/rei04240.pdf

Reilly, Lucy, Anne Chapman, and Thomas O'Donoghue. 2002. "Home Schooling of Children With Disabilities." *Queensland Journal of Educational Research*, 18(1): 38–91.

Roache, Leo E. 2009. "Parental Choice and Education: The Practice of Homeschooling in New Zealand." EdD, partial fulfillment, Massey University, Palmerston, New Zealand. Accessed April 28, 2015. http://mro.massey.ac.nz/bitstream/handle/10179/1227/02whole.pdf?sequence=1&isAllowed=y

Roberts, Helen, 1999. "Home Based Child Care: A Parent's Perspective: An Option for Children with Special Needs." Dip in Early Intervention: 55, Auckland College of Education, New Zealand.

Rockliff, Jeremy, and Department of Education, Tasmanian Government. 2014. *Review of the Tasmanian Education Act*, 23. Hobart: Tasmanian Department of Education.

Ross, John (2015). "NSW Home-school Students Face High Fees for Vocational Training." *The Australian*, April 29. Accessed April 30, 2015, http://www.theaustralian.com.au/higher-education/nsw-home-school-students-face-high-fees-for-vocational-training/story-e6frgcjx-1227325422842

Rowntree, Suzannah. 2012. "Home Schooling: Education Outside the Box." *Quadrant*, 56(6): 74–78.

Sansom, Marie. 2014. "Home Schooling Surge Put Under the Microscope. Government News. Sydney, Education & Training, Health & Social Services, Law State." Accessed April28,2015.http://www.governmentnews.com.au/2014/08/home-schooling-surge-put-microscope/

Select Committee on Home Schooling, Legislative Council of the New South Wales Parliament. 2014. *Home Schooling in NSW*. Sydney, NSW. Accessed April 28, 2015. http://www.parliament.nsw.gov.au/homeschooling?open&refnavid=CO4_1 http://www.parliament.nsw.gov.au/Prod/Parlment/committee.nsf/0/3A5B892FF6C728B6CA257DA50019B2D0?open&refnavid=CO5_1

Shim, Hee Kyung 2000. "ESL Reading Tutoring at Home Using 'Pause, Prompt and Praise' and Pre-Reading Activities." MA diss., University of Auckland, New Zealand.

Simich, Melinda. 1998. "How Parents who Home School Their Children Manage the Process." Med, Nedlands, University of Western Australia.

Simpson, Andrew P. 1999. "Literacy, Learning and Funds of Knowledge in Alternative Families." BEd (Hons), Southern Cross University, Lismore, NSW.

Smith, Alexandra. 2016. "Home-schooled Kids Perform Better in NAPLAN: Report." *The Sydney Morning Herald,* February 7. Accessed February 9, 2016 http://www.smh.com.au/nsw/homeschooled-kids-perform-better-in-naplan-report-20160204-gmlgu9.html#ixzz3zTETJf71

Smith, Craig S. 2003. A Brief History of Home Education in New Zealand (Parts 1–4). *TEACH Bulletin*, 73(4): 2. Accessed April 28, 2015. http://hef.org.nz/about-us/a-brief-history-of-home-education-in-new-zealand-by-craig-smith/

Stroobant, Emma. 2006. "Dancing to the Music of Your Heart: Home Schooling the School-Resistant Child. A Constructionist Account of School Refusal." PhD: 265. University of Auckland, New Zealand. Accessed April 28, 2015. http://hdl.handle.net/2292/2429

Stroobant, Emma, and Alison Jones 2006. "School Refuser Child Identities." *Discourse: Studies in the Cultural Politics of Education*, 27(2): 209–223.

Symes, Colin. 2012. "Remote Control: A Spatial-History of Correspondence Schooling in New South Wales, Australia." *International Journal of Inclusive Education*, 16(5): 503–517.

Thomas, Alan. 1998. *Educating Children at Home*. London: Cassell.

Thomas, Alan. 2014. "Home Education and Unschooling or Autonomous Learning." *Select Committee on Home Schooling,* 159.4. Legislative Council of New South Wales. Parliament House, Sydney, NSW. Accessed April 28, 2015. http://www.parliament.nsw.gov.au/prod/parlment/committee.nsf/0/d3400b443652ded0ca257d540082fd2f/$FILE/0159%20Dr%20Alan%20Thomas.pdf

Thornton-Smith, Marie-Louise. 1989. "John Holt: Radical Romantic: A Study of His Educational Writings." MEd. University of Melbourne, Victoria.

Tomazin, Farah. 2015. "Homeschool Parents Deserve State Vouchers to Teach Kids, Says Key Crossbencher. *The Age,* April 26. Accessed April 26, 2015. http://www.theage.com.au/victoria/homeschool-parents-deserve-state-vouchers-to-teach-kids-says-key-crossbencher-20150425-1msm3z.html?stb=fb

Townsend, Ian. 2012. Thousands of Parents Illegally Home Schooling. *Background Briefing,* January 30. Accessed April 13, 2014. http://www.abc.net.au/news/2012-01-28/thousands-of-parents-illegally-home-schooling/3798008

Trevaskis, Rosanne. 2005. *Home Education – The Curriculum of Life*. MEd, Faculty of Education, Monash University, Melbourne, Victoria.

Varnham, Sally. 2008. "My Home, My School, My Island: Home Education in Australia and New Zealand." *Public Space: The Journal of Law and Social Justice*, 2(Art 3): 1–30.

Varnham, Sally, and Joan Squelch. 2008. "Rights, Responsibilities and Regulation – The Three Rs of Education: A Consideration of the State's Control Over Parental Choice in Education." *Education and the Law*, 20(3).

Wallace, Brenda. M. 1999. "Home Schooling: Why Do Families Choose to Homeschool Their Children?" BEd. Dunedin College of Education, New Zealand.

Welner, Karianne M., and Kevin Welner. 1999. "Contextualising Homeschooling Data: A Response to Rudner." *Education Policy Analysis Archives*, 7(13).

White, E. Jayne. 2003. "In search of quality: a journey for family day care." Master of Arts in Ed: 246, Victoria University of Wellington, New Zealand.

White, Richard T. 1983. "The End of Schools as We Know Them?" Faculty of Education, Monash University, Clayton, Victoria.

Whitehead, Lisa. 2006. "Government's Controversial Plan to Regulate Home Schooling. 1–3."

Wight, Susan. 2006. "Home Education and Bureaucracy." *Directions in Education: Australian Council for Educational Leaders*, 15(6), 1.

Williams, Rose. 2004. Accelerated University Access. *Mindscape*, 24(1): 7–11.

15

Theories, Practices, and Environments of Learning and Home Education in Latin America

Erwin Fabián García López, Diego Fernando Barrera Tenorio, and Wills Emilio Alejandro Fonseca
Translated by Robert Lyon

Introduction

This text brings together several different perspectives on home education and descholarization in Latin America, movements that continue to grow throughout the region. The purpose of the text is to review and question the traditional theories, practices, and environments of learning and education. We justify the relevance of the topic from social and pedagogical perspectives, and we also present an overview of the legal status of the issue in several Latin American countries, a philosophical reflection on the future of home education in Latin America, and a Brazilian case study. In Latin America, the origins of the educational thought known as descholarization can be traced to the works of Tomás Amadeo Vasconi during the 1960s, particularly *School As a Social Institution* (1963) and *Education, Social Structure, and Change* (1964). Through a sociological perspective rooted in structural functionalism, Vasconi shows how schools and teachers tend to make decisions that prepare students for a certain professional status in the future. By doing this, they are also preparing students for a specific socioeconomic status (Suasnábar and Isola 2011). In the 1970s, this first sociological insight into the role of schooling was further developed with the founding of the Center for Intercultural Documentation (CIDOC) in Cuernavaca, directed by Valentina Borremans and coordinated by Ivan Illich (Zaldivar 2012). Nevertheless, our analysis and the autoethnographic processes that we discuss only cover a shorter period of about fifteen years.

Descholarization is a dynamic, complex, and problematic concept. The editorial request from the United States from which this text originates uses the term "home education," an important term in academic literature today (Knowles, Marlow, and Muchmore 1992). The action-research group that we are a part of considers

The Wiley Handbook of Home Education, First Edition. Edited by Milton Gaither.

descholarization to be a comprehensive concept that covers and includes various terms and concepts that have emerged in Latin America. These include homeschooling, liberatory education, natural learning, self-teaching, and self-directed learning (García López 2011). The term "unschooling" seems to exclude or just not emphasize some ideas that we have come to believe about these forms of education that take place away from the traditional school. Beyond just a combination of different educational practices, the descholarization movement can also be thought of as a category in which to group the things that people learn outside of traditional schooling. There have been several attempts to institutionalize the principle of descholarization as a "method" by calling it "indirect instruction" in which, "the teacher becomes an observer and companion" (Rodríguez 2013). Nevertheless, in these methods there is still a "teacher," an authority figure. This is a hierarchical structure that goes against what these practices are intended to challenge. One of the primary objectives of the descholarization movement is to minimize the institutionalization of human beings. Some of the underlying questions of the descholarization movement include:What is education? What is schooling? How far removed from traditional schooling are each of the terms and practices embodied within the descholarization movement? Why should society move away from schooling? What are the religious, political, ethical, and ideological motivations that make families want to join the descholarization movement, to teach their children in various ways, or even to not teach them at all? The term "teaching" should be questioned since it involves an imposition. As such, we prefer to speak of accompanying learning. "To teach" means "to show something" and etymologically comes from the Old English *tǣcan,* "to show, present, point out," of Germanic origin. It is related to *token*, from an Indo-European root shared by the Greek *deiknunai,* "to show," and Latin *dicere,* "to say." The Spanish verb *enseñar* comes from the Vulgar Latin insignāre, the present active infinitive of *insignō*, from Latin *signō* (Wiktionary 2015). If "to teach" means "to show something," (that is, a piece of culture) then it should not be taken to mean "to *impose* something." Teaching must not mean the imposition of content, but rather the facilitation of learning. In our experience, conventional forms of education do not facilitate learning. As a phenomenon, education can occur in spite of school. That is, even a person who attends school and endures conscious learning may also consciously or unconsciously learn things outside of school and outside of the ways that society indoctrinates people through hierarchies, regulations, and guidelines that force others to behave "properly." In the words of Albert Einstein, "The only thing that interferes with my learning is my education."

The descholarization movement is as complex as the human beings that take part in it (Morin 1999a). It is a relational form of education in which parents accompany their children in their learning. Although we have mentioned that the concept of descholarization can be used to refer to various terms and practices, it can also be used as a category for the things that people learn when they are removed from the practices of traditional schooling. Without trying to generalize about this inherently heterogeneous phenomenon, we believe that the best forms of descholarization include accompanying the learning of the children without imposing culture, directions, goals, or ideological concepts. By characterizing the descholarization movement as a collection of complex processes, we are trying to get across that "its various components are inseparable. There is an interdependent, interactive, and retroactive connection between the object of knowledge and its context" (Morin 1999b). We also mean that despite the seemingly inescapable need to find similarities, common themes, guidelines, and the causes of the social phenomena that we observe, we cannot predict the kind of results that will come from them. While we are constantly on alert against the mental enslavement that permeates daily life, we cannot avoid acknowledging that the proliferation of information and communications technology that allows both rapid and wide dissemination of ideas is a real factor in the development of communities of parents that take part in the descholarization movement. It is also a real factor in structuring virtual communities regardless of geographic location. However, we must not think that the descholarization movement should solely rely on the existence of these technologies.

One of the most important things about the descholarization movement is its fluidity. Our intent is not to create a static or all-encompassing pedagogical model, but rather to encompass the forms of education that some families follow in order to preserve their children's right to play freely, to freely develop their own interests, and the opportunity to freely make mistakes and learn from their errors. The definition of the descholarization movement cannot become a mold or a mental prison for those who participate in it. Nor can it become a set of methods that promote the isolation and indoctrination of human beings. In relation to this idea, Pedro García Olivo (2014) defends the fluid conception of the descholarization movement in an interesting way. He says that if the freedom of those who choose to join the movement can only be maintained by avoiding the development of a fixed mindset and panoptic institutionalization, the concept of descholarization will continue to elude us.

When one reviews the sociohistorical origin of an emerging movement like the descholarization movement that has such potential to impact social structures and that arises from the very core of the mechanisms that sustain these structures, it would seem like common sense to say that the movement stems from a social problem. Latin American countries have traditionally been identified in the social sciences as supporters of leftist libertarian ideals which thrive thanks to the magnitude of social inequality that exists in the region. However, it is important to note that the individuals and families of the communities that practice forms of descholarization should not be identified with these stereotypes. The Latin American leftists, although numerous and diverse, generally still cling to the belief that physical schooling is a sign of progress and development. They subject the masses to the standards and norms of traditional education. It would almost be too optimistic to think that these leftists could desire the freedom that the descholarization movement considers as something inherent to the human condition.

It is interesting to compare the growth of the descholarization movement in Latin America with the growth of homeschooling in the United States. In 1992, Knowles, Marlow, and Muchmore published a description of the beliefs of homeschoolers in the US. They say, "Our general understanding is that the extensive expansion of this population is largely a result of the growth of a segment of the movement with powerful religious and ideological underpinnings." Although these claims cannot be considered entirely valid for Latin America, it is worth noting that there is a certain similarity. While an American newspaper described homeschoolers in 1986 as, "an odd mixture of ex-hippies and straight arrow conservatives" (Knowles, Marlow, and Muchmore 1992), in Latin America it is a family's economic condition that determines whether a family will adhere to the ideas of descholarization. Although the upper-middle class families of the movement are usually more visible, there are many lower-class families who inquire about these alternatives for various reasons. In some cases, they do not have the financial means to continue paying for the education of their children. There are also cases of families who have minimal or no belief in schooling. Likewise, there are many groups, either vulnerable or marginalized because of their ethnicity, culture, or political beliefs, that have distanced themselves from the school.

Another common misconception from the social sciences is that Catholicism, a fundamental part of education across all of Latin America and long considered the perpetuating force of Spanish colonial structures, could be a relevant part of the descholarization movement given that it has historically represented tension in the region between the trends of secularization and confessionalism since the beginning of the nationalist movements during the nineteenth century (Ossenbach 1993). However, evidence shows that the dominant factor in the search for alternatives to traditional schooling in the region is not the rejection of religious education itself. In fact, the descholarization movement in Latin America is growing rapidly because of Christian families, both Catholic and non-Catholic, approaching these forms of education from their religious points of view. They are trying to avoid things at school, intentional or not, that are contrary "to the fundamental principles of a Christian worldview," or more generally, "to the good of the children" (Hijos del Altísimo 2013). Most families who homeschool due to religious beliefs are not motivated by a desire to change the form of teaching that we see as indoctrination. Instead, they want to change where the schooling takes place. In the words of Christopher J. Klicka (2002):

> The teachers in a home school are the parents, and these parents have a commitment to make the necessary career sacrifices in order to personally provide an education for their children. For the majority, their primary reason to homeschool is to teach their children Christian principles and give them a thorough education – a reaction to the steady academic and moral decline in the public schools. Furthermore, these homeschooled children are protected from negative socialization, such as drugs, sexually transmitted diseases, and violence present in the public schools. Instead, the homeschooled child is trained in the traditional values on which our country was founded.

With the idea of sacrifice, the teaching of religious principles, the barrier against a corrupt society, and the continuation of traditional values, this behavior has more to do with millennialism (Cohn 1993) than a new perspective on learning or the descholarization movement.

One of the most important things to understand about the people and families that take part in the descholarization movement in Latin America is that, whether they are in favor of homeschooling or unschooling, they recognize that people have a right to knowledge and that knowledge can mean power in society. Nevertheless, our particular form of descholarization does question why educational institutions must intervene in child development. In our opinion, children are fully developed, and they should not be considered adolescent or lacking in some way. They should have legal rights starting from childhood. Studies show that the evolutionary psychology theories of authors like Piaget are quite wrong because babies have a very pronounced ability to abstract from the first months of life. They use counterfactual conditionals to imagine different possible realities and to apply statistical probability models to establish laws on the functioning of reality. They are thus able to anticipate events (Dragow 2014). Moreover, the rights of children constitute an area that is constantly in flux. This is a battleground between different points of view. The existence of a universal declaration of the rights of children has not changed or overthrown traditional parenting practices. Some families think that the government and the community (that is, society as a whole) should have no power over the lives of their children. Other families believe that children are virtually the property of their parents. We have encouraged discussion on these issues in order to establish the extent of society's responsibility, even in extreme cases where the government has the need to intervene when there is a high risk of infringement of the rights of children.

While those who home educate and those who study this issue can agree on the argument of Sugata Mitra and Nicholas Negroponte that as a species we have made knowledge obsolete (Mitra 2013), it is important to emphasize that this claim involves the basic assumption that access to knowledge is universal and easily accessed through information and communications technology (ICT). These are not always the prevailing conditions of Latin America (Raygada Watanabe 2003). The sociospatial population distribution, gaps in local coverage and infrastructure, and the things that traditional schools are responsible for, such as the possibility of offering distance education, are reasons that families opt for alternative forms of education like homeschooling. Although we cannot determine how much of an impact these factors have on the growth of the descholarization movement, our opinion is that many field laborers believe in traditional education and that if they do believe in some form of descholarized education, they are not doing it for a specific educational or learning purpose.

Besides the lack of resources and the digital divides which exist not only between developed and developing countries, but also between social classes and urban and rural populations within countries of the region (Chaparro 2007), there are other factors that give the descholarization movement its unique sense of rebellion and unavoidable change. This character that is expressed and required in some cases is closely related to the breakdown of the cultural processes that create poverty. Institutionalized education involves the intentional subduing of the freewill of children, even though their right to self-determination is said to be defended, ironically, through the imposition of compulsory schooling. These individuals are being taught poverty, a modernized poverty that is developed by comparing standards of living and levels of consumption by favoring the majority that are eager to be educated at the expense of minorities. Thanks to the institutionalized system that makes education a luxury good, society has set itself toward the inevitable decision to end school (Illich 1971) as an instrument of social cohesion and as a way to transmit and acquire culture. This is because school by nature tends not only to promote inequity but ultimately to create a climate of violence (Gómez Arévalo 2010).

In the social sciences, education ends up either being represented by economic variables like GDP growth or by the reproduction of social structures and patterns of social behavior. There are families who homeschool with tutors and who often do not pay attention to their children. They only want their children to be sufficiently competitive in the labor market or in another area. Some families, by trying to be unique and innovative, inadvertently end up preparing their children for the neoliberal system of economics and the demands of control societies as mentioned by Deleuze (2006). However, in our opinion, any learning process or process of accompanying such learning should have emotions as a central component. In the forms of descholarization that we consider to be most appropriate, the parents and children are compelled by something that no quantitative argument manages to take into account: the joy of parenting, learning, and co-learning that one experiences as a parent when one discovers one's own enthusiasm and that of one's children, something that seems to be increasingly lost today in our inflexible society that values "productivity." While neuroscience continues to unravel the complex biochemical mechanisms that trigger this joy and that indicate that enthusiasm is the engine of brain development, developing countries appear to be focusing on turning off those mechanisms of joy and enthusiasm in order to focus on a quantitative productivity that is cost-efficient but sterile in the qualitative dimensions of human life. In the words of anthropologist Dr José María Garrido Mayo:

> In the industrialized countries of the West, independence, individual success, private property and competitiveness are encouraged, while in traditional cultures, the concept of community prevails over the individual, so that social cohesion is promoted. Therefore, the values that are encouraged are reciprocity, mutual aid, cooperation, and social solidarity. There is no doubt that parenting standards such as breastfeeding, nutrition, sleeping arrangements, attitudes towards crying children, the amount of physical contact with babies, etc. are not the result of chance, but rather they have a social function. [...] As such, changing parenting practices could change society (Garrido Mayo 2013).

Because of this, the research in Colombia has been conducted from an autoethnographic perspective that revolves around the questions: is it possible to educate without indoctrination?; and do we want our children to serve others or do we want them to be happy? (Rodrigañez 2010). This brings us to another consideration: where does the indoctrination of our children begin? Child development is delicate and worthy of consideration because it is misunderstood. If we conceive of children as empty vessels, it implies that every parent has an obligation and a right to fill that void with their own opinions, to make their mark, and to teach rather than accompany. Any epistemology that disregards humans' intrinsic drive to learn makes us suspicious of indoctrination and that the student's creativity is being constrained. This can lead to the limitation and stereotyping of people in an ideological, political, economic, religious, or cultural manner. In his book *Sweet Leviathan: Critics, Victims and Antagonists of the Welfare State*, Pedro García Olivo (2014) presents a form of descholarization which seems to promote the resistance to indoctrination that we suggest. The most important aspects of his educational philosophy include community education in which people are educated by everyone in society throughout their lives, and free education which occurs through spontaneous relationships, informality, and a lack of administrative regulation. Another important aspect of his educational philosophy is education without self-problematization. This is education that is not looked at as a separate part of life or that segregates specific knowledge. In this form of education it is not possible to separate learning from play or work. Finally, García Olivo also discusses education that corresponds with a more egalitarian society and traditional practices of direct democracy or openly anti-political arrangements that negate assumptions of the rule of law and the liberal concept of "citizenship" (188).

Another form of descholarization that is crucial for us to mention involves the work of Arno Stern at The Research Institute for the Semiology of Expression and his own experiences with his son André Stern, a man who never went to school. The father discovers what, from a structuralist perspective, would be called an "invariant" in some places, or as he calls it, "formulation." Formulation is an observable phenomenon, yet also a "complex, original, structured, and universal" practice (Stern 2000). Formulation happens when there is no pressure or outside influence, when the presence of others only involves having playmates and not spectators, and when the accompanying practitioner facilitates formulation and is not a referential or receptive figure. It is a nonverbal phenomenon that happens naturally. It is like a collection of homemade art that is drawn, captured, or represented as if it were separated from true art and lacking the elements, laws, and habits of it. Play, to a greater extent than the therapeutic practice of Stern's formulation, frees the individual from depending on external models. Play also develops a positive self-esteem. In the words of Martín Vega and José Miguel Castro, "when we are free of structure, comparisons, and judgment, fear disappears, boundaries are broken, and we evolve beyond what we imagine to be possible. One can then improvise, explore, create, and take part in the most serious and rigorous activity that exists: play" (Martin and Castro n.d.). André Stern is living testimony to this practice. He has spent his entire life playing without pressure, without structure, without people telling him what to do, and without positive reinforcement. As a musician, composer, luthier, journalist, and author of the book *I Never Went to School*, at his conferences André Stern describes spontaneous enthusiasm as the central element off which his learning was built. He presents himself as a representative example of the theory of the German neurobiologist Gerald Hüther whose proposals on brain development seem to involve a reaffirmation and extension of theories by researchers such as Piaget and Bruner. To Hüther, learning is a physical and emotional experience that is successfully achieved through the release of chemical messengers from the neuroplastic emotional centers. We are able to learn thanks to the chemical reaction that enthusiasm produces. As a structure, Hüther says that, apart from the oldest structures and those that are indispensable to survival, the brain is not "finished." Connections are established through use. Use is promoted through novelty and interest since these things expand existing connections. When connections are not used, they are dismantled. These connections represent certain bodily and mental states that Hüther calls "inner images," patterns or plans of action that help an organism respond to change." The mental state that develops from these experiences is what people use to evaluate their sensory perceptions (input). One's mental state determines what one pays attention to, what is not noticed, what is cared about, and what is feared." That is how this mechanism influences learning. It forms attitudes towards it (Hüther 2012).

When we stop considering education to be an intentional and forced attempt to teach something and when we open ourselves to a constructive social conception of it, it becomes clearer that wanting to be educated is an inherent part of human social-structure and that it is an integral part of humanity's inherent social dimension. It is important to make clear that we are not trying to support the descholarization movement with a constructivist educational foundation. Rather, we are trying to show that all forms of education can be understood as a constructive social interaction that involves peers, not hierarchical relationships. In the words of De Zubiría (2004), "it is impossible to discuss human culture without mentioning people teaching each other." Jerome Bruner, one of the psychologists who led the cognitive revolution under the simple and powerful principle that "learning and thinking are never isolated from each other" (Bruner 2006), states that "we educate children by expressing the main goals of our culture, the highest aspirations that they can reach for, and a sense of the limits of human possibility" (2). Nowadays cultures cannot be unambiguously associated with a country, territory, ethnic group, or socioeconomic condition. New cultural groups are being formed as communities that share common interests are connected by various means of communication.

The essential characteristic of the learning process is what we call the trigger of learning, a difficulty or simple imbalance that alters the condition of tranquility or homeostasis. Bruner (2006) describes the trigger of learning as young people "entering a state on the brink of anxiety." This is created when adults put young people in new situations. Although both the desire for novelty and curiosity can be considered biological characteristics since they are shared by primates in general, only humans structure play and rituals for children with an end goal in mind (149). The subtle difference between intrinsic curiosity and curiosity that is channeled into socially acceptable activities constitutes the distinctive essence of humans, the social component of education that acts as a means of transmission and acquisition of culture.

A similar theory is central to the learning theory of Jean Piaget. According to Piaget, "There is something innate that motivates us to look for order, structure, and predictability in the things around us. When our internal structures explain our surroundings, there is balance. When they are unable to explain an occurrence, there is imbalance, and the struggle to regain balance begins. Learning only occurs when the imbalance is introduced" (Escamilla 2000, 52). This imbalance can be understood from the perspective of human evolution as adapting to the habitat. In other words, the intelligence involved in learning, understood as a strategy for human survival, is the opportunistic kind of knowledge, not the specialist kind like the two modes of adaptation to a habitat identified by Desmond Morris (Bruner 2006). "The non-specialized rely [for survival] on their high flexibility rather than morphological or behavioral specialization" (148). Learning is our essential survival strategy.

From an anthropological point of view, Bruner (2006) affirms the difficulty of discussing the teaching of prehominids and "primitive" man. One must look at the hunter-gatherer societies existing today in order to gain some understanding. Bruner finds it significant that in the extensive film documentation on the !Kung bushmen, a population of hunter-gatherers living in the isolated northwest of Botswana, the northeast of Namibia, and southern Angola (Barnard 2007), one virtually never finds an instance of teaching that takes place outside of the situational context in which the learning behavior is relevant. "No one teaches outside of the situation where the learning is relevant like in a school setting. Actually, there is nothing like a school" (Bruner 2006). In any case, as long as we understand that among the bushmen there are instructional interactions between adults and children (148), we can say that schooling is just an institutionalized form of a natural process, a product of the decontextualization of the human educational process. Language, especially written language, plays an important role in this since it is a means of transmitting knowledge. It is written language that legitimizes the storage of decontextualized information since it can be retrieved asynchronously and universally. It shifts the emphasis from "know how" to "know what" (153).

This question of what school teaches us brings to mind the famous phrase of Seneca, "Non scolae sed vitae discimus," which translates to "We learn not for school but for life." This serves as the title of an essay by Engeström (1996) in which the author presents the acquisition of knowledge in school as a "historically formed process." By focusing on correcting a misconception about the cause of the phases of the moon (which, according to his research, was entirely confused with the cause of lunar eclipses), Engeström explains that in this historically formed process, experiences are encapsulated to the point that people have difficulty questioning what is taught in textbooks. It impedes them from doubting the textbook or at least recognizing it as "trying to fix and crystallize certain generally accepted conceptions of an era."

The Legality of Descholarization in Latin America

Its questionable legality is a fundamental part of the descholarization movement. All social institutions depend on education in order to persist through future generations. How much of an impact could the descholarization movement have on social structures? In the future, its impact could be considerable. Although the goal is to get away from the established forms of schooling, this phenomenon (just like many others) could easily be assisted by the status quo. The descholarization movement is growing, especially in Latin America, but it is still new enough that governments have not tried to explicitly ban it through some kind of regulation. When we speak of the "status quo," we are actually employing a euphemism. We are speaking of the post-imperialist empire as understood by Hardt and Negri (2002). The new decentralized and de-territorialized form of sovereignty that is permanently transforming the capitalist system tries to turn anything fluid into a way to make money. The descholarization movement is not unaffected by this dynamic. That is why in the introduction we mentioned the need to keep considering descholarization as a fluid concept and that the political left of Latin America does not desire the freedom that is such an integral part of the movement. It would be easier from a political point of view for nation-states, although in decline, to build a legislative wall so that they can act fairly autonomously. However, today García Olivo's "Sweet Leviathan" has become tangible. It was established, without notice, through cultural mechanisms and promises of material welfare which are very difficult to escape. Since the main form of institutionalized sociocultural control is the school itself, the descholarization movement tries to keep its opposition in plain sight. The risk is that as a teaching method it could become even more useful to capitalist logic than the traditional school itself.

In Colombia as in other Latin American countries (except Brazil, a country which explicitly prohibits descholarized education, collaborative self-directed learning, and homeschooling), the freedoms to teach, learn, research, and give lectures are fundamental rights and principles of education that go hand in hand with the cultural and social diversity. These federal laws explicitly establish the parents' right to choose the education that will be given to their children. Furthermore, beyond the family, the law states that the government and society are also responsible for the care and education of children. In Colombia, some rulings (such as, among others, the ruling SU-337 of 1999) of the Constitutional Court, the main protector of the integrity and the supremacy of the Constitution, reaffirm that it is primarily the role of the family to choose their child's education. However, fighting for alternative schooling is a complicated issue in a country like Colombia where basic human rights are not guaranteed for most people. In Colombia, as in other Latin American countries where educational research is conducted, most parties involved (meaning family, government officials, teachers, researchers, and the administrative staff of educational institutions) believe that education is equivalent to schooling. What is even more shocking is that most of these people also believe that the school is the main institution responsible for child welfare. With regards to education, some of the required standards and basic educational regulations that specifically aim to reduce the growing dropout rates are actually decreasing the chances of official accreditation for descholarized education, collaborative self-directed learning, and homeschooling before 18 years of age. The most explicit example of this kind of regulation is the Ministry of National Education's Decree 299 of 2009 which "regulates some aspects related to the validation of the high school diploma in one exam." While education experts from both teaching and legal perspectives accept that descholarized education, collaborative self-directed learning, and homeschooling are valid alternatives to school, the message spread by government authorities has been that school is a mandatory part of a child's education. This point of view violates the rights of children and causes both confusion and worry among families that practice descholarized education, collaborative self-directed learning, or homeschooling.

In the diversity that exists in Latin America, it is important to notice how legislation evolves along with society's level on the Kelsen pyramid. Their constitutions defend the freedoms to teach and learn, but lower laws do not recognize the distinction between schooling and education. These laws can be shocking and controversial since there are laws that permit the choice of education for minors. Furthermore, there are other provisions that should provide a legal basis for descholarized forms of education.

Colombia

Articles 27 and 71 of Columbia's constitution mention, among other regulations, the freedoms to teach, learn, and pursue knowledge. Paragraph 3 of Article 26 of the Universal Declaration of Human Rights and paragraph 4, Article 68 of the Constitution give parents the right to choose the kind of education they want for their children. At the same time, paragraph 3 of Article 67 of the Constitution charges the government, society, and the family with education, "which is mandatory between five and fifteen years of age and must include at least one year of preschool and nine years of general education" (it indicates mandatory education, not schooling). Furthermore, Article 37 of Law 1098 of 2006, The Code of Children and Adolescents, provides several fundamental freedoms for children and adolescents such as the free development of personality and personal autonomy, and the freedom to choose a profession or occupation. Finally, the decrees 2832 of 2005 and 299 of 2009 deal with the validation of grades in formal education and the validation of studies for people who have not completed one or more grades of any level of education.

However, in the relation to this, the following laws can restrict what is described. For example, Article 7 of Law 115 of 1994 designates the family as being primarily responsible for the education of their children, but it outlines that this is accomplished by "enrolling their children in educational institutions." Article 10 of the same law states that formal education takes place in official educational institutions. Furthermore, Article 52, paragraph 8 of The Code of Children and Adolescents orders the appropriate authority to verify that the right to education is being upheld by enrolling all children and teenagers in the educational system. Finally, subsection 2 of Decree 1860 of 1994 states that authorities may require the presentation of student ID to verify compliance with the constitutional and legal obligation of enrollment in educational institutions. In other words, Colombia makes school attendance explicitly mandatory. To add some additional context, note that in accordance with Article 9 of Law 715 of 2001, "an educational institution is referred to as a group of people and resources that is offered by public authorities or private individuals whose purpose is to provide one year of preschool and at least (and on average) nine grades of general education. In order to provide educational services, they must be licensed for operation or have official recognition."

Ecuador

In agreement No. 067-13, dated April 8, 2013, Ecuador's Minister of Education, Monica Franco Pombo, issued regulations on homeschooling. This is a form of education that is, according to Article 1 of the agreement:

> partially in-person and rather unusual. Its implementation is based on one or several assumptions which the law takes into account. As such, this legal precept is based on legal and political provisions. The first of these is the constitutional articles 26 and 29. Article 26 recognizes education as essential to a good life. Therefore, it is a priority for public policy. Article 29 declares that the government guarantees the freedom of education, "and the right of people to learn in their own language and cultural atmospheres. Parents, or guardians, are free to choose an education for their children that is consistent with their principles and beliefs."

However, the Organic Law of Intercultural Education in Article 2, paragraph s, states that one of the principles of educational activity is flexibility. In conclusion, a political argument would be to respond to the request from some parents for authorization to take the education of their children into their homes.

Quality assurance In order to achieve quality homeschooling, the aforementioned agreement declares, among other things, that:

- It is only applicable for the basic, general level of education.
- The child's legal guardian must explicitly request permission to homeschool from the District Director of Education. A specialized committee will consider the request.
- The District Director of Education shall assign an educational institution that will support and monitor the homeschooling children.
- The parents, guardians, or representatives of the students must demonstrate sufficient teaching ability through certified coursework in education or a related area.
- The parents must either have enough time to assist the child themselves, or they must guarantee the assistance of a tutor.
- The home must have a computer and internet access.

- Each month, the children must visit the school so that a teacher can counsel and perform pedagogical monitoring. In addition, every two months, they must sit for the exams required by the educational system.
- The academic goals should adhere strictly to the official curriculum.

Current discussion Milton Luna, coordinator of the citizens' movement The Social Contract for Education which was cited by the news station Explored in Ecuador, notes that "this form of education gives the family back the responsibility of educating their children. However, the risk still remains that parents could become overbearing and not allow the child to develop their skills and abilities" (Explored 2009). Nevertheless, there are dissenting voices. Miriam Aguirre, dean of the Faculty of Education at The Catholic University, said "I do not agree with that form of education because it does not develop a child's socialization" (Mena Erazo 2010).

Argentina

Legal status On the blog "The Choice of Homeschooling," lawyer Madalen Goiria (2009) presents the compulsory schooling law. Article 129 of the National Education Law of Argentina says that parents must ensure that their children attend school. However, there is an advisory board, The Provincial Council of Education, that has the power to permit homeschooling. The legal basis of this allowance can be found in Article 26 of the Regulatory Decree 572/62 that, "provides three means of ensuring the compulsory education of school age children: public school, private school, and the home itself."

Current discussion Two opinions of the subject are found on the La Nación webpage (2016). Both agree that school is the ideal place for children to socialize. This is contrary to the descholarization movement which is thought to prevent this interaction. According to the psychologist Ana Caraballo, "homeschooling prevents children from having the opportunity to share time and activities with other children, to compete, and to (among other things) learn to accept differences." Meanwhile, Ana Ravaglia, Buenos Aires' undersecretary of education, notes that, "Going to school is more than a routine. It is access to an atmosphere of socialization and collective construction of knowledge" (Premat 2012).

Despite this statement, Ravaglia does not reject home education. As a result she finds it essential that children can verify their grades. She says that in order to do this, one must either find the relevant legal standard or create it. According to Ravaglia, "the important thing is that the child has a certificate that substantiates the validation by law of a compulsory level of education and that we as the Ministry of Education can meet the occasional needs by framing it within legislation that, if not existing, must be thought to be implemented." Nevertheless, the official ends by say saying that there is insufficient documentation of the phenomenon.

Chile

Legal status Chile and Colombia have similar policies on home education. For example, the constitutions of both countries establish that parents have the preferential right to educate their children. The constitutions also establish the freedom of teaching (Chile: Article 19 paragraphs 10 and 11), and they declare that general education is mandatory (Chile: General Law of Education, 20370, 2009, Article 4). However, their constitutions do not limit education to attendance at a school. Finally, both countries accept the validation of studies (Chile: Article 7, Exempt Decree 2272 of 2007).

According to the blog, *The Black Sheep Group*, Chile's Ministry of Education does not systematically monitor home education (Colectivo Oveja Negra 2011).

Current discussion Andrea Precht, Doctor of Educational Science and Director of the School of Education at the University of St Thomas, encourages people to think critically about this form of education since it could easily turn into a flexible way to acquire knowledge that still does not require them to critically reflect on their surrounding world. It is an example of "liquid modernity" as Zygmunt Bauman, the Polish sociologist, would say.

If, and only if, homeschooling families accept their position in a countercultural movement can we explore and problematize this new way of thinking. We must ask ourselves if we are not facing an illusory resistance given that the managerial thinking of post-Fordist societies actually requires forms of education that are localized, liquid, fluid, flexible, and focused on expanding capabilities, the continuous development of one's potential, and that have a concept of children that involves constant activity and exploration. In short, post-Fordist societies need independent individuals who can think for themselves and who understand planning, personal initiative, communication, and self-motivation (Precht 2011, 192).

Mexico

Legal status Article 3 of the Mexican Constitution recognizes every person's right to receive education, which is mandatory at the primary and secondary levels. However, going to school is not mentioned. The General Education Act of 1993 orders the government to promote and supervise all forms of education (Article 9). In addition, in Article 64 of the same law, the Ministry (of public education or federal education authority) is granted the power to "issue certificates, verification, or diplomas to prove a level of knowledge acquired through self-learning, work experience, or other forms of education that correspond to a certain educational level or grade in school."

Current discussion As the website Lemonhass recorded in an interview posted on YouTube in 2011, Mexico's Secretary of Education, Fernando González Sánchez, said that "Home education is a new experiment. It is unregulated; however, it is beginning to emerge as an adaptable form of education." Note that the representative from the Colombian Ministry of Education, Heublyn Castro Valderrama, also said that home education is one of the "forms of flexible schools" (Barrera Tenorio 2011).

The Current State of the Descholarization Movement

The following discussion is part of a collaborative effort led by Alejandra Jaramillo Morales, PhD in Latin American Literature and Cinema and MA in Latin American Literature from Tulane University, New Orleans.

1. The way of life that school imposes

Regarding the role of schooling in human development, Ernesto Sábato says "education always suggests a model for how we should be and how we should live together." In other words, schools are governed by the "dominant system of beliefs" (Sábato and Catania 1989). Every form of government, whether it is oppressive or not, clearly uses schools to transmit and, in some cases, impose the government's understanding of the world, its idea of how people should live together, its way of understanding the use of resources, and its method of organizing society. The problem with using school in this way lies in the fact that these ideas become so commonplace that people try to write them into an unquestioned official discourse. In light of this, we believe that knowledge, education, and training should enable people to identify the government's hidden curriculum, the dominant system of beliefs, just as these things should enable them to understand the diverse sociocultural groups that exist today. This is one of the primary reasons that we have chosen to distance ourselves from school. It is not because we believe in an education free of ideology. In truth, every action is inherently ideological. It is instead because we believe that every form of education should make us question our beliefs, particularly those that are being forced upon us at every moment. The idea is not to set ourselves apart from the modern world, but rather to recognize the consequences of, and the alternatives to, the beliefs commonly held in modern society so that we and our children can grow independently of the way of life that school imposes.

2. In relation with nature

Since the Renaissance, as Sábato says in his essay "Man and Mechanism," western societies have assumed a relationship with nature that has resulted in a desire for more individual control over it. Unfortunately, in their quest for understanding, school and science are becoming ignorant of our connections with the planet and of our codependency with the environment. Our educational philosophy seeks to distance itself from "the inventors and positivists of the industrial revolution that studied nature just so that they could exploit it as they desecrated and destroyed it."

We think that it is important to teach our children about planetary awareness, that is, the recognition of the sociocultural, spiritual, genetic, and natural diversity that surrounds us and that, above all, makes us feel responsible for our surroundings and ourselves.

3. Distancing ourselves from technological developments for the sake of development

The governments and economic systems that control global geopolitics today have great confidence in science and technology. This confidence is a chief cause of the dehumanization that is prevalent in these fields. As Sábato said, science is not unethical anymore because it rests in the hands of the government and the economy. From there it can be as much of a nuisance as an assistance. Technological progress can thus be seen as a goal in itself. However, technology should instead be reconsidered from a human standpoint so that it helps us to be better people, to understand our place in the world, and to better understand who we are. We have questioned how the speed of the modern world can help us, but also how it can harm us. We have questioned the role that medicine plays in our lives. When people go to the doctor, they typically do what the doctor prescribes without realizing that this "specialist" could be wrong, that they have the right to seek different opinions, and that, above everything else, they have the right to make their own decisions about their bodies whether certain doctors are in agreement or not. Knowledge of science and technology is important in our educational philosophy because we believe that all knowledge that humans have obtained is important. However, in light of everything, it is necessary to question the use of science and technology since they are imposed on us as facts of life. We must be constantly critical so that we use science and technology with the responsibility that we believe is necessary.

4. A true codependence between the individual and the community

During the 20th century we witnessed totalitarian, capitalist, and socialist governments. Sometimes the community was forgotten in the name of the individual. For example, capitalist legislation generally defends personal freedoms that are to the detriment of the community. People protect their own assets and their right to have what is theirs. Everyone else could die of hunger for all they care. On the other hand, in socialist governments, the focus on the community grew so oppressive that the individual nearly disappeared. For example, the People's Education Army in China homogenizes children. They become practically identical so that they do well on the state exam that finishes their secondary schooling. This is an unhealthy collective obsession that is caused by the inability to think differently on this exam. This obsession has also served to produce depression and emotional problems in thousands of Chinese teenagers. Sábato instead proposes an education that is capable of strengthening the individual and the community at the same time. In other words, he proposes an education that creates people who recognize that their development and their identity are dependent on their relationship with the community in which they live. This is a fundamental premise of our decision to home educate. We believe that schools in capitalist countries like those of Latin America tend to promote a form of individuality that treats freedom as part of the free market. This leads to perverse forms of society in which nothing will stop people from reaching their own particular goals. While it is clear that governments try to protect the community from these selfish impulses of capitalism to a certain point, this protection is almost nonexistent since economic powers have been stronger than the government for some time and since the government also depends on these economic powers. Therefore, school is an inherent part of having and living in a capitalist society. While we are also led by these acts of selfishness, when people are at least more willing to think, to throw doubt on these economic models, and to hopefully consider more communal and cooperative forms of owning possessions, it is possible to achieve an education that can question these methods of appropriating goods.

5. Recognizing the difference between savant and sage

Sábato says "we must reconsider knowledge. Instead of only studying the knowledge of men in laboratories, we must learn to value the wisdom that people gain throughout their lives. Unfortunately in Spanish we do not have the distinction between *savant* and *sage* that the French have. I am referring to the necessity of *sagesse* [wisdom]. This is the wisdom that existed with the Councils of Elders in ancient societies before people knew how to read or write." We have the same words in Spanish: *sabiente* and *sabio*. Sábato defends sages, which are people who navigate through life with the ability to use their gifts and talents to "understand people that are both similar and different to themselves, to accept misfortune with courage, to have restraint in triumph, to know what must be done with the world, to age with greatness, and to die humbly." However, we nevertheless believe that the savant is also important. The savant would be someone who dedicates part of their life to mastering something such as engineering, art, mathematics, architecture, or law. The sage would then be someone who dedicates part of their life to learning to live, to reflecting on themselves in order to make the most of their abilities, and to managing the uncertainties that life imposes on them in the most adequate ways possible. We believe that our society has forgotten the sage's wisdom in order to focus on the savant's knowledge. Schools focus the majority of their time on developing knowledge. They usually do not offer classes for special talents or classes for self-reflection, or allow for moments of overflowing emotions to be dealt with in school. Instead these moments are usually viewed as a unnecessary distractions that takes time away from math, chemistry, or physics. If we, people that were raised to be savants, could learn to mix the savant with the sage, we would probably be less unhappy, less demoralized, less lost to the drift of a world that boasts of its advances in knowledge (that is, the savant's knowledge) and that is decreasing in its knowledge of life, of joy, of death, and of immanence (wisdom).

6. A formative education, not informative

Ricardo Piglia, another Argentinian writer, was asked about the responsibility of Latin American writers in the the new millennium in a text that was titled, "Three Proposals and Five Difficulties" (2001). He says that writers must expose the fact that there is a great deal of darkness behind the immense amount of information surrounding us. Thus, illuminating what is hidden behind this overwhelming amount of information is one of the most important things that we can do. Sábato also proposed that education should focus more on training than information. During the years that we have practiced home education, we have seen how easy it is to find information. Our children are surrounded by sources of information such as libraries, the internet, grandparents, and intelligent people, but we are also increasingly conscious that the accumulation of knowledge, a side-effect of capitalism, is unnecessary. How many of us could today pass the standardized tests that we took when we finished our schooling, whether it be college or high school? Surely if we took these tests today our degrees would have to be revoked since when we take them the first time, we do it with our minds full of the information that was accumulated throughout our schooling. Over time this information quickly becomes unnecessary. Having said that, children who do not go to school have already demonstrated that the information taught in school over a period of several years can be learned in several months, especially when one has learned how to learn. This is the main goal of the descholarization movement.

To summarize, while information (that is, knowledge) is necessary, it can be learned without forcing people to attend school and without the paradigms that school imposes. Furthermore, information can only be acquired when it is needed or wanted. Information must also be subject to doubt. Everyone knows that things that used to be considered the truth are only partially true today. Therefore, they should constantly be called into question and removed from the norm.

Nevertheless, education is important because through education one gains wisdom and above all the ability to learn, which is actually part of wisdom itself. In other words, education helps us to understand ourselves so that we may connect with all the people who learned before us.

Related to this topic is an interesting passage by Sugata Mitra (2013) who claims that a child can learn with a computer. This is a questionable premise for those of us who believe that learning happens naturally and uniquely for each child. A child who gets information off the internet without being able to doubt and question what they read could come to believe, for example, that the main solution to a pandemic like swine flu is to get vaccinated with medicine from a big pharmaceutical company. Do the majority of Google searches regarding this topic recommend vaccination as the only option? For us, learning to doubt and question is the main purpose of education and of all information.

7. Freedom with accountability

In a 1987 interview Sábato says, "modern schools should be microcosms that prepare children for real communities. In other words, schools should prepare children for societies that are based in dialogue, social justice, freedom, and the common good where people have individual freedom but are also respectful of their fellow man." When people ask us, as they do everywhere we go, why we decided to home educate our children, this is one of the main reasons we tell them. As much as we would like to believe otherwise, it appears to us that the schools in our countries, even the seemingly good ones, are not managing to recognize that freedom cannot be separated from accountability. This is because, as Edgar Morin (1999b) suggests, we will only be able to inhabit this planet in a poetic, wonderful, political, rational, and pleasureful manner if we recognize that as a species we are in a constant flux between unity and diversity.

In that case, there is hope. As Sábato would say, "I have always had hope, maybe because I believe that life is tragic and gloomy. In a perfect world there would be no spiritual or psychological need of hope. If hope reappears after every disaster it is because we generally have a desperate desire to live."

Education (both for our children and ourselves) is the search for freedom with accountability, an independent and considerate critical-thinking ability, and a relationship with nature that values it like life and death. Education should be something that makes us both individuals and community, something that teaches us how to learn in an adequate manner. All of these things keep us connected to life and to hope.

Descholarization in Brazil

In November 2011, José Aravena Reyes participated in the third international conference on descholarization, collaborative self-directed learning, homeschooling, and flexible school models with the presentation, "Distance Education in Brazil: A Flexible and Emancipating Education" (Aravena 2011). Using this presentation as a reference we will discuss some similarities between the descholarization movement and distance education. We will also mention some other points as a continuation of the discussion that began a year before the conference in order to generate mutual support between the two communities that will hopefully lead to better understanding and research.

First we must say a little about distance education in Brazil. To begin, what stands out is the critical outlook that the movement is trying to assume. It is notable that the people practicing distance education are raising questions about "using classrooms as geographic spaces of power, institutions as political spaces of domination, and school as the main form of education and source of information" (4).

Nevertheless, by defining distance education as a form of education that someone does to "teach and learn without being restricted by time or space," it is clear that they are looking for flexibility. It is likely true that this search for flexibility is related to the need to decentralize (on a large and small political scale). In terms of distance education in Brazil, one will note two principal characteristics: (1) the geography when trying to deal with areas that are far from the big academic centers and even physical spaces for education; (2) the curriculum when one looks for greater student autonomy by trying to confront the progression and hierarchy of access to and control of information (1).

It is also necessary to consider that distance education can give way to critical thinking since such forms of education originate from the need to promote free thought. Nevertheless, we concede that distance education in itself is not able to create critical thinking (8). When combined with what we know about micro-politics, distance education strengthens what is recognized as the need to "give more attention to the daily work of institutions and the political aspect of technology instead of concentrating on the analysis of abstract topics or the analysis of topics with purely technological goals" (2). Doing this would bring us closer to the understanding that in education, individuals and their practices are more important than their methods.

Other aspects of distance education in Brazil could be surely considered to emphasize certain truths, but nevertheless, it is necessary to keep in mind that the truth must always be put into context and thought through carefully. Therefore, we will try to outline just some of the similarities and differences between distance education and descholarization.

However, before we do this, it is necessary to say why we use the term descholarized learning: our conception of descholarization arises out of the need to capture the diversity of practices and understandings that are included in this philosophy. There are probably as many different forms of descholarization as there are families and communities that choose these practices. One must keep in mind that while this idea includes homeschooling, it also includes the learning that happens in non-traditional contexts like out in the community or in unique situations in which there is no access to traditional schooling.

Flexibility

Many forms of flexibility are appearing in education movements such as active education, progressive pedagogy, and student-centered learning, among others. These movements have increased, largely due to what Deleuze (2006) identifies as the crisis caused by confinement centers such as prisons, hospitals, factories, schools, and families. This crisis is part of the transition from a disciplinary society to a control society (1).

Identifying the impact of the surge of control societies demonstrates the need to question the celebrated flexibility that is common to both the descholarization and distance education movements. Andrea Precht presented a warning that is equally relevant to both movements at the second international conference on descholarization, collaborative self-directed learning, homeschooling, and flexible school models. She said, "Neoliberal thinking has become more critical. It is transforming the meaning of critical thinking; it is absorbing it, and it is channeling it towards the deregulation of work, education, and society; [...] We can call ourselves the abolition of the old school order, but at the same time, we could potentially be supporting the creation of a new political thought" (2011, 188). Thus it is necessary to keep in mind that although flexibility can be closely tied to autonomous learning, it can also be tied to wide-reaching methods of control and domination.

Times and rhythms

The presentation of José Aravena Reyes demonstrates the way in which distance education can make the school day more flexible. To do this he draws on the experience of a graduate course of the Federal University of Juiz de Fora (UFJF) in which "they could not require synchronous learning or demand too much time from the students" (2011, 5). In this example it is clear that there is flexibility in both the times that the students complete the work and the intensity of time dedicated by the students. By doing this, the choices offered complement the freedom of the students to determine their dedication to the course.

The flexibility of distance education can be compared to night education for illiterate adults since, in most cases, it is also offered at different times from those of their work. Furthermore, in some cases there are flexible schedules and differing levels of commitment required. One could examine the extent that distance education questions its part in the creation of skilled labor. Does it question the increased exploitation of and the obsession with job qualifications that are based on degrees? Deleuze raises two important points when he considers the question: "Is it not strange that so many young people have such a lack of motivation that they demand workshops and ongoing training? They must discover for themselves how such things will be of use to them, just as their predecessors laboriously discovered the disciplines."

We can also ask these questions of practitioners of the descholarization movement. Among the diversity that exists, there are families, communities, and forms of descholarization that maintain practices of formal schooling. These can include schedules that are even more exhausting than those of conventional schools. This is to prepare students to be sufficiently competitive in the labor market. It is also common to find images on social networks like Facebook that try to associate descholarization with success stories like those of Steve Jobs that are rather overblown. This even happens among those who promote natural learning where the subject determines a good amount of the dynamics, times, and rates of learning.

Regarding this situation it is pertinent to cite Peter McLaren who, in an interview by Marcia Moraes in Brazil (2004), uses the ideas of Paulo Freire to show that in any educational movement, a critical assessment of society must be conducted. The assessment must first focus on pedagogy. This interview again mentions the role that Freire played in the teaching of adult literary, but it also mentions the number of questions that he had of his own method of teaching when it considers that "the first requirement of the Freirean practice of 'humanization' is a radical imagination focused on getting away from an education that has become rather domesticated" (10).

In addition to thinking about when learning happens, it is also necessary to consider the rate at which things are learned. In this sense, some forms of distance education and descholarized education that reproduce certain practices of formal schooling such as set curriculums, degrees, and deadlines demonstrate the need to reflect on assessment.

Flexible assessments

Using Brazil as an example, José Aravena highlights that "for education that depends on diplomas, distance education can add flexibility to the assessments" (5). The teachers who participated in the course by the UFJF had a noteworthy idea about this. They thought that having more flexibility led to more assessments and a greater focus on diplomas. We might gain support for more comprehensive learning assessments when we consider that "evaluating by means of grades at predetermined points of the course (like photographs of learning) makes it unlikely that teachers will return to content that has already been covered. Students probably will not be able to return to the content and understand it later on in the course" (6).

It is curious that given this situation they promoted the alternative of a sole final exam since even though they were given various formative assessments on topics that arose in the course, these formative assessments were not considered part of the formal assessment process of the learners. Additionally, we should stress the value that is given to the content. When speaking about assessments, people usually discuss evaluating learning from the point of view of the degree that is being completed. This includes the goals of the degree, its curriculum, its syllabi, and the content. In the case of the descholarization movement, there are segments of the movement that assess based on what is wanted to be taught. In other words, the assessments are still determined by "content," but it is content that is supposedly wanted to be learned. It may be necessary to ask: How can we assess the learnings that take place outside of the curriculum but that are equally as important and relevant?

In some segments of the descholarization movement there is an obvious preoccupation with getting degrees and validating learning with formal exams. This is the opposite of the opinion of other segments of the movement that oppose any kind of assessment since they believe that assessments limit holistic learning. For the action-research project on descholarization, collaborative self-directed learning, homeschooling, and flexible school models, the explanation given by Bajtín and Medvédev (1993) has been of great help. They explain that we are constantly evaluating and assessing through language and conversations.

As we advance alternative ideas of assessing learning, we must keep in mind what Deleuze proposes with respect to degrees, exams, and the training that big corporations are doing nowadays since, "just as the company replaces the factory, ongoing training tends to replace the exam. This is the surest way to put schools in the hands of businesses (2006, 2).

Spatial flexibility

We previously emphasized the importance of questioning schools' use as a geographical space of power. It is necessary to complement this with a discussion that considers the rise of distance education as a response to an increased demand for education in general. Colleges like distance education because their campuses cannot support the demand, and they only need to generate a minimal amount of infrastructure to support the in-person activities for distance courses (mainly for assessments). In addition, we should remember that José Aravena Reyes also emphasizes the use of podcasts (audio through the internet). These are not just used when time is limited, but also space. As a result, students can study and cook at the same time.

Although these ideas indicate the possibility of physically distancing oneself from the school, they do not necessarily indicate a separation from the practices of formal schooling. These are practices that believe that learning is subject to fluid dynamics or that it is a construction of knowledge established through the institution of school without caring where it takes place. As such, we will focus on the methods and only touch on how physical spaces make learning possible.

Javier de Nicoló Sr who worked with the homeless on the streets of Bogotá emphasizes how it is now critical to not just recognize the importance of "street smarts." It is also critical to recognize the importance of things learned in other spaces apart from those of formal schooling (De Nicoló et al. 2009). We could again consider the tragedy of the confinement centers and think about the changes that they are causing. Even though what we call the street is frequently the opposite of confinement centers because of the types of relationships that are made there, it is possible to decrease the misuse of the street and its contributions to learning. One can find different ways of approaching and dealing with public spaces. Some prefer the popular thought where the "street" acquires greater relevance in learning, while others favor the use of different spaces (large community rooms, cultural spaces, etc.). Therefore, one might have to turn to a more territorial point of view and consider that it is not the physical space in itself that determines the learning.

For the descholarization movement, the topic of spaces has become especially relevant when discussing homeschooling, since the child's education is said to be limited to the physical space of the home. We should emphasize that electronic groups of people interested in the descholarization movement are beginning to see the value of various spaces like parks, libraries, cultural centers, etc. Nevertheless, one of the issues that the action-research group has investigated is the possibility that these spaces can be imbued with practices influenced by traditional schooling. Ivan Illich (1985) is an essential reference for questioning how school can be associated with something more than physical spaces. Thus, this idea is relevant for more than just homeschooling. Every form of education should question its use of spaces.

In spatial or territorial terms, it is also appropriate to discuss the similarities between distance education and studies on digital segregation since "the digital world, which is governed by the rules of the current economic and political structure, is rooted in various forms of segregation" (Chaparro 2007). These studies seek to concentrate in part on the capabilities of digital technologies and the application of knowledge rather than just the physical and material aspects. On this subject, Chaparro describes four main points regarding the access to and use of technology: (1) motivation for access (wanting to use technology, motivation, and desire); (2) material access (resources, finances, web access); (3) access to the skills (strategic, informative, instrumental, formal education, informal education, expertise); (4) real usage (forms of use and application which may differ depending on multiple personal, social, and organizational factors).

Critical Individuals

In order for autonomous learning to occur, the individuals that take part in these forms of education must be able to think critically. Some of the previously discussed ideas are based on this assumption since the flexibilities that we have discussed can have nuances and these can be linked to several sophisticated mechanisms (both conscious and unconscious) of domination, control, and heteronomy. Therefore we are trying to emphasize some other factors that can be considered important in discussing education, especially the idea that when discussing learning and education, the important thing is to consider the individuals and their practices before their methods.

What Should be Taught?

Before discussing autonomy, it may be important to discuss the topic of who decides what content is taught. There are many approaches to curriculum development. Before a curriculum is released, a group of experts discusses what they consider to be the most important information. From the get-go it is necessary to question why content and "knowledge" are frequently just information. This is particularly relevant when we consider new technologies. Nevertheless, the difference between information and knowledge is not questioned very often. It is also necessary to consider that approaches to the curriculum continue to be presented in which the acquisition of information could be compared with the capitalist philosophy of accumulation. People forget that if one learns how to learn information, one can acquire it as needed and desired. This has become even more true with the amount of sources of information that are currently available.

Martín-Barbero (2006) attempts to make the case that the new information and communications technologies are becoming a challenge because they are bringing about "the temporary and systematic nature of new jargon and the new ways of producing, ordering, saving, and publicizing knowledge" (17). By doing this he is approaching the understanding that we are in a new age of learning that does not revolve around a book. Nor does it require the sequence of schooling nor giving out assignments (18).

Based on these thoughts, Martín-Barbero also questions the use of technology in certain educational environments when he emphasizes how teachers are failing to integrate it well into the educational system. This demonstrates the challenge of "overcoming an idea that is still remarkably common." The challenge is getting past the idea of simply learning what the teacher says without understanding "the cultural challenge that permeates the media and the effect on learning that the media is causing" (19).

The idea of the "alma profesoral" as presented by Victor Florían can be linked with Gaston Bachelard's argument on the philosophy and epistemology of teaching. From this argument, one can see how even when changes are made to government policy, there are individuals that continue their teaching practices and repeat, "their knowledge every year like an Aristotelian pedagogic who firmly clings to their teaching principles as part of their identity" (4).

Hernán Prieto (2011) has developed various arguments to question the common idea of, "making students believe that they are the teacher even though you are the teacher in reality" that is held in many forms of education. To do this, he goes through several educational movements that promote ideas related to autonomous learning and different teaching methods that seek to focus on the student. We must emphasize that there are currently forms of education that do not teach content but rather a way to carry out any plan or process that one undertakes. However, we must also thoroughly question these forms of education. The question rises of who decides the content in programs like the distance education course in Brazil. Although it offers certain flexibilities, it still has to deal with the problem of demand and coverage.

In order to stop considering content from the perspective of "knowledge," it must first and foremost be clarified that while technology and the knowledge of science are important, their use must be denaturalized. Thus it is noteworthy how in his presentation, José Aravena Reyes demonstrates that, "many of the students got to the end of the course with the feeling that the real use of advanced degrees is the ability to concretely influence life in schools and not just the acquisition of highly specialized knowledge." Even though technical and scientific things are important, it is possible that they are not the only things that should be valued with regards to education and learning. They probably should not even be priorities.

Sources of Information

It cannot be denied that there are currently many sources of information and that they are becoming easier to access with new technologies. José Aravena Reyes emphasizes these ideas with the distance education course for teachers when he explains that, "when they learned to use the internet as a source of information and when they discovered that there are a vast number of such sources, the teachers realized how school was imprisoning their students and how they, as the teachers of these students, were the primary promoters of these prison-like behaviors" (2011, 5).

In Aravena Reyes' study one can read that the teachers thought critically about how schools concentrate on information. They also thought about how the internet can be used as a gateway to access many sources of information. However, it is necessary to keep in mind that there are powerful mechanisms on the internet that prioritize information that is in line with the dominant political and social thought. The information can be noticeably biased. Castells (1999) considers this situation when he says that "a sociological theory of information that is not based on the new economic interdependence of the world is simply irrelevant for the purpose of understanding the new social structure of our societies" (44).

Going back to Victor Florián (1993), we see that he identifies knowledge's dynamic nature. Therefore, the discussions that we considered to be true before are now only versions of the truth. There should always be a doubt about what we know or what we think we know. Furthermore, we have to keep in mind that while it is important to remove school as the primary source of information for children, it is even more important to not adopt other sources of biased information without the ability to question them. It is necessary to keep in mind that even with everything that the new technologies of information make possible, the rise of technology, as Deleuze would say, "is more than a technological evolution; it is a profound mutation of capitalism" (2006, 3).

One prevalent concern throughout the action-research project was that such a diversity of opinions permeate these forms of education. We have tried to ensure that we present many different points of view, not just the views of the people who are responsible for teaching the information. The number of opinions should not just be noticeable in the relationships in which the acquisition of information is particularly relevant. We must also remember that there are many relationships and practices that make it possible to educate at different levels. Then there are concerns about the operational goals that accompany educational processes. Regarding the relationship between distance education and state institutions, this relationship must be looked at with caution until there is mutual understanding with the administrators who look to further their points of view and who avoid criticizing the established forms of education.

Teaching and Learning

Regarding new technology, Martín-Barbero poses several questions, even to university-level departments of education, about what it means to learn and how school can attempt to be, "an authentic social and cultural space of learning," or in a simple question: How does school have to change to be able to communicate with society?

(2006, 16). These concerns surface several times in this text because it is so important to think about how and why learning transcends technology. Furthermore, Martín-Barbero emphasizes the importance of communication and relationships in education.

One must remember the teaching and learning ideas that Gabriel Restrepo (2010) lays out in his groundbreaking sociological theory. In this theory he considers that all social processes teach under the assumption that "enseñar [to teach] derives from *in signum*, a permanent demonstration of the signs" (158). This perspective is the opposite of what continuously theoretically and practically develops from the forms of teaching that conceive pedagogy as pushing specific content. These ideas imply an instructional dynamic that is based on an asymmetrical relationship between the teacher and the student (101). On the other hand, Restrepo says that that the word *aprender* [to learn] derives from the root *apprehendere*, which means "to incorporate what is taught," keeping in mind the idea of *in signum*. This connects it to the idea of "meaningful teaching" and also with how to make sense of something that is taught to us, whether that be skills, abilities, knowledge, behaviors, or values.

It is important to consider and to constantly reevaluate the practices and perspectives of both the descholarization and distance education movements. For example, there are several things that a critical person would consider when questioning the true autonomy of a form of education that values teaching over learning. The first thing they would consider would be their own beliefs on teaching and learning. Then they must question where everyone else in education falls on the spectrum and how their beliefs are related to student autonomy. Doing this questioning can be important to the forms of education that seek "emancipation" and/or more flexible schooling regulations.

Socialization and Affection

The sociological nature of learning as developed by Restrepo is another approach to the topic of relationships. In order to internalize knowledge and to create autonomous learners, it is necessary to recognize that context and interest play a part. People must acknowledge that learning and education happen in many moments, spaces, and relationships. This means that socialization could be considered a broad education and that communication is one of the means of achieving it.

Consequently, we must do away with the view of socialization that approaches children as malleable individuals. Instead we should do more with the intergenerational relationships that are common in education and recognize that, in general, people are educated and socialized throughout their lives and through different means. These means are independent of our age. If these ideas were accepted, schooling and family would not be the only forms of socialization in a child's education. Instead, socialization would also occur through the media (communication methods and ICT), through the community and/or neighbors, through work, and by gender, among others.

To establish just one way that socialization occurs through the media, Martín-Barbero explains that the media "is not just disrupting the traditional forms of transmitting and disseminating knowledge. In fact, nowadays it constitutes the principal means of socialization. That is to say, the media is the principal identification mechanism and the main source of teenagers' worldview, their ways of life, their preferences, and their fears" (2006, 16).

One thing that worries people about some forms of home education is the possible isolation of the community or, in some cases, the family. It is necessary to resume the topic of diversity, dealing with the selection of sources of information, in order to explain this. One should keep in mind that a wide socialization could allow for deeper analysis and various points of view to consider, not just those of their own learning process. It is essential to emphasize a couple of examples dealing with this. The first is that of José Zuleta Ortíz, the son of Estanislao Zuleta, an important intellectual leader that took an interest in education, among other topics, because of his own experience with the descholarization movement. In an interview he explains that his family was isolated due to the discomfort created when the educational perspectives of the family were questioned. Furthermore, he explains that there was no possibility for him to choose whether to continue schooling or not, and that, perhaps to avoid the discomfort that these questions of his childhood caused, he was bound to the countryside, and his friends were mostly the friends of his father. In addition, José Zuleta Ortíz explains that these dynamics where some points of view are homogenized were also prevalent in some communal, alternative forms of education. The second example is that of some religious American families who raised controversy for their resolution against the teaching of evolution. Their intention was to present intelligent design and/or creationism to the exclusion of other theories on the origin of life.

Although it is quite difficult to try and restrict socialization, we must question the impact that these restrictive practices can have on the autonomy and critical formation of the students. It is also necessary to question the types of learning that formal schooling regards as scholarly. To do this, one must remember the spatial and territorial contexts of learning. An example of this has already been outlined regarding the street as a place of spatial flexibility. Additionally, in the case of distance education, we have to question the dynamics of socialization that the combination of schooling and ICT promotes.

Affection is another relevant aspect of socialization. To just touch briefly on its influence on the learning process we can mention what Bowlby (2001) describes in his attachment theory. In his theory he believes that affection is related to autonomy, and he describes it as vital to the process of continually evaluating the internal and external conditions of the individual that are reflected in one's method of deciding, acting, and evaluating communication with other people. Bowlby explicitly relates affection with two basic functions: socialization and physical protection/emotional security. Furthermore, he discusses that affection determines if a person tends to be calmer (secure) or more anxious (insecure). In this sense, we can say that affection, as well as knowledge and willpower, are determinants of learning and change. Once again we must question the descholarization and distance education movements. This time we must question the extent that they create affectionate relationships that result in more diverse and profound learnings.

Basic Questions

The action-research group on descholarization, collaborative self-directed learning, homeschooling, and flexible forms of schooling has sought to critically explore the dynamics of these movements and other alternatives to formal schooling. We must repeat that while these alternatives were formerly only thought of for the potential emancipation that they offer, it has been found that they also offer a powerful, complex, and well thought-out way to create people that are more interconnected. Although the text has touched on this idea in part, it is worth emphasizing two matters relating to it.

The first relates to keeping in mind the hidden curriculum that can permeate education and that is reproduced (whether consciously or unconsciously) in even supposedly "alternative" forms of education. This hidden curriculum is frequently related to changes in corporations and the global economy. For example, these things are reflected in the growing trend of descholarized training that is causing the significant reduction of funding for centers of education by said corporations. As such, under the guise of "better" views on learning, they are seeking to generate greater effectiveness to blur the lines between what Gabriel Restrepo would call the worlds of life and the worlds of the social system. By doing this, the end goal becomes maximizing production. The goal of maximizing production increasingly permeates daily life, private moments, and the minds of every individual. It defines their lives.

It does not hurt to repeat that it is becoming necessary to question the way that transnational capitalism is using flexibility. Without attempting to discuss technology in itself, Castells offers a guide for questioning the flexibility of the distance education movement when he says that "technology is not just science and machines; it is also social and organizational technology" (39). Deleuze considers that there is a correlation between the type of society and the type of technology (machines) since the types of technology "express the kind of society that created the technology and that also uses the technology." This is what leads us to believe that control societies tend to focus on information (2006, 3).

To summarize, the second question seeks to emphasize that education has little to do with methods. It has more do with the people that are directly or indirectly involved (their characteristics, behaviors, and abilities). How do we respond to the fact that these people, even in rather alternate forms of education, keep following erroneous educational practices such as purchasing expensive textbooks, strictly adhering to protocol, and spending money on training for different methodologies?

The book *Street Pedagogy*, an investigation conducted by the Childhood Protection Institute (IDIPRON), evaluates certain evolutions in the field of research previously led by Javier de Nicoló. The book stresses that all the individuals involved (social workers, administrators, teachers, students, etc.) must play an active part in the education of children, teenagers, and young people on the street.

It may be necessary to consider that every ethical form of education should involve critical thinking and self-reflection on behalf of the involved individuals. This would cause people to reevaluate their actions in personal and private situations as well as their hidden beliefs. In other words, it would make them "open the black box."

How will descholarization and distance education affect our understanding of our "black box"?

Acknowledgment

This chapter was developed in collaboration with the action-research group on descholarization, collaborative self-directed learning, homeschooling, and flexible forms of schooling from the Faculty of Human Sciences, National University of Columbia: Julián Ernesto Ramirez Caballero, Researcher, MEd candidate; Laura Córdoba, Volunteer Coordinator for Reevo Colombia.

References

Aravena, José. 2011. November 2–4. "Educación a distancia en Brasil: por una educación flexible y emancipadora." Presented at the Tercer Congreso Internacional sobre Educación sin Escuela (ESE), Autoaprendizaje Colaborativo (AC), Educación en Familia (EF), Modelos de Escuelas Flexibles (MEF). Universidad Nacional de Colombia, Facultad de Ciencias Humanas, Instituto de Investigación en Educación, Bogotá.

Barnard, Alan. 2007. *Anthropology and the Bushman*. Oxford, UK: Berg Publishers.

Barrera Tenorio, D. 2011. "Análisis jurídico y político sobre la Educación Sin Escuela (ESE) en Colombia." In *Un mundo por aprender: Educación sin Escuela (ESE), Autoaprendizaje Colaborativo (AC), Educación en Familia (EF), congresos de 2009 y 2010,* edited by Erwin Fabián García López, 255–261. Bogotá: Universidad Nacional de Colombia. Facultad de Ciencias Humanas. Instituto de Investigación en Educación.

Basham, Patrick, John Merrifield, and Claudia Hepburn. 2007. "Educación en casa: De lo extremo a lo corriente." *Estudios de Política Educativa*. Vancouver: The Fraser Institute. http://www.altisimo.net/escolar/InstitutoFraser-Homeschooling.pdf

Bajtín, Mijaíl, and Pável Medvédev. 1993. "La evaluación social, su papel, el enunciado concreto y la construcción poética." Translated by Desiderio Navarro. *Criterios* 9–18. http://www.criterios.es/pdf/I391medvedev.pdf

Bowlby, John. 2001. *La separación afectiva*. Translated by I. Pardal. Barcelona, Buenos Aires: Paidós.

Bruner, J. 2006. *In Search of Pedagogy, Volume I: The Selected Works of Jerome S. Bruner*. New York: Routledge.

Cabo, Carlos. 2012. "El homeschooling en España: descripción y análisis del fenómeno." Doctoral thesis, Universidad de Oviedo, España. http://encina.pntic.mec.es/jcac0007/indice.htm

Castells, Manuel. 1999. "Flows, Networks, and Identities: A Critical Theory of the Informational Society." In *Critical Education in the New Information Age*, edited by Manuel Castells, Ramón Flecha, Paulo Freire, Henry A. Giroux, Donaldo Macedo, and Paul Willis. Boston: University of Massachusetts. http://es.scribd.com/doc/53792254/22678017-Manuel-Castells-Ramon-Flecha-Paulo-Freire-Henry-A

Chaparro, Jeffer. 2007. "La segregación digital en contexto." *Ar@cne: Revista electrónica de recursos en internet sobre geografía y ciencias sociales* 95. http://www.ub.edu/geocrit/aracne/aracne-095.htm

Cohn, N. 1993. *En pos del Milenio: Revolucionarios milenaristas y anarquistas místicos de la Edad Media*. Madrid: Alianza Editorial.

Colectivo Oveja Negra. 2011. "Homeschooling en Chile." *Colectivo Oveja Negra,* October 24. https://ovejanegracolectivo.wordpress.com/2011/10/24/homeschooling_en_chile/

Deleuze, Gilles. 2006. "Post Scriptum sobre las sociedades de control." *Polis,* April 14, 2006. http://polis.revues.org/5509

De Nicoló, J., I. Ardila, C. Castrillon, and G. Mariño. 2009. *Musaráñas. Programa de intervención con niños de la calle*. Bogotá: Idipron.

De Zubiría, Miguel. 2004. "Introducción a las pedagogías y didácticas contemporáneas." In *Enfoques pedagógicos y didácticas contemporáneas*. Bogotá: Fundación Internacional de Pedagogía Conceptual Alberto Merani.

Dragow, A. 2014. "De certezas, terremoto y miga de pan." *Educación sin Escuela - Columbia,* December4.https://educacionsinescuelacolombia.wordpress.com/2014/12/04/de-certezas-terremoto-y-miga-de-pan-ponencia-de-anna-dragow/

Engeström, Yrjö. 1996. "*Non Scholae sed Vitae Discimus:* Toward Overcoming the Encapsulation of School Learning." In *Introduction to Vygotsky*, edited by Harry Daniels. London: Routledge, Taylor & Francis Group.

Escamilla, J. 2000. *Selección y uso de tecnología educativa*. México: Trillas, ITESM, Virtual University.

Explored. 2009. "Colegio ya no es la única opción."

Florian, Victor. 1993. "El alma profesoral : filosofia y epistemologia de la pedagogia." *Pedagogía y Saberes,* 4: 27–32. http://www.pedagogica.edu.co/storage/ps/articulos/pedysab04_06arti.pdf

García López, Ervin Fabián. 2011. "Reflexiones y valoraciones comparativas de la Educación sin Escuela, Autoaprendizaje Colaborativo, Educación en Familia, en tres familias colombianas." In *Un mundo por aprender: Educación sin Escuela (ESE), Autoaprendizaje Colaborativo (AC), Educación en Familia (EF), congresos de 2009 y 2010,* edited by Erwin Fabián García López. Bogotá: Universidad Nacional de Colombia. Facultad de Ciencias Humanas. Instituto de Investigación en Educación.

García Olivo, Pedro. 2014. *Dulce Leviatán: Críticos, víctimas y antagonistas del estado del Bienestar*. Bardo Ediciones. http://bardoediciones.noblogs.org/files/2014/04/libro_final.pdf

Garrido Mayo, M. J. 2013. "Antropología de la infancia y etnopediatría." *Etnicex: Revista de estudios etnográficos* 5. http://dialnet.unirioja.es/descarga/articulo/4761662.pdf

Goiria Montoya, Madalen. 2009. "Educar en casa en Argentina." *La opción de educar en casa,* September 3. https://madalen.wordpress.com/2009/09/03/edycar-en-casa-en-argentina/

Goiria Montoya, Madalen. 2012. *La Apción de Educar en casa: Implantación social y encaje del homeschool en el ordenamiento jurídico español*. Universidad del País Vasco. http://www.unav.edu/matrimonioyfamilia/b/uploads/31378_Goiria_Opcion-educar-2012.pdf

Gómez Arévalo, Amaral Palevi. 2010. "Ideas y pensamientos educativos en América Latina: de la escolástica colonial al posneoliberalismo educativo." *Revista Latinoamericana de est Illich, Ivan.udios educativos (México)* 40. http://www.redalyc.org/articulo.oa?id=27018884006

Hardt, M., and A. Negri. 2002. *Imperio*. Buenos Aires: Paidós.

Hijos del Altísimo. 2013. *Manifiesto pedagógico Cristiano alternativo*. Perú. http://www.altisimo.net/escolar/Manifiesto%20pegagogico%20cristiano%20alternativo.pdf

Hüther, Gerald. 2012. "Learning Enthusiastically: A Conversation with Prof. Dr. Gerald Hüther." *Televizion*, 14–15. http://www.br-online.de/jugend/izi/english/publication/televizion/25_2012_E/huether_learning.pdf

Illich, Ivan. 1971. *Deschooling Society*. New York: Harper & Row.

Illich, Ivan. 1985. *La sociedad desescolarizada*. Mexico.

Klicka, Christopher. 2002. *The Right to Home School: A Guide to the Law on Parents' Rights in Education*. Durham, NC: Carolina Academic Press.

Knowles, J. Gary, Stacy E. Marlow, and James A. Muchmore. 1992. "From Pedagogy to Ideology: Origins and Phases of Home Education in the United States, 1970–1990." *American Journal of Education*, 100: 195–235. http://www.jstor.org/stable/1085568

La Nación 2016. Accessed May 1, 2016. http://www.lanacion.com.ar/1480720-educarse-sin-ir-a-la-escuela-es-posible

Mitra, Sugata. 2013. "Build a School in the Cloud" Presented at *TED 2013*. http://www.ted.com/talks/sugata_mitra_build_a_school_in_the_cloud/transcript?language=en

Martín, V., and J.M. Castro. n.d. "La educación creadora." En *Diraya*.

Martín-Barbero, Jesús. 2006. "La educación en el ecosistema comunicativo." *Comunicar*, 13: 13–21.

Mena Erazo, Paúl. 2010. "Ecuador: primeros casos de escuela en casa." *BBC Mundo*, June 6. http://www.bbc.co.uk/mundo/cultura_sociedad/2010/06/100604_0224_ecuador_educacion_casa_lav.shtml

Moraes, M. 2004. "El sendero del disentimiento: Entrevista a Peter McLaren." Translated by M. González and M.A. Muñoz. *Revista de Reflexión Socio-educativa* 4. http://www.barbecho.uma.es/DocumentosPDF/BARBECHO4/A1B4.PDF

Morin, Edgar. 1999a. "L'intelligence de la complexité." *Gazeta de Antropología*, 20: 43–77. http://hdl.handle.net/10481/7253

Morin, Edgar. 1999b. "Los siete saberes necesarios para la educación del futuro." Paris: UNESCO.

OFTP. 2015. "Homeschooling FAQ." *The Ontario Federation of Teaching Parents*. http://ontariohomeschool.org/homeschooling-faq/

Ossenbach, Gabriela. 1993. "Estado y Educación en América Latina a partir de su independencia (siglos XIX y XX)." *Revista Iberoamericana de Educación* 1. http://www.rieoei.org/oeivirt/rie01a04.htm

Piglia Ricardo y León Rozitchner. 2001. *Tres propuestas para el próximo milenio (y cinco dificultades)*. Fondo de Cultura Económica.

Precht, Andrea. 2011. "La educación casera como resistencia. Paradojas, tensiones y desafíos." In *Un mundo por aprender: Educación sin Escuela (ESE), Autoaprendizaje Colaborativo (AC), Educación en Familia (EF), congresos de 2009 y 2010*, edited by Erwin Fabián García López. Bogotá: Universidad Nacional de Colombia. Facultad de Ciencias Humanas. Instituto de Investigación en Educación.

Premat, Silvina. 2012. "Educarse sin ir a la escuela, ¿es posible?" *lanación.com*, June 10. http://www.lanacion.com.ar/1480720-educarse-sin-ir-a-la-escuela-es-posible

Prieto, Hernán. 2011. "Citando a la escuela." In *Un mundo por aprender: Educación sin Escuela (ESE), Autoaprendizaje Colaborativo (AC), Educación en Familia (EF), congresos de 2009 y 2010*, edited by Erwin Fabián García López. Bogotá: Universidad Nacional de Colombia. Facultad de Ciencias Humanas. Instituto de Investigación en Educación.

Raygada Watanabe, Rosemary. 2003. "La educación rural a distancia en Latinoamérica." Paper presented at the Foro OEA Virtual Educa, Miami. http://www.red-ler.org/educacion_rural_distancia_AL.pdf

Restrepo, G. 2010. "Teoría dramática de la sociedad." http://www.slideshare.net/educacionsinescuela/teora-dramtica-de-la-sociedad

Rodrigañez, Casilda. 2010. "Poner límites o informar de los límites." https://docs.google.com/a/agenciauno.com/viewer?a=v&pid=sites&srcid=ZGVmYXVsdGRvbWFpbnxjYXNpbGRhcm9kcmlnYW5lenxneDozOWQxZDFiNTU0MmRhNGYx

Rodríguez, Pau. 2013. "Crece el modelo de escuelas libres en Cataluña." *El diari de l'educació*, July 5. http://www.eldiario.es/catalunya/diarieducacio/Crece-modelo-escuelas-libres-Cataluna_6_150544947.html

Sábato, Ernesto R., and Carlos Catania. 1989. *Entre la letra y la sangre: Conversaciones con Carlos Catania*. Barcelona: Seix Barral.

Stern, Arno. 2000. "Formulation." *Arno Stern Official Website*. http://www.arnostern.com/en/en_formulation.htm

Suasnábar, C., and N. Isola. 2011. "Tomás Amadeo Vasconi y la radicalización del pensamiento político-pedagógico en las décadas del sesenta y setenta." *Revista Colombiana de Educación*, 61.

Valero Estarellas, J. 2012. "Homeschooling en España." *Revista General de Derecho Canónico y Derecho Eclesiástico del Estado*, 28.

Wolcott, H.F. 1994. "Education as Culture Transmission and Acquisition." In *The International Encyclopedia of Education. Second Edition. Volume 3*, edited by T. Húsen and T. Postlethwaite. Oxford: Pergamon

Zaldivar, Jon. 2012. "The Deschooling Theories: Forty Years of Historical Perspective." *Social and Education History*, 1: 28–57. DOI: 10.4471/hse.2012.02

16

The Legal Situation of Home Education in Europe

Henk Blok, Michael S. Merry, and Sjoerd Karsten

Introduction

The story of home education in Europe is a complex one. One of the reasons is that Europe comprises more than fifty different nations, some quite sizeable – such as Germany, France, and the United Kingdom, with tens of millions of inhabitants – others much smaller, down to the likes of Andorra, Liechtenstein, and Vatican City, with populations of less than 100 000. Some, like Italy and Spain, have existed for more than a century; others have appeared only relatively recently. Take modern Germany, formed in 1990 with the reunification of East and West. Or Macedonia, which came into being after the break-up of Yugoslavia in the 1990s. Another complication is that many countries do not regulate education nationally or federally, but at the state, provincial, or regional level. That is the case in Belgium's separate language communities, for instance, and in the constituent nations of the United Kingdom. Perhaps the most compounding factor of all, however, is that educational systems reflect both historical developments and recent changes. The dissolution of the Soviet Union on December 26, 1991, for example, sparked major transformations of the systems across the former Communist bloc (Kostelecká 2010).

Educational systems, including those elements related to home education, are constantly changing. This has made it difficult for the authors to present a comprehensive picture of the situation across Europe, and we realize that forming a good overview will thus require some perseverance on the part of the reader.

Our goals in this chapter are twofold. First, we want to provide a general insight into the legal framework governing home education in a broad selection of European countries. The questions we address here include the following. Is home education regulated by law? What conditions are attached to it? Does the government monitor

The Wiley Handbook of Home Education, First Edition. Edited by Milton Gaither.

it? And, if so, how? Initially, these questions are taken up by looking at aspects on a country-by-country basis. But then – and this is our second goal – we examine the similarities and differences between them. Are there any generalizations we can make? And, if so, in what respects?

Finally, in our closing discussion, we put forward some general principles and objectives that governments might consider when further developing legislation and regulations with respect to home education. International treaties like the 1989 United Nations Convention on the Rights of the Child (UNCRC) are important here, since they have legal force in the signatory countries. But we also mention considerations of a sociological nature, not least the fear that widespread home education might create some form of parallel society with the potential to undermine national unity. A good understanding of policy intentions is important in this regard – partly in order to make home education policy in individual countries more appropriate to their particular situations, but also so as to achieve greater European harmonization. Considering the huge differences in current national legal and regulatory regimes, harmonization is certainly desirable.

The Beginnings of Contemporary Home Education in Europe

Home education – or homeschooling, as it commonly called in North America – concerns the education of children outside school, chiefly under the responsibility of their parents. We prefer the term home education, which is widely used in Europe, as it does not necessarily imply that parents follow a "schoolish" approach. It can also refer to learning in the home, under the supervision of distance or internet schools.

Present-day home education in Europe started to develop from the late 1970s onwards. The movement began in the United Kingdom, where one particularly significant event was the creation in 1977 of a support organization named Education Otherwise, by a small group of parents in the town of Swindon. The British movement was inspired by developments in the United States, where home education had been gaining ground since the early 1970s (Gaither 2008). There were two distinct driving forces behind the renewed interest there. One was evangelical Christians opposed to public schooling, not least because the curriculum included the teaching of Darwin's theory of evolution. The other centered on the writings of sociologists, psychologists, and educationalists like Ivan Illich, John Holt, and Raymond and Dorothy Moore, who were worried about the negative effects of school education on the normal development of children. In 1977 Holt began producing *Growing without Schooling*, a newsletter promoting home education. The fact that the US and the UK have strong cultural and social ties, including a common language, no doubt helped the movement gain its first European foothold in Britain.

Since then, however, other European nations have also seen active debates about the pros and cons of home education. The rise of the internet from the early 1990s onwards greatly facilitated interaction between proponents in different countries. As a result, home education is now an established phenomenon in many parts of

Europe. However, this is not to say that it has retained or gained legal status everywhere, as we shall see in subsequent sections.

Selection of Countries

It would not be feasible to include all fifty or more European nations in our review. In some there is little information available about home education, especially where it is not a widespread phenomenon. There are also translation problems if information is not available in English. We have therefore restricted ourselves to a more or less representative selection of fourteen countries (Table 16.1) of different sizes, in different regions (North, East, South, West), with different levels of prosperity, and with different home education histories. Two nations, the UK and the Czech Republic, were excluded because other chapters in this handbook take up these cases. All the selected countries are member states of the European Union, the political community currently made up of twenty-eight European nations.

Descriptive Framework

In developing a framework to describe the differences in national regulations, we considered three main issues of relevance: the general context, the legal framework, and the inspection regulations.

Table 16.1 Selected European countries.

Country	*Region*	*Population (x 1000)*	*Gross domestic product per capita (US$)*
Austria	West	8223	44 208
Belgium	West	10,449	39 778
Bulgaria	East	6925	15 933
Estonia	North	1258	23 065
France	West	66,259	36 104
Germany	West	80 997	40 901
Hungary	East	9919	22 119
Italy	South	61 680	33 111
The Netherlands	West	16 877	43 198
Norway	North	5150	65 640
Poland	East	38 814	22 162
Portugal	South	10 814	25 411
Spain	South	47 738	32 682
Sweden	North	9724	43 180

Note: Reference year 2012.

General context

One important question here is whether parents have a free choice between school and home education. If they do, we consider the prevalence of home education to be an important aspect of the general context. Registration requirements are essential to reliable estimates, and so we sought to ascertain whether such requirements exist. In some countries the position of home-educating parents is currently uncertain, due to pending changes to the law. If and when that is the case, we indicate this accordingly.

Legal framework

The main question in this respect is whether a government has enacted legislation relevant to home education. This may cover the requirements home educators have to satisfy, for example, and establish inspection regimes and procedures. We recognize a distinction between high, moderate, and low regulation by the authorities (Basham, Merrifield, and Hepburn 2007). High regulation requires parents to inform authorities about their wish to start home education, involves requirements concerning the curriculum, entails home visits or compulsory testing, and may even demand that homeschooling parents be qualified teachers. Moderate regulation requires notification and asks for some sort of progress record, such as regular test reports. Low regulation does not require parents to have contact with the authorities.

Inspection regulations

Inspections of school education may serve two functions: compliance or implementation. *Compliance inspection* concentrates on observance of the applicable legislation and regulations, so that the public knows that they are being enforced. This is relevant if the government bears legal responsibility for the institutions concerned. *Implementation inspection* focuses on whether the taxpayers are "getting their money's worth." This means that institutions have a certain degree of autonomy and the government cannot be held directly accountable for their functioning, but still government has a certain involvement – through funding, say, or because the institutions provide essential public services. The criteria in this case focus on the community value of the school's provision. Are the teachers competent? Are students advancing properly? And so on.

With home education, parents take direct responsibility for the costs of educating their own child. Accordingly, there is no basis for implementation inspections. Whether such a basis exists for compliance inspections depends on the legislation. Governments may impose separate rules for home education, such as determining what subjects are taught, or what results need to be achieved. There may also be other applicable legislation, not specifically concerning education. Many countries have laws on child welfare, which set out parents' responsibilities for their child's upbringing and education. In this case, the inspection may focus on checking compliance with these obligations. International treaties may also be relevant. For example, the 1989 United Nations Convention on the Rights of the Child (UNCRC) contains provisions concerning the right to education (Article 28), and setting out its goals (Article 29): these should focus on ensuring the best possible development of the child's personality, talents, and mental and physical abilities. In the case of home education, parents are responsible for achieving this. If they fail to do so, the government is required to provide the child with the necessary protection and care, as set out in Article 3. The state may thus establish compliance inspections to ensure that the rights of the child are observed.

Regardless of the functions they serve, inspections of home education may either be delegated to the same agency that oversees school education or entrusted to a more specialized organ. Alternatively, local schools may play a role. Various forms of data collection are also an option, including self-reporting, home visits, and face-to-face contacts with the child. Another issue is whether children should take achievement tests. For example, the authorities may have set standards for schools against which progress of homeschooled students can be judged.

Sources

Much of the data we have used was obtained from the internet. Public and private organizations publish a wide range of information online. Academic sources have been used, too, but to a lesser extent as there are no available handbooks or encyclopedias, and very few relevant scholarly articles. We also approached local correspondents, who were often able to supply us with detailed and reliable information obtained from local sources. One striking uncertainty concerns the number of children actually receiving home education. Governments sometimes present lower figures than those provided by advocacy groups. In such cases, we present both estimates.

Home Education in Selected European Countries

Our country descriptions are presented both in text and table format (Table 16.2), with the former more elaborate than the latter.

Austria

Home education (*häuslicher Unterricht*) is a legal option: parents can comply with the compulsory schooling requirement by educating their child at home. However, they do have to meet certain conditions. At the beginning of each school year, for

Table 16.2 Overview of national regulations on home education (HE).

General context	*Legal framework*	*Inspection/monitoring*
Austria		
HE has been a legal option for many years. Its prevalence amounts to 0.20% of the school-age population (this figure includes an unknown proportion of children in authorized private schools). Learning materials are available to parents free of charge.	Moderate regulation. Parents have to apply to the education inspectorate for permission. HE must be equivalent to school education. Parents can appeal if the inspectorate turns down their application.	At the end of the school year, the child takes the regular school examinations (99% of HE children pass these). If a child does fail, parents must return them to school education.
Belgium		
Parents are free to provide HE. They must notify the authorities annually. In both Flanders and Wallonia, current prevalence is about 0.10% and climbing steadily. Using new, stricter requirements, the authorities are trying both to raise the quality of HE and to discourage its take-up.	High regulation. The parental right to HE is enshrined in the Constitution. Inspection regulations are governed by education laws, which are different in Flanders and Wallonia.	At specified ages, children must sit national examinations. Supervision has been assigned to the education inspectorate, which operates differently in each community. **Flanders:** The inspectorate conducts home visits and analyzes documentation submitted by parents. In the event of negative assessments, parents must enroll the child for school education. **Wallonia:** The inspectorate conducts home visits on an irregular basis, but always when the child is 8 and 10 years old. Methods include examining teaching materials and testing the child. If progress is not deemed adequate, parents may have to enroll the child in school.
Bulgaria		
HE is not a legal option. If school attendance is not possible – for medical reasons, say – the school may offer individual education or tutoring at home, provided by a teacher. However, about 400 children (0.05% of the school-age students) receive HE from their parents, mostly without official consent.	Low regulation. As HE is not allowed, no regulations are in force.	Not applicable.

Estonia		
Parents opting for HE must apply to the school at which the child is registered. School choice is free. In collaboration with the school, parents develop an individual curriculum that more or less follows the school curriculum. The school provides learning materials free of charge. In 2012, 300–400 children received education outside school, either on medical grounds or for specific reasons advanced by parents (0.30% of the student population, ages 7–17). The government has been positive about HE in general, and the public has become more aware of this option.	High regulation. Since 2010, HE has been regulated under a specific law covering education outside school, both on medical grounds and because parents have chosen HE for other reasons.	The school monitors academic progress through semi-annual testing. If it is not satisfied with learning outcomes, and the child falls behind the individual curriculum plan, it may demand that the child return to school.
France		
HE is permitted by law. Parents must notify the local authority and the national inspectorate annually. Subjects to be taught are prescribed by law. At the age of 16 the child must have attained the same standard as one educated in school. Prevalence is about 0.26% (ages 6–11).	High regulation. HE is explicitly permitted by the legislation, which also requires that the education inspectorate conduct annual inspections, and defines how they should take place.	The inspector checks annually that all subjects are being taught, typically by means of a home visit. If results are unsatisfactory, a second visit follows shortly afterwards. If this again produces a negative outcome, parents must send the child to school.
Germany		
HE has been practically non-existent for a long time. Children are required by law to attend a certified school, or to be taught at home by a qualified teacher. HE provided by parents without a teaching license is a criminal offence. Prevalence is less than 0.01%.	Low regulation. All children must attend school. Exceptions are possible only for those with a long-term illness and for immigrant children living in Germany for a short period.	Not applicable.

(Continued)

Table 16.2 (Continued)

General context	*Legal framework*	*Inspection/monitoring*
Hungary		
HE is not mentioned in law, but parents are allowed to provide their child with "individual education." Permission has to be obtained from a local school. The HE child is not obliged to attend any school classes, but has the right to do so. It is estimated that 5632 children (0.70% of the school-age population) receive individual or home education.	High regulation. Dispensation from school attendance for children aged 6–16 must be obtained from the local school. Parents have to follow the state curriculum, and children are tested once or twice a year.	Supervision is the responsibility of the school at which the child is registered. It assesses whether the family's resources and the child's progress are sufficient. In addition, from 2015 onwards local government and health officials must agree that HE is not detrimental to the child.
Italy		
HE is a recognized way for parents to fulfill their duty to educate their child. Prior authorization by a local school is required. The number of children receiving home education is very low; reliable statistics are unavailable.	Low to moderate regulation. Under Article 30 of the Constitution, parents have the right and duty to educate their child. Act 53/2003 states that parents wanting to home educate their child must prove their "economic and didactic capability."	There is hardly any monitoring. Examinations are optional, except when the child is transferring to school education, or to obtain a qualification.
The Netherlands		
HE is not legally recognized. It is an option only for parents with religious or philosophical objections to school education. Numbers rose (by 15% a year) to a prevalence of about 0.02% in 2012 (400–500 children). In June 2013 the government tabled proposals for severe restrictions on HE opportunities.	Low regulation. There is no specific regulation of HE. Instead, child protection legislation has occasionally been used to restrict the practice. Enforcement is the responsibility of the Council for Child Protection, part of the Ministry of Justice.	As HE is not recognized by law, there is no supervision. In individual cases, such as when accusations of child abuse have been made, the Council for Child Protection conducts an investigation and may take legal action to demand specific measures, including removal of the child from their parents' custody. This is very rare, but not unknown, in cases of HE.
Norway		
HE is legally recognized. Parents must notify the local authority that they intend to provide it. Prevalence was about 0.07%, as of 2014.	High regulation. The law states that HE must be equivalent to school education. Inspection is the responsibility of local authorities.	Inspection determines whether the child is receiving an education equivalent to that provided by schools. Usually, a supervisory teacher visits the family twice a year to evaluate the quality of the HE. The law allows local authorities to test the child's progress. If this is deemed insufficient, the child must attend school.

Poland		
Following the collapse of the Communist Eastern Bloc in 1990, new legislation on education and schooling was introduced. This recognized HE as a legal option. Currently, parents must ask the principal of the local school for permission to educate their child at home. They also have to file a declaration that they will follow the compulsory core curriculum. There is growing public interest in HE. Its prevalence as of the 2013–2014 school year was 0.03% (about 1500 children).	High regulation. The Education System Act allows parents to apply for home education. Approval must be obtained from a local school. Parents have to follow the core curriculum, and the child has to take the annual national examinations.	Supervision is the responsibility of the school at which the child is registered. Its principal assesses progress through the annual examinations. Schools receive a monthly grant for each home-educated child.
Portugal		
HE is legally recognized in two forms: education by the parents themselves, and by a licensed teacher at home. Parents simply declare they wish to provide HE, with a statement regarding their own or the teacher's qualifications. The declaration must be renewed each year. The number of home-educated children has risen to about 0.02% of the school population.	High regulation. Parental choice is a legal right established in the Constitution and education law.	Monitoring occurs at the end of fourth, sixth, ninth, eleventh, and twelfth grades, with the child sitting national examinations in Portuguese and mathematics. In other subjects they take examinations organized by a school, usually at the end of the school year.
Spain		
HE is neither legal nor illegal: it is simply not mentioned in either the Constitution or education law. Prevalence is about 0.07% (2000–4000 families). Despite its uncertain legal status, most families providing HE are undisturbed by the authorities. Advocacy groups are lobbying for HE to be made an explicitly legal option, but so far to no avail.	Low regulation. In December 2010 the Constitutional Court ruled that current education law provides no basis for parents to offer HE instead of school education. This ruling leaves them in an insecure legal position.	As HE is not recognized by law, no supervision exists.
Sweden		
Until 2011, HE was a legally recognized way to provide compulsory education. Since then, however, it has been possible only "if special circumstances exist." This change in the law has effectively made HE impossible.	High regulation. The law requires a fully satisfactory alternative to school education, to be monitored by authorities on an unspecified way.	Court cases have made it clear that providing HE without permission can result heavy fines, and interventions by social services. It is not specified how HE is to be supervised, but this is hardly an issue as it is so rarely permitted.

instance, they must apply to the education inspectorate for permission (and they can appeal if that is refused). Education at home must be equivalent to that provided in school. At the end of the year the child takes the regular school examinations, at a school of the parents' own choosing. It has been established that 99% of home-educated children passed these examinations in the 2010–2011 school year – as did the same percentage of school-educated students (derStandard 2011). Learning materials are available free of charge. The number of home-educated children amounts to about 2000 annually (Els Hoendervoogt, personal communication), representing 0.20% of the school-age population. This figure includes an unknown number of children receiving their education in authorized private schools.

Belgium

The federal constitution states that parents are entitled to provide their child with home education. Further regulations operate at the community level (that is, in the Dutch-speaking community in Flanders and the French-speaking community in Wallonia).

Flanders At the beginning of the school year, parents are required to notify the authorities that they intend to give their child home education (*huisonderwijs*). In their notification they must declare that the teaching they provide focuses on developing the child's full personality and talents and on preparing her or him for an active life as an adult. Since 2003, parents must also declare that they comply with the UNCRC requirements concerning education. Following the latest available official statement, the prevalence of home education remains low, at around 0.10% in 2009–2010, but is climbing steadily (Vlaams Ministerie van Onderwijs en Vorming 2011). According to research by the Flemish education inspectorate, for a good proportion of parents and children home education is a "flight" option: they choose it because the child has not been doing well at school, either emotionally or academically. Many children receive home education for a few years only, then return to school. Supervision is in the hands of the education inspectorate: an inspector carries out home visits and asks parents to submit all relevant documents. The child's presence is desirable but not required. The inspector assesses whether parents are complying with the obligations set out in the UNCRC. If they do not cooperate, or if the inspector repeatedly reaches negative conclusions, parents must register the child for school education. Biannual reports show that the inspectorate issues more negative assessments in respect of children of secondary education age than for those of elementary age (Vlaams Ministerie van Onderwijs and Vorming 2011). Since 2013, children educated at home have been required to sit school examinations for 12–15-year-olds. The Flemish government introduced this measure in an effort both to improve the quality of home education and to put a brake on the number of parents choosing it.

Wallonia The law states that parents wishing to give their child home education (*enseignement à domicile*) must notify the authorities on an annual basis. There are no restrictions concerning their reasons for doing so. Reliable data about the number of children being educated at home is difficult to obtain. According to a newspaper report, the figure rose from 189 in 2000 to 504 in 2007 (7SUR7 2008). This amounts to an incidence of about 0.09%. Inspection of home education in Wallonia is the responsibility of a specialized task force or inspectorate. It conducts home visits, reviews the educational materials used and questions the child. Inspectors then assess whether the education provided at home is equivalent to school education. After two successive negative judgments, parents must enroll the child in school. Inspections take place when the child turns 8 and 10 but can also be performed at other times. Wallonia has a so-called "certification requirement." From the age of 12, home-educated children must sit the same examinations as those attending school. These are held at the ages of 12, 14, and 16, with a certificate awarded in each case if they are passed. Should a child receiving home education fail to obtain such a certificate at any stage, their parents are required to enroll her or him at a school.

Bulgaria

The current Bulgarian legislation leaves no scope for the home education of children aged 6–16. All those within this range are subject to mandatory education in one of the legally recognized school types. According to Article 78(1) of the Regulations on the Implementation of the Public Education, the following six legitimate forms of education are available: morning, evening, part-time, individual, independent, and remote. Students in morning, evening and part-time education are organized into classes and groups. In the other forms, instruction is on an individual basis (Article 79). Individual education is intended for students unable to attend school for more than thirty consecutive school days for health reasons, and also for talented students and for those who, for family reasons, wish to complete their education in one or more grades outside standard term times. In these cases the school organizes individual tutoring at home, as determined by the principal or – for those children with health problems – a medical advisory committee.

The state requirements for education at home are based on the student's individual curriculum, which is developed by and has to be approved by the school concerned. Its content and requirements are derived from those of the school curriculum. Education at home is possible only if the child is registered with a school, public or private, and is no longer allowed if the requirements of the approved curriculum are not observed.

Over the past few years there has been active public debate about both the advantages and disadvantages of home education and its legalization as an alternative to public and private schools. The discussion is led by the Bulgarian Homeschool Association. According to information provided by this organization, there are currently about 400 children receiving education from their parents at home.

They represent 0.05% of the total student population. Usually, parents circumvent the law in a covert fashion by, for example, enrolling their children for distance education in a school in another European country, or the United States. Most who do this are well-educated, with specific and deeply held religious beliefs. The mothers uphold traditional values and combine home education with home-making. The fathers are professional men, who have succeeded in life and typically hold a traditional attitude towards marriage and family (Petar Balkanski, email message to authors, October 6, 2014).

Estonia

Since 2010, home education (*Koduõpe*) has been explicitly regulated under a law covering all forms of schooling outside the classroom – in hospitals, for instance, as well as in the home. Local education authorities are responsible for the tuition of hospitalized children and those being educated at home for medical reasons. This instruction is provided by qualified teachers at the hospital, in the home or at another agreed location that has been deemed suitable.

Parents wanting to educate at home for reasons other than medical grounds must apply to the school at which the child is registered. This registration is compulsory for all children aged 7 and up, but parents can do it at any school. Most of those wanting home education choose small, independent institutions like Waldorf schools. Permission to home educate is granted one year at a time. In collaboration with the school, the parent has to draw up an individual curriculum that follows the school's. The school monitors academic progress with semi-annual testing. The parent can be present when assessments take place. If the school is not satisfied with the learning outcomes and the child falls behind the individual curriculum plan, it may demand that the child return to the classroom. The school has to provide, free of charge, any textbooks, workbooks and worksheets it is using, if the parents wish to use the same materials. In 2012, according to the government, 88 children were being home educated by parental wish and 255 for medical reasons. In total, that amounts to about 0.30% of the student population (ages 7–17). For various reasons, however, the official statistics are not entirely reliable. In reality, it is estimated that about 100 children are home educated by parental wish every year (Tiia Leis, email message to authors, September 17, 2014). This form of education is allowed throughout the compulsory schooling period, between the ages of 7 and 17.

The government has been very positive about home education in recent times and every few years has relaxed the law. The general public is much more aware of this option than it was in 2005, when a group of parents started an association for home education. However, many schools still find it difficult to comprehend and approve parental requests. Some smaller schools have been very positive, though, and have established good working relationships with parents that keep both sides happy. For example, there is one small Waldorf school that has registered about twenty home-educated children from all over Estonia. It has appointed a special coordinator to deal with these families so that classroom teachers are not involved. This has proven a sensible solution, since the person concerned has experience with both school and home education (Tiia Leis, email message to authors, September 17, 2014).

France

Parents have a legal right to provide home education (*instruction en famille*), as laid down in Article 131(2) of the Education Act. They must register annually with their local authority and the French inspectorate of education. The law requires that parents offer a broad range of subjects, including French, mathematics, at least one foreign language, arts and sports education. They are free to choose their methods, but children are expected to attain a level comparable to school education at age 16. Since March 5, 2009, and with effect from the 2009–2010 school year, a more rigorous regime has been enforced. This defines objectives students must have reached at the end of the compulsory education period (Ministère de l'Éducation Nationale, de la Jeunesse et de la Vie Associative 2012). According to official figures from Miviludes – an interdepartmental task force to combat "sectarian aberrations" – 13547 children aged 6–11 were home educated in 2009 (Les Enfants d'Abord 2010a). They represent about 0.26% of this age group.

Inspection of home education is regulated by law. Children must be interviewed by an inspector once a year. This is usually done at home. Parents have to show that they are teaching the subjects required by law. Inspectors must respect educational freedom, including variations in progress. There is no legal obligation to test children in different subjects. In practice, however, some inspectors do conduct specific written tests. Exact practices in this respect vary by region and have sparked debate as to whether inspectors are biased against home education (Les Enfants d'Abord 2010b). If a negative assessment is issued, a second inspection follows soon afterwards. If this is also negative, parents must enroll their child in school. In 2009, some 1626 families were inspected and school attendance orders were issued in 45 cases (Le Figaro 2010).

Germany

Compulsory education has been in place since the 19th century, but laws in force prior to 1938 allowed for the attendance stipulations to be satisfied through private or home education (Spiegler 2003). Legislation introduced in 1938, by the Nazi regime, banned home education, and that remains the case to this day. The current German constitution gives parents primary responsibility over their children and their education (Article 6.2: "The care and upbringing of children is the natural right of parents and a duty incumbent upon them"). However, the state (read: the Federal government) has the same duty as parents to educate children. When the interests of parents and the state collide, "any purported parental rights wilt in the face of State control" (Martin 2010, 237). All relevant passages about education and schooling are contained in the laws of Germany's constituent states, the sixteen Bundesländer. All of these demand compulsory school attendance (Spiegler 2003, 2009). Commonly, home education (*Hausunterricht*) is simply not thought to be a legal alternative, although some scholars argue that this mainstream interpretation of state laws is unconvincing and not in line with legal reasoning in German constitutional law in general (Reimer 2010). Exemptions are possible only for children who are ill for long periods and for immigrant children who will remain in Germany only for a short period of time. Education for the former group is provided by a teacher from a public school, who visits the family home two or three times a week. Penalties for evading compulsory school attendance vary by state. They may include fines, prison sentences, and even loss of parental authority. There is no established inspection of home education. It is estimated that some 500 children receive home education despite the restrictions, a prevalence of 0.005%. Our local correspondent has the impression that the subject attracted growing interest in the early 2000s but has not increased in prevalence in the past decade (Thomas Spiegler, personal communication).

Hungary

In Hungary, home education (*otthonoktatás*) is not mentioned in the law. However, parents are allowed to provide "individual education" to a child aged between 6 and 16 years old (the period of compulsory schooling). Effectively, then, individual education is the Hungarian label for what elsewhere is called home education or homeschooling. Parents wanting to home educate have to register the child with a school, public or private. If the child has already been a school student, the principal may grant her or him individual student status and exemption from attending lessons. Individual students have to take examinations, usually once or twice a year, at the school where they are registered. In exceptional cases, parents may request intervention by independent examining boards. The individual student is not obliged to attend classes but has the right to do so. It is thus possible for a child to take part in some school lessons or study groups, but not others. However, preparing children for examinations is the responsibility of the parents, who for this reason have to follow the state curriculum and use the same books as the students in the school of registration.

Under the latest legislation, which took effect in September 2015, children are obliged to attend nursery school from the age of 3. Also new was the provision that local government and health officials must agree that individual or home education would not be detrimental to the child. This condition was added to prevent the abuse or neglect of minority ethnic children under the pretext that they are receiving home education. It has been estimated that 5632 students, about 0.70% of the school-age population, received individual or home education for some reason in the 2007–2008 school year (Mrs. Földi, email correspondence with authors, between August 27 and September 19, 2014). Grounds for home education include parental request, illness, learning difficulties or residency abroad.

Italy

Home education (*educatione parentale*) is legal in Italy but not widely known. This entitlement is derived from articles 30 and 33 of the Constitution, under which it is the parents' right and duty to maintain, instruct, and educate their children, including those born out of wedlock. The compulsory education requirement can be fulfilled either by attendance at a public or private school or through home education, subject to authorization by the appropriate school authorities. Parents must notify the authorities annually of their intention to educate their child at home. They must also demonstrate that they have the didactic and economic capability to do so. Didactic capability means that the parent must have completed two full academic years of schooling beyond the level of the children they are currently teaching. Economic capability simply refers to adequate financial means. Most home-educating families are able to demonstrate their compliance with these criteria. Children are not required to sit for annual examinations; whether they do so is up to the parents. Examinations are required only if and when the child wants to enter the school system, or obtain a qualification. There is hardly any monitoring by state or school officials of the effectiveness of the education parents provide. The number of children receiving home education is so low that it does not appear in the statistics (Controscuola, n. d.).

The Netherlands

The Netherlands is one of the few European countries with no legal recognition of home education (*thuisonderwijs*). Consequently, it is not deemed an acceptable means of satisfying compulsory education requirements. The only way to do that is to enroll the child in a school. The law on compulsory education does, however, contain a provision under which parents can be exempted if there is no school appropriate to their religious or philosophical conviction within a reasonable distance. Since this legislation says nothing further about how the children concerned are to be educated, exempted parents are free to teach them at home (Sperling 2010). The parents of between 400 and 500 children, about 0.02% of the total, were exempted in this way in 2011–2012. According to official figures, this number grew by some 15% per annum between 2000 and 2012 (Christenen voor Onderwijsvrijheid 2013). Because the central registration system is known to be rather unreliable, however, these statistics are somewhat uncertain. As home education is not mentioned in any educational law, there is at present no provision for the inspection of the children concerned. Occasionally, though, the Council for Child Protection, which operates nationally, has investigated families to determine whether children should be enrolled in school despite their having an exemption. The jurisdiction of this body is based on a provision in the Dutch Civil Code, which states that parents are responsible for the upbringing of their children. The service takes action only if it has been reported that a child's well-being is in danger. In the past this regularly led to lawsuits, as the service considered home-educated children to be in danger by definition. But in recent years there have been virtually no legal actions of this kind, since several courts have ruled that the sole fact that a child is not enrolled in school, but instead is receiving an alternative education from their parents, does not constitute a danger to the child's development (Blok and Sperling 2012).

In 2003 the government initiated a parliamentary debate about the status of home education. Its proposal was that exemptions to the compulsory schooling requirement be granted only when parents were able to provide an appropriate alternative form of instruction, such as home education. They would also be required to submit to monitoring by the Inspectorate for Education. Over the next few years the government has amended its proposals several times, but no version has yet been adopted. The latest initiative dates from November 2015 and would legalize home education, irrespective of religious or philosophical motives of parents. A stringent inspection regime would advance the quality of the parents' provision of education and promote the child's development. Advocacy groups remain afraid that the strictness of the inspection regime might deter prospective parents.

Norway

In Norway it is education that is obligatory, not school. This means that a child need not attend school in order to be educated. It is the parents' responsibility to ensure that their children receive the instruction to which they are entitled. This can be accomplished by sending them to a public or private school, or by home education (*hjemmeundervisning*). But that must be equivalent to school education, as defined in the Norwegian educational legislation (Beck 2001). Parents have to inform the local authority if they do provide home education. Prevalence is low, at around 0.07% of all school-age children. That represents 200–400 individuals each year, a number that has been more or less stable in the past decade (Christian Beck, email message to the authors, September 16, 2014). Inspection of home education is required by law and delegated to local authorities, who have some freedom with respect to its organization. A typical approach involves home visits by a supervisory teacher from a local school, twice a year. Based on an interview with the parents, the teacher forms an opinion about the quality of the home education. When in doubt, the teacher can have the child take an achievement test. If it emerges that the quality of their education is unsatisfactory, the child must start attending school. No data is available on the outcomes of such visits.

Poland

In the aftermath of the post-1989 political transformation made possible by the collapse of the Soviet Union and the dissolution of the Communist Eastern Bloc, Poland introduced new educational regulations. Under Article 70 of the Constitution, enacted on May 25, 1997, education is compulsory up to the age of 18. The means whereby this obligation is fulfilled are specified in the Education System Act. The original version of that law, which entered force on September 7, 1991, stated that, "at parents' request, the school principal may give his or her permission to fulfill the schooling obligation for their child out of school" – thereby permitting home education (*edukacja domowa*). In the years following 1991, the conditions for obtaining dispensation from school attendance were heavily debated between a growing group of parents interested in home education on the one hand and, on the other, politicians, government officials, and legal authorities. As a result, the relevant provisions of the Education System Act were substantially amended. The latest requirement is that a parental request for out-of-school education be accompanied by the following documents: "an opinion from a psychological and pedagogical counseling center, [a] parents' statement about providing the child with conditions enabling the completion of core curriculum obligatory for the specific level of education and a parents' commitment, that while fulfilling the school obligation… their child would take an annual classification examination during each school year" (Paciorkowski 2014, 158). Since June 2014, parents have been allowed to file their request at any time, even during the course of the school year. In the past, school officials could be rather reluctant to agree to parents educating their child at home. But nowadays many of them take a fundamentally positive attitude towards this option, since they receive a monthly grant for each home-educated child. The number of such children is clearly rising, too, from 40–50 in 2009 to 1500 (about 0.03% of the student population) in the 2013–2014 school year – although the reader should be warned that these figures may not be totally reliable, as there is no central registration of home-educated children (Marek Budajczak, email message to authors, September 8, 2014). Overall, then, not only has the legal position evolved considerably since 1991, but society at large – including the media, schools, and government officials – has become increasingly well-disposed towards home education.

Portugal

Compulsory education lasts twelve years, starting when the child turns 6 years old. Parents are free to choose between school and non-school education. Non-school education exists in two forms: parental education (*ensino doméstico)* and individual education (*ensino individual*). The difference is that parents assume responsibility for educating the child in the former, whereas in the latter it is a licensed teacher who does so. Parents' educational rights are established in the constitution and in legislation. They do not have to ask for permission to choose parental or individual education: they simply declare each year that they want it, and provide a statement describing their own qualifications or those of the teacher they have appointed. Parental qualifications are deemed sufficient if they exceed the level at which they are educating the child. At the end of each school cycle – that is, upon completion of the fourth, sixth, and ninth grades at the elementary level, and the eleventh and twelfth grades at the secondary level – the child takes the same compulsory examinations in Portuguese and mathematics as those attending school. In other subjects, such as sciences, history and foreign languages, parentally or individually educated children sit tests organized by schools at the end of each cycle. Curriculum documents are published on the Ministry of Education website, along with past national examination papers. Schools must provide access to documentation relevant to the tests they organize. Although home education remains rare, it is growing. Between 2009 and 2014 the number of children involved quadrupled from 82 in 2009–2010 to 338 in 2013–2014, according to official figures (Claudia Sousa, email message to authors, October 31, 2014). The 2013–2014 number represents a prevalence of 0.02%.

Spain

The Spanish constitution (Article 27.1) states that every child has the right to education, and acknowledges "freedom of instruction." Strictly speaking, home education (*educar en casa*) is not illegal in Spain, but neither is it recognized legally as a viable alternative to conventional schooling. In December 2010 the Constitutional Court ruled that there is nothing unconstitutional about home education in itself, but that the law currently provides no legal basis for a parental decision to choose it (for a comprehensive commentary on this ruling and the current legal situation see Valero Estarellas 2013). In its judgment the court invited the Spanish government to develop legislation covering alternative educational options, including home education. The ruling also stated that there is no legal loophole that would allow parents to home educate. Rather, the Education Act imposes an explicit obligation that school be attended between the ages of 6 and 16, and so non-compliant parents can be prosecuted and forced to school their children. The Constitutional Court ruling leaves home-educating families in a precarious legal position. Advocacy groups are urging the government to declare home education an explicitly legal alternative, but as yet without success. The number of home-educating families is currently estimated at about 2000–4000, roughly 0.07% of all school-aged students (Madalen Goiria, email message to authors, September 9, 2014). There is little firm data, but most parents in Spain report pedagogical motivations behind their choice to homeschool, and very few political or religious reasons (Elizalde, Urpí, and Tejada 2012). According to local information, the vast majority of these families are continuing their home education undisturbed by the authorities (Madalen Goiria, September 9, 2014). Understandably because home education is not a legal alternative, there exists no formal supervision or monitoring.

Sweden

In the recent past, Swedish law did allow for home education (*hemundervisning*). Parents had to apply for permission, which was granted by some – but not all – local authorities for up to one year at a time. The law required a fully satisfactory alternative to school education, and regular monitoring by the state. Children had to be assessed after each school year, before continuing home education in the following year could be considered. Prevalence was about 0.01% (approximately 100 children in 2001). In 2011, however, the law was tightened. Since then, home education has been permitted only "if special circumstances exist." Religious or philosophical convictions are no longer valid reasons for choosing it (Riksorganisationen för Hemundervisning I Sverige 2010). The thinking behind this change is that school education is comprehensive and objective, and so allows all students to participate, regardless of their own or their parents' religious or philosophical values. Unauthorized home education can result in heavy fines and intervention by social services. The effective ban under the 2011 law has led many of the families affected to leave Sweden for neighboring Nordic countries or elsewhere. However, a handful are still trying to educate at home despite legal harassment. Although home education has been practically wiped out in Sweden, interest in it is growing and there is still an active political pressure group trying to strengthen the position of parents and children who, for whatever reason, prefer it to school education (Jonas Himmelstrand, email message to the authors, August 27, 2014).

A Few Generalizations on Home Education in Europe

An advance warning is needed here. The fourteen countries included in this chapter in no way constitute a representative sample in the statistical sense – they are merely an "opportunity sample." Despite this limitation, there are certainly some general lessons to be drawn from the overview we have provided. For example, it is remarkable how widely the nations of Europe differ in their approach to, and regulation of, home education. In ten of the fourteen countries that we have reviewed, it is a legal right. But that does not always mean that it is easily accessible for parents. Some countries are far stricter in their requirements than others. The least stringent include Austria, France, Belgium, and Poland. Sweden is a special case, because home education is subject to such restrictive conditions that it is effectively outlawed. In Italy it is a legal option, but one so little-known that few, if any, parents take it up. Four of our countries – Bulgaria, Germany, the Netherlands, and Spain – provide no legal right to home education. Bulgaria does allow individual and distance education, but this has to be given under the supervision of a school and leaves parents with only a subordinate responsibility for provision. The Netherlands is another special case: home education is not a legal option in itself, but in certain cases parents can invoke their specific religious or philosophical convictions to obtain a complete exemption from compulsory schooling, thus paving the way for home education as an alternative. In Spain home education is tolerated, although the Constitutional Court has ruled that there is no legal basis for that approach. Of the countries we have discussed in this chapter, Germany is the only one where home education is prohibited outright. Moreover, that ban is strictly enforced; German parents who do not send their children to school can expect to be prosecuted.

All countries with home education as a legal option have a registration requirement, usually with the local authorities or a school, and in some cases with the inspectorate as well (France). One interesting finding is that in many countries, despite such a requirement, it is still not clear how many children are receiving home education. This means that these countries are not making effective use of the registration data. This might be a problem of aggregation, with local records not being combined systematically to form a wider or national register. With the caveat that there is some uncertainty about the estimates available, the prevalence of home education in every single country discussed is far below 1%. Hungary has highest estimated incidence, at 0.7% of the school-age population, with home education most uncommon in Germany, Italy, and Sweden. Significantly, in several European countries the numbers of home-educated children are reported as rising: Belgium, Estonia, the Netherlands, Poland, and Portugal. Falling numbers are reported only in Sweden, where recent legislation has imposed severe restrictions.

Not much is known about the general characteristics of home-educating families. We found that in several countries, including Bulgaria, Estonia, Germany, and Hungary, medical grounds are seen as a valid reason for choosing home education. Most students in this category have serious illnesses or disabilities, for which schools are unable to cater sufficiently. In the Netherlands, many families have religious or philosophical reasons for avoiding school education. Home educators in Spain are supposedly motivated by pedagogical reasons. Similar or quite different motivations may play a role in other countries, meaning that home-educating families might represent an atypical sample of the general population. However, more research is needed to verify this supposition.

Many countries have established some form of inspection or monitoring, but Germany, Italy, the Netherlands, Spain, and Sweden have not. Usually, this is because home education is not an option recognized in law. Overall, the most common form of supervision is by a school. Usually, this means that parents must enroll their child at a school, and that he or she has to sit its end-of-year examinations. In the event of particularly disappointing results, the authorities can then issue a school attendance order. This is the approach taken in Austria, Bulgaria, Estonia, Hungary, Poland, and Portugal. In Portugal, and also in Belgium, there is an additional requirement: the child must sit the official national examinations held at particular ages. Another, less common form of supervision is home visits. They are standard practice in Belgium and France, where the visits are conducted by a school inspector, and in Norway, where the task is entrusted to a supervisory teacher from a nearby school. Most countries require parents to follow the compulsory or standard school curriculum.

It is difficult to predict how the future of home education will unfold in the countries we have reviewed. Whilst it has a long history and a more or less legal standing in most of them, that status is by no means secure. Recent years have seen attempts in several countries to tighten up, and to enforce more strictly, the requirements imposed upon families educating at home, with greater or lesser success. This has been the situation in Germany, France, Hungary, the Netherlands, and Sweden. Indeed, in Germany and Sweden the restrictions have effectively eliminated home education. Certainly, in none of the reviewed nations has it yet attained the status of a familiar and widely accepted form of schooling, as it has done, for example, in North America (Gaither 2009).

To conclude, we have observed wide differences between European countries with respect to home education regulations. It is difficult to determine why this is. Geographical factors seem to have little significance: in all four of the regions we have defined (North, South, East, and West), we find some nations open to home education and others where it is not a legal option. In northern Europe, for example, Norway and Estonia allow parents to educate their children at home whereas Sweden does not. Nor, apparently, is the size of population a significant factor. Relatively large countries like Germany and France differ widely in their attitudes. Whilst German home educators run a high risk of prosecution, their French counterparts are acting entirely within the law. Prosperity also seems not to come into it. Rich Norway has a positive policy, while the Netherlands – a society not much less prosperous – has a very suspicious approach. Even neighbors with close ties, and sometimes a more or less common history – the Netherlands and Belgium, for example, or Germany and Austria – can be poles apart when it comes to official attitudes towards home education.

Discussion

Knowing that all fourteen countries covered in this review are members of the European Union raises an obvious question: is the time not ripe for greater policy harmonization when it comes to home education? Regulatory concordance is an essential aspect of the principle of free movement between member states, which extends to students and the labor force. The wide legislative discrepancies with respect to home education can create an impractical situation for migrant workers, many of whom are parents with young children. Many of them want to keep in touch with their home culture, including their native language, and in many cases home instruction offers a better chance to do that than the conventional schooling available in their host country. From a more or less similar perspective, Koons argues that member states of the European Union should seek a unified policy regarding home education (Koons 2010).

International treaties provide an important comparative basis for the national regulation of home education. Particularly important here is the 1989 United Nations Convention on the Rights of the Child (UNCRC), which has been signed by all the countries we have discussed. Article 28 affirms every child's right to education, whilst Article 29 states that education should foster the development of the child's personality and talents, their preparation for a responsible adult life, and their respect for human rights, as well as the cultural and national values of the child's own country and those of others. In addition, the 1950 European Convention on

Human Rights (ECHR), also signed by every country covered in this chapter, contains relevant provisions (Sperling 2015), including:

> No person shall be denied the right to education. In the exercise of any functions which it assumes in relation to education and to teaching, the State shall respect the right of parents to ensure such education and teaching in conformity with their own religious and philosophical convictions" (ECHR, Protocol 1, Article 2).

It is not impossible for the rights of the child to conflict with those of his or her parents. In their domestic law, individual nations must therefore find an appropriate balance between these two considerations: a child's right to development of his or her talents and personality, as fully and broadly as possible, versus the parents' right to provide an education that conforms to their own religious and philosophical convictions. States also need to formulate their legislation in such a way that it enables the effective exercise of these rights, on both sides. Among other things, this means making sure that children who do not go to school still receive a form of education that complies with the provisions of the international treaties. Few countries refer explicitly to these in their national legislation, although Belgium – and Flanders especially – is one positive exception. Flemish parents opting for home education must declare that they comply with the UNCRC requirements, and local education inspectors check that they do.

As we noticed in the preceding section, a number of social concerns about home education have been raised across Europe. In France, for example, suggestions have been made that religious sects may exploit it for their own purposes. In Hungary, voices have been heard raising the possibility that certain ethnic minorities – notably the Roma – may choose home education, exacerbating segregation. In the Netherlands, critics have suggested that home-educated children will grow up sheltered, having lacked the opportunity to cultivate the social skills necessary to interact with others. And in Flanders, Belgium, concerns have been raised about parents lacking the competencies needed to teach subjects at the high-school level. Each of these worries expresses a general level of anxiety about what home education may portend for the children themselves, for others, and for broader society. Moreover, many of these issues boil down to concern that home education will not serve the child's best interests (Merry and Karsten 2010; Petrie 2001).

Let us consider these criticisms more closely. First, the argument is that home-educated children miss the opportunity to mix with their peers, and thus are denied the chance to have their experiences and opinions expanded or challenged by encounters with others different from themselves (Apple 2006; Beck 2001; Kunzman 2009; Stevens 2001). This implies that home-educated children are less likely to develop tolerance towards others and the views they hold. Concomitantly, home education is also more likely, critics argue, to prevent children from developing the critical thinking skills necessary for autonomous decision making (Reich 2002a, 2002b). Second, and related to this worry, is the belief that home education, if taken up by too many parents, threatens to undermine the social cohesion needed to forge shared political trust and commitment in a society (Beck 2015; Lubienski 2000; Monk 2004). Both of these views stress the importance of bringing children from different backgrounds together under one roof in order to learn about, with, and from each other. These attractive aims express an important socializing goal of schooling, one with the potential to reduce prejudice, foster critical thinking, and encourage a sense of shared concern with fellow citizens. Promoting a sense of mutuality and shared concern is a worthy goal. Moreover, raising children to be open-minded, respectful of differences, and inclined to cooperate with others with whom they do not share similar ideas or experiences is commendable, and ought to be encouraged and supported. Parents who fail in these endeavors may indeed be said to fail in educating their children well. But that is not the whole story.

Home-educated children typically participate in a variety of learning and social activities with other home-educated children. Indeed, home-educating parents are often keen to develop social networks, both as a means to organize shared learning activities and as a way of promoting social interaction; for reviews of the socialization topic see Medlin (2013) and Murphy (2014). Furthermore, the motivations for educating at home are highly diverse (Rothermel 2003). Just as we find a wide range of family backgrounds and perspectives in a school, so we are also likely to encounter a fair amount of diversity among home educators and their families. To be sure, parents and their children are far more likely to organize activities with others more like themselves than not, but the same is also true of parents with children attending school. It may also be the case that conservative religious parents are more likely to opt for home education; yet even when home education is disallowed or not an option, this fact does not prevent religious parents from selecting religious schools that conform to their personal beliefs. And in Europe, most religious schools are in fact heavily subsidized by the state. Of course, indoctrination of the child should not be the aim of a religious upbringing, but the point is simply that it is not a foregone conclusion that attending a school will diminish the likelihood of this outcome. A third consideration is that it is equally fair to ask whether schools are more likely to succeed in fostering the outcomes for which home educators are so often criticized. Too often, critics of home education make hypothetical claims about it – what *might* happen – and pit these against the most idealized aims of schools: what *should* happen. We can probably all agree that tolerance, critical thinking, and political trust are worthwhile goals, yet still find that they are quite difficult to foster within a school given the way schools sort and select their students, considering how parents themselves select schools, and bearing in mind how pupils express preferences vis-à-vis their own peer group.

Finally, with respect to worries about social cohesion, it must be said first that the meaning of this term is almost never clearly defined by its advocates. More often than not, it appears to denote a compliance with dominant behavioral and attitudinal norms. But these are norms that many parents have good reason to avoid, certainly when they veer toward consumerist or conformist ways of thinking and behaving. Second, the idea that shared school attendance fosters greater cohesion – however that is defined – has never been proven convincingly. In any case, all democratic societies facilitate a plurality of ways in which persons may pursue their life projects in exercise of their own freedom of conscience. Correspondingly, this freedom is frequently coupled with freedom of association: people can choose who to spend their time with. And that, more often than not, means with those of a similar background. Third, in the field of education specifically, all democratic societies make provision for a variety of options, which effectively means that interactions in school between, say, children from different ethnic or religious backgrounds are already limited. But even where schools are not segregated along lines of ethnicity and religion, so that their composition is more mixed, children from different groups are not necessarily more likely to interact (New and Merry 2014). As we have already pointed out, schools themselves use grouping strategies, and their students also tend to succumb to peer preferences. So neither the mitigation of prejudice nor the common purpose and political trust that advocates of schooling claim is a foregone conclusion. These outcomes must be consciously cultivated, under conditions that are not always favorable to them.

But nor should any of the foregoing trivialize fair criticism of home education, where applicable. No doubt, some home educators *are* ill-equipped for the task they have taken on for their children. They can be academically underprepared, poorly organized, emotionally unstable, or intent on indoctrinating their children with unshakable beliefs (Merry and Howell 2009). Each of these conditions warrants disallowing home education in particular cases. But it seems to us that any or all of them could apply in a school setting, too. Moreover, and regardless of the type of education children receive, favorable outcomes invariably rely heavily on their parents. Naturally, teachers and peers also play a role insofar as they can offer a different point of view for children to consider. But a child who learns from her parents that racial prejudice is wrong, for instance, or that we ought to care about others as well as ourselves, is more likely to practice these virtues in interactions with others, irrespective of whether or not they are reinforced in school.

Two final considerations need to be borne in mind. First, if we consider the individual needs and interests of children themselves, we quickly realize that a one-size-fits-all approach to education is not only going to be unpopular with parents, not to mention highly impractical given the range of underlying differences children display and the accommodations educators thus need to make, but is also likely to be viewed as unjust. As we have seen, most European governments by and large recognize that a state monopoly on education is undesirable and so make a variety of educational options available to their citizens, even in nations where home education is forbidden. Second, however we may feel about home education, it will continue to be the case that parents in most countries continue to enjoy legal protections that entitle them to choose an education for their own child in accordance with their own conscience. This does not mean that parents' wishes are always paramount: as we have seen, states have an important regulatory function to play, specifically in ensuring that children are educated in a safe environment, that their learning materials are adequate, and that their instructors are properly qualified to offer instruction in a specific subject. Even so, parents generally enjoy considerable authority in deciding where and how their child will be educated. And this is something the framers of the ECHR and the UNCRC understood very well, that *most* parents are best placed to make good - not perfect - choices for their own children. In Europe, different states interpret and facilitate this freedom in various ways, but the basic principle remains unchanged. Unsurprisingly, then, countries that aim to ban or severely restrict home education often have difficulty justifying this policy in the light of the more basic moral and constitutional freedoms of education that all parents are guaranteed.

Acknowledgments

We wish to thank Petar Balkanski (Bulgaria), Christian Beck (Norway), Marek Budajczak (Poland), Mrs. Földi (Hungary), Jonas Himmelstrand (Sweden), Madalen Goiria (Spain), Els Hoendervoogt (Austria), Tiia Leis (Estonia), Claudia Sousa (Portugal), and Thomas Spiegler (Germany) for their help in locating and checking national information. It is the authors' responsibility if any information is incorrect.

References

7SUR7. 2008. "La Scolarité à Domicile en Augmentation en 2007." Accessed March 24, 2015. http://www.7sur7.be/7s7/fr/1502/Belgique/article/detail/124848/2008/01/07/La-scolarite-a-domicile-en-augmentation-en-2007.dhtml

Apple, Michael W. 2006. *Educating the "Right" Way: Markets, Standards, God, and Inequality*, 2nd ed. New York, NY: Routledge.

Basham, Patrick, John Merrifield, and Claudia, R. Hepburn. 2007. *Home Schooling: from the Extreme to the Mainstream*, 2nd ed. Vancouver, Canada: The Fraser Institute. Accessed February 24, 2015. https://www.fraserinstitute.org/sites/default/files/Homeschooling2007.pdf

Beck, Christian W. 2001. "Alternative Education and Home Schooling in Norway." *Childhood Education*, 77: 356–359.

Beck, Christian W. 2015. "Home Education and Social Integration." In *International Perspectives on Home Education*, edited by Paula Rothermel, 87–98. Basingstoke, UK: Palgrave Macmillan.

Blok, Henk, and Joke Sperling. 2012. "Thuisonderwijs in Nederland en Vlaanderen: een Review" [Home Education in the Netherlands and in Flanders: a Review]. *Pedagogiek*, 32: 234–250.

Controscuola, n. d. "Homeschooling in Italy." Accessed March 24, 2015. http://www.controscuola.it/english/

derStandard.at. 2011. "Häuslicher Unterricht ist in Österreich äuszerst Selten," 22 November. Accessed March 24, 2015. http://derstandard.at/1319183480065/Anfrage-Haeuslicher-Unterricht-ist-in-Oesterreich-aeusserst-selten

Elizalde, María, Carme Urpí, and María Tejada. 2012. "Diversidad, Participación y Calidad educativas: Necesidades y Posibilidades del Homeschooling" Diversity, Parent Involvement and Quality Education: Needs and Possibilities of Homeschooling]. *Estudios Sobre Educación*, 22: 55–72.

Gaither, Milton. 2008. *Homeschool: An American History*. New York, NY: Palgrave Macmillan.

Gaither, Milton. 2009. "Homeschooling in the USA: Past, Present and Future." *Theory and Research in Education*, 7: 331–346.

Home Education in the Netherlands. 2013. "State Secretary Dekker's Ban on Home Education is Behind the Times." Accessed February, 2015. http://www.home-education.nl/press-release-nvvto-state-secretary-dekkers-ban-on-home-education

Koons, Colin. 2010. "Education on the Home Front: Home Education in the European Union and the Need for Unified European Policy." *Indiana International and Comparative Law Review*, 20: 145–174.

Kostelecká, Yvona. 2010. "Home Education in the Post-communist Countries: Case study of the Czech Republic." *International Electronic Journal of Elementary Education*, 3(1): 29–44.

Kunzman, Robert. 2009. *Write These Laws on Your Children: Inside the World of Conservative Christian Homeschooling*. Boston, MA: Beacon Press.

Le Figaro. 2010. "13.500 Enfants ne Vont pas à l'École," July 4. Accessed March 24, 2015. http://www.lefigaro.fr/flash-actu/2010/04/07/97001-20100407FILWWW00520-13500-enfants-ne-vont-pas-a-l-ecole.php

Les Enfants d'Abord. 2010a. "Rapport 2009 de la Miviludes et Instruction en Famille; un Amalgame de Trop!" [Report 2009 of Miviludes on Home Education: a Superfluous Melting Pot]. Accessed February 24, 2015. http://www.lesenfantsdabord.org/wp-content/uploads/2012/06/reactionrapportMIVILUDES1.pdf

Les Enfants d'Abord. 2010b. "Les Contrôles Pédagogiques État des Lieux" [Inspections at Home]. Accessed February 24, 2015. http://www.lesenfantsdabord.org/wp-content/uploads/2012/06/Controles_pedagogiques-Etat_des_Lieux-2010.pdf

Lubienski, Christopher. 2000. "Whither the Common Good? A Critique of Home Schooling." *Peabody Journal of Education*, 75: 207–232.

Martin, Aaron T. 2010. Homeschooling in Germany and the United States. *Arizona Journal of International and Comparative Law*, 27: 225–282.

Medlin, Richard G. 2013. "Homeschooling and Socialization Revisited." *Peabody Journal of Education*, 88: 284–297.

Merry, Michael S., and Charles Howell. 2009. "Can Intimacy Justify Home Education?" *Theory and Research in Education*, 7: 363–381.

Merry, Michael S., and Sjoerd Karsten. 2010. "Restricted Liberty, Parental Choice and Homeschooling." *Journal of Philosophy of Education*, 44: 497–514.

Ministère de l'Éducation Nationale, de la Jeunesse et de la Vie Associative. 2012. "Bulletin Officiel n° 3 du 19 Janvier 2012". Accessed February 24, 2015. http://media.education.gouv.fr/file/3/46/0/instruction_famille_204460.pdf

Monk, Daniel. 2004. "Problematising Home Education: Challenging Parental Rights and 'Socialisation'." *Legal Studies*, 24: 568–598.

Murphy, Joseph. 2014. "Social and Educational Outcomes of Homeschooling." *Sociological Spectrum*, 34: 244–272.

New, William S., and Michael S. Merry. 2014. "Is Diversity Necessary for Educational Justice?" *Educational Theory*, 64: 205–225.

Paciorkowski, Szymon. 2014. "Homeschooling in Poland? Legal Status and Arguments Used in Polish Debate over Home Education." *Social Transformations in Contemporary Society*, 22: 153–162.

Petrie, Amanda. 2001. "Home Education in Europe and the Implementation of Changes to the Law." *International Review of Education*, 47: 477–500.

Reich, Rob. 2002a. "Opting out of Education: Yoder, Mozart, and the Autonomy of Children." *Educational Theory*, 52: 445–461.

Reich, Rob. 2002b. *Bridging Liberalism and Multiculturalism in Education*. Chicago, IL: University of Chicago Press.

Reimer, Franz. 2010. "School Attendance as a Civic Duty vs. Home Education as a Human Right." *International Journal of Elementary Education*, 3(1): 5–15.

Riksorganisationen för Hemundervisning I Sverige. 2010. "How the Swedish Government Voted Against a Human Right." Accessed February 24, 2015. http://hemundervisning.org/en/?English_information

Rothermel, Paula. 2003. "Can We Classify Motives for Home Education?" *Evaluation and Research in Education*, 17(2&3): 74–89.

Sperling, Joke. 2010 *"Moet jij niet naar School?" Een Onderzoek naar de Juridische Aspecten van Thuisonderwijs vanuit Nederlands en Rechtsvergelijkend Perspectief ["Don't you have to go to School?" A Study into the Legal Aspects of Home Education in the Netherlands]*. Rotterdam, The Netherlands: Erasmus University.

Sperling, Joke. 2015. "Home Education and the European Convention on Human Rights." In *International Perspectives on Home Education*, edited by Paula Rothermel, 179–188. Basingstoke, UK: Palgrave Macmillan.

Spiegler, Thomas. 2003. "Home Education in Germany: An Overview of the Contemporary Situation." *Evaluation and Research in Education*, 17: 179–190.

Spiegler, Thomas. 2009. "Parents' Motives for Home Education: The Influence of Methodological Design and Social Context." *International Electronic Journal of Elementary Education*, 3: 57–70.

Stevens, Mitchell L. 2001. *Kingdom of Children: Culture and Controversy in the Homeschooling Movement*. Princeton, NJ: Princeton University Press.

Valero Estarellas, María J. 2013. "The Long Way Home: Recent Developments in the Spanish Case Law on Home Education." *Oxford Journal of Law and Religion*, 2: 1–25.

Vlaams Ministerie van Onderwijs and Vorming. 2011. *Huisonderwijs; Evaluatie 2008–2009 en 2009–2010 [Home Education; Annual Report 2008–2009 and 2009–2010]*. Brussels, Belgium: Agentschap voor Onderwijsdiensten. Accessed February 24, 2015. http://www.vlaanderen.be/nl/publicaties/detail/huisonderwijs-evaluatie-2008-2009-en-2009-2010

17

Home Education Experience in Selected Post-Communist Countries

Yvona Kostelecká

Introduction

Since the late 18th and early 19th centuries, dedicated educational institutions (i.e. schools) have been the dominant sites for children's education in most industrialized societies. However, an opposing trend emerged in the United States in the 1970s and 1980s, when parents began protesting against compulsory school attendance and fighting for their right to choose the manner of educating their children. Similar tendencies emerged shortly after that in other Anglo-Saxon countries, and also in other developed countries in Western Europe and the rest of the world (Kostelecká 2014a).

Following the fall of the Iron Curtain, similar tendencies appeared in the so-called post-communist countries in Central Europe and eventually resulted in incorporating the home education option into said countries' legislation. Even though homeschooling has become legal in Central European countries, creating the ideal legislative framework for it is an ongoing process. So far, there has been a shortage of comprehensive research reports that describe the situation in these countries in a systematic manner and present the acquired data and practical home-education experience to both experts and the general public, as has long been the case in developed Western countries, where intensive research has been conducted for many years (Beck 2002, 2008, 2010; Blok 2004; Brabant 2009; Dalahooke 1986; Gaither 2008; Kunzman 2012; Martin-Chang, Gould, and Meuse 2011; Morton 2010; Murphy 2014; Petrie 1995, 2001; Ray 1994, 1997; Reimer 2010; Rothermel 2002; Sheng 2014; Thomas 1998; Van Pelt 2015 and more). Several articles have so far been published on the issue in the Czech Republic.

The first text to introduce home education into the public debate was an article published in a professional teaching magazine by Jiří Tůma (2001), a mathematician

The Wiley Handbook of Home Education, First Edition. Edited by Milton Gaither.

and associate professor at Charles University in Prague. Tůma, one of the first promoters of home education in the country, opened the discussion about home education among teachers by providing information about the existence of home education in some EU states. As Tůma himself homeschooled his own children during his research stay at a university in Australia in the early 1990s, he was also able to share some of his personal insights into the practical aspects of homeschooling.

A study on the educational and psychological aspects of home education that was published in the leading Czech scientific journal *Pedagogika* by the well-known Czech psychologist Václav Mertin (2003), introduced the subject of home education to academia. Comparing home education with education in schools, Mertin concluded that the conditions in contemporary schools do not enable them to provide pupils with an environment as supportive of child learning as the environment that can be provided at home. He cited large classes, lack of emotional support for individual children, and a process of learning that separated academic disciplines into poorly linked individual entities as the main weaknesses of schools. Although the conclusions of Mertin's study have been cheered by proponents of home education in the Czech Republic, they have spurred great debate within the academic community. In reaction to Mertin's article, the journal published a second article on home education written by another well-known Czech psychologist, Stanislav Štech (2003). Contrary to Mertin, Štech was critical to the idea of a family as the "optimal environment" for development and education of children and did not see school as an impersonal institution incapable of providing effective education. In his theoretical study Štech stressed that individuals need both primary socialization in the family as well as subsequent secondary socialization in school for their healthy development. He considered home education as one of the "second order" options for educating children, not really a full-fledged alternative to education provided by schools. Both articles attracted a lot of attention and contributed to a division within the professional community into two opposing groups: supporters and opponents of home education.

The first empirically based study on home education in the Czech Republic was published by Kostelecká (2003). Based on a survey of homeschooling families, interviews with both homeschoolers and their supervisors, studying academic results of home-educated children, and actively observing the learning process in families, this the study provided basic information about the "pioneers" of homeschooling in the Czech Republic. It shed light on who the homeschooling parents were and revealed their motives for homeschooling, along with their attitudes, opinions, and teaching methods, their experience concerning the cooperation with schools overseeing the process of education, and so on. The research revealed that most homeschooling parents were well educated couples with an above average number of children. Most of them followed the traditional model of a family, with fathers working long hours as the primary breadwinners while the majority of mothers, who served as principal educators of their children, were not involved in paid jobs and concentrated on childcare and homecare.

Kostelecká's next article (2005) compared the practical aspects of home education in the Czech Republic with that in the most developed countries. She concluded that the regulation of the home education by the state was substantially stricter in the Czech Republic than in most Western countries. Extending this research to the situation in other post-communist states (Kostelecká 2010) revealed that the Czech Republic was not an atypical example but rather a typical case in this respect. The general features and the basic principles of home education in the post-communist countries of Central East Europe can be found in an article published in the *International Review of Education* (Kostelecká 2012).

Some of the studies published in the Czech Republic have devoted attention to the specific methodological aspects of home education. The methodological aspects of environmental education in the curricula of homeschooling families was researched by Jančaříková (2008). More recently, Pražáková (2012) studied the teaching styles of math among homeschoolers. She has pointed out that the teaching styles of homeschoolers tend to change over time and are highly dependent on the level and type of education of the home-educating parents. Parents with a higher level of education tended to be more flexible as far as the teaching methods were concerned. They also used less structured and less rigidly organized time schedules for the math lessons than parents with lower levels of education. The study also revealed that home-educating parents tend to use different situations in their daily lives as an opportunity to teach math, including informal conversation with their children. Pražáková estimates that such teaching methods bring about a high proportion of implicit and unintended learning. The study, however, did not pay attention to the academic results of such education. In this chapter, we will attempt to add to the existing knowledge by providing a detailed analysis of the legislation on home education in the following Central European post-communist countries: Czech Republic, Poland, Slovakia, Slovenia, and Hungary. All of these were first established as independent countries following the dissolution of the Austro-Hungarian Empire. After World War II, all of them fell into the Soviet Union's sphere of influence and remained there until the late 1980s, when communist regimes across Europe collapsed. In the 1990s, society in the five countries experienced profound transformation, resulting in their accession to the European Union in 2004. They are currently striving to complete the transformation of all aspects of their social system, including education, and to create a coherent, functioning democratic regime in all respects. We will provide a detailed description and analysis of home education legislation in the above countries, partly to identify some characteristic trends but also to discover certain differences based on the countries' unique national attributes.

Homeschooling as Part of Compulsory School Attendance, or Compulsory Education?

It is worth mentioning that not all countries use the term "homeschooling/home education" in their legislation. In fact, the only country currently using it is Slovenia. Czech and Slovak legislation uses the term "individual education"; Polish legislation speaks of "out-of-school education"; Hungary describes homeschoolers as "private students." Regardless of the term used, it is obvious the legislation refers to more or less the same thing. Therefore, we have decided to use the generally accepted term "homeschooling/home education" in this chapter.

First attempts to legalize home education in Central European countries occurred in the early 1990s. However, countries interested in offering the option after the fall of the Iron Curtain had to figure out a way of doing it that would not clash with existing legislation. The process was easier for those post-communist countries that amended their legislation, replacing the notion of compulsory school attendance, typical for the former Eastern Bloc countries, with compulsory education (Petrie 1995, 2001). Such transformation in education legislation happened in Hungary and Slovenia. The remaining three countries (Czech Republic, Poland, Slovakia) retained the legislative concept of compulsory school attendance and subsequently had to decide whether to pass an amendment allowing homeschooled children to be exempt from compulsory school attendance or to introduce home education as a legitimate form of compulsory school attendance. All three countries eventually decided to go with the second option.

Countries with compulsory education

In countries with compulsory education, i.e. Hungary and Slovenia, the legalization of homeschooling was an easier process. Home education was simply listed among the legitimate forms of compulsory education. Therefore, home education legislation in these countries appears logical and consistent. Article 6, section 1 of the Hungarian Public Education Act of 1993 states that "every child is obliged to participate in education in the Republic of Hungary, as prescribed by this Act" (Act No. LXXIX, 1993). Article 7, section 1 further states that "compulsory education may be completed by school attendance or as a private student, on the basis of the choice of the parents." The wording of the Act makes it clear that school attendance is only one of the forms of compulsory education. Parents are therefore allowed to choose the manner of educating their children. The private student status, which also includes homeschooling, is included explicitly. In Slovenia, the situation is similar. The Slovenian Elementary School Act of 1996 is even clearer on the issue, stating explicitly in Article 5 that "parents have the right to choose elementary education for their children either by means of public or private schools or by means of home education" (Elementary School Act, 1996).

Countries with compulsory school attendance

The situation is far more complicated in countries with compulsory school attendance. Homeschooling has been introduced as one of the forms of compulsory school attendance, albeit sometimes in a very peculiar way. Article 19, section 1 of the Slovak Education Act states that "nobody can be exempted from obligatory school attendance" (Act 245/2008, 2008). Article 20, section 1 further states that "obligatory school attendance is fulfilled in elementary schools, secondary schools..." Nevertheless, Article 23 names "individual education" as one of the forms of compulsory school attendance: "individual education that is realized without regular participation in education in a school..."

In the Czech Republic, the situation is similar. Compulsory school attendance is confirmed by the Charter of Fundamental Rights and Freedoms, a constitutional act (Charter, 1993). Article 33, section (1) of the Charter states that "everybody has a right to education. School attendance is obligatory for the period regulated by the law." Article 36, section (1) of the Education Act also states explicitly that school attendance is compulsory (Act 561/2004, 2004). In spite of that, Article 40 of the Act defines an "other way" of completing compulsory education, defined as "individual education that is realized without regular participation in education in school..."

In Poland, the state of affairs is similarly complicated. An amendment to the Polish Constitution of 1997 states in Article 70, section (1) that "everybody has a right to education. Education is obligatory till the age of eighteen (Act No. 483/1997, 2007). The manner of fulfilling the compulsory schooling is regulated by law." The Polish Constitution thus mentions the right to receive education and the compulsory nature of education, but also compulsory school attendance, which should be further regulated by law. The Polish Education System Act of 1991 states in Article 16, section (5) that compulsory education may be completed by "attending elementary and secondary school, public and private" (Act No. 425/1991, 1991). The Act mentions no other manner of obtaining compulsory education. However, section (8) of the Article 70 mentions "out of school" education as an alternative manner of compulsory school attendance.

Even though we might expect that countries with compulsory education would be able to legalize homeschooling more swiftly and easily, that has not been the case. On the contrary: the first post-communist Central European country to legalize home education was Poland, which prescribes compulsory school attendance. The option to homeschool children was explicitly mentioned in the Education Act No. 425/1991 adopted by the first post-communist parliament in 1991 (Dueholm 2006). The second country to legalize home education was Hungary: in the Public Education Act of 1993, it introduced the status of a private student who may be educated individually, outside of an educational institution (Act No. LXXIX, 1993). Slovenia made homeschooling legally possible in 1996 (Elementary School Act, 1996). In the Czech Republic, the situation was rather specific. Home education had been legally permitted since the school year 1998–1999, but only as an experimental assessment of home education as a distinct way of organizing elementary education, meant exclusively for pupils in lower elementary schools (P. Kolář 2000). Officially, such education was only made legal in 2004 (Act 561/2004, 2004). Slovakia only legalized home education nearly twenty years after the fall of the communist regime, by the Education Act of 2008 (Act 245/2008, 2008).

Homeschooling Legislative Framework: A Detailed Description

Over the past 20 years, homeschooling legislation has gradually developed in most of the countries in question. What is the current situation? Who may receive home education in each of the five countries? What conditions must be met in order to be allowed to homeschool one's children? How does the state monitor home education and evaluate its results? We shall attempt to provide answers to all of these questions.

Home education target groups

In general, the target groups allowed to receive home education are different in each country (Petrie 1995, 2001; Kostelecká 2003, 2012). Some countries allow homeschooling for all children within the compulsory education age group, while others limit homeschooling to specific target groups. Hungary, Slovenia, and Poland are among the former; the Czech Republic and Slovakia impose an age limit. In the Czech Republic, the Education Act of 2004 states in Article 41, section (1) that "individual education is only permitted for pupils at the lower elementary school level" (Act 561/2004, 2004). Even though the Act does not allow individual education at the upper elementary school level, it is available in the form of experimental testing, introduced by the ministry of education on May 23, 2007. Of the five countries analyzed in this chapter, Slovakia is the most restrictive in its legislation concerning homeschooling: individual education is only allowed for pupils unable to attend school due to health reasons, pupils at the lower elementary school level, and students held in custody or serving a prison sentence, who are therefore unable to attend school. Homeschooling is therefore available to a considerably limited target group.

Prerequisites for homeschooling

Some countries prescribe certain conditions that must be met for the child to be allowed homeschooling. In this respect, the five countries in question fall in two groups again: those which allow homeschooling without the need to obtain approval from an authorized institution, and those where parents have to apply for permission to homeschool their children. The former group includes countries with compulsory education, i.e. Hungary and Slovenia; and the Czech Republic, Poland and Slovakia, which prescribe compulsory school attendance, belong to the latter.

Parents in Slovenia need not apply to be able to homeschool their children, since it is a legitimate option granted by law. Article 5 of the Elementary School Act states that parents have the right to either send their children to a public or private school, or to educate them at home (Elementary School Act, 1996). Article 88 of said Act states that "parents have the right to organize home education for their children at the elementary school level." Parents who wish to homeschool their children have to meet a single, albeit formal, condition: Article 89 of the Education Act requires that parents wishing to homeschool their children notify the principal of the school at which the child has been accepted, no later than three months prior to the start of the school year (Elementary School Act, 1996). Such a notification must include the public education program the parents have chosen to follow, the child's full name, the address at which home education will take place, and a full name of the person teaching the child.

Hungary has a similar, but slightly more restrictive legislation. The state imposes no restrictions regarding the start of home education and does not require the parents to justify their reasons for choosing homeschooling; the choice to homeschool is left solely at the parents' discretion (Education Hungary… 2008): "Compulsory education may be completed by school attendance or as a private student, based on the parents' choice." (Article 7, section (1)) (Act No. LXXIX, 1993). Article 11, section (1) of the Education Act also defines the rights of the students: letter (n) mentions the students' right to be exempt from curricular activities: "they might become private students and apply for exemption from curricular activities". There are certain legal prerequisites for homeschooling, albeit only of a formal nature. Article 16 of the Ministerial Decree of 1994 states that all children within the compulsory education age group must enroll at a school (Ministerial Decree, 2004). Parents who wish to homeschool their children must notify the principal of the school where the child has been enrolled and Article 23, section (1) of the Decree states that the principal must contact the local child welfare service to ascertain that homeschooling would not be harmful for the child.

On the other hand, countries with compulsory school attendance have a more or less stringent approval process. In Poland, the parents' wish alone is not deemed sufficient reason for homeschooling. Permission to homeschool must be granted by the principal of the school where the child has been enrolled. The Polish Education Act of 2009 states that at the parents' request, the principal of the school where the child has been enrolled may allow the child to be educated outside of the school (Act No. 458/2009, 2009). The permission to homeschool a child may be granted provided that the parents file the application by May 31, with the following documents attached: opinion of the local education advisory center; the parents' declaration promising to assure adequate conditions for following the relevant compulsory curriculum; and the parents' assurance that the child will sit all the required exams every year. However, the principal of the school where the child has been enrolled may not grant the parents' request even if all of the above conditions have been met.

In the Czech Republic, home education is governed by the Education Act of 2004 (Act 561/2004, 2004). Article 41, section (1) states that parents may apply to the school principal to allow "individual education": "The school principal has the power to authorize home education." Article 41, section (3), letter a) states that the principal may authorize home education, provided that "relevant reasons for home education exist." However, the Act does not state explicitly which reasons may be considered relevant, and leaves the decision at the principal's discretion. Unusually, the Education Act also requires that in order to obtain permission for homeschooling, parents need to provide a description of the space, materials, and technologies used for homeschooling, and to prove that they have met the conditions for adequate health protection. This implies that the truthfulness of such information may be verified by an "inspection visit" to the applicant's home, which may entail a number of problems. Where the parents' application was denied due to "insufficient space, materials, and technologies," or "inadequate health protection," it would lead to an absurd situation: the state would not allow the child to be educated at a place they live and spend most of their time outside of school. Another major prerequisite for allowing homeschooling is that the home educator has completed at least secondary education with a "Maturita" (exit examination comparable to high school graduation).

Home education legislation in Slovakia is similarly complicated. Article 24 of the Slovak Education Act of 2008 refers to homeschooling as "individual education" (Act 245/2008, 2008). Section (1) states that individual education may be permitted by the principal of the school where the child has been enrolled for compulsory school attendance. The Education Act stipulates a number of prerequisites that must be met in order to be allowed to homeschool one's child. The decision is made by the school principal based on an application by the child's legal representative. Article 24, section (4) of the Education Act states that "education of a pupil who has been allowed to receive individual education … is guaranteed by the legal representative of the child, and must be provided by a person qualified as a certified teacher at lower elementary school level." This condition considerably limits the number of people who may be allowed to homeschool their children. In order to homeschool, parents have to be qualified lower elementary school teachers, otherwise they have to hire a qualified teacher at their own cost. Article 24, section (14) states: "The legal representative shall pay 'financial remuneration' to the person providing individual education to the pupil." Article 24, section (5) of the Education Act stipulates further prerequisites that must be met in order to be allowed homeschooling: full name of the child; date of birth; birth registration number; address of permanent residence; school year; reasons for seeking home education; description of an individual education program, the principles and objectives of which must comply with the Education Act; description of the space, material, and technical conditions in which homeschooling will be provided, as well as adequate health protection; full name of the educator and proof of qualification; list of textbooks and other learning materials; and any other information relevant for the pupil's individual education.

Home education evaluators

Countries that offer home education as a legal alternative to school attendance usually appoint certain institutions as guarantors that the contents and results of home education comply with all legal requirements. In Slovenia, Hungary, Poland, and the Czech Republic this responsibility has been assigned to schools in which the child has enrolled for compulsory school attendance or compulsory education. Slovakia is more restrictive: in addition to schools, the homeschoolers' performance is also assessed by the school inspection service.

In Slovenia, the school is responsible for maintaining all required documentation regarding the progress of the child's homeschooling. Hungary has a similar arrangement. Article 66, section (1) of the Hungarian Education Act states explicitly that homeschooled children are in a legal relation to the school they have enrolled at or transferred to. The school's responsibility is to evaluate the child's progress. In certain specific circumstances, parents may request that the child's education results be evaluated by an independent committee; however, final assessment is still within the school's authority. In Poland, home education is also tied to the school the child has enrolled at for compulsory school attendance. School principals are responsible for overseeing that all legal prerequisites have been met. The same is true for the Czech Republic. Slovakia is the only post-communist Central European country where the school principal is not the only one responsible for overseeing home education. Article 24, section (10) of the Slovak Education Act states that "quality of the individual education is verified by the State School Inspection… Educational, material, technical, and health conditions of individual education are supervised by the school where the pupil is enrolled (Act 245/2008, 2008). The legal representative of the pupil is obligated to enable on-site inspections by an authorized school inspector and an authorized employee of the school."

Home education evaluation methods

The methods of evaluating the results of homeschooling vary considerably from country to country, depending mainly on the extent to which evaluation methods are prescribed by current legislation or left at the discretion of the school principals. In this respect, the five countries in question can be divided into two complementary groups: those where legislation does not specify the form and frequency of homeschooling evaluation (Hungary), and those where the national Education Acts prescribed both the frequency and method of evaluation (Slovenia, Poland, Czech Republic, Slovakia).

Of the five countries in question, Hungary is the only one where the law does not prescribe any specific method of homeschooled pupils' evaluation or the intervals at which they should be evaluated. Article 23, section (2) of the Regulation on Educational Institutions states explicitly that decisions regarding the child's advancement, evaluation methods, and frequency are fully within the schools' competence.

In contrast, Slovenian law prescribes a specific evaluation method. Article 90 of the Elementary School Act states that homeschooled children must pass an evaluation exam in order to establish whether they have achieved the same level of education they would have attained by attending school. Such an exam is repeated at the end of each school year. If pupils fail to demonstrate the required level of knowledge, they have the right to retake the exam. In case of a repeatedly failed exam, the pupil has to start attending school in the next school year.

Polish law also prescribes the method for evaluating the results of home education. Article 16, section (12) of the Polish Education Act states that every homeschooled child must pass a final exam for each school year, which is conducted by the school where the child has been enrolled for compulsory school attendance (Act No. 458/2009, 2009). If the child passes the final exam, he/she will receive a school report for the given year. The final exams include both written and oral examination, held at the date agreed upon by the pupil and his/her parents. The final exam is conducted by a committee appointed by the school principal. The principal or his/her deputy also acts as chair of the committee, which consists of teachers for each subject that is included in the respective school year's curriculum. The committee chair, the pupil and his/her parents agree on the number of subjects in which the pupil will be examined in one day. Section (13) of the Education Act states that "during the graded exam, parents (legal representatives) of a child can be present as observers." The school must then issue an exam report with the following information: pupil's full name; exam committee members; date of exam; exam content, results, and final evaluation. The pupil's written test and a short description of the oral exam are also attached to the exam report, which is then handed out to the pupil together with their regular school report. If the curriculum includes vocational training, and the pupil is therefore unable to obtain a grade in the practicals, the school should organize substitute activities that will allow the pupil to complete their curriculum and obtain a grade.

In the Czech Republic, Article 41, section (4) of the Education Act states that a homeschooled pupil must take an exam at the end of each term comprised of that term's curriculum (Act 561/2004, 2004). The exam is conducted at the school where the pupil has enrolled for compulsory school attendance. If it is not possible to evaluate the pupil at the end of a term, the school principal will set up an alternative date for the exam, which must take place no later than two months after the end of the respective term. In case the child's legal representative has any misgivings regarding the exam result, he/she may ask the school principal for a re-examination. If the principal agrees, the pupil will be re-examined by a committee. In case the school principal also acted as the examiner, the child's legal representatives have the right to ask the relevant regional authority for re-examination. In case the regional authority decides to grant the legal representatives' request, a new committee will be established to re-examine the pupil.

The Slovak Education Act states in Article 24, section (6) that a homeschooled pupil must take an exam twice a year consisting of the relevant curriculum. The exam is conducted at the school where the pupil has enrolled for compulsory school attendance. If the child passes the exam, he/she will receive a school report. However, the school principal has to take the child's health into account. Article 57 of the Act also stipulates the exam format. The examination committee must have at least three members, with the school principal or another teacher appointed by the principal serving as committee chair. Other committee members include the examiner and an assessor, who must possess the required qualifications for the exam subject or a related subject. The committee chair announces the exam result on the same day the exam has been taken, and the grade the pupil receives is final. The principal may allow the child's legal representative to be present at the exam. It is quite evident that Slovak home education legislation is in many aspects the strictest of the five countries in question. The wording of the law rules out virtually all parents as educators of their own children, since it prescribes unusually strict and specific qualification prerequisites. Parents interested in homeschooling are more or less forced to hire a certified teacher at their own cost. The law also partially intrudes on family privacy by demanding that the parents allow inspection visits of authorized personnel from the State Inspection Commission and staff of the school where the child has been enrolled for compulsory school attendance. Last but not least, children must sit for exams before a committee to which their teachers and legal representatives may not be admitted. The child's legal representatives merely have the right to request permission to be present at the examination by committee. The exam grade is final and may not be disputed.

Subject of evaluation

As in the previous instance, the situation in the five countries in question varies in the extent to which the subject of evaluation is prescribed by law or left at the school principal's discretion. Again, the countries fall into two categories. In the first group, the subject of evaluation is prescribed by legislation (Slovenia, Poland, Czech Republic, Slovakia); in the second, evaluation is left at the school principal's discretion (Hungary).

The Slovenian Education Act provides the most detailed description of subjects evaluated in each school grade. In grades one to three of elementary school, pupils are tested in math and their mother tongue. In grades four to seven, they are also tested in a foreign language. In grades seven to nine, the examination involves a number of subjects: mother tongue, math, foreign language, history, civics and ethics, physical education, etc. All of these subjects are prescribed in Article 28 of the Act.

Article 17 of the Polish Education Act of 2007 also prescribes the form and content of the homeschoolers' examination (Ministerial Decree, 2007). The examination of homeschooled children does not include certain subjects that are compulsory under "normal" circumstances, such as technology, arts and crafts, music, physical education or any other elective subjects; neither does it include the pupils' conduct.

Czech legislation does not explicitly state which subjects shall be involved in the examination; it merely stipulates that homeschooled pupils should take an exam twice a year in the "relevant curriculum." Similarly, homeschooled pupils in Slovakia must take an exam in the "relevant curriculum" before a committee.

Prerequisites for continued home education

In all of the five countries, parents are allowed to continue homeschooling their children provided they meet certain legally defined prerequisites. However, such requirements vary greatly from country to country. Article 90 of the Slovenian Education Act states that in order to be allowed continued homeschooling, "a pupil must receive education of at least comparable quality to the education provided by the educational program of the public school". If a pupil fails to meet this condition in a given school year, even after a repeated examination, he/she must start attending school in the next year. In Hungary, an assessment is performed to ascertain whether home education is suitable for the given child. Article 7, section (2) of the Education Act of 1993 (Act No. LXXIX, 1993) states that "if the head teacher or the office of the public guardian or the child welfare service deems it disadvantageous for a student to complete their compulsory education as a private student, or the student may be expected not to complete their studies begun as a private student, they are obliged to inform the public administration officer of the competent council where the student's domicile or, in default of this, place of residence is. The public administration officer decides in which manner the student should complete their compulsory education."

Polish law stipulates that school principals may withdraw their permission for a child to be educated outside of school if a child fails to attend the graded examination without a justified reason or fails the exam.

The Czech Republic deals with the issue in a similar manner. Article 41, section (7) of the Education Act lists the circumstances under which a school principal may withdraw their permission for a child to be homeschooled: the child's legal representatives have failed to ensure suitable conditions for home education (poor material conditions, insufficient teacher qualification, inadequate health protection); the child's legal representatives have not complied with the prerequisites prescribed by law; the child fails the examination at the end of the second term of the school year, or cannot be evaluated.

Slovakia also leaves the decision to allow a child to continue home education to the school principal or the school inspector. Article 24, section (11) of the Slovak Education Act stipulates the circumstances under which a school principal may withdraw his/her permission for a child to be homeschooled. Individual education may be discontinued if the child's legal representative has failed to comply with the prerequisites prescribed by law, if the child has failed the examination at the end of an evaluation period, or at the school inspector's suggestion.

Reasons for Choosing Homeschooling

Why do parents choose to educate their children at home? In answering this question we cannot compare the situation across different post-communist countries in Central Europe, since we only have the required data for the Czech

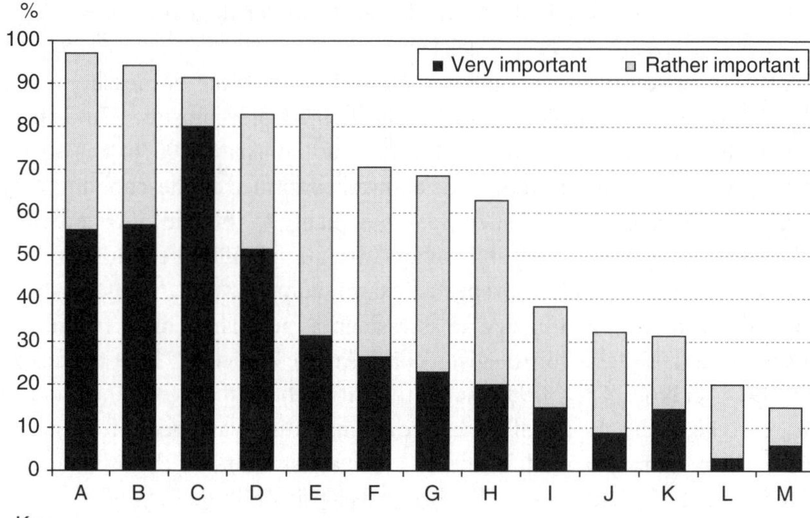

Key

A. Homeschooling allows our family greater freedom.
B. I want to spend as much time with my children as possible.
C. Homeschooling allows us to adjust the speed and content of learning to suit the child's needs.
D. I want to retain as much influence on my child's upbringing as possible, until he/she is mature enough to form his/her own judgment.
E. I am afraid my child will imitate his/her schoolmates' behavior, and our influence as parents will be limited.
F. I am afraid of possible pathological social behavior in a school (bullying, smoking, drinking, drugs, etc.).
G. I want to protect my child from the stress and tension school work may bring.
H. I am afraid that school will reinforce stereotypes, and cause my child to lose his/her identity, creativity, and initiative.
I. I am convinced that homeschooling is the best way to obtain good education.
J. I am afraid that school would hold my child back.
K. Religious reasons.
L. I have doubts concerning the quality of education at the school my child is (was) supposed to attend.
M. I am afraid of my child's failure at school.

Figure 17.1 Reasons for homeschooling in the Czech Republic.

Republic (Kostelecká 2003). In a survey conducted shortly after the introduction of home education in the Czech Republic, parents were offered thirteen possible reasons that might have played a more or less significant role in deciding whether or not to homeschool their children. Parents were asked to determine how important each reason was for them, on a scale of 1 to 4: 1 = not important at all; 2 = not very important; 3 = rather important; 4 = very important (Figure 17.1 shows results for ratings 3 and 4).

Figure 17.1 clearly indicates that when deciding to homeschool, parents placed different weight on the proposed reasons. First of all, it appears that most parents were not motivated by doubts as to the quality of school education, fear of the child's failure, or fear that school would hold their child back. Academic reasons in general seemed to have played a minor role. On the other hand, most respondents put great emphasis on the reasons related to their desire to retain as much influence on the child's upbringing as possible and for the family to remain the primary place to instill values they consider important. It seems that parents had no objections against school as an institution of learning, but they did not wish to allow the school to share the influence on their child's upbringing. Surprisingly, these homeschooling parents did not list fear of pathological social behavior among the most important reasons, even though the situation in Czech schools in this respect is far from ideal. M. Kolář (2000) estimates that "20 percent of children at all school levels have been subject to bullying, which amounts to approximately 300000 students." Factor analysis offers a more in-depth understanding of the parents' responses. We have used factor analysis from the SPSS statistical program, principal components method, Varimax rotation. Results indicate that there are five primary reasons which might lead parents to homeschool their children. The first probable reason is the parents' desire to build a strong, cohesive family unit. Other reasons include a desire to tailor instruction to the child's developmental needs, protection of the child from some of the school's negative characteristics, fear of the child's negative socialization, and the belief that individualized instruction offers benefits to the child.

Considering that the above survey might not have covered all reasons leading parents to choose homeschooling and could not have taken into account specific cases that do not fit a predefined scale, a subsequent survey was conducted to gain deeper insight into the issue. To obtain the desired information, an in-depth guided interview with the parents was used. In-depth interviews precluded a large respondent sample, and the results obtained therefore cannot be quantified; they merely provide a better qualitative insight. In-depth interviews regarding the parents' motivation to homeschool their children basically indicate that there are two types of homeschooling families:

1. Those who have been forced to choose homeschooling "due to circumstances": they usually included families with a previous negative schooling experience.
2. Those who might be called "homeschoolers by conviction." Their children had not been forced to start homeschooling due to poor schooling experience. Most of them have never attended school and if they did, they did not have any serious problems.

The two groups of parents usually gave vastly different reasons for their decision to homeschool. They tended to give more than one reason that motivated them to start – usually, it was a combination of several reasons, some of them more decisive, others less important.

Families whose children had attended school in the past usually listed as their main reason the child's negative experience at school (stress; bad treatment by teachers; troubles with schoolmates; frequent absences and health issues; the school's inability to fulfill the child's special needs; long commute, etc.). Some children had only had a bad experience in a single school during their first years of school attendance; others changed schools several times before the parents decided to homeschool them. The parents started to feel that the school institution available to their child did not/could not meet their expectations. The parents were often afraid that staying in school could have a negative impact on their child's healthy development. Such parents cannot be labeled as typical homeschooling advocates: home education had been the means of escape from the system, and one of the possible alternatives they decided to try. They would probably never have decided to homeschool their children if a suitable school had been available within a reasonable commuting distance. They chose homeschooling as an alternative to the school system that did not work for their children, for one reason or another. Sometimes, homeschooling was only a temporary solution until they found a suitable school for their child. This group includes children who suffered from undue stress at school.

Some parents were driven to homeschooling due to the child's frequent non-attendance caused by his/her poor health condition, such as a weakened immune system. Such children are always threatened by infection in a large group of their peers. They may not suffer from any life-threatening illnesses, but insufficient treatment could lead to permanently damaged health. Frequent illnesses and absences may negatively affect the child's relationship with his/her schoolmates (the child is "out of the loop," is perceived as different, and may be envied by his/her classmates if the absence is "convenient" for some reason), but also with his/her teachers: he/she may be labeled as a malingerer, too delicate or pampered, etc.). The child may also have large gaps in the curriculum. All of these factors may impair the child's success at school and his/her attitude toward it. Little Aneta is a typical example of such a child:

> Aneta was frequently ill. In Slovakia, where she is from, a child may only be excused from school by a doctor's note. Her mother was forced to visit the doctor's office, which was several kilometers away, with even the slightest problems (such as a mild fever) that could have abated on their own after a few days' rest. The doctor frequently prescribed antibiotics, which, the mother was convinced, further weakened her daughter's immune system, leading to yet more absences. In the end, the family decided to withdraw Aneta from school, claiming that the main reason was to prevent her from everyday contact with a large group of children. The family had then moved to the Czech Republic and started homeschooling Aneta. After three years of homeschooling, Aneta started attending school again. Temporary isolation from a large group of children helped boost her immune system, and she had returned to school without any difficulties. The positive experience with Aneta's homeschooling has led the parents to start homeschooling her younger siblings as well (Kostelecká 2003).

Homeschooling was also much sought after by parents whose children suffered from specific educational needs. Such children require a lot of patience, a one-on-one approach, and skilled guidance. However, even special schools often lack sufficient resources to meet the parents' expectations. The story of little David is a good example:

> David suffered from cerebral palsy, epilepsy, and mental retardation. He started homeschooling in fourth grade. Up until then, he went through three schools, but none of them were suitable. David's mother was convinced that school could not help David realize his full potential. David was under constant stress. His mother was very disappointed by the school's attempts to turn over David's education to his family. David was forced to study in the afternoon in order to keep up with the pace in class, which was extremely draining for both him and his family. David's mother was convinced that even even a child with learning disabilities can be educated, and decided to start homeschooling David. In retrospect, she is very positive about her homeschooling experience. She believes that virtually any child can benefit from homeschooling, but doubts that every parent could manage it. From her own experience, she is aware that home education is a great strain on the family: it is time-demanding, it poses financial difficulties since the parents are forced to live on a single income, and requires a lot of effort on the parents' part, since they need to be willing to keep educating themselves (Kostelecká 2003).

A quite different group consisted of the families of homeschoolers whose parents chose the option not because their child had a bad school experience, but out of conviction that home education was the best form of education available. They did not start homeschooling to solve a specific problem with school attendance but to retain exclusive influence on their child's upbringing and education. Such parents usually emphasized such things as the nurturing of family ties, the possibility to maintain influence on the child's socialization, greater chance of instilling the family values, one-on-one approach, a chance to allow the child to mature in a secure environment before starting to attend school, and more time to nurture the child's unique interests. Some parents were not happy with the values their child's school was teaching, or they were afraid that their child would spend too much time outside of the home due to a long commute to school. Little Filip provides a good example of this type:

> Little Filip is a dyslexic, but that was not the primary reason his parents decided to homeschool him. They were great supporters of home education and wished to test its effectiveness themselves. While homeschooling Filip, they came to the conclusion that he has learned a lot more at home than was the required standard for his age. They explained this by the fact that they had imposed no artificial limits on what a child was allowed to learn at a certain age, and so Filip had the chance to learn freely, limited only by his own abilities and interests. Since Filip was able to master the curriculum much more effectively at home, he had enough time for his hobbies, especially his beloved chess. According to his mother, Filip had no difficulty adapting to being in class, and he behaved much more freely than many of his peers (Kostelecká 2003).

Parents who had homeschooled their children from the start were often unable to estimate how their children would have developed in school, and it was therefore difficult for them to decide what the benefits or shortcomings of home education were. On the other hand, parents whose children had attended school prior to starting homeschooling, or had other children who attended regular school, were able to compare the effectiveness of home education with that of standard school attendance and evaluate the influence of homeschooling on the child's cognitive, social, and emotional development much more specifically.

Conclusion

In all of the countries in question, attempts to legalize home education emerged shortly after the fall of the Iron Curtain. In Poland, the option was introduced as early as the adoption of the first post-communist Education Act; in other countries, parents had to wait much longer for homeschooling to become legal. Home education was only legalized in Slovakia nearly twenty years after the revolution.

Once a decision had been made to legalize homeschooling in some form, legislators had to find a way to incorporate home education into the existing legislation, which prescribed compulsory school attendance. One of the options was to change compulsory school attendance to compulsory education, which eventually happened in Hungary and Slovenia. In one sense, this represented a minor "technical" change in terminology; however, we may interpret such a change as a potentially major shift in understanding the role of schools in education – in other words, schools are no longer exclusive providers of education. In the remaining researched countries, legislators were more careful. In the Czech Republic, for example, compulsory school attendance is explicitly set down in the Charter of Fundamental Rights and Freedoms (Charter, 1993). Changing the legislation to prescribe compulsory education rather than compulsory school attendance would have required amending this constitutional act, a rather improbable event since such a step requires a wide political consensus. It was therefore easier to adopt an amendment which would either have allowed homeschooled children to be exempt from compulsory school attendance, or would have established homeschooling as an accepted form of compulsory school attendance. In the end, Czech legislators went for the second option, and a similar development occurred in Poland and Slovakia. In all of these three countries, home education was legalized as one of the accepted forms of compulsory school attendance. Legislators had therefore allowed the possibility of homeschooling without undermining the crucial role of schools in the education system.

Interestingly, the process of introducing home education in the countries' legislation differed considerably from country to country. Some countries, like Slovenia or Hungary, adopted new legislation concerning home education that has remained virtually unchanged since then; in others, home education legislation has undergone quite a dramatic development over the years. This has been the case in Poland; at first, the rules for homeschooling were quite liberal, only to get more rigorous over the years, introducing still more and more prerequisites that parents have to meet to be allowed to homeschool their children. The requirements have also become stricter over time. The Czech Republic has undergone similar development. In the

1990s, home education was introduced as part of an experimental testing project, with fairly liberal rules; these have been replaced by a much more stringent legislation that now governs home education. In spite of that, we should not generalize and claim that following a short period of liberalization in the 1990s, legislation in these countries had gradually become ever stricter in all respects. Studying the relevant legislation in Central European post-communist countries, we have rather identified two parallel trends. Firstly, home education has gradually become available to an ever wider group of children and students in more and more countries. An amendment to the Polish Education Act of 2009 has made homeschooling available to a much wider group of children, from preschoolers to tertiary professional school students, and home education may now be conducted under the patronage of private schools. In 2007, the Czech Republic has allowed home education for children at the upper elementary school level, even if only in the experimental testing phase. Slovakia incorporated home education into its legislation in 2008 – for the first time in its modern education history. However, as homeschooling becomes available to a widening target group, countries have shown a tendency to restrict this form of education by prescribing increasingly strict conditions under which parents are allowed to start and continue homeschooling their children.

Twenty-five years after the fall of the communist regimes in Central Europe, we may say that in all of the above respects, the situation in the countries in question is not markedly different from that in other developed democracies. Even though there are some developed countries where home education is not a legal alternative (e.g. Germany), it is legally permitted in most developed countries. This includes both countries and states with compulsory school attendance (e.g. New Zealand, Ontario, Quebec, certain US states) and those with compulsory education (e.g. UK, France). Many countries are still in the process of developing their home education legislation, especially as regards offering the option to a wider group of children, even if the conditions for homeschooling may be modified. According to the annual report *Freedom in the 50 States,* published by George Mason University, most US states have been gradually simplifying the rules governing homeschooling.

Home education in the post-communist countries in Central Europe, including the five countries examined in this chapter and others, such as Estonia (Leis 2005), Romania (Pasztor 2008), Latvia (Kolasińska et al. 2007) and Lithuania (Kolasińska et al. 2007), has a certain specific trait: due to the legislation governing home education, parents who decide to homeschool their children are forced to maintain intensive contact with the school, more likely much closer contact than if their child attended the school. This applies even to countries with compulsory education, not just countries with compulsory school attendance. Such a paradox is a consequence of the fact that in all the countries surveyed for this chapter, supervision over home education has been entrusted to the schools in which the children must enroll to fulfill compulsory education/compulsory school attendance. This puts the parents in a highly subordinate position in relation to the schools. In some countries, parents may merely notify the school of their intention to homeschool their child; in others, they must actually ask the school for permission. The schools may only grant such permission if all the legal prerequisites have been met, leaving the final decision as to whether all conditions have been fulfilled at the school principal's discretion. In some cases, the principal may decide not to grant permission even if the parents have met all the legal requirements. When Portuguese parents decide to homeschool their children, they must register with the local *ensimo basico* (elementary school), which then oversees the children's education (Petrie 1995) but such supervision is generally rare. In this respect, the situation in post-communist countries differs considerably from that in developed democracies. In many countries (e.g. certain US states, England), parents need not even report their intention to homeschool their children; in others, they are merely obligated to report their intention to the authorities, such as the local educational authority (France). Only a few countries demand that parents apply for permission to homeschool their children (Kostelecká 2003). Compared to this, home education legislation in the countries considered here seems exceedingly strict.

Post-communist countries are also very particular about the method of evaluating home education results. Almost all of the countries included in this chapter prescribe a detailed manner of evaluating homeschooled children. Legislation usually requires that children take an exam once or twice a year, often in a number of subjects. Some countries even require exams by committee. Ironically, this creates a situation in which the parents, as the primary educators, have no say regarding the evaluation of their children's results, and the child's evaluation depends on a series of one-shot exams. Slovakia has by far the strictest regulations, stipulating that a person may only become a home educator if he/she possesses the qualifications required for lower elementary school teachers. In schools, teachers with such qualifications are allowed to evaluate a whole class of children, but a child educated by a similarly qualified teacher at home must pass an exam before a committee twice a year, in all the subjects prescribed for their respective grade.

The homeschooling evaluation process varies from country to country: from countries where continued homeschooling is not contingent on evaluation results, to countries with exacting evaluation methods. The post-communist countries examined in this chapter rank among the strictest in this respect.

Even though home education legislation in the five post-communist Central European countries shares certain common aspects, it may come as a surprise how different it actually is. Legislation has clearly been influenced by a number of concurrent factors, some of which contribute toward a greater convergence of legislative solutions; others tend to lead toward divergence. Convergent factors include such things as shared historical experience, namely communist rule, which has universally led to the fact that barring certain exceptions, home education was not legally possible until the late 1980s, and has thus been legalized much later than in developed Western countries. Similarly, all of the five countries shared the notion that education should be provided exclusively by schools, resulting in the requirement for compulsory school attendance. In all of these countries, the exclusive role of schools has persisted even for homeschooled children – the school continuously monitors the homeschooled children's results, issues the standard certifications, and has a final say in deciding whether a child will be allowed to continue homeschooling. The actual geographical proximity of the five countries offers further convergence potential: it allows closer contact between local experts and makes it easier to share experience and good practice. Unfortunately, this potential has not yet been fully realized. Our analysis has shown that despite geographical proximity and certain language similarity, information exchange among these countries has so far been fairly limited (with the exception of the Czech Republic and Slovakia, who have established a certain level of cooperation and information exchange).

However, there are also factors contributing to a greater divergence of home education legislation in the different countries. One of the most important factors in this respect is the fact that there is no widely accepted consensus as to whether homeschooling should be a full alternative to school education or not. For example in 2015, the proposal to fully legalize home education in the Czech Republic at the upper elementary school level has become an unexpected source of controversy within the coalition government regarding the new Education Act. The Minister of Education spoke against the proposal, which was in turn supported by the Chairman of the parliament's Education Committee, and a former rector of one of the country's most prestigious universities. First, the disputed section was omitted from the draft bill under pressure from the Minister. Later, however, several MPs again included the disputed section into the draft of the bill despite the disagreement of the Minister. The approved version of the bill thus legalized home education at upper secondary school level. But the whole bill was eventually vetoed by the president, albeit for reasons unrelated to home education. Under the Czech Constitution the President's veto could be outvoted by the majority of the entire membership of the Lower Chamber of the Parliament. The repeated voting about the vetoed bill is scheduled for June 2016, so the legal status of home education at the upper elementary level remains unresolved for now.

Due to this lack of consensus, the European Union, which otherwise tends to support harmonization of education systems, has decided not to comment on the issue of home education at all, leaving it entirely within the competence of the member states. This means that if a family interested in homeschooling gets into a clash with local legislation, and the case is referred to the European Court of Human Rights, the court regularly rules in favor of the defendant, i.e. the member state (Reimer 2010).

In order to bring the debate on home education in the Czech Republic to a higher level, to make it more factual and less ideological it is necessary to conduct research that systematically maps the current situation and makes the information and expertise available to both experts and the general population. This should include topics that have not been researched systematically so far, such as: the relationship between homeschooling families and the schools overseeing their results; the role of schools in homeschooling; the role of homeschooling support organizations; educational/didactic aspects of home education like methods and forms of education, the number of lessons devoted to each subject and the daily/weekly teaching schedule. Proper attention should also be paid to the social and psychological aspects of homeschooling, namely to the study of parents' reasons for choosing homeschooling, and to socialization issues such as homeschoolers' ability to integrate into the school environment later on and the self-perception of homeschooled children.

Acknowledgments

This chapter was written with the support of the Czech Science Foundation through a project entitled "Home Education – Facts, Analyses, Diagnostics" registration number: 16-17708S.

The chapter is an extended version of the article "Domácí vzdělávání a legislativa. Studie postkomunistických států střední Evropy" published in Czech in the journal *Orbis Scholae* in 2014.

References

Beck, Christian W. 2002. "Home Education – New Political Tension?: The Case of Northern Europe." Paper presented at the Comparative Education Society of Europe Conference, July, London, UK.

Beck, Christian W. 2008. "Home Education and Social Integration." *Outlines: Critical Social Studies*, 10(2): 59–69. PsycInfo, EBSCOhost.

Beck, Christian W. 2010. "Home Education: The Social Motivation." *International Electronic Journal of Elementary Education*, 3(1): 71–81.

Blok, H. 2004. "Performance in Home Schooling: An Argument Against Compulsory Schooling in the Netherlands." *International Review of Education*, 50(1): 39–52.

Brabant, C. 2009. "Imagining Each Other: Educated at Home in the United States." In *The Child: An Encyclopedic Companion*, edited by R.A. Shweder, T.R. Bidell, A.C. Dailey, S.D. Dixon, P.J. Miller and J. Modell. Chicago, IL: University of Chicago Press.

Dalahooke, M.M. 1986. *Home Educated Children's Social/Emotional Adjustment and Academic Achievement: A Comparative Study*. PhD diss., California School of Professional Psychology.

Dueholm, Natalia. 2006. "History of Homeschooling Movement in Poland." Accessed December 12, 2014. http://www.hslda.org/hs/international/Poland/200612191.asp

Gaither, Milton. 2008. *Homeschool: An American History*. New York, NY: Palgrave Macmillan.

Jančaříková, Kateřina. 2008. "Význam environmentální výchovy v individuálním (domácím) vzdělávání." In *Tři cesty k pedagogice volného času*, edited by Jan Činčera, Michal Kaplánek, and Jan Sýkora, 75–80. Brno: Tribun.

Kolář, Michal. 2000. *Skrytý svět šikanování ve školách: příčiny, diagnostika a praktická pomoc [The Hidden World of Bullying in Schools: causes, diagnosis and practical assistance]*. 2nd ed. Praha: Portál, 2000. Pedagogická praxe.

Kolář, Petr. 2000. "Systém domácího vzdělávání v USA a ve vybraných zemích Evropy. [Home Education in the US and Selected European Countries]." *Informační studie* 5(155). Praha: Parlamentní Institute.

Kolasińska, Ewa, Joanna Kuźmicka, and Anna Smoczyńska. 2007. *Edukacja domowa*. Warszawa: Polskie Biuro Eurydice.

Kostelecká, Yvona. 2003. "*Domácí vzdělávání*." PhD diss., Univerzita Karlova v Praze, Pedagogická fakulta.

Kostelecká, Yvona. 2005. "Legislativní úprava domácího vzdělávání v zahraničí a její komparace se situací v České republice." *Pedagogika*, 55(4): 354–67.

Kostelecká, Yvona. 2010. "Home Education in the Post-Communist Countries: Case Study of the Czech Republic." *International Electronic Journal of Elementary Education*, 3(1): 29–44.

Kostelecká, Yvona. 2012. "The Legal Status of Home Education in the Post-Communist Countries of Central Europe." *International Review of Education*, 58(4): 445–63. DOI: 10.1007/s11159-012-9298-0

Kostelecká, Yvona. 2014a. "Doma, nebo ve škole." *Studia paedagogica*, 19(1): 65–82. http://www.phil.muni.cz/journals/index.php/studia-paedagogica/article/view/704

Kostelecká, Yvona. 2014b. "Domácí vzdělávání a legislativa. Studie postkomunistických států střední Evropy." *Orbis scholae*, 8(1): 9–26.

Kunzman, R. 2012. "Education, Schooling, and Children's Rights: The Complexity of Homeschooling." *Educational Theory*, 62(1): 75–89.

Leis, Tiia. 2005. "Home Education in Estonia." Accessed December 12, 2015. http://folk.uio.no/cbeck/Estonia.htm

Martin-Chang, S., Odette N. Gould, and Reanne E. Meuse. 2011. "The Impact of Schooling on Academic Achievement: Evidence from Homeschooled and Traditionally Schooled Students." *Canadian Journal of Behavioural Science/Revue Canadienne des Sciences du Comportement*. 2011, vol. 43, issue 3, s. 195–202. DOI: 10.1037/a0022697

Mertin, Václav. 2003. "Pedagogicko-psychologické aspekty individuálního vzdělávání/Individual education from the point of view of educational psychology." *Pedagogika*, 53(4): 405–17. Accessed December 12, 2014. http://pages.pedf.cuni.cz/pedagogika/?p=1969

Morton, Ruth. 2010. "Home Education. Construction of Choice." *International Electronic Journal of Elementary Education*, 3(1): 29–44. Accessed May 7, 2016. https://homeeducation.files.wordpress.com/2008/03/final-bsa-paper.doc

Murphy, Joseph. 2014. "The Social and Educational Outcomes of Homeschooling." In *Sociological Spectrum* 34(3): 244–272.

Pasztor, Gabriella. 2008. The Secretary of the Ministry of Education and Research. Interpellation presented by MP Andrian-Sirojea Mihei on March 10. http://www.cdep.ro/pls/steno/steno.stenograma?ids=6451&idm=9,01&idl=1

Petrie, Amanda J. 1995. "Home Educators and the Law within Europe." *International Review of Education*, 41(3/4): 285–96. DOI:10.1007/BF01255557

Petrie, Amanda J. 2001. "Home Education in Europe and the Implementation of Changes to the Law." *International Review of Education*, 47 (5): 477–500. DOI:10.1023/A:1012260228356

Pražáková, Dana. 2012. "*Matematika v domácím vzdělávání: charakteristiky vzdělávacího stylu rodin*." PhD diss., Univerzita Karlova v Praze, Pedagogická fakulta.

Ray, Brian D. 1994. *A Nationwide Study of Home Education in Canada: Family Characteristics, Student Achievement, and other Topics*. Salem, OR: National Home Education Research Institute.

Ray, Brian D. 1997. *Strengths of Their Own – Home Schoolers cross America: Academic Achievement, Family Characteristics, and Longitudinal Traits*. Salem, OR: National Home Education Research Institute.

Reimer, Franz. 2010. "School Attendance as a Civic Duty v. Home Education as a Human Right." *International Electronic Journal of Elementary Education*, 3(1): 29–44. Accessed May 7, 2016. http://files.eric.ed.gov/fulltext/EJ1052397.pdf

Rothermel, Paula. 2002. "*Home-Education: Rationales, Practices and Outcomes.*" PhD diss., University of Durham. Accessed December 12, 2014. http://pjrothermel.com/phd/Home.htm

Sheng, X. 2014. "*Learning with Mothers: A Study of Home Schooling in China.*" Rotterdam: Sense Publishers.

Štech, Stanislav. 2003. "Škola, nebo domácí vzdělávání?: Teoretická komplikace jedné praktické otázky." *Pedagogika*, 53 (4): 418–36. Accessed December 12, 2014. http://pages.pedf.cuni.cz/pedagogika/?p=1966

Thomas, Alan. 1998. *Educating Children at Home*, London: Continuum.

Tůma, Jiří. 2001. "Domácí vzdělávání v zemích EU a u nás." *Učitelské listy*, 8(1): 14.

Van Pelt, Deani Neven. 2015. "Home Schooling in Canada: The Current Picture - 2015 Edition." Barbara Mitchell Centre for Improvement in Education.

Appendix: Reference List of Laws and Other Regulations

Czech Republic

Announcement of experimental testing, as specified in Article 171, section (1) of Act 561/2004 on preschool, elementary, secondary, tertiary professional and other education (the Education Act)

Charter of Fundamental Rights and Freedoms: Constitutional Act 2/1993 Sb. [Listina základních práv a svobod. Ústavní zákon č. 2/1993 Sb.]

Act 561/2004 on preschool, elementary, secondary, tertiary professional and other education (the Education Act) [Zákon 561/2004 Sb. o předškolním, základním, středním, vyšším odborném a jiném vzdělávání (školský zákon)]

Hungary

Act No. LXXIX of 1993 on Public Education (1993. évi LXXIX. Törvńy a közoktatásról).

Ministerial Decree on Educational Institutions 11/1994. (VI.8) (MKM rendelet a nevelési - oktatási intézmén yek müködéséről)

Poland

Act No. 425/1991 on the System of Education (Ustawa 425 z dnia 7 września 1991 r. o systemie oświaty, Dz. U. z 2004 r. Nr 256, poz. 2572 z późn. zm).

Act No. 483/1997 Constitution of Republic of Poland (Konstytucja Rzeczypospolitej Polskiej z dnia 2. kwietnia 1997 r, Dz.U. 1997 nr 78 poz. 483).

Act No. 458/2009 on the Changes of the Act on the System of Education and Some Other Acts (Ustawa 458/2009 z dnia 19 marce 2009 r. o zmiane ustawy o systemie oświaty oraz o niektórych innych ustaw)

Ministerial Decree on Conditions and Forms of Evaluation of Students in Public Schools No. 562/2007 (Rozporządzenie ministra edukaci narodowej 562/2007 z dnia 30. kwiernia 2007 r. w sprawie warunków i sposobu oceniania, klasyfikowania i promowania uczniów i słuchczy oraz przeprowadzania sprawdzianów i egzaminów w szkołach publicznych)

Slovakia

Act 245/2008 on Education and Training (the Education Act), amending and superseding certain other acts, adopted on 22 May 2008 [Zákon 245/2008 Z. z. o výchove a vzdelávaní (školský zákon) a o zmene a doplnení niektorých zákonov z 22. mája 2008]

Slovenia

School Act 1996 [Zakon o osnovni šoli - ZOsn (Uradni list RS, št. 12/96 z dne 29. februarja 1996)]
Elementary School Act No. 3535/2006 [Zakon o osnovni šoli 3535- ZOsn - UPB3 (Uradni list RS, št. 81/06 z dne 31. 7. 2006)]

18

Home Education in Asia Minor

Elife Doğan Kılıç

Introduction

In the globalization process, a new union of multinational states (European Union) has been formed as various countries have come together in economic, political, and cultural senses in the world. With the political formation of the European Union, education has become increasingly homogenized among the union countries. It has tended toward raising monotype people in education as a result of accreditation. In addition, all states specify their expectations of the performance of their education system through schools in education laws. States have aimed at raising good people, good citizens, good producers, and good consumers (Aydın 2012). Alternatives to schools started to be put forth with this global balance.

Informal education practices in Europe date back to the 8th century. Jean Jacques Rousseau's *Emile* may be counted among the first examples. Bertrand Russell seriously criticized schools in 1935. Feyerabend made harsh criticism of science and modern schools in the 1960s, rejecting the theory of information that forms science, and trying to define a new mission of information in changing the understanding of science. He asserted that scientific knowledge would eliminate human diversity and individuality (Sağsan 2003).

Ivan Illich's idea of "Deschooling Society" started to be discussed as an alternative to formal education in the 1970s. According to Illich, schools limit the behaviors and living spaces of individuals (Şişman 2000). Catherine Baker (1995) stated her reasons for unschooling her 14-year-old daughter in "Refusing Submission to the Obligatory School System." She argued that school is an institution organized for raising slaves for itself and that adults cannot notice this hidden agenda because they successfully completed this slave education themselves. According to Baker, "school

The Wiley Handbook of Home Education, First Edition. Edited by Milton Gaither.

is an institution where children are guarded, it keeps a close watch on children while their parents work; it teaches children necessary information for operating the social-financial machine; it instils obedience and distributes roles." She says that education for increasing production and ensuring obedience is practiced at school instead of "idleness," which is what is needed to improve intuition and imagination, and to allow passion and thoughts to acquire a creative quality.

Should we have an anarchist opinion of science and school like Feyerabend? Should we adopt Ivan Illich's idea of "Deschooling Society"? Or should we unschool our children by "Refusing Submission to Obligatory School Systems" like Baker? Many wonder which one is the better approach. Home education studies must be reviewed to answer these questions.

Historical Development and Definition of Home Education

Compulsory education emerged in the West for the first time in the 17th century and then started to be practiced in Gotha, Calemberg, and particularly Prussia in Germany in the 18th century. The first legal regulation was enacted in Massachusetts in the United States in 1789. Griswold suggested his book *Fireside Education* for child education in 1828. In addition, Warren Burton tried to support home education with his work, *Helps to Education in the Homes of Our Country*. A.A. Berle introduced his book, *The School in Your Home* at the Paris Peace Conference in 1912 and tried to give information to the participants and parents on home education. Leaders of the Modern Home Education movement are John Caldwell Holt and Raymond and Dorothy Moore. Holt published his book *How Children Fail* for the first time in 1964 (Kılıç et al. 2008). There are many well known bureaucrats, scientists and artists who were taught at home, including George Washington, Thomas Edison, Mozart, Patrick Henry, and Ansel Adams (Terry 2011).

John Stuart Mill made the first studies on home education (Terry 2011). When the academic literature is examined, there were two different views at the origin of home education. The first of these views was that, according to Raymond and Dorothy Moore, home education aims at raising individuals in accordance with Christianity. It was adopted by traditional middle-class families (Lyman 1998) and rightist, fundamentalist North American families who wanted their children to be raised in accordance with the Christian tradition. The second view was that, according to Holt, home education was adopted by ex-hippies, immigrants, and multinational leftist groups, who came together under the name of New Age Devotees (Lyman 1998), leftist families alleging that they had problems with how, where, and with which methods information was delivered in schools (Snyder 2011).

Home education is referred to by many different names in the literature, with labels including "homeschooling," "education without school," "comfortable or flexible homeschool," (Murphy 2012) "education at home," and "home-based education" (İbrahim Bajunid 2002). In this chapter, the term "home education" has been used.

Home education has been defined various ways. Some see it as a favorable learning method allowing children to learn at their own pace, in their own ways (Bajunid 2002). Some define it as education provided at home without schools (Stafford 2012). Others consider it to be an active and deliberate educational program arranged by parents (Broadhurst 1999). Home education is also defined as a systematic model where the learner is valued, where self-actualization is prioritized, and where learning commensurate with ability is possible.(Taştan and Demir 2013).

Based on these definitions, in this chapter home education will be defined as education that allows children to learn at their own pace, in their own ways, is provided at home, and in which parents have the right to arrange an active and deliberate program for their children's education.

Reasons for Practising Home Education

Nowadays many observers of children attending school find that children are labeled, experience social isolation problems, display antisocial behaviors, and are at increased risk of drug addiction (Seitz et al. 2013).

For this reason, families at different socioeconomic levels look for options to provide education other than traditional schooling for their children. They draw attention to the failures of schools and embark on a quest for an approach to education that matches their own standards (Hetzel, Long, and Jackson 2001). One of these options is home education. It provides free education for students, freedom to embrace change, and the opportunity to use technology more comfortably and is thus rapidly becoming more popular (Belfield and Levin 2005). However, parents are practicing home education and educating their children in homeschools mostly for economic and ideological reasons (Green-Hennessy 2013).

Themes such as students with special needs, the success level of students, student qualifications, social development levels of students (French, Walker, and Shore 2011; Jackson 2009), legal regulations on home education, and policies related to family were at the forefront of parents preferring home education until the early 1990s (Chapman and O'Donoghue 2000).

According to John Stuart Mill, who described his own home-based education in his 1873 *Autobiography* (Terry 2011), individualized education programs can be specifically scheduled for the children at home. Parents can implement programs suitable for their children's temperament cost-effectively. The child is educated in a freer and safer environment compared to school, and homeschooled children can develop tighter family ties by avoiding peer pressure. They can learn their own customs and traditions. (Terry 2011).

In the US, many homeschooling mothers do not want their children to be affected negatively in terms of religion and morality and to experience academic failure (NCES 2008). In Canada, mothers prefer educating at home in order to provide moral and religious education (Basham, Merrifield, and Hepburn 2007).

In Malaysia, families prefer home as they find the curriculum implemented at schools to be lacking and the teachers unqualified, and they believe that practices at schools do not comply with family values (Rajamony 2008). In the study of home education in Malaysia, because techonogy is used more often in home education compared to in the classroom environment it is thought that different learning environments can evolve education practice. Therefore, the effects of present and future teachers' services to the home is that they are going to change the dimension of instructional services and to change the responsibilities of teachers at school (Alias et al. 2013).

A significant body of academic research indicates that students with learning disabilities frequently take advantage of home education. These studies reveal that mothers of students with learning disabilities want their children to be educated at home due to the difficulties they face in public schools (Reilly, Chapman, and O'Donoghue 2002). Religious education is the motivating factor for some mothers to provide home education to their children (Penn-Nabrit 2003). Particularly in North America, fundamentalist families prefer home education (Hanna 2012; Rothermel 2003). Lack of confidence is observed in parents and children who turn to home education, with problems faced by parents in their own school life becoming a significant factor in deciding to homeschool (Atkinson et al. 2007). Besides, some mothers state that they do not want their children to experience disappointment at school and therefore argue that their children should be home educated (Llewellyn 1998). Network connections, family and groups of friends, local organizations, some local administrations, and schools all offer support to children being home educated (Atkinson et al. 2007).

Home Education in Turkey

It is stated that while there were 850 000 homeschooled children in the US in 1999 (NCES 2008; Princiotta, Bielick, and Chapman 2006), the number increased during 2005– 2006 and current estimates vary from 1.9 million to 2.4 million (Ray 2015). Home education continues legally in all 50 US states (Yuracko 2008) and is increasingly being considered as an alternative to formal education elsewhere (Snyder 2011). Not only has it been adopted in the US, but also in countries such as South Africa, Canada, Mexico, Columbia, India, Thailand, Austria, Belgium, the Czech Republic, Finland, the Netherlands, Poland, Luxembourg, UK, France, Ireland, Italy, Israel, New Zealand, People's Republic of China, and Switzerland (McIntyre-Bhatty 2007). In countries such as Scotland and Switzerland, there was a dramatic increase in home education between 2005 and 2006.

Education is carried out under the supervision and control of the State in Turkey. Article 42 of the Constitution of the Republic of Turkey, states that every Turkish boy and girl has the right to be educated free of charge in state schools. According to Article 6 of Basic Law of National Education no. 1739 (Law No: 1739 Adoption Date: 14.6.1973 Official Gazette: 24.6.1973/14574), individuals are directed to various programs or schools within the capabilities of and in line with their interests, tendencies, and competencies during their education. According to Article 17, the objectives of national education are to be carried out not only in public and private educational institutions but also at home, in working places, and anywhere else and at every opportunity. In addition, a "Circular on Education Services at Home and in Hospitals," which is based on providing education services at home for those who cannot directly benefit from formal education institutions implementing any of the programs of preschool, primary school or special education, due to their health problems, was issued by the Ministry of National Education in 2010. This Circular covers the related procedures and principles on planning and implementing education services that should be provided for the duration of treatment for those who are being treated at home or are staying in the hospital and so cannot directly benefit from formal education institutions due to health problems. The Circular also applies to individuals at the preschool and primary school level in need of special education. Supportive education services for the individuals in need of special education are provided by the teacher(s) visiting the children's home and/or the hospital. In order to provide the home education service, there needs to be a medical report stating that it is impossible for the student to benefit from any formal education institution for at least four months or that adverse outcomes outweigh the benefits of the formal education. The report includes an application petition from the parents, a student certificate, issuance of the report of due diligence, evaluation of the home environment and parents' contract, and the report of the evaluation council. In addition to these, student information including the relevant doctor's and parents' approval for the inpatient student to have the education service is needed (MEB 2010).

Home education in Turkey has been arranged – as just described – only for people who are ill and in need of special education. In addition, the Turkish Statistical Institute (TurkStat) has found that there are still illiterate individuals over the age of 15 in Turkey. It has been ascertained through the examination of demographic information based on the Central Population Management System (MERNIS) by the TurkStat that 443640 men and 2 200 072 women aged 15 and over are illiterate. It has also been found that 1 203 461 men and 2 626 492 women aged of 15 and over are literate but have not graduated from any school (Table 18.1). The number of people who are literate without attending a school but who learned through the help of a relative is 3 829 953 in total. When these data are scrtunized it becomes clear that about 4 000 000 people in Turkey have become literate thanks to home education in an illegal way.

The aim of this chapter is to take the opinions of fourth-year students studying primary school teaching and preschool teaching at the Faculty of Education, Sinop University on "Home Education and the Reasons for Selecting School in Formal Education". We adapted the scale used by Klein and Poplin (2008) in their study "Families Home Schooling in a Virtual Charter School System" adapting the criteria for our Turkish research.

Table 18.1 Distribution statistics of the population (over age 15) by completed education level and gender in Turkey.

Completed Education Level	*Total*	*Males*	*Females*
Illiterate	2 643 712	443 640	2 200 072
Literate but not graduated from any school	3 829 953	1 203 461	2 626 492
Primary school graduate	14 994 232	6 454 722	8 539 510
Primary education graduate	11 959 942	6 783 011	5 176 931
Junior high school or equivalent school graduate	2 828 299	1 720 425	1 107 874
Secondary education or equivalent school graduate	12 085 335	6 976 694	5 108 641
Bachelor's degree	6 706 780	3 762 530	2 944 250
Master's degree	532 757	313 397	219 360
Doctoral degree	154 180	93 407	60 773
Unknown	1 683 918	862 885	821 033
Total	**57 419 108**	**28 614 172**	**28 804 936**

Non-Turkish citizens were not included.

Source: TUİK 2013.

Methodology

Working group This study was descriptive research. It included 108 voluntary participants, all prospective teachers studying at the Faculty of Education, Sinop University: 65 senior students from primary school teaching, and 43 students from preschool teaching, who studied during the spring semester of 2013. Thirty-six of the participants were male and 72 were female. The data of this research was collected through the literature review and the scale.

Instrument We employed the scale used by Klein and Poplin (2008) in "Families Home Schooling in a Virtual Charter School System," adapting it for the students of the Faculty of Education, Sinop University. This 37-item scale was translated from the original English text and compared in terms of "language and meaning" by experts with a good knowledge in both languages. Then experts were consulted about compliance with the aim and adequacy of the expressions. In line with the suggestions of these experts, expressions in the Turkish scale were corrected and the items to be removed were eliminated from the survey instrument form, which was then prepared as a 31-item draft. This draft form of the "Scale of Home Education and Reasons for Choosing School in Formal Education" was applied to fifty third grade students studying Social Sciences Teaching, at the Faculty of Education, Sinop University in order to get feedback on the clarity of expressions, questions, and the timeframe of the survey instrument. At the end of survey, prospective teachers stated their verbal opinions and suggestions, and made minor corrections in two items. The scale used to collect data in the research consisted of two parts: the first part included demographic information; the second part included thirty-one items related to home education. The scale was prepared as a five-point Likert scale ranging from Strongly Agree (5) to Strongly Disagree (0).

Item–total point correlations, which indicated whether each item in the scale measured the same thing as the total scale, were calculated. This correlation coefficient also allowed individuals to be distinguished from each other in terms of measured features with the scale. Cronbach's Alpha coefficient for internal consistency was examined for reliability of the scale.

Factor structure Validity and reliability studies on the scale of Home Education and Reasons for Choosing School in Formal Education (HE) were conducted in this research. Three subdimensions of the HE scale were determined as: Reasons for Choosing Home Education (RCHE); Reasons for Choosing School (RCS); and Evaluation of School Experience (ESE).

First of all, Exploratory Factor Analysis (EFA) was made on data applied to all groups. While making EFA, Mahallanobis distances ($p = 0.05$, sd:31) were taken into account, finding the Kaiser-Meyer-Olkin value as 0.729, Bartlett's Test of Sphericity value ($\chi^2 = 1342{,}649$, $p < .05$') was significant. Inter-item correlation values were found below 0.80. Three-factor structure could not be found in the operations conducted after the elimination of unrotated operations made over 108 individuals in EFA and cyclical items. The same operation did not display three-factor structure when it was applied with rotation. EFA was made by dealing with each of three subdimensions in the HE scale.

Factor structure of the Turkish adaptation of the HE scale was determined by making EFA. According to the initial outcomes of EFA, items 26, 27, 28, and 31 of which factor load values are below 0.30 were eliminated and the analysis was redone. In consequence of the second factor analysis, it was discovered that the scale was a three-factor scale. Dimension of RCHE was calculated as $\alpha = 0.70$, dimension to RCS as $\alpha = 0.85$, and dimension of ESE as $\alpha = 82$. The HE scale was calculated as $\alpha = 0.84$. Common factor variants of HE vary between 0.515 and 0.824. In the second factor analysis, factor load values of RCHE vary between 0.300 and 0.695, factor load values of RCS between 0.603 and 0.802, and factor load values of ESE between 0.335 and 0.750. EFA results are given in Table 18.2.

As Confirmatory Factor Analysis (CFA) is shown as the proof of the validity of the measured structure, a model concordant with the three-factor original model of the scale was structured and CFA was made (using the LISREL 8.7 program). In the measurement model, the factor load value regarding an indicator for latent variables representing factors was equalized to (λ) 1.00 (MD1, MD11, MD18).

Many fit indexes are used to determine the adequacy of the tested model in CFA. In this study, Chi-Square Goodness of Fit Test, Goodness of Fit Index (GFI), Adjusted Goodness of Fit Index (AGFI), Comparative Fit Index (CFI), Non-Normed Fit Index (NNFI) and Root Mean Square Error of Approximation (RMSEA) of Fit Index were examined for the CFA.

After the CFA was applied to the 31-item scale, factor load value of item 9 of the RCHE subdimension was 0.12 and factor load value of item 28 of ESE subdimension was 0.11. As the related items should be removed from the scale if factor load values of scale items are below 0.30 (Kline 2016), item 9 and item 28 were removed from

Table 18.2 Outcomes of exploratory factor analysis of the home education scale.

	Item	*Common Factor Variant*	*Factor Load Values*	*Factor Load Values*	*Factor Load Values*
Reasons for choosing home education	1. Providing high academic facilities	0.824	0.572		
	2. Creating high expectations at the excellence level in education	0.742	0.662		
	3. Providing a safe environment for learning	0.518	0.682		
	4. Increasing the opportunities needed to instill moral values	0.652	0.565		
	5. Meeting unique learning needs	0.767	0.695		
	6. Strengthening family ties	0.573	0.546		
	7. Being flexible while programming the lessons	0.616	0.356		
	8. Parents becoming efficient role models	0.734	0.329		
	9. Finding some activities in state schools inappropriate for children	0.811	0.300		
	10. Children having religious freedom	0.609	0.500		
	11. Children having the opportunity to access educational tools, materials and resources free of charge	0.803		0.603	
	12. Increasing direct participation of children in education	0.717		0.684	
	13. Enjoying easy accessibility to supportive technology for education at school	0.695		0.801	
	14. Receiving updated feedback on learning progress at schools	0.640		0.802	
	15. Belonging to a respectable community of learners	0.743		0.788	
	16. Students being able to receive professional support on educational problems	0.603		0.768	
Evaluation of school experience	17. Receiving individualized support for studnets' special needs (for example learning disabilities)	0.572		0.637	
	18. Ensuring saving more time than one would spend gathering resources related to curriculum together on his/her own	0.562			0.600
	19. Being satisfied with having the possibility for access to high quality learning materials	0.665			0.750
	20. Meeting academic needs of students	0.608			0.684
	21. Maintaining learning process at home by regulating	0.717			0.335

(*Continued*)

Table 18.2 (Continued)

Item	*Common Factor Variant*	*Factor Load Values*	*Factor Load Values*	*Factor Load Values*
22. Having enjoyment in learning through technology provided by technology within education program at schools	0.545			0.697
23. Appreciating responsibility undertaken by school for learning	0.664			0.705
24. Compatibility of parents' needs regarding planning and flexibility for home education with each other0.	0.637			0.445
25. Having immediate assistance when encountering technological problems at school	0.551			0.620
29. Thinking that social needs of students are met at schools	0.619			0.642
30. Parents using the opportunities provided by communication network established with other parents	0.623			0.695
31. Limitation of students by home education				

Table 18.3 Significant values for the model data fit after the Confirmatory Factor Analysis.

Values	*χ^2/sd*	*RMSEA*	*GFI*	*AGFI*	*NNFI*	*CFI*
31 items	1.94	0.058	0.65	0.59	0.91	0.91
29 items	1.42	0.052	0.73	0.67	0.94	0.95

Note: Results of the CFA shows that the scale has a three sub-dimensional construct. The associated Path Diagram is given in Figure 18.1.

the scale. Changes in the values of RMSEA, GFI, AGFI, NNFI and CFI were observed after excluding the related items from the analysis (Table 18.3).

When the related literature was examined, it was observed that if the value obtained by dividing Chi-square (χ^2) value into degree of freedom was below (χ^2/sd) 3, it would be an acceptable level for data-model fit (Schermelleh-Engel, Moosbrugger, and Müller 2003). After CFA, GFI, AGFI, CFI and NNFI >0.90 and RMSEA <0.06 are usually the criteria (Hu and Bentler, 1999). But both GFI and AGFI values are affected from the sample size. Interpreting these values is more meaningful if the sample size is at least tenfold the parameter number to be estimated. But in this study, when the estimated parameter number (item loads, item errors, factor number and inter-factor correlation) is considered, GFI and AGFI values are low as the sample size could not reach the desired level. If the sample size is not adequate and

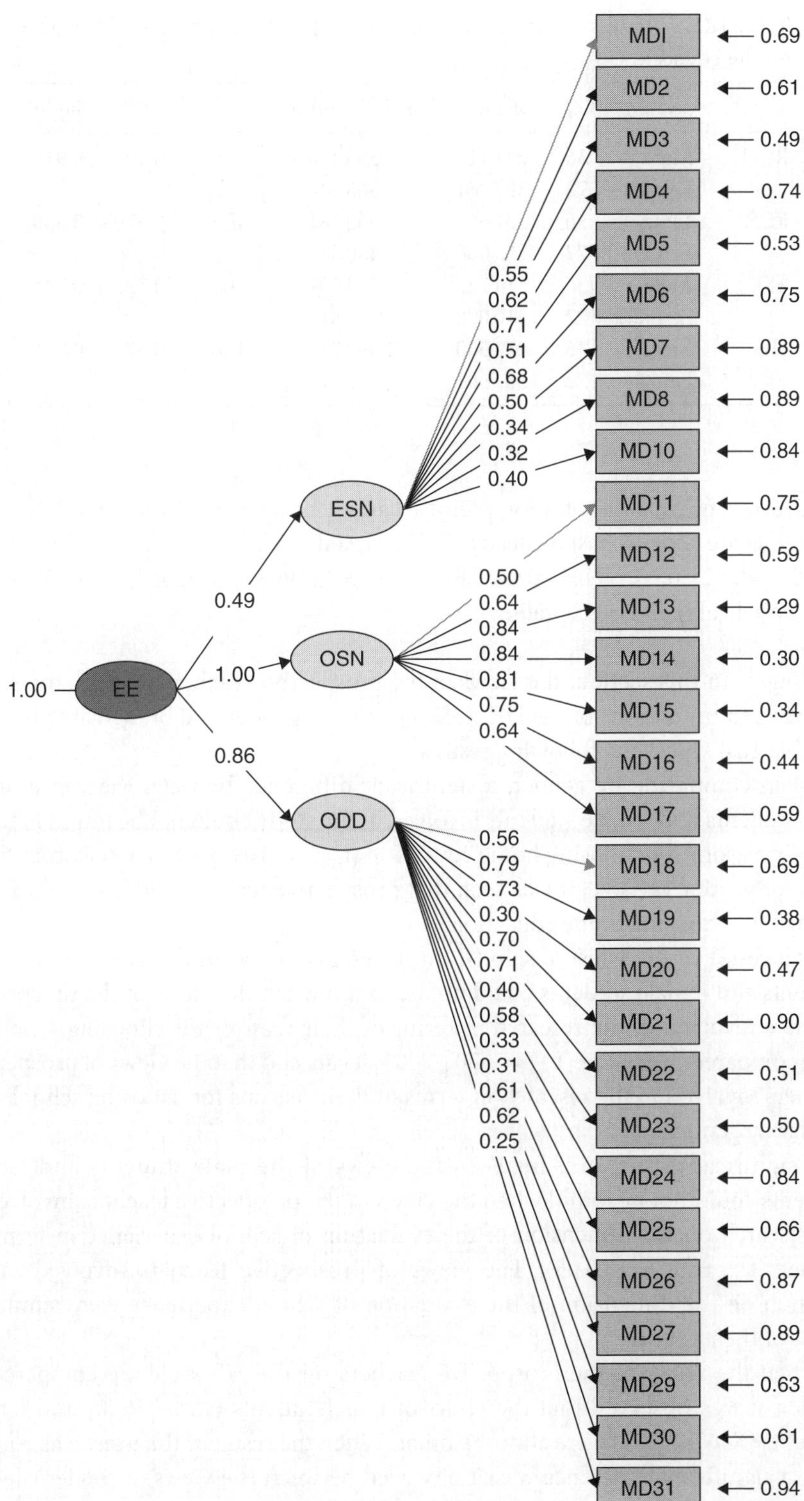

Figure 18.1 Path Diagram of CFA results.

Table 18.4 Results of t-test regarding views of prospective teachers by gender on the HE scale.

	Section	*N*	*Mean(X)*	*Std. Deviation*	*df*	*t*	*Sig.(p)*
RCHE	Male	36	231 111	553 316	106	−0.109	0.914
	Female	72	232 361	568 044			
RCS	Male	36	131 667	502 281	106	0.670	0.505
	Female	72	125 000	480 317			
ESE	Male	36	314 722	753 084	106	0.327	0.744
	Female	72	310 000	683 817			
HE	Male	36	677 500	1 398 239	106	0.378	0.706
	Female	72	667 361	1 268 579			

multivariate normal distribution premise cannot be obtained from data, NNFI and CFI values are taken as basis instead of GFI and AGFI. After the CFA, $(\chi^2/sd) = 1.42 < 3$, RMSEA = 0.52 < 0.60, NNFI = 0.94, CFI = 0.95 > .90 values shown in Table 18.3 indicate that model value fit is acceptable.

Findings In this section, the views of the prospective teachers on the expressions of three subdimensions of the HE scale in terms of gender and branch are given.

Table 18.4 shows the following results.

When comparing by gender, a significant difference between the views of the male students and female students involved in the study could not be found in terms of their reasons for choosing home education ($t_{(106)} = -.109$ $p > .05$). Concordantly, in terms of gender variable, it was seen that prospective teachers did not differ in the reasons for choosing home education.

As a result of the t-test, a significant difference between the views of the male students and female students could not be found when the views of the prospective teachers involved in the research in terms of their reasons for choosing schooling were compared by gender ($t_{(106)} = .670$ $p > .05$. It can said that the views of prospective teachers involved in the research in terms of their reasons for choosing school were similar by gender.

A significant difference between the views of the male students and female students could not be found when the views of the prospective teachers involved in the research on the dimension of the evaluation of school experience in terms of gender ($t_{(106)} = .327$ $p > 0.05$). The views of prospective teachers involved in the research on the dimension of the evaluation of school experience were similar in terms of their gender.

When the views of the prospective teachers on the HE scale are compared by gender, it was observed that the views of male students (X: 67,7500) and female students (X: 67,75361) were almost similar. When the result of the t-test was considered, a significant difference wasn't observed between the views of the female and male students ($t_{(106)} = 3$ $p > 0.05$).

Table 18.5 Results of t-test regarding views of prospective teachers by their branches on the HE scale.

	Branch	*N*	*Mean(X)*	*Std. Deviation*	*df*	*t*	*Sig.(p)*
RCHE	Primary school teaching	65	224 462	601 049	106	−1,721	0.141
	Preschool teaching	43	24 325 581	477 952			
RCS	Primary school teaching	65	12 538 462	499 711	106	−0.481	0.516
	Preschool teaching	43	130 000	470 056			
ESE	Primary school teaching	65	205 385	641 063	106	−0.294	0.167
	Preschool teaching	43	208 837	524 726			
HE	Primary school teaching	65	555 231	1 307 563	106	−1,142	0.053
	Preschool teaching	43	582 093	1 004 646			

The results of the t-test with regards to the views of the prospective teachers' reasons for choosing home education by their branches are given in Table 18.5.

Table 18.5 shows the following results.

When the views of the prospective teachers involved in the research on the reasons for choosing home education by their branches were compared, a significant difference was not observed between the views of students of the primary school teaching and preschool teaching ($t_{(106)}$ = -1,721 p > .05). It was deduced that the students of preschool teaching and primary school teaching hold similar opinions.

When the views of the prospective teachers regarding choosing the school by their branches were compared, a significant difference between the views of the students of primary school teaching and preschool teaching was not observed according to the t-test results ($t_{(106)}$ = -481 p > .05). It could be said that the students of preschool teaching and primary school teaching hold similar opinions.

When the views of the prospective teachers involved in the research on the ESE dimension by their branches are compared, a significant difference was not observed between the views of the students of the preschool teaching and primary school teaching according to the t-test results ($t_{(106)}$ = -, 294 p > .05). It can be said that the views of the students of the preschool teaching (X: 20, 8837) and primary school teaching (X: 20, 5385) were similar.

When the views of the prospective teachers involved in the research on the HE scale were compared within the whole, as a result of the t-test analysis, a significant difference between the students of the primary school teaching and preschool teaching was not found ($t_{(106)}$ = -1,142 p > .05). The views of prospective teachers involved in the research on "Home Education and the Reasons for Choosing School in Formal Education" did not differ in terms of gender and branch variables.

Discussion

In this section, RCHE sub-dimension, RCS sub-dimension and ESE sub-dimension of the HE scale were discussed in the light of the other works.

Sub-dimension: Reasons for Choosing Home Education (RCHE) As the reasons for choosing home education the following were arranged in the scale for the prospective teachers: providing high academic facilities (i1), creating high expectations at the excellence level in education (i2), providing a safe environment for learning (i3), increasing the opportunities needed to instill moral values (i4), meeting unique learning needs (i5), strengthening family ties (i6), being flexible while programming the lessons (i7), parents becoming efficient role models (i8), finding some activities in state schools inappropriate for children (i9), and children having religious freedom (i10).

It was seen that the views of the female and male prospective teachers accumulated around the mostly disagree option based upon the answers they had given to the items related to the RCHE dimension by the gender variable. When the views of the prospective teachers involved in the research on the RCHE dimension by their branches were compared, it was observed that the views of the students of the primary school teaching and preschool teaching were similar. It was observed that both the students of the primary school teaching and preschool teaching mostly disagreed with the items in the scale for RCHE.

The reason why prospective teachers mostly disagree with the RCHE dimension based on gender and branch variable is because of the statements specifying "Home education is essential for the individuals needing private education who are at the age of preschool, primary school, secondary school and high school education and who are not in a position to have direct education at education and training institutions" and "The individuals cleared to be educated at home by the Committee of Private Education Services are registered to a primary school, secondary school or private education center (school). They are not obliged for attendance" in the "Circular for Education at Home and Hospital of the Ministry of National Education" numbered 5212 and dated November 25, 2009 and "Regulations on the Amendments on the Regulation for Private Education Services" numbered 28360 and dated July 21, 2012 by the Directorate General of Private Education Guidance and Counseling Services, in the relevant articles. The individuals who prefer home education are defined by the legal texts in Turkey. Home education cannot be provided to anyone other than the individuals with the conditions defined by the laws.

When the literature was reviewed, it was found in Collom's work (2005) that the reasons for choosing home education abroad were different from those in Turkey. In this work Collum revealed that the education of the family, gender, income level, and political character had nothing to do with preference of home education. Medlin (1994) found that 61% of his sample of 27 homeschooling families employed a pedagogy and curriculum not substantially different than those of traditional state schools, while only 19% employed less structured pedagogies or full unschooling.

Thorpe et al. (2012) included parents of 707 home education students in research they conducted in Western Pennsylvania. In this research, most of the parents pointed out that they chose home education in order to increase family time and parents' influence and decrease peer pressure and the effect of other negative factors in the lives of their children.

In research conducted on the parents choosing home education for their children, it was found out that the fathers achieved the goal of home education in terms of ethical socialization and were less political while mothers had difficulty in undertaking the role teacher (Vigilant, Trefethren, and Anderson 2013).

In addition to this, in another work conducted on the socialization of the children of the families choosing home education, the families accepted that their children were socialized through the internet (Atkinson et al. 2007). Likewise, Ray (2015) noted that 24% of the parents of the home-educated children involved in his research used packaged programs on a computer.

Clements (2002) conducted a qualitative work on three families to define the method they used in home education. In this work, curriculum, computer, video, and education based on workbooks were handled. Clements determined that all parents used firstly their own methods and then other curricula.

The motivations expressed by the homeschooling families involved in a study in South Dakota were as follows: to strengthen family ties, the inadequacy of the state schools in teaching the love of God, to prevent peer pressure, the inadequacy of state schools in assisting the children in terms of character development, and public school classes being very crowded. Home education was preferred by mostly married women. Distance of the school to the home was not very important. The families expected their children to have religious education at least once a week. Most of the teachers providing home education were parents who were university graduates while a small of them were teachers. According to the research works, homeschools were accepted as the alternative to state schools (Boschee and Boschee 2011).

Families prefered home education where richer materials (radio, television, computer, etc.) were used. Also, they controlled their students easily (Dumas, Gates, and Schwarzer 2010).

Sub-dimension: Reason for Choosing School (RCS) The following were arranged for the prospective teachers as the reason for choosing a school in the scale: providing the child with access to the educational tools, materials, and resources free of charge (i11); increasing direct participation of children in education (i12); enjoying easy accessibility to supportive technology for education at school (i13); receiving updated feedback on learning progress at school (i14); belonging to a respectable community of learners at school (i15); students being able to receive professional support on educational problems (i16); receiving individualized support for students' special needs of student (i17).

It was seen that the views of the female and male prospective teachers involved in the research were strongly negative with regards to the reasons for the dimension of choosing a school, by gender. Likewise, based on the branch variable, while the students of the primary school teaching strongly disagreed on the items regarding the dimension of choosing a school, students of the preschool teaching noted that they mostly disagreed. Prospective teachers of both branches held negative opinion concerning the reasons for choosing a school.

The reason why the prospective teachers disagreed with the items concerning choosing a school stipulated within the scale was that registrations of the students for the first class of all official primary schools, for the fifth class of all official secondary schools, and for the ninth class of all official high schools are executed over the Electronic School Management Information System (e-school) by the Ministry of National Education to the most appropriate school based on home address, without any application and depending on the students' MERNIS (Central Population Management System) information. These results indicate that there are still shortcomings regarding the infrastructure of the Turkish educational system and that students are limited in their choice of school.

In Turkey, the government has made it mandatory for parents and students to choose the nearest state schools to their home addresses. They have to be content with the facilities they are provided. Glasman and Besson (2004) have pointed out in their research that families accessed the new information more easily through using different disciplines technically at school. Those who are not content with the facilities in public schools send their children to private schools and make them take private courses at home. Literature covering the difference in terms of education between the public-schooled students and the homeschooled students, includes the study by McKinley et al. (2007) who carried out research on home-educated students, students at public school and students at private school. A significant difference was not found statistically when the points of the students at the private school were compared with the points of the home-educated students and students of public schools, although the students of the private school defined themselves as important in terms of cooperation, claims, self-control and being more talented at social skills compared to the other students, in this research. A significant difference was not observed when the development level of the social skills of the public school students was compared with the level of the students of the private school in the work conducted by Wharfe (as in cited Medlin 2013). An American researcher noted that schools increasingly place so much stress on homework and on the results of standardized tests that students and parents have been expressing increasing frustration and opposition (Kravolec and Duell 2001, cited in Glasman and Besson 2004).

Sub-dimension: Evaluation of School Experience (ESE) The items on the scale related to the evaluation of school experience are the following: it provides the prospective students with more time instead of the time to be spent while gathering resources supplied with the curriculum on their own with regards to the evaluation of the school experience (i18), being satisfied with having the possibility for access to high quality learning materials (i19), meeting the academic needs of students (i20), the motivating reasons for home education in general and maintaining home education by regulating the its process (i21), having enjoyment in learning through technology provided within education programs at school (i22), appreciating responsibility undertaken by school for learning (i23), compatibility of parents' needs regarding the planning and flexibility for home education with each other (i24), having immediate assistance when encountering technological problems at school (i25), thinking that social needs of students are met at schools (i29), parents using the opportunities provided by the communication network established through the education at school (i30), limitation of students by home education (i31).

The average of the female and male prospective teachers involved in the research for the evaluation of the school experience based on the gender variation demonstrated that they mostly disagreed. When the views of the prospective teachers with regards to the dimension of the evaluation of school experience were compared by their branches, it was seen that the students of the primary school teaching and preschool teaching were the same and they strongly disagreed. The evaluation of success or failure of the students of the formal education or students of the home education are determined only through the Upgrading Exam from Primary Education to Secondary Education (TEOG), Upgrading Exam for Higher Education (YGS) and Placement Exam for Undergraduate Programs in Turkey.

The education is received mostly in public schools in the Turkish educational system. In addition, in order to promote private schools, the private schools are subsidized by the government. The feedback from the students at public and private schools, and homeschooled students (in spite of being few in number) are provided via exams such as TEOG, YGS and LYS (Transition to Higher Education Examination). The available literature shows that the achievement of homeschooled students was the same as for those in schools (e.g. Staehle 2000). Staehle (2000) asserted in his work that the school was necessary for most of the children. However, when the home-educated children were studied it was seen that home education also provided the same opportunities for the children as the school (Staehle 2000). In literature, there are some studies that disagree with these findings. Welner and Welner (1999) note that parents and homeschooling advocates often claim that home education produces superior academic results, but the data presented to defend this claim suffers from profound methodological problems, making true comparisons between home and institutionally schooled children impossible.

Views of prospective teachers on "Home Education and the Reasons for Selecting School in Formal Education"

When the responses of the female and male prospective teachers involved in the research regarding home education scale based on gender variable were scrutinized, it was seen again that they mostly chose the option of "I am hesitant." When the average of the views of the female and male prospective teachers were compared on the whole in terms of the reasons for choosing school in home education and formal education, based on the branch variable, it was found that students of preschool teaching mostly disagreed with the articles within the home education scale while students of primary school teaching strongly disagreed. There was no difference in the views on "Home Education and the Reasons for Selecting School in Formal Education."

When the field work conducted in Turkey with regards to the home education scale was studied, it was seen that that kind of work was very limited. "Homeschooling in Turkey (Focus Group Interviewing Method) by Kılıç Doğan and Önen (2012) was published in the *US-China Education Review*. In this work, group focus discussion was performed. The result of this work demonstrated that it was not possible to carry out home education in Turkey. In the work of Taştan and Demir (2013), which supported the previous work, research was conducted on thirty academics serving at five different education faculties. As a result of the research, it was determined that the academics did not have an adequate understanding of the factors involved in the decision to homeschool. Moreover, it was found that most academics placed a high priority on the educational level of the parent as the determinative factor in the viability of home educaiton as a method of instruction in Turkey.

When the works outside of Turkey were studied, home education was shown to provide an alternative option for the establishment of psychological, physical, and academic requirements. In addition to this, the opinion that the educational environment for the children of parents who opposed the general educational system was provided through suitable pedagogic applications (Norlidah, et al. 2013; Rajamony 2008; Collom, 2005).

When the literature with regards to the home education was studied, deficiency of socialization opportunities, inadequacy of the parents in all intellectual areas, especially material deficiency in scientific areas and lack of attention regarding basic skills, was stipulated as the negative side of home education (Nelson 1986). On the other hand, Olivos (2009) criticized home education in terms of its ability to deal with cultural differences, questioning how intercultural issues would be reflected and taught. Also Trainor (2010) argued that the adequacy of parents' social, economic, and pedagogic capital resources should be examined.

Future Research

In this work, firstly the scale for HE was adapted. In the next stage, the views of the senior students of preschool teaching and primary school teaching were asked using the HE scale. This and similar research could be adjusted and expanded to include other prospective teachers in other classes and other branches and applied comparatively. Besides this, a work to compare the students with a teaching certificate in the Science-Literature Faculty and Theology Faculty and the students of the Faculty of Education could be planned. This work could also be carried out comparing the views of teachers and school administrators. Informative meetings on home education for parents could be arranged and their views on the applicability of home education could be ascertained. Also a comparison could be made by asking the views of parents and teachers of different ethnic origins (e.g. Kurds, Cherkes, Arabs) and of different sects (e.g. Alevists).

Conclusion

This work aimed to put forward the views of the senior students of the primary school teaching and preschool teaching at the Faculty of Education at Sinop University on "Home Education and the Reasons for Selecting School in Formal Education". Firstly, the scale of Klein and Poplin (2008) in the essay titled "Families Home Schooling in a Virtual Charter School System" was adapted into Turkish. The adapted scale consists of two parts: (1) demographic factors; (2) the reasons for choosing home education, including three different sub-dimensions consisting of reasons for choosing school and evaluation of school experience. First Exploratory Factor Analysis and then Confirmatory Factor Analysis of the scale used in this research was conducted. After the final form of the scale was established, the scale was applied to the senior students of primary school teaching and preschool teaching. The views of the prospective teachers on "Home Education and the Reasons for Selecting School in Formal Education" differed little based on gender and branch. The reasons for choosing home education, reasons for choosing school, and evaluation of school experience did not differ in terms of gender. Likewise, the reasons for choosing home education, reasons for choosing school, and evaluation of school experience did not differ based on branch.

In conclusion, our data suggest that Turkish educators do not have a high view of the decision to home educate, which only adds to the difficulty of families who might choose this strategy for their children. To the degree that home education is accepted, our subjects would want clear defintions and parameters for the content and type of education being offered at home and especially would want prospective home-educating parents to be well educated themselves (Atkinson et al. 2007).

Due to the geographical conditions in the Eastern and Southeastern part of Turkey and the patriarchal structure perpetuated in these regions, education in these regions is needed much more, particularly for female students who are not sent to school here. When the initiative is given to the families, especially in rural areas, in Eastern and Southeastern Turkey, unfortunately the children are made to work in the fields; they are made to marry at a very early age; and they are left vulnerable. Home education runs the risk of killing the childhood of the child through power rather than ensuring her/him their childhood in an atmosphere of enjoyable learning and happiness. Besides, families from different ethnic origins (Kurds, Arabs, Cherkes, Lazs, etc.) may wish to stand up for home education in order to teach their own cultures. Also, Alevis in Turkey may wish to support home education to provide their children moderate Islam instead of strict Islam, while extreme conservative Sunni families may wish to have home education in order to teach strict Islam to their children. Although we are not satisfied with the current educational system in Turkey, the education even in its present form can prevent small children from being used as laborers, being child brides, and being abused by terrorist organizations. Educated families and a developed understanding of democracy are needed for home education; otherwise, if home education is applied in Turkey, the children can be left vulnerable and uneducated.

References

Alias, Norlidah, Saedah Siraj, Mohd, Nazri Abdul Rahman, and Dorothy Dewitt. 2013. "Homeschooling in Malaysia: The Implications for Teacher Services." *Malaysian Online Journal of Educational Management*, 1(2): 10–18.

Aydın, İ. 2012. *Alternatif Okullar*. Ankara: Pegem A Yayınları.

Atkinson, M., et al. 2007. *Support for Children Who are Educated at Home*. Slough, UK: National Foundation for Educational Research.

Bajunid, Ibrahim. 2002. "Changing Mindsets: Lifelong Learning for All." Kuala Lumpur: International Conference On Life Long Learning.

Baker, C. 1995. *Insoumission à l'école Obligatoire*.Translated by Ayşegül Sönmezay: Istanbul.

Basham, P., J. Merrifield, and C.R. Hepburn. 2007. *Home Schooling: From the Extreme to the Mainstream*, 2nd ed: Studies in Education Policy.

Belfield, C.R., and H.M. Levin. 2005. *Privatizing Educational Choice*. Denver, CO: Paradigm Publishers.

Broadhurst, D. 1999. *Investigating Young Children's Perceptions of Homeschooling*. Paper presented at the AARE Annual Conference Melbourne. Accessed May 3, 2016. http://www.aare.edu.au/data/publications/1999/bro99413.pdf

Boschee, B.F, and F. Boschee. 2011. "A Profile of Homeschooling in South Dakota." *Journal of School Choice: Research, Theory, and Reform*, 5 (3): 281–299.

Chapman, A., and T.A. O'Donoghue. 2000. "Home Schooling: An Emerging Research Agenda." *Educational Research and Perspectives*, 27(1): 19–36.

Clements, A.D. 2002. "Variety of Teaching Methodologies Used By Homeschoolers: Case Studies of Three Homeschooling Families." Paper presented at the annual meeting of the Eastern Educational Research Association. Sarasota, FL: 1–8. Accessed May 3, 2016. https://scholar.google.com/scholar_lookup?title=Variety%20of%20teaching%20methodologies%20used%20homeschoolers%3A%20Case%20studies%20of%20three%20homeschooling%20families&author=A.%20Clements&publication_year=2002

Collom, E. 2005. "The Ins and Outs of Homeschooling: The Determinants of Parental Motivation and Student Achievement." *Education and Urban Society*, 37(3): 307.

Dumas,T.K., S. Gates, and D.R. Schwarzer. 2010. "Evidence For Homeschooling: Constitutional Analysis In Light Of Social Science Research." *Widener Law Review* 16(63): 63–87. Accessed May 3, 2016. http://widenerlawreview.org/files/2011/02/02-GATES_final.pdf

French, L.R., Walker, C.L., and Shore, B.M. 2011. "Do Gifted Students Really Prefer To Work Alone?" *Roeper Review*, 33 (3): 145–159.

Glasman, D, and Besson.L. 2004. "Le travail des élèves pour l'école en dehors de l'école." *Rapport Établi à la Demande du Haut Conseil de l'Évaluation de l'École*, No .15 Paris. Accessed May 3, 2016. http://www.cndp.fr/bienlire/04-media/documents/rapport_Glasman_Besson.pdf

Green-Hennessy, S. 2013. "Homeschooled Adolescents in the United States: Developmental Outcomes." *Journal of Adolescence*, 37(4): 441–449.

Hanna, L.G. 2012. "Homeschooling Education: Longitudinal Study of Methods, Materials, and Curricula." *Education and Urban Society*, 44(5): 609–631. DOI: 10.1177/0013124511404886

Hetzel, J., M. Long, and Jackson, M. 2001. "Factors that Influence Parents to Homeschool in Southern California." *Home School Researcher*, 14: 1–11.

Hu, Li-Tze, and Peter M. Bentler. 1999. "Cutoff Criteria for Fit Indexes in Covariance Structure Analysis: Conventional Criteria versus New Alternatives." *Structural Equation Modeling: A Multidisciplinary Journal*, 6(1): 1–55.

Jackson, G. 2009. "'More than One Way to Learn': Home Educated Students' Transitions between Home and School." Unpublished PhD thesis, Monash University, Clayton. Accessed May 3, 2016. http://arrow.monash.edu.au/hdl/1959.1/83110

Kılıç Doğan, E., et al. 2008. "Küreselleşme Sürecinde Ev Eğitimi." *İlköğretmen Dergisi*, Sayı 17.

Kılıç Doğan, E., and Önen, Ö. 2012. "Homeschooling in Turkey (Focus Group Interviewing Method)." *US-China Education Review*, B 8.

Klein, C. and Poplin, M. 2008. "Families Home Schooling in a Virtual Charter School System." *Marriage & Family Review*, 43(3/4): 369–395. DOI: 10.1080/01494920802073221

Kline, Rex B. 2016. *Principles and Practice of Structural Equation Modeling*, 4th ed. New York: Guilford.

Llewellyn, G. 1998. *The Teenage Liberation Handbook: How to Quit School and Get a Real Life and Education* (revised and expanded ed.). Eugene, OR: Lowry House Publishers.

Lyman, I. 1998. "Homeschooling: Back to the Future." *Cato Policy Analysis*, No. 294. Accessed May 3, 2016. http://www.cato.org/pubs/pas/pa-294.html

McIntyre-Bhatty, K. 2007. "Interventions and Interrogations: An Analysis of Recent Policy Imperatives and their Rationales in the Case of Home Education." *Education, Knowledge & Economy*, 1: 241–259. DOI: 10.1080/17496890701580507

McKinley, M.J., et al. 2007. "Social Skills and Satisfaction with Social Relationships in Home-Schooled, Private-Schooled, and Public-Schooled Children." *Home School Researcher*, 17(3): 1–6.

MEB. 2010. "Evde ve Hastanede Eğitim Hizmetleri Yönergesi." Ministry of National Education, Circular on Education Services at Home and in Hospitals.

Medlin, R.G. 1994. "Predictors of Academic Achievement in Home Educated Children Aptitude, Self Concept, and Pedagogical Practices." *Home School Researcher*, 10 (3): 1–7.

Medlin, R.G. 2013. "Homeschooling and the Question of Socialization Revisited." *Peabody Journal of Education*, 88(3): 284–297, DOI: 10.1080/0161956X.2013.796825

Murphy, Joseph. 2012. *Homeschooling in America: Capturing and Assessing the Movement*, Thousand Oaks, CA: Corwin.

NCES. 2008. "1.5 Million Homeschooled Students in the United States in 2007." Jessup, MD: National Center for Education Statistics.

Nelson, E. 1986. Home Schooling. *ERIC Clearinghouse on Educational Management, 15.* University of Oregon, Washington. Accessed May 3, 2016. https://ia801004.us.archive.org/19/items/ERIC_ED282348/ERIC_ED282348.pdf

Norlidah, A., et al. 2013. "Homeschooling in Malaysia: The Implications for Teacher Services." Malaysian Online *Journal of Educational Management* 1(2): 10–18. Accessed May 3, 2016. http://mojem.um.edu.my

Olivos, E.M. 2009. "Collaboration with Latino Families: A Critical Perspective of Home- School Interactions." *Intervention in School and Clinic*, 45(2): 109–115. DOI: 10.1177/1053451209340220

Penn-Nabrit, P. 2003. *Morning by Morning: How we Homeschooled our African American Sons into the Ivy League*. New York: Villard Books.

Princiotta, D., S. Bielick, and C. Chapman. 2006. "Homeschooling in the United States: 2003." Statistical Analysis Report. Accessed May 3, 2016. http://nces.ed.gov/pubs2006/2006042.pdf

Rajamony, Ebinezar John A/L Y. 2008. "The Malaysian Experience in Home Schooling." PhD thesis, Universiti Putra Malaysia.

Ray, B.D. 2015. "Research Facts on Homeschooling." Accessed February 27, 2015. http://www.nheri.org/ResearchFacts.pdf

Reilly, L., A. Chapman, and T. O'Donoghue. 2002. "Home Schooling of Children with Disabilities." *Queensland Journal of Educational Research, 18*(1), 38–61.

Rothermel, P. 2003. "Can we Classify Motives for Home Education?" *Evaluation and Research in Education*, 17(2-3): 74–87. Accessed May 3, 2016. http://www.tandfonline.com/doi/abs/10.1080/09500790308668293#.VO7vTU05mcw

Sağsan, M. 2003. "Epistemolojik Anarşizmi Karşısında Feyerabend'ı Yeniden Anlama Üzerine Düşünceler.(Epistemological Anarchism Against Feyerabend: Thoughts on Re-understanding.)" *TKD Ankara Şubesi Yayın Organı*, 59: 14–30. Accessed May 3, 2016. http://staff.neu.edu.tr/~msagsan/publications.html

Schermelleh-Engel, K., H. Moosbrugger, and H. Müller. 2003. "Evaluating the Fit of Structural Equation Models: Tests of Significance and Descriptive Goodness-of-Fit Measures," *Methods of Psychological Research*, 8(2): 23–74.

Seitz,C. M., et al. 2013. "Coverage of Adolescent Substance Use Prevention in State Frameworks for Health Education: 10-Year Follow-Up." *Journal of School Health*, 83(1): 53–60 Accessed May 3, 2016. http://onlinelibrary.wiley.com/doi/10.1111/j.1746-1561.2012.00747.x/epdf

Şişman, M. 2000. "Öğretmenlik Mesleğine Giriş (Introduction to Teaching Profession)." Ankara: PEGEM A yayıncılık.

Snyder, M. 2011. "An Evaluative Study of the Academic Achievement of Homeschooled Students Versus Traditionally Schooled Students Attending a Catholic University." Nova Southeastern University: Unpublished PhD thesis. Accessed May 3, 2016. http://files.eric.ed.gov/fulltext/ED533544.pdf

Staehle, D. 2000. "Taking a Different Path: A Mother's Reflections on Homeschooling." *Roeper Review*, 22 (4): 270–271. DOI: 10.1080/02783190009554051

Stafford, B. 2012. "Bad Evidence: The Curious Case of the Government-Commissioned Review of Elective Home Education in England and How Parents Exposed Its Weaknesses." *Evidence and Policy*, 8(3): 361–381. DOI: 10.1332/174426412X654077

Taştan, M., and Ö. Demir. 2013. "The Views of Academic Staff in Turkey On Home Schooling Programs: A Qualitative Study." *The Journal of Academic Social Science Studies*, 6(5): 1085–1103. Accessed DOI: 10.9761/JASSS1426

Terry, B.K. 2011. "Homeschooling in America a Viable Option." Accessed May 3, 2016. http://files.eric.ed.gov/fulltext/ED517220.pdf

Thorpe, L.T., et al. 2012. "Homeschooling Parents' Practices and Beliefs about Childhood Immunizations." *Vaccine*, 30: 1149–1153. DOI: 10.1016/j.vaccine.2011.12.019

Trainor, A.A. 2010. "Diverse Approaches to Parent Advocacy During Special Education Home-School Interactions: Identification and Use of Cultural and Social Capital." *Remedial and Special Education*, 31(1): 34–47. DOI: 10.1177/0741932508324401

TUİK. 2013. Okullaşma Oranı: Accessed May 3, 2016.http://www.turkstat.gov.tr/UstMenu.do?metod=temelist

Vigilant, G.L., L.V. Trefethren, and T.C. Anderson. 2013. "'You Can't Rely on Somebody Else to Teach Them Something They Don't Believe': Impressions of Legitimation Crisis and Socialization Control in the Narratives of Christian Homeschooling Fathers." *Humanity & Society*, 37(3): 201–224. DOI: 10.1177/0160597613495841

Welner, K.M., and K.G. Welner, 1999. "Contextualizing Homeschooling Data: A Response to Rudner." *Education Policy Analiysis Archives*, 7(13): 1–13. DOI: 10.14507/epaa.v7n13.1999

Yuracko, K.A. 2008. "Education Off the Grid: Constitutional Constraints on Homeschooling." *California Law Review*, 96(1): 123–184. Accessed May 3, 2016. http://scholarship.law.berkeley.edu/californialawreview/vol96/iss1/3

19

Home Education in China

Xiaoming Sheng

Introduction

Since the initiation of market-oriented reforms in 1978, Chinese society has been experiencing a period of transition from a planned, centrally controlled economy to a market economy. From the mid-1980s this process of transition has had a great influence on both income inequality and social stratification mechanisms in China (Bian 1994; Li 2000; Bian 2002). The radical changes in the area of economics have resulted in dramatic changes in social stratification (Lu 1989); for instance, in the middle of the 1990s, a new middle class emerged in China (Li 2000). The relevant literature indicates that social transformation is an impetus for, and is reflected in, educational changes (Fagerlind and Saha 1989; Carnoy and Samoff 1990). Parents, particularly middle-class parents, are more likely to pursue a better education for their children, which has led to a noticeable change in parents' choices regarding their children's education. It is becoming varied and diversified. In this respect, home education, as an educational phenomenon, has emerged in Beijing, Shanghai, and Guangzhou. However, as a marginal educational phenomenon, the development of home education has been ignored by Chinese educational research, perhaps because homeschooling families generally have felt dissatisfied with mainstream schooling. Policymakers and education officials have access to little substantive information in relation to home education. This chapter reports the findings of my data-based research study of homeschooling families in China, which was carried out in order to provide in-depth information regarding the demographic characteristics of homeschooling parents, the motivation for home education, and the teaching style and teaching content of home education in present-day China. In what follows, firstly the background to the homeschooling movement throughout the world will

The Wiley Handbook of Home Education, First Edition. Edited by Milton Gaither.

be briefly described. Then an introduction focusing on the current status of home education in China will be provided, followed by a description of the Chinese legal situation of home education. The primary types of Chinese home education will be summarized and then a brief description focusing on the characteristics of homeschooling families will be given. The chapter will then briefly describe the reasons for parents choosing home education, and this will be followed by a discussion of the teaching styles and content of home education in China. In particular, the chapter will consider the relationship between religious belief and Confucian studies and the development of home education. Finally, the challenges and concerns of home education will be discussed.

Background to the Homeschooling Movement Across the World

The homeschooling movement in the Western context

In the past few decades, there has been rapid and dramatic growth of home education throughout the world. As an important educational phenomenon, home education has achieved rapid growth in countries such as the United States, Britain, Canada, Australia and China. In the US, the rapid growth of the home education movement has inspired academic researchers to investigate this phenomenon (Knowles 1991a, 1991b; Knowles, Marlow, and Muchmore 1992; Ray 1994, 1997, 2000, 2003, 2005, 2009a, 2009b, 2010; Rudner 1999; McDowell and Ray 2000; Klicka 2002, 2007; Gross 2003; Spiegler 2003; Villalba 2003, 2009; Brabant, Bourdon, and Jutras 2003; Sampson 2005; Bunday 2006; Ellin 2006; Princiotta and Bielick 2006; Princiotta et al. 2004, 2006; Glenn 2005; Hopwood et al. 2007; Ray and Eagleson 2008; Murphy 2012; Kunzman and Gaither 2013). Since the emergence of modern home education in the late 1970s, a growing number of British scholars have paid attention to its rapid development in the UK (Meighan and Brown 1980; Meighan 1981, 1984a, 1984b, 1996, 1997; Rothermel 1999a, 1999b, 2002, 2004, 2010, 2011; Hopwood et al. 2007; Webb 1989, 1997, 2011; Jennens 2011; Lees 2014). In Canada, several studies have documented the rapid growth in home education and explored parental motivations to home educate (Common and MacMullen 1986; Luffman 1997; Arai 2000; Tator 2001; Dahlquist 2002, 2005; Dahlquist, York-Barr, and Hendel 2006; Fairchild 2002; Brabant, Bourdon, and Jutras 2003; Aurini and Davies 2005; Brabant and Bourdon 2012). In China, a few studies have focused on the exploration of the demographic aspects of, motivation for, and academic results of home education (Sheng 2013, 2014).

As Collom (2005) asserts, in the US home education has become an increasingly popular alternative educational path to that of conventional school education. Similarly Klein (2006) indicates that home education has become one of many educational choices available to parents today in the US. At the beginning of the 1980s, nearly all children and young people between the ages of 6 and 18 were in formal and institutional schools (Ray 2000, 73). On September 16, 1999, the US Senate passed a resolution designating the week of September 19–25 that year, as "'National Home Education Week" (Basham 2001; Basham, Merrifield, and Hepburn 2007). As Isenberg (2007, 390) states, the data from the National Household Education Surveys (NHES) are "large enough to include a sufficiently large sample of homeschooled children and a comparison group of children who attend a conventional school" in the US. Data from the 1999 NHES stated that home education in the USA in 1999 was estimated to involve approximately 850 000 students (Bielick, Chandler, and Broughman 2001), which was about 1.7% of students nationwide aged from 5 to 17 in grades K–12 (Lawrence 2007, 2). For the 2001–2002 school year, the NHES estimated that there were around 1.1 million American students in grades K–12 who were being educated at home (Lines 2000; Dennis 2000; Houston and Toma 2003; Princiotta et al. 2004), which represents a 29% increase on the estimated 1999 number. Over the 2005–2006 school year there were thought to be between 1.9 and 2.4 million students who were being educated at home in the United States (Ray 2007). However, the data from the 2007 NHES offered a different figure: they indicated that around 1.5 million students (1 508 000) were being home-educated, which was about 2.9% of the school-aged population in the US (Princiotta et al. 2004; Bielick 2008). This is a significant increase from the NHES 2003 estimate (Princiotta et al. 2004; Bielick 2008). With figures from 2011 showing an estimated 1.77 million (Noel, Stark, and Redford 2013), it is clear that homeschooling continues to grow at a fast pace in the United States.

The increasing development of home education in East Asia

According to the Ministry of Education in Japan, more than 120000 children are reportedly avoiding or refusing school at the primary and middle school levels in Japan (Kugai 2014). According to Kugai (2014) who is a Japanese homeschooling parent and advocate of homeschooling in the city of Himeji, it is difficult to estimate how many homeschoolers are currently active in Japan, since there is no official research that has been done to determine their numbers. However, as estimated unofficially by Kugai (2014), the number is around 2000 to 3000.

In Vietnam, the Education Law does not make any specific reference to home education. If parents choose to home educate, they are only required to reassure the government that they are fully complying with the "requirements on contents and methods of general education" as outlined in Article 28 of the Education Law.

In Taiwan, since the end of the 1990s, home education has undergone dramatic growth, and a number of home education associations have been established. For example, Mu Zhen Home Education Association was established in 1998 in Xin Zhu. In 1998, seven homeschooling families set up a homeschooling community, which aimed to broadcast ideas and views about home education and enhance communication between homeschooling families (Mu Zhen 2014).

The status of home education in China

Generally speaking, the modern development of home education in China is at an early stage and so far constitutes only a marginal educational phenomenon within the education system. Before the end of the 1990s, the majority of participants in home education could generally be considered to be "passively involved" in it. Some of the parents, particularly mothers, were forced into home educating because their children had experienced academic difficulties or psychological problems, such as MBD (Minimal Brain Dysfunction) or ADHD (Attention-Deficit Hyperactivity Disorder), which made it impossible for them to benefit from conventional classroom-based education. However, since the beginning of the 21st century, a growing number of parents in Beijing, Shanghai, and Guangdong have been enthusiastically practicing home education for their children.

In comparison to the Western context, there have been relatively few academic studies on the topic of home education in China (Sheng 2013, 2014). From my studies, I have documented the rapid growth in the country's home education since 2000, and there is also a small but growing body of media reports regarding its development. The *China Youth Paper* in 2013 reported that a growing number of homeschooling families had emerged in Beijing, Shanghai, Guangdong, Zhejiang, Jiangshu, Hubei, and Yunnan. The majority of such families are located in Beijing, Shanghai and Guangdong. According to the website of the China Home Education League in 2013, there were over 1000 members of the League who were practicing home education. The dramatic increase in the number of homeschoolers in Beijing and Shanghai, reported by this website, is a surprising phenomenon in a country like China, where the possession of a diploma is so important in the labor market.

An accurate number of homeschoolers is difficult to obtain because in China the government does not allow home education, and thus parents who conduct home education are not required to register with the authorities. In previous decades, journalists reported a few isolated groups of families who were practicing home education in certain regions in China. Table 19.1 illustrates the number of home-schooled children reported by media. On the basis of the results of my surveys of home-educated children in China, I estimate that there are currently around 25000 homeschooling children nationwide. In particular, there was a significant growth from 2005 to 2014, rising from less than 8000 in 2005 to over 25 000 in 2014, involving children at both primary and secondary school levels. At the primary level, the age of home-educated children is usually between 5 and 12 years.

Many home educators and advocates of home education have produced and published specific textbooks regarding traditional Chinese literature (e.g., Confucian works) for home-educated children, and several homeschooling parents have established an online homeschooling website, the Home Education League, which aims to build up a support network for families practicing home education. To some extent, this can be seen as a kind of original homeschooling industry. The homeschooling parents and organizers are able to generate a large amount of money from this new educational industry through selling textbooks and online courses.

Table 19.1 The estimated number of homeschooled children reported by media.

Name of Place	*Home education*	*Homeschoolers*	*Sources*
Guangzhou, Gugangdong	Home Education League	408	*Nan Fang Du Shi Paper*, 2013
Beijing	Christian Home Education	200	Sheng, 2014
Shanghai	Meng Mu Tang	12	Sheng, 2014
Shenyang, Liaoning	Guo Xue Home Education	50	Sheng, 2014
Nanjing, Jiang Shu	Nanjing Home Education League	15	*Yang Zhi Evening Paper*, 2011
Beijing	Ri Ri Xin Home Education	148	163.net, educational channel, 2013
Nanchang, Jiangxi	Confucian Home Education	8	*Jiangxi Daily*, 2013
Nationwide	China Home Schooling League	1000	163.net, 2013
Haikou, Hainan	Confucian Home Education, Du Jing Xue Tang	22	163.net, educational channel, 2011

Legal Situation of Home Education

Legal situation of home education in East Asia

In Japan, under the current School Education Law, home education is not illegal. As Kugai (2014) states, people in Japan who choose home education are not being prosecuted or sent to jail. As indicated by Kugai (2014), "While it is a fact that there is no law in Japan that concretely provides for home-based learning, it is also a fact that there is no provision under law at present that expressly prohibits it. For those families in Japan who do pursue home learning as an alternative to school, the Ministry of Education generally does not stand in their way. At this stage, the ministry neither discourages nor encourages home learning in Japan." Further, Ohkubo (2014) explains " Even so, there are lots of people in society who believe that children are required to attend school and many cases where boards of education possess no understanding of what home education is about. Thus we still see cases, depending on the local area or district, of interference by boards of education in trying to make children go to school."

Similarly in South Korea there is no provision under law that prohibits home education, neither is there any law that specifically permits home education. As in Japan, if parents remove their child from conventional schools and educate them at home, there will be no intervention from the government.

In Taiwan, the number of families who choose to educate their children at home has increased steadily since the Legislative Yuan admitted the legal status of home education in Taiwan through an Attachment to the Education Law on June 23, 1999. (Mu Zhen 2014). With the amendment legally permitting families to educate their children at home, more and more people have participated in the Mu Zhen Home Education Association, although they are still expected to fulfill the requirements of conventional school education.

Legal situation of home education in China

In 1951, the Chinese government published a law entitled "The Decision on the Reform of the Education System." Since then, the education system in China has gradually developed into a complete system which comprises four stages: preschool education (three years), junior education (six years), middle education (six years), and higher education (four to ten years) (Chen 2000). Preschool education refers to that which children aged 3 to 5 receive in kindergarten/nursery school. Junior education is the education which students aged 6 to 12 receive in elementary schools. Middle education refers to the educational process which students aged 13 to 18 undergo in junior secondary schools (three years) and senior secondary schools (three years). The time spent in elementary education and junior secondary education forms the period of compulsory education in China, the duration of which is nine years (Chen 2000). When the nine-year period of compulsory education has been completed, the next stages involve both mainstream education and vocational education (Chen 2000). The regular education system is comprised of senior secondary schools, mainstream colleges providing undergraduate education, and technological academies and institutions of higher education (Chen 2000).

As of this writing, China has no special law relating to home education, but it is illegal because it contravenes the provisions of the "China Compulsory Education Law." In July 2006, the full-time Shanghai homeschool called Meng Mu Tang, in which twelve children followed a Confucian reading course (called Du Jing education in Chinese), was declared illegal and ordered to close by the local educational authority in Shanghai. The educational authority stated that the act of practicing homeschooling contravenes the provisions of the China Compulsory Education Law with regard to Items 2, 4 and 35. Items 2 and 4 require that parents should be responsible for sending their school-age children to receive compulsory education at school – education is seen as a kind of national responsibility rather than that of the citizen.

According to Item 35, educating children at home contravenes the specific principles regarding the school curriculum, teaching content, and curriculum setting. A school such as Meng Mu Tang breaks the laws that require permission to be granted to run schools; the owners of Meng Mu Tang should have applied for such permission from the local educational authority in Shanghai. Since the teaching content of Meng Mu Tang was only concerned with Confucian works it also broke several of Item 35's specific principles.

However, the person legally responsible for Meng Mu Tang claimed that it was not an educational institution, it was only a form of modern home education that several parents had organized voluntarily and should not be regarded as an official educational institution – consequently it was not necessary to apply for permission to run it. All the fees and costs relating to Meng Mu Tang had been shared by the parents participating in it. Furthermore, as a form of home education, Meng Mu Tang should be given official recognition and legal permission to operate. The works of Confucius are one of the treasures of Chinese traditional culture, and reading them should be central to the teaching content of home education. Since in most Western countries, home education is permitted, Shanghai should likewise permit home education by law. On February 10, 2009 Meng Mu Tang, which had continued to operate surreptitiously, was closed by the Shanghai Educational Authority again, for the same reasons as its closure in 2006. The educational authority claimed that if the parents were to send their children to study at Meng Mu Tang, it would be regarded as an illegal action.

Main Types of Home Educators in China

The primary types of home educators in present-day China are shown in Table 19.2 and can be summarized as follows: homeschoolers who have strong religious motivations, such as the Christian homeschoolers in Beijing (Sheng 2014); homeschoolers who advocate and encourage the study of Confucian works and Chinese traditional culture (e.g., Meng Mu Tang) (Sheng 2013); homeschoolers who regard home education as a kind of pedagogy (e.g., Ri Ri Xin Xue Tang, aiming to provide a superior education to maximise their children's talents, and using both English literature and Chinese literature); families forced to choose to educate their children at home because of illness or psychological problems; those educating children who were born and educated abroad; and others. My surveys found that Confucian home education, which emphasizes the transmission of Confucian studies and Chinese traditional culture, has been developed using the methods of business. For example, these parents have established a homeschooling website and published a series of textbooks to provide a basis for their children's day-to-day learning. Unlike the development of home education in the US, Canada and Australia, home education in China is still at an immature stage. Curricular development of home education is still insufficient.

The Characteristics of Homeschooling Families

Homeschooling families are distinctive not only in terms of high academic achievement, but also family characteristics (Martin-Chang, Gould, and Meuse 2011). As described earlier in this chapter, comprehensive demographic data in relation to homeschoolers are difficult to obtain. The most reliable estimate of the characteristics of homeschoolers in China is primarily drawn from my previous empirical studies on home education in China.

Table 19.2 The primary types of home schooling in China.

	Christian home education	*Meng Mu Tang*	*Ri Ri Xin Xue Tang*	*Home education because of illness*	*Home education for children who were born and educated abroad*	*Others*
Teaching patterns	Mothers are involved in everyday teaching	Employing professional teachers in the area of Confucian theory	Self-designed teaching context and style; unschooled, child-centered learning	Mixed teaching methods including both conventional teacher-centered teaching style and child-centered teaching style	Child-centered teaching style; unschooled; mother-/father-centered teaching style	Mixed methods including child-centered and teacher-centered teaching style
Organizational patterns	Cooperative study activities organised by the church once a week	Purchasing a villa as the study environment with; 12 students living and studying together	Teaching at a house	At home individually	At home individually	At home individually or learning together in a small group
Parents' belief	Christian	Confucian theory and its works	Various and multiple	Various and multiple	Various and multiple	Various and multiple
Educational idea	Focus on children's mental growth, rather than academic results; emphasis on the learning of Christian	Emphasis on the learning of Chinese traditional culture	Providing a superior education to maximize children's talents	Providing children with a normal and regular education which they cannot obtain at conventional schools	Providing their children high-quality English-language teaching to improve their chances of being admitted by an overseas institution	Providing an education which individually matches children's learning needs and study interest

Generally speaking, home education in China is small-scale, unregulated, unorganized and largely unnoticed. It has emerged mainly in the big cities where people's economic resources are superior, and its modern development can be regarded as being in its initial phase, in which there seems to be escalating tension and hostility between homeschooling families and educational officials. As mentioned earlier, China has no special law relating to home education, but the practice is illegal because it contravenes the provisions of the China Compulsory Education Law.

The interview data generated from my studies indicated that mothers are the primary homeschooling educators. Only a few fathers have resigned from their jobs and stayed at home to practice home education for their children. It is noted that the participants in home education in China are middle-class with a good educational background, relatively high economic income and high expectation of their children's education. The data show that there are a number of Chinese Christian families providing their children with Christian home education in the city of Beijing. Although my own study included all the grade levels with a total range of 4–18 years, the vast majority of homeschooled children are primarily concentrated in the elementary levels – aged between 5 and 13 years – with only a few homeschoolers in the secondary school grades. There were no significant gender differences between male and female homeschooled students.

In brief, the study revealed the following primary characteristics of homeschooling families: the mothers fulfilled the role of teacher or educator in the process of home education; the majority of parents were dissatisfied with contemporary school education in China; the majority of the mothers came from a privileged educational background; most of the parents were Christian, with strong religious beliefs; religion had an important influence on their everyday teaching at home; and all the homeschooling families came from the middle classes, and were relatively wealthy and well educated.

Education

All the parents who were engaged in home education in the sample were mothers who were well educated, holding a bachelor's degree or higher: 58% of the parents in the sample possessed a PhD degree, while 41.6% of the parents were holders of a master's degree. This finding is consistent with the results of studies conducted in the Western context. Many academics have observed that homeschooling parents seemed to be better educated as a group as compared with the general population (Ray 1990; Bieklick, Chandler, and Broughman, 2001; Bauman 2002; Dahlquist 2005; Planty et al. 2009). The interview data revealed that the privileged cultural and economic resources of the middle-class homeschooling parents in the sample provided them with the means, in terms of time, energy, and the ability to stay at home, to practice home education. As in other East Asia countries such as Japan and South Korea, there exist in China traditional values and norms which emphasize high academic achievement of offspring. Nearly all the parents who were practicing home education for their children in my study had high expectations for their children's educations.

The income of homeschooling families

Studies have observed the correlation between family income and the parental decision to homeschool (Ray 2004; Belfield and Levin 2002; Belfield 2004; Bauman 2001; Goyette 2008). However, these studies have been inconclusive, and there exists a disagreement regarding the influence of economic factors on parents' decision to homeschool. Belfield and Levin (2002: 5) observed that the homeschooling families are at the mid-point of the distribution of household incomes: when household income falls below a certain threshold, both parents must work; when it rises above a threshold, private schooling options can be financed more readily. He argued that homeschooling families that are "in the middle of the distribution of household incomes" would be more likely to choose to educate their children at home (Belfield and Levin 2002: 5). Similarly, Lips and Feinberg (2008) found that socioeconomic status may be a factor that influences parents to choose home education for their children. They discovered that the homeschoolers whose families received annual household incomes of less than US$75 000 were more likely to choose to home educate than those whose families had a higher annual income. In Canada, Faris (2006, 15) claimed that "almost 70 per cent of Canadian homeschooling families live with an annual household income of less than C$65 000 and two-thirds of the homeschooling households report having only one income earner." However, several scholars observed that there was no typical demographic of homeschooling families, and that socioeconomic status or family structure had no significant correlation with parents' choice to educate their children at home (Yang and Kayaardi 2004; Essenberg 2004). Nevertheless, Goyette (2008) observed that lower-income families were statistically more likely to educate their children at home, "with 11.4 percent of those making less than US$40000 reporting home education as compared to 1.3 percent of those families making between US$40 000 and US$80 000 and no families who made more than US$80 000' (as cited in Jorgenson 2011, 30).

In contrast to earlier studies, the results of my survey on home education in China illustrated that there existed a close correlation between family income level and parents' decisions to homeschool and that economic situation was a determining factor in parents choosing to educate their children at home (Sheng 2014, 94). This result is similar to the findings of one of the earlier studies that actually did suggest a correlation between income and homeschooling (Lubienski 2000, 29), which suggested that parents' decision to educate their children at home represents a sacrifice on their part in terms of time and energy and requires them to relinquish the opportunity of a second income. The vast majority of parents in the study possessed privileged economic resources, which permitted the mother to stay at home to educate the children. I would suggest that in my study the parents' choice to homeschool was primarily dependent on their economic resources, which were sufficient to ensure that one parent – always the mother – would have the time to stay at home. The data from this research indicated that covering the cost of home education required considerable financial resources. In summary, I would say that the families in China who are capable of practicing home education are usually middle-income, two-parent families with mothers who are full-time housewives.

The structure of homeschooling families

As mentioned earlier, all the home-educated children in this research came from urban, middle-class, two-parent families in which the mother was almost always the parent who stayed at home and practiced home education. The studies' data showed that all the Christian homeschooling children had grown up in two-parent families.

The Reasons for Home Education

From the interviews that were conducted in my empirical studies, it was noticeable that the majority of homeschooling families were motivated by a combination of both pedagogical factors and, to a lesser extent, religious preferences. The reasons that parents make the choice to homeschool are complex in a transitional society like that of China. All the homeschooling educators in the study felt dissatisfied with the present examination-oriented education system and considered that schools had lost sight of moral concerns, focusing on standard examination results to the exclusion of all else. The middle-class parents in the sample showed a particular concern about whether conventional school education could teach their children the specific values and philosophy that they themselves espoused. They looked at education at school in terms not only of the training that the school provided but also the values and norms that were promoted. I found that a variety of Christian families in Beijing in China were practicing home education in order to transmit certain ethical values and beliefs to their children. I discovered that a number of home educators in China had chosen to homeschool because home education was better able to transmit their preferred Chinese traditional culture and knowledge of Confucian works to their children (Sheng 2013, 2014). It was also noticeable that a growing number of homeschooling parents had made such a choice because home education was able to meet their children's physical needs and the specific needs of gifted children in Beijing, Shanghai, and Guangdong. Nearly all the parents who were practicing home education for their children had high expectation of their children's education. For these homeschooling parents, their first concern was the pursuit of educational excellence.

It is clear that the parents in my studies felt very uncomfortable with the teaching purposes of the present education system, which did not always work for their children's academic benefit. For a significant majority of the parents, their decision to homeschool was primarily framed by their academic and pedagogical concerns, and the other focus, namely, the transmission of religious values, was a secondary consideration. Many parents in my study reported that their motivation to homeschool was that they wanted to have more control over the content of what their children were studying (Sheng 2014).

As mentioned earlier in this chapter, a number of parents were forced to choose to homeschool because their child had physical or mental health problems, while others chose to home educate because their children were born abroad and could not easily adapt to the current educational system in China. In addition, dissatisfaction with the current examination-oriented educational system, religion, and specific values regarding Confucian studies and Chinese traditional culture have all played their part

It was also noticeable to me that the vast majority of homeschoolers had suffered as a result of the current examination-oriented education system. In general, all the homeschooling children had had unhappy or even painful experiences at conventional schools and had found the learning environment stressful. To some extent, for the families interviewed, the negative experiences at public schools could be seen as the most important motivating factors in them choosing to educate their children at home in modern-day China. In addition to some homeschooling families claiming that their motivation to home educate was to ensure their child's achievement of high academic results, some middle-class parents wanted to provide their children with home education in order to strengthen the parent–child relationship (Dahlquist, York-Barr, and Hendel 2006; Kunzman 2009; Kunzman and Gaither 2013).

Teaching Styles in Home Education

A number of studies have focused attention on the exploration of the teaching style used in home education in the United States (Thomas 1998; Ray 2000; Lowe and Thomas 2002; Pearson 2002; Saba and Gattis 2002; Huber 2003; Trevaskis 2005; Hoffman 2006; Klein 2006; McKeon 2007; Anthony 2009; Kunzman and Gaither 2013). Lowe and Thomas (2002) and Klein (2006) have found that the majority of homeschooling families have periods of both informality and structure in the arrangement of their home education. Medlin (1994) observed that 61% of the homeschooling parents surveyed reported that they used the traditional methods, and 82% of them used structured approaches in their practice of home education. In New Jersey, Davenport (2001) revealed that homeschooling parents primarily used direct tutorial instruction or individual work activities. Lowe and Thomas (2002, 10) have claimed that "the homeschooling parents use a variety of methods and approaches. These range from formal, structured arrangements to informal approaches which are completely child-led." Clements (2002) summarized four primary types of curricula that were commonly used by homeschooling families, including textbook-based (prepackaged) curricula, literature-based (parent-designed) curricula, computer-based curricula, video/satellite-based curricula and unschooling curricula (as cited in McKeon, 2007, 36). Huber's (2003) study also reveals several teaching strategies and approaches, namely, instruction-based skills, traditional classroom instruction, classical education writing instruction, learner-structured instruction and unschooling methodology (as cited in McKeon 2007, 38).

As shown by the qualitative data from my surveys, the primary teaching style in China could be divided into three categories: a structured teaching style, a flexible teaching style, and unschooling. The homeschooling parents who emphasized the transfer of Confucian work and Chinese traditional culture primarily adopted a structured style, which included a schedule and planned teaching content. Many homeschooling parents used a kind of teaching style that was entirely child-centered. For example, as shown by the interviews provided by Christian home educators, most of the Christian homeschooling families preferred to adopt a flexible teaching style, which is entirely children-centered. According to the Christian homeschooling families, the flexible pedagogy had led to better academic results in both subject study and other areas in which the child was interested. Some of the homeschooling parents used a mixed teaching pattern that included both structured and flexible teaching patterns.

It was clear from the interview data that the vast majority of the homeschooling parents had experienced a transition from a commitment to the fixed structure provided by the textbooks to making their own curriculum decisions according to their children's capabilities and study needs. Most of the homeschooling families in the survey reported a similar change or transfer from a fixed/structured teaching style to a flexible teaching pattern. According to the parents, in the initial period they usually used traditional teaching approaches with fixed schedules and designed teaching plans. As the year progressed and according to the experiences and educational skills that they had acquired from their daily home teaching, they were likely to engage with the design and planning of a curriculum that aimed to meet their children's individual needs and learning interests. At this stage, the parents usually used a flexible pedagogy, which allowed their children to participate in decisions about the pace of learning and to lead the learning activities. This finding is consistent with what the scholars in the Western context have found. McKeon (2007) has observed that most of the parents in his survey started out as traditional homeschoolers and evolved into eclectic home schoolers. He suggested that the homeschooling parents were making changes to their teaching methods in line with the perceived needs of their child. As I argue, "the changes in their teaching strategies indicated that the values and attitudes that homeschooling parents had acquired as a result of their own conventional school education had negatively influenced their initial choice of teaching methods for home education." (Sheng 2014, 72)

My previous research recognized similar findings in studies conducted in the Western context. It has been frequently noted that a family's religion is strongly associated with the types of teaching style that the parents use (Hood 1990; Huber 2003; McKeon 2007). McKeon (2007) found that a parent's religion was linked to "the style of homeschool a parent runs, the type of teacher he or she is, and the reading method used in the homeschool" (136). He suggested that parents with a strong faith may use that faith to determine the ways in which they choose to manage their home education. It has been found that those parents professing to be Catholic or Protestant engage in either authoritative type teaching styles or delegative styles more frequently than those categorized as adherents of other religions (McKeon 2007, 93).

Teaching Content of Home Education

As I have presented in previous research, it is important to note that parents' values, beliefs, and religion determined the types of home education they chose, and I have focused attention on the exploration of the teaching style that homeschooling families used. Further, my studies found that the types of home education were strongly associated with the teaching content the parents wanted to transfer to their children on a day-to-day basis. Thus, the homeschooling families who were keen to transmit Chinese traditional culture preferred Confucian works and Chinese traditional literature for their daily teaching content. For example, Meng Mu Tang concentrated on Chinese Confucian studies and works. Homeschooling families who were Christian, on the other hand, generally purchased and used a packaged English-language Christian homeschooling curriculum and textbooks that were published in the US in order to transmit specific ethical values to their children, choosing, in general, to teach Christian beliefs and related values in their daily teaching. Many parents, who wished to satisfy the needs of their talented children, usually chose both English literature and traditional/classical Chinese literature. Some families, whose children were ill and could not receive conventional education at school, chose to use the same curriculum and textbooks provided by public schools. Many families whose children were born and grew up in Western countries decided to use the same English-language curriculum and textbooks as those of the public/state schools in the US and the UK.

Unexpectedly, it was noticeable that apart from those parents who were forced to home educate because of children's health problem, the other types of homeschooling family intended that their children should move on to secondary school or a university education abroad. From this perspective, the majority of homeschooling families chose the teaching content entirely on the basis of their values, beliefs and religion, rather than the consideration of moving on to further levels within the conventional school system. Those homeschooling families who planned for their children to return to conventional schools following a period of home education, wanted to use the same curriculum teaching content and textbooks as those of the public schools. It was also noticeable that some parents used a parent-designed curriculum in order to control what their children should learn and pursue the academic excellence of their children. As indicated above, it is clear that the educational goals of homeschooling families were strongly associated with the types of curriculum that they chose for their daily teaching. Some parents who were unhappy with what the public schools taught preferred to teach their child using an individual/parent-designed curriculum. Those parents who were practicing Christian home education for their children usually preferred to purchase and use published curriculum packages. Table 19.3 summarises the teaching content of home education in China.

In my studies, one of the aspects I focused on exploring was whether there is a correlation between the academic results of homeschooled children and the parents' possession or otherwise of a teaching certificate. The data indicated that there was no significant correlation between them, a result that is in accord with the findings of studies conducted in the US that have also indicated that there is no significant

Table 19.3 Teaching content of home education in China.

Christian home schooling	*Meng Mu Tang*	*Ri Ri Xin Xue Tang*	*Home schooling (because of ill health)*	*Homeschooling for children who were born and educated abroad*	*Others*
Christian homeschooling text books and related reading materials: • Sunlight homeschooling textbooks. • Preston homeschooling textbooks. Bible study was conducted on every Thursday afternoon of each week.	Confucian theory and its works: • Confucius Analects. • Shan Zhi-jing.	Confucian works and Chinese traditional culture. English literature, and English textbooks.	Primarily the school curriculum teaching content and textbooks that were being taught in the current schools at both elementary and secondary level.	English-language textbooks which were used in the US, UK and Hong Kong. English-language homeschooling textbooks that were introduced from the US.	The curriculum teaching generated from the current conventional schools; self-chosen textbooks. Primarily the curriculum content and textbooks that were being taught in the current schools at both elementary and secondary levels.

correlation between whether or not parents possessed teaching qualifications and a homeschooled child's academic achievement (Rakestraw 1988; Ray 1990, 1991, 1994; Havens 1991; Medlin 1994; Duvall and Ward 1997). Duvall and Ward (1997) have observed that special needs children were successfully home educated by their parents, none of whom were government-certified teachers. The results of studies by Rakestraw (1988), Havens (1991) and Ray (1991) reveal similar outcomes in Texas, Alabama and Oklahoma.

Religious Beliefs and Home Education

In my studies, I have looked at the relationship between religion and home education and at the role of religious belief in home education in the Chinese context. Those parents in my study who were Christian reported that their religious beliefs had had a strong influence on their practice of home education. There is evidence that the influence of their religious beliefs, the church and their church friends played an important role in the whole process of their practice of home education, including their initial decision to homeschool, their choice of curricula and textbooks, and their participation in relevant training programs. The vast majority of mothers reported that the training program provided by the church had been of great assistance to them in teaching their children at home. Nearly all the parents reported a close correlation between their decision to homeschool and their religious faith, and they mentioned home education in terms of divine will. As stated by a Christian home educator, "Everything has always been instructed and guided by God" and "It was the instruction and guidance of God that contributed to my children's lives."

Confucian works and home education

Home education is not a new educational phenomenon. In the history of China, the use of home education, *shi shu*, has been a very common educational pattern. *Shi shu*, a style based on an old-style homeschool with a private tutor, arose more than 2000 years ago in the Spring and Autumn Period (770–476 BC). *Shi shu* existed continuously from this time – apart from a temporary abatement during the Qin Dynasty (221–206 BC) – until it was gradually abandoned at the end of Qing Dynasty. In the middle of the 1950s, this old-style education pattern was entriely eliminated. *Shi shu* had several types and included, for example, schools set up by tutors, and others sponsored and developed by wealthy families. Since 1949, the government gradually reformed and replaced it and by the the middle of the 1950s, this old-style education pattern was entirely eliminated. While *shi shu* as a kind of education was abandoned, *shi shu* as a kind of educational style emerged in contemporary Chinese society in the form of private classes (*bu xi ban*) and private tutors.

Since the middle of the 1990s, with the rapid growth of the economy and the emergence of the Chinese middle class, diversity in parental choice regarding their children's education arose and led to an increasing amount of Confucian home education that emphasizes the learning of Confucian studies, such as in the Meng Mu Tang and Ri Ri Xin Xue Tang, in Shanghai, Beijing, and Guangzhou. By 2014, Confucian studies and Du Jing education (in which a Confucian reading course is followed) had become one of the primary teaching contents of home education in China.

Meng Mu Tang, named after the mother of a Chinese ancient academic, Meng Zhi, can be seen as a kind of modern *shi shu*, like the private academies that existed in ancient China. The teaching content at Meng Mu Tang focused only on Confucian studies and works. From then on, a growing number of similar private Confucian academies emerged across China.

Confucian home education has experienced a change from being less accepted by the public and media to being a widely acknowledged alternative form of education. The renaissance of Confucian home education in China has given rise to a nationwide discussion as to whether or not this full-time private academy, which merely focuses on Confucian studies and works, is appropriate for the healthy development of a child.

It is essential to explore the reasons for Confucian home education becoming more and more popular in contemporary China, looking in particular at the educational phenomena such as Meng Mu Tang and Ri Ri Xin Xue Tang and why they emerged in Shanghai and Beijing. The city of Shanghai is a large international city in which new theories and ideas arising from Western contexts, as well as foreign languages, are very popular. In this respect, it is interesting that in such an international city, Confucian home education has become very popular among certain middle-class parents. When considering the reasons for the renaissance of Confucian reading courses and modern *shi shu*, it is necessary to acknowledge that it is likely that all educational phenomena are generated from the particular sociocultural context of China. I suggest that the rapid growth of the economy since 1978 and the emergence of a new middle class in China since the mid-1990s have given rise to socially polarizing effects in terms of parental choice concerning their children's education. In general, the rebirth of Confucian education and particularly Confucian home education are due to the multiple educational choices available to parents for their children. Rapid economic development over the past few decades has brought about the emergence of home education in China in that, without strong economic support, the middle-class parents who are practicing Confucian home education may have found it impossible to make such a choice.

It is interesting to witness the dramatic growth of Confucian home education in big Chinese cities such as Beijing and Shanghai. With the rapid economic development, Beijing and Shanghai have become international cities in which the newest theories arising from the Western context are very popular. As a young sociologist, I place specific attention on exploring why traditional Confucian studies are popular among the middle classes in international cities like these. Firstly, the emergence of the new social class (i.e., the middle class) has generated multiple education needs. This middle class is not satisfied with being marginalized in its choice of conventional schools. In order to increase their offspring's competitive opportunities in the future labor market, middle-class parents are eager to invest heavily in their children's education. Secondly, middle-class parents want their children to be educated individually according to their individual learning needs. However, the teaching styles and teaching content provided by conventional schools cannot adequately respond to such needs. In their eyes, home education can promise them much more than what is offered by conventional schools. Thirdly, a growing percentage of the middle class is eager to instruct its children about traditional Chinese culture, which promises an appropriate and happy learning environment that will ensure their children's achievement of academic excellence.

As I have discussed elsewhere in my research (Sheng 2013, 2014), in contemporary Chinese traditional society, the different social groups are conducting a hegemonic battle of classificatory struggle in order to distinguish themselves from each other. In the competition to provide a better education for their children, the different economic, social, and cultural resources that parents possess has resulted in their differing ability to mobilize their children's educational success, which in turn is embodied in the varying social statuses of parents located within different fractions of the middle classes in contemporary China. In this respect, many middle-class parents who are providing their children with Confucian homeschooling (e.g. Meng Mu Tang, Ri Ri Xin Xue Tang) have prioritized their preference for distinguishing themselves in terms of social class. This is evident in the comments provided by a middle-class parent: "…the education of Meng Mu Tang is different from the education at school. It belongs to someone who really understands education and Chinese traditional culture…However, the school teachers do not know this…" (Sheng 2014, 120).

When we look back over the Chinese history of more than 5000 years, we see that a historical form of home education, *shi shu* existed for over 2000 years. China's current sociocultural situation has arisen as a result of Chinese traditional culture, norms, and values (e.g. Confucian studies and works). From this perspective, I would suggest that in East Asian countries, such as China, South Korea and Japan, the home education which emphasizes Confucian studies and works may undergo increased development, when compared with the form which advocates Christian beliefs and values.

Challenges and Concerns of Home Education in China

The first concern is whether the scope and depth of the curriculum that home-educated children have studied at home in their junior years will fulfill the requirements of conventional schools when these children move into secondary education. Another question arises: will it be possible for homeschooled children to be admitted to university and college in China? The majority of homeschooling families in my study who were interviewed claimed that they would like the children to study abroad when they reached the appropriate age for university education.

Because home education is illegal, the homeschooling parents are not required to register in China. In this context, the educational quality at elementary and secondary level that the homeschooling families provided could not be monitored or supervised by the government authority. It is suggested that the Chinese government should admit the legal status of home education. If the practice of home education in China were legal, the government authority would be able to supervise and monitor the quality of education which the homeschooling families provide for their children. It would also make it possible for home education in China to develop rapidly and successfully.

In the past decade, home education has grown dramatically in China. It has been noted that the rapid growth of home education in urban areas of China has resulted in an emergence and increase in the special curricula for home education, including those independently created by homeschooling parents themselves and packaged as commercially produced curricula. The development of home education shows a commercial trend. It is noteworthy that the homeschoolers who advocated the teaching of Chinese traditional culture and Confucian studies and works have written and published a series of textbooks specially designed for homeschooled children's daily learning. Related teaching software and online courses have also emerged as items produced commercially by the members of the Home Education League. Since 2012, homeschooling parents and advocates have promoted the rapid development of home education from a commercial point of view. Homeschooling families have usually adopted special textbooks (e.g., Confucian textbooks or Christian textbooks). The English-language textbooks that have been imported from the US or other Western countries are very expensive, as are the textbooks that emphasize Confucian studies and works and Chinese traditional culture, since the print run is limited. With the rapid growth of home education in China, it is estimated that more and more commercial and business agencies will participate in and advocate the development of home education in China.

As presented previously, it is necessary for the government authority to supervise or monitor whether a homeschooled child is being properly educated both academically and socially. In this context, it is suggested that the education authority should establish relevant regulations in order to ensure that home-educated children both obtain outstanding academic results and experience healthy social development. In modern-day China there has to date been no direction or guidance in relation to home education from the government authority. It is suggested that the local educational authority should focus on establishing regulations to govern home education in order to achieve a balance between protecting the well-being of the students and the rights of parents to direct their children's education themselves.

As I have pointed out elsewhere (Sheng 2013, 2014), currently nearly all homeschooling parents have chosen English-language Christian textbooks or Confucian-centered textbooks. The teaching and learning content, curriculum content, and language used in home education may prove disadvantageous to home-educated children when continuing their secondary education or higher education within the current Chinese education system. If the homeschooled children have not studied a similar curriculum or course to those of their peer groups at the keypoint secondary schools in China, it may be not possible for them to achieve success in the competition for places at one of the selective or top Chinese universities or colleges. Even a graduate from a private school or an international school in China finds it more difficult to be admitted to a top university. The majority of homeschooling families have tried to deal with this dilemma by sending their children to study abroad. Similar problems have emerged when the curriculum and teaching content that homeschooled children have received in China do not match the curriculum requirements of the schools in overseas countries. If they do not, it is also difficult for these homeschooled children to be admitted by a selective secondary school or institution.

The educational authority should allow and encourage home-educated children to register at a public school while they are being educated at home by their parents. Given that the practice of home education is illegal in China, the significant majority of home-educated children cannot legally be registered at a school. Because of this, most of the children cannot take advantage of the opportunity to continue their education at conventional schools when they are ready to return to mainstream education and, moreover, those home-educated children aged less than 15 may not have the chance to take the entrance examination for universities in China.

When compared with their peer groups, there are only a small number of homeschooled children in China. Contemporary society does not recognize home education and regards conventional schools as the only way for children to be educated. In this context, children who are educated at home seem likely to become isolated. Although the homeschooling families create their own networks and communities, which help them to avoid this isolation, it is necessary for them to gain access to many more of the academic and social resources of public schools. I therefore suggest that the resources of public schools, such as libraries and gyms, should be open to homeschoolers. In addition, home-educated students should be encouraged to take part in a variety of musical activities, speech competitions, sporting events, and science competitions.

Homeschooling parents generally show dissatisfaction with the examination-oriented system of education at school. They feel that contemporary school education is driven entirely by whether a student can achieve outstanding academic results rather than whether a child is being properly educated about ethical and moral concerns. I suggest that the criticisms of homeschooling parents raise a crucial question about the purpose of schooling and serve as an important reminder that policymakers may lose sight of moral concerns, focusing merely on standardized academic scores. I suggest that schools should take into account suggestions from these parents. It is necessary for public schools to listen to the actual needs of parents and ensure that schools are much more responsive to the students' needs.

Areas for Future Research

In closing I would like to suggest several areas for future research of home education in the context of China. Firstly, with regard to demographic characteristics of homeschoolers, future research should enlarge the number of sample students in order to provide a broad understanding of this research area. Secondly, there seems to be a need for further investigation into the motivation for home education and teaching process. Thirdly, future research should strive to obtain in-depth information in relation to teaching content of home education in China.

References

Anthony, K.V. 2009. *Educational Counter Culture: Motivations, Instructional Approaches, Curriculum Choices, and Challenges of Home School Families*, Unpublished doctoral diss., Mississippi State University.

Arai, A.B. 2000. "Reasons for Home Schooling in Canada." *Canadian Journal of Education/ Revue Canadienne de l'éducation.* 25 (3): 204–217.

Aurini, J., and S. Davies. 2005. "Choice without Markets: Homeschooling in the Context of Private Education." *British Journal of Sociology of Education, 26*: 461–474.

Basham, P. 2001. "Home Schooling: From the Extreme to the Mainstream." *Public Policy Sources*. Vancouver, BC: Fraser Institute.

Basham, P., J. Merrifield, and C. R. Hepburn. 2007. "Home Schooling: From the Extreme to the Mainstream." *Studies in Education Policy*, 2nd ed. A Fraser Institute Occasional Paper, 3:1–24.

Bauman, K.J. 2001. *Home Schooling in the United States: Trends and Characteristics*. Working Paper Series No. 53. Washington, DC: US Census Bureau. http://www.census.gov/population/www/documentation/twps0053.html

Bauman, K.J. 2002. "Home-schooling in the United States: Trends and Characteristics." *Education Policy Analysis Archives*, 10(26).

Belfield, C.R. 2004. *How Many Homeschoolers are There?* New York: National Center for the Study of Privatization in Education.

Belfield, R., and H.M. Levin. 2002. "The Effect of Competition on Educational Outcomes: A Review of the US Evidence." *Review of Educational Research*, 72: 279–341.

Bian, Y. 1994. *Work and Inequality in Urban China*. Albany, NY: Suny Press.

Bian, Y. 2002. "Chinese Social Stratification and Social Mobility" (in Chinese)." *Annual Review of Sociology*, 28:91–116.

Bielick, S. 2008. *1.5 Million Homeschooled Students in the United States in 2007: (NCES 2009-030)*. Washington, DC: National Center for Education Statistics, US Department of Education.

Bielick, S., K, Chandler, and S. Broughman. 2001. *Homeschooling in the United States: 1999 (NCES 2001-033)*. Washington, DC: National Center for Education Statistics, US Department of Education.

Brabant, C., S. Bourdon, and F. Jutras. 2003. "Home Education in Quebec: Family First." *Evaluation and Research in Education*, 17(2&3):112–131.

Brabant, C., and S. Bourdon. 2012. "Le Changement en Éducation et la Gouvernance réflexive. Expérimentation d'un Modèle d'Appropriation du Changement pare des Groupes de Parents-Éducateurs au Quèbec." *Education et Francophonie XL*, 1: 32–55.

Bunday, K. 2006. "Homeschooling in the 1980s". Accessed April 5, 2008. http://learninfreedom.org/sidlif1980sgrowth.html

Carnoy, M., and Samoff, J. (1990). *Education and Social Transition in the Third World*. Princeton, NJ: Princeton University Press.

Chen, G. (2000) *Educational Principle* (Jiao Yu Yuan Li) (in Chinese) (2nd Edition) (Shanghai, China East Normal University Press).

Clements, A.D. 2002. "Variety of Teaching Methodologies used by Home Schoolers: Case Studies of Three Homeschooling Families." Paper presented at the annual meeting of Eastern Educational Research Association, Sarasota, FL.

Collom, E.2005. "The Ins and Outs of Home Schooling: The Determinants of Parental Motivations and Student Achievement." *Education and Urban Society* 37: 307–335.

Common, R., and M. MacMullen. 1986. "Home Schooling: A Growing Movement." *Education Canada*, 26(2): 4–7.

Dahlquist, K. 2002. "Home Schooling in Minnesota from the Perspective of Home School Educators." *ProQuest Digital Dissertations*. UMI No. 3059922

Dahlquist, K.L. 2005. *The Choice to Home School: Home Educator Perspectives and School District Options*. Department of Educational Policy and Administration, University of Minnesota-Twin Cities, MN.

Dahlquist, K.L., J. York-Barr, and D.D. Hendel. 2006. "The Choice to Homeschool: Home Educator Perspectives and School District Options." *Journal of School Leadership*, 16: 354–385.

Davenport, A.M. 2001. *Homeschooling: A Descriptive Study of Educational Practice and Climate in Selected Settings*, Unpublished doctoral diss., New York: Seton Hall University.

Dennis, G. J. 2000. *Homeschooling High School: Planning Ahead for College Admission*. YWAM Publishing.

Duvall, S.F., and D.L. Ward. 1997. "An Exploratory Study of Homeschool Instructional Environments and their Effects on the Basic Skills of Students with Learning Disabilities." *Education & Treatment of Children*, 20(2):150–173.

Ellin, A. 2006. "Physical Culture: Home Schoolers Learn ABC's of Keeping Fit." *The New York Times*.

Essenburg, Wendy. 2004. "Parent Personality and the Decision to Homeschool." Ohio: Union Institute and University.

Fagerlind, I., and Saha, L. J. 1989. *Education and National Development: A Comparative Perspective*. Oxford: Pergamon.

Fairchild, E. 2002. "Home Schooling and Public Education in Iowa: The Views of Rural Superintendents." *ProQuest Digital Dissertation*.

Faris, P. 2006. "Home Education in Canada: National Poll of Home-Schooling Families Shows Startling Results." Accessed December 10 2014. www.imfcanada.org/sites/default/files/Home_Education.pdf

Glenn, C.L. 2005. "Homeschooling: Worldwide and Compulsory State Education." In *Homeschooling in Full View*, edited by B.S. Cooper, 45–68. Greenwich, CN: Information Age Publishing.

Goyette, K.A. 2008. "Race, Social Background, and School Choice Options." *Equity & Excellence in Education*, 41(1), 114–129.

Gross, J. 2003. "Unhappy in Class, More are Learning at Home." *The New York News*.

Havens, J.E. 1991. "A Study of Parent Education Levels as They Relate to Academic Achievement Among Home Schooled Children." Unpublished doctoral diss.,, Southwestern Baptist Theological Seminary, Fort Worth, TX.

Hoffman, B. 2006. *Homeschooling Methods: The Various Types of Homeschooling Methods in Existence Today*.

Hood, M. K. (1990). Contemporary philosophical influences on the home-schooling movement (Doctoral dissertation, University of Alabama at Birmingham, 1990). *Dissertation Abstracts International*, 51, 4056.

Hopwood, V.,L. O'Neill, G. Castro, and B. Hodgson 2007. "The Prevalence of Home Education in England: A Feasibility Study (No. PR827)." UK Government, Department for Education and Skills.

Houston, G.R., and Toma, E.F. 2003. "Home Schooling: An Alternative School Choice." *Southern Economic Journal* 69(4), 920–935.

Huber, E. 2003. "Unexplored Territory: Writing Instruction in Pennsylvania Homeschool Settings, Grades 9–12." *Home School Researcher*, 15 (4): 1–10.

Isenberg, E. 2007. "What Have we Learned about Homeschooling?" *Peabody Journal of Education*, 87(2–3): 387–409.

Jennens, R. 2011. "Professional Knowledge and Practice in Health, Welfare and Educational Agencies in England in Relation to Children Being Educated at Home: An Exploratory Review." *Child Care in Practice*, 17(2):143–161.

Jiangxi Daily. 2013. "Advantages and Disadvantages of Home Schooling, How Long Shi Shu Can Work? (in Chinese)." Accessed December 10 2014. http://www.jxnews.com.cn/jxrb/system/2013/09/26/012675276.shtml

Jorgenson, T. M. 2011. "Homeschooling in Iowa: An Investigation of Curricular Choices Made by Homeschooling Parents." PhD diss., University of Iowa. http://ir.uiowa.edu/etd/1235.

Klicka, C. 2002. *Home Schooling: The Right Choice*. Nashville, TN: Broadman & Holman Publishers.

Klein, C. 2006. *Virtual Charter Schools and Home Schooling*. Youngstown, NY: Cambria Press.

Klicka, C.J. 2007. "Home Schooling in Poland." *The Home School Court Report*, 23: 30–31.

Knowles, J.G. 1991a. *Now We Are Adults: Attitudes, Beliefs, and Status of Adults Who Were Home-educated as Children*. Paper presented at the annual meeting of the American Educational Research Association. Chicago, IL. April 3–7.

Knowles, J. G. 1991b. "Parents' Rationales for Operating Home Schools." *Journal of Contemporary Ethnography*, 23: 203–230.

Knowles, J.G., S. Marlow, and J. Muchmore. 1992. "From Pedagogy to Ideology: Origins and Phases of Home Education in the United States, 1970–1990." *American Journal of Education*, 100:195–235.

Kugai, T. 2014. "Homeschooling in Japan: Frequently asked questions regarding home learning (homeschooling) in Japan.",Accessed September 20, 2014. http://www.asahi-net.or.jp/~ja8i-brtl/faq.html

Kunzman, R. 2009. *Write these Laws on your Children: Inside the World of Conservative Christian Homeschooling*. Boston, MA: Beacon Press.

Kunzman, R., and M. Gaither. 2013. "Homeschooling: A Comprehensive Survey of the Research." *Other Education: The Journal of Educational Alternatives*. 2(1): 4–59.

Lawrence, M.J. 2007. *Home Schooling: Status and Bibliography*. New York: Nova Science Publisher, Inc.

Lees, H.E. 2014. *Education Without Schools: Discovering Alternatives*. Bristol, UK: Policy Press.

Li, Q. (2000) *Social Stratification and Disparity between the Rich and Poor* (in Chinese), (Xiamen, Lujiang Press), 82–104.

Lines, P. 2000. "Homeschooling Comes of Age." *The Public Interest*. 140: 74–85.

Lips, D., and Feinberg, E. 2008. *Backgrounder*. Washington DC: The Heritage Foundation; Palo Alto, CA: Hoover Press.

Lowe, J., and A. Thomas. 2002. *Educating your Child at Home*. London: Continuum.

Lu, X. 1989. "Rethinking the Peasant Problem (in Chinese)"*Sociological Research*, 6, 1–14.

Lubienski, C. 2000. "Whither the Common Good? A Critique of Home Schooling." *Peabody Journal of Education*, 75(1/2): 207-232.

Luffman, J. 1997. "A Profile of Home Schooling in Canada." *Education Quarterly Review*, 4(4): 30–47.

Martin-Chang, S., O. Gould, and R. Meuse. 2011. "The Impact of Schooling on Academic Achievement: Evidence from Homeschooled and Traditionally Schooled Children." *Canadian Journal of Behavioural Science*, 43(3):95–202.

McDowell, S.A., and B.D. Ray. 2000. "The Home Education Movement in Context, Practice, and Theory: Editors' Introduction." *Peabody Journal of Education*, 75(1/2): 1–7.

McKeon, C.C. 2007. *A Mixed Methods Nested Analysis of Homeschooling Styles, Instructional Practices, and Reading Methodologies*, Unpublished doctoral diss.

Medlin, R. G. 1994. "Predictors of Academic Achievement in Home Educated Children: Aptitude, Self-concept, and Pedagogical Practices." *Home School Researcher*, 10(3): 1–7.

Meighan, R. 1981. "A New Teaching Force? Some Issues Raised by Seeing Parents as Educators and the Implications for Teacher Education." *Educational Review*, 33: 133–142.

Meighan, R. 1984a. "Home-based Educators and Education Authorities: The Attempt to Maintain a Mythology." *Educational Studies*, 10(3): 273–286.

Meighan, R. 1984b. "Political Consciousness and Home-Based Education." *Educational Review*, 36: 165.

Meighan, R. 1996. "Home-Based Education: Not Does it Work, but Why Does it Work so Well? In SET Research Information for Teachers." *Australian Council for Educational Research*, SET two, 12. Melbourne, Victoria.

Meighan, R. 1997. *The Next Learning System: And Why Home Schoolers are Traiblazers*. Nottingham, UK: Educational Heretics Press.

Meighan, R., and C. Brown. 1980. Locations of Learning and Ideologies of Education. In *Schooling, Ideology, and the Curriculum*, edited by L. Barton, R. Meighan, and S. Walker, 131–152, Brighton, UK: Falmer.

Murphy, J. 2012. *Homeschooling in America: Capturing and Assessing the Movement*. Thousand Oaks, CA: Corwin.

Mu Zhen. 2014. "Mu Zhen Home schooling Association (in Chinese)." Accessed December 15. http://www.mujen.org.tw/

Nan Fang Du Shi Paper. 2013. "Guangzhou Parents who are Concerned Low Quality of Education at School Establish 'Home Schooling League' (in Chinese)." Accessed November 12. http://zgcf.oeeee.com/html/201309/26/302071.html

Noel, A., P. Stark, and J. Redford 2013. Parent and Family Involvement in Education, from the National Household Education Surveys Program of 2012. Accessed October 12, 2014. http://nces.ed.gov/pubs2013/2013028rev.pdf

Pearson, R. 2002. *The Worth of a Child: Rural Homeschooling/Public School Partnerships Are Leading the Way*. 1–13. Accessed February 1, 2010. The ERIC database.

Planty, M., et al. 2009) *The Condition of Education 2009* (NCES 2009-081). National Center for Education Statistics, US Department of Education. Washington, DC.

Princiotta, D., & Bielick, S. 2006. *Homeschooling in the United States: 2003 (*NCES 2006-042) National Center for Education Statistics, US Department of Education. Washington, DC.

Princiotta, D., Bielick, S., & Chapman, C. (2004). *1.5 Million Home Schooled Students in the United States in 2003 (NCES 2004-115)*. National Center for Education Statistics, US

Department of Education. Washington, DC. Accessed June 15, 2008. http://nces.ed.gov/pubs2004/2004115.pdf

Princiotta, D., and S. Bielick. 2006. *Homeschooling in the United States: 2003, (*NCES 2006–042). National Center for Education Statistics, US Department of Education. Washington, DC.

Rakestraw, Jennie F. 1988. "Home Schooling in Alabama." *Home School Researcher*, 4(4): 1–6.

Ray, B.D. 1990. "Social Capital, Value Consistency, and the Achievement Outcomes Of Home Education." Paper presented at the annual meeting of the American Educational Research Association, Boston.

Ray, B.D. 1994. *A Nationwide Study of Home Education in Canada*. Salem, OR: National Home Education Research Institute.

Ray, B.D. 1997. *Home Education Across the United States: Academic Achievement, Family Characteristics, and Longitudinal Traits*. Salem, OR: National Home Education Research Institute.

Ray D.B. 2000. "Home Schooling: The Ameliorator of Negative Influences on Learning?" *Peabody Journal of Education*, 75(1/2): 71–106.

Ray, B.D. 2000. "Home Schooling for Individuals' Gain and Society's Common Good." *Peabody Journal of Education*, 75(1/2): 272–293.

Ray, B. D. 2003. *Worldwide Guide to Homeschooling*. Nashville, TN: Broadman & Holman Publishers.

Ray, B.D. 2004. *Home Educated and Now Adults: Their Community and Civic Involvement, Views About Home Schooling, and Other Traits*. Kearney, NE: Morris Publishing.

Ray, B. 2007. "The Evidence Is So Positive, What Current Research Tells Us About Homeschooling." Accessed August 30, 2010. http:www.christianbook.com/Christian/Books/cms_content?page=1812612&sp=102656 & event=1016ToS%7C1806673%7C102656

Ray, B.D. 2009a. "Research Facts on Homeschooling."Accessed July 10, 2010. http://www.nheri.org/research/Research-Facts-on-Homeschooling.html

Ray, B.D. 2009b. *Homeschool Progress Report 2009: Academic Achievement and Demographics*. Purcellville, VA: Home School Legal Defense Association.

Ray, B.D. 2010. "Academic Achievement and Demographic Traits of Homeschool Students: A Nationwide Study." *Academic Leadership*, 8(1): 1–44.

Ray, B.D., and B.K. Eagleson. 2008. "State Regulation of Homeschooling and Homeschoolers' SAT scores." *Academic Leadership*, 6(3): 1–14.

Rothermel, P.J. 2004. "Home Education: Comparison of Home – and School-Educated Children on PIPS Baseline Assessments." *Journal of Early Childhood Research*, 2(3): 273–299.

Rothermel, P. 1999a. "A Nationwide Study of Home Education: Early Indications and Wider Implications." *Education Now*, 24.

Rothermel, P. 1999b. *Home-education: A Critical Evaluation*. Paper presented at the British Psychological Society annual conference, Belfast, NI.

Rothermel, P. 2010. "Home Education: Practising Without Prejudice?" *Every Child Journal*, 1(5): 48–53.

Rothermel, P. 2011. "Setting the Record Straight: Interviews with a Hundred British Home Educating Families." *Journal of Unschooling and Alternative Learning*, 5(10).

Rudner, L.M. 1999. "The Scholastic Achievement and Demographic Characteristics of Home School Students in 1998." *Education Policy Analysis Archives*, 7 (8). Accessed April 24, 1999. http://epaa.asu.edu/ojs/article/view/543

Saba L., and J. Gattis. 2002. *The McGraw-Hill Homeschooling Companion*. Chicago, IL: R.R. Donnelley & Sons Company.

Sampson, Z.C. 2005. "Home Schools are Becoming More Popular Among Blacks." *The New York Times*.

Sheng, X. 2013. "Confucian Work and Homeschooling: A Case Study of Homeschooling in Shanghai." *Education and Urban Society*. DOI: 10.1177/0013124513489707

Sheng, X. 2014. *Learning with Mothers: A Study of Home Schooling in China*. Rotterdam: Sense Publishers.

Spiegler, T. 2003. "Home Education in Germany: An Overview of the Contemporary Situation." *Evaluation and Research in Education*, 17(2&3):179–190.

Tator, A. 2001. "Home Schooling: Parent Choice and Student Needs." *ProQuest Digital Dissertations*. UMI No. 3036926

Thomas, A. 1998. *Educating Children at Home*. London: Cassell Education.

Tomiko Kugai. 2014. "Homeschooling in Japan: Frequently Asked Questions Regarding Home Learning (Homeschooling) in Japan." Accessed September 20 2014. http://www.asahi-net.or.jp/~ja8i-brtl/faq.html

Trevaskis, R. 2005. *Home Education – The Curriculum of Life*. Unpublished MEd, Monash University, Clayton.

Villalba, C.M. 2003. "Creating Policy from Discursive Exchanges on Compulsory Education and Schooling in Sweden." *Evaluation and Research in Education*, 17 (2&3): 191–205.

Villalba, C.M. 2009. "Home-based Education in Sweden: Local Variations in Forms of Regulation." *Theory and Research in Education*, 7(3):277–296.

Webb, D.L. 1997. "Home Schools and Interscholastic Sports: Denying Participation Violates United States Constitutional Due Process and Equal Protection Rights." *Journal of Law and Education*, 26(3), 123–132.

Webb, J. 1989. "The Outcomes of Home-based Education: Employment and Other Issues." *Education Review*, 41(2):121–133.

Webb, S. 2011. *Elective Home Education in the UK*. Stoke-on-Trent, UK: Trentham Books.

Yang, P.Q., and Kayaardi, N. 2004. "Who Chooses Non-public Schools for Their Children?" *Educational Studies*, 30, 231–249.

Yang Zhi Evening Paper. 2011. "Other Education of Full-time Mothers and Fathers: Resignation and Educating Children at Home (in Chinese)." Accessed December 12 2014. http://edu.sina.com.cn/zxx/2011-09-23/1048313704.shtml

20

Contemporary Homeschooling and the Issue of Racism

The Case of South Africa

Michael Olalekan Olatunji

Introduction

Homeschooling is a form of education steered by parents, based within the home (Jayawardene 2015). Owing to this, homeschooling does not rely on either institutional private schooling or state-run public schooling (Ray 2013). According to Hill (2010), homeschooling is not a new phenomenon in the United States because in the colonial days families, including wealthy ones, educated their children at home combining the efforts of parents, tutors, and older children. Distefano, Rudestam and Silverman (2005) have also made it known that prior to the introduction of compulsory school attendance laws in the United States, most childhood education took place within the family or community. They explained that for much of history and in many cultures, engaging the services of trained teachers was an option available only to the privileged few in the society. As a result of this, until relatively recently, most people were educated by family members (especially during early childhood), family friends or anyone with useful knowledge.

According to Louw (1992) cited in Olatunji (2014), homeschooling in South Africa dates back to the days of the early Trekboers and Voortrekkers. He argued that it can be regarded as the most traditional form of education and says the essential difference is that, in those days, parents were compelled to homeschool, while in the contemporary sense of the word, parents homeschool their children by choice. In addition, Magida (2008) explained that the component of non-formal education is such that it goes beyond a focus on the adult only. According to him, early childhood or children's education is an integral component of non-formal education in many countries of the world and is even backed by law. This non-formal component addressing children's education, says Magida, is homeschooling

The Wiley Handbook of Home Education, First Edition. Edited by Milton Gaither.

and is similar to correspondence education experienced by adults except for some differences such as:

- The nomenclature: "correspondence education" on one hand and "homeschooling" on the other.
- One focuses on adults and the other on children or adolescents.
- One involves self-learning and the other utilizes the parent as teacher.
- One involves certification and the other does not.

Brynard (2007) also pointed out that homeschooling is one of the modes of education regarded as an open learning educational approach in that it is a learning experience that is devoid of conventional structures and limitations. The extent of openness in homeschooling, however, will depend on the modality of its implementation. In the same vein, Ray (2010) emphasized the fact that homeschooling, which a decade earlier appeared to be cutting-edge and "alternative," is now bordering on "mainstream" in the United States. Ray argued further that homeschooling may be the fastest- growing form of education in the United States, and it has also been growing in countries such as Australia, Canada, France, Hungary, Japan, Mexico, South Korea, Thailand and the United Kingdom.

While homeschooling is receiving wide acceptability in many nations, with the US taking the lead, Olatunji (2014) reported that his correspondence in 2013 with Pestalozzi Trust (a legal defense fund for home and civil education) in South Africa revealed that African countries have not generally shared in this growth and acceptability. Apart from a relative handful of families in the Republic of South Africa and an even smaller number of families in Botswana, Kenya and Uganda, contemporary homeschooling is not common in African countries. He also pointed out that this observation was confirmed in another correspondence of his with the Home School Legal Defense Association in the US in 2013. Similarly, Magida (2008) cited in Olatunji (2014) stated that homeschooling is little or not known in Nigeria. When compared to countries such as the US, Australia, Canada, France, Hungary, Japan, Mexico, South Korea, and the UK, South Africa can be said not to have made much progress in homeschooling. Nevertheless, in the context of Africa, South Africa is indisputably at the forefront.

Ray (2010) correctly pointed out that the body of research on home-based education has expanded dramatically since the late 1970s when the first studies and academic articles dealt with the modern homeschool movement. He rightly observed further that numerous researchers have examined the academic achievement of home-educated children and youth, their social, emotional, and psychological development, their success into adulthood, and various aspects of homeschooling families in general. While these research efforts are highly commendable, there is a gap in the sense that they have not included Africa in their focus. One of the consequences of this is that there are relatively few research reports on homeschooling in Africa. This chapter is an attempt to contribute to ongoing efforts to fill this gap.

Contemporary Homeschooling in the Republic of South Africa

Olatunji (2014) citing Pistorius (1970), pointed out that homeschooling was fundamental to civilization in South Africa as the only form of education for many years. According to him, parents had a unique right to and responsibility for their children's education. However, when state schools were established in the late 19th century, they took over the parents' unique position; school attendance was made compulsory thus making homeschooling, without exception, illegal. The government of South Africa was so resolute in its stand that in 1994 Andre and Bokkie Meintijies were brought before the court of law for homeschooling their children. As a result of this development, Graham and Allison Shortridge, Directors of Theocentric Christian Education in South Africa, got Chris Klicka at the American Home School Legal Defense Association (HSLDA), with the support of the 40 000 members of his organization in America and Canada, to intervene. This family was eventually released, though given a suspended sentence (Van Oostrum 1997, 1). According to Graham and Allison Shortridge (2013), in 1994 there were only three families homeschooling that they knew of, themselves being one of them.

As the shortcomings of the state education system continued to increase, many parents started to agitate for their rights as primary educators of their children to homeschool them. The activities of these parents were carried out underground for many years, and during this period they also worked hard towards securing legal recognition by the government. With the assistance of Louis Green (the then vice president of the African Christian Democratic Party (ACDP)), Graham and Allison Shortridge made a presentation on homeschooling to the South African Parliament. Olatunji (2014) citing Graham and Allison Shortridge (2013), pointed out that, up to this point in time, the concept of homeschooling was virtually unheard of in South Africa, so the education committee at parliament needed to be "educated" about it. The ACDP through Louis Green assisted these parents by placing a pile of literature on homeschooling at the parliament library and giving copies to members of the education committee. This pile of literature had been sent by Chris Klicka at the American HSLDA, who had earlier been contacted by Graham and Allison Shortridge for assistance. According to Durham (1996: 77), by 1996 about 1300 South African children were being taught at home. However, she also drew attention to the possibility of a large number of parents operating homeschools that were unregistered out of fear that they might be prosecuted by the government.

Van Oostrum and Van Oostrum (1997, 1) reported that the National Coalition of Home-Schoolers, one of South Africa's homeschooling Associations, estimated that in 1997 there were approximately 2000 children being homeschooled in South Africa and that this represented a vast increase in number compared with the previous years. They, however, gave their own estimation of the figure to be 2400 homeschoolers in 1997. These figures were based on surveys of curriculum suppliers nationally and homeschoolers in the Pretoria area. The problems with this estimation are that not all homeschoolers make use of curriculum suppliers and that, on occasion, more than one family may make use of one subscription. As part of the effort to secure government approval of homeschooling in South Africa, several associations were formed, including the Association for Home-schooling, founded in 1992, and the National Coalition of Homeschoolers, established in 1996 (Van Oostrum and Van Oostrum 1997a: 33). Other associations include the Eastern Cape Home Schooling Association, the KwaZulu Natal Home Schooling Association, and the Western Cape Home Schooling Association. In addition, the Pestalozzi Trust was founded in 1998 as a legal defense fund for home education.

The Trust made itself available to represent members' families on matters ranging from consultation to correspondence and negotiation with local officials, and in court proceedings as a way through the appellate courts. The Trust takes responsibility for the payment of all litigation cost for homeschool cases it undertakes. The American HSLDA, Canada Home School Legal Defense Association, the African Christian Democratic Party of South Africa, Homeschooling Associations in South Africa, and several individuals played active roles for years in the bid to get homeschooling legalized in South Africa.

The South African Schools Act (No. 84 of 1996) went into effect in January 1997, and on July 28, 1998 the first draft of the National Policy guidelines for homeschooling was published. These guidelines included information regarding homeschool registration, conditions for registration, and withdrawal of registration. The second draft was published on April 9, 1999. On November 23, 1999, in accordance with the National Education Policy Act (NEPA, No 27 of 1996), the final policy for the Registration of Learners for Home Education was passed. This document states that home education is:

a. A program of education that a parent of a learner may provide to his/her own child at home. In addition, the parent may, if necessary, enlist the specific services of a tutor for specific areas of the curriculum, or
b. A legal, independent form of education, alternative to attendance at a public or an independent school.

The NEPA (No 27 of 1996) furthermore stipulates that parents "may not instill unfair discrimination, racism or religious intolerance in learners." In addition, several conditions for registration of a learner have to be complied with. The Head of Department must be content that:

a. The home education "is in the best interest of the learner", is beneficial to the learner; complies with the fundamental right of the learner to education; and will be taught at least as persistently and to the same standard as in public school;
b. The number of learning hours, available learning resources and highest education standard achieved by the learner is declared, the proposed learning program is submitted, and the learning program suits the age and ability of the learner, meets the minimum requirement of the Curriculum and is not of an inferior standard to that of the public school education;

c. The language policy and specified outcomes of the eight learning areas are complied with;
d. A learner receives a minimum of three hours contact teaching per day;
e. The parent will protect the learner from any form of abuse or unfair discrimination and will not promote racism or religious intolerance with the learner; and
f. The values of the constitution of the Republic of South Africa prevail in the education which is provided at home.

The policy for the Registration of learners for Home Education (November 1999) outlines duties of the parents for monitoring of home education. Such duties include:

a. Keeping a record of attendance, building up a portfolio of a learner's work, including up-to-date records of progression, providing evidence of intervention and educational support, and making all of the above available for inspection by an education official;
b. Keeping evidence of continuous assessment for a period of three years;
c. Providing for mandatory assessment of a learner's progress, upon completion of each phase, by an independent and suitably qualified person who has been approved by the department.

Guidelines for the withdrawal of registration are also included in the policy. In addition, there is a *pro forma* application for the registration of a learner for home education.

According to Olatunji (2014), the Eastern Cape Home Schooling Association (ECHSA) in 2001, estimated that there were in excess of 10 000 home learners in South Africa, a considerable increase over the number quoted for 1997. Mufweba (2003:15) reported that Leendert Van Oostrum, President of the Pestalozzi Trust, estimated the number of home learners in South Africa at between 30 000 and 50 000 in 2003. In an interview conducted by Olatunji (2014) through correspondence in October 2013 with Van Oostrum, the latter pointed out that there were just over 65 000 home learners in South Africa according to the 2011 census. He cautioned, however, that the figure was not accurate, as it was almost certainly a substantial overcount in some respects and a substantial undercount in others. The figure, he said, would fall very near the middle of the range of his own estimation which he said was between 30 000 and 100 000. Though the exact figure is not known, it is very obvious that the number of home learners in South Africa has been increasing dramatically, an indication that it is an increasingly popular education alternative. It can also be expected that the number of homeschoolers in the Republic of South Africa and the desire to know about this mode of education will continue to grow. Bouwe Van der Eems (2013) alluded to this in his assertion that South Africa is ranked second after the US in the list of countries where most searches for the word "homeschooling" is done through Google search.

Olatunji (2014), citing Brynard (2007) argued that homeschooling should never be regarded as a threat to any existing system of education in South Africa but rather as complementary. Like any past, present or future system, maintained Brynard, homeschooling has shortcomings. However, in an interview that Brynard conducted with a chief Education Specialist (Special Needs in Education) of the Free State Department of Education, it was pointed out that homeschooling does offer possible educational solutions in certain circumstances, as well as relief from the pressure on an overburdened South African School System. Brynard (2007) reported the view of the chief Education Specialist that the many advantages of homeschooling could be used to the benefit of the South African educational system. Furthermore, Olatunji (2014) citing Morgenrood (1997) highlighted the opinion of the Society for Home schooling in South Africa that a free, affordable system of private education (including homeschooling) will offer the kind of competition that will make the quality of education in public schools improve. According to the society, homeschooling could be pivotal not only to the freedom of all learners, but also to affordable quality education.

Why Some Parents Prefer Homeschooling in South Africa

Brynard (2007) interviewed a wide spectrum of South Africans which included parents, education specialists, university lecturers, secondary school teachers and child psychologists on the reasons for homeschooling in South Africa. She revealed that the reasons given by the interviewees for homeschooling corresponded with views held in the US and other countries where homeschooling is being practiced. Some of the reasons that emanated from the interviews are:

- Parents are in a position to use their discretion concerning the type and the depth of exploratory and play-oriented childhood for their wards.
- Education can be planned in such a way that will allow each child to work at his or her own pace.
- Subjects that parents adjudged as useful but which are not available in conventional schools can be taught. These include: ethics, commitment to God, commitment to legally instituted authorities, some major world languages (English, French, Chinese), music, and money management.
- The child can be introduced early enough to family values that are deemed as essential.
- Homeschooling prevents premature and dangerous parent–child separation.
- Homeschooling enables parents to give adequate protection to their children from molestation and abuse that they may face in or around public schools.
- Parents and adults of integrity serve as primary role models.
- Homeschooled children are predominantly free from negative peer pressure.
- Homeschooling children have the opportunity of enjoying relatively more resources as they have the community and the entire world as their resources.

In addition to the above reasons cited by Brynard (2007), Jayawardene (2015) pointed out that among the frequently cited reasons by parents for homeschooling as reported by the National Home Education Research Institute in the United States, is a desire for a safer learning environment free of the racism associated with institutional schools. In a similar perspective, Fields-Smith and Williams (2009) identified racism as a key determinant in parents' decision to homeschool in the US. In their study, many Black parents expressed the belief that the institutional norms and structures of traditional schools fostered destructive rather than supportive learning environments for Black students. Similarly, Mazama and Lundy (2012) emphasized the fact that research suggests that Black families in the United States increasingly choose to homeschool their children as a means of protecting them from the deleterious effects of school-based racism. In the light of these US findings, this chapter examines the phenomenon of racism in post-apartheid South Africa and its effects on homeschooling.

Racism in Post-Apartheid South Africa

According to Rasekgala et al. (2011), racism can be described as a "prejudice or animosity against people who belong to other races." Based on this prejudice there is a belief that people of different races have different qualities and abilities, and that some races are inherently inferior or superior to the others. Racism can masquerade as creedal, cultural, or religious practices that are distinct to a particular grouping of people to the exclusion of others. Similarly, Taylor (2004) explained racism as ethical disregard for people who belong to a particular race. Disregard in this context, he says, means the withholding of respect, concern, goodwill or care from members of a race. He pointed out that disregard in this context covers a range of attitudes all at once, from outright hatred, to the simple failure to notice that someone is suffering, to the related failure to notice that there is a person in front of you, as opposed to the personification of a pre-existing stereotype.

In the same vein, (Blum 2002) pointed out that there are three general categories of racism: *Personal racism* – racist acts, beliefs, attitudes, and behavior on the part of individual persons; *Social* (or sociocultural) *racism* – racist beliefs, attitudes, and stereotypes widely shared within a given population and expressed in cultural and social modes such as religion, popular entertainment, advertisements, and other media; *Institutional racism* – racial inferiorizing or antipathy perpetrated by specific social institutions such as schools, corporations, hospitals, or the criminal justice system as a totality. Each of these categories, he says, interacts in a complex manner with the other categories. It is the view of Matolino (2013) that racism is a universal problem. In a similar perspective, Rasekgala pointed out that throughout the world many countries have been and are still battling issues of racism and equal treatment of children in schools. He emphasized that South Africa is not alone in this struggle. Too many, however, prefer to deny the existence of racism or presume a superficial tolerance (South Africa Human Right Commission 1999: vii).

According to Durrheim and Dixon (2005) cited in Mtose (2011), the experiences of many Black people in post-apartheid South Africa who continue to suffer or suffered the effects of racism further suggest that racism is alive, active, pervasive, and no less damaging. Following a study, Mtose (2011) presents accounts of the lived experiences of racism of Black people as recounted in their talk about living their everyday lives in post-apartheid South Africa. Some of the extracts from the study are presented below:

Extract 1

Yonda: X town [name of place] is still a very much a racialist town but I feel like these little comments little back chatting and how we still have to bow down to the white man sometimes when especially it comes to the police I feel like the white police do not even want to listen to you because automatically if you black they just do not want to hear your story...if they believe you are wrong because you are black you remain wrong no matter what.

According to Mtose (2011), extract 1 shows that in post-apartheid South Africa, racism is ingrained in blackness.

Extract 2

Nontaba: We walked into this shop to buy some things, we walked in as a group mixed group… they looked at us in weird way like, how can they hang around with white girls they were just very very confused and they treated us with less respect than they did to the white people and that made me feel bad that there are still people like that around why should I be treated less why should I be made to feel less because of the colour of my skin? … we were there first but they decided to help the white people before us and even when they were helping the customer service was very bad it was like they are doing because they have to do it.

According to Mtose (2011), in extract 2 above, Nontaba interprets the racist treatment that she received from white people as situating her as inferior and white people as superior.

Extract 3

Sifiso: When you get to the University there are still these courses and degrees which were previously not opened to the black guys like the Civil Engineering Electrical Engineering and I recognized that the University especially the previously predominantly white institutions… after 1994 to enter Engineering Degree you will need say 75% and considering where we come from as black students it is difficult for you to achieve that 75% which means these were reserved for white people so in my view that was also racism in a special type which was carefully and cautiously constructed by the university itself.

Mtose (2011) pointed out that in extract 3, Sifiso had to work very hard in order to resist discrimination and prove that he was worthy and able to compete and match

White standards. According to him, Sifiso's reports confirm discrimination against Black people at predominantly White institutions. He claims that the requirements for access to certain degrees and courses are high in order to limit Black people's access to them.

Extract 4

Mon: Today we still find pockets of racism …in my church in the Methodist church the services are divided into two separate meetings. Nobody has declared which meeting should each race group attend but you find that the morning service is for whiter people then at 11 o'clock when the black service starts there is not even a single white only the black people …this is the trend.

Supporting his view with extract number 4, Mtose (2011) concluded that although segregation is no longer a policy, White people and Black people choose to self-segregate by associating racially with other White people or Black people only.

Extract 5

Zifiki: when I got to X [name of school] I befriended a lot of white people and I still have a lot of very good white friends right now… so what used to happen is whenever we used to talk to the white people they would be like to us I know I am friends with you because you are like a clean black…you are one of those clean blacks and stuff and you do not speak with an accent….you do not have that accent that black people have in common …and you have got money as well you know so yeah you are like better you are a cultured black.

Extract 6

Sana: I had a white friend her name is Amy like we would walk to school together … this one time we are walking together to our classroom and there is a 'riot'[noise] as girls walk kuyakhulunywa kudiscuswa amasopizi ayizolo [girls are chatting and discussing previous day's 'soapiest'] and then we in and then she says "yhoo black people are loud" and I looked at her and then she realised that she is talking to me she has a black friend Sana and then she says to me but you are not like them …then I told her that I don't want you to be my friend because its scary because I am black what's wrong with being black and being loud ? …I felt she has been racist and I was angry to know that side of her actually I was very disappointed because she could have said girls are so loud why black?…I noticed that she is being racist she did not even see who she was talking to there were probably coloureds and Indians in the discussion or white people or white girls.

In extracts 5 and 6, Zifiki and Sana make claims to be friends with White people. Zifiki reports that her friendship with White people differentiated her from other Black people. In her talks with her friends the other Black people were generally constructed as deficient in comparison to her as an individual Black. She reports she has been told that she is able to be friends with White people because she is a clean Black, she speaks good English and she has money. In essence she understands her inclusion in whiteness as based on her ability to manage to shed race-typical characteristics and become like Whites. Not only is Black identity individualized and treated as an exception, but in extract 6, Sana is invited to and expected by a White friend to criticize other Black people. She is required to substitute her Black culture for a White culture. While the White friend criticizes Black people for being loud, she is expected to be a different, civilized Black who does not shout whilst other Black students are criticized for failing to adapt to the civilized White culture.

While commenting on the issue of racism in South African schools, Msila (2015) has this to say: "We have to be afraid, very afraid that 20 years after democracy we are still bickering on issues of race and racism in schools." Msila made specific reference to Roodepoort Primary School episode which he said clearly reflects a small incident that displays deep gashes in the rainbow nation. According to Msila (2015), when a Black principal and her deputies were appointed at Roodepoort primary school, the colored parents cried foul and demanded that a colored principal be appointed. The colored parents also prevented children from entering the school premises. In the subsequent week, Msila explained further that nineteen colored teachers did not report for duty and only Black teachers were on the school premises. As a result of this development, the police had to be brought into the school in order to defuse the tension. Msila observed that the events at Roodepoort Primary school are detrimental to all pupils and destructive to their futures, including how they should view others. According to him, when the police have left the school and probably a new "acceptable principal" is appointed by the School Governing Body what remains in the school will be pupils schooled to embrace social stereotypes. Msila (2015) argued that xenophobia is one factor that pupils may see as positive because communities magnify their hatred against the foreigner. He was quick to point out that soon the children at Roodepoort Primary will learn to be negative toward "The Other." Msila (2015) argued further that the events at Roodepoort Primary are just a small example of how our communities fail at fairness, respect, and equality. According to him, pupils' motivation and commitment will be negatively affected in a school where they are judged by the language they speak or the color of their skin, yet racism still continues to manifest itself in our schools. Msila pointed out that it is appalling to find racism coming from various role-players. In this connection, he cited recent incidents at Curro Roodeplaat Foundation School which according to him also display how racism can be coated with other reasons as pupils are segregated according to their "cultures." He also cited the case of a new Black pupil at Northern Cape Agricultural School who was raped with a broom on school premises on the pretext of initiation. According to him, this was clearly a racist crime although pupils of other race groups witnessed this as spectators, some even laughing. The four boys who did this were doing it to a Black pupil.

Similarly, Sehoole (2012) reported that at the end of 2011, the University of Pretoria was hit by allegations of apparent racism among its staff, where a Black engineering professor alleged systematic harassment and victimization, on racial grounds.

According to Banda (2009: 5) cited in de Klerk (2011), at Rhodes University in September 2009, a huge furor followed a very public and offensive use of the word "nigger" on the campus. The incident took place during the annual intervarsity sporting competition against sister institutions. A Black professor and his wife and child were driving slowly past a group of drunken White students on campus and one of them shouted out the word "Niggers!" at them. The professor (who was not a South African) was extremely distressed; as he put it in a subsequent article "The racist indignity to which a white Rhodes University student subjected my family ignited conflicting emotions and thoughts in me. Such is the psychological violence engendered by racism. Feelings of outrage engulfed me, followed by thoughts of vengeance.... As a black person, I felt racially violated. My family and I longed for restorative justice."

In a similar perspective, Terblanche (2012) pointed out that during his teaching career in South Africa that spans fifteen years, he had a brief teaching experience at a White school and some colored schools. According to him, while these schools usually have a reasonable percentage of Black learners, the acts of racism toward them are appalling. Furthermore, subsequent to allegations of differential treatment of learners based on race at Hoerskool Ellisras in South Africa, an investigation was carried out. Some of the key findings of the investigation according to the report presented by Rasekgala et al. (2011) are as follows:

1. Management of the school has not done much in bringing about racial integration among learners. White learners keep their place and so do Black learners, and this cannot be attributed simply to cultural differences. In most cases Black teachers teach Black learners and the same applies to their White counterparts.
2. The admission policy of the school allows Black learners to be admitted, but the school's transformation agenda and efforts towards school desegregation are very limited. There is little evidence that suggests the school is making an effort to transform from its racial past to reflect the principles enshrined in the Constitution of the Republic of South Africa of non-racialism and access to education by all.
3. Annual school fees are set at ZAR900.00 per month per learner, and when this is added together with miscellaneous fees charged by the school, it becomes impossible for families that are not well-to-do to have their children in this school. The school has a curriculum policy which prevents English-speaking learners in general but Blacks in particular to access certain subjects such as Electrical Engineering and Mathematics. Prior to 2011 no Black learner could register for an Information Technology class.
4. Fights in the school have racial overtones, as in most cases it is between Black and White boys.

Moreover, the report showed that one of the School Management Team members had this to say concerning School Integration (transformation):

> For many years, the school was run in a particular way and it is difficult to change from this. Many unpleasant things were said about our school and I think we need to appreciate

> the issues raised by the Concerned Parents. Maybe we have been slumbering. But we are definitely making an effort. But the problems we experience in the school are the problems experienced in the community.

The report also revealed that the main thrust of the explanation by the member of the School Management Team is an acknowledgment of the problems experienced in the school as problems faced by the wider community. This, according to them, is important in that attempts to address racial issues at the school should be broadly conceived to include analysis of the broader community and South African society. Mechanisms restricted to the school are bound not to achieve much. The team reported further that the principal of the school was quite scathing about the home environment: "The problem is at home. Our communities are at fault. Racial issues start at home and then come to our schools. Start with the home". They also made mention of a different perspective that emerged from the views of the Black parents:

> The school is still stuck in the past, hence our demands submitted to the MEC [Member of the Executive Council]. When we were co-opted in the SGB [School Governing Board], we thought they want to change but after one meeting of the SGB, where we were told that everything will be communicated in Afrikaans, we have serious doubts about transformation. We came out of that meeting really exhausted and could not function properly for two days. And there were issues we wanted to discuss but were told no. Worse we were told we have no voting rights.

According to the report, the views expressed by the co-opted member of SGB were shared by four others. These four other members said they thought the new SGB was serious about working towards truly transforming the school and turning the school into a fully racially integrated school. But to their surprise, their first meeting gave them a different conclusion. The co-opted members said they got a message in the meeting that the school belongs to Whites, but as Blacks they are accommodated.

In addition, the report presented by Rasekgala et al. (2011) indicated that comments by some of the teachers on the issue of school integration and transformation suggest practices that predominantly keep Black learners together and away from their White counterparts. According to them, one of the teachers said that in the few cases where you find White learners mixing freely with Black learners, often this is because they started at the primary school and both are in the English classes. It is rare to find learners in the Afrikaans classes interacting freely with learners in the English classes. The same report also revealed that members of the task team had an opportunity to observe practices/interaction during break, and in the majority of cases White learners keep to themselves, and the same applies to Black learners. There was only one case where a group of young boys included Blacks and a White learner. Rasekgala et al. explained further in their report that during interviews with teachers, the task team members were told that these learners are in grade 8 and the White learner is in an English class, not Afrikaans, as the latter are exclusively for Whites.

According to the report, one of the co-opted members of the SGB commented as follows on fighting:

> Racial conflict at the school is very bad. What is the school doing to eradicate this? My son cannot go into the restrooms, if there are white kids in there. If he goes he has to have his friend. He is scared to go alone in there when there are white kids. This is not good at all. Black kids are not allowed to walk in certain areas. On the school buses it is worse. The bus issue is a story of its own.

The report also indicated that the views expressed above by the co-opted parent were shared by many Black parents. This according to them is also reflected in the letters submitted to the school and MEC by one Mr. Sithole in which he laments continued fights at the school. According to Mr. Sithole as reported by Rasekgala et al., at some point his daughter called panicking and saying she needed to be picked up from school immediately. Rasekgala et al. (2011) in their report also mentioned the case of a Black child who had had his jaw broken by one White learner and his parents had to take him to hospital in Pretoria for an operation. They observed further that racism in schools could lead to tragic ends, where a learner loses his or her life simply because he/she is attacked on the basis of skin color. In the same vein, the report showed that in addition to the fact that some Black learners were turned away from school on the basis of being Black, although under the pretext of there not being teachers to teach the subjects they require in English, racism also manifests itself at Hoerskool Ellisras in the following ways:

- dissemination of messages in Afrikaans more than in English;
- separate seating arrangements in buses during sporting trips;
- inculcation of fear amongst Black learners and hence separatist arrangements during breaks and on trips;
- employment of predominantly white staff.

Furthermore, Adjai and Lazaridis (2013) pointed out that while post-apartheid South Africa was built on a culture of inclusiveness, tolerance, and human rights, embodied in its 1996 Constitution, Black South African citizens in particular exhibit high levels of xenophobia towards fellow Africans, subjecting them to different forms and degrees of prejudice and discrimination.

The World Conference Against Racism, Racial Discrimination, Xenophobia and Related Intolerance (WCAR, 2001) as cited in Adjai and Lazaridis (2013) defined xenophobia as attitudes, prejudices, and behaviors that reject, exclude, and often vilify persons, based on the perception that they are outsiders or foreigners to the community, society or national identity. Unlike *old racism* which is based on discriminatory treatment at the hands of a race (a biological group) different to one's own, xenophobia can be linked to *new racism* which is based on the discriminatory treatment of the other on the basis of the other's national origin or ethnicity (Adjai and Lazaridis 2013).

Singh (2013) citing Osman (2009) made it known that immigrant learners in South Africa do experience xenophobia-based attacks. He expounded further that since the xenophobic violence of 2008, there have been constant flare-ups of xenophobia across South Africa. As the result of this, foreign nationals, including students, live in constant fear of attacks by local people. Xenophobic attacks may take the form of verbal abuse, indirect insulting or direct physical attack.

Contemporary Homeschooling in Post-Apartheid South Africa

As pointed out in the earlier paragraphs, racism is not yet a thing of the past in post- apartheid South Africa. Given the relatively recent instances of racism and xenophobia both in the larger society and in the schools, one opines that it is only reasonable for many parents in South Africa to develop cold feet about sending their children to conventional schools and to opt for homeschooling as a panacea for an unsafe learning environment that is characterized by racism and its related ills. It follows, therefore, that racism may be a contributory factor to homeschooling and its growth in South Africa. While there is a dearth of recent literature on the linkage of racism to homeschooling in South Africa, Jensen (1998), Durham (1996) and Eloff-Vorster (2000) cited in Van Schoor (2005) pointed out that cruel social environments in many public schools in South Africa, and specifically racism in schools, is a major reason why parents opt for homeschooling. They mentioned further that whether parents are equipped for this task, in terms of ability and qualifications, does not seem to influence their decision at all.

Moreover, Olatunji (2014) reported that an interview he had in 2013 by correspondence with Graham and Allison Shortridge revealed that one of the reasons for homeschooling in South Africa is the bullying that is prevalent in state schools. However, the "Racism in Schools" report presented by Rasekgala et al. (2011) shows that bullying is not limited to state schools and that in some cases bullying and its associated ills in schools have racist undertones. For example, Olatunji (2014) while citing Molosankwe (2012) made mention of an incident in which a grade 10 pupil called Nkululeko Ndlovu, 18, of Phineas Xulu Secondary School in South Africa, was allegedly shot dead by a fellow student, a grade 11 pupil in the same school. Ndolvu had been shot in the classroom as he sat waiting to write an examination. Furthermore, Molosankwe observed that no one was prepared to shed a tear for Ndolvu. The general feeling was that he had got what he deserved. According to Molosankwe, one teacher was overheard saying "minus one problem" while some other teachers conceded privately that he had been troublesome and that he had scared them too. In addition, Mosolamkwe gathered that Ndolvu's classmates at the school all knew he was a bully and preyed on the other children with his gang and that the other schoolchildren felt no grief, only freedom that his reign of terror had been brought to an end. Furthermore, Abraham, Mathew, and Ramela (2006) cited in Olatunji (2014) pointed out that research carried out by the Medical Council of South Africa showed a high level of sexual abuse of girls in South African schools. Similarly, studies by the African Child Policy Forum (2010) showed that 32% of reported child rape cases in South Africa were carried out by teachers. If the importance of a safe learning environment cannot be over-emphasized (and normally it cannot) it follows therefore that learning environments that are susceptible to events of this nature will normally make parents wary of sending their children to such places. Where these events have racist and or xenophobic undertones, they give parents additional reasons to opt for homeschooling as a safer alternative.

Instances of bullying and sexual abuse that have racist undertone include the case cited by Msila (2015) in which a new Black pupil of Northern Cape Agricultural School in South Africa was raped with a broom on the school premises by four White learners. Another instance was the case cited by Rasekgala et al. (2011), in which a Black learner at Hoerskool Ellistras in South Africa had his jaw broken by one White learner. According to Raskgala et al., the parents of the Black learner had to take him to a hospital in Pretoria where he was operated on. They pointed out that the parents of the Black learner had to institute legal proceedings because of their belief that the school does not have an effective disciplinary procedure. Rasekgala et al. rightly observed that the school should be an environment where learners interact without fear and socialize freely across racial boundaries. According to them, failure in this regard has adverse effect on educational outcomes. They argue further that one cannot learn in a hostile environment that is racially charged. These submissions lend further credence to the idea that the prevalence of racism in South African conventional schools could be among the factors motivating parents' to homeschool their children.

Msila (2015) pointed out that what happened at Roodepoort Primary School reflects the struggles that South African schools have in addition to their pedagogic challenges. He reiterated the fact that racism in schools will limit the real function of schools as they continue to engender inequality. He opined that these institutions are a reflection of an ailing society that is trying to stand up. Msila explained further that many schools in South Africa lack the exercise of the functional paradigm of portraying schools as democratic institutions that promote humane and social justice goals. According to Msila, the fact that racism is still prevalent in South African schools demonstrates how education has failed to lead in deconstructing inequality and promoting quality of life for all.

The Good and the Bad Sides of Contemporary Homeschooling in South Africa

Homeschooling in post-apartheid South Africa has come to be one reliable means of avoiding racism in conventional schools. To the concerned parent, at least, there is a respite. Homeschooling has also proven to be a way for parents to ensure that their children avoid some other challenges facing South African public education system. For example, Modisaotile (2012) pointed out that the dropout rate in South Africa is very high, and literacy and numeracy levels are low. According to him, other challenges that the public education system faces include poor teacher training, unskilled teachers, lack of commitment to teaching by teachers, and a shortage of resources in education despite the large budgetary commitments by government. As reported by Modisaotile (2012), Bloomberg News in 2011 showed that over the past five years the Republic of South Africa had seen a doubling of the education budget to 165 billion rand, but still the system had failed to reverse unacceptably low examination results or to improve the standard of teaching. Olatunji (2014) citing Modisaotile (2012) also revealed that the quality of education in the Republic of South Africa remained very poor, and the output rate had not improved. In addition, classrooms were still overcrowded, with the ratio of teachers to learners being 1 to 32 in South African public schools. According to Blach (2011) cited in Modisaotile (2012), Annual National Assessments (ANANs) for grade 3 and 6 learners have found low levels of literacy and numeracy for South African learners. In addition, the assessments found that only 35% of learners could read, with results ranging from 12% per cent in Mpumalanga to a "high" of 43% in the Western Cape. In a press statement before the Annual National Assessment for 2011, the Minister of Basic Education, Mrs. Angie Motsshekga, indicated her concern over the standard of South African education by stating:

> This is worrying precisely because the critical skills of literacy and numeracy are fundamental to further education and achievement in the worlds of both education and work. Many of our learners lack proper foundations in literacy and numeracy and so they struggle to progress in the system and into post-school education and training.

According to a June 2011 diagnostic overview cited in Olatunji (2014), the National Planning Minister was reported to have observed that the quality of schooling was substandard, especially in the township schools. Drug abuse was also highlighted as one of the major causes of class repetition at school in South Africa. Olatunji (2014) citing McEntire (2011) pointed out that drugs are easily obtainable by students, and their use is prevalent even at the primary school level. The substance most abused by students is alcohol, followed by cigarettes and marijuana. According to a 2011 report from the Bureau of Justice, 85% of teenagers claim that they know where to obtain marijuana, while 29% state that someone has offered or sold them illegal substance at school (McEntire 2011). While South Africa is working round the clock to see that the aforementioned challenges in her public education system are surmounted, homeschooling is performing a key function of being a "refuge" for a teeming population of students that continues to increase by the day.

It is obvious that homeschooling in South Africa is of immense benefit to many parents and their wards; however there is the challenge of ensuring that the reemergence of racism in post-apartheid South Africa is nipped in the bud. Furthermore, notwithstanding the strengths of homeschooling in South Africa, there is still that serious downside of the dearth of scholarship and accurate data. The implications of the non-availability of accurate data on homeschooling in South Africa are enormous. Among other things, it means that accurate planning and accurate policy decisions for and about homeschooling can hardly be possible; neither can optimum development of homeschooling in South Africa or optimum benefit from this mode of education.

Some Lessons for Other African Nations

As discussed earlier in this chapter, the public school system in the Republic of South Africa is facing many challenges. However, the reality of challenges facing the public education system is a common feature in countries around the world. For example, in her submission on the reasons why some parents are opting for homeschooling in the United States, Leiding (2008) argued that American education is facing challenges characterized by negative social pressure (such as bullying, crime, drugs, and other school related problems). Like America and other non-African countries, South Africa has been exploring the homeschooling option as one of the ways of getting around the challenges in its public education system. Ironically, in terms of progress in education (both quality and quantity) the Republic of South Africa is very much ahead of most, if not all the other African countries, where contemporary homeschooling is still largely unknown, widely unpracticed and or not recognized by the authorities. It is noteworthy also that many of the factors that made some parents in South Africa opt for homeschooling are also not only common in these other African countries but present in greater dimensions. An attempt is made in the ensuing paragraphs to highlight some examples.

When it comes to education, Africa is running a twin deficit in access to school and learning in school. Far too many children are out of school, and far too many of those in school are not learning. What is happening in education in Africa merits the description of a regional emergency. The emergency is fueling poverty and inequality, compromising economic growth, and setting Africa on course for a potentially destabilizing crisis of youth unemployment (Watkins 2013). Watkins pointed out, for example, that despite its vast oil wealth, Nigeria has 10 million children out of school. That shocking figure puts the country in the unenviable position of topping the world rankings for out-of-school children. Many of Africa's children are denied an education because they are working as child laborers. According to the International Labour Organization, sub-Saharan Africa is now the only region in which the proportion of children defined as "economically active" is rising (2010). Alarmingly, around one in three children of primary school age in Africa is involved in hazardous employment, working in dangerous environments for pitifully low wages instead of nourishing their minds at school. When it comes to enrollment and years in school, Africa is a world apart. Only around one third of children make it to secondary school, compared to over half in South Asia. Just 6% make it through to university, and 38% of young adults aged 20–25 have less than four years of education (Van Fleet, Watkins, and Greubel 2012). If the current trends continue, there will be more than 2 million children out of school in Africa in 2016, and the figure will be on the increase in subsequent years. Why the slowdown? In large measure, governments across the region have systematically failed to put in place the policies needed to reach the most marginalized children – the rural poor, young girls from disadvantaged homes, slum dwellers, pastoralists and others (UNESCO 2010).

Learning outcomes are similarly bleak. Millions of children across the African region are suffering from what amounts to a "zero-value-added" education. They are spending several years in school and progressing across grades without acquiring even the most basic learning competencies (Watkins 2013). Research at the Brookings Institution's Center for Universal Education (CUE) has helped to provide a window into the learning deficit. Covering 28 countries that are home to over three-quarters of Africa's primary school-age population, CUE reviewed a range of regional learning assessments, national surveys and examination results. The aim was to develop a new policy tool – the Africa Learning Barometer – to identify the proportion of children falling below an absolute minimum level of competency for literacy and numeracy (Van Fleet, Watkins, and Greubel 2012). The bar was set at a very low level. Most of those falling below the threshold were unable to read a simple sentence or successfully complete basic addition. The Africa Learning Barometer points unequivocally to an education and learning crisis. Over one-third of the pupils covered in the survey – 23 million in total – fell below the minimum learning threshold. In the cases of Ethiopia, Nigeria and Zambia, the share was over 50%.

If the aim of education systems is to enable children to realize their potential, escape poverty, and gain the skills that they and their countries need to build shared prosperity, much of Africa scores an "F-minus." Today there are 127 million children of primary school age in sub-Saharan Africa. The cumulative effect of a large out-of-school population, high dropout rates and low levels of learning is that some 61 million of these children – almost half of the total – will reach their adolescent years without having gained basic literacy and numeracy skills, let alone 21st-century learning skills.

No education system is better than its teachers – and nowhere is this more evident than in Africa. Many countries in Africa are facing an epidemic of teacher absenteeism, and as a result of this, schoolchildren are being denied their most valuable learning resource. Part of the problem can be traced to low morale and legitimate grievances over pay and conditions. The major problem, however, is that the systems for teacher recruitment, training and support are hopelessly out of touch with national learning needs (Watkins 2013). Studies in countries such as Uganda, Nigeria, and Mozambique have found that fewer than half of their teachers are able to score in the top band on a test designed for 12-year-olds (Africa Progress Panel, 2012)

Training and classroom delivery is geared toward mind-numbing rote learning, rather than problem-solving. To make matters worse, few countries in Africa have functioning national learning assessment systems, depriving policymakers of the flow of information needed to guide reform (Watkins 2013). In addition, as Dume et al. (2010) revealed, sexual abuse of students by teachers and others is not uncommon in Ghana and also in Nigeria. Similarly, studies by the African Child Policy Forum (2010) show that more than 84% of girls in Ethiopia, 94% in Uganda, and 99% in Kenya have experienced some form of physical abuse at school. A large proportion of girls – 42% in Uganda, 40% in Burkina Faso and Nigeria, 30% in Cameroon and Ethiopia, 27% in DRC, 26% in Kenya, and 17% in Senegal – are also reported to have been victims of rape either in school, on the way to school, or when coming from school. The studies further reveal that 72% of school children in Ethiopia report to have been slapped while at school, while 67% of school girls in Botswana were sexually harassed by teachers. Bandason and Rusakaniko (2010) as cited by Olatunji (2014) confirm the prevalence of smoking among secondary school students in Harare, Zimbabwe. In the multivariate analysis, smoking was found to be statistically associated with having a friend that smoked, getting involved in a physical fight, alcohol use, marijuana use, and having had sexual intercourse.

As Leiding (2008) has argued, teaching children at home is not for everyone, and clearly not every parent in Africa should opt for homeschooling. Furthermore, the thrust of this chapter is not that education should be moved from school to the home en masse; neither should we deny the reality that the home is not perfect or that poor and illiterate parents exist across Africa. The argument, however, is that, in light of the prevailing challenges confronting the public school system across Africa coupled with the aforementioned examples, parents in other African nations who are in a position to make use of homeschooling should follow the example of South African parents by embracing the option as a personal initiative in salvaging their children from paying so dearly for the problems that they did not cause. In so doing however, there will be the need to work out a way to avoid the shortcomings of this mode of education as implemented and operated in South Africa while capitalizing on its strengths. The South African public school system is currently relieved of the burden of between 30 000 and 100 000 children (as explained earlier in this chapter) who are being homeschooled; it is worth the effort for various governments in the rest of Africa to consider working hand in hand with parents in their respective countries to see how they can similarly make the best use of home education to relieve their own overburdened public education systems and provide an equally good alternative for parents who cannot afford to send their children to private schools.

Suggestions and Conclusion

According to Olatunji (2014), the fact that there are between 30 000 and 100 000 home learners in the Republic of South Africa must be a relief either overtly or covertly to the public education system, which has frequently been described as overburdened. At the same time, homeschooling assures that the private education system in South Africa will not become overstretched for the next several years. This measure of relief recommends homeschooling to other African countries where the public school system is not only overburdened but overburdened to the extreme and where the private school system is beyond the reach of many due to the very high school fees relative to the poverty of the masses. Homeschooling, therefore, is a possible panacea for "rescuing" at least some children in the African countries where the relevant authorities are still unaware of the benefits of this form of education or undecided about it. Homeschooling would go a long way to complement whatever the governments in these African nations might have been doing to solve the problem of an overburdened school system but which have not yet brought any appreciable result.

Olatunji (2014) observed that there is a major problem of awareness of the whole idea of homeschooling and its prospects on the part of parents in African countries, as shown by the fact that nothing very substantial is happening across the continent concerning homeschooling. It is therefore suggested that organizations such as the Pestalozzi Trust and other homeschooling associations in South Africa that are actively pursuing the course of homeschooling should begin to see the whole of Africa as their terrain and not just the Republic of South Africa, though they still have an "unfinished war" concerning homeschooling in South Africa. It is not just the children in the Republic of South Africa who need a future but the children in the whole of Africa. What the Pestalozzi Trust and other homeschooling associations have done and are doing to gain and maintain a foothold for homeschooling in South Africa should be extended to the whole of Africa, starting with a dynamic awareness campaign.

Associations like Elimu Nyumbani (meaning "home school" in Kiswahili – the commonest language spoken in East Africa) in Kenya coordinating the few families who are homeschoolers, and the individuals that are struggling to make meaning out of homeschooling in Botswana, Namibia, Tanzania and Uganda should learn from the successes and challenges of homeschoolers and homeschooling associations in the Republic of South Africa and seek possible assistance.

The persistence of racialized asymmetrics and differentiations in various forms pose a significant potential for social crisis in South Africa if left unchallenged and uncontested (Puttick 2011). There is a need, therefore, for South Africa to redouble its efforts in combating racism in all its forms head-on. Other African nations would also do well to learn from the Republic of South Africa how to safeguard themselves against racism and xenophobia so that these issues do not become part of the factors that inform, sustain or promote homeschooling in their countries if and when it is embraced.

References

Abraham, N., S. Mathew, and P. Ramela. 2006. "Intersection of Sanitation, Sexual Coercion and Girls Safety in Schools." *Tropical Medicine and International Health*, 11(5): 751–756.

Adjai, C., and G. Lazaridis. 2013. "Migration, Xenophobia and New Racism in Post-Apartheid South Africa." *International Journal of Social Studies*, 1: 192–205.

Africa Progress Panel. 2012. "Seizing Opportunities in Times of Global Change." Africa Progress Report 2012: Jobs, Justice and Equity.

African Child Policy Forum. 2010. "Violence against Children in Africa: The Challenges and Priorities for Action." Document prepared for the 15th session of the African Committee of Experts on the Rights and Welfare of the Child, March 15–19, Addis Ababa, Ethiopia.

Bandason, T., and S. Rusakaniko. 2010. "The Prevalence and Associated Factors of Smoking among Secondary School Students in Harare Zimbabwe." *Tobacco Induced Disease*, 8: 12–20.

Blach, G. 2011. "A Weak Foundation for Pupils." *The Star*, July 5. Accessed October 20, 2015. http://www.iol.co.za/the-star/a-weak-foundation-for-pupils-1.1093347#.ViaOMNKrTIU

Blum, L. 2002. *"I'm not a Racist But …": The Moral Quandary of Race*. New York: Cornell University Press.

Brynard, S. 2007. "Homeschooling as an Open-Learning Educational Challenge in South Africa." *South African Journal of Education*, 27: 83–100.

de Klerk, V.A. 2011. "A Nigger in the Woodpile? A Racist Incident on a South African University Campus." *Journal of Languages and Culture*, 2: 39–49.

Distefano, A., K.E. Rudestam, and R.J. Silverman. 2005. *Encyclopedia of Distributed Learning*. London: Sage.

Dume M., C. Bosumtwi-Sam, R. Sabates, and A. Owosu. 2010. "Bullying and School Attendance: A Case Study of Senior High School Students in Ghana." *Research Monograph* 41, July. University of Sussex Center for International Education.

Durham, K. 1996. "Learning the Home Way: Homeschooling and the South African Schools Bill." *Indicator SA*, 13, 3: 76–79.

Hill, P. 2010. "How Home Schooling Will Change Public Education." *Hoover Digest Research and Opinion on Public Policy*.

International Labour Organization. 2010. "Accelerating Action Against Child Labour." ILO Global Report on Child Labour 2010. International Labour Conference, 99th Session. Accessed November 30, 2012. http://www.ilo.org/ilc/ILCSessions/99thSession/reports/WCMS_126752/lang--en/index.htm

Jayawardene, S. 2015. "Black Homeschooling: Racial Protectionism, Cultural Relevance, and Favorable Social and Academic Outcomes." *Afrometics*. July 4. Accessed October 20, 2015. http://www.afrometrics.org/black-homeschooling-racial-protectionism-cultural-relevance-and-favorable-social-and-academic-outcomes.html

Leiding, D. 2008. *The Hows and Whys of Alternative Education – Schools where Students Thrive*. Lanham, MD: Rowman & Littlefield Education.

Louw, G.J.J. 1992. "Die Huisskool – n' Vormvan Alternatiewe Onderwys." *Koers*, 57: 355–372.

Magida, A.Y. 2008. "Homeschooling in the Non-Formal Education of Nigeria: A Mechanism for Sustainable Development." *International Journal of Literacy*, 3(1).

Matolino, B. 2013. "'There is a Racist on my Step and He is Black': A Philosophical Analysis of Black Racism in Post-Apartheid South Africa." *Alternation*, 20(1).

McEntire. 2011. "Drugs in Schools. SA Private Schools." No longer available online.

Modisaotsile, B.M. 2012. "The Failing Standard of Basic Education in South Africa." Policy Brief. Africa Institute of South Africa. Briefing N0 72, March.

Molosankwe, B. 2012. "Joy after Bully Shot." *The Star Newspaper*, November 22: 1, 16.

Msila, Vuyisile. 2015. "Racism Resurfacing in our Schools." *The Sunday Independent*, March 1. Accessed October 20, 2015. www.iol.co.za/sundayindependent/racism-resurfacing-schools-1.1825153

Mtose, X. 2011. "Black Peoples' Lived Experiences of Everyday Racism in Post-Apartheid South Africa." *The Journal of International Social Research*, 4: 325–338.

Mufweba, Y. 2003. “Families Who choose Home School.” *Saturday Star,* February 22.

Olatunji, Michael. O. 2014. “Contemporary Homeschooling in South Africa: Some Lessons for other African Nations.” *Middle Eastern & African Journal of Educational Research*, 9: 4–16.

Pestalozzi Trust. 1998. “Copy of Draft Guidelines for the Registration of Learners for Home Education.” No longer available online.

Pistorius, P. 1970. *Gister en Vandag in Die Opvoeding*. Potchefstroom: Pro Rege Pers Beperk.

Puttick, Kirstan. 2011. “First Year Students’ Narratives of “Race” and Racism in Post-Apartheid South Africa.” Unpublished Masters Thesis, Faculty of Humanities, University of Witwatersrand, Johannesburg.

Rasekgala, M. et al. 2011. “Report of Racism in Schools: The Case of Hoerskool Ellisras.” Limpopo Provincial Government. Republic of South Africa. Accessed October 20, 2015. http://policyresearch.limpopo.gov.za/handle/123456789/793

Ray, B.D. 2010. “Academic Achievement and Demographic Traits of Homeschool Students: A Nationwide Study.” *Academic Leadership*, 8, February.

Ray, B.D. 2013. “Homeschooling Associated with Beneficial Learner and Societal Outcomes but Educators do not Promote It.” *Peabody Journal of Education*, 88: 324–341.

Sehoole, C, 2012. “South Africa: Challenges of Racism and Access.” *International Higher Education*, 68: 20–21.

Shortridge, Graham, and Allison Shortridge. 2013. “History of Theocentric Christian Education.” *Theocentric Christian Education*. Accessed October 22, 2015. http://www.homeschool-tce.co.za/pages.php?id=71

Singh, S.K. 2013. “Zimbabwean Teachers’ Experiences of Xenophobia in Limpopo Schools.” *Alternation*, 7: 51–66.

South African Schools Act No. 84 of 1996. Government Gazette, No. 17579. Pretoria Government Printer.

Taylor, Paul C. 2004. *Race: A Philosophical Introduction*. Cambridge: Polity.

Terblanche, W.R. 2012. “Racism in Schools: A Teacher’s Perspective.” *Thought Leader*, February 10. Accessed October 20, 2015. http://thoughtleader.co.za/readerblog/2012/02/10/racism-in-schools-a-teachers-perspective/

UNESCO. 2010. *Reaching the Marginalized. EFA Global Monitoring Report*. Paris: UNESCO.

Van der Eems, Bouwe. 2013. “How Many Homeschoolers are there in South Africa?” *Association for Homeschooling,* February 8. Accessed October 22, 2015. http://www.tuisskolers.org/home/entry/hoeveel-tuisskolers-is-daar-in-suid-afrika.html

Van Fleet, J.W., K. Watkins, and L. Greubel. 2012. “Africa Learning Barometer,” September 17. Washington DC: The Brookings Institution. Accessed November 30, 2012. http://www.brookings.edu/research/interactives/africa-learning-barometer

Van Oostrum, L.J., and K. Van Oostrum. 1997. “Loaves for Life.” *Home Education – A Way to Freedom and Equality*. Totiusdal: The Association for Homeschooling.

Van Oostrum, L.J. 1997. “Tuisonderwys: n’Didaktiese en Etiese Perspektief.” Unpublished MEd diss., University of Pretoria.

Watkins, K. 2013. “Narrowing Africa’s Education Deficit.” *Foresight Africa: Top Priorities for the Continent in 2013*, 17–21. Accessed October 20, 2015. http://www.brookings.edu/research/reports/2013/01/~/media/103D2A7A566648CAA6998469292 E891C.ashx

Index

The Wiley Handbook of Home Education, First Edition. Edited by Milton Gaither.